CHILDREN AND YOUTH IN SPORT

A Biopsychosocial Perspective
2nd Edition

Frank L. Smoll
University of Washington

Ronald E. Smith
University of Washington

KENDALL/HUNT PUBLISHING COMPANY
4050 Westmark Drive   Dubuque, Iowa 52002

Contents

PART THREE
Social Processes

PART FOUR
Anatomical and Physiological Concerns

PART FIVE
Psychological Issues

PART SIX
Future Directions

Contributors

The Editors

Frank L. Smoll, Ph.D., Professor, Department of Psychology, University of Washington, Seattle

Ronald E. Smith, Ph.D., Professor, Department of Psychology, University of Washington, Seattle

The Authors

David I. Anderson, Ph.D., Assistant Professor, Department of Kinesiology, San Francisco State University, and Institute of Human Development, University of California, Berkeley

Donald A. Bailey, Ph.D., Professor Emeritus, College of Kinesiology, University of Saskatchewan, Saskatoon, Canada, and Continuing Visiting Professor, School of Human Movement Studies, University of Queensland, Brisbane, Australia

Jack W. Berryman, Ph.D., Professor, Department of Medical History and Ethics, University of Washington, Seattle

Brenda Light Bredemeier, Ph.D., Co-Director, Mendelson Center for Sport, Character and Culture, University of Notre Dame, Notre Dame

Robert J. Brustad, Ph.D., Professor, School of Kinesiology and Physical Education, University of Northern Colorado, Greeley

Michael A. Clark, Ph.D., Assistant Professor, Institute for the Study of Youth Sports, Michigan State University, East Lansing

Joan L. Duda, Ph.D., Professor, School of Sport and Exercise Sciences, University of Birmingham, Edgbaston, Birmingham, United Kingdom

Martha E. Ewing, Ph.D., Associate Professor, Department of Kinesiology, Michigan State University, East Lansing

Karen E. French, Ph.D., Professor and Chair, Department of Physical Education, University of South Carolina, Columbia

Jere D. Gallagher, Ph.D., Associate Professor and Chair, Department of Health, Physical and Recreation Education, University of Pittsburgh, Pittsburgh

Daniel Gould, Ph.D., Professor, Department of Exercise and Sport Science, University of North Carolina, Greensboro

Susan L. Greendorfer, Ph.D., Professor Emerita, Department of Kinesiology, University of Illinois, Urbana-Champaign

Amy Harris, M.S., Teacher, Lakota Public Schools, Westchester, Ohio

John L. Haubenstricker, Ph.D., Professor and Director, Institute for the Study of Youth Sports, Michigan State University, East Lansing

Thelma S. Horn, Ph.D., Associate Professor, Department of Physical Education, Health, and Sport Studies, Miami University, Oxford

Mimi D. Johnson, M.D., Clinical Assistant Professor, Division of Adolescent Medicine, Department of Pediatrics, University of Washington, Seattle

John H. Lewko, Ph.D., Director, Center for Research in Human Development, Laurentian University, Sudbury, Ontario, Canada

Robert M. Malina, Ph.D., Professor, Department of Kinesiology, Michigan State University, East Lansing

Siobhain McArdle, M.S., Doctoral Student, University of Birmingham, Edgbaston, Birmingham, United Kingdom

Lyle J. Micheli, M.D., Director, Division of Sports Medicine, Children's Hospital Boston, Associate Clinical Professor, Department of Orthopaedic Surgery, Harvard Medical School, Boston

Norman N. Morra, Ph.D., Associate, LaMarsh Centre for Research on Violence and Conflict Resolution, York University, North York, Ontario, Canada

Terry Orlick, Ph.D., Professor, School of Human Kinetics, University of Ottawa, Ontario, Canada

Julie A. Partridge, M.S., Doctoral Candidate, School of Kinesiology and Physical Education, University of Northern Colorado, Greeley

Michael W. Passer, Ph.D., Senior Lecturer, Department of Psychology, University of Washington, Seattle

F. Clark Power, Ed.D., Chair, Program of Liberal Studies, University of Notre Dame, Notre Dame

Lynda B. Ransdell, Ph.D., Assistant Professor, Department of Exercise and Sport Science, University of Utah, Salt Lake City

Karl S. Rosengren, Ph.D., Associate Professor, Department of Kinesiology, University of Illinois, Urbana-Champaign

Peter A. Salob, M.D., Fellow, Division of Sports Medicine, Children's Hospital Boston, Boston

Tara K. Scanlan, Ph.D., Professor of Psychology and Director of the International Center for Talent Development, University of California, Los Angeles

Vern Seefeldt, Ph.D., Professor and Director Emeritus, Institute for the Study of Youth Sports, Michigan State University, East Lansing

David Light Shields, Ph.D., Co-Director, Mendelson Center for Sport, Character and Culture, University of Notre Dame, Notre Dame

Michael D. Smith (deceased), Ph.D., Former Professor of Sociology and Physical Education and Director of the LaMarsh Centre for Research on Violence and Conflict Resolution, York University, North York, Ontario, Canada

Jerry R. Thomas, Ed.D., Professor and Chair, Department of Health and Human Performance, Iowa State University, Ames

Katherine T. Thomas, Ph.D., Associate Professor, Department of Health and Human Performance, Iowa State University, Ames

David A. Van de Loo, M.D., Pediatrics and Adolescent Medicine, Midelfort Clinic Ltd., Eau Clair, Wisconsin

David K. Wiggins, Ph.D., Professor, Department of Health, Fitness and Recreation Resources, George Mason University, Fairfax

Beverly J. Wilson, Ph.D., Assistant Professor, Department of Graduate Psychology, Seattle Pacific University, Seattle

Preface

The vast degree of involvement in sport, both vicariously and directly, is one of the most notable features of contemporary Western society. Indeed, sport has been an increasingly integral part of American culture and must be considered a major social institution. This is particularly true for children and youth, as more and more youngsters participate in athletics each year. The phenomenon termed *youth sports* refers to adult-organized and controlled athletic programs for young people in the age range 6 to 18 years. The participants are formally organized into teams and leagues, and they attend practices and scheduled competitions under the supervision of an adult leader. These programs not only have clear popularity in the United States, but also have attained acceptance on a worldwide basis.

Although youth sports are firmly entrenched in our social and cultural milieu, they are the focus of considerable controversy. Those who favor sport programs emphasize that there are many aspects of the experience that contribute to personal development. They generally view youth sports as a microcosm of society where participants can learn to cope with many of the important realities of life. Within sport, youngsters can compete and cooperate with others, they can learn risk taking and self-control, and they can deal with success and failure. Important attitudes are formed about achievement, authority, and persistence in the face of difficulty. In addition, the advocates point out, lifelong patterns of physical activity that promote health and fitness can be initiated through involvement in youth sports. Critics counter with claims that excessive physical and psychological demands are placed on young people, and that programs exist primarily for the self-serving needs of coaches and parents. They suggest that children and youth would benefit far more if adults simply left them alone to participate in their own games and activities.

A realistic appraisal of youth sports acknowledges both the benefits and the harm that can be done. We are convinced that the sport environment affords a strong *potential* for achieving important objectives. The question is not whether youth sports should continue to exist. They are here to stay, in spite of the criticisms that are sometimes leveled at them. The real question is how the programs can be effectively structured and conducted in ways that ensure attainment of positive outcomes.

One of the keys to unlocking the potential of youth sports lies in understanding their physical, psychological, and sociological dimensions. Since the mid-1970s, the scientific community has directed attention to studying the impact of highly structured sports on young athletes and on the complex social network comprising coaches, parents, and peers. The proliferation of research has given rise to youth sport conferences and symposia as well as academic courses on the subject at colleges and universities. The accumulation of empirical evidence has also resulted in a body of knowledge that spans several disciplinary areas, including psychology, sociology, and the sport sciences.

Children and Youth in Sport provides a multidisciplinary perspective of youth sports. It is well-known that human behavior is determined by interacting causes that operate at many levels of influence: biological, psychological, and sociological. For example, biological principles sometimes appear to explain behavior, but they themselves are inadequate. Those who focus on any one type of influence tend to lose sight of the fact that young athletes' development is determined by interaction among all levels of influence. Therefore, our goal has been to produce a volume that provides readers with an up-to-date survey of current scientific knowledge of the multifaceted nature of youth sports. It is our ultimate hope that *Children and Youth in Sport* will foster a better understanding of critical issues, and that the specific recommendations offered by our panel of experts will stimulate and guide changes in current policies and practices. Improving the conditions under which youth sports are conducted should ultimately prove beneficial to all individuals involved—young athletes and adults alike!

Profile of the Second Edition

As a text, the second edition of *Children and Youth in Sport* is directed toward upper-level undergraduate or graduate youth sport courses. Students from physical education, kinesiology, psychology, and many other fields should find the information valuable. We have sought to develop a pedagogically sound package, with coverage that is comprehensive, current, and cohesive yet economic of space. The chapters from the first edition have been reworked and updated by the authors, adding significant material published since our first edition. Yet, the basic format of the chapters and discussions of works of enduring importance remain unaltered. Moreover, two entirely new chapters have been added on the topics of overuse injuries and motivational climate. In addition to serving as a text for youth sport courses, the book serves as a comprehensive reference for youth sport administrators, coaches, and parents.

Acknowledgements

For whatever virtues are found in this volume, many people share the credit. First and foremost, we are greatly indebted to the authors for contributing up-to-date syntheses of the literature in their respective areas of expertise. We would also like to express our gratitude to the editorial and production staffs of Kendall/Hunt Publishing Company for their roles in designing and producing the book.

Frank L. Smoll and Ronald E. Smith

Part One

History and Current Status

Children and youth have engaged in play and informal games throughout the course of human history. However, the past century has witnessed the development of increasingly organized youth sports as an integral part of American culture. The beginning of the youth sport movement in the United States actually dates back to the early 1900s. The first programs were instituted in public schools when it was recognized that physical activity was an important part of education. The programs emerged as after-school recreation activities, but they soon acquired a highly competitive "win at all costs" orientation. This change resulted in condemnation and subsequent withdrawal of support by educators. Over time, sponsorship and control of some sports shifted to a host of local and national agencies. The diversified mix of autonomous organizations offered a wide array of sport programs that grew in scope and popularity.

In moving from the sandlot to the more elaborate venues that now exist, the youth sport explosion has touched youngsters and adults in astonishing numbers. For example, a report presented at the 1984 Olympic Scientific Congress indicated that, of the 45 million young people (ages 6 to 18 years), about 20 million participated in nonschool athletics in the United States. At the same time, nearly 2.5 million men and women volunteered their time as coaches, league administrators, and officials. Youth

1

sports have continued to flourish during the past two decades, and many millions more youngsters are now participating (see Chapter 3). Today there are more opportunities to play a greater variety of sports than ever before. This is not only true for young males, but the rise of sport programs for girls and young women has been a relatively recent and highly significant development.

The growth of youth sports and the importance of their role in child and adolescent development is undeniable. But this expansion has generated persisting and, at times, bitter debate. Thoughtful persons have raised questions about the desirability of adult-organized sports. However, the answers to their queries are not simple. Just as medical doctors must have thorough histories of their patients, so must we understand the evolution of youth sports. By analogy, this knowledge assists us in effectively dealing with both the maladies and well-being of contemporary athletics, and in contributing to a healthy and happy future.

The opening chapter by Jack W. Berryman provides a historical account of the growth of highly organized sport programs for young boys. In tracing the rise of boys' sports, Berryman focuses on two separate but interrelated developments in the social and cultural milieu of U.S. society at the turn of the twentieth century. The first was the inclusion of sport in the school curriculum, which brought organized athletics closer to the children of the nation than ever before and established the rationale for their acceptance and promotion. The second factor influencing the growth of boys' sports was recognition that childhood is an important stage in the development of an adult and that measures must be taken to ensure a happy and profitable period of growing up. As a result, an entirely new branch of social welfare, called boys' work groups, began using sports to provide wholesome leisure-time pursuits for young boys and to keep them out of trouble. Of particular interest are the alterations of philosophies and attitudes of professional educators and the associated shifts in sponsorship of youth sports to community-based organizations.

David K. Wiggins' chapter begins with an overview of the boys' playground movement of the mid-nineteenth century. He then chronicles the late-nineteenth-century transition from participation in less organized and more informal games to competing in highly organized sports directed by adults. Similar to Berryman's work, Wiggins' historical analysis indicates that despite the early influence of educational institutions, the highly competitive programs that emerged in the 1920s and 1930s were primarily in the hands of various churches, boys' work groups, civic groups, and community councils. Professional educators eventually relinquished any control they had over youth sports because of their growing belief that highly competitive athletics exposed children to great risks. It is important to note that participation was initially confined to White males, and that attempts to eliminate racial and sexual discrimination did not begin until the mid-1950s and the early 1970s, respectively. In this regard, Wiggins describes the changing status that occurred for African American boys in southern Little League Baseball programs. Significant legal cases are then reviewed that led to more equitable treatment for girls and young women in sport. The trend toward gender equity coincided with revised interest in youth sports on the part of academicians and professional educators. Among the most visible indications of this concern was the organization of conferences, the establishment of institutes, and the formulation of coach-training programs devoted specifically to youth sports. The final part of the chapter focuses on the growth in publications and research studies on both the benefits and hazards of highly competitive youth sport programs.

In the final chapter of this part, Martha E. Ewing and Vern Seefeldt examine the current status of youth sport programs in America. Alarming reports from the Federal government have created a sense of urgency about the declining fitness level of children and youth. There is also realization that the promotion of physical activity and sport participation is paramount in reducing the trend toward inactivity and increased obesity. In addressing the changes in participation rates since 1990, the authors focus on programs conducted under the auspices of agency-sponsored organizations, where the largest number of youngsters participate. Citing data compiled from a national survey conducted by the Sporting Goods Manufacturers Association, Ewing and Seefeldt note that only the team sports of soccer and basketball increased their number of participants from 1987 to 1999; whereas, organizations that sponsor team sports all reported substantial gains in participation. Several plausible explanations for the discrepant phenomena are offered. With respect to the continued growth in interscholastic sport programs, figures from the National State High School Associations indicate that the largest growth has occurred for girls. However, one of the unfortunate aspects of participation in school-sponsored sports is the variance in participation for people of color. Specifically, Ewing and Seefeldt report that White youth continue to be most highly involved, and Hispanic students and Black female students remain under-represented. A unique feature of the chapter is the inclusion of information pertaining to youngsters' participation in what the authors label a major threat to community-based sport programs, namely, the emergence of elite sport camps. These commercial enterprises have placed a greater financial burden on parents and created greater expectations and greater discontent with sport. In addition to presenting a comprehensive picture of participation, Ewing and Seefeldt identify barriers to participation in programs in urban environments, such as lack of qualified leaders, safety at program sites and facilities, economics/affordability, and lack of cooperation among program providers. Recommendations for overcoming the barriers are included.

The Rise of Boys' Sports in the United States, 1900 to 1970

Jack W. Berryman, University of Washington

The rise of highly organized competitive sport programs[1] for boys under the age of 12 was a phenomenon of the first half of the twentieth century and indicated that sport had finally penetrated all levels of the American population.[2] To be sure, young children played games and enjoyed a variety of sports throughout America's history, but regulated and administered sport programs by interested individuals and organizations solely for the use of small boys did not begin until after 1900. In fact, the first instances of sport teams, leagues, championships, and other examples of highly organized children's sports outside of the schools were not evident until the 1920s and early 1930s. Even then, the programs were only local affairs, usually established by communities who wanted to provide something different and special for their children. Little did they know that in another 10 to 15 years nationally organized and administered sports for children would be spreading throughout the country to eventually become one of the most pervasive forces in the lives of many American youngsters.

Two separate but interrelated developments in the social and cultural milieu of American society during the early twentieth century provided the most direct influence on the rise and growth of boys' competitive sport programs. The first, of course, was the rise of sport itself in all parts of the country and the subsequent desire to

---

1. Highly organized competitive sports have been defined as: "any athletic activity which involves a considerable amount of the leisure time of the youngster in formalized practice, which encourages extensive attendance by adult spectators, which is limited to the outstanding players, and which involves the selection of winners on a state, regional, or national basis" (National Recreation Congress, 1952, p. 423).
2. This chapter is a revised and condensed version of an article titled "From the Cradle to the Playing Field: America's Emphasis on Highly Organized Competitive Sports for Preadolescent Boys," by J. W. Berryman, 1975, *Journal of Sport History, 2,* 112–131. The reader is directed to the original publication for a more detailed account of the trends and factors under discussion as well as for supporting documentation.

participate and spectate by large numbers of the population. More specifically, though, the inclusion of sport in the school curriculum brought organized sport closer to the youth of the nation than ever before. Along with school sports came the rationale for their acceptance and promotion. This was most often provided by professional physical educators, recreation people, playground directors, and athletic coaches who were responsible for the majority of competitive sport situations during the first three decades of the twentieth century.[3] But when philosophies changed within this group during the 1930s, educators dropped any sponsorship of children's sport they had previously provided and refused to condone high-level competition for preadolescents. This change of outlook by professionally trained educators who were deeply involved with the early stages of sport competition for children was the first important development in conjunction with the overall rise of sport. Although it seemed to be antagonistic to the growth and development of children's sport, the alteration of philosophy would eventually lead to bigger, better, and more highly organized programs.

The second development influencing the growth of boys' sport programs was that Americans began to realize the need and importance of protecting and providing varied opportunities for children. Childhood became recognized as an important stage in the development of an adult, and concerned individuals and organizations took measures to ensure a happy and profitable period of growing up. By means of a variety of laws and policies enacted by national, state, and community organizations, children were provided with an abundance of free time, parents took a different view of their offspring, and national programs were organized to protect the child's welfare. An entirely new branch of social welfare, called boys' work, originated in the last decade of the nineteenth century.[4] Boys' work groups, originally composed of all voluntary members, were organized specifically to provide wholesome leisure-time pursuits for young boys and keep them out of trouble. These social workers began using sports and other recreational activities very early in their work and realized the importance of reaching the youthful minds and bodies of preadolescent boys. Leaders of this movement advocated the usefulness of sport for many of the same reasons that schools turned to sport. But when the schools refused to sponsor competitive sports for the young boys, the task was left to the voluntary boys' work groups. Therefore, the linking of the overall popularity of sport and its believed values, many of which were established by school personnel in the early twentieth century, as well as the sport

---

3. By the close of the 1920s, sport had become quite popular in the United States. However, with few exceptions, organized sport competition was still for the middle-aged adult population, college students, and high school students in the upper grades. Organized competitive sport had not yet developed for the elementary school-aged population.

4. One person directly associated with the movement defined boys' work as "social engineering in the field of boyhood motivation . . . supervised leisure-time education, the purpose of which is social adjustment and creative living" (Stone, 1931, p. 28).

sponsorship of boys' work agencies (along with the work groups' own modifications and gradual growth) did more to promote boys' sport competition than any other factor and led directly to America's emphasis on highly organized competitive sports for preadolescent boys.

Before the 1930s, the responsibility for providing recreational activities and organized sports for small children was shaped by the schools, playgrounds, and a few nationally organized youth membership agencies such as the YMCA, Boy Scouts, and Boys' Clubs. As specific alterations of goals and purposes occurred within the physical education and recreation profession, however, the provision of sport competition for preadolescent boys became more and more a primary function of national voluntary boys' work agencies. Beginning in the 1930s, physical educators and professional recreation leaders denounced the overt emphasis placed on winning, the physical and emotional strain that sport placed on children, and the attempt to organize competition into leagues for championship play, which were becoming common in many children's sport programs. Professionals also disagreed with providing competition for only the best athletes instead of allowing all children to participate. As a result, professionally trained leaders in sports and recreation retracted their support and relinquished their hold on organized competition for young boys.

By allowing highly organized children's sport to leave the educational context, professional educators presented a golden opportunity to the many voluntary youth-related groups in America. These groups had no educationally imposed restrictions on their work for children and many times had the funds and support from parents and communities to provide elaborate and well-organized sport programs. The volunteer workers and members of these groups often had no educational training in child development or child psychology and operated with little or no restraints in providing the best for the children. Consequently, by giving up their support of youth sports, school personnel could no longer enforce their rules and regulations for competition. Accordingly, the outside agencies capitalized on children's free time from school during the evenings, weekends, and summer months and provided numerous opportunities for competition. With very few limitations and a single goal of serving children and making them happy, boys' work groups saw no end to the sport situations they could provide.

The withdrawal of the schools' sponsorship came at a time when the values inherent to sport and its benefits to both children and society were becoming firmly established in the beliefs of most Americans. Parents, child welfare workers, and organizations established to serve youth were not easily convinced of what they believed were questionable detriments of sport competition for children. Therefore, child-related organizations, and specifically boys' work groups, stepped in to fill the void created by professional educators. The schools continued to be paramount in their sponsorship of interscholastic athletics for youth beyond the age of 12, but sport competition for preadolescent boys became the responsibility of child-oriented organizations outside of the educational framework. Their main objective was to provide wholesome character-building activities to occupy the leisure time of children to better enable them to make the transition from childhood to adulthood. Sport, these organizations believed, was the one activity that was capable of providing all of the necessary conditions for this successful growth and development. Thus, it was during the 1930s, under the sponsorship of boys' work organizations outside of the educational context, that highly organized sport competition for preadolescent boys began its ascendance to present-day heights.

Educators Discourage Highly Competitive Sports

The policy statements of the professional physical education and recreation groups, as well as other leading educators from the 1930s to the 1960s, illustrated their discouragement of highly competitive sports for children. A steady stream of proposals, guidelines, speeches, manuals, and periodical articles containing warnings against too much competition for elementary school children flowed from the ranks of professional educators. The statements reinforced their refusal to condone and administer such programs and were released at various times during the 1930s, 1940s, 1950s, and 1960s when children's sport in association with boys' work groups was making rapid progress.

The first formal statements by professional physical educators and recreational leaders declaring their concern about organized sports for elementary school children came during the early 1930s. The sport programs that were already in the schools came under attack because they were not in line with educational objectives, and only a few of the highly skilled students were able to compete. Later in the decade, a determined effort was made to establish official policies to eliminate all interscholastic competition for elementary-age children both within and outside of the school ("Mid-West District News," 1937). The American Association for Health, Physical Education and Recreation (AAHPER) was quick in approving a resolution against highly organized sports for children at its 1938 convention in Atlanta, Georgia. Its statement, like many of the ones to follow, was based on the strenuous nature of competitive sports.

> Inasmuch as pupils below tenth grade are in the midst of the period of rapid growth, with the consequent bodily weaknesses and maladjustments, partial ossification of bones, mental and emotional stresses, physiological adjustments, and the like, be it therefore resolved that the leaders in the field of physical and health education should do all in their power to discourage interscholastic competition at this age level, because of its strenuous nature. ("Two Important Resolutions," 1939, pp. 488–489)

Before the end of the decade, the Society of State Directors of Physical and Health Educators also prepared a formal statement on the subject. Its policy statement was directed to school board members and school administrators and suggested that interscholastic athletics had no place in elementary schools. The Society specifically discouraged postseason games and championships, extensive travel and "all star" teams, all of which were becoming attractive aspects of organized sport programs outside of the school (Moss and Orion, 1939).

During the 1940s educational psychologists spoke out against the emphasis placed on competition for rewards (Duncan, 1951; Skinner, 1945), and AAHPER adopted another resolution condemning interscholastic competition for the first 8 grades ("Recommendations," 1947).[5] In 1947 a Joint Statement of Policy on Interscholastic Athletics by the National Federation of High School Athletic Associations and AAHPER recommended that the competitive needs of elementary-age children be met with a balanced intramural program (AAHPER and the National Education Association, 1947).[6] Finally, in 1949 AAHPER and its Society of State Directors of Health, Physical Education and Recreation joined with representatives from the Department of Elementary School Principals, National Education Association, and the National Council of State Consultants in Elementary School Principals to form the Joint Committee on Athletic Competition for Children of Elementary and Junior High School Age. Their recommendations were more extensive than any of the previous statements but stayed with the same overall policy of no highly organized competitive programs (AAHPER, 1952).[7] They made an attempt to influence community agencies as well as school personnel but failed to realize that the very aspects of competitive sport they were condemning were the interesting and unique features that were attracting young, enthusiastic, and energetic boys. Leagues, championships, tournaments, travel, spectators, and commercial sponsors were viewed by parents, community leaders, and the boys' work agencies as examples of doing a great service for the children. In addition, young boys wanted to play on a level as close to the "big leagues" as possible and enjoyed the new form of attention provided by sport competition.

Evidence that the formal resolutions and professional policies that were passed during the 1930s and 1940s had some impact on school-sponsored programs became noticeable by the 1950s. Specifically, surveys reflected the transfer of sponsorship

---

5. For a survey of common activities in elementary schools during this time see Schmidt (1944, p. 130).
6. Also see Lowman (1947, p. 635). A large percentage of orthopedists surveyed believed interscholastic competition should be discouraged for young boys because of its strenuous nature. They were particularly critical of swimming, tackle football, wrestling, and ice hockey.
7. They believed elementary schools should only provide intramural playdays, sportsdays, and informal games.

for children's sport programs from the schools to independent boys' work agencies. A National Recreation Association survey in 1950 of 304 departments throughout the United States indicated only 36 approved of high-level competition and championship play ("Competitive Athletics," 1951). The President's Committee on Interschool Competition in the Elementary School, representing AAHPER, found that 60% of the schools surveyed in 1950 had no competition for elementary-age children. Of the 40% that did sponsor some competitive sports, none had competition below the fourth-grade level (Wayman et al., 1950). The shift of support for children's programs was finally recognized and alluded to in a professional recreation journal in 1952, whereby the author successfully captured the nature of the contemporary scene.

> Although elementary schools continue to feel pressure to adopt the characteristics of the high school and college interscholastic sports program, most of the recent developments have taken place outside of the school system. . . . As a result, the recent development of "highly organized competitive athletics" for the elementary school age child has been sponsored largely by private independent groups not connected with the schools or the public recreation department. (National Recreation Congress, 1952, pp. 422–426)

Another survey conducted by Scott (1953) focused on the attitudes of adults toward athletic competition for young children. The results illustrated one of the major reasons that highly organized programs were growing rapidly outside of the educational realm. From a group of more than 1,000 respondents from seven states, which included parents, teachers, and administrators, the majority of all three groups were in favor of intensive competition. The parents were the most favorable, however, and within this group, the fathers were overwhelmingly supportive.[8] With this type of support from parents and even some school personnel, it was evident that professional physical education and recreation groups were competing against unfavorable odds.[9]

Boys' Work Groups Assume Leadership

Although organized sport competition at the elementary school level failed to gain support and therefore faltered after its seemingly robust beginnings during the first decades of the twentieth century, youth sport programs outside of the school grew

---

8. Similar results were found in a survey of parents having boys in Little League Baseball in Fresno, California, in 1951 (Holman, 1951). One hundred percent of the parents regarded the program as beneficial to their sons and repudiated the claims that competition was harmful physically, psychologically, or socially.
9. It should be noted that parents were very concerned that their sons excelled and held their own among the peer group. Sport competition offered a unique setting where young boys could be compared and evaluated with others of the same age.

rapidly in the number of total participants and in the variety of sports offered. With few exceptions, the stimuli behind these programs that arose all over the United States were parents and other interested adults associated with boys' work. Organizations identifying with the boys' work movement selected the promotion, sponsorship, and organization of sports as one of the best things they could do for children. To make children happy and to give them what they wanted became one of their major objectives. They progressed by paying little or no attention to the warnings from professional educators.

The boys' work movement had its beginnings in the last decade of the nineteenth century and resulted from efforts of concerned adults to improve the total environment for children. Citizens of the larger cities became greatly concerned with the effects of industrialization, urbanization, and immigration and, as a result of the general child study movement, were also beginning to realize the basic needs of children. Welfare and reform programs were therefore instituted to improve or alleviate such social problems as child labor, public health and sanitation, lack of wholesome play facilities, crime and delinquency, orphan and dependent children, and crowded housing. But the main factors that led adults to establish programs and organizations to aid the plight of the child were the increased amount of leisure and delinquency and a growing population of underprivileged and neglected children.[10] Leaders of the boys' work movement during the late nineteenth century explored the ideas of organizing boys into clubs and groups to better carry on training programs. These early programs were designed to occupy leisure time to keep the boys out of trouble, keep them off the streets, and evangelize them. Most of these early programs operated under the auspices of a religious education group or the social welfare program of agencies.[11] However, by the beginning of the twentieth century, the boys' work movement developed and achieved separate status from other welfare movements. This development represented the fact that at least a portion of American society had seen the need and value of special agencies to act as conservators and curators of child life.[12]

---

10. Directly related to these developments were the play movement and the child welfare movement. The combination of objectives included in each of these two distinct aspects of the overall childhood reform movement assisted the development of organized sports and additional play facilities for young children.
11. It was realized early in boys' work that sport-related clubs and teams served as a better medium for organization than the earlier attempts at trying to reach large masses of boys at one time.
12. Basically, the boys' work groups aided the overall society by protecting children through their dependency period, including children into the culture, and supplementing the family by providing for special needs and by sponsoring specific services. The work groups were committed to a specific social obligation toward children not yet accepted by the whole society. Consequently, boys' work agencies began to provide services in education, health, and recreation, all of which they believed could be improved by organized sport programs. See Mangold (1924) and Wickenden (1960).

The use and encouragement of play, games, sports, and general recreational activities began quite early in the boys' work programs. As the emphasis moved from soul saving to one of boy guidance and concern for the "whole person" during the 1920s, organized sports became more and more popular as an acceptable method of filling leisure-time hours.[13] New organizations for boys came into existence as separate enterprises. They were recreational rather than evangelical in nature, primarily because of the character-building values thought to be inherent to play, games, and sport. The concepts of clean fun as a character builder and of play as creative education, rather than just something to keep boys out of trouble, led to the formation of more playgrounds, gymnasiums, swimming pools, and outdoor athletic fields. Accordingly, civic groups, fraternal orders, and businesses joined the ranks of established boys' work organizations that already included religious bodies, philanthropic groups, national and state governments, and general child welfare groups in sponsoring and promoting sporting activities for the younger set. The primary objective of the new sponsors was to use sport as a preventive measure for juvenile delinquency.[14]

During the 1920s and 1930s highly organized competitive sport programs for young boys began to be established outside the realm of the educational system by local groups representing the fundamental boys' work beliefs. As early as 1924 the Cincinnati Community Service started city baseball tournaments for boys under 13. Likewise, Milwaukee organized its "Stars of Yesterday" baseball leagues and began sponsoring a "Kid's Baseball School" in 1936. The *Los Angeles Times* conducted its Junior Pentathlon for the first time in 1928, the Southern California Tennis Association established its junior program two years later, and tackle football for boys under the age of 12 began in the Denver area in 1927 and in Philadelphia three years later. Two further developments that occurred in 1939, however, did more for the overall growth of this new trend in sport than the others.

---

13. Sport competition was believed to enhance personality adjustment and creative living in society. In addition, since boys' workers wanted to aid the transition from childhood to adulthood, they sponsored sport programs that combined association on a peer basis with adult leadership. See DeGraff (1933, p. 2) and Stone (1932, p. 5).

14. The belief that a boy busy with sports had little time to get into trouble influenced many organizations in local communities to begin sponsoring boys' sports. Psychological and sociological knowledge of the time indicated that problems of delinquency originated in early childhood and not during the actual time of delinquent acts. Therefore, it was deemed important to extend the age range lower for a positive delinquency prevention program. Civic clubs such as Rotary, Lions, Kiwanis, and Jaycees; fraternal orders like the Elks and Moose; and businesses such as Winchester, Curtis Publishing, General Electric, Pratt and Whitney, and John Wanamaker all turned to sport sponsorship in the interest of protecting young children from crime and providing them with wholesome alternatives for gang life in the streets. For more information, see Engle (1919), North (1931), Reckless and Smith (1932), and Shanas (1942).

The first development was an article entitled "*Life* Goes to a Kid's Football Game" that appeared in *Life* magazine. It concerned the Denver Young American League and included color photographs and descriptions depicting the values of such an activity. Themes such as nationalism, courage, character, the need for similar programs in other communities, and the disgrace of "turning yellow" were discussed in the article. The second major development in 1939 was the introduction of Little League Baseball in Williamsport, Pennsylvania. Formed by Carl Stotz, a local businessman, the organization grew from a few local teams at its inception to more than 300 leagues in 11 states by 1949. Part of Little League's success can also be linked to the publication of an article entitled "Small Boy's Dream Come True" in the *Saturday Evening Post* (Paxton, 1949). This article, like the *Life* article 10 years before, included beautiful colored photographs, proclaimed the values of such a program for small boys, and emphasized the rewards reaped by communities that had already established Little League teams. The author was correct in observing that "the Little League's chief mission in life is to give a lot of pleasure to a lot of little boys. With its realistic simulation of big-league playing conditions, with its cheering crowds, it is a small boy's baseball dream come true" (p. 140). From this point on, the "little league" concept spread to almost every sport on the American scene.

Interest in providing sporting competition for young children began to spread to a variety of other youth-related agencies after the 1940s. As continued emphasis was placed on providing fun and amusement for young boys and as organizations found ulterior motives for promoting sport competition, the sponsorship of children's sports began to come from previously unexpected sources. Nationally known business firms, professional sport organizations, Olympic committees, and colleges initiated particular aspects of sport sponsorship for young boys. Sponsorship came in the form of funds, facilities, workers, advertisements, and equipment. These new sponsors joined previously established sponsors such as civic groups, churches, community councils, local merchants, and some of the older youth membership organizations. They saw a chance to assist the development of young boys but, at the same time, realized that boys' sport programs could help them as well. This new sidelight to sponsorship, the idea of a "two-way-street" or what could be termed a form of "ludic symbiosis" in this context, differed radically from the earlier voluntary groups' support and added the aspects of big business and more-pronounced competition to sport for young boys.

By the 1960s highly organized sport competition for preadolescents had grown to encompass millions of American boys. Little League Baseball, Pop Warner Football, and Biddy Basketball were joined on the national level by similar developments in other sports, such as Pee Wee Hockey and Little Britches Rodeo.[15] Most of these national sporting bodies had member teams and leagues throughout the United States,

---

15. Some of the other children's sports were Midget Lacrosse, Junior Ski Jumping, Junior Nordic Skiing, National Junior Tennis League, Junior National Standard Racing, and the Junior Special Olympics for retarded children.

but the youthful participants in baseball, football, basketball, and other sports did not necessarily have to belong to one of the national controlling bodies. When this occurred, local boys' sports organizations were often just referred to as midget leagues, the "lollypop set," boys' leagues, youth leagues, junior leagues, small fry leagues, or tiny tot leagues. The important factor, however, was that regardless of title, sponsor, or organizational structure, young boys below the age of 12 were being introduced to highly organized competitive sports in just about every community in the United States.

As indicated, radical changes occurred in the sponsorship of boys' sports programs. By the 1960s the most prominent sponsors could be classified in six different categories: (a) private national sport bodies such as Little League Baseball; (b) youth-serving organizations composed of adult members such as the Jaycees; (c) youth membership organizations composed of child membership such as the YMCA; (d) youth sport development organizations such as Junior Golf; (e) quasi-commercial organizations like Ford's Punt, Pass and Kick; and (f) an individual or community like Jim's Small Fry's or Riverdale Junior Baseball. An analysis of each sponsor's stated objectives revealed the same idea of sport's inherent values that had existed since the turn of the century. Each sponsor claimed to support children's sport for one or more of the following reasons: physical fitness, citizenship, character, sportsmanship, leadership, fair play, good health, democratic living, and teamwork. It also was evident that a few of the sponsors took advantage of the "two-way-street" concept. Boys' sports were used as training grounds for future athletes, as methods to prevent juvenile delinquency, as proselytizing agents to attract new members, as methods of advertisement, as means of identification and glory, and as methods for direct financial gain.

Parents, too, began to get more deeply involved than ever before with the sports of their children. Eager mothers and fathers devoted more time to sports and actually began to take part in the sports themselves. Many reasons could be given to explain this increased interest of parents, but three major causes were believed to be the increasing awareness of the athlete as a viable professional endeavor, overly competitive mothers and fathers, and parents' desire of "sure victory" for their children. Earlier in the history of children's sports, parents were content to be only spectators, but the decades of the 1950s and 1960s became an era of parental entrance, with their child, into competition. Instances of parents constructing racers for the Soap Box Derby, fine-tuning engines for youthful go-cart drivers, and engineering new gear ratios for bike racers appeared as boys' sports became increasingly important to the entire family. This new emphasis placed on children's sport by the family unit, combined with the entrance of big business and other high-pressure tactics after the early 1950s, caused even the most avid sponsors to begin to take a serious look at what they had developed.

The literature after 1950 concerning highly organized competitive sports for young boys reflected the growing concern for the welfare of the young competitors.[16]

Nationally circulated journals, magazines, and newspapers carried articles emphasizing the pros and cons of children's sport in an attempt to illustrate the current status of the ever-growing youth leagues and to present the most recent findings related to the subject. Similarly, those in favor of the highly competitive situations used the mass media to advertise the goodness and need for such programs and even went so far as to suggest new organizations in previously unchildlike sports such as yachting, motor boating, and airplane flying. Likewise, those strongly opposed to highly organized sports attacked their obvious detriments via the printed word. The issue became increasingly visible as the debate continued, but even in the 1970s, youth sport programs were showing no signs of decline. In fact, the decade of the 1970s ushered in a new and eager generation of youthful competitors.

Conclusions

The rise of highly organized sport competition for preadolescent boys was an important phase of the total involvement of Americans with sport and has blossomed into a new national sporting trend. Lowering the age for entrance into sport indicated the faith Americans had in it and reflected a desire to provide the young with something thought to be beneficial for their overall development. Besides illustrating the breadth and depth of the nation's involvement with sport, the guided entrance of children into sporting competition also influenced the overall growth of sport. Young children carried their interests and desires with them into adult life and subsequently passed them along to their own children. In addition, the joy, freeness, and innocence of the youthful competitors came to be seen as desirable characteristics of sport itself. These attributes were sought as highly desired traits by the adult population. The older portion of the population attached sport to the image of youth and consequently engaged in a variety of sports beyond the time when they normally would have ceased participation.

The provision of highly organized competitive sports for boys below the age of 12 and the accompanying introduction of more sporting opportunities and facilities for all young children was one of the most significant social and cultural events of recent times. It contributed an additional dimension to the age of childhood and marked the beginning of a new era in American sport. An analysis of the origins of this trend, however, is also important outside of its contributions to the realm of sport because the history of the developments in childhood is central to the study of overall social change and human behavior. The growth of sport for young boys illustrated a change in parental authority as well as an alteration in general child-rearing practices. The fact that sport teams were usually organized by age or weight groupings indicated

---

16. It is interesting to note that the *Readers' Guide to Periodical Literature* did not include a topical heading for "Sports for Children" until Volume 22 (March 1959–February 1961), p. 1564.

the increased sensitivity to the various stages of childhood and became an important step in the growth of child welfare. Children's sport organizations led to changes in the American family structure and, in many instances, added a new aspect to the socialization of children. In addition, the sponsorship and use of sport by boys' work agencies contributed to the belief that Americans should organize the life and activities of their children. Finally, the degree to which children's sports became organized mirrored an often-proclaimed American characteristic of being overly regimented, businesslike, and competitive.

References

American Association for Health, Physical Education and Recreation and the National Education Association. (1947). *Cardinal athletic principles*. Washington, DC: Author.

American Association for Health, Physical Education and Recreation (Joint Committee on Athletic Competition for Children of Elementary and Junior High School Age). (1952). *Desirable athletic competition for children*. Washington, DC: Author.

Competitive athletics for boys under twelve—Survey. (1951). *Recreation, 45*, 489–491.

DeGraff, H. O. (1933, March). Social factors in boys' work. *Association Boys' Work Journal*, p. 2.

Duncan, R. O. (1951). The growth and development approach. *Journal of Health, Physical Education and Recreation, 22*, 36–37.

Engle, W. L. (1919). Supervised amusement cuts juvenile crime by 96%. *American City, 20*, 515–517.

Holman, H. (1951). *Play ball: A study of Little League Baseball in operation*. Fresno, CA: Recreation Department.

Life goes to kid's football game. (1939, October), *Life*, pp. 90–93.

Lowman, C. L. (1947). The vulnerable age. *Journal of Health and Physical Education, 18*, 635; 693.

Mangold, G. B. (1924). *Problems of child welfare*. New York: Macmillan.

Mid-west district news. (1937). *Journal of Health and Physical Education, 8*, 382.

Moss, B., and Orion, W. H. (1939). The public school program in health, physical education, and recreation. *Journal of Health and Physical Education, 10*, 435–439; 494.

National Recreation Congress. (1952). Are highly competitive sports desirable for juniors? Conclusions from the committee on highly organized sports and athletics for boys twelve and under. *Recreation, 46*, 422–426.

North, C. C. (1931). *The community and social welfare*. New York: Recreation Department.

Paxton, H. T. (1949, May). Small boy's dream come true. *Saturday Evening Post*, pp. 26–27; 137–140.

Reckless, W. C., and Smith, M. (1932). *Juvenile delinquency*. New York: Recreation Department.

Recommendations from the Seattle convention workshop. (1947). *Journal of Health and Physical Education, 18*, 429–432; 556–557.

Schmidt, C. A. (1944). Elementary school physical education. *Journal of Health and Physical Education, 15*, 130–131; 161.

Scott, P. M. (1953). Attitudes toward athletic competition in elementary schools. *Research Quarterly, 24*, 352–361.

Shanas, E. (1942). *Recreation and delinquency*. Chicago: Recreation Commission.

Skinner, C. E. (1945). *Elementary educational psychology*. New York: Prentice-Hall.

Stone, W. L. (1931). *What is boys' work?* New York: Recreation Department.

Stone, W. L. (1932). *The place of activities in boys' work. Work with boys*. New York: Recreation Department.

Two important resolutions. (1938). *Journal of Health and Physical Education, 9*, 488–489.

Wayman, F., Hager, R., Hartwig, H., Houston, L., LaSalle, D., and McNeely, S. (1950). Report of the President's Committee on Interschool Competition in the Elementary School. *Journal of Health, Physical Education and Recreation, 21*, 279–280; 313–314.

Wickenden, E. (1960). Frontiers in voluntary welfare services. In E. Ginzberg (Ed.), *The nation's children: Vol. 3. Problems and prospects* (pp. 124–147). New York: Columbia University Press.

A History of Highly Competitive Sport for American Children

David K. Wiggins, George Mason University

American children have always participated in their own play activities, games, and sports. Regardless of their economic station in life, living conditions, and physical abilities, children in this country carved out a world of sport that contributed to their overall growth as human beings while providing the sense of accomplishment and enjoyment necessary to be functioning members of society. Children of both sexes in such diverse settings as New York City, Puritan New England, southern slave communities, and western frontier towns organized sporting activities free from the surveillance of adults who did not exercise the same degree of control over young people as their contemporary counterparts. Marbles, crack-the-whip, capture-the-flag, soccer, variations of baseball, and a host of other games were played with unabated enthusiasm by children on city streets, urban sandlots, and open fields.

Children in this country could eventually choose between their own organized sports and those directed and controlled by adults. By the latter stages of the nineteenth century, adults were abandoning their traditional laissez-faire approach toward children's activities and establishing large-scale sport programs for America's youth (particularly boys). These initial programs came about largely through the efforts of the Young Men's Christian Association (YMCA). Established by evangelical Protestants in England in 1851 and transported to this country prior to the Civil War, the YMCA eventually responded to the precarious position of children in an increasingly industrialized American society by organizing sport leagues for boys and offering classes in physical culture.

By the beginning of the twentieth century various agencies—including playgrounds, schools, and national youth organizations—followed the YMCA's example and began sponsoring recreational activities and sport programs for children. These programs were part of the progressive era's effort to control the behavior and contribute to the moral development of children through organized play activities and sports administered by reform-minded adults. The public school athletic league and other reformist organizations established by various educators, recreation leaders, and philanthropists were intentionally designed to inculcate children with a particular set of values necessary to function properly in a democratic society.

The 1920s witnessed the emergence of children's sport programs that were decidedly different from those progressive reformers established. These programs, rather than ideologically based or intentionally reformist, were usually highly competitive and geared toward elite performers and championship play. Tellingly, the movement toward increased competitiveness drew heavy criticism from professional recreation leaders and physical educators who had previously been supporters of youth sport programs. The disenchantment of professional educators resulted in their eventual relinquishment of highly organized youth sport programs to various business firms, colleges, Olympic committees, professional sport organizations, and individual or community service groups. The withdrawal of professional educators' support from youth sport programs did not curb the debate over the value of highly competitive athletics for children. On the contrary, the last several decades have seen a continuing dialogue, centering on the negative effects or positive outgrowths of youth sport programs, among medical doctors, professional educators, and other sundry groups.

Christian Manliness, Playgrounds, and Reform Minded Adults

In the mid-nineteenth century, American Protestants ignited a movement commonly known as Muscular Christianity. Alarmed by the debilitating effects of industrialization and other changes in American life, well-known clergymen and eastern intellectuals abandoned their traditional animosity toward vigorous physical activity and promoted the interconnectedness between sport and spiritual sacredness. Thomas Wentworth Higginson, Oliver Wendell Holmes and other advocates of Christian manliness associated achievement with a vigorous childhood that stressed the Greek ideal of the harmonious development of mind, body, and spirit. It was imperative for "manly" youth to participate in sport while exercising Christian virtues and such character habits as self-control, candidness, and honesty (Lewis, 1966; Lucas, 1968; Rader, 1983).

The transmission of Christian manliness to American boys took place primarily through such well-known pieces of sports fiction as Thomas Hughes's *Tom Brown's School Days* (1857); G. W. Bankes's *A Day of My Life; or, Everyday Experiences at Eton* (1877); Bracebridge Heming's *Eton School Days* (1864); and Robert Grant's *Jack Hall, or The School Days of an American Boy* (1887). The YMCA, however, was the most important institution associated with the Muscular Christianity movement. Originally opposed to organized sport for children, the YMCA was luring more young men and boys into its program toward the latter years of the nineteenth century by establishing classes in gymnastics and promoting highly competitive athletics (Boyer, 1978; Forbush, 1901, 1904; Rader, 1983).

Although several people would be responsible for this transformation within the YMCA, it was Luther Gulick who spearheaded the organization's new interest in games and highly competitive sport. Born of missionary parents in Honolulu in 1865, Gulick was always committed to the basic tenets of Muscular Christianity and the compatibility between physical development and spiritual sacredness. Gulick's belief in Christian manliness was largely an outgrowth of the evolutionary theory of play he developed with his former mentor, G. Stanley Hall, the famous genetic psychologist from Clark University. The two men theorized that play activities of preadolescent children consisted of the same physical activities that had allowed primitive men and women to survive in a hostile environment. Such individual activities as running and hurling objects at targets were both relics of the struggle for survival and natural acts necessary for the physical and psychological development of young children. Older children's more-advanced games, such as football, basketball, and baseball, combined the earliest hunting instinct and the more recent instinct of cooperation while serving as the primary vehicle in developing moral character. Participation in team sports, therefore, provided an ideal opportunity for adults to develop in boys self-control, loyalty, obedience, selflessness, and other character traits rapidly vanishing from the increasingly industrialized American society (Dorgan, 1934; Forbush, 1901; Gerber, 1971; Gulick, 1898, 1899).

Gulick incorporated the new evolutionary theory of play in different ways at the YMCA Training School in Springfield, Massachusetts. He spearheaded the establishment of a graduate diploma in physical education. He also organized a sport program at the school for young men and adolescent boys. Perhaps most important, Gulick developed a pioneering course in the psychology of play, a class in which students were encouraged to create new games and sports appropriate for specific age groups (Dorgan, 1934; Forbush, 1901; Gerber, 1971).

Gulick did not expend all his energy on the YMCA. He also contributed mightily, along with such other reform-minded adults as Joseph Lee, Henry Curtis, Jane Addams, and Clark Hetherington, to the playground movement in the early twentieth century. Resulting primarily from rapid urbanization and its attendant problems, the playground movement had as one of its primary purposes the moral development of children through sports. Progressive reformers, through the Public School Athletic League and a variety of other programs, organized play and sports activities to develop character among young people of both sexes and different ethnic groups while socializing them into an increasingly complex industrialized society (Cavallo, 1981; Goodman, 1979; Guttmann, 1988; Hardy, 1982; Jable, 1979).

Highly Competitive Sport Outside the Educational Domain

The sport programs established for children by progressive reformers were idealistic in nature and intentionally designed to influence social behavior and moral development. The same cannot be said of the highly competitive youth sport programs that emerged during the 1920s and 1930s. A result of both the continuing interest of adults in the welfare of children and increasing popularity of sport in American society, these programs were organized for boys only and usually involved elite championships, all-star play, and close parental involvement. Examples of these programs are many and varied. In 1924 the Cincinnati Community Service organized a Junior Baseball tournament for boys under age 13. The tournament involved 84 teams and received endorsement from Judge Kenesaw Mountain Landis, the Commissioner of Major League Baseball. In 1927 Denver organized a tackle football program for boys under age 12. The *Los Angeles Times* established its Junior Pentathlon program a year later. In 1930 Pop Warner began play in Philadelphia and the Catholic Youth Organization began its junior tennis program with sponsorship from the Southern California Tennis Association. The Milwaukee Recreation Department established its "Stars of Yesterday" baseball program in 1936 for boys under 15. Finally, in 1939 Carl Stotz founded his famous Little League Baseball program in Williamsport, Pennsylvania (Berryman, 1975; Cloyd, 1952; Monroe, 1946; Paxton, 1949).

No sooner had these programs been established when professional educators, particularly those from the health, physical education, and recreation fields, began criticizing and passing resolutions condemning highly competitive sports for children. Their concerns usually revolved around questions of notoriety, commercialism, intensity of competition, elite championship play, and emotional and physiological damage incurred by young athletes. For example, in 1938 the American Association for Health, Physical Education and Recreation (AAHPER) passed a resolution at its national convention disapproving of youth sport programs. The Society of State Directors of Physical and Health Education made official announcements in both 1938 and 1946 denouncing highly competitive sport in elementary and junior high schools. In 1947 AAHPER issued another resolution condemning interscholastic sports for children below the ninth grade and also made a joint policy statement with the National Federation of High School Athletic Associations arguing for the development of intramural programs at the elementary school level. The following year the Joint Committee on Athletic Competition for Children of Elementary and Junior High School Age—an organization made up of representatives from AAHPER and other groups—recommended the abolishment of highly competitive youth sport programs. In the early 1950s similar proclamations were made by such groups as the National Recreation Congress, National Conference on Physical Education for Children of Elementary School Age, and National Conference of Program Planning in Games and

Sport for Boys of School Age (AAHPER, 1938,1947,1952; Lowman, 1947; Moss and Orion, 1939; National Recreation Congress, 1952; Wayman et al., 1950).

The policy statements of professional educators ultimately contributed to the elimination of children's interschool athletic competitions. Professionals did not stop, however, the growth of already existing youth sport programs or the creation of new ones outside the educational setting. By the latter half of the 1960s, children's highly competitive sport programs were being sponsored by such organizations as business firms, religious groups, community service organizations, Olympic committees, colleges, and professional sport organizations (Berryman, 1975).

The continuing support of youth sport programs outside the educational setting resulted from a number of interrelated factors. One of the primary reasons was the lasting belief of parents that children benefited in a number of different ways from participation in highly competitive sport programs. Although cognizant of some of the negatives associated with youth sport programs, the large majority of parents believed that highly competitive athletics contributed to the fitness level, overall character development, and sportsmanship of children (Scott, 1953; Seymour, 1956; Skubic, 1955, 1956). Another factor in the continued growth of youth sport programs was the increased media coverage and adulation enjoyed by outstanding athletes, and American society's obsession with highly competitive sport. Children, and their parents, were aware of this adulation and the logical consequence was an early involvement in sport that might ultimately lead to their own fame and fortune.

The Quest for Racial and Gender Equality in Youth Sport

The growth of highly competitive youth sport programs during the middle decades of the twentieth century was not a uniform development or devoid of the racial and gender realities of American culture. African American boys in the south were similar to the older members of their community in that the majority of their sport programs were conducted on a segregated basis. The region's rigid caste system and tradition of racial segregation forced African American boys to participate on their own teams and in their own leagues in virtually every sport. The unfortunate consequence of these programs were that African American boys were denied the opportunity to participate in championship tournaments sponsored by national youth sport organizations.

Perhaps the most visible example of the obstacles faced by African American boys in southern youth sport programs occurred in Little League Baseball. In the first 15 years of its existence, Little League Baseball seemingly made no effort to ensure that African American children in the south were allowed the same opportunities to play as their white counterparts. Adopting the approach of most national organizations during this period, Little League Baseball allowed its southern chapters to bar African American children from state and regional tournaments without any signs of protest.

This approach did not change until 1955 (just a year after the passage of the famous Brown v. Board of Education desegregation case) when National Little League officials interceded on behalf of African American players from Pensacola, Florida. Sam Lacy, the well-known sportswriter of the *Baltimore Afro-American*, explained in his autobiography that 11 teams in northwest Florida that year refused to play the All-Black Pensacola J.C.'s. Almost immediately, National Little League officials disqualified the 11 teams and declared the Pensacola J.C.'s the district champions. The result was that the Pensacola J.C.'s traveled to Orlando where it became the first African American team to ever play in a Little League state tournament in the south (Lacy, 1998).

The path to equality in highly organized youth sport was even a longer process for girls than it was for African American boys. For years, girls were not allowed to participate in youth sport programs because of the continuing belief about their supposed emotional and physiological weaknesses. That would all begin to change during the 1970s, however, as a result of a combination of the Equal Rights Amendment, Title IX and a host of changing social forces pervading American society. Again, Little League Baseball serves as the most visible example of the obstacles girls had to overcome in order to participate in highly organized sport. In May 1973 Jenny Fuller, a young ballplayer from California, wrote a letter to President Richard Nixon lamenting the fact she was not allowed to participate on her local Little League team because of gender. The Office of Civil Rights responded to Fuller by explaining that steps were being taken to handle such discriminatory practices. Coinciding with Fuller's letter were a number of unsuccessful lawsuits brought against the National Little League by girls who had been denied an opportunity to participate for their local teams. The strongest of these suits was filed by a young girl named Carolyn King and the Ypsilanti, Michigan, American League and the city of Ypsilanti. This particular suit, like so many of those involving Little League Baseball and questions of sexual discrimination, centered on local and national jurisdiction. After King beat out more than 100 boys for a position as center fielder, the Ypsilanti City Council ordered the local League to either let her participate or suffer the loss of city financial aid, staff, and facilities. The local League acceded to the Council's order. The National Little League responded, in turn, by revoking the local League's charter (Jennings, 1981).

The Carolyn King affair in Ypsilanti preceded by a couple of months the sexual discrimination case that would ultimately lead to the desegregation of Little League Baseball. Maria Pepe, a young player from Hoboken, New Jersey, experienced the same pangs of discrimination many other girls suffered when she was denied the opportunity to participate on her local Little League team. The uniqueness of this case, however, is that it would culminate in an investigation by the New Jersey Division of Civil Rights and eventually in the integration of Little League Baseball. The Civil Rights Division, at the request of the Essex Chapter of the National Organization for Women (NOW), conducted an investigation in November 1973 on behalf of Pepe and a number of other girls who wanted to participate in Little League Baseball. During six days of deliberation, the National Little League defended its segregationist policies by having expert witnesses present evidence confirming that highly competitive sport was harmful to girls both emotionally and physiologically. The key witness for the National Little League was Creighton Hale, who was executive vice-president of the organization and an exercise physiologist. Hale cited a number of studies claiming that girls had slower reaction time and weaker bones than those of boys and, therefore, were unsuited for vigorous competitive sport. Hale also argued that girls could harm their breasts while participating in competitive athletics (Jennings, 1981).

The Civil Rights Division countered with its own expert testimony. Psychiatrist Antonia Giancotti claimed that mutual participation in sport by boys and girls contributed positively to the development of mental health. Joseph Torg, a pediatric-orthopedic surgeon, contended that the bone strength of preadolescent girls was actually greater than that of boys of comparable age. Torg also criticized Creighton Hale for basing his testimony on studies that examined adult cadavers rather than those of children (Jennings, 1981).

The testimony given by Torg and others proved crucial in the decision handed down by Sylvia Pressler, the Division's hearing officer. Pressler concluded that differences in athletic performance between girls and boys under the age of 12 resulted from an individual rather than "sexual class basis." Most important, she ruled that because Little League Baseball was given public financial support and used public accommodations, "it was indeed subject to state and federal laws preventing discrimination" (Jennings, 1981, p. 85).

Little League Baseball challenged Pressler's ruling by appealing to New Jersey's superior court in March 1974. Little League argued that its federal charter officially prohibited girls from participation and that New Jersey law allowed only boys on its local teams. Little League Baseball's arguments proved futile and ultimately unconvincing. The state's superior court ruled on March 29, 1974, that a local league chartered by Little League, Inc. was not exempt from federal legislation barring sexual discrimination. The conflict was finally put to rest in December 1974 when Congress amended the National Little League Charter, allowing girls as well as boys to participate (Jennings, 1981).

The decision Congress handed down did not translate into immediate desegregation of leagues across the country or stop people from expressing their opposition to girls' participation in highly competitive sport programs. Increasingly, however, girls found their way onto both integrated and nonintegrated teams in a variety of different sports at various levels of competition. The last two decades have seen a growth in the number of girls participating in youth sport programs sponsored by such diverse organizations as the United States Olympic Development Committee, Amateur Athletic Union, and the American Alliance for Health, Physical Education, Recreation and Dance (Figler and Whitaker, 1991).

Academicians, Professional Educators, and the Youth Sport Phenomenon

The desegregation of youth sport programs would coincide with an outpouring of interest in children's sport on the part of academicians and professional educators. The expansion of youth sport programs, combined with recognition of the importance of sport as a social institution, caused educators and scholars from such disciplinary areas as sport psychology and sport sociology to consider the implications of children's participation in highly competitive athletics. One of the most visible indicators of this interest was the increasing number of conferences that included posters, verbal presentations, and symposiums devoted specifically to youth sport participation. Such national organizations as the North American Society for the Psychology of Sport and Physical Activity (NASPSPA), the North American Society for Sport Sociology (NASSS), the National Association for Physical Education in Higher Education (NAPEHE), and the American Alliance for Health, Physical Education, Recreation and Dance (AAHPERD) began including sessions at their annual conferences devoted to some aspect of children's involvement in sport. The 1989 NASPSPA Conference, as just one example, devoted a session to "children in sport and physical activity." Included in the session were presentations on topics ranging from the relationship of parental attitudes and levels of intrinsic motivation in young athletes to reasons for dropping out of youth sport programs (NASPSPA, 1989).

Even more significant were the organization of conferences and workshops devoted exclusively to children's participation in sport. In 1973 a conference was held at Queens University in Canada entitled "The Child in Sport and Physical Activity." Organized by John Albinson and George Andrew, two physical educators from the host university, the conference took a multidimensional approach in that it included papers from such disciplinary areas as motor learning, exercise physiology, motor development, psychology of sport, sports medicine, and sport sociology (1976). Four years later a similar conference was organized by Frank Smoll and Ronald Smith at the University of Washington entitled "Contemporary Research on Youth Sports." The conference was unique for a number of reasons, including the fact it was jointly sponsored and partly financed by the Safeco Insurance Company and involved all data-based presentations rather than speculative or opinion-oriented studies. Although business organizations had always provided financial support to youth sport programs, very seldom had a company such as Safeco helped fund a research conference devoted to the subject. The conference presentations touched on various topics dealing with youth sport participation and included as participants such well-known academicians as Jerry Thomas, Glyn Roberts, Lawrence Rarick, Tara Scanlan, Robert Malina, and Michael Passer (Smoll and Smith, 1978).

In 1985 the Big Ten Committee on Institutional Cooperation held a symposium at Michigan State University entitled "Effects of Competitive Sports on Children and Youth." Conceived of by leaders of the Youth Sport Institute at Michigan State and supported by several of the university's academic units, this symposium brought together noted scholars from several disciplines to share their research and knowledge relating to the effects of highly competitive sport on children (Brown and Branta, 1988). In the same year, the American Orthopaedic Society for Sports Medicine (AOSSM) held a workshop in Indianapolis, Indiana, entitled "Strength Training for the Prepubescent Athlete." This workshop, which included as participants physicians, physiologists, and other sports medicine professionals, focused on the ramifications of youth strength-training programs from a variety of disciplinary perspectives (Cahill, 1988). In 1990 the AOSSM held yet another workshop in Peoria, Illinois, addressing intensive training and participation in youth sports. Perhaps broader in scope and certainly different in format from its symposium three years earlier, this workshop included as participants some of the most noted scholars in the country who analyzed the various risks and benefits of youth sports from psychological, sociological, physiological, and clinical viewpoints. Participants intended to maximize the positive contributions and minimize the negative outcomes of highly competitive youth sport programs (Cahill and Pearl, 1993).

Another indication of professional interest in youth sports was the establishment of guidelines and conduction of large-scale legislative studies. In 1976 AAHPERD led the drive toward healthier and more educationally sound youth sport programs by establishing the National Association for Sport and Physical Education Youth Sports Task Force. Made up of experts from the recreation, medical, and physical education professions, the task force analyzed the effects of children's participation in highly competitive sport programs and provided suggestions as to how those programs could be more satisfying and beneficial. Perhaps the most notable and far-reaching accomplishment of the task force was the drafting of a "Bill of Rights for Young Athletes," a document that attempts to guarantee, among other things, that children are given the right to have fun, enjoy equitable treatment, and share in the administration of youth sport programs (Martens and Seefeldt, 1979).

Larger in scope than AAHPERD's Task Force was Michigan's Joint Legislation Study Committee (JLSC) on Youth Sport Programs. An outgrowth of the state's concern about the educational value of youth sport participation, this special six-member committee conducted, in collaboration with several Michigan universities, a longitudinal study assessing the impact of highly competitive sports on the development of children. The results of the study, which were announced in November 1978, indicated that enjoyment and the chance to increase skill level were children's primary motivations for participation in youth sport programs. Coaches, administrators, and other support personnel indicated that their involvement in youth sports came about either because of their children's participation in the program or because they provided special skills needed by the particular organization (JLSC, 1976, 1978a, 1978b).

Among the most significant outgrowths of the longitudinal study was the establishment of the Youth Sport Institute at Michigan State University in 1978. Under the leadership of Vern Seefeldt, the institute was founded to ensure that children benefited positively from participation in youth sport programs. In an effort to achieve that goal, the institute has conducted scientific research on children's sport participation; provided in-service education, clinics, and workshops for youth sport administrators; and disseminated educational materials to parents, coaches, and officials involved in children's competitive sport programs (JLSC, 1976, 1978a, 1978b).

The Youth Sport Institute at Michigan State set the stage for similar types of programs both inside and outside the formal educational setting. The National Council of Youth Sports Directors (NCYSD) was established in 1979 to secure mutual cooperation among executives of youth sport programs. Originally sponsored in cooperation with the Athletic Institute, the NCYSD included on its membership roll such groups as the American Amateur Baseball Congress, American Youth Soccer Organization, Babe Ruth Baseball, National Federation of State High School Associations, National Junior Tennis League, Pop Warner Football, U.S.A. Wrestling, U.S. Field Hockey Association, and YMCA (NCYSD, n.d.). The North American Youth Sport Institute (NASYSI) was organized the same year as the NCYSD in Kernersville, North Carolina. The NAYSI took on a number of projects, including the sponsorship of research studies and clinics for youth sport coaches (Cox, 1982). The National Youth Sports Coaches Association (NYSCA), the officially endorsed program of the National Recreation and Parks Association, was organized in 1981 to train youth sport coaches, educate the general public about youth sport programs, and conduct research on all aspects of youth sports (NYSCA, n.d.). Finally, in 1981 Rainer Martens, a well-known sport psychologist and now head of Human Kinetics Publishers, officially founded the American Coaching Effectiveness Program (ACEP). Certainly one of the most extensive coaching education programs in the country, ACEP offers courses that provide both the theoretical underpinnings and knowledge of sport techniques and fundamentals (ACEP, 1984).

Informing Parents, Participants, and the Public through Publications and Research

A growth in publications and research studies dealing with various aspects of highly competitive sports for children coincided with the establishment of institutes and coaching programs. Included in these studies and publications were a plethora of popular essays on youth sports written by well-known sportswriters, Little League parents, and famous professional athletes. These articles, which usually centered on questions concerning the value of youth sport programs, have appeared in such popular magazines as *Ladies Home Journal*, *The Atlantic Monthly*, *U.S. News and World Report*, *Today's Health*, *Sports Illustrated*, *Changing Times*, *Better Homes and Gardens*, *Look*, *Life*, and *New York Times Magazine* (Feller, 1956; Roberts, 1975; Tarkenton, 1970; Underwood, 1975).

Just as informative as the aforementioned essays were several reminiscences and popular books written on various aspects of youth sport programs. Catherine and

Loren Broadus, parents of three former Little League players, describe the problems associated with youth sport programs in their book *Laughing and Crying with Little League* (1972). Al Rosen, a former major league player, provides a personal view of Little League Baseball in his book *Baseball and Your Boy* (1967). Rosen argues, among other things, that Little League Baseball can be a very positive experience for children who have supportive parents and enthusiastic as well as competent coaches. Emily Greenspan provides an insightful analysis of highly competitive youth sport programs in her book, *Little Winners: Inside the World of the Child Sports Star* (1983). She describes in detail the trials and tribulations of young athletes, including the effects of sport participation on family relationships. Martin Ralbovsky, a writer for the *New York Times*, provides a provocative oral history of the Schenectady, New York, Little League champions of 1954 in his book, *Destiny's Darlings* (1974). Ralbovsky's story of the Schenectady Club, which was based on interviews with nine players and the manager of the team 20 years after they captured the championship, was a mixture of positive reminiscences and lasting disillusionment. Larry Yablonsky and Jonathon Brower provide a journalistic summary of a Little League program in California in their 1979 book, *The Little League Game*. The authors suggest that changes should be made in Little League, including restrictions on the number of innings pitched by one player, elimination of scorebooks, and players' selection of coaches.

The more popular literature on children's sport was counterbalanced by a large body of publications emanating from previously mentioned conferences, professional organizations, institutes, and coaching education programs. For instance, John Albinson and George Andrew took seven papers from the conference they organized at Queens University in 1973 and edited a book entitled *Child in Sport and Physical Activity* (1976). In a similar vein, Frank Smoll and Ronald Smith published a collection of papers from their 1977 youth sport conference at the University of Washington. Entitled *Psychological Perspectives in Youth Sports* (1978), the book includes essays on everything from "Social Learning of Violence in Minor Hockey" to "Children's Assignment of Responsibility for Winning and Losing." Rainer Martens and Vern Seefeldt summarized the results of AAHPERD's 1976 Youth Sports Task Force in a book entitled *Guidelines for Children's Sports* (1979). Michigan State's Youth Sport Institute has put together an impressive list of titles, including Daniel Gould's *Motivating Young Athletes* (1980); Vern Seefeldt, Frank Smoll, Ronald Smith, and Daniel Gould's *A Winning Philosophy for Youth Sports Programs* (1981); and Frank Smoll and Ronald Smith's *Improving Relationship Skills in Youth Sport Coaches* (1979). One of the first youth coaching manuals published by a national association was Jerry Thomas's *Youth Sports Guide for Coaches and Parents* (1977). Published by AAHPERD, the manual discusses such topics as instructional strategies, motivating young athletes, psychological issues, physiological development, and philosophy of winning and losing. In 1981 Rainer Martens, Robert Christina, John Harvey, and Brian Sharkey came out with their *Coaching Young Athletes*, a book that served as the sports medicine and science resource book for ACEP. The following year Richard Cox edited another AAHPERD publication on youth sport entitled *Educating Youth Sports Coaches: Solutions to a National Dilemma* (1982).

Maureen Weiss and Daniel Gould (1986) provided an international perspective on youth sport participation with their edited proceedings of the 1984 Olympic Scientific Congress titled *Sport for Children and Youths*. The text, which included as contributors a number of well-known scholars from around the world, covered such topics as game modification, perceptions of stress, and injuries in youth sports. Eugene Brown and Crystal Branta (1988) edited the papers from the 1985 Big Ten Conference on Youth Sport at Michigan State in a book entitled *Competitive Sports for Children and Youth: An Overview of Research and Issues*. Included in the book are chapters dealing with such topics as psychological stress, physiological characteristics, strength training, and body composition among young athletes. Finally, Bernard Cahill and Arthur Pearl edited the papers from the 1990 youth sport conference organized by the American Orthopaedic Society for Sports Medicine (AOSSM) in Peoria, Illinois. Entitled *Intensive Participation in Children's Sports* (1993), the book includes eight chapters and topics ranging from competitive stress and burnout among young athletes to pathoanatomic change in youth sport participants.

A number of other specialized monographs have provided data and much needed insights into various aspects of children's highly competitive sport programs. These works, while varying in style and format, generally take a multidisciplinary approach to the study of youth sports by employing different methodologies and asking a host of questions. Terry Orlick and Cal Botterill analyze the importance of athletic competition for young children in their 1975 book *Every Kid Can Win*. The authors provide a number of practical suggestions for adults interested in changing the structure of organized games. Thomas Tutko and William Bruns provide a critique of sport programs, with special emphasis on youth sports, in their 1976 book *Winning Is Everything and Other American Myths*. In 1978 Rainer Martens came out with his well-known anthology, *Joy and Sadness in Children's Sports*. The book consists of 38 articles from both popular and scholarly sources and a number of practical applications drawn by Martens. Frank Smoll, Richard Magill, and Michael Ash provide a close look at youth sports from a variety of different perspectives in their 1988 book, *Children in Sport*. A compilation of 22 essays written by some of the best-known sport studies scholars in the country, the book includes topics ranging from the growth and development of young athletes to family influences in sport socialization of children. A similar type of publication is Daniel Gould and Maureen Weiss's 1987 *Advances in Pediatric Sport Sciences*. The second volume in a series by Human Kinetics Publishers, the book includes as contributors such noted academicians as Jay Coakley, Thelma Horn, Shirl Hoffman, Marjorie Woollacott, and Brenda Bredemeier. Perhaps more than any other work on the subject, the book integrates the scholarly literature from several behavioral science disciplines dealing with sport participation of children. Patricia and Peter Adler, well-known for their work on college basketball, provide excellent data on how informal play, recreational activities, and highly organized sport fit into the lives of upper-middle-class children in one town in their 1998 book, *Peer Power: Preadolescent Culture and Identity.* Jay Coakley and Peter Donnelly's 1999 book *Inside Sports* includes insightful essays that focus directly on various aspects of youth sport. Paul DeKnop, Lars-Magnus Engstrom, Berit Skirstad, and Maureen Weiss provide an international perspective on youth sport in their 1996 *Worldwide Trends In Youth Sport.* A collaborative effort of the sport and leisure committee of the International Council of Sport Science and Physical Education (ICSSPE), the book explores various aspects of youth sport in 20 countries. Finally, Shane Murphy takes a critical look at highly organized youth sport programs in his 1999 *The Cheers and the Tears: A Healthy Alternative to the Dark Side of Youth Sports Today.*

Providing additional insights into highly competitive children's sports are surveys and textbooks from the sport studies and exercise science fields. Sport sociology surveys perhaps serve as the best examples among this genre; virtually all of them include a chapter or section on some aspect of children's highly competitive sport programs. Jay Coakley, for instance, takes an interesting look at children's sport participation in his well-known text, *Sport in Society: Issues and Controversies* (2001). Coakley discusses, among other things, the differences between informal games and adult-directed sport programs for children, possible reasons for "dropping out" of youth sport programs, and the concept of idiocultures as described by Gary Fine (1987) and other academicians. Howard Nixon discusses such items as adult values in youth sports, the success ethic in "Little Leaguism," and girls' participation in competitive sport in his 1984 survey, *Sport and the American Dream.* Wilbert Leonard examined the emphasis on winning, elimination from participation, levels of maturity, influence of adults, and psychological ramifications of youth sport participation in his 1988 text, *A Sociological Perspective of Sport.* In their 1991 survey, *Sport and Play in American Life: A Textbook in the Sociology of Sport,* Stephen Figler and Gail Whitaker analyze the advantages and disadvantages of youth sports, alternative models for children's sports, and a host of other issues. Stanley Eitzen and George Sage examine the socialization process, sports alternatives, and other concerns in their 1991 text, *Sociology of North American Sport.*

Serving as theoretical underpinnings for the aforementioned works are a plethora of quantitative and qualitative research studies on youth sports published in academic journals and other outlets representing various disciplinary areas. Although defying easy classification, these studies fall most neatly into the psychological, sociological, physiological, anthropological, and motor development domains. Within these domains, the studies are further delimited to such topics as moral growth through physical activity, children and the sport socialization process, attrition in children's sport, motor skill performance in children, gender differences in sport participation of children, influence of coaching behavior on the psychological development of children, physiological impact of intensive training on young athletes, and self-esteem and achievement in children's sport (Nash, 1987; Scanlan and Lewthwaite, 1986; Weiss, Weise, and Klint, 1989; Horn, 1985; Harris, 1984; Fine, 1985; Gill, Gross, and Huddleston, 1983; Burton and Martens, 1986; Rejeski, Darracott, and Hutslar, 1979; Passer, 1983; Duda, 1987; Donnelly, 1993; Hasbrook and Harris, 1999).

Summary

The involvement of children in highly competitive sport has, as we have seen, changed dramatically over the course of American history. Initially participants in games and sports among themselves, American children could eventually choose between informal games and adult-directed sport programs both within and outside the educational domain. The organization of adult-directed sport programs resulted from a combination of factors, including concerns about the health and moral development of American children. Professional educators, however, would eventually relinquish any control they had over youth sport programs to nonschool agencies and business organizations because of their belief about the harmful effects of intense competition on children. Relinquishing control of youth sport programs to other organizations only seemed to intensify the interest of professional educators and academicians in children's sport participation. This was most evident in the establishment of youth sport institutes and coaching clinics as well as the publication of a myriad of studies dealing with highly competitive sport programs for children.

References

Adler, P. A., and Adler, P. (1998). *Peer power: Preadolescent culture and identity*. New Brunswick, NJ: Rutgers University Press.

Albinson, J. G., and Andrew, G. M. (Eds.). (1976). *Child in sport and physical activity*. Baltimore: University Park Press.

American Association for Health, Physical Education and Recreation. (1938). Two important resolutions. *Journal of Health and Physical Education, 9,* 488–489.

American Association for Health, Physical Education and Recreation. (1947). *Cardinal athletic principles*. Washington, DC: Author and National Education Association.

American Association for Health, Physical Education and Recreation. (1952). *Desirable athletic competition for children*. Washington, DC: Author.

American Coaching Effectiveness Program. (1984). *Brochure*. Champaign, IL: Human Kinetics,

Bankes, G. W. (1877). *A day of my life; or everyday experiences at Eton*. London: Stanley Paul.

Berryman, J. W. (1975). From the cradle to the playing field: America's emphasis on highly competitive sports for pre-adolescent boys. *Journal of Sport History, 2,* 112–131.

Boyer, P. (1978). *Urban masses and moral order in America, 1820–1920*. Cambridge, MA: Harvard University Press.

Broadus, C., and Broadus, L. (1972). *Laughing and crying with Little League*. New York: Harper and Row.

Brown, E. W., and Branta, C. F. (1988). *Competitive sports for children and youth: An overview of research and issues*. Champaign, IL: Human Kinetics.

Burton, D., and Martens, R. (1986). Pinned by their own goals: An exploratory investigation into why kids drop out of wrestling. *Journal of Sport Psychology, 8,* 183–197.

Cahill, B. R. (Ed.). (1988). *Proceedings of the conference on strength training and the prepubescent*. Chicago: American Orthopaedic Society for Sports Medicine.

Cahill, B. R., and Pearl, A. J. (1993). *Intensive participation in children's sports*. Champaign, IL: Human Kinetics.

Cavallo, D. (1981). *Muscles and morals: Organized playgrounds and urban reform 1880–1920*. Philadelphia: University of Pennsylvania Press.

Cloyd, J. (1952). Gangway for the mighty midgets. *American Magazine, 154,* 28–29; 83–85.

Coakley, J. J. (2001). *Sport in society: Issues and controversies*. St. Louis: Times Mirror/Mosby.

Coakley, J., and Donnelly, P. (1999). *Inside sports*. London: Routledge.

Cox, R. (Ed.). (1982). *Educating youth sport coaches: Solutions to a national dilemma*. Reston, VA: American Alliance for Health, Physical Education, Recreation and Dance.

DeKnop, P., Lars-Magnus, E., Skirstad, B., and Weiss, M. (1996). *Worldwide trends in youth sport*. Champaign, IL: Human Kinetics.

Donnelly, P. (1993). Problems associated with youth involvement in high-performance sports. In B. R. Cahill and A. J. Pearl (Eds.), *Intensive Participation in children's sports* (pp. 95–126). Champaign, IL: Human Kinetics.

Dorgan, E. J. (1934). *Luther Halsey Gulick, 1865–1918*. New York: Teachers College, Columbia University.

Duda, J. L. (1987). Toward a developmental theory of children's motivation in sport. *Journal of Sport Psychology, 9,* 130–145.

Eitzen, D. S., and Sage, G. H. (1993). *Sociology of North American sport*. Dubuque, IA: Brown and Benchmark.

Feller, B. (1956, August). Don't knock Little Leaguers. *Colliers*, pp. 78–81.

Figler, S. K., and Whitaker, G. (1991). *Sport and play in American life*. Dubuque, IA: Wm. C. Brown.

Fine, G. A. (1985). Team sports, seasonal histories, significant events: Little League Baseball and the creation of collective meaning. *Sociology of Sport Journal, 2,* 219–233.

Fine, G. A. (1987). *With the boys: Little League Baseball and preadolescent culture*. Chicago: The University of Chicago Press.

Forbush, W. B. (1901). *The boy problem: A study in social pedagogy*. Boston: Pilgrim Press.

Forbush, W. B. (1904). Can the Y.M.C.A. do all the street boys' work? *Work with Boys, 4*, 182.

Gerber, E. W. (1971). *Innovators and institutions in physical education*. Philadelphia: Lea and Febiger.

Gerber, E. W., Felshin, J., Berlin, P., and Wyrick, W. (1974). *The American woman in sport*. Reading, MA: Addison-Wesley.

Gill, D. L., Gross, J. B., and Huddleston, S. (1983). Participation motivation in youth sports. *International Journal of Sport Psychology, 14*, 1–14.

Goodman, C. (1979). *Choosing sides: Playground and street life on the lower east side*. New York: Schocken Books.

Gould, D. (1980). *Motivating young athletes*. East Lansing, MI: Youth Sport Institute.

Gould, D., and Weiss, M. (Eds.). (1987). *Advances in pediatric sport sciences* (Vol. 2). Champaign, IL: Human Kinetics.

Grant, R. (1887). *Jack Hall, or the school days of an American boy*. New York: Scribner.

Greenspan, E. (1983). *Little winners: Inside the world of the child sports star*. Boston: Little, Brown.

Gulick, L. H. (1898). Physical aspects of group games. *Popular Science Monthly, 53*, 793–805.

Gulick, L. H. (1899). Psychological, pedagogical, and religious aspects of group games. *Pedagogical Seminary, 6*, 144.

Guttmann, A. (1988). *A whole new ball game: An interpretation of American sports*. Chapel Hill: The University of North Carolina Press.

Hardy, S. (1982). *How Boston played: Sport, recreation, and community*. Boston: Northeastern University Press.

Hasbrook, C. A., and Harris, O. (1999). Wrestling with gender: Physicality and masculinities among inner-city first and second graders. *Men and Masculinities, 1*, 302–318.

Harris, J. (1984). Interpreting youth baseball: Players' understanding of fun and excitement, danger and boredom. *Research Quarterly for Exercise and Sport, 55*, 379–382.

Hemings, B. (1864). *Eton school days*. London: Hutchinson.

Horn, T. (1985). Coaches feedback and changes in children's perceptions of their physical competence. *Journal of Educational Psychology, 77*, 174–186.

Hughes, T. (1857). *Tom Brown's school days*. New York: Harper and Brothers.

Jable, J. T. (1979). The public school athletic league of New York City: Organized athletics for city school children, 1903–1914. In W. M. Ladd and A. Lumpkin (Eds.), *Sport in American education: History and perspective* (pp. ix-18). Washington, DC: American Alliance for Health, Physical Education, Recreation and Dance.

Jennings, S. E. (1981). As American as hot dogs, apple pie and Chevrolet: The desegregation of Little League Baseball. *Journal of American Culture, 4*, 81–91.

Joint Legislative Study Committee. (1976). *Joint legislative study on youth sports: Agency-sponsored sports—Phase I*. Lansing, MI: State of Michigan.

Joint Legislative Study Committee. (1978a). *Joint legislative study on youth sports: Agency-sponsored sports: Agency—Phase II*. Lansing, MI: State of Michigan.

Joint Legislative Study Committee. (1978b). *Joint legislative study on youth sports: Agency-sponsored sports: Agency—Phase III*. Lansing, MI: State of Michigan.

Lacy, S., with Newson, M. J. (1998). *Fighting for success: The life story of Hall of Fame sportswriter Sam Lacy*. Centreville, MD: Tidewater Publishers.

Leonard, W. M. (1988). *A sociological perspective of sport*. New York: Macmillan.

Lewis, G. (1966). The Muscular Christianity movement. *Journal of Health, Physical Education and Recreation, 37*, 27–28.

Lowman, C. L. (1947). The vulnerable age. *Journal of Health and Physical Education, 18*, 635; 693.

Lucas, J. A. (1968). A prelude to the rise of sport: Ante-bellum America, 1850–1860. *Quest, 2*, 50–57.

Martens, R. (1978). *Joy and sadness in children's sports*. Champaign, IL: Human Kinetics.

Martens, R., Christina, R. W., Harvey, J. S., Jr., and Sharkey, B. J. (Eds.). (1981). *Coaching young athletes*. Champaign, IL: Human Kinetics.

Martens, R., and Seefeldt, V. (1979). *Guidelines for children's sports*. Washington, DC: American Alliance for Health, Physical Education, Recreation and Dance.

Monroe, K. (1946). Hothouse for tennis champs. *Readers Digest, 49*, 22.

Moss, B., and Orion, W. H. (1939). The public school programs in health, physical education, and recreation. *Journal of Health and Physical Education, 10*, 435–439; 494.

Murphy, S. (1999). *The cheers and the tears: A healthy alternative to the dark side of youth sports today*. San Francisco: Jossey-Bass.

Nash, H. L. (1987). Elite child-athletes: How much does victory cost? *The Physician and Sportsmedicine, 15*, 129–133.

National Council of Youth Sports Directors. (n.d.). *Brochure*.

National Recreation Congress. (1952). Are highly competitive sports desirable for juniors? *Recreation, 46*, 422–426.

National Youth Sport Coaches Association. (n.d.). *Brochure*. West Palm Beach, FL: Author.

Nixon, H. L. (1984). *Sport and the American dream*. New York: Leisure Press.

North American Society for the Psychology of Sport and Physical Activity. (1989). *Program bulletin*. Kent, OH: Kent State University.

Orlick, T., and Botterill, C. (1975). *Every kid can win*. Chicago: Nelson-Hall.

Passer, M. W. (1983). Fear of failure, fear of evaluation, perceived competence and self-esteem in competitive trait anxious children. *Journal of Sport Psychology, 5*, 172–188.

Paxton, H. T. (1949). Small boy's dreams come true. *Saturday Evening Post, 221*, 26–27; 137–140.

Rader, B. (1983). *American sports: From the age of folk games to the age of spectators*. Englewood Cliffs, NJ: Prentice-Hall.

Ralbovsky, M. (1974). *Destiny's darlings*. New York: Hawthorne Books.

Rejeski, W., Darracott, C., and Hutslar, S. (1979). Pygmalion in youth sports: A field study. *Journal of Sport Psychology, 1*, 311–319.

Roberts, R. (1975, July). Strike out Little League. *Newsweek*, p. 11.

Rosen, A. (1967). *Baseball and your boy*. New York: Funk and Wagnall.

Scanlan, T. K., and Lewthwaite, R. (1986). Social psychological aspects of competition for male youth sport participants: IV: Predictors of enjoyment. *Journal of Sport Psychology, 8*, 25–35.

Scott, P. (1953). Attitudes toward athletic competition in elementary schools. *Research Quarterly, 4*, 352–361.

Seefeldt, V., Smoll, F. L., Smith, R. E., and Gould, D. (1981). *A winning philosophy for youth sports programs*. East Lansing, MI: Youth Sport Institute.

Seymour, E. (1956). Comparative behavior characteristics of participant boys in Little League Baseball. *Research Quarterly, 27*, 338–346.

Skubic, E. (1955). Emotional responses of boys to Little League and Middle League competitive baseball. *Research Quarterly, 26*, 342–352.

Skubic, E. (1956). Studies of Little League and Middle League baseball. *Research Quarterly, 27*, 97–110.

Smoll, F. L., Magill, R. A., and Ash, M. J. (1988). *Children in sport* (3rd ed.). Champaign, IL: Human Kinetics.

Smoll, F. L., and Smith, R. E. (1978). *Psychological perspectives in youth sports*. Washington, DC: Hemisphere.

Smoll, F. L., and Smith, R. E. (1979). *Improving relationship skills in youth sport coaches*. East Lansing, MI: Youth Sport Institute.

Tarkenton, F. (1970, October). Don't let your son play smallfry football. *Ladies Home Journal*, pp. 146–147.

Thomas, J. (Ed.). (1977). *Youth sports guide for coaches and parents*. Washington, DC: National Association for Sport and Physical Education.

Tutko, T., and Bruns, W. (1976). *Winning is everything and other American myths*. New York: Macmillan.

Underwood, J. (1975). Taking the fun out of games. *Sports Illustrated, 43*, 86–98.

Wayman, F., Hager, R., Hartwig, H., Houston, L., LaSalle, D., and McNeely, S. (1950). Report of the President's Committee on Interschool Competition in the Elementary School. *Journal of Health, Physical Education and Recreation, 21*, 279–280; 313–314.

Weiss, M. R., and Gould, D. (Eds.). (1986). *The 1984 Olympic scientific congress: Vol. 10. Sport for children and youths*. Champaign, IL: Human Kinetics.

Weiss, M. R., Weise, D., and Klint, K. (1989). Head over heels with success: The relationship between self-efficacy and performance in competitive youth gymnastics. *Journal of Sport and Exercise Psychology, 11*, 444–451.

Yablonsky, L., and Brower, J. (1979). *The Little League game*. New York: Times Books.

Patterns of Participation in American Agency-Sponsored Youth Sports

Martha E. Ewing, Michigan State University
Vern Seefeldt, Michigan State University

The belief that participation in sports and other physical activities provides many benefits for youth and adults is long-standing. For children, one of the main benefits derived from sport participation is learning sport skills that can be used to further participation in activities as adults. Participation in sport contributes to increases in children's perceptions of competence (Horn and Weiss, 1991), self-esteem (Barnett, Smoll, and Smith, 1992; Smith, Smoll, and Curtis, 1979), emotion management (Gould, Eklund, and Jackson, 1993; Hanin, 1997), and moral development (Bredemeier and Shields, 1987). In addition, participation in sport and physical activity has been associated with reducing risk factors for health problems in later life (Baranowski et al., 1992; Williams, Carter, and Wynder, 1981). For instance, active adolescents are less likely to smoke cigarettes than their sedentary counterparts (Vidmar, 1992) and use drugs (Escobedo, Marcus, Holtzman, and Giovino, 1993). Likewise, active adolescents are more likely to stay in school, have good conduct, and higher academic achievement (Jeziorski, 1994; Zill, Nord, and Loomis, 1995). In addition, for adolescent females, involvement in sport programs has been associated with a reduction in sexual activity and pregnancies (Sabo, Miller, Farrell, Barnes, and Melnick, 1998).

Given all these benefits to participation in sport, a paradox exists. In a recent report to the President, the Secretary of Health and Human Services and the Secretary of Education state the following: "Our nation's young people are, in large measure, inactive, unfit, and increasingly overweight. Physical inactivity threatens to reverse the decades-long progress in reducing deaths from cardiovascular diseases" (Shalala and Riley, 2000, p. 1). The report acknowledges that it is paramount that we "enhance efforts to promote participation in physical activity and sports among our young people." This chapter will address the changes in participation rates since 1990.

When viewing participation patterns, the expedient approach is often followed. That is, reviewers will look at participation rates of all youth in certain age groups or involved in certain sports. However, this approach has masked many discrepancies in participation patterns particularly among minority youth and females. Therefore, this chapter will provide data for minority youth and females to show where inconsistencies exist and where efforts of youth sport providers need to be aimed to enhance the number of youth participating in sports and physical activity.

The assumption surrounding youth sport participation has been that 100% of the youth in a community should be participating in sport programs. Obviously, many factors preclude all youth from participating, such as direct and indirect costs, practices and games held at times that are inconvenient to the prospective participants, and diverse interests of today's youth. Therefore, this chapter will address the inclusion of physical activities or unstructured activities to the discussion, since many youth will find ways within their local neighborhoods to engage in sports and physical activities that are not organized or supervised by adults.

Participation in Organized Youth Sports

The term *youth sports* has been collectively applied to any of the various athletic programs that serve individuals who are under 18 years of age in which a systematic sequence of practices and contests is supervised by adults (Seefeldt, Ewing, and Walk, 1992). The sports under this rubric differ greatly in competitive level, length of season, cost to competitors, qualifications of coaches and officials, and skill levels of the athletes. However, the constant operative within this process is the advancement by age group and skill level which signifies that even the most unskilled 5-year-old child is able to enroll in a procedure for developing athletic talent that could eventually propel him/her to Olympic stardom. Unfortunately, by age 15 as many as 75% who have selected a specific sport at a younger age may no longer be participating in it (Ewing and Seefeldt, 1989). Who participates in youth sports in the United States and what is the organizational structure that supports this immeasurable mass of athletic talent?

For purposes of this discussion youth sports in the United States have been divided into five categories, based on the philosophies that define the various programs. The five categories are agency-sponsored sports, club sports, recreational sports, interscholastic sports, and intramural sports. A brief description and the estimated enrollments in each category are provided in Table 3.1. Unfortunately, there is no precise accounting of the number of children and youth who participate in organized sports. Estimates of enrollees in team sports are generally obtained by multiplying the number of registered teams by an allocated number of names on a roster. An exception to this custom occurs in USA Hockey, where each member is individually recorded and counted in the total enrollment figures. The current method of determining the total participants in youth sports is likely to over-estimate those who participate because the organizational structure and reporting systems do not permit the identification of those who participate in more than one sport. Thus, multiple sport participants may be counted numerous times in the annual total.

Table 3.1 Estimated Percent of Youth Enrolled in Specific Categories of Youth Sports[1]

Category of Activity	% of all Eligible Enrollees[2]	Approximate N of Participants
Agency-Sponsored Sports (e.g., Little League, Pop Warner	Little League, Pop Warner)	50
Club Sports (pay for services— gymnastics, ice skating, swimming, tennis)	5	2,550,000
Recreational Sports Programs (everyone plays— sponsored by recreation departments)	30	15,300,000
Intramural Sports (middle, junior, senior high schools)	10	510,000
Interscholastic Sports (middle, junior, senior high school)	50	6,000,000

[1]Total population of eligible participants in the 5–17 year age category (in 2000) was estimated to be 51,500,000 by the United States Census Bureau.

[2]Total does not equal 100% because of multiple-category entries for some youth.

Note that the largest number of participants in Table 3.1 are found in the category titled agency-sponsored sports, and the smallest number of participants are enrolled in intramural sports. Only approximately 6 to 7 million of the 47 million who participate in youth sports (14%) do so under the auspices of the school systems. Although the number of students who participated in the ten most popular interscholastic sports has grown by nearly one million since 1975–76, the increase was primarily due to the greater opportunities available to girls (National Federation of State High School Associations, 2001).

Youth Sports and the Year 2000 Census

The year 2000 census and its projections for the population of youth in 2010 provides valuable information and future challenges for promoters of youth sports. The census data affirm that the population of 5- to 17-year-old children and youth increased from 45,325,000 in 1990 to 51,507,000 in 2000, resulting in a gain of 9%. However, the projected gain for this age group is a mere 899,000 from the years 2000 to 2010. Of even greater interest are the data on gender and ethnicity. The numbers of 5- to 17-year-old males and females are both projected to increase by only one percent during the first decade of the new century. The greatest changes are destined to occur in ethnicity (see Table 3.2), where youth of Hispanic and Asian/Pacific Islander descent will increase, proportionately, by 32% and 33.6%, respectively. Youth classified as White, Black, and Native American will all decrease, proportionately, with the greatest decreases in numbers (-2,440,000) and proportion (-7.3%) projected to occur among White children and youth.

Table 3.2   Population Projections (in Millions) of the 5 to 17 Age Group, by Ethnicity[1]

	White	Black	Hispanic	Asian/Pacific Islander	Native American
2000	33.4	7.6	7.9	2.1	0.5
2010	30.9	7.3	10.4	2.8	0.5
% Change	−7.3%	−3.7%	32.0%	33.6%	−3.9%

[1]U.S. Census Bureau population projections at http://www.census.gov/population/www/projections/natsum.html (January 30, 2001).

Participation in Nonschool-Sponsored Sports

In a world where predictions translate into reality the 9% increase in numbers of 5- to 17-year-old children and youth during the 1990s would have resulted in an equal increase of participants in the various youth sport programs, but the data compiled from a survey conducted by the Sporting Goods Manufacturers Association (SGMA, 2000) suggest otherwise. Data based on a self-administered questionnaire returned by 14,891 householders, designed to reflect the demography of the United States, revealed that only the team sports of soccer and basketball increased their number of participants from 1987 to 1999 (see Table 3.3). It should be noted, however, that national organizations that sponsor youth softball, football, soccer, and baseball all reported substantial gains in youthful participants during the years from 1992 to 1999.

Table 3.3 Trends in Participation (in Millions) in Team Sports from 1987 to 1999[1]

Sport	Rank	Participation	% Change
Basketball	1	39.4	10
Volleyball	2	24.2	−33
Softball	3	19.8	−36
Football	4	18.7	N/A
Soccer	5	17.6	14
Baseball	6	12.1	−20
Ice hockey	7	2.4	0

[1]Calculated from data presented in U.S. Trends in Team Sports, The SGMA Report 2000, North Palm Beach, FL, 2000.

The decrease in overall participation in sports for the 5 to 17 year age group (i.e., SGMA data) and the increase reported by youth sport organizations have several plausible explanations. First, children and youth are more attracted to organized activities, at the expense of spontaneous, free-play types of activities. Social conditions such as fear for the safety of youth in unsupervised situations and the lack of access to suitable play spaces may have been determining factors that influenced the move toward organized sports (Seefeldt, 1995; Weiler, 1998). Secondly, organizers of youth sports may have become more deferential to the needs of younger athletes by offering programs at younger ages and providing children with greater choices of activities. Thirdly, the reported decline in sports participation may reflect the popularity of video games, television and the sedentary life styles that have led to the tremendous increase in weight gain and obesity among younger Americans during the 1990s (Shalala and Riley, 2000).

The propensity of children and youth who seek organized sports in lieu of engaging in spontaneous play places a greater burden on the organizers of sports for youth. Will there be opportunities for all levels of ability in the future, or will the desire to serve only the highly skilled athletes reduce the opportunities for those less skilled or for those in developmental programs? Advocates of "sports for all" will have to become increasingly vigilant in the future if youth sports are to continue as a place where children of all ability levels can learn skills in a variety of competitive settings.

Participation in School-Sponsored Sports

Interscholastic sports in the United States are conducted under the auspices of the State Associations who are members of the National Federation of State High School Associations (2001). For information regarding the demography, enrollments, and projected involvement of boys and girls in interscholastic sports, see Chapter 24 by Seefeldt and Clark (this volume).

Despite the turbulence in youth sports during the 1990s, involvement in interscholastic sports remained relatively stable. The overriding events centered on the emergence of girls as equal participants in school-sponsored sports (see Figure 3.1.). Although the eligible enrollees to interscholastic programs favor boys by approximately one million members, girls increased their participation from 1,892,000 in 1990 to 2,676,000 (41.4%) in 2000. Participation by boys increased from 3,406,000 in 1990 to 3,862,000 (13.4%) in 2000. Thus, approximately 40.9% of interscholastic athletes in 2000 were girls.

Nationwide, the participation in interscholastic sports remained high during the 1990s. Kann and co-workers (2000) found that 55.1% of all high school students played on one or more interscholastic teams in the previous 12 months. Male students were significantly more likely (61.7%) than female students (48.5%) to have played on a school-sponsored sport team. The significant sex difference in sport participation was also evident across all ethnic groups. Overall, White students (56.9%) were more likely than Hispanic students (50.8%) to have played sports. White female students (50.5%) were more likely than Black female students (36.3%) to have played on sports teams. Female students, regardless of ethnicity, decreased their participation across the grades (freshmen = 53.4% and seniors = 42.3%). In a longitudinal study spanning 32 years, and including 21 local school districts in the Lansing, Michigan area, Haubenstricker, Seefeldt, Branta, and Wisner (2001) reported that 75.4% of boys and 61.6% of girls participated in interscholastic sports. These data suggest that interscholastic sports are accommodating a large proportion of high school enrollees.

Data on enrollments in interscholastic sports also indicate their independence from the overall participation in sports by all age groups. Table 3.3 indicates that participation in team sports by the total population decreased, with the exceptions of basketball and soccer, while Table 3.4 shows increases in the six most popular team sports for the age group 12 to 17 years (SGMA, 2000). Data from the National Federation of State High School Associations (2000) indicate that from 1990–91 to 1998–99 participation in football increased by 7%, in basketball by 11%, track and field by 22%, soccer by 65%, baseball by 9%, volleyball by 33% and fast pitch softball by 55%. Thus, a comparison of sports participation by high school athletes to that of the total population provides strikingly different results. Equally apparent is the realization that the decrease in sports participation has occurred in the age groups beyond the high school years. Table 3.4 indicates that large percentages of current sports participants are included in the 6 to 17 year age group. For example, 53% of

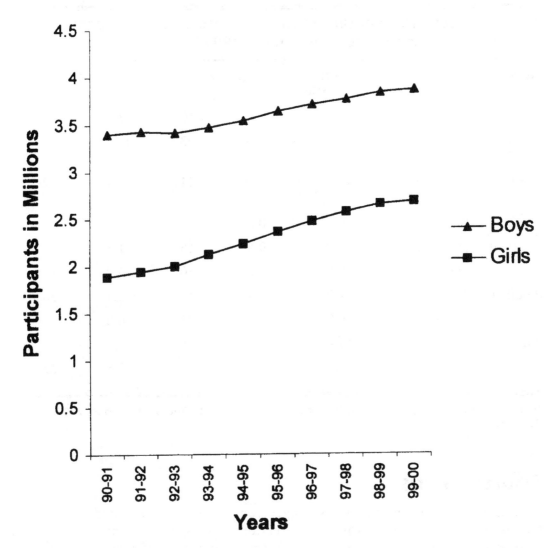

Figure 3.1. Participation patterns of boys and girls in high school sports from 1990–2000. Source: National Federation of State High School Associations (2001).

the 39.4 million individuals who play basketball are 17 years or younger; 73% of all soccer players in the United States are 17 years or younger. These data suggest that the decline in numbers of participants has occurred beyond the years when youth sports agencies sponsor and control the programs.

Table 3.4 Total Number (in Millions) and Percent of Participants, by Team Sport, in Various Age Categories in 1999[1]

Sport		Total Participation	Ages 6–11		Ages 12–17	
			N	%	N	%
Basket-ball		39.4	9.0	23	11.8	30
Volley-ball	Court/Grass	19.1	2.1	11	6.1	32
	Beach	9.5	0.8	8	1.7	18
Softball	Fast Pitch	3.2	0.5	15	1.3	40
	Slow Pitch	18.0	3.6	20	3.2	18
Football	Tackle	4.9	0.8	17	2.7	56
	Touch	16.7	3.8	23	6.0	36
Soccer		17.6	8.0	45	5.1	29
Baseball		12.1	4.6	38	3.5	29

[1]Calculated from data presented in U.S. Trends in Team Sports, The SGMA Report 2000, North Palm Beach, FL, 2000.

Sports Camps

Descriptions of sports camps range from their relatively benign characterization as programs that provide a recreational atmosphere in which children of similar ages learn sports-specific skills under the guidance of a coach or athletic trainer to the more malicious portrayal as a marketplace where sporting goods manufacturers and college coaches congregate for the purpose of promoting products, either human or material, under the guise of providing college scholarships and/or futuristic contracts related to the endorsement of wearing apparel. In reality, the majority of sports camps, clinics and combines probably function near the middle of these extremes (Author, 1996).

Perusal of advertisements in journals devoted to athletics confirms that children and youth have abundant opportunities to obtain special instructions in sports skills away from their communities. Solicitations via print and electronic media tell parents and aspiring athletes that special instruction is available to individuals of various skill levels, in co-educational or gender-specific settings, during the summer months or at times surrounding holiday and school vacations, at various locations throughout the United States, from a duration of several days to year-around sessions, for fees that include scholarships for the indigent to camps that are affordable only to the wealthy. Clearly, this synopsis of sports camps is a marked departure from a time when children and youth received their out-of-school instruction in sports within their own communities, by instructors who were also local residents.

The earliest versions of sports camps embraced two concepts that were especially appealing to parents and administrators of interscholastic athletic programs: (a) the camps were organized and conducted by coaches from the local community, for youth in the local community, and (b) the availability of wholesome activities, supervised by qualified, trusted instructors, provided a healthy alternative to a potentially sedentary lifestyle during the summer months when the unencumbered time of youth was at a premium.

The popularity and unrestricted operation of summer sports camps soon gravitated to excesses that trammeled the concepts of amateurism, education and parity; concepts held in high regard by the National Federation of State High School Athletic Associations (NFHS) and its State Associations. Directors of sports camps began recruiting attenders from distant geographical areas, selecting professional athletes and coaches as instructors in order to attract more enrollees and limiting enrollments to elite athletes.

Manufacturers of sports shoes and athletic apparel soon realized that identification with a known brand of equipment or apparel during the formative years was an effective technique for establishing loyalty to a product. When the athletes reached adulthood and were able to endorse products, their earlier exposure to the representatives of the manufacturer became an important inducement for endorsing the now familiar product. Thus, the community-based sports camps soon gravitated to the point where they only accommodated those who were not sufficiently skilled to be invited to the more prestigious camps.

The NFHS and its State Associations soon realized that the unrestricted actions of those who conducted sports camps posed a threat to the concepts of educational athletics and amateurism, two pillars of interscholastic athletics. By enacting legislation to curb the travel of individuals and teams during the interscholastic sports seasons and limiting enrollment in athletic events to those sanctioned by the NFSH and its State Associations, the NFSH forced athletes to choose between participation in interscholastic sports and association with independent sponsors of organized athletics.

The profusion of sports camps and their discriminative nature inevitably displeased a number of parents, primarily because they felt misled by the advertisements that attracted their sons and daughters to the camps. These malcontented parents of campers paved the way for a mini-industry of consultants who established referral services that were designed to match the talents and desires of the athletes with the types of camps that provided the necessary atmosphere and services (Grossman, 1998). The demand by parents for referral services became so great that within years numerous agencies opened their doors, many offering evaluations of hundreds of camps, from which the aspiring athlete could choose (see Directory of Athletic Camps [2001] and Directory of National Camps [2001]). Thus, the inability of sports camps to control their actions from within resulted in an external assessment that they neither requested nor willingly accepted.

Today the industry of sports camps for children and youth seems to be thriving, if an example in a local newspaper is any indication of success ("Area Sports," 2000). The feature listed 22 camps available in Michigan, most with multiple sports offerings, repeated for durations of from 5 to 7 weeks during the summer months. Fourteen of the camps were offered by institutions of higher education, and the rest were by agencies such as YMCAs or Fitness Centers. Excluded from the list were the numerous camps offered by local high schools and agencies within local communities. It is not possible to determine how many of the estimated 47 million children and youth who participate in youth sports also enroll in sports camps, but their popularity suggests that the numbers are substantial.

Participation Patterns of Females and People of Color

Participation in school-sponsored sports by females has increased dramatically during the 1990s. Basketball, track and field, volleyball, and softball are the most popular sports (SGMA, 2000). Table 3.5 provides information by sport for changes in the number of girls participating in selected high school sports from 1990 to 1999. Soccer has grown the fastest with a 112% increase, followed by softball (55%) and swimming and diving (51%). Females are clearly increasing in numbers in all sports which would negate the assertions of critics who argue that girls are not interested in playing sports.

While participation patterns are improving for females, particularly at the high school level, the pattern of participation for minorities is not as encouraging. For example, African-American females represent less than 5% of all high school athletes (Women's Sports Foundation, 2001). According to data supplied by the U.S. Department of Health and Human Services (1996), the participation pattern for males in both school-sponsored and agency-sponsored programs is higher for males than females regardless of race. The data presented in Table 3.6 clearly show that women of color are underrepresented in both school-sponsored and agency-sponsored sport programs.

Table 3.5 Number of Female Participants in Selected High School Sports from 1990 to 1999

	1990–1991	1998–1999	Change
Basketball	387,802	456,873	+18%
Track and field	320,763	405,163	+26%
Volleyball	300,810	380,994	+27%
Softball (fast pitch)	219,464	380,994	+55%
Soccer	121,722	257,586	+112%
Tennis	132,607	156,505	+18%
Cross country	106,514	155,529	+46%
Swimming and diving	88,122	133,235	+51%
Competitive spirit squads	N/A	74,462	N/A
Field hockey	43,348	57,980	+20%

Table 3.6 Percentage of Participation by Sex Among Minorities in High School and Other Agency-Sponsored Sport Programs

Race	School-sponsored Programs		Agency-sponsored Programs	
	Males	Females	Males	Females
White, non-hispanic	59.9	47.1	47.2	29.9
Black, non-hispanic	57.9	34.9	46.8	21.1
Hispanic	48.6	27.3	43.2	21.2

In general, the participation pattern of females shows a steady increase. As noted earlier, female participation in school-sponsored sports continues to rise. Participation in soccer, arguably the hottest sport in the 1990s, illustrates this trend well. The 1999 National Soccer Participation Survey reports that 7.5 million females played soccer at least once during 1998, representing a 5% gain from 1997 and a 34% increase over 1991. However, these results vary based on the age of the participant. Among girls 6 to 11, participation was down 10% to 3.2 million from 3.5 million. For girls 12 to 17 years of age, participation rose 37% to 3.0 million from 2.2 million from 1997 to 1998. Females, ages 6 to 17, now represent 45% of the player population. Commitment, as measured by the average days played per year, is very similar between males and females. Females averaged 38 playing days per year compared to 42 for males (SGMA, 2000).

Female participation has also shown a steady increase in softball during the 1990s. Participation in school softball rose from 256,000 in 1990 to 369,000 in 1999 (SGMA, 2000). Likewise, in the agency-sponsored softball leagues dramatic increases can be observed (see Table 3.7). Although it is unclear what is precipitating the revival of softball participation for females, it is possible that the success of the USA Softball team in the 1996 and 2000 Olympics may have provided some of the impetus.

Table 3.7 Participation Trends in Agency-Sponsored Youth Softball Leagues

	1992	1994	1996	1999
Little League	299,910	365,685	404,535	392,370
Dixie Softball	47,040	64,605	71,775	78,720
PONY Softball	29,715	31,140	37,545	47,280
Babe Ruth Softball	34,470	49,515	53,655	61,080
Total	411,135	510,945	567,510	579,450

Very few agency or school-sponsored programs monitor the race of their participants. However, in 1992 and again in 1995, the Centers for Disease Control and Prevention surveyed students ages 12 to 21 years to determine participation in selected physical activities (U.S. Department of Health and Human Services, 1996). The percentages of students who reported participating in dance or aerobics; baseball, softball, or frisbee; and basketball, football or soccer for one or more times during the week preceding the survey are presented in Table 3.8. Although the interaction of sex and race are not reported, the percentage of participants by sex clearly show that many more females participate in aerobics and dance than males, who report participating more in the team sports. With respect to race, White, non-Hispanic students report lower rates of participation in aerobics or dancing while Black, non-Hispanic students are under-represented in baseball, softball, or frisbee. Participation rates for other activities and groups are very similar.

Table 3.8 Percentage of Participants in Selected Physical Activities by Race and Sex

Sex	Aerobics or dancing	Baseball, softball or frisbee	Basketball, football or soccer	Tennis, squash or racquetball
Males	22.6	27.2	61.7	11.7
Females	53.9	17.5	29.7	9.3
Race				
White	35.0	23.6	44.7	11.4
Balck	49.4	16.6	49.5	5.4
Hispanic	42.0	23.4	47.1	8.0

Barriers to Participation

Although there are many opportunities for youth to participate in sport, these opportunities are unevenly distributed. The variance in opportunities to participate in sport programs or other physical activity has resulted in a call to action by the Secretaries of Health and Human Services and Education. Shalala and Riley (2000) have identified several changes in the activity of youth that contributes to both the lack of physical activity and an increase in the number of youth aged 6 to 11 years who are overweight. Specifically, by age 11, 9.7% of girls and 11.3% of boys are overweight. Based on fitness tests administered in California in 1999, only 20% of the students in grades 5, 7, and 9 met the standards for all health-related fitness components. Unfortunately, more than 40% failed to meet the minimum requirement for cardiorespiratory endurance (cited in Shalala and Riley, 2000)!

Most striking is the discrepancy found between youth in suburban communities versus those in urban communities. Seefeldt (1995) reported that less than 5% of the youth in Detroit, Hamtramck, and Highland Park, Michigan, participated in organized sports or swimming. Compare this number with the estimated 75% to 80% of youth living in suburbs who are involved in organized sport activities. The vast majority of youth in the urban setting did participate in special events and informal recreation programs sponsored by local recreation centers. While children may appear to be somewhat active in these programs, they are experiencing little structure and supervision from adults.

Barriers to participation in successful programs in urban environments include (a) lack of qualified leaders, (b) inadequate sites and facilities, (c) inaccessibility to neighborhood schools, (d) inappropriate programming by age and gender, (e) safety at program sites and enroute to sites, (f) affordable, accessible transportation, and (g) lack of cooperation among program providers (Seefeldt, 1995). Each of these barriers will be discussed briefly. Program administrators would be well-advised to assess their own community in terms of these barriers.

The need for trained adult leaders for youth sport programs is critical. In order for youth to learn appropriate skills and have fun learning skills, adults must understand how to organize practices and to conduct practices and games in developmentally appropriate and safe environments. With the reduction in physical education instruction, many youth have no basis for learning sport skills. This puts the pressure on youth sport coaches to become better teachers in order to help all youth on their teams, not just the youth who already know the skills. If youth are not learning skills or deriving other positive benefits from their participation in sport, they will drop out. Many of these youth will turn to video and computer games as entertainment which perpetuates inactivity and puts them at risk in terms of health and fitness.

Many of the sites and facilities used for youth sport activities are old and run down. Communities must assess community centers for their location and their general condition. Two issues that arise can be captured in two questions. First, are the community centers and recreational areas located where the youth are? Secondly, are current sites adequate for the types of programming that appeal to today's youth? As people move and communities change, many of the recreation facilities are located away from the current population or fail to provide for a myriad of activities that appeal to youth. Simply putting in hiking and biking trails through parks could increase the activity of many youth.

Parents perceive that one of the safe areas for youth is the local school. When parents are not close to a park or community recreation center, the schools became the logical choice for activity. Many schools discourage the use of their facility or associated playgrounds. Some of the reasons given by school principles for disallowing their facilities to be used for recreation include (a) facilities are not compatible with the groups' need, (b) schools cannot provide adult supervision, (c) safety concerns, and (d) no one asked to use the school building (Seefeldt, 1995). Clearly, through cooperation of recreation program leaders and school administrators, most of these reasons could be resolved through community discussion and sport organizers working together to share space.

Youth of today are interested in more than just competitive programs. Community recreation leaders must broaden programs to meet the interests of the citizens of the community. Girls and boys who do not perceive themselves to be skillful enough to participate in competitive programs could benefit from instructional leagues or in programs where the competition is focused on one's own previous performance rather than in comparison to the skills and abilities of other youth. Such activities might include dancing, hiking, canoeing, or other lifetime activities. Our society has made the emphasis on winning so compelling that many youth are discouraged from even trying out for sport because of their low ability or low esteem.

Safety is the number one concern of parents in urban areas with respect to their children. As communities have grown and major streets dissected communities, access to play grounds and recreation centers has become very dangerous. Transportation that is affordable must be sought to move youth to the safe facilities in order to participate. Adults want to know that their children will be safe from drug dealers and adults who prey on young children. Many community centers have started providing a bus service to move youths from their homes to the recreation areas or have contracted with city buses to move children at a reduced rate. Access to available sport venues is a major issue that community and sport leaders must take very seriously.

The last barrier in urban environments is the lack of cooperation and collaboration among program providers. Many youth are excluded when sport providers do not work together to assure that youth of all ages as well as both sexes and all races are provided with appropriate activity. For example, many of the sport providers will curtail their programs when youth reach the age of 13 or 14. For the youth who are not sufficiently skilled enough to qualify for the interscholastic team at their school, the opportunity to engage in physical activity is lost. This is occurring at the very age when youth may benefit most from adult supervision and programs that allow them to engage in meaningful activity with their friends.

Another obvious barrier to participation in organized sports is economics. The percentage of youth participating in selected sports by household income was provided by *The SGMA Report 2000* (SGMA, 2000). For youth living in households whose annual income was less than $35,000, participation rates were among the lowest. For example, in soccer, a sport that is relatively inexpensive for participants, only 13% to 14% of the youth participated compared to 20% to 28% participants in other income categories. Very similar patterns were found in softball, baseball, and volleyball. For the team sports of basketball and football, participation rates were more equitable with participants in households whose annual income exceeded $35,000.

Finally, it would be short-sighted not to recognize two elements related to families that contribute to a lack of physical activity. First, parents who do not engage in physical activity often serve as poor role models for their children. Parents need to recognize the need for their children to be physically active and encourage and support their children's desires to be active. Secondly, electronic media has made sedentary activities more appealing. Video games, cable and satellite television are appealing sedentary activities. Parents must monitor their children's use of these electronic toys and insist that physical activity be a part of each child's day.

Summary

There is a new sense of urgency about the fitness level of youth in America. Accompanying this sense of urgency is the realization that the role of sports, physical education, and alternative physical activity programs is paramount in reducing the trend towards inactivity and increased obesity. Patterns of participation in sport are on the increase in most agency-sponsored and school-sponsored sports. However, the pattern of participation is quite variant with females, people of color, and particularly, females of color being under-represented in our sport programs. Communities and schools must address the needs of these youth before we become a more sedentary society. Active parents are critical to getting youth involved in an active lifestyle. We cannot afford to lose a generation of youth who will then become the role models of future generations. Many barriers to participation have been identified. Costs associated with participation in sports plus lack of safe playgrounds, inaccessibility of schools for sport and activity programs in the nonschool hours, playgrounds and recreation centers that are no longer located where the children are living, and the attractiveness of video and computer games are but a few of the barriers. These barriers can be overcome if community recreation departments, agency-sponsored programs, and school-sponsored programs would unite to offer a diverse, instructive program. One major threat to the youth sport programs for all children is the emphasis on elitism that is fostered through the numerous sport camps.

As the fabric of the American society changes, including the shifts in populations in the near future, it is incumbent upon the organizations sponsoring youth sport programs to include youth in their planning of programs. The pendulum must swing back towards an emphasis on skill development and the teaching of life skills, such as respect for authority and individual differences. Sport can be a catalyst for helping youth develop into productive adults, but we must protect youngsters from overzealous adults who would promote elitism as the future of youth sports. Perhaps the single most important factor in providing a quality experience for youth in sports is the coach. At the youth level, it may be more important than ever to provide coaches with more education if they are to meet the needs of today's youth.

References

Area sports camps. (2000, May 7). *Lansing State Journal*, p. C12.

Author. (1996). Camps, clinics, combines. *Athletic Management, 8*, 14–15.

Baranowski, T., Bouchard, C., Bar-Or, O., Bricker, T., Heath, G., Kimm, S. Y. S., Malina, R., Obarzanek, E., Pate, R., Strong, W. B., Truman, B., and Washington, R. (1992). Assessment, prevalence, and cardiovascular benefits of physical activity and fitness in youth. *Medicine and Science in Sports and Exercise, 24* (Suppl.), S237–247.

Barnett, N. P., Smoll, F. L., and Smith, R. E. (1992). Effects of enhancing coach-athlete relationships on youth sport attrition. *The Sport Psychologist, 6*, 111–128.

Bredemeier, B. J., and Shields, D. (1987). Moral growth through physical activity: A structural developmental approach. In D. Gould and M. R. Weiss (Eds.), *Advances in pediatric sport sciences: Behavioral issues* (Vol. 2, pp. 143–156). Champaign, IL: Human Kinetics.

Directory of National Camps. (2001). [On-line]. Available: http://www.national-camps.com/main.cfn

Directory of Athletic Camps. (2001). [On-line]. Available: http://www.athleti-camps.com/

Escobedo, L. G., Marcus, S. E., Holtzman, D., and Giovino, G. A., (1993). Sports participation, age at smoking initiation and the risk of smoking among US high school students. *Journal of the American Medical Association, 269*, 1391–1395.

Ewing, M., and Seefeldt, V. (1989). *Participation and attrition patterns in America's agency-sponsored and interscholastic sports: An executive summary.* North Palm Beach, FL: Sporting Goods Manufacturers Association.

Gould, D., Eklund, R., and Jackson, S. (1993). Coping strategies used by U.S. Olympic wrestlers. *Research Quarterly for Exercise and Sport, 64*, 83–93.

Grossman, C. (1998, February 20). Happy campers, unhappy camps. *USA Today*, p. 12D.

Hanin, Y. L. (1997). Emotions and athletic performance: Individual zones of optimal functioning. *European Yearbook of Sport Psychology, 1*, 29–72.

Haubenstricker, J., Seefeldt, V., Branta, C., and Wisner, D. (2001, March). *Relationships of participation in interscholastic athletics to adult physical activity.* Paper presented at the National Convention of the America Alliance for Health, Physical Education, Recreation and Dance, Cincinnati, OH.

Horn, T. S., and Weiss, M. R. (1991). A developmental analysis of children's self-ability judgements in the physical domain. *Pediatric Exercise Science, 3*, 310–326.

Jeziorski, R. M. (1994). *The importance of school sports in American education and socialization.* Lanham, MD: University Press of America, Inc.

Kann, L., Kinchen, S., Williams, B., Ross, J., Lowry, R., Grumbaum, J., and Kolbe, L. (2000). Participation on sports teams. In Center for Disease Control, *Surveillance Summaries*, June 9: 49 (No. 55-5D) p. 26.

National Federation of State High School Associations. (2001). *1999–2000 athletics participation summary.* [On-line]. Available: http://www.Nfhs.org/part_survey99-00.htm

Sabo, D., Miller, K., Farrell, M., Barnes, G., and Melnick, M. (1998). *The Women's Sports Foundation Report: Sport and Teen Pregnancy.* East Meadow, NY: Women's Sports Foundation.

Seefeldt, V. (Ed.). (1995). *Recreating recreation and sports in Detroit, Hamtramck and Highland Park: Final report to the Skillman Foundation*. Detroit, MI: The Skillman Foundation.

Seefeldt, V., and Clark, M. A. (2002). The continuing evolution in youth sports: What does the future hold? In F. L. Smoll and R. E. Smith (Eds.), *Children and youth in sport: A biopsychosocial perspective* (2nd ed., pp. 591–627). Dubuque, IA: Kendall/Hunt.

Seefeldt, V., Ewing, M., and Walk, S. (1992). *Overview of youth sports programs in the United States*. Washington, DC: Carnegie Council on Adolescent Development.

Shalala, D., and Riley, R. (2000). *Physical activity and health: Adolescent and young adults*. Washington DC: U.S. Department of Health and Human Services.

Smith, R. E., Smoll, F. L., and Curtis, B. (1979). Coach effectiveness training: A cognitive-behavioral approach to enhancing relationship skills in youth sport coaches. *Journal of Sport Psychology, 1*, 59–75.

Sporting Goods Manufacturers Association. (2000). *The SGMA report 2000: U.S. trends in team sports*. North Palm Beach, FL: Author.

U.S. Census Bureau. (2001). *Population projections*. [On-line]. Available: http://www.census.gov/population/www/projections/natsum.html.(January 30)

U.S. Department of Health and Human Services. (1996). *Physical activity and health: A report of the Surgeon General*. Atlanta, GA: U.S. Department of Health and Human Services, Centers for Disease Control and Prevention, National Center for Chronic Disease Prevention and Health.

Vidmar, P. (1992). The role of the federal government in promoting health through the schools: Report from the Presidents' Council on Physical Fitness and Sports. *Journal of School Health, 62*, 129–130.

Weiler, J. (1998). The athletic experience of ethnically diverse girls. *ERIC Clearinghouse on Urban Education*, No. 131. New York, NY.

Williams, C. L., Carter, B. J., and Wynder, E. L. (1981). Prevalence of selected cardiovascular and cancer risk factors in a pediatric population. *Preventive Medicine, 10*, 235–250.

Women's Sports Foundation. (2001). [On-line]. Available: http://www.womenssportsfoundation/results_topics2.html?article+45&record=1

Zill, N., Nord, C. W. and Loomis, C. A. (1995). *Adolescent time use, risky behavior and outcomes: An analysis of national data*. Rockville, MD: Westat.

Part Two

Readiness for Participation

Over the past few decades, there has been a trend toward entering youth sport programs at earlier ages. Often as a result of parental coercion, boys and girls as young as 3 and 4 years of age now compete in a broad range of activities, including swimming, gymnastics, and figure skating. The advent of early childhood education programs, expanded media coverage of youth sports, and schemes for the early identification of athletic talent undoubtedly have contributed to the situation. Consequently, one of the most common questions about youth sports is "When should children begin competing?" The significance of this query is that it reflects a concern for the welfare of the child. Given that the overall objective of youth sports is to provide positive developmental experiences, it follows that the issue of readiness is of paramount importance.

In our society, as in others, many significant life events are organized according to chronological milestones. For example, initiation of formal education and attainment of voting privileges are geared solely to the amount of time that an individual has lived since birth. Yet it is well-known that chronological age alone is a rather poor indicator of an individual's degree of progress toward maturity. Because biological clocks run at different rates, children of the same chronological age may differ tremendously. More exactly, boys in the age range 10 to 16 years may vary as much as 60 months in their physiological maturity, which translates into differences as great as 15 inches in height and 90 pounds in weight.

Biological processes obviously play a primary role in determining readiness for sport. But other characteristics, such as children's cognitive and perceptual abilities and their interests and motivation, must be taken into account. The demands of the task/sport and the nature of the learning environment are also major factors to consider. For these reasons, it is impossible to recommend a specific age for participation of all children in all sports. In this part of the book, three chapters provide different perspectives of the complex process of readiness.

Chapter 4, by John L. Haubenstricker and Vern Seefeldt, focuses on the determination of readiness as a function of (a) the environmental context in which a motor skill is to be learned, (b) the demands of the skill, and (c) the degree to which the learner possesses the critical antecedents that are essential if the skill or activity is to be learned efficiently and effectively. After an overview of environmental factors and task demands that impact motor skill acquisition, consideration is given to the learner's biological attributes, perceptual abilities, and cognitive abilities underlying readiness. Biological attributes include the physical aspects of the body (e.g., height, weight, limb lengths) and the motor abilities (e.g., strength, balance, coordination) associated with them—all of which change with age and maturation. With respect to perceptual abilities (vision, audition, touch-kinesthesis), the authors stress that instructors must be able to assess the capabilities and limitations of their students so that appropriate challenges can be proposed and met. The ensuing discussion of cognitive demands of learning a motor task is limited to developmental processes involved in the expansion of selective attention, the ability to process information, increases in memory and the learner's ability to use stored information, and the use of language to enhance learning. As noted above, however, developmental considerations in readiness are commonly overriden by the predilection of adults to classify children according to chronological age. Three topics associated with this problem are addressed in the final sections of the chapter; specifically, the interrelationship between cognitive and motor functions, the orderly sequence of motor development and necessary antecedent behaviors, and predicting the rate of motor skill acquisition. Haubenstricker and Seefeldt thus provide a maturational approach for determining readiness to participate in sports. Indeed, they point out that inherent defects of classification systems based on linear time can be overcome by instructors who are knowlegeable about the developmental phases that govern the dimensions of human learning.

Michael W. Passer and Beverly J. Wilson deal directly with the age-based question of psychological readiness for participation in youth sports. To establish age guidelines, three criteria are examined: motivational readiness, cognitive readiness, and potential harmful consequences. Motivational readiness, which includes emotional reactions to competition, is seen as an aspect of children's development of an orientation toward social comparison. More exactly, motivational and emotional factors address the extent to which youngsters are attracted to and seek out opportunities to compare their physical abilities against those of peers. The discussion of cognitive readiness focuses on children's capacity for self-evaluation, information-processing capabilities, ability to attribute causality for their performance, and role-taking capabilities. In relation to the preceding, harmful consequences that may result from a lack of motivational and cognitive readiness are highlighted. Based on these criteria, Passer and Wilson conclude their chapter by recommending that children not participate in youth sports until they are 6 or 7 years old. Arguments for setting lower or higher age guidelines are also discussed.

Is there an optimum age at which to introduce children to a sport? In a provocative counterpoint to traditional views, David I. Anderson challenges the conviction that experiences can have a greater influence at some times during life than at others and that such times must be taken advantage of for optimum skill development. To begin, the author posits that there is little evidence to suggest that opportune times, referred to as critical periods, exist for learning the myriad of cultural skills required to function in contemporary society. He also notes that these periods appear to have little relevance to behavioral changes that are as complex and multiply determined as those associated with sport skill learning. The next issue addressed is the concept of readiness, which implies that certain physical, psychological, and behavioral prerequisites must be present before a child can profit from practice on a skill. Again, Anderson concludes that despite the intuitive appeal of the concept, evidence to support the importance of readiness for learning is limited and practical issues, such as how to measure readiness, make it difficult to specify an appropriate age at which to expose a child to a sport. Indeed, the complexity of human development and the diversity of children's interests, motivations, abilities, and prior experiences further complicate the issue. The critique of the critical period and readiness concepts does, however, provide insight into the multitude of factors that must be considered when deciding the appropriate time to initiate sport skill learning. In summarizing his treatise, Anderson asserts that researchers and practitioners might profit most from focusing less attention on the age of first exposure and more attention on other variables that influence learning, such as the quality of experiences, if facilitating skill acquisition and retention is the primary goal.

The Concept of Readiness Applied to the Acquisition of Motor Skills

John L. Haubenstricker, Michigan State University
Vern Seefeldt, Michigan State University

Specialists in human development use the word *readiness* to indicate that an individual has reached a certain point in an ongoing process. With regard to learning, readiness is that point in the life history of an individual at which the critical elements or antecedents necessary for acquiring specific knowledge, skills, values, or behaviors are present. Because the life histories of individuals differ, readiness to learn is unique to each individual.

Individuals are always in a state of readiness to learn something at any point during their life span. The challenge is to match an individual's readiness with appropriate learning tasks. For example, would we expect a 4-year-old to be *ready* to acquire the knowledge and skills necessary to play first base on an adult baseball team, or to play goalie on a high school soccer team? Obviously not! Why not? We would be quick to identify a number of prerequisites or critical elements that would be necessary to successfully perform at these positions, such as physical size, hand-eye-foot coordination, agility, mental alertness, knowledge of situational play, the reaction time and movement time needed to respond to balls in flight, and the specific motor skills associated with the positions. Should we expect a 4-year-old to be *ready* to play first base on a competitive softball team comprised of other 4-year-olds? Probably not, because a 4-year-old does not possess the critical antecedents necessary to play this complex position, and the child may experience even less success because his or her teammates also lack the prerequisites for their positions.

In contrast, after adjusting the size and weight of equipment, and distances, can we expect a 4-year-old to learn to hold a bat properly, hit a ball off a "T," and then run to "first base" as part of a drill? Can we expect the child to catch a ball tossed softly from a short distance; or, to field a ball that has been carefully rolled, and then run to tag a base? We would expect most 4-year-olds to be able to learn these tasks because we believe that they possess the prerequisites to perform them.

Determining the readiness of individuals to learn motor skills is a complex process, and it requires analysis of three major interrelated dimensions: (a) the environmental context in which the skill is to be learned or performed, (b) the demands or requirements of the skill or activity itself, and (c) the degree to which the learner possesses the critical antecedents necessary to learn the skill or activity (Shumway-Cook and Woollacott, 1995). A schematic representation of these relationships is presented in Figure 4.1. Research and experience have provided information about the growth and development of children and youth (Breckenridge and Murphy, 1969; Malina and Bouchard, 1991), some general benchmarks for the acquisition of fine and gross motor skills during infancy and childhood (see reviews by Haubenstricker and Seefeldt, 1986; Haywood and Getchell, 2001; Payne and Isaacs, 1999), and teaching/learning progressions for fundamental motor and basic sport skills (Blakemore, Hawkes, and Burton, 1991; Michigan's Exemplary Physical Education Curriculum Project, 2000). Knowledge of such information can provide the basis for teachers and coaches to determine the readiness of individual learners to acquire specific motor skills.

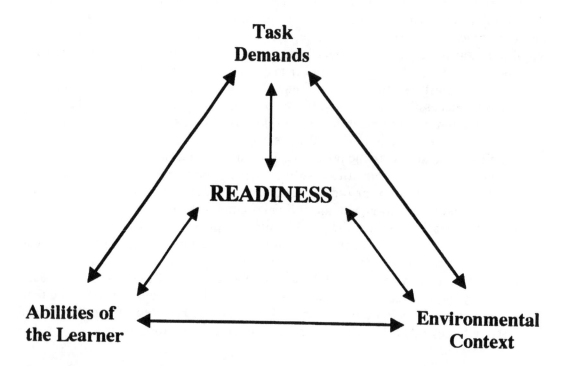

Figure 4.1. Model of readiness for the acquisition of motor skills.

Complexity of the Environmental Context

The environmental context in which a motor skill is to be learned can have a significant impact on the success or failure of the learner in acquiring the skill. Some teachers and coaches prefer that children learn requisite sport skills by having them play "the game." This approach provides a very complex environment because the learner must not only learn the skill, but must concurrently attempt to apply it in a purposeful way. Few, if any, individuals benefit from this approach. However, placing novices in a game setting may be useful for one reason, and that is to show them that they, indeed, are novices.

Other teachers and coaches may focus on skill drills followed by game play. While this approach has some merit, it leaves out two essential components—the key elements of the skill itself, and transitional or lead-up activities that permit the use of a skill in increasingly complex contexts. Setting up an appropriate learning environment should be based on a thorough understanding of the skill itself and the ultimate (game) context in which it is to be used, as well as knowledge of the readiness of the learner to benefit from each context.

A suggested progression of environmental contexts against which the readiness of an individual can be compared is as follows:

1. Have the learners practice the key components of specific skills alone until they can demonstrate the skills using appropriate form. The learners must possess the antecedents necessary to learn the skill.

2. Use drills to practice the skills until they are habituated, and then to develop variations of the skills. Repetitions are needed to fixate form in environments that are relatively simple, but which may include limited elements of cooperation and/or competition to facilitate learning.

3. Use drills to practice and become proficient in skill combinations. For example, in basketball, skill combinations might include catch and pass; catch, dribble while moving, and shoot (or pass); dribble, pivot, and pass; and, catch and shoot.

4. Use lead-up activities and situational play to introduce rules of the sport, offensive and defensive concepts, position play, teamwork, strategies, and the performance of individual and combination skills in a competitive setting.

5. Play the actual sport. The assumption is that when arriving at this point of the progression, the learner is *ready* to participate effectively, and will experience positive outcomes through participation in the sport.

The progression suggested above implies that youth sport programs should be prepared to accommodate individuals in various states of readiness. Thus, children and youth whose readiness precludes successful participation in a highly competitive sport environment should be offered opportunities to learn sport skills in a less threatening developmental or instructional environment.

Requirements of the Skill

In order to identify the critical antecedents of a motor skill, the coach or teacher must be able to determine the requirements of the skill when it is used in various contexts. A skill that is practiced in isolation will have fewer critical antecedents than when the skill must be performed in an actual game. For example, knowledge of when and where to use a particular skill in a game, and how to execute it with opponents attempting to interfere with its performance are critical antecedents for success in a game, but not necessarily when practicing the skill alone.

The first task of the teacher or coach is to determine the key elements of the task itself. In other words, what sequence of movements is involved in the task? What type of coordination and how much of it is required (hand-eye, foot-eye, hand-eye-foot)? What are the strength demands? What are the energy demands for performing the skill in a simple environment? Do these demands change as the learning environment becomes more complex; and, to what extent do other antecedents such as pattern recognition (of players), field of vision, working memory, and decision-making become important? Conducting a careful analysis of a motor skill will enable the teacher or coach to make a better determination of the readiness of an individual to learn the skill.

Attributes and Abilities of the Learner

The readiness of an individual to learn a particular motor skill is dependent on how well the abilities of the learner match the requirements of the skill and the contextual demands of the environment. Although it may be impossible to identify all the attributes and abilities that influence the learning of a motor skill by an individual, some of the more obvious ones include biological attributes, perceptual abilities, cognitive abilities, antecedent motor skills, and prior experiences with motor skills. The status of most, if not all, of these attributes and abilities in children is immature when compared to that of adults.

Biological Attributes

Biological attributes include the physical aspects of the body and the motor abilities associated with them. Examples of physical aspects are height, weight, limb lengths, body shape or physique, body proportions, and tissue composition. Motor abilities, defined by Magill (2001) as "an ability that is specifically related to the performance of a motor skill" (p. 16), include abilities such as muscular strength and endurance, cardio-respiratory endurance, agility, static and dynamic balance, flexibility, and neuromuscular coordination.

The acquisition or performance of motor skills requires strength and energy expenditure, more in some skills than in others. Physical size and body shape often provide an advantage in skills such as the spike in volleyball or rebounding in basketball (being tall and muscular), a routine on the uneven bars in gymnastics (being short and muscular), and the lineman's block in football (having a large body frame, muscle, and weight). Guarding in basketball and defending against the pass in football require agility. Distance running requires cardiovascular endurance.

Because biological attributes change with age and maturation, the essential question becomes, "Does the learner possess the critical biological antecedents (basic movements, neuromuscular coordination, agility, strength, energy, flexibility, etc.) necessary to learn a specific motor skill within a particular environmental context?" For a detailed description of the biological growth and motor performance of children and youth, see Malina and Bouchard (1991).

Perceptual Abilities

The acquisition of a motor skill is a complex process that is the result of perception, cognition, and action (Shumway-Cook and Woollacott, 1995). Perceptual abilities are critical to the acquisition of motor skills because they provide information that is essential to the planning of purposeful movement. Through perception we determine our orientation in the environment with regard to posture and balance, and our relationship to objects and individuals. Perception enables us to compare and integrate input from the various sensory modalities, and it is the process through which we recognize the form, flow, and pattern of movements within a skill, as well as those of movements within the environment (Smith, 1984).

The process of perception is dependent upon sensory information provided by various receptors in the body. Sensory receptors provide information about the physiological status of the body (e.g., chemoceptors and pain receptors); the orientation of the body to gravity, the relative position of body parts to each other, and the movement of body parts (proprioceptors); the location of the body in the environment (visual and tactile receptors); and the nature of the environment itself (visual, auditory, tactile, and perhaps olfactory and gustatory receptors). Perception involves not only the gathering of information, but synthesizing it, and comparing it with previously stored information (Williams, 1983). Thus, through the process of perception the learner attempts to derive meaning from current information available in the internal and external environment so that appropriate actions can be taken to achieve a particular goal or objective, such as learning a new motor skill.

The status of the perceptual abilities of the learner, and the ability of the coach or instructor to construct an appropriate learning environment to match those abilities, will determine the readiness of the learner to acquire a specific motor skill. However, there are many perceptual abilities and most are developmental in nature. Therefore, the teacher or coach must not only be aware of various perceptual abilities, but also of the changes that they undergo in children and youth.

Visual abilities. Perceptual abilities associated with vision, hearing, touch and proprioception (kinesthesis) are the most directly related to learning motor skills. Of these, we tend to depend on our visual abilities the most (Magill, 2001). Visual abilities important to motor skill acquisition include static and dynamic acuity, depth perception, peripheral vision, figure-ground perception, and the perception of movement. *Visual acuity* is the clarity with which we can see the details of objects. *Static visual acuity* (SVA) refers to the sharpness of vision when the individual and what is being viewed are both stationary. Most children acquire 20/20 static distance vision by 5 years of age (Payne and Isaacs, 1999), but maturation of the macula of the eye does not occur until age 6 years (Lowrey, 1986). SVA can improve up to about 10 years of age, with periods of rapid improvement occurring from 5 to 7 years and again from 9 to 10 years (Williams, 1983). SVA becomes less precise as the distance between the learner and the object is increased, when illumination is decreased, and when the contrast between the object and its background is diminished (Sage, 1984).

Dynamic visual acuity (DVA) is the ability to see detail in objects that are moving. Although DVA can improve up to age 20 years (Morris, 1977), major periods of improvement occur from 5 to 7 years, 9 to 10 years, and from 11 to 12 years (Williams, 1983). DVA is inversely related to the speed of moving objects; the faster objects are moving, the more difficult they are to track and the harder it is to identify details about them. Teachers and coaches should consider the DVA of children when teaching them motor skills that require efficient visual tracking of rapidly moving objects.

The visual perception of depth is a requisite for learning most motor skills, because it provides information about the distance between the learner and stationary or moving objects in the environment. *Depth perception* also yields information about relative distances between objects in the environment. The perception of depth is dependent on binocular vision. A three-dimensional view of the environment is the result of the integration by the cerebrum of slightly different flat images provided by each eye. Individuals with one functional eye are dependent on monocular cues to depth such as proximal size, brightness, partial overlap, shading, texture, and linear perspective (Sage, 1984). The ability to perceive depth is usually mature by 6 years of age (Payne and Isaacs, 1999); however, the ability to judge specific distances (such as required by a golfer in order to select the appropriate club) reaches adult capacity by about 12 years of age (Williams, 1983). Accuracy in judging absolute distances apparently can be improved with practice. The capacity of children to judge distances, particularly of moving objects, with speed and accuracy should be addressed by teachers and coaches when teaching new skills to them.

Another visual ability related to skill acquisition and performance is *peripheral vision*. Peripheral vision refers to the ability to see moving objects or people in the lateral areas of the visual field while the eyes are fixed on a central point in the environment. Good peripheral vision is necessary in dynamic sport situations where one's relationship to other players and to the flow of play is important. Peripheral vision is also helpful in providing information about the position of limbs or implements in skills such as catching a ball or throwing a javelin (Sage, 1984). Functionally, effective use of peripheral vision may not mature until the teen years. In a study by Davids (1987), cited in Payne and Isaacs (1999), 9-year-old children made more catching errors than 12- and 15-year-old subjects when presented with peripheral visual information in a dual-task setting. Thus, the size of the peripheral visual field, as well as use of information in the field, may be limitations for children in learning motor skills that demand simultaneous monitoring of a moving target and the avoidance of objects in the environment. For example, a child learning to catch a fly ball must not only keep track of the flight of the ball, but must also avoid obstacles while moving to intercept the ball.

The human brain tends to organize information in visual space to bring order out of chaos. During the process of organizing visual information in the environment, some features of the environment become focal points or "figures" and are separate from the rest of the environment, which becomes the "ground." This is known as the *figure-ground* principle (Sage, 1984). Figure-ground perception improves through the childhood years, with substantial refinement between 8 and 13 years of age, and it undergoes continued enhancement through the teen-age years (Williams, 1983).

One of the responsibilities of the teacher or coach is to help the learner identify the "figure" or "figures" in a skill-learning situation. This may be relatively easy when the figures are objects such as bats, balls, sticks, and pucks. It may be more difficult when it involves the placement of body parts on less specific "figures," like the placement of the hands on specific areas of a vaulting horse, or the positioning of a foot on a mat. Sometimes the "figure" can be enhanced through the use of added tape marks to aid in learning a skill. In dynamic sport contexts, the "figure" may change from moment to moment (e.g., from a ball to an opponent to a teammate). Color is often used to create contrast between figure and background. For example, in baseball a green background is used to provide contrast to a white ball for the safety of batters. Members of sports teams and officials wear uniforms of different colors to avoid confusion and to enhance safety and performance. Relevant environmental and task cues are "figures" for motor skill acquisition. Children usually need greater assistance than teenagers and adults in identifying and using these "figures."

An ability that requires visual acuity, figure-ground perception, depth perception and peripheral vision is *perception of movement* or visual tracking. Although infants have the capacity to track slowly moving objects, it is not until about 12 years of age that children can make both quick and accurate judgments about objects moving in space (Williams, 1983). Motor skills that require visual tracking and movement of the body or its parts to intercept a moving object are complex. Consider the case of an 8-year-old female goalie attempting to intercept a soccer ball being kicked toward the goal area. First, she must locate the ball. This may require repositioning the body. If the ball is already in flight, she must quickly determine its distance, speed, and angle of approach, and predict its time and the location of its arrival. Almost simultaneously, she must plan and then implement a movement response so that she gets to the intercept point on time and is positioned so that she can catch, kick, or deflect the ball to prevent it from crossing the goal line. If the dimensions of the goal are designed for adult play, her task becomes all the more ominous because she has to protect a greater area.

The key issues for the teacher or coach with regard to visual perception of motion is the ability of the learner to identify what movement is to be observed and then respond quickly and accurately to the movement perceived. For example, we have learned that young children cannot react successfully to baseballs that are pitched overhand; therefore we place the ball on a "T" so that they can strike a stationary ball. Older children may be able to hit a ball pitched by an adult who adjusts the speed of the ball to the ability of the batter. Children 10 to 12 years of age may be ready to strike balls pitched by their peers. The task of the teacher or coach is to optimize the visual learning environment so that the learner can make progress in acquiring motor skills. Additional examples of the role of vision in the acquisition and performance of various types of motor skills are provided by Magill (2001).

Auditory abilities. Most teachers and coaches recognize the importance of hearing or audition in the acquisition and performance of motor skills. We expect children and youths to listen when we provide instructions on how to perform a skill, when we inform them of relevant movement and environmental cues, and when we provide feedback after an attempt at performing the skill. We want them to learn to respond to auditory signals for starting, maintaining, or stopping movements. For example, we use speech, whistles, and even guns (in track and swimming) to start and/or stop the performance of skills. The dance teacher may rely on beating a drum or on music to assist individuals in learning and performing dance skills. We become aware of auditory feedback inherent in performing skills such as the "clank" of a basketball against a rim as opposed to the "swish" of the ball going through a net, or the "crack" of the bat on a well-hit ball. We may use either familiar or novel sounds in the environment to orient our bodies for visual input.

Despite the obvious importance of audition in learning motor skills, little research has been conducted on the role of auditory abilities in sport. The capacity to hear is present at birth and attempts at localizing sounds occur within the first few months after birth. Basic listening skills in conjunction with language development are well established by the fourth year (Lowery, 1986). Common auditory abilities associated with information-processing tasks include auditory acuity, sound localization, auditory discrimination, auditory memory, and auditory figure-ground (Williams, 1983). *Auditory acuity* is the ability to detect the presence or absence of sound. This ability appears to mature during the early childhood years. *Sound localization* refers to the ability to identify the spatial orientation of sounds in the environment. Williams (1983) reported that little is known about developmental changes in this ability during the early and middle childhood years. However, the ability of young children to orient their bodies to sounds within their immediate environment indicates a readiness to listen to verbal instructions or feedback from a parent, teacher, or coach.

Three auditory perceptual abilities that seem critical to motor skill acquisition are auditory discrimination, auditory memory, and auditory figure-ground. *Auditory discrimination* is the ability to differentiate between two sounds, particularly with regard to the sounds of speech. Because of the use of speech in motor skill acquisition, it is important that the learner be able to correctly hear and understand the words that are spoken. The vocabulary used by the instructor or coach also must be appropriate. Auditory discrimination skills continue refinement until age 12 or 13 (Williams, 1983). *Auditory memory* refers to remembering sequences or patterns of auditory stimuli. The capacity to remember sequences of words and sentences is important when receiving verbal instructions or feedback during skill acquisition. Available data suggest that complex auditory memory skills reach maturity around 14 to 15 years of age (Williams, 1983). *Auditory figure-ground* is analogous to visual figure-ground in that it refers to selecting relevant sounds from sounds that are distracting or not useful. The time course for the development of this ability in children and youths is not clearly established. However, most teachers and coaches are aware of instances where children selectively attend to other sounds rather than to their instructions. Examples of this are listening to the conversation of teammates while the coach is speaking to the team, or attending to the sirens of police cars or fire trucks that are passing nearby. In contrast, while learning and performing motor skills the young athlete must learn to selectively attend to critical information such as auditory signals, instructions, and feedback while blocking out distractions such as crowd noise and "advice" from others.

Tactile-kinesthetic abilities. The sensory modalities of touch and kinesthesis or proprioception usually function together during purposeful movement. The sense of touch is derived primarily from receptors located in the skin. These receptors provide information about the presence and location of contact between two or more body parts, or between the body and another object or surface in the environment. They also provide information about the intensity of contact (pressure) and vibration, the texture (smoothness, roughness) and consistency (hardness, softness) of objects or surfaces, and contribute to the perception of size and shape. Proprioceptive sensations are largely generated by receptors located in muscles, tendons, joint tissues, and the vestibular apparatus of the inner ear (Sage, 1984). Collectively, proprioceptors provide information about the position and movement of the body and its parts, the orientation of the body in space, as well as the muscular tensions and forces created within the body. Sage also cited evidence that receptors in the skin overlying joints may contribute to awareness of joint position.

Developmentally, tactile-kinesthetic abilities appear to develop relatively early. For example, by the age of 5 years, children can accurately localize single points on the body where they have been touched; the ability to identify the location of simultaneous or sequential touching of two body parts is mature by 6 years of age;

and, the ability to accurately identify, discriminate, or recognize shapes or forms manually is complete by age 8 (Williams, 1983). The ability to replicate the extent of movement of limbs (position memory) improves at least through the age of 10 years. Four tests of proprioception were administered by Haubenstricker (1971) to kindergarten, first, and second grade children (ages 5–7 years). The children were blindfolded for all the tests. Improvement in performance was noted across the grades on three of the four tests—one-foot balance, thickness discrimination, and weight discrimination. No significant improvement was noted on a task requiring dual-limb positioning.

Although the tactile-kinesthesis system tends to be subservient to vision, its importance in motor skill acquisition is recognized by motor learning theorists (Magill, 2001; Sage, 1984; Shumway-Cook and Woollacott, 1995). Proprioceptive feedback resulting from movement provides important information to the central nervous system concerning the execution of planned movements, and it undoubtedly plays a role in corrective adjustments during slow movements and movement sequences. It may also influence the timing of the initiation of motor commands, and plays a role in the coordination of body and limb segments. However, little is known about the effectiveness of consciously focusing on kinesthetic awareness in order to facilitate motor learning.

Because some components of tactile-kinesthetic perception are still improving during early and middle childhood, teachers and coaches may assist readiness for skill acquisition with some of the following practices. Permit young children to manipulate equipment related to the skill. For example, when working on kicking skills, permit children to handle the ball to become aware of its size, shape, consistency, and weight. It also may be helpful to have available balls of varying sizes, weights, and composition, and let children practice kicking balls that feel most comfortable to them. When teaching batting skills, have a variety of bats and balls available so that children can explore various combinations. Determine how many of the children are ready to use the equipment required by the rules of the game.

Another approach is to manually assist children who cannot respond appropriately to visual modeling and/or verbal instructions. They may benefit from being manually placed in the appropriate postural stance, manually guided to a proper grip, or physically guided through a movement pattern.

Summary. Many of the perceptual abilities related to vision, audition, and touch-kinesthesis are still developing during the childhood years. Research suggests that many of these abilities do not reach maturity until 12 or 13 years of age. In addition, there is substantial individual variation in the perceptual abilities of similarly aged children. The teacher or coach of motor skills should be cognizant of differences in perceptual abilities within and between ages during the childhood years, and seek ways to accommodate the various states of perceptual readiness by modifying task demands and contextual complexity.

Cognitive Abilities

The acquisition of a motor skill does not occur without cognitive involvement. Initially, a mental structure or image of the skill must be developed; otherwise, there is no framework or blueprint from which to develop a movement plan. Fitts and Posner (1967) referred to this early phase of skill acquisition as the "cognitive phase." Bernstein (1967) stressed the importance of the establishment of a "motor image" based on sensory information and perceptual processing. In other words, the learner must understand the nature of the skill and its objective, and develop an "executive plan" or "motor program" before an effective attempt at performing a skill can be made. Once the first attempts have been made, cognitive processes are involved in evaluating various types of feedback regarding the performance, and in making decisions regarding changes for the next attempt at performing the skill. Language and vocabulary are important when instructions and feedback are provided verbally. Mental rehearsal of motor skills also has been found to be effective in enhancing skill acquisition. In addition, cognitive processing is crucial when decisions are to be made regarding the use of a particular sport skill in the context of playing a sport.

Because of the involvement of cognition throughout the process of motor skill acquisition, the readiness of children for the cognitive demands of skill learning must be addressed. Do the cognitive abilities of children differ from those of adults? When are children cognitively ready to learn a certain motor skill? These questions are not easy to answer. Moreover, due to the extensive literature on the cognitive development of children, the discussion in this section will be limited to some of the cognitive abilities associated with the processing of information for skill acquisition. These abilities include selective attention, processing information, memory, making decisions, feedback, and language.

Selective attention. The capacity to selectively attend is present early in life. For example, young infants can visually attend to objects moving through their visual space. They tend to focus on familiar faces or novel stimuli. Thus, the problem for the coach of young athletes is not the athletes' ability to attend, but rather to what they are attending and for how long they can attend. Young athletes, unless highly motivated, tend to be easily distracted. They may focus on a dog running across the playing field rather than watching a demonstration or listening to instructions; and then be thoroughly confused when they are instructed to begin practicing what has been demonstrated. They typically also have a shorter attention span than adolescents or adults.

From a cognitive perspective, readiness to learn may be as much a function of the environment created by the coach, as it is a function of the intellectual capacity of the athlete. In order to maintain the attention of young athletes, the coach must seek to reduce distractions (e.g., positioning players so that all can see and hear), keep demonstrations and explanations short, change drills frequently, focus only on the most relevant cues, and positively redirect attention when distractions occur or concentration is lost.

Processing information. The ability to process information is related to age, experience, and the nature of the information to be processed. Children do not have the cognitive resources of adolescents and adults to process information. Even though the sensory receptors of children are nearly mature by six years of age, their perceptual abilities are not (as discussed in the previous section). As a result, their information processing skills are less accurate and slower than those of adolescents and adults (Thomas, Thomas, and Gallagher, 1981). Children cannot label, code, and organize information as rapidly as adults. Because of their limited experiences, they have less stored information against which they can make comparisons and subsequent judgments. In addition, if the information they are receiving is too complex in difficulty or detail, the wrong information may be processed, leading to inaccurate decisions.

The coach can facilitate readiness by adjusting the speed, amount, and complexity of information provided to young athletes. By using appropriate vocabulary, keeping instructions and demonstrations simple, allowing athletes to ask for clarification, simplifying the practice environment, anticipating slower response times, and showing patience when incorrect responses occur, the coach can enhance skill learning in young athletes.

Memory. Information processing involves the use of memory. Memory influences readiness to learn in at least two ways. The first is the amount of knowledge and experience stored in memory that can be drawn upon to learn motor skills. In general, children have less knowledge and experience than adults so they are limited in what they can retrieve from their long-term memory to apply to new learning situations. The second influence of memory is the amount of information that can be held in short term or "working memory" when performing mental operations (Hitch and Towse, 1995). Working memory is needed to respond to instructions, to keep demonstrated movement patterns in consciousness, and to compare sensory information with long-term memory. Research has shown that young children generally can only keep two or three items in their working memory compared to the capacity of adolescents and adults to maintain from five to nine items (Dempster, 1981). The implication for coaches is that instructions involving sequential behavior should be limited to one or two steps, and that children should not be required to attend to more than one or two movement cues during a practice trial. In addition, providing specific knowledge, relevant cues, and concrete examples should enhance working memory.

One strategy that may positively influence readiness is mental rehearsal—mentally repeating new information in order to remember it. This ability develops around age 7 (Kail, 1990) and has been shown to enhance the acquisition of skill in children (Thomas et al., 1981). Asking children to repeat verbal instructions and movement cues out loud, or to repeat them silently to themselves, are two ways to use mental rehearsal.

Decision-making. Because their perceptual skills and their information processing abilities are limited when compared to adults, young athletes are also less adept at making timely and accurate decisions. Sometimes decisions are delayed or inappropriate because they do not have enough information in memory to make an accurate decision rapidly. At other times, the demands for a response may be too fast and the learner cannot process available information fast enough to make an appropriate response. Motor skills can be learned more readily when the demand for quick responses is removed and when instructions are related to past experiences. A simplified learning environment where the amount of information provided and demands for speed in decision-making are gradually increased can facilitate readiness for skill acquisition in young athletes. Furthermore, coaches must exercise patience and have realistic expectations when placing young athletes in competitive practice and game situations where rapid responses are required.

Feedback. Limitations in information processing skills also apply to the use of feedback in young athletes. Young athletes often are not aware of feedback information available to them following a performance and are dependent on guidance from the coach. They need to know what feedback is important and how to use it to improve their next performance. If a shortstop throws the ball out of the reach of the first baseman, what feedback is available to the shortstop? Why didn't the ball reach its target? Did the shortstop not look at the target? Was the shortstop off balance when the throw was made? Was the throw made too rapidly? Was there too much or not enough force in the throw? What will I do the next time if the ball is hit to me? Young athletes may not reflect about these questions. The coach can facilitate learning by helping young athletes to recognize and use the feedback available to them following a trial or performance, and by providing additional cues to improve performance. Keeping in mind the cognitive limitations of young athletes, feedback should be kept simple and focused on what changes need to be made rather than on what was done incorrectly. In addition, interactions with young athletes in the form of feedback should be positive so that they view their unsuccessful attempts at performing a skill as learning and not as failure situations.

Language. A key factor in skill learning is communication between the teacher or coach and the learner. Certified teachers and parents of young children usually are familiar with the vocabulary and comprehension of young children, and consequently use a vocabulary that can be understood by the children. However, the young volunteer coach may use a vocabulary that is too difficult, or may resort to using "Baby talk" in an attempt to adjust his or her communication to the level of the young athlete. One solution to this problem is for the coach to request that the athletes tell him or her when they don't understand a certain word or a set of instructions. Another approach is for the coach to ask the athletes if they understand what was said, or to have them repeat the instructions in their own words.

Coaches also must be cognizant of the "tone" they use in communicating with young athletes. The same words, such as "Come over here," can be expressed in a harsh and punitive tone or in a friendly and supportive tone. A positive tone can influence the readiness of young athletes to learn new skills, whereas a negative approach may create fear and decrease the desire (and thus the readiness) to learn a new skill.

Sometimes coaches have the opportunity to teach young athletes who speak a different language, or have little command of the prevailing language in the country. Under these circumstances, the coach may need to use gestures or even manually guide the young athlete to positions in situations where visual demonstrations don't provide sufficient information.

Summary. The concept that "Children are not miniature adults" applies to the cognitive development of children as well as to their biological development. Most cognitive abilities continue to develop during childhood and reach adult capacity during the early teenage years. With practice and experience, they may continue to improve into the adult years. The coach who is aware of such developmental changes, and attempts to adjust the learning environment to match the capabilities of the young athletes, can have a strong, positive influence on their "readiness" to acquire new skills.

Interrelationship Between Cognitive and Motor Functions

The teaching of motor skills has traditionally ignored the importance of learning styles and cognitive functions that may influence the rate of learning (Connolly, 1970). Attempts to identify and incorporate the hierarchy of cognitive structures into situations that involve motor skill learning are a welcome addition to the literature (Kelso and Clark, 1982; Kugler, Kelso, and Turvey, 1982; Schmidt, 1975; Smith and Thelen, 1993). The relatively late incorporation of cognitive information into the theory and practice of motor skill acquisition may have been due to the strong influence that biologists had on the field during the first part of the twentieth century. For example, Piaget's developmental sequence, originally presented in 1952, received only scant attention in the United States for nearly two decades. Hebb's (1949) attempt to explain readiness to learn by incorporating earlier experiences into present actions is still a fundamental part of most theories of skill acquisition. Hebb's model suggests that experience in a variety of tasks aids the performer in (a) selecting more appropriate stimuli, (b) making finer discriminations concerning the accuracy of the response, (c) attending to a task for a longer period of time, (d) being able to depend more on transfer of elements, (e) being able to retain more of what was learned by integrating it with previous experience, and (f) eliminating faulty responses from alternatives available.

The concurrent and inseparable development of cognitive and motor processes in early life were emphasized by Bruner (1969), who affirmed this relationship as a result of extensive research with children below 6 months of age. He noted that the ability to solve problems that require a motor response is a process that begins soon after birth. According to Bruner, the infant's initial movements are not random responses but represent the answers to hypotheses that are formed by problems that are unique to early development. Out of these early movements the infant develops a hierarchy of functions that provides the basis for future learning. The reflexes and reactions that are present at birth provide the repertoire from which the infant learns to *differentiate* the actions that are effective and efficient in completing a specific task. The second mechanism, which Bruner termed *modularization*, permits the infant to partition and recombine the movements into additional patterns. *Substitution* is a means whereby one action is used in place of another, thus adding variety to the responses available. *Sequential integration* permits the selection of a variant order, in lieu of solving the same problems with a rigid sequence of movements. *Place holding* permits the infant to carry on two motor skills while devoting alternate degrees of attention to both of them. *Internalization of action* is the ability to carry out behavior symbolically.

The ability to perform complex motor operations and the transferability of these mechanisms to many motor tasks during the first 2 years of life underscore the importance of abundant stimulation in early infancy. This definition of abilities also illustrates the need for additional studies of cognitive and motor development during the periods of early and middle childhood.

Perhaps the most recent of the paradigm shifts to emerge in viewing the concept of readiness was that of dynamical systems, introduced by Kugler et al. (1982) in a book edited by Kelso and Clark (1982). The theory of dynamical systems evolved from contemporary theories of motor control. *Dynamical systems* theory suggests that the emerging movement is a product of the individual's cognitive status, neural maturation, and all the environmental elements to which the individual has been and is being exposed. The theory of dynamical systems views the contributing systems, whether neurological, biological, psychological, or environmental, as equally important, with no single factor being ultimately more important than any of the others. This all-encompassing theory combines the ontogenetic with the phylogenetic forces that influence the acquisition of motor skills. Its primary contribution may be the attention it focuses on variables that have heretofore been ignored as contributors to enhanced motor function.

The onset of locomotion increases the opportunities for sensory stimulation available to the child (see Haywood and Getchell, 2001; Keogh and Sudden, 1985). The motor repertoire is expanded when responses are made to an incessant desire for sensory stimulation. A cyclic process is initiated whereby an increase in sensory experiences contributes to the variety and frequency of motor responses. An enlarged repertoire of motor patterns provides more options to the performer, and a greater proportion of successful responses contributes to a desire for additional stimulation.

This cycle is self-sustaining, with the provision that the environment contains appropriate stimuli and the child has the opportunity to formulate the motor responses. On the basis of this proposed sequence, it is evident that an abundance of experiences that culminate in successful motor responses early in life is an efficient way to establish the readiness necessary for subsequent learning.

Order and Sequence in Motor Skill Acquisition

The orderly nature of early motor behavior has frequently led to the erroneous impression that infants or young children acquire their motor repertoires at approximately the same chronological age. However, because genetic endowment determines the boundaries within which the skills are expressed, a wide range exists in the ages at which children learn basic motor skills (Roberton and Halverson, 1988; Haubenstricker and Seefeldt, 1986). Consequently, classification of motor skills by age has less utility for teachers of movement than having them know the developmental sequences and the ability to provide the appropriate experiences when the child is ready for the next step toward maturity (Payne and Isaacs, 1999). Also, many scales that purport to assess motor performance for compensatory or remedial motor education lack the specificity that is necessary for prescriptive teaching. These scales were developed primarily by psychologists and physicians and have basic problems in defining the specificity in developmental patterns that are common to children beyond one year of age (Bruner, 1969).

The identification of an orderly sequence of development in various fundamental movement skills has provided teachers with practical guides concerning the readiness of children to move on to the next level of a particular skill. However, we do not yet have sufficient evidence to suggest when the introduction of specific skills should occur; nor do we have sufficient evidence to know which antecedent conditions are essential or helpful in moving the child into a position of readiness for specific skills. Apparently these movements have their origins in the reflexes and reactions displayed during the first year of life.

Predicting the Rate of Motor Skill Acquisition

The concept of maturation and the use of skeletal age and body size as criteria for readiness to engage in certain activities are discussed by Malina (this volume). Even though research evidence suggests that the selection and classification of performers for subsequent competition in sports and dance be determined by variables such as biological maturity, skill, body size, and experience, the grouping of young athletes has been primarily a season-by-season procedure based solely on chronological age, thereby ignoring the time-honored admonition of C. W. Crampton (1908) who stated, "All observations, records and investigations of children, and all treatments of children, whether pedagogical or medical, social or ethical, must regard physiological age as a primary and fundamental basis" (pp. 235–237).

Virtually all of the investigators whose work was reviewed for this topic reported the retrospective prediction of success, often through the use of regression equations that were obtained from cross-sectional studies or computed at the termination of longitudinal studies. None of the investigators attempted to predict the success of individuals in specific athletic endeavors prior to their involvement in activity programs, nor did they conduct a longitudinal follow-up to determine the accuracy of the original predictions. In no case were the predictive equations applied to other samples as a test of their validity. This neglect is unfortunate in light of the national interest that is currently focused on organized sports and dance for young children, the well-defined objectives for success that are commonly associated with these programs, and the desire on the part of most coaches and teachers to foretell the success of their clients at the earliest possible age. Perhaps the most useful function of predictive criteria would be the determination of relative success, thus eliminating the need for children to engage in tasks with which they have a relatively low level of success.

The relationship between the various indicators of biological maturity, commonly classified under the phrase *primary* and *secondary sex characteristics*, is modest to high, depending on whether individuals mature early or late in relation to their chronological age peers. As might be expected, the relationship between skeletal age and the primary and secondary sex characteristics is also in the modest-to-high range. Thus, if skeletal age has a high positive relationship with height, weight, breadth, and measures of circumference, and also with the primary and secondary sex characteristics, it seems ironic that some form of predictive equation that incorporates some indicator of maturational age is not used more frequently as a means of predicting the readiness of children to engage in various sports. However, the ease of grouping children by chronological age and the expertise that is required to classify them by any other technique or formula causes the promoters of youth sports to routinely revert to the qualifying criterion of chronological age.

The practice of using chronological age as a criterion for eligibility to enrollment in educational settings has been subject to question for decades (Uphoff and Gilmore, 1986; Sweetland and DeSimone, 1987). Educators realized that chronological age was merely a measure of time, and not of maturity, physical ability or cognitive function. More recently, reliance on chronological age as the sole criterion for eligibility in age-group sports has also been challenged, because of the inherent inequity in such a procedure. Typically, the first day of the calendar year, January 1st, is the reference date for eligibility. Under this system of eligibility, some individuals may be 9, 10, or 11 months older than their teammates by the time teams are selected. If team membership includes a 2-year age range, there may be as much as a 24-month difference in age between teammates.

The influence of *relative age*, the vernacular used to describe the inequities built into the calendar-age method of determining eligibility in youth sports, has been studied in ice hockey and soccer (Daniel and Janssen, 1987; Barnsley and Thompson,

1988; Boucher and Mutimer, 1994; Montelpare, Scott, and Pelino, 1997). Clearly, the occurrence of a birth date early in the calendar year was an advantage in being selected for team membership. Individuals on rosters of select or elite teams disproportionately had birthdays during the first four months of the calendar year. To circumvent the influence of relative age, Boucher and Halliwell (1991) recommended a 9-month rotational system to be completed every 3 years, wherein each athlete would have the advantage of being the oldest in his/her age group once every 2 years. The 3 x 3 month rotation system seems unnecessarily confusing and impractical for sponsors of sports programs who have heretofore had difficulty implementing any system of age-group eligibility that was more complicated than use of the standard calendar year as a reference.

The influence of relative age can be markedly diminished by adopting a system that identifies the most important date in the sports year (usually the date on which rosters are completed) and designating that date as the reference point for eligibility. The date of age determination (DAD) is then set 3 months prior to the reference date (Seefeldt, 1992). This method of determining eligibility on the basis of chronological age results in 50% of any class having birth dates within 3 months of the most important day in the sport year. It also has the advantage of stability, because the DAD remains the same from year to year unless the date on which rosters are determined also changes.

Part of the reluctance to use skeletal age as a predictor of motor performance is that teachers and coaches cannot easily obtain such an assessment. The determination of skeletal age requires special competencies in its procurement and assessment that are not required when obtaining other growth data. Additional deterrent may result from a reluctance to expose children to X-irradiation except for diagnostic purposes. However, the most logical reason for its exclusion from predictive equations involving motor performance is its high positive relationship to parameters that are considerably easier to assess. If it can be demonstrated that height, weight, or other bodily dimensions account for most or all of the variance in performance attributable to physical growth, there is no need to include an estimate of biological maturity. This is precisely what research reports have indicated. Espenschade in 1940, Rarick and Oyster in 1964, and our own longitudinal data (Howell, 1979; Seefeldt, Haubenstricker, and Milne, 1976) confirm that skeletal age adds little to the prediction of motor performance if chronological age, height, and weight are already part of the equation.

The difficulty in classifying children and youth for physical activity by criteria other than chronological age does not excuse promoters of youth sports from making an attempt to equalize competition as much as possible. Young athletes who dominate competitive situations or whose size is a threat to the safety of teammates or opponents should be reclassified according to criteria that include an estimate of biological age, body size, playing experience, skill level, and social maturity in relation to the youth of their age group and those in the age category to which the athlete is to be promoted.

Concluding Comments

There is still little evidence to suggest that the readiness to learn specific motor skills can be identified with accuracy through a combination of chronological age, body size, or the various assessments of biological maturation. The most feasible procedure for ensuring that young performers will be ready to learn motor skills involves a task analysis of the skills to be learned, accompanied by an opportunity for the learner to acquire the requisite antecedent skills. Although the order in which children learn the sequence in fundamental motor skills is invariant, great variation exists in the rate at which they move through the sequences to maturity.

References

Barnsley, R. H., and Thompson, A. H. (1988). Birthdate and success in minor hockey: The key to the NHL. *Canadian Journal of Behavioral Sciences, 20*, 167–176.

Bernstein, N. (1967). *The co-ordination and regulation of movements*. Oxford: Pergamon Press.

Blakemore, C., Hawkes, N., and Burton, E. (1991). *Drill to skill: Teacher tactics in physical education*. Dubuque, IA: Wm. C. Brown.

Breckenridge, M. E., and Murphy, M. N. (1969). *Growth and development of the young child*. Philadelphia: W. B. Saunders.

Bruner, J. (1965). *The process of education*. Cambridge, MA: Harvard University Press.

Bruner, J. (1969). Processes of growth in infancy. In A. Ambrose (Ed.), *Stimulation in early infancy* (pp. 205–225). New York: Academic Press.

Boucher, J., and Halliwell, W. (1991). The Novem System: A practical solution to age grouping. *Canadian Association of Health, Physical Education, and Recreation Journal, 57*, 16–20.

Boucher, J., and Mutimer, B. (1994). The relative age phenomenon in sport: A replication and extension with ice hockey players. *Research Quarterly for Exercise and Sport, 65*, 377–381.

Connolly, K. (Ed.). *Mechanisms of motor skill development*. New York: Academic Press.

Crampton, C. W. (1908). Physiological age: A fundamental principle. *American Physical Education Review, 13*, 235–237.

Daniel, T. E., and Janssen, C. T. L. (1987). More on the relative age effect. *Canadian Association of Health, Physical Education, and Recreation Journal, 53*, 415–419.

Demster, F. N. (1981). Memory span: Sources of individual and developmental differences. *Psychological Bulletin, 89*, 63–100.

Espenschade, A. (1940). Motor performance in adolescence. *Monographs of the Society for Research in Child Development, 5*, 1–127.

Fitts, P. M., and Posner, M. I. (1967). *Human performance.* Belmont, CA: Brooks/Cole.

Haubenstricker, J. L. (1971). *The relationship of selected measures of proprioception to the physical growth, motor performance, and academic achievement in young children.* Unpublished doctoral dissertation, Michigan State University, East Lansing.

Haubenstricker, J., and Seefeldt, V. (1986). Acquisition of motor skills during infancy and childhood. In V. Seefeldt (Ed.), *Physical activity and well being* (pp. 41–104). Reston, VA: American Alliance for Health, Physical Education and Dance.

Haywood, K. M., and Getchell, N. (2001). *Life span motor development* (3rd ed.). Champaign, IL: Human Kinetics.

Hebb, D. (1949). *The organization of behavior.* New York: Wiley.

Hitch, G. J., and Towse, J. N. (1995). Working memory: What develops? In F. E. Weinert and W. Schneider (Eds.), *Memory performance and competencies: Issues in growth and development* (pp. 3–22). Mahwah, NJ: Lawrence Erlbaum Associates.

Howell, R. (1979). *The relationship between motor performance, physical growth, and skeletal maturity in boys and girls nine to twelve years of age.* Unpublished master's thesis, Michigan State University, East Lansing.

Kail, R. (1990). *The development of memory in children* (3rd ed.). New York: Freeman.

Kelso, J. A. S., and Clark, J. E. (Eds.). (1982). *The development of movement control and co-ordination.* New York: Wiley and Sons.

Keogh, J., and Sugden, D. (1985). *Motor skill development.* New York: Macmillan.

Kugler, P. N., Kelso, J. A. S., and Turvey, M. T. (1982). On the control and co-ordination of naturally developing systems. In J. A. S. Kelso and J. E. Clark (Eds.), *The development of movement control and co-ordination* (pp. 5–78). New York: Wiley and Sons.

Lowrey, G. H. (1986). *Growth and development of children* (8th ed.). Chicago: Year Book Medical Publishers.

Magill, R. A. (2001). *Motor learning: Concepts and applications* (6th ed.). Boston: McGraw-Hill.

Malina, R. M. (2002). The young athlete: Biological growth and maturation in a biocultural context. In F. L. Smoll and R. E. Smith (Eds.), *Children and youth in sport: A biopsychosocial perspective,* (2nd ed., pp. 261–292). Dubuque, IA: Kendall/Hunt.

Malina, R. M., and Bouchard, C. (1991). *Growth, maturation, and physical activity.* Champaign, IL: Human Kinetics Books.

Michigan's Exemplary Physical Education Project. (2000). *EPEC lessons— Grades K, 1, 2, 3, 4, 5 and User's Manual.* Available from The Michigan Fitness Foundation, P.O. Box 27187, Lansing, MI 48909.

Montelpare, W. J., Scott, D., and Pelino, M. (1997, May). *Tracking the relative age effect across minor, amateur and professional ice hockey*. Paper presented at the Third Symposium on Safety in Ice Hockey, St. Louis, MO.

Morris, G. S. D. (1977). Dynamic visual acuity: Implications for the physical educator and coach. *Motor skills: Theory into Practice, 2*, 15–20.

Payne, V. G., and Isaacs, L. D. (1999). *Human motor development: A lifespan approach* (4th ed.). Mountain View, CA: Mayfield.

Rarick, G. L., and Oyster, N. (1964). Physical maturity, muscular strength and motor performance of young school-age boys. *Research Quarterly, 35*, 523–531.

Roberton, M. A., and Halverson, L. E. (1988). The development of locomotor coordination: Longitudinal change and invariance. *Journal of Motor Behavior, 20*, 197–241.

Sage, G. H. (1984). *Motor learning and control: A neuropsychological approach*. Dubuque, IA: Wm. C. Brown.

Schmidt, R. A. (1975). A schema theory of discrete motor learning. *Psychological Review, 82*, 225–260.

Seefeldt, V. (1992, September). *Date of age determination and its potential influence on the selection of athletes in USA Hockey programs*. Paper presented at the annual meeting of USA Hockey, Lake Placid, NY.

Seefeldt, V., Haubenstricker, J., and Milne, C. (1976, March). *Skeletal age and body size as variables in motor performance*. Paper presented at the Third Symposium on Child Growth and Motor Development, University of Western Ontario. London.

Shumway-Cook, A., and Woollacott, M. (1995). *Motor control: Theory and practical applications*. Baltimore: Williams and Wilkins.

Smith, L. B., and Thelen, E. (Eds.). (1993). *A dynamic systems approach to development: Applications*. Cambridge, MA: MIT Press.

Smith, M. M. (1984). Perception and action. In M. M. Smith and A. M. Wing (Eds.), *The psychology of human movement* (pp. 119–152). London: Academic Press.

Sweetland, J. D., and DeSimone, P. A. (1987). Age of entry, sex, and academic achievement in elementary school children. *Psychology in the Schools, 24*, 406–412.

Thomas, J. R., Thomas, K. T., and Gallagher, J. D. (1981). Children's processing of information in physical activity and sport. *Motor Development: Theory into practice* (pp. 3–8). Monograph 3. Newtown, CT: Motor Skills: Theory into Practice.

Uphoff, J. K., and Gilmore, J. (1986). Pupil age at school entrance: How many are ready for success? *Young Children, 41*, 11–16.

Williams, H. G. (1983). *Perceptual and motor development*. Englewood Cliffs, NJ: Prentice-Hall.

CHAPTER 5

Motivational, Emotional, and Cognitive Determinants of Children's Age-Readiness for Competition

Michael W. Passer, University of Washington
Beverly J. Wilson, Seattle Pacific University

As the signal sounded to start the race, most of the contestants seemed frozen in time. Barely advancing past the starting line, they stood no chance as the winner finished the race at breakneck speed to collect $3,200 toward a future college scholarship. Adding fame to fortune, the race was videotaped and broadcast on the evening TV news. Never had we seen a baby crawl a few yards so quickly. Fortunately, the other contestants seemed to take their loss in stride, and there were no pouts, protests, or tantrums.

From time to time the news media feature physical contests that adults have organized for infants: from crawling races and "decathlons" (including such wondrous events as the "baby toss") to 10-yard "dashes" for 1-year-olds. In one sense these events are so ludicrous as to be funny, but in reality, they are not amusing. Sport scholars note that the dominant sport culture in contemporary western society emphasizes achievement and winning, materialism, commercialism, and the view that sport performance is a means to an end (e.g., Bar-On, 1997; Ingham and Hardy, 1993; Lucas, 2000; Swain, 2000). Events such as the "baby crawl" take these societal themes to an absurd extreme. While other infant "competitions" may not link material rewards to performance, they provide an equally telling commentary on just how eager some parents are to give their children an early thrust into the world of competition. The irony, however, is that from the participants' point of view these events do not represent sports, races, or contests of any kind. As our subsequent comments will indicate, however noble or benign the parents' intentions and motives for organizing such events may be, any belief that their babies or toddlers really are "competing" simply is misguided.

Criteria for Determining Age-Readiness for Competition

Estimates suggest that, within the United States alone, about 45 million children and teenagers participate in some form of youth sports or organized physical activities (Weinberg and Gould, 1999). To our knowledge, infant and toddler competitions thankfully are rare, but it is not too far a climb up the age ladder before we find very young children competing in formal youth sport programs. For example, in the United States 3-year-olds compete in organized swimming and gymnastics, 5-year-olds participate in track and field, wrestling, and baseball programs, and 6-year-olds compete in youth soccer and bowling (Martens, 1988). Some 4-year-old Australian children become involved in youth sports (Robertson, 1986), in Brazil 6-year-olds compete in swimming, soccer, and gymnastics (Ferreira, 1986), and in Canada competition for 6- to 8-year olds is offered in some sports as high up as the provincial level (Valeriote and Hansen, 1988). Although most children join the ranks of youth sport at a later age, participation by 3- to 6-year-olds in some sports has become accepted across the globe.

Should very young children compete in youth sports? If not, then at what age are children ready and able to compete? What criteria can be used to make such a determination? Whether viewed at the level of the individual child or in terms of general age guidelines, children's readiness for competition depends on many factors: the child's level of physical, psychological, and social development, the task demands of the particular sport, parental readiness, and broader cultural and socialization factors (see reviews by Coakley, 1986; Haubenstricker and Seefeldt, this volume; Malina, 1986; Sharkey, 1986).

In this chapter we examine several psychological issues relevant to forming general age guidelines for participation in youth sports. The first issue concerns children's motivational readiness for competition. Whether in sports, academics, music, or other domains, competition gives children the direct opportunity to test and evaluate their abilities against those of other youngsters. This is important to children because it is a key means by which they assess their competence (Butler, 1996; Scanlan, this volume). This process of learning about our characteristics (e.g., gauging the level of our abilities or the accuracy of our opinions) by comparing ourselves to other people is called social comparison (Festinger, 1954). From a social comparison standpoint, motivational readiness for competition occurs when children become attracted to, seek out, and take advantage of opportunities for comparing their own abilities with those of their peers.

Because the concepts of motivation and emotion are closely intertwined (Edwards, 1998; Lazarus, 1991), we will examine children's emotional reactions to competition as an important criterion for judging motivational readiness. The words *motivation* and *emotion* are derived from the Latin term *movere*, meaning "to move," and we can think of emotions as reactions to events that involve important motives and goals (Passer and Smith, 2001). Thus, children's emotional responses (or lack thereof) to winning or losing can provide important clues as to whether they are responding to the social comparison information inherent in competitive situations.

Children's cognitive readiness for competition represents another general issue that will be examined to establish age guidelines for youth sports. It is all too easy for adults to take for granted the numerous reasoning skills and cognitive abilities that come into play during competition and that help make competition a psychologically meaningful and maximally rewarding experience. Among others, these cognitive factors include the ability to organize and store information (e.g., a coach's instructions, set plays, an opponent's behavioral or strategic tendencies) in memory and retrieve that information later on, the ability to accurately identify the causes of why one has performed well or poorly so that future adjustments can be made, and the ability to understand situations from another person's (e.g., a coach, teammate, or opponent) point of view.

Finally, parents, coaches, and administrators often ask about age guidelines for youth sport participation because they are concerned that children's involvement at too early an age might produce harmful physical or psychological consequences. Some of these potential negative consequences will be addressed as a third criterion for judging children's age-readiness for formal athletic competition.

Motivational Readiness for Competition

At its heart, competition is a social comparison process. To determine whether you have the ability to run or swim a certain distance, or shoot or kick a ball into a net, you need only make the attempt and observe the outcome. To determine whether you run or swim *quickly*, or are *good* at shooting or kicking a ball into a net, you must gauge how your performance compares to the performance of other people (Festinger, 1954).

Motivationally it makes sense to delay children's entrance into organized sports until they reach an age where the unique opportunities for ability comparison provided by competition become attractive and important to them. In other words, once children develop the motivation to compare their skills with those of their peers, participating in competition begins to serve a special psychological function for them. Several investigators have emphasized that very young children cannot and do not compete because they are either incapable of or uninterested in social comparison (Roberts, 1980; Scanlan, this volume; Sherif, 1976). Therefore, to assess children's motivational readiness for competition we must determine the age at which their social comparison motivation develops.

Before doing so, we wish to emphasize a critical point. Children who are too young to engage in social comparison surely can participate in athletic activities, have fun, learn skills, attempt goals, and gain feedback about their abilities by examining whether they can physically accomplish certain tasks (e.g., hitting a ball). For that matter, we suppose, even infants placed in a "crawling race" may find it a pleasurable experience. Thus, it might be argued that it is inappropriate to equate motivational readiness for competition with the development of social comparison motivation. This stance, however, fails to take into account one important fact: Every one of these benefits—pleasure and fun, skill development, goal accomplishment—can be obtained from noncompetitive instructional or play settings. If the activity truly is being conducted for the child's benefit and enjoyment, rather than for the satisfaction of parents or other adults, then there is absolutely no need to formalize and structure physical activities into highly organized competitive games for children to whom social comparison is meaningless or of little importance.

The Preschool Years

At what age do children become oriented toward social comparison? When they are about 2 to 2 1/2 years old, children develop a well-organized, autonomous achievement orientation that evolves from a more basic mastery or competence motivation (Veroff, 1969; White, 1959). The child masters new skills via exploration and play and readily evaluates the outcome of mastery attempts. Competence is judged based on autonomous standards, and satisfaction is derived from successful mastery attempts. From 3 1/2 to 5 1/2 years of age children increasingly act to maximize their self-gain at the expense of others when placed in conflict of interest situations (see Pepitone, 1980). For example, naturalistic observations made during indoor and outdoor free play periods indicate that preschoolers periodically initiate attempts to take objects away from other children and defend themselves against such attempts by other children (Weigel, 1984).

To adults it often appears that these children are "competing" rather than sharing or cooperating because they vie with peers for desired objects or limited rewards. But this typically is not competition in a true social comparison sense. Rather, these children simply act to acquire or hold on to something they value (Pepitone, 1980), and in essence they are still pursuing autonomous achievement goals. Similarly, while they are working on achievement tasks very young children often may look at their peers' work, a behavior that adults may perceive as reflecting competitive interests. However, such looking primarily stems from children's desire to gain information that helps them complete or improve their performance rather than a desire for relative ability comparison (Butler, 1989, 1996).

Although achievement motivation strongly centers around autonomous goals between the ages of 2 to 5, some naturalistic observation studies of preschoolers at play indicate that they begin to engage in some types of social comparison when they are about 4 years old (Chafel, 1986, 1987; Mosatche, 1981). Much of this social comparison centers around rudimentary differences or similarities that children share (e.g., "My hair is brown, your's is red," "We are both 4 1/2 years old."), and while some preschoolers engage in "besting statements" or verbal boasts their comparisons often pertain to simple object possession (e.g., "My toy is bigger than yours," "I've got the most and you don't."). Some besting statements, however, do seem to serve a competitive function related to ability (e.g., "I can run faster than you.").

Other researchers have placed children of varying ages into competitive situations to determine whether they use social comparison information to assess their competence. For example, Ruth Butler (1996) asked Israeli children in kindergarten (average age = 5 years, 10 months) and fourth grade (average age = 9 years, 9 months) to create some artwork under competitive or noncompetitive conditions. The children worked independently while a same-sex, same-age peer (a confederate) performed the same task next to them. Bulter later showed the children a videotape of their session, focusing on instances where they had glanced at the peer's artwork. When asked to explain why they had glanced during the middle to latter part of the session, older children were much more likely to cite social comparison motives (e.g., "I wanted to see whose picture was best.") in the competitive situation rather than the noncompetitive situation. In contrast, kindergarteners were much less responsive to these situational differences: None cited social comparison in the noncompetitive situation, and only about 15% mentioned social comparison motives for glancing in the competitive situation (compared to about 55% of the fourth graders). In sum, at least at this task, most of the younger children seemed uninterested in using social comparison information to assess their competence. Overall, the studies discussed above suggest that most 4- and 5-year-olds do not spontaneously exhibit a consistent motive toward social comparison.

Preschoolers' emotional responses to competition. Children typically exhibit a number of emotions, such as pride and shame, in competitive situations. When experiencing pride children often look at another and smile, point out their accomplishments, puff out their chest, hold up their head, and make eye contact with others. When children experience shame they tend to avoid eye contact, lower their eyes, hang their head, or cover their faces with their hands. Unlike basic emotions such as anger, fear, sadness, or happiness, pride and shame are self-conscious emotions that occur when children evaluate their behavior relative to some standard (Lewis, 1997, 1998). Self-conscious emotions emerge after children have developed certain basic cognitive abilities, such as the ability to reflect upon themselves and their behavior. Research indicates that children are capable of self-evaluative behavior between 2 and 3 years of age (Stipek, 1995; Stipek, Recchaia, and McClintic, 1992; Veroff, 1969; White, 1959).

As noted earlier, children's emotional responses (or lack thereof) to winning or losing a competition can provide important clues as to whether they use social comparison information inherent in competitive situations as a basis for forming such self-evaluations. For example, in a study by Pascuzzi (1981), second graders and preschoolers participated in races with two other children of the same sex and age. After each race children's emotional responses, self-concept of ability, and expectancy of future success were measured. All of these psychological variables had been shown in earlier research to be influenced by perceptions of success and failure. Thus,

Pascuzzi reasoned that if the children's psychological responses after the race differed according to whether they finished first, second, or third, this would indicate that they judged their own performance relative to how well their peers did. If the children did not engage in social comparison, then the order of finish would have no bearing on their postrace responses. As predicted, second graders' responses varied according to their place of finish. The results for the preschoolers, however, depended on gender: the psychological responses of the preschool boys varied according to their order of finish but those of the preschool girls were similar regardless of placement.

In a subsequent study by Reissland and Harris (1991), younger boys and girls (mean age 34 months) competed against their older siblings (mean age 58 months) in a "race" to fit objects into a wooden board. For each pair of siblings their mother was present during the race and the task was rigged so that the younger children would win the first race, with the older children winning the second. The results indicated that all of the 4- to 5-year-olds exhibited pride when they won and almost all of the approximately 2- to 4-year-olds did likewise; the few who didn't exhibit pride were quite young (mean age 23 months). Further, the younger children drew as much attention to their achievement as the older children.

At first glance the Reissland and Harris (1991) findings suggest the remarkable possibility that most preschoolers—even as young as 2 1/2 to 3—use social comparison to judge whether they have "won" and gauge their emotional response accordingly. Unfortunately, the researchers note that the task of completing the puzzle elicits pride, yet there was no control group to examine children's pride reactions when they successfully completed the task in the absence of a "race" situation. It is entirely possible that the "race" meant nothing or little to the children, and that their pride and desire for their mother's attention was based only on their individual achievement of completing the task. Stated differently, their pride may have been an indicant of autonomous achievement motivation, not social comparison motivation.

Other research, however, supports the hypothesis that children become increasingly aware of competitive aspects of tasks by the age of three years. Stipek and her colleagues (Stipek, 1995; Stipek et al., 1992) established a competitive goal structure by asking two children to place a set of balls on five poles of varying length as quickly as they could. The researchers specifically told children that this was a race and that they wanted to see who could finish the task first, and the children were seated so that they could see each other's performance. Children younger than 33 months old appeared to be oblivious to the competitive nature of the task. They expressed as much pride in their work when they finished after the other child as when they finished before the other child. Even when these children were the first to complete the task, they were not able to report that they had won above the level that would be expected by chance. After 33 months of age, children appeared to become more aware of competitive standards and showed more pleasure when they completed the task first than when the other child finished second.

Finally, a more recent study by Donzella, Gunnar, Krueger, and Alwin (2000) provides additional evidence that preschoolers are aware of the competitive structure of tasks. Physiological responses (e.g., salivary cortisol, vagal tone) of 3- to 5-year-olds were recorded during a competition for a prize with an adult experimenter whose performance intentionally varied, thereby allowing each child to win and lose certain games. Donzella et al. (2000) found that many children showed greater stress when they were losing rather than winning

Summary of findings on preschoolers' social comparison motivation. Studies of children's emotional responses to winning and losing in staged competitive situations suggest that around 3 years of age some children become aware of and influenced by competitive aspects of tasks. Moreover, this awareness grows significantly between the ages of 3 to 5 years. For example, on the "place the balls on the poles" race described above, Stipek and her colleagues (Stipek, 1995; Stipek et al., 1992) found that 24-month-olds to 41-month-olds continued to work on the task even after the other child finished, whereas older children were increasingly likely to slow or stop their own work after the other child finished. Approximately 25% of the 42- to 50-month-olds and 50% of the 51- to 60-month-old children slowed or stopped working completely when the other child finished first. In addition, naturalistic observations indicate that some preschool-age children spontaneously engage in simple ability comparisons and make use of social comparison information to assess their abilities when placed in competitive situations (Chafel, 1986, 1987; Mosatche, 1981). At the same time, however, these findings suggest that, overall, most preschoolers are not strongly oriented toward seeking out social comparison for the purpose of assessing their abilities. Rather, individualistic or autonomous achievement motivation is predominant during this age period.

Elementary School Years

Children's social comparison motivation develops significantly during the early elementary school years. Veroff (1969) notes that in general children do not begin to spontaneously compare themselves with peers for purposes of ability assessment until they are about 5 to 6 years old. Frey and Ruble (1985) conducted classroom observations and found that as children progressed from kindergarten to first grade there was a sharp increase in social comparison related to performance assessment. Using a different methodology, other researchers have exposed children to achievement tasks and found that at around ages 7 through 9 they use or seek out social comparison information more consistently to judge their own abilities (Butler, 1989, 1996; Ruble, Boggiano, Feldman, and Loebl, 1980).

This rise in social comparison behavior during the early elementary school years corresponds nicely with other findings which show that, in contrast to preschoolers who generally value individualism and have difficulty understanding the concept of social comparison, early elementary school age children place greater social value on superiority (Knight, Dubro, and Chao, 1985) and have a better understanding of social comparison (Schoeneman, Tabor, and Nash, 1984). There is also evidence that children's interest in competition stems directly from this burgeoning desire for social comparison. Naturalistic observation research (Rowen, 1973) indicates that around the ages of 6 or 7 children begin to transform all sorts of situations into competitive ones to determine who is "the best." Other research has found that around the age of 7 children will increase their competitive behavior when social comparison information is made available (Toda, Shinotsuka, McClintock, and Stech, 1978).

In sum, findings from diverse lines of research suggest that the early elementary school years are when most children develop an interest in social comparison for purposes of assessing their ability and begin to seek out competitive situations specifically for their social comparison value. During the middle and late elementary school years children's interest in social comparison continues to grow (Butler, 1989, 1996; Keil, McClintock, Kramer, and Platow, 1990; Stipek, 1995).

Although numerous qualities can serve as focal points for youngsters' social comparison interests, physical and athletic ability typically are valued attributes among children of elementary and secondary school age, particularly so for boys (Adler, Kless, and Adler, 1992; Buchanan, Blankenbaker, and Cotten, 1976; Landers-Potts and Grant, 1999). Therefore, as social comparison motivation strengthens during the elementary school years, it would be expected that an increasing number of youngsters would seek out sport opportunities to develop and assess their athletic skills relative to their peers. This is, in fact, what happens. Depending on the sport, the average beginning age of participation in nonschool (i.e., nonmandatory) youth sport programs typically ranges from 8 to 12 years (Martens, 1988; Valeriote and Hansen, 1988), and the total number of participants across most sports grows steadily until peaking at around the ages of 11 to 13 (State of Michigan, 1976).

This analysis suggests two conclusions. First, if motivational readiness for competition is the main criterion upon which general age guidelines in youth sports are to be based, then participation should not begin until children are about 6 to 7 years old. At this age the desire for and ability to use social comparison information should be developing steadily in most children. Second, for the vast majority of children, their age of initial involvement in youth sports currently falls well within this guideline.

Cognitive Readiness for Competition

Capacity for Self-Evaluation

Participation in sports requires a host of cognitive skills and abilities, and the capacity for self-evaluation is one of the most basic. For self-evaluation to occur, children must first develop self-awareness; i.e., the ability to reflect upon themselves and their behavior (Lewis, Sullivan, Stanger, and Weiss, 1989). Self-evaluation also involves the ability to maintain internalized standards against which children can compare their behavior. Self-awareness and the ability to maintain standards for behavior develop between 18 to 24 months of age (Bullack and Lukenhaus, 1989; Kagan, 1981), and the capacity for self-evaluation emerges shortly thereafter, usually by the age of 3 (Stipek, 1995; Stipek et al., 1992; Veroff, 1969; White, 1959).

For example, Stipek and her colleagues (Stipek, 1995; Stipek et al., 1992) observed 13- to 39-month-old children's reactions when either the child or an adult knocked over a pin with a ball. Because children tended to smile whenever a pin was knocked over regardless of the identity of the initiator, they concluded that smiles in this context were just as likely to reflect the child's pleasure in the outcome itself as a positive evaluation of self. In contrast, by 22 months children were more likely to look up at the adult when they had knocked over the pin than when the adult had knocked it over. By 2 to 3 years only 10% of the children looked at the adult after the adult knocked over the pin, whereas 65% of the children looked at the adult after they themselves knocked over the pin. Although seeking the attention of another does not necessarily indicate the ability to understand others' evaluations, it does suggest that young children anticipate or possibly desire that others respond to their work.

Lewis, Alessandri, and Sullivan (1992) also examined children's self-evaluation and found that 3-year-olds varied their expression of shame and pride based on the difficulty level of the tasks they completed. These children were more likely to express pride when they completed a difficult than an easy task and were more likely to express shame when they failed at an easy versus difficult task.

Information Processing Abilities

One very important set of cognitive factors concerns the child's information processing capabilities. Young athletes must be able to attend to and remember considerable amounts of information such as rules of the sport, skill techniques and lessons, game or performance strategies, and specific instructions from coaches during practice and competition. In many sports athletes also need to learn and remember various plays or performance options, as well as the characteristic strategies or plays used by one's opponent.

Children's memory capabilities, ability to attend to and process information, and metacognitive abilities (i.e., their awareness of their own cognitive processes) improve substantially as they age (Gathercole, 1998; Flavell, 1970, 1999). Before the age of 4 most children have relatively short attention spans and are easily distracted from achievement-related activities in which they are engaged (Ruff and Lawson, 1990; Shaffer, 1993). As they progress through elementary school children are able to focus their attention on tasks for longer periods of time and they become better at paying attention to and searching for task-relevant information. Research suggests that around the late elementary or early secondary school years children become much more sophisticated in gathering relevant information and ignoring task-irrelevant information.

Even if young athletes successfully attend to task-relevant information they must be able to retain and retrieve it later on. Sometimes this time duration is short (e.g., as when a baseball coach sends a player up to the plate with instructions to "bunt," or a wrestling coach discusses a last minute change in strategy with an athlete) and at other times the needed retention period is long (e.g., as when players learn rules or various plays or formations that will be used throughout a season or beyond).

Children's memory capabilities also improve as they grow older. These changes appear to be brought about in large part by increases in the speed and efficiency with which children process information into memory and by their use of more sophisticated rehearsal and retrieval strategies (Gathercole, 1998; Kail, 1991. For example, one of the most common strategies that people use to remember information is to rehearse it. Another strategy is to group bits of information together into clusters or "chunks" (e.g., in trying to learn a play diagram of "X's" and "O's," a player would group related "letters" into larger units rather than trying to individually memorize the location of each one). Although children as young as 2 or 3 may use rehearsal and clustering under very simple and carefully arranged task conditions, these strategies are primitive and rarely appear spontaneously. Between the ages of 5 to 8 children use rehearsal more regularly but not in the same way as older children do. Further, they often have trouble using clustering and if they do use this strategy in one situation, they typically fail to generalize it to other situations. By late childhood and into adolescence it takes progressively less time to process information, memory strategies become more sophisticated, and they are used more flexibly (Case, 1996; Gathercole, 1998).

Attributional Abilities

The capacity to understand causal relationships is another cognitive ability highly relevant to the competition process. As noted earlier, children seek out competition because it provides social comparison information that helps them assess their competence. Yet, competence cannot be judged accurately until one becomes aware that performance outcomes such as winning and losing are the product of interactive causal factors such as (but not limited to) physical skill, strategy, preparation, effort, task (opponent) difficulty, and luck. A number of studies suggest that it may not be until the late elementary and early secondary school years that this cognitive ability becomes well developed (Nesdale and Pope, 1985; Nicholls, 1978; Roberts, 1980, 1986; Weiner and Kun, 1978). For example, Nesdale and Pope (1985) found that 4- to 7-year-old children attributed their successes and failures to the difficulty of the task and generally did not view ability, effort or luck to be responsible for their performance outcomes. In fact, many of the explanations given by preschool and kindergarten aged children for why they can or cannot accomplish something bear little resemblance to the traditional attributional categories employed by adults or older children (see Burgner and Hewstone, 1993). Research by Ewing, Roberts, and Pemberton (cited in Roberts, 1986) with 9- to 14-year-old youth sport participants found that children younger than 12 were not able to differentiate between the relative contributions of effort and ability as determinants of success and failure.

These developmental shifts in causal reasoning influence not only how children of different ages will assess their competence based on performance outcomes, but also how they will respond emotionally to those outcomes, what their future perform- ance aspirations and success expectancies will be, and how they will approve or disapprove of other children based on those children's outcomes. For example, Stipek and DeCotis (1988) studied 6- through 13-year-olds and concluded that not until age 12 were pride-shame reactions to success-failure exclusively linked to ability and effort attributions. Similarly, whereas by age 6 children's expectancies of future success begin to be influenced by their past success-failure outcomes, it may not be until 10 to 12 years of age that their success expectancies become linked to the diverse attributions they make for these outcomes (Weiner and Kun, 1978). As Weiner and Kun note, in order to develop realistic performance expectancies and achievement goals, children may first need to understand that how well one does in the future depends on the cause of having done well or poorly in the past. In this vein, Roberts (1986) suggests that children's attributional capacities influence their general achievement goals in sports.

Role-Taking, Theory of Mind, and Other Cognitive Abilities

A host of other cognitive abilities are called into play during organized sport participation; among them are simple logical reasoning and problem solving skills, the capacity to understand situations from various perspectives or roles, language comprehension, and the ability to judge other people's emotions and thoughts from their nonverbal behavior. Similar to the age-related changes that occur in children's information processing and attributional capabilities, these other cognitive abilities develop dramatically and become much more sophisticated by the end of the elemen- tary school years.

For example, a person's beliefs about the "mind" and ability to understand other people's mental states—to infer what someone else "must be thinking" in a given situation—reflects what developmental psychologists call "theory of mind." As de- velopmental psychologist John Flavel (1999) notes, preschoolers tend to be relatively poor judges of when other people are thinking and of what other people are thinking about. As one example, preschoolers often assume that a person who is sitting quietly is not engaged in any thinking at all. Moreover, although preschoolers are capable of some introspection, they are much less aware of *their own* thoughts than are older children. Preschoolers often have trouble remembering and describing their own current and recent thoughts (Flavell, 1999; Flavell, Green, and Flavell, 2000), an obvious limitation in sport-related situations where a coach (or parent) might ask their young athletes to "explain what they were thinking about" when the athlete failed to execute some skill or strategy on a recent play.

More generally, several sport scientists propose that children's cognitive abilities are such that they do not develop a mature overall understanding of the competition process until they are about 12 years old (Coakley, 1986; Roberts, 1980). Coakley (1986), for example, proposes that full comprehension of what it means to compete against an opponent cannot occur until children possess the ability to put themselves into the point of view or role of other participants. Coakley argues that before the age of 6 children's thinking is egocentric and from 6 to 8 years of age children begin to understand others' viewpoints. Between the ages of 8 to 10 children's role taking abilities are sufficiently developed so that they can understand and accept another person's viewpoint. Finally, when they are 10 to 12 years old, children develop the capacity to comprehend more than just one other viewpoint and can readily adopt a group perspective. Based on more recent developmental research than that cited by Coakley, the specific ages at which these perspective-taking abilities develop may be subject to some debate; some studies show, for example, that even 3-year-olds are capable of adopting another child's perspective at very simple tasks (Shaffer, 1993). Nevertheless, the overall age-progression and implications of Coakley's analysis remain intact: In team sports young children will have difficulty understanding that a team is comprised of interdependent positions that must simultaneously respond to each others' and the opposing players' movements (Coakley, 1986). Anyone who has watched 7-year-old youth soccer players continually swarm to the ball from across the field like bees to nectar, rather than maintain field position and focus on strategically passing the ball as repeatedly instructed by the coach, can bear witness to Coakley's general point.

Potential Harmful Consequences

Are young children at risk for psychological harm when they participate in youth sports? Yes, they are. Among other risks, it is possible that their self-perceptions of physical competence may suffer, that their short-term and long-term competitive anxiety may increase, that they will be unpopular with teammates, and that their general self-esteem may decrease because of their sport involvement.

It is absolutely essential, however, to keep two points in mind. First, other achievement activities in which young children participate—including typical academic experiences in elementary school—carry analogous risks. Second, even among older children sport competition can have negative psychological effects if the setting is aversive or managed inappropriately by coaches or parents (Tofler, Knapp, and Drell, 1998). Sport psychologists estimate that for "every 10 children who begin a sport season, 3 to 4 of them will drop out by the start of the next season" (Weinberg and Gould, 1999, p. 456). Although benign reasons such as "having other things to do" or "becoming more interested in other activities" seem to account for most children's decision to drop out of youth sports, in perhaps up to 25% of cases a sport-specific negative factor plays a key role. For example, the psychological stress brought about by an overemphasis on competition and winning can adversely affect older children's and young adolescents' physical and psychological health, enjoyment of sports, and athletic performance (see Passer, 1988; Smith, Smoll, and Passer, this volume). Further, among both younger and older children, those who are poorer performers athletically usually will be less popular among their teammates or other peers in the sport setting (Passer and Scanlan, 1980; Weiss and Duncan, 1992). There simply is no magic age beyond which participation in youth sports can be delayed so as to guarantee that such outcomes will not occur.

Still, there are some special hazards that must be considered prior to involving young children in organized sports, and many of them are an outgrowth of children's lack of motivational and cognitive readiness for competition. Several negative consequences may arise when children who are not motivationally ready are placed in competitive events. At best, the physical activity will be enjoyed, but the competitive component simply will be meaningless or irrelevant to children who are not oriented toward social comparison; they will focus instead on autonomous individual achievement goals. At worst, the children will not enjoy the activity for intrinsic reasons and may find themselves involved in youth sports, not because they want to be, but because others—such as their parents—have decided they ought to be. In turn, research suggests that children who feel it is not their own decision to participate in youth sports are less likely to be satisfied with their sport experience and more likely to discontinue their involvement (McGuire and Cook, 1983). Children who report participating in youth sports to please their parents have also been found to have higher competitive stress (Scanlan and Lewthwaite, 1984).

As noted earlier, young children do not understand complex causal relationships and may be especially likely to form inaccurate assessments of their physical competence based on success-failure outcomes in sports. Indeed, the correlation between perceived and actual competence is weaker among younger children (see Roberts, 1986). Inaccurate perceptions of ability subsequently may cause children to develop unrealistically high or low achievement goals.

This difficulty in assessing competence and the true causes of performance outcomes increases young children's dependence on performance-related feedback from adults. Thus, young children are especially sensitive to comments and reactions by adults, sometimes in ways that adults do not realize. For example, constructive mild criticism from adults may be perceived by young children as evidence of failure rather than as helpful advice, the result being that the children experience stress (Roberts, 1986). Young children also may misinterpret adults' lack of reaction. Smith, Smoll, and Curtis (1978) studied 8- through 15-year-old Little League Baseball players; their findings suggested that when 8- to 9-year-olds performed well or did something positive and coaches ignored it (e.g., they failed to offer praise), the children interpreted the coaches' neutral behaviors as aversive or negative responses.

Youth sport participants also obtain considerable performance feedback by observing coaches', parents', and each other's nonverbal responses, such as facial expressions. Numerous studies indicate that young children are less skilled than older children in accurately inferring people's emotions from facial expressions. In particular, 3- through 8-year-olds are most accurate in identifying happiness from facial expressions, but have more difficulty distinguishing between negative emotions (Fabes, Eisenberg, Nyman, and Michealieu, 1991; Gross and Ballif, 1991). Preschoolers tend to confuse expressions of anger and sadness, anger and disgust, and perceive neutral facial expressions as indicating sadness; even third-graders often confuse anger and sadness and misjudge neutral expressions. Younger children are also more likely than older children to infer someone else's emotion based on the simple outcome of a situation (e.g., incorrectly judging that a coach looks angry because the player or team lost) rather than taking into account other situational factors or the other person's attribution for that outcome (e.g., correctly judging that a coach looks sad, not angry, because the child tried hard but was up against a superior opponent or had bad luck). Moreover, children are less accurate in using facial expressions to identify more complex emotions (e.g., pride, shame, guilt) than basic ones (see Gross and Ballif, 1991). Thus, there is considerable potential for young children to misread coaches', parents', and teammates' nonverbal reactions to their performance. The finding that children have relative difficulty reading neutral facial expressions is especially interesting because it fits in with Smith et al.'s (1978) observation that young children may perceive a coach's nonresponse to positive player performance as punitive. Thus, coaches may feel that they are verbally and nonverbally responding to players in a neutral fashion, but this may not be the players' interpretation.

Another potential hazard of sport participation at an early age is that young children, limited by language capacity and other relatively immature cognitive skills, cannot understand the directions or instructions of adults as well as older children can. This inability may cause frustration and stress not only for the child, but also for parents and coaches who feel they are communicating clearly and become annoyed when their instructions are not obeyed. In some cases these adults may have unrealistic expectations of children's cognitive abilities and speak to them as if they are miniature adults (a tendency facilitated, perhaps, by the stylish uniforms and other adult trappings of many youth sport programs). In other cases, well-meaning parents and coaches may do a good job of adjusting task demands and their level of speech to the age of the child, but may not be fully aware of the sometimes subtle limitations in children's cognitive abilities (e.g., very young children find it more difficult to understand negative instructions [Don't do X] than positive instructions [Do Y]). Thus, the readiness of parents and coaches to work within the level of youngsters' cognitive abilities becomes another important consideration in determining the age at which children should become involved in youth sports (Malina, 1986).

Age Guidelines and Conclusions

Three broad issues bearing on children's preparedness for participating in youth sports have been discussed: motivational readiness, cognitive readiness, and potential harmful consequences. Of these, we view motivational readiness as the starting point for formulating age guidelines. As the "infant scholarship crawl" contest mentioned at the beginning of this chapter illustrates, children of virtually any age can be placed in athletic events or physical contests that are organized and labeled by adults as "competition." But it is not until the early elementary school years that most children will have a fairly well developed orientation to respond to these contests as representing competition in a social comparison sense, much less spontaneously seek out competitive sport situations for their social comparison value. Based solely on the criterion of motivational readiness, we suggest that adults should delay children's participation in youth sports until the early elementary school years.

Several arguments can be made for setting a younger age limit, while others can be given for establishing an older one. With regard to a lower age limit, the first argument is that involving preschoolers in sport competition is necessary if the children are to become highly skilled performers or possibly champions when they grow older. However, we do not know of any good, nonanecdotal data to support this argument. In fact, even in countries such as Russia, where elite training programs in some sports begin as early as age 4 or 5, many sport specialists have begun to doubt whether the final level of skill achieved by athletes is proportional to the number of years spent in training (Jefferies, 1986). If preschool age children are to be involved in adult-supervised physical activity—even for the alleged purpose of "grooming" them for potential elite performance—their time would be better spent on skill development than on competition.

A second argument for lower youth sport age limits is that some preschoolers are oriented toward social comparison and competition, as suggested by the studies we presented earlier. The counterpoint is that there is no consistent evidence that even a large minority of preschoolers are oriented toward socially comparing their physical abilities, and those who are typically make very basic comparisons.

A third and related argument is that involving very young children in organized sports will facilitate their interest in social comparison. Veroff (1969) contends that young children may become intrinsically socially comparative if their environment orients them toward this, and recent research indicates that children's understanding and use of social comparison is influenced by the degree of competitiveness in their general social-educational environment (Butler and Kedar, 1990; Butler and Ruzany, 1993). Whether accelerating children's interest in social comparison and competition is an inherently wise developmental goal can only be answered in relation to one's personal values about childhood. But even if the answer is affirmative, the potential costs must be weighed, and this is precisely where children's cognitive readiness and the potential harmful consequences of early involvement in sport competition must be considered.

Research on children's cognitive abilities suggests they typically will not have a reasonably mature understanding of the competition process until the middle to late elementary school years. Although numerous studies over the past two decades have shown that many cognitive abilities develop more quickly than previously believed (Baillargeon, 1987; Ritblatt, 2000), it is clear that during the elementary school years children's information processing capabilities, attributional processes, role-taking abilities, and skill in inferring other people's emotional reactions all become much more sophisticated. When they compete older children will have a better understanding of what they are doing, why they are doing it, the causes of their success-failure, and how other people feel about it.

The issue of readiness is complicated by the differences that exist in the rate of children's psychological development and in the kinds of sport environments to which they are exposed. Nevertheless, based on criteria considered in this chapter, we recommend that children younger than 6 or (perhaps more appropriately) 7 be discouraged from participating in youth sports. By this age most children should have a general motivational readiness for competition and cognitive abilities sufficient for a basic understanding of the competition process. Even so, the competitive emphasis of sport should be phased in gradually as children get older, and it is essential that the parents and coaches of youth sport participants—especially 6- to 9-year olds—be made aware of the ways in which children's cognitive capacities differ from those of adults. This educational goal should be a key component of coach and parent training programs.

References

Adler, P. A., Kless, S. J., and Adler, P. (1992). Socialization to gender roles: Popularity among elementary school boys and girls. *Sociology of Education, 65*, 169–187.

Bar-On, T. (1997). The Ambiguities of Football, Politics, Culture, and Social Transformation in Latin America. *Sociological Research Online, 2*, <http://www.socresonline.org.uk/socresonline/2/4/2.html>

Baillargeon, R. (1987). Object permanence in 3 1/2- and 4 1/2-month-old infants. *Developmental Psychology, 23*, 655–664.

Buchanan, H. T., Blankenbaker, J., and Cotten, D. (1976). Academic and athletic ability as popularity factors in elementary school children. *Research Quarterly, 3*, 320–325.

Bullack, M., and Lukenhaus, P. (1989). The development of volitional behavior in toddler years. *Child Development, 59*, 664–674.

Burgner, D., and Hewstone, M. (1993). Young children's causal attributions for success and failure: 'Self-enhancing' boys and 'self-derogating' girls. *British Journal of Developmental Psychology, 11*, 125–129.

Butler, R. (1989). Mastery versus ability appraisal: A developmental study of children's observations of peers' work. *Child Development, 60*, 1350–1361.

Butler, R. (1996). Effects of age and achievement goals on children's motives for attending to peers' work. *British Journal of Developmental Psychology, 14*, 1–18.

Butler, R., and Kedar, A. (1990). Effects of intergroup competition and school philosophy on student perceptions, group processes, and performance. *Contemporary Educational Psychology, 15*, 301–318.

Butler, R., and Ruzany, N. (1993). Age and socialization effects on the development of social comparison motives and normative ability assessment in kibbutz and urban children. *Child Development, 64*, 532–543.

Case, R. (1996). Modeling the process of conceptual change in a continuously evolving hierarchical system. *Monographs of the Society for Research in Child Development, 61*, 283–295.

Chafel, J. A. (1986). A naturalistic investigation of the use of social comparison by young children. *Journal of Research and Development in Education, 19*, 51–61.

Chafel, J. A. (1987). Achieving knowledge about self and others through physical object and social fantasy play. *Early Childhood Research Quarterly, 2*, 27–43.

Coakley, J. (1986). When should children begin competing? A sociological perspective. In M. R. Weiss and D. Gould (Eds.), *Sport for children and youths* (pp. 59–63). Champaign, IL: Human Kinetics.

Donzella, B., Gunnar, M. R., Krueger, W. K., and Alwin, J. (2000). Cortisol and vagal tone responses to competitive challenge in preschoolers. *Developmental Psychobiology, 37*, 209–220.

Edwards, D. C. (1998). *Motivation and emotion: Evolutionary, physiological, cognitive, and social influences.* Thousand Oaks, CA: Sage.

Fabes, R. A., Eisenberg, N., Nyman, M., and Michealieu, Q. (1991). Young children's appraisals of others' spontaneous emotional reactions. *Developmental Psychology, 27*, 858–866.

Ferreira, M. B. R. (1986). Youth sport in Brazil. In M. R. Weiss and D. Gould (Eds.), *Sport for children and youths* (pp. 11–15). Champaign, IL: Human Kinetics.

Festinger, L. (1954). A theory of social comparison processes. *Human Relations, 7*, 17–140.

Flavell, J. H. (1970). Developmental studies of mediated behavior. In H. W. Reese and L. P. Lipsett (Eds.), *Advances in child development and behavior* (Vol. 5). New York: Academic Press.

Flavell, J. H. (1999). Cognitive development: Children's knowledge about the mind. *Annual Review of Psychology, 50*, 21–25.

Flavell, J. H., Green, F. L., and Flavell, E. R. (2000). Development of children's awareness of their own thoughts. *Journal of Cognition and Development, 1*, 97–112.

Frey, K. S., and Ruble, D. N. (1985). What children say when the teacher is not around: Conflicting goals in social comparison and performance assessment in the classroom. *Journal of Personality and Social Psychology, 48*, 550–562.

Gathercole, S. E. (1998). The development of memory. *Journal of Child Psychology and Psychiatry and Allied Disciplines, 39*, 3–27.

Gross, A. L., and Ballif, B. (1991). Children's understanding of emotion from facial expressions and situations: A review. *Developmental Review, 11*, 368–398.

Haubenstricker, J. L., and Seefeldt, V. (2002). The concept of readiness applied to the acquisition of motor skills. In F. L. Smoll and R. E. Smith (Eds.). *Children and youth in sport: A biopsychosocial perspective* (2nd ed., pp. 61–81). Dubuque, IA: Kendall/Hunt.

Ingham, A. G., and Hardy, S. (1993). Introduction: Sport studies through the lens of Raymond Williams. In A. G. Ingham and J. W. Loy (Eds.), *Sport in social development: Traditions, transitions, and transformations* (pp. 119–145). Champaign, IL: Human Kinetics.

Jefferies, S. C. (1986). Youth sport in the Soviet Union. In M. R. Weiss and D. Gould (Eds.). *Sport for children and youths* (pp. 35–40). Champaign, IL: Human Kinetics.

Kagan, J. (1981). *The second year: The emergence of self-awareness*. Cambridge, MA: Harvard University Press.

Kail, R. (1991). Processing time declines exponentially during childhood and adolescence. *Developmental Psychology, 27*, 259–266.

Keil, L. J., McClintock, C. G., Kramer, R., and Platow, M. J. (1990). Children's use of social comparison standards in judging performance and their effects on self-evaluation. *Contemporary Educational Psychology, 15*, 75–91.

Knight, G. P., Dubro, A. F., and Chao, C. (1985). Information processing and the development of cooperative, competitive, and individualistic social values. *Developmental Psychology, 21*, 37–45.

Landers-Potts, M., and Grant, L. (1999). Competitive climates, athletic skill, and children's status in after-school. *Social Psychology of Education, 2*, 297–313.

Lazarus, R. S. (1991). Progress on a cognitive-motivational theory of emotion. *American Psychologist, 46*, 819–834.

Lewis, M. (1997). The self in self-conscious emotions. *Annals of the New York Academy of Sciences, 818*, 119–142.

Lewis, M. (1998). Emotional competence and development. In D. Puschkar, W. M. Bukowski, A. E. Schwartzman, D. M. Stack, and D. R. White (Eds.), *Improving competence across the lifespan: Building interventions on theory and research* (pp. 27–36). New York: Plenum Press.

Lewis, M., Alessandri, S., and Sullivan, M. W. (1992). Differences in shame and pride as a function of children's gender and task difficulty. *Child Development, 63*, 630–638.

Lewis, M., Sullivan, M. W., Stanger, C., and Weiss, M. (1989). Self-development and self-conscious emotions. *Child Development, 60,* 146–156.

Lucas, S. (2000). Nike's commercial solution: Girls, sneakers, salvation. *International Review for the Sociology of Sport, 35,* 149–164.

Malina, R. M. (1986). Readiness for competitive youth sport. In M. R. Weiss and D. Gould (Eds.), *Sport for children and youths* (pp. 45–50). Champaign, IL: Human Kinetics.

Martens, R. (1988). Youth sport in the USA. In F. L. Smoll, R. A. Magill, and M. J. Ash (Eds.), *Children in sport* (3rd ed. pp. 17–23). Champaign, IL: Human Kinetics.

McGuire, R. T., and Cook. D. L. (1983). The influence of others and the decision to participate in youth sports. *Journal of Sport Behavior, 6,* 9–16.

Mosatche, H. S. (1981). An observational study of social comparison in pre-schoolers. *Child Development, 52,* 376–378.

Nesdale, A. R., and Pope, S. (1985). Young children's causal attributions and performance expectations on skilled tasks. *British Journal of Developmental Psychology, 3,* 183–190.

Nicholls, J. G. (1978). The development of the concepts of effort and ability, perception of own attainment, and the understanding that difficult tasks require more ability. *Child Development, 49,* 800–814.

Pascuzzi, D. L. (1981). Young children's perception of success and failure. Abstract in *Psychology of Motor Behavior and Sport—1981*: 97.

Passer, M. W. (1988). Determinants and consequences of children's competitive stress. In F. L. Smoll, R. A. Magill, and M. J. Ash (Eds.), *Children in sport* (3rd ed., pp. 203–227). Champaign, IL: Human Kinetics.

Passer, M. W., and Smith, R. E. (2001). *Psychology: Frontiers and applications.* Boston: McGraw-Hill.

Passer, M. W., and Scanlan, T. K. (1980). *A sociometric analysis of popularity and leadership status among players on youth soccer teams.* Paper presented at the meeting of the North American Society for the Psychology of Sport and Physical Activity, Boulder, CO.

Pepitone, E. A. (1980). *Children in cooperation and competition.* Lexington, MA: D.C. Heath.

Reissland, N., and Harris, P. (1991). Children's use of display rules in pride-eliciting situations. *British Journal of Developmental Psychology, 9,* 431–435.

Ritblatt, S. N. (2000). Children's level of participation in a false-belief task, age, and theory of mind. *Journal of Genetic Psychology, 161,* 53–64.

Roberts, G. C. (1980). Children in competition: A theoretical perspective and recommendations for practice. *Motor Skills: Theory Into Practice, 4,* 37–50.

Roberts, G. C. (1986). The perception of stress: A potential source and its development. In M. R. Weiss and D. Gould (Eds.), *Sport for children and youths* (pp. 119–126). Champaign, IL: Human Kinetics.

Robertson, I. (1986). Youth sport in Australia. In M. R. Weiss and D. Gould (Eds.), *Sport for children and youths* (pp. 5–10). Champaign, IL: Human Kinetics.

Rowen, B. (1973). *The children we see: An observational approach to child study.* New York: Holt, Rinehart, and Winston.

Ruble, D. N., Boggiano, A. K., Feldman, N. S., and Loebl, J. (1980). Developmental analysis of the role of social comparison in self-evaluation. *Developmental Psychology, 16,* 105–115.

Ruff, H. A., and Lawson, K. R. (1990). Development of sustained focused attention in young children during play. *Developmental Psychology, 26,* 85–93.

Scanlan, T. K. (2002). Social evaluation and the competition process: A developmental perspective. In F. L. Smoll, R. E. Smith (Eds.), *Children and youth in sport: A biopsychosocial perspective* (2nd. ed., pp. 393–407). Dubuque, IA: Kendall/Hunt.

Scanlan, T. K., and Lewthwaite, R. (1984). Social psychological aspects of competition for male youth sport participants: I. Predictors of competitive stress. *Journal of Sport Psychology, 6,* 208–226.

Schoeneman, T. J., Tabor, L. E., and Nash, D. L. (1984). Children's reports of the sources of self-knowledge. *Journal of Personality, 52,* 124–137.

Shaffer, D. R. (1993). *Developmental psychology: Childhood and adolescence* (3rd ed.). Pacific Grove, CA: Brooks/Cole.

Sharkey, B. J. (1986). When should children begin competing? A physiological perspective. In M. R. Weiss and D. Gould (Eds.), *Sport for children and youths* (pp. 51–54). Champaign, IL: Human Kinetics.

Sherif, C. (1976). The social context of competition. In D. Landers (Ed.), *Social problems in athletics* (pp. 18–36). Urbana: University of Illinois Press.

Smith, R. E., Smoll, F. L., and Curtis, B. (1978). Coaching behaviors in Little League baseball. In F. L. Smoll and R. E. Smith (Eds.), *Psychological perspectives in youth sports* (pp. 173–201). Washington, DC: Hemisphere.

Smith, R. E., Smoll, F. L., and Passer, M. W. (2002). Sport performance anxiety in young athletes. In F. L. Smoll and R. E. Smith (Eds.), *Children and youth in sport: A biopspychosocial perspective* (2nd ed., pp. 501–536). Dubuque, IA: Kendall/Hunt.

State of Michigan (1976). *Joint legislative study on youth sports programs: Phase I.* East Lansing, MI: Author.

Stipek, D. (1995). The development of pride and shame in toddlers. In J. P. Tnagney and K. W. Fischer (Eds.), *Self-conscious emotions: The psychology of shame, guilt, embarrassment and pride.* New York: Guilford Press

Stipek, D. J., and DeCotis, K. M. (1988). Children's understanding of the implications of causal attributions for emotional experiences. *Child Development, 59,* 1601–1610.

Stipek, D., Recchia, S., and McClintic, S. (1992). Self-evaluation in young children. *Monographs of the Society for Research in Child Development, 57* (Serial No. 226).

Swain, J., (2000). The money's good, the fame's good, the girls are good: The role of playground football in the construction of young boys' masculinity in a junior school. *British Journal of Sociology of Education, 21*, 95–109.

Toda, M., Shinotsuka. H., McClintock, C. G., and Stech, F. J. (1978). Development of competitive behavior as a function of culture. age, and social comparison. *Journal of Personality and Social Psychology, 36*, 825–839.

Tofler, I. R., Knapp, P. K., and Drell, M. J. (1998). The achievement by proxy spectrum in youth sports: Historical perspective and clinical approach to pressured and high-achieving children and adolescents. *Child and Adolescent Psychiatric Clinics of North America, 7*, 803–820.

Valeriote, T. A., and Hansen, L. (1988). Youth sport in Canada. In F. L. Smoll, R. A. Magill, and M. J. Ash (Eds.), *Children in sport* (3rd ed., pp. 25–29). Champaign, IL: Human Kinetics.

Veroff, J. (1969). Social comparison and the development of achievement motivation. In C. P. Smith (Ed.), *Achievement-related motives in children* (pp. 46–101). New York: Russell Sage Foundation.

Weigel, R. M. (1984). The application of evolutionary models to the study of decisions made by children during object possession conflicts. *Ethology and Sociobiology, 5*, 229–238.

Weinberg, R. S., and Gould, D. (1999). *Foundations of sport and exercise psychology* (2nd ed.). Champaign, IL: Human Kinetics.

Weiner, B., and Kun, A. (1978). *The development of causal attributions and the growth of achievement and social motivation.* Unpublished manuscript, University of California, Los Angeles.

Weiss, M. R., and Duncan, S. C. (1992). The relationship between physical competence and peer acceptance in the context of children's sports participation. *Journal of Sport and Exercise Psychology, 14*, 177–191.

White, R. W. (1959). Motivation reconsidered: The concept of competence. *Psychological Review, 66*, 297–334.

CHAPTER 6

Do Critical Periods Determine When to Initiate Sport Skill Learning?

David I. Anderson, San Francisco State University
and University of California, Berkeley

Do Critical Periods and Readiness Determine When to Initiate Sport Skill Learning?

If you want your child to succeed in sports and academics, it is important to expose the child to appropriately stimulating experiences very early in life, preferably within the first three years. At least, that's the claim made by many parents and educators in response to the recent surge of interest in brain research shown by popular magazines and newspapers. The notion that "earlier is better" has become somewhat entrenched in our popular culture (Elkind, 1990), despite a glaring lack of evidence to support any firm conclusions about the appropriate time to expose children to the myriad of cultural skills that will be critical for their functioning in contemporary society. The lack of evidence is even more apparent in the field of sports, where we see numerous examples of individuals who are able to achieve considerable success despite initiating practice in their respective sports at ages that vary considerably. In the game of golf, for example, it is widely known that Tiger Woods, the current number one golfer in the world, was introduced to golf clubs before his first birthday and had developed a competitive game by the age of 5. Yet, it is less well known that Karrie Webb, who, at the same age as Tiger, is the world's number one golfer in the woman's game and has a record as accomplished as that of Tiger, did not begin to play golf until she was 8 years of age. Then there is Greg Norman, another Australian, who was one of the professional golf tour's leading money winners, despite not having picked up a golf club until he was 16 years old. Anecdotal evidence such as this makes it bewilderingly complex to determine the appropriate age to initiate sport skill learning.

The problem of determining the appropriate age at which to initiate sport skill learning is compounded by the lack of scientific research on this intriguing topic. Nevertheless, there is a wealth of research in other fields of inquiry, such as the neurosciences, developmental psychology, and ethology (the study of animal behavior) that can provide insights into the problem. We will draw upon research from these areas as well as from the more closely related fields of motor learning and motor development to analyze the arguments that have been made for and against the importance of early exposure to sport skill learning for ultimate success. Much of our understanding of when to initiate skill learning comes from work that was done in the 1930s by the well-known developmental psychologist, Myrtle McGraw. That McGraw's ideas are still highly relevant to our understanding of skill development is a testament to the excellence of her original work, but also to the dearth of contemporary research in this area. While the issues addressed in this chapter are equally relevant to the development of basic competence in movement as they are to the development of expertise in sport, it will become apparent that the recent burgeoning of interest in expert performance will also make a contribution to an understanding of when to initiate sport skill learning.

The discussion will revolve around two important concepts in human development—critical periods and readiness. The critical period concept suggests that there are "windows of opportunity" or specific periods during which experiences have a much greater influence than they do at other times in development. Many people believe that certain skills cannot be accomplished or might never reach their full potential if learning is undertaken outside of a critical period. In contrast, the readiness concept implies that certain physical, psychological, and behavioral prerequisites must have been acquired before the child can profit from practice on a task. The readiness and critical period concepts are very closely linked and many people, inappropriately, use the terms synonymously. The concepts are extremely important for our discussion because they provide the basis for arguing both for and against early exposure to sport skill learning. Those who adhere to the importance of early experiences for learning often argue their case (at least implicitly) on the basis of the critical period concept. Those who argue against early exposure often cite the readiness concept to support their case. What then are the implications of the two concepts for our understanding of when to initiate sport skill learning? Are there certain periods in development that must be taken advantage of if the child is to reach his or her full potential in a sport or physical activity? Can a child's chances of success be harmed by exposure to a skill before he or she is ready to learn? Or, is there a balance that can be reached between these two competing outcomes?

It will become apparent that there are no simple answers to these questions. Human development is extremely complex and difficult to predict. The critical period and readiness concepts are themselves complex and, ultimately, I will question their relevance for determining when to initiate sport skill learning. Nevertheless, an understanding of these concepts can provide insight into the myriad of factors that must be taken into account when deciding the appropriate time to expose a child to a sport. Furthermore, it must be stated at the outset that, while the focus of this chapter is on the age at which sport skill learning should be initiated, I will also question whether this is the most appropriate focus. Age at first exposure is an important variable, but no more important than a host of other factors that influence learning. When all is said and done, readers will have to make their own decisions about when to initiate sport skill learning and how to facilitate the learning process. It is hoped that this chapter will contribute to decisions that are, at the very least, well informed.

The Critical Period Concept

A Brief Historical Perspective

The critical period concept is ubiquitous in the physical and behavioral sciences and to review the idea thoroughly requires a working knowledge of fields as separate as cell biology and canine socialization. While some question the utility of the concept for behavioral development (McGraw, 1985; Moyer, 1999; Thelen and Smith, 1998), the conviction that experiences can exert a greater influence at some times during life rather than at others has a long history in conventional thinking (Bateson, 1979). Furthermore, the conviction has inspired consideration of early intervention in areas as diverse as education (e.g., government sponsored Head Start programs) and ophthalmology (Colombo, 1982). Historically, some argue that the notion can be traced back to ancient times (Hess, 1973), though, for the present purposes, it is insightful to consider the scientific development of the concept from the turn of the 20th Century.

Freud is perhaps the best-known proponent of the view that early experiences are critical for subsequent behavior (e.g., Freud, 1910). Although he didn't explicitly make reference to critical periods, Freud implied their existence by maintaining that the origins of neuroses could be found in experiences that occurred at certain times during early development. Experimental embryologists made the first formal reference to the critical period concept. Certain cell masses were found to be affected by specific chemicals during a particular stage in their development but not earlier or later, and some cells transplanted at a particular time in their development were found to assume the characteristics of host location cells and thrive but to wither if transplanted at other times (Spemann, 1938; Stockard, 1921). For example, with the introduction of chemicals at specific times during development, Stockard (1921) was able to produce horrible abnormalities in fish embryos. At other times the chemicals had little or no effect. One of the most widely cited examples of a critical period in mammalian development is the observation that surgical closure of one eye during a brief period after birth causes a severe visual impairment in species such as cats and monkeys when the eye is later reopened (Wiesel and Hubei, 1963). Since these early findings, critical periods have been postulated for a variety of biological and non-biological phenomena yet, despite its ubiquity (or perhaps because of it), the critical period concept has not reached a high level of theoretical development (Bornstein, 1989).

Critical Period Effects

Scott, Stewart, and DeGhett (1974) have generically defined a critical period as a time during which an organizational process can be most easily altered or modified. In other words, it is a time during which an organizational process has the greatest degree of plasticity. Bateson (1979) has likened a critical period to a brief opening of a window where experience influences development only while the window is open. With this conceptualization in mind, two types of critical period effects have been proposed. First, there are periods during which normative experience is expected for normal to advantageous development (e.g., Spemann, 1938) and second, there are periods during which some type of noxious experience can produce irreversible harm to the individual (e.g., Stockard, 1921). Some researchers have suggested that the term *critical period* be used to label the former effects and the term *sensitive period* be used to refer to the latter (Fox, 1971). Others argue that a distinction be made between periods in which experience is necessary for continued normal development and periods in which experience is not necessary but nevertheless beneficial (e.g., Moltz, 1973). Because these arguments have not been settled formally, I will follow the lead provided by Scott et al. (1974) and use the term critical period to refer to a time during which an organizational process can be most easily altered or modified, knowing full-well that many would refer to such a time as a sensitive period.

Greenough and colleagues (e.g., Greenough, Black, and Wallace, 1987) have put these semantic arguments in perspective by suggesting that regardless of the preferred label, the terms do very little to explain the underlying mechanisms. Instead, Greenough makes reference to an experience-expectant phase of development during which an organism has come to count on information that is ubiquitous in the environment and that has been so throughout much of the evolutionary history of the organism. We will return to this idea later when considering the utility of the critical period concept for sport skill development, particularly with reference to those who maintain that the first three years of life are critical for the development of numerous cultural skills such as those associated with language, reading, mathematics, music, and the basic motor skills that are thought to serve as the foundational building blocks for sport skill development,

Identifying Critical Periods

Two popular research designs have been used to identify critical periods (Colombo, 1982). In the first, several groups of participants are exposed to some form of stimulation or deprivation such that each group receives the manipulation at a different age. The groups are followed longitudinally over a period of time and assessed on whatever variables are of interest. The critical period is the period during which the manipulation produced the greatest effect. Ideally, the duration of treatment should also be varied systematically. The second research design is based on the correlation method and it relies on naturally occurring abnormal or pathological conditions that prevent an individual from having certain experiences. An excellent example of this type of research was conducted by Banks, Aslin, and Letson (1975) who determined from follow up examinations of patients who had had surgery at various times during their lives to correct congenital eye problems that a critical period for normal visual development exists between birth and approximately three years of age.

It is appropriate for us to think about how one might use these research designs to determine if critical periods exist for the development of sport skills. What factors might compromise the interpretation of data gathered using one of these types of designs? For example, how would one control for possible additive effects of experience in those individuals exposed to the skill at later chronological ages? These are just some of many questions that must be addressed when considering the utility of the critical period concept for understanding and facilitating sport skill learning.

Critical Periods for Motor Skill Development

The person generally credited with first noticing the phenomenon of critical periods for children learning motor skills was Myrtle McGraw (1935, 1939). Her study of the twin boys Johnny and Jimmy are well known to all who have studied motor development. In the initial period of the study, both boys were observed in McGraw's laboratory five days a week for the first 22 months of life. During this time, Johnny was challenged by a variety of stimulating motor activities while Jimmy was left relatively unhindered to play with a few toys in his crib. When the twins were 22 months old, Jimmy was given a period of two and a half months of intensive practice in the same activities to which Johnny had been exposed earlier. Johnny's early exposure was beneficial for the development of some skills but detrimental for others. McGraw's findings have important implications for our understanding of critical periods for sport skill development and we will consider specific findings throughout this chapter. For now, however, it is appropriate to consider the general conclusions drawn at the end of the study as well as McGraw's interpretation of those conclusions some time later. Toward the end of the now classic monograph that described the study in detail, McGraw wrote:

> While there are critical periods in the development of any behavior-pattern when it is most susceptible to modification, it must not be inferred that behavior-patterns can be modified through exercise only during these critical periods of susceptibility. It means merely that these are the most economical periods of achievement. To delay beyond the period of greatest susceptibility means that other factors which have begun to grow will act as interferences and distractions, thereby rendering the achievement of the particular pattern more difficult. (McGraw, 1935, p. 310).

Given arguments about the appropriate use of the critical period label, it is interesting to note that later in her career McGraw lamented using the term critical period, a term she acknowledged picking up from her extensive readings in embryology. In an attempt to clarify what she meant by the term, McGraw noted:

> Being impressed with the disarray that is manifest as a newborn's reflexes begin to decline when the signals of new behavioral traits emerge, and with the fact that those signals indicate a readiness of challenge or practice, I referred to that type of transition as "critical periods" for advancing behavior. But in the course of events I discovered that many writers were assuming that if opportunity was not provided at that time the behavior would *never* be achieved. It was certainly not my intention to imply that if a particular trait was not encouraged at the "critical" time it would never be achieved. I did write an article admitting the misapplication of the term and suggesting instead an "opportune time" as an appropriate label for the nurturing of a particular trait. (McGraw, 1985, p. 169).

Having some sense of McGraw's concerns about the term critical period, it is worth returning now to the questions posed in the discussion of the research designs used to identify critical periods. To those questions we could add—"Did McGraw's research design permit the identification of critical periods for motor skill development?" Shortly, we will consider this question with reference to the concept of "readiness" in motor development. To fully appreciate this future discussion, however, it is important first to look at the physical and behavioral signs that have been proposed to permit identification of the onset of a critical period.

Determinants of Critical Periods

Is Maturation of the Nervous System the Primary Determinant?

Most investigators believe that critical periods for physical and behavioral development are confined to early development and many suppose that they occur only once during the lifetime (Bornstein, 1989; Scott, 1962). It should not be surprising then that McGraw (1935) picked up the idea of critical periods from her observations of Jimmy and Johnny. During McGraw's era, the prevailing theoretical view of development was largely unidimensional. New skills were thought to emerge from maturation of the central nervous system and maturation was presumed to be directly controlled by genetic factors (Clark and Whitall, 1989). In harmony with the prevailing view, McGraw initially stressed the importance of neuromuscular maturation as a primary determinant of critical periods for motor skill acquisition (e.g., McGraw, 1935). However, in subsequent writing she expressed a much more contemporary developmental perspective:

> The major factor contributing to an alteration in behavior may at one time be the status of neurostructural components, at another time variations in anatomical dimensions, and at another time personal or individual experience. In fact, it probably is the interrelationship of a multitude of factors which determines the course of behavior development at any time. (McGraw, 1946, p. 364).

Such a view is surprisingly similar to contemporary systems theories of development. These theories put forward a multiply determined, historical, and contextually dependent view of development where the emergence of new skills is constrained by interactions among numerous task, environmental, and organismic constraints (Higginis, 1977; Kelso, 1995; Kugler, Kelso, and Turvey, 1980, 1982; Newell, 1986; Thelen and Smith, 1994; Thelen and Smith, 1998; Turvey and Fitzpatrick, 1993). Thus, critical periods are determined by the interactions among numerous factors. However, although behavior is organized from a number of different anatomical, physiological, and psychological subsystems, it is generally acknowledged that the slowest maturing system can hold back the emergence of a new behavior. This system has been referred to as a *rate limiter* for skill development (Thelen and Smith, 1994; Thelen and Ulrich, 1991).

The rate limiter concept can be understood by looking at motor skills that suddenly appear or disappear. For example, newborns demonstrate a stepping pattern that disappears a few months later only to return when the child begins to walk. Thelen proposes that the disappearance of newborn stepping is the result of rapid weight gain, primarily in the form of fat (e.g., Thelen, 1983). Because the rapid weight gain is not accompanied by a proportionate gain in muscle strength, lifting the legs against gravity becomes difficult for the child. Support for this proposal comes from the observation that infants who gain weight the most rapidly also show the most rapid disappearance of the stepping reflex as well as the finding that adding weights to the infant's legs inhibits stepping, whereas submerging the infant's legs in water facilitates stepping (Thelen, 1983). Thus, insufficient strength to lift the legs can be viewed as a rate limiter to the re-emergence of infant stepping. The relevance of this example here is that it stands in direct contrast to previous accounts of the disappearing stepping reflex which maintained that the brain's maturing cortex inhibited control of more primitive brain areas (thought to control the immature movement pattern) before bringing the behavior back under voluntary control (e.g., Touwen, 1976). Consistent with a multidimensional view of development, many factors in addition to nervous system maturation can contribute to the emergence and disappearance of motor skills. Thus, many factors determine the opportune times to learn sport skills.

Potential Behavioral Clues to Critical Periods

A systems approach to development provides some clues as to what might be the behavioral markers of a critical period. This perspective views movement production and skill as a process of pattern formation (Kelso, 1995). Motor development can be viewed then as the progressive change in behavioral patterns that vary in stability. The concept of stability is very important here because stable patterns of behavior are very resistant to change whereas change can be induced with relative ease when the system is less stable (Kelso, 1995). As a result, new skills are thought to emerge as previous skills lose stability (Thelen and Smith, 1994) and a loss of stability is marked by an increase in behavioral variability. Loss of stability is characteristic of a system in transition and, according to Thelen (1995), "Knowing when systems are in transition is important because theory predicts that interventions can only be effective when the system has sufficient flexibility to explore and select new solutions" (p. 94).

Ideas about the role of instability or variability in behavioral development are not new in the literature on critical periods. McGraw (1935) argued that to be most effective, stimulation should be introduced at the point when partial aspects of a total pattern were perceptible but intermittent or inconsistent within a background of diffuse activity. Such periods were presumed likely to occur just before the onset of cortical inhibition during infancy. The notion is a corollary to the idea that integrated behavior patterns often are not achieved until after temporary set backs that involve regression to less mature forms of behavior (e.g., Bernstein, 1967, 1996; Gesell, 1954). A general systems perspective has been used to account for why critical periods are thought to occur primarily during early development (e.g., Scott et al., 1974). Again, the argument is based on the idea that systems in a state of flux are more open to external influences than are organized and fixed systems and that a state of flux is characteristic of early development. Furthermore, organizational processes are thought to be most easily modifiable when the process is occurring most rapidly and again, change is typically most rapid at the beginning of the process (Scott, 1962).

Recently, Tucker and Hirsh-Pasek (1993) have adopted a systems approach to explain critical period phenomena in language learning. Language learning is very relevant to a discussion of sport skill learning because very complex patterns of muscular coordination underlie the ability to speak. Not only must control be developed over the vocal chords, the mouth, lips, jaw, and tongue but also over the diaphragm so that airflow and air volume can be regulated. Furthermore, language specialization is very closely tied to specialization in handedness and the development of manual skills (Provins, 1997a). Lenneberg (1967) was the first to propose a critical period for language development. He suggested that language is innately determined and that its acquisition is dependent on both necessary neurological events and some unspecified minimal exposure to language. (The lack of specificity regarding the stimulus or experience to which the individual must be exposed is a frequent criticism leveled at research on critical periods, e.g., Colombo, 1982.)

Lenneberg suggested that the critical period occurred between the ages of two and puberty, assuming that language acquisition was impossible before two due to maturational factors and after two because of lack of cerebral plasticity resulting from the establishment of cerebral dominance or lateralization of the language function. Subsequent researchers have suggested that the critical age ending the opportune period for language acquisition might be as early as seven (e.g., Johnson and Newport, 1989) and others have suggested that there might be different critical periods for different aspects of language such as pronunciation and grammar (e.g., Long, 1990). The presence of critical periods in language acquisition is a hotly debated topic and while it is beyond the scope of this chapter to enter into the debate, it is instructive to return to the insights that have been revealed into the critical period concept by using a systems approach to study language development.

Tucker and Hirsh-Pasek (1993) maintain that developmental systems begin in a relatively undifferentiated state and, as such, the system's learning potential (degrees of freedom) is much greater than at later periods of development. As each successive, systemic reorganization takes place, the system becomes more rigid, less flexible, more automatic, and less susceptible to environmental perturbations. In other words, the system becomes more "mechanized" to borrow a term from von Bertalanffy (1968). Tucker and Hirsh-Pasek (1993) believe that the difficulties most adults have in acquiring a second language can be explained by the highly differentiated and integrated nature of the first language. Adapting the first language to accommodate a second language requires a major reorganization and, therefore, considerably more conscious effort on the part of the adult than the child.

Though not all researchers agree that critical periods exist for language development, it is useful to consider a quote by Scott et al. (1974) linking critical periods in language development to the general concept of critical periods as viewed from a systems perspective. The authors state:

> It is a continuing scandal of our educational system that this period is not utilized for the teaching of foreign languages. This finding is not unconnected with the fact that the critical period of organization of our educational system is long since past. Like any other well-organized system, it is extremely resistant to change. (Scott et al., 1974, p. 510)

Despite the authors' strong stance on the issue, great caution is needed when attempting to leap from basic research to educational policy implications.

Application to Sport Skills

How might we apply the concepts of stability and instability to the identification of a critical period for the learning of a new sport skill? At first blush, the answer seems relatively straightforward. The period when the behavior appears most disorganized or variable is the time when some type of intervention is likely to be most successful. But, won't this time almost always be during the very initial phase of learning a new skill? Not necessarily. Anderson (2000) recently reported evidence for a sudden reorganization of a movement pattern following an increase in movement pattern variability on the third day of practicing a new skill. The participants' goal was to learn a modified gymnastics stunt referred to as a mat kip or kip up. This task requires the performer to project the body from a supine position on the floor to a standing position. The skill is a favorite in martial arts movies when one or other of the fighters is knocked to the ground and springs back to an upright position.

Two of the learners were unsuccessful at the task after four days of practice. However, consistent with the notion of systems becoming more stable over time, these two learners showed a clear tendency over the first two days of practice to repeat the same unsuccessful pattern of motion to solve the movement problem. Variability was introduced on the third day by slightly modifying the environment in which the skill was performed and providing videotape feedback from the previous days of practice. Following this intervention, both learners spontaneously shifted to a new pattern of interlimb coordination on the fourth day of practice, although neither learner was able to achieve the goal of the task. It must be noted with this example that variability in the movement pattern was introduced by the intervention; it did not occur as a natural consequence of learning the skill. Yet, consistent with predictions from a dynamic systems perspective, the rapid transition from one movement pattern to another was preceded by a period of instability.

Consideration of different levels on which development can occur adds further complexity to the potential identification of critical periods by elevated variability in behavior. The movement outcome was highly consistent for the two performers alluded to in the previous example—neither performer successfully achieved the goal of the task. However, variability was very apparent at the level of the movement pattern where motions among body segments and joints are of primary interest. A better illustration of the complexity introduced by different levels of analysis comes from the extensive research on postural development conducted by Marjorie Woollacott and her colleagues (e.g., Woollacott and Shumway-Cook, 1991). The development of postural control is an extremely important area of study in motor behavior because postural control is vital to nearly all goal-directed motor activity (e.g., Rochat and Bullinger, 1995; Stoffregen and Riccio, 1988; Stoffregen, Pagulayan, Bardy, and Hettinger, 2000).

There appears to be an important transition in the development of postural control between the ages of four and six years. According to Woollacott, Debû, and Shumway-Cook (1987), it is during this time that the child learns to overcome reliance on visual information for postural control and integrate information from the visual, vestibular, and somatosensory perceptual systems. Most importantly, this period is characterized by a regression in postural control at the level of neuromotor processes; patterns of muscular activation are longer in latency and higher in variability (clear indicators of a system in transition). However, children sway less during this period compared to earlier ages! Thus for the teacher, parent, or coach who does not have access to the sophisticated equipment needed to measure muscle activity, the transition would proceed unnoticed. Nevertheless, the concepts of instability and variability might be the best indicators we have of the periods during which interventions are likely to be most successful. It is important to keep in mind, though, that instability is just as likely to follow an intervention as it is to precede one. Again, there are no simple answers to the questions posed in this chapter!

In summary, the notion that experiences can have a greater influence at some times during life than at others has broad intuitive appeal as does the idea that such periods are likely to exist early in development and to occur only once. However, there is simply too little evidence to conclude that these popular beliefs are true. The lack of evidence is due in large part to the difficulty of conducting ethical and well-controlled research to identify critical periods in human development, a situation that is further compounded by the assumption that critical periods are multiply determined. Despite these limitations, the concept of instability, which has emerged from a systems perspective on critical periods, might provide a useful indicator of opportune times for facilitating skill learning. An implication that stems from this suggestion, as well as the discussion so far, is that if critical periods exist, they might be context dependent rather than age dependent. It is appropriate to consider this idea here because the readiness concept is addressed in the next section. In contrast to the critical period concept, readiness suggests that initiating learning is not bound by an age period but, instead, is determined by whether the learner has had specific experiences or acquired certain prerequisites.

The Readiness Concept

The Relationship Between Readiness and Critical Periods

An implication from the previous discussion is that critical periods will not be apparent until after the skill has been introduced to the child, insinuating that the child has already demonstrated readiness to begin practice. In other words, readiness is a prerequisite to the demonstration of critical periods. It is very difficult to define the term readiness precisely because the concept of readiness is used so broadly and so frequently in such a wide variety of fields. Furthermore, the readiness and critical period concepts are often very difficult to dissociate (as may be apparent already) because of the loose way in which the critical period concept is applied in the physical and behavioral sciences. In any case, readiness is associated with the idea of prerequisites or substrates for learning (e.g., Arend, 1980). The concept is based on the hierarchical and integrated nature of development, a theme that is apparent in both contemporary (e.g., Lerner, 1998) and traditional (e.g., Hebb, 1949; Piaget, 1952, 1954) theories of development.

According to Hebb (1949), much early learning is foundational because it provides the organism with essential perceptual and motor skills that form the framework within which subsequent learning takes place. Subsequent learning stems from earlier learning in this scheme. Robert Gagné (1968, 1970) has also stressed the cumulative nature of development by stating that the "child progresses from one point to the next in his development . . . because he learns an ordered set of capabilities which build upon each other in progressive fashion through the process of differentiation, recall, and transfer or learning" (1968, p. 181). The idea that new forms of behavior are assembled from earlier forms of behavior is also a central tenet of systems approaches to development (Thelen and Smith, 1998). The reorganizations at each successive level of development emerge from components and organizations among components that were present earlier. The systems perspective is useful here because it suggests that there are numerous properties of the individual and the environment that contribute to the emergence of new forms of behavior. Any component, if not present or not present in sufficient quantity or quality, could act as a rate limiter and hold back the development of a new motor skill.

Recently, my colleagues and I (Campos, Anderson, Barbu-Roth, Hubbard, Hertenstein, and Witherington, 2000) have suggested that the hierarchical integration and organization of development can explain why precocious exposure to a particular experience can fail to produce developmental change. Our work focuses on psychological changes in infancy and their relationship to locomotor experience (namely in the form of hands-and-knees crawling). Assuming that development is multiply determined and hierarchically organized, locomotor experience will not bring about a change in a psychological skill if the skill in question is dependent on other skills that have not yet fully developed. Other examples that support this notion are introduced in the next section.

Readiness for Learning Motor Skills

It is appropriate to return to a question posed earlier in the chapter, "Did McGraw's research design permit the identification of critical periods for motor skill development?" In her 1935 monograph, McGraw spoke at length about both the critical period and readiness concepts. You will recall, however, that later in her career she expressed some remorse about adopting the term critical period from the embryologists and applying it to human motor development. While some of her observations on Johnny and Jimmy revealed characteristic patterns of developmental change that share many similarities with the concept of critical periods, her research design did not permit determination of whether such changes were a function of critical periods in development or readiness. For example, Johnny was given considerable practice on tricycle riding when he was 11 months old whereas Jimmy was not exposed to tricycling until he was 22 months old. Johnny struggled for eight months before showing any improvement on the task while Jimmy, despite his later exposure, mastered the task very rapidly. McGraw (1939) accounted for the ineffectiveness of early tricycle practice for Johnny by stating that the "activity was initiated before his neuro-muscular mechanisms were ready for such a performance" (p. 3).

Later, McGraw stated rather definitively that it is simply wasted effort to begin training before adequate "neural readiness." Gesell and Thompson (1929) reached a similar conclusion in their study of identical twin girls. In the study, one twin was given special training between the ages of 46 and 52 weeks in locomotor activities related to stair climbing. The other twin did not receive such training until she was 53 weeks of age. At 53 weeks, the untrained twin did not climb the stairs as well as the trained twin. However, following only two weeks of training, which was five weeks less than the previously trained twin had received, the untrained twin surpassed the performance of her sister in climbing the stairs. Again, Gesell and Thompson concluded that better learning with less training results when the child's maturation level is adequate for the skill being learned. A similar conclusion could be drawn from a study by Hilgard (1932) in which two-year-old children were given 12 weeks of instruction in buttoning, cutting with scissors, and climbing. After the training period, the children were significantly more proficient than a control group; however, the control group was able to reach the same level of proficiency on the skills after only one week of intensive training.

It is readily apparent that the rapid learning observed in the above-mentioned examples was a result of readiness rather than a function of the children being in a critical period. Furthermore, in a multidimensional view of development, the ineffectiveness of practice could be a function of many or any one of many factors that constrain learning in addition to neural maturation. Much of the confusion about the critical period concept has stemmed from the use of the terms readiness and critical periods to account for the same phenomena—namely rapid change in behavior or in the systems that underlie behavior. Because change is most rapid during the initial phase of learning any new motor skill (or in the initial phase of any system's organization), that phase could be considered a critical period for learning. It appears to be the period during which the new behavior is least stable and interventions have the greatest impact. However, this is not the way in which the critical period concept traditionally has been applied.

Many years ago, Scott and Marston (1950) reinforced the above view by maintaining that the time immediately after the onset of a learning ability should be critical for a large number of phenomena that are organized by learning. Subsequently, Scott (1962) maintained that the time when maximum sensory, motor, motivational, and psychological capacities were first present was the critical period for any type of learning. Richard Magill and I capitalized on this idea to suggest that critical periods might be appropriately viewed as periods of optimal readiness for learning sport skills (Magill and Anderson, 1996). These are periods when the child's maturation level is appropriate for the skill to be learned, when he or she has acquired the necessary prerequisite skills to be learned, and when he or she is adequately motivated to learn the skill. This perspective implies that exposure to learning a sport skill should be delayed past the point when the child shows minimal readiness to learn the skill, to the point when he or she shows optimal or maximal readiness. However, following this idea, how does one determine when the child has reached a point of minimal or optimal readiness? What factors about the task and the environment in which the skill will be learned must be taken into account when determining minimal or optimal readiness for learning? These are two of many questions that will be addressed in the next section, which considers when a child should be exposed to learning a new skill.

When Should Motor Skill Learning Be Initiated?

In the introduction, we saw that arguments for and against early exposure to skill learning are based largely on the critical period and readiness concepts. Now that the reader has a greater appreciation for both of these concepts, we will consider how each has been used to determine the appropriate time to initiate skill learning. Consistent with my position at the beginning of the chapter, it will become more apparent that, due to the myriad of factors that contribute to behavioral change, the critical period and readiness concepts provide little in the way of clear guidance about when to initiate sport skill learning.

A Case for Early Exposure

The brain develops very rapidly during early childhood. The introductory paragraph of this chapter noted that "earlier is better" has become a rather ingrained viewpoint in our popular culture. The viewpoint can likely be traced to at least two related factors: First, interest in brain and child development has recently surged among policy makers and the popular media and, second, the critical period concept is still firmly established within many circles in the neurosciences. With respect to the first point, it is interesting to note that in 1991 the Carnegie Corporation of New York formed a task force to address what was referred to as a "quiet crisis" afflicting children from birth to age three. According to Bruer (1998a), the task force's report, *Starting Points* (1994) was the seminal document that spurred interest in brain science and child development. Following *Starting Points,* the Carnegie Corporation and several other foundations sponsored a conference in Chicago in 1996 that led to the publication, *Rethinking the Brain* (Shore, 1997). The publication was released at the same time as a 1997 White House conference on brain and early childhood development. Both the publication and the conference were designed to supplement *Starting Points* as a means to encourage parents, educators, and Congress to reformulate educational policies and priorities (Bruer, 1998a).

With reference to the second point about the view of critical periods in the neurosciences, it is pertinent to note that at about the same time the Carnegie Corporation and its collaborators were having their conference in Chicago, a similar conference on the "Critical" Period of Brain Development was being held by a group of neuroscientists in Washington. In a telling introduction to the report on the conference, Wynder (1998) stated:

It is the consensus of the participants that a "critical" period exists during which the synapses of the dendrites are most ready for appropriate stimulation, be it through words, music, love, touch, or caring. If these synapses are not so stimulated early, they may never fully develop. The deliberations of this conference need to be closely examined by all segments of society so as to decide how we can best develop the cognitive, emotional, and behavioral nature of our children to their optimal level, which if done well is a wise and economically sound investment in our future. (p. 166)

It is necessary to consider how this conclusion emerged before we can grasp the implications for sport skill development.

Earlier in the chapter, allusion was made to Wiesel and Hubei's (1963) classic work on the role of visual experience during an early period in development for subsequently normal visual functioning. This work stimulated considerable research on the interaction between internal and external factors on brain development in a number of animal species. Based on this work, it is now well established that a common feature of brain development in mammals, including humans, is the early overproduction of synapses followed by a substantial decrease in their number (Black, 1998; Greenough et al., 1987). Synapses refer to the connections that allow nerve impulses to travel from one neuron (nerve cell) to another. Huttenlocher has shown that the number of synaptic connections in the human cerebral cortex increases dramatically after birth and reaches a maximum value between about 6 months and 7 years of age (depending on the cortical region studied) after which it decreases to adult levels by about 15 to 16 years of age (Huttenlocher, 1979, 1990, 1992, 1994). More recent research that has studied the cortex by way of glucose utilization suggests that a variety of neural processes, including synapse formation, rise from birth to age 4, remain high until the age of 10 and gradually decline to adult levels by 16 to 18 years of age (Chugani, 1998). Synapse elimination is considered the final step in neural circuit formation because this process leads to a refinement of redundant connections formed at earlier developmental stages (e.g., Kakizawa, Yamasaki, Watanabe, and Kano, 2000). Not coincidentally, the pruning of synapses is critically dependent on experience, particularly experience generated by self-produced activity (e.g., Greenough et al., 1987; Inglis, Zuckerman, and Kalb, 2000).

The period of rapid synapse formation across the first years of life has been championed as the critical period for learning a host of different skills (Wynder, 1998), with the assumption that a child will be permanently handicapped if he or she is not provided with the appropriate experiences during this period (Lindsey, 1998/99) because synapses will be either lost forever or committed to other functions. Recently, Gabbard (1998) has applied this line of thinking to the learning of motor skills. He suggests that the window of opportunity for the development of basic motor skills extends from the prenatal period to approximately the age of 5. The suggestion is in agreement with the notion that children have the potential to demonstrate "mature" performance in a host of "fundamental" motor skills such as running, jumping, throwing, and catching by the age of 6 (Gallahue and Ozman, 1995). Gabbard suggests that basic gross-motor activities (activities such as climbing, running, and kicking that use large muscle groups) should be encouraged before the age of 2 and that a flood of sensory-motor experiences from a wide range of motor activities that stimulate visual, tactile, and kinesthetic awareness should be provided from that point onward.

Some skills appear more difficult to learn later in life. Reference was made earlier to Lenneberg's (1967) critical period hypothesis for language learning and the relevance of language learning to sport skill learning was noted. Though there is much debate about critical periods for language acquisition, from personal experience, many people would acknowledge that learning a second language as an adult is a very challenging task. The difficulty seems to vary with the language. Adult Japanese learners, for example, have a very difficult time making the distinction between "r" and "l" in English (Yamada, 1991).

Young children's acquisition of language is curiously similar to the ease with which they can acquire a musical capability referred to as perfect pitch or absolute pitch (AP). AP is the ability to identify the pitch of a tone or produce a tone at a given pitch without the use of an external reference pitch (Takeuchi and Hulse, 1993). Most researchers agree that AP can be learned by anyone but it is most easily acquired before the ages of 5 or 6 (Takeuchi and Hulse, 1993). Apparently, the skill can be acquired by adults but only with considerable effort (Brady, 1970; Takeuchi and Hulse, 1993). Consistent with the importance of experience in brain development, the organization of the brain is different in musicians with perfect pitch versus non-musicians and musicians without perfect pitch (Schlaug, Jäncke, Huang, and Steinmetz, 1995). (Though one could argue that musicians gravitate towards music because their brains are already organized in a particular way.) On a related but somewhat tangential point, it is interesting to note that differences in brain organization have been observed between musicians who play stringed instruments and non-musicians. The extent of reorganization is related to the age at which music practice began, with an earlier start associated with a larger amount of cortical representation of the fingering digits (Elbert, Pantev, Wienbruch, Rockstroh, and Taub, 1995).

Takeuchi and Hulse (1993) have put forward a very interesting hypothesis to explain why children are capable of acquiring AP before 5 or 6 but not afterward. According to the hypothesis, AP may only develop if early musical training includes the association of pitch names with absolute pitches, rather than on the relational aspects of pitch. Once the relative features of a melody are noticed, it is very difficult to distinguish absolute features. The significance here is that there is presumed to be a general shift between three to six years of age in the extent to which a child notices the relative features of auditory stimuli. The shift in perception from absolute features of a stimulus to relative features among stimuli is a common theme in the developmental literature (Pollack, 1969). The shift from absolute to relative features of auditory stimuli is thought to be a byproduct of learning to understand speech (Terhardt, 1974). Children learn to ignore the absolute pitches of the partials of a tone because to identify speech sounds, they must recognize the frequency relations among the partials of voiced speech sounds. Thus AP can be developed easily prior to relative pitch but not afterwards because the latter tendency to notice the relations among stimuli interferes with the former requirement to attend to the absolute features of a stimulus. This phenomenon is curiously similar to the concept of field dependence and independence in the visual processing literature (e.g., MacGillivary, 1980). Field independent individuals can easily separate the foreground of a figure from the background whereas field dependent individuals find it very difficult to achieve such separation.

Interference between early and later learning. The notion of interference between earlier and later learning is interesting to raise here given the previous discussion on the hierarchical and integrated nature of development and the importance of mastering prerequisites before attempting to learn more challenging tasks. Interference from one task to another is not incompatible with a cumulative view of development; in fact, it would be predicted from such a view. From a learning theory perspective, acquisition of new skills proceeds most easily when there are no competing tendencies (Bornstein, 1989) and the case with which subsequent tasks are learned depends on what has been learned previously. Recently, Kelso and his colleagues have attempted to formalize this view in motor learning by introducing the concept of *intrinsic dynamics* (Kelso, 1995; Zanone and Kelso, 1992). Intrinsic dynamics refer to the spontaneous coordination tendencies among body parts that exist prior to the learning of a new task (Kelso, 1995). The ease with which learning proceeds can be predicted on the basis of whether the learner's intrinsic dynamics either compete or cooperate with the dynamics of the task to be learned. For example, for many of us it is difficult to rub our head and pat our belly (or vice versa) at the same time. The difficulty arises because the arms seem to want to move together, to mirror each other's movements. This common coordination tendency between human limbs (e.g., Kelso, Southard, and Goodman, 1979) must be overcome if we are to master the task of rubbing our head and patting our belly. However, Kelso maintains that learning the new pattern of coordination modifies the learner's intrinsic dynamics. In other words, a new pattern of coordination cannot be established or changed independently of other patterns of coordination as all patterns emerge from the same anatomical and physiological substrate.

The intrinsic dynamics concept reinforces the idea that new skills are acquired on the background of existing skills and capacities. However, the usefulness of the concept for determining the ease with which new sports skills can be learned is, at this point, questionable. A strategy for determining a learner's intrinsic dynamics has been described for tasks that require the coordination between two limbs (Kelso, 1995), however, the strategy is difficult to apply to sport skills because such skills require coordination among many body parts and researchers have not yet determined how to succinctly describe the patterns of coordination in the majority of these skills. Instead, researchers have addressed the relationship between what are supposed to be the prerequisite sub-skills and abilities for a given skill and the performance on that skill by examining correlations between the former and the latter (see Schmidt and Lee, 1999 for a comprehensive discussion of this strategy).

How important are prerequisite sub-skills and capacities? The strategy of focusing on correlations between a skill and its hypothesized prerequisites has been overwhelmingly *unsuccessful* at predicting performance in a wide range of tasks (Ericsson and Charness, 1994; Ericsson et al., 1993; Ericsson and Lehmann, 1996; Howe, Davidson, and Sloboda, 1999). In the realm of sports, experts' superior performance in their domain of expertise does not transfer to general tests of speed, such as simple reaction time, or to general tests of perception (Starkes, 1987; Starkes and Deakin, 1985). For example, the speed with which a performer reacts to an opponent's play in racquet sports such as badminton and tennis is crucial to successful performance. However, Abernethy and his colleagues have shown that there are no differences on laboratory tests of reaction time between experts in racquet sports and novices (e.g., Abernethy, 1991; Abernethy and Russell, 1987). Instead, experts have developed visual search strategies that allow them to anticipate what their opponents will do and plan actions in advance. In another example, a longitudinal study of elite German tennis players found no early capacities that predicted tennis performance in early adulthood (Schneider, 1993). Thus, motor skills appear to be highly specific (a suggestion that is not new, e.g., Henry, 1958, 1968) and seem to become more specific with practice given the lack of correspondence that has been observed between expert and initial performance (e.g., Chase and Simon, 1973), early and later learning (Magill, 2001), and performance in early and later childhood (Haubenstricker and Seefeldt, 1986).

Further evidence for the highly specific nature of motor skills has recently been provided by Provins (1997a, 1997b) who notes that the correlations between tasks performed on either side of the body are low and insignificant. One of the most compelling examples, however, comes from the developmental literature where Karen Adolph has shown that what infants learn about their ability to negotiate sloping surfaces while crawling shows no transfer at all to the negotiation of slopes when the child begins to walk (Adolph, 1997, 2000). Initially, infants will plunge down almost any degree of slope, but with experience they learn to avoid those slopes that are risky for descent. When the child starts to walk, he or she will once again plunge down the slopes that had been avoided when crawling. The child must learn all over again what slopes to avoid from the walking posture and the learning period is as long as it was when the child first learned what slopes to avoid from the crawling posture. One suggestion that might help to explain this counter intuitive finding is that the perceptual processes supporting the control of different movement patterns like crawling and walking might be mapped onto highly specific motor response loci (Goodale, 1988; Milner and Goodale, 1995).

What do all of the above-mentioned findings have to say about when children should be exposed to sport skills? What do the findings suggest about the concept of readiness? The examples seem to seriously challenge the view that later learning is a function of prerequisites that were developed at earlier phases of learning, but do they imply that earlier is better? Before answering this question, it is worth spending a little more time looking at evidence that tends to undermine the importance of prerequisites for the learning of sport skills. The evidence is related to the idea that motor skills are highly specific and it implies that the capacities believed to underlie performance are not necessarily apparent prior to learning but can be developed by practicing the task.

Joint mobility is often cited as an important prerequisite for successful performance in a number of sports and performing arts. Yet research shows that ballet training must start before dancers reach age 11 to gain the necessary flexibility to perform at elite levels. Stress associated with intensive training at young ages appears necessary for dancers to gain sufficient "turn out" in different positions at adult ages (DiTullio, Wilczek, Paulus, Kiriakatis, Pollack, and Eisenhardt, 1989; Klemp and Charlton, 1989; Watkins, Woodhull-McNeal, Clarkson, and Ebbeling, 1989). Similarly, flexibility in the ankles and shoulders differentiates swimmers from non-swimmers and provides an excellent predictor of swimming speed (Poppleton and Salmoni, 1991). Ericsson et al. (1993) argue that swimmer's flexibility is also a function of intense training at a young age and they suggest further that anatomical and physiological adaptations occur most rapidly when training overlaps with physical maturation. This finding supports the idea that systems are most responsive to external influences during periods of rapid change (e.g., Scott, 1962) and it also tends to support those who maintain that critical periods are much more apparent for anatomical and physiological development than for behavioral development (e.g., Colombo, 1982).

There is anecdotal evidence that lacking prerequisites may, in some cases, have beneficial effects on later skill development. In a recent *Time* magazine article on Tiger Woods, Goodgame (2000) notes that Tiger was first introduced to the game of golf at 10 months of age. His father taught him the basics but because Tiger lacked size and strength he was unable to hit the ball very far and so he learned to score with putts and delicate wedge shots. His first coach noted that, at age 5, Tiger had the imagination to hit a wide range of different wedge shots. In contrast, Goodgame points out that Jack Nicklaus (touted as the best golfer ever) felt he never developed first-rate shots from off the green because he didn't start playing golf seriously until he was 10. At that age Nicklaus was already big for his age and intent on smashing the ball. Thus, the inability to drive the ball long distances forced Tiger to concentrate on an aspect of his game that many believe is crucial for success.

Do children learn motor skills differently than adults? Most researchers would agree that the process by which motor skills are learned is similar for both adults and children. For example, Jane Clark has observed that if one carefully watches an infant struggling to take his or her first walking step, the similarities with an adult challenged to learn a new sport skill are striking (Clark, 1995). However, the noted Russian physiologist Bernstein, whose work (e.g., Bernstein, 1967, 1996) has had a tremendous impact on contemporary theorizing in the field of motor behavior, has suggested that children might have an advantage over adults for learning many motor skills. Bernstein's (1996) argument is based on a hierarchically organized motor system composed of levels A, B, C, and D. Level A supports the spinal column and provides the muscles of the limbs with background tone. Level B is concerned with basic patterns of coordination among groups of muscles and level C adapts movements to the temporal and spatial characteristics of the environment surrounding the individual. Finally, level D, what Bernstein has described as the level of actions, is the leading level where whole sequences of movements are chained together to solve a motor problem.

The leading level possesses the resourcefulness and maneuverability that separates humans from all other species of animals and, not surprisingly, it is considered to be evolutionarily younger than the other levels. Because level D always takes the leading role at the beginning of learning a new skill, even though control will inevitably pass to level C, Bernstein maintains that "skills like swimming take much more time and more effort to become automated in adults than in children, because in children such skills are immediately put under the control of the level of space (C)" (1996, p. 182). Thus, he suggests that "spatial" skills like swimming should be learned during childhood, "just to save this effort." Though Bernstein has raised a fascinating hypothesis, there is no direct evidence to unequivocally support the presumed levels of the motor system nor is there any evidence to support the assertion that children might acquire certain skills faster than adults because those skills are controlled by a different level of the motor system. Nevertheless, this hypothesis provides much food for thought and is ripe for investigation. It is also of interest to note that some contemporary researchers believe that the learning of motor skills is much more effectively accomplished when cognitive activity (that which Bernstein would associate with level D) is minimized. There is even some support for this assertion (Masters, 1992).

A Case Against Early Exposure

The former discussion appears to present a fairly compelling case for exposing children to skills at an early age. However, final judgment on the issue will be reserved until the end of the chapter. As we shall see in the next section, there are just as many arguments for not exposing the child to early experience as there are for exposing the child to early experience.

The relevance of rapid brain development during early childhood. One of the most vocal critics of the notion that children should be exposed to a host of specific skills early in life is John Bruer (1998a, 1998b, 1999). Bruer's arguments can be summarized along three major lines. First, there is no evidence that the period of rapid synapse formation in the brain is the optimal time for learning. Increases in synaptic densities in the brain are associated with the initial emergence of skills and capacities but these skills and capacities continue to develop after synaptic densities have decreased to adult levels. Thus, there is no simple relationship between the number of synapses and the ability to learn. In fact, some neuroscientists and developmental psychologists argue that it is only after the neural processes begin to stabilize at puberty that we are ready to engage in high-level learning (e.g., Goldman-Rakic, Bourgeois, and Rakic, 1997; Rakic, Bourgeois, and Goldman-Rakic, 1994).

Bruer's second line of argument speaks directly to the critical period hypothesis. Drawing upon the work of Wiesel and Hubel (1963), Greenough and colleagues, and subsequent work on the visual system (e.g., Daw, 1995), Bruer notes that the known complexity of the critical period concept makes it very difficult to speak of a critical period for vision or any other sensory system, let alone of a critical period for brain development. The concept of experience-expectant brain plasticity introduced by Greenough et al. (1987) is most relevant here because the concept provides an intuitive understanding of why animals might have evolved to take advantage of critical periods and why critical periods are likely to be highly circumscribed and largely irrelevant for most aspects of behavioral development, particularly those that are the focus of this chapter. It is worth quoting Bruer's explanation of the relationship between brain development and experience directly here:

> Relying on the environment to fine-tune the system results in neural circuits that are more sensitively tuned than they ever could be if they were hardwired by genetic programs at birth. Relying on the presence of certain kinds of stimuli just at the right times would seem to be a highly risky developmental strategy, especially for a system like vision that is fundamental to survival. The reason it is not risky is that the kinds of stimuli needed during critical periods—patterned visual input, the ability to move and manipulate objects, noises, the presence of speech sounds—are ubiquitously and abundantly present in any normal human environment. Nature has made a bet that the stimuli will be present, but nature has placed its money on an almost sure thing. The brain expects certain kinds of stimuli to be present for normal development, and they almost always are, unless a child is abused to the point of being raised in a deprivation chamber. (1998b, p.16)

Accordingly, then, neuroscientific research on critical periods is likely to have little relevance for formal education if critical periods are based on information that has been ubiquitously present throughout our evolutionary history. On the basis of this argument, there is no reason to expect that critical periods exist for highly specific socially or culturally transmitted skills such as those involved in sport.

The final point in Bruer's argument is that the adult brain remains plastic throughout life (e.g., Nelson and Bloom, 1997). Even in adulthood, new experiences and learning result in synapse production (Greenough et al., 1987) and changes in patterns of stimulation that result from amputation and nerve damage lead to relatively rapid and substantial cortical reorganization (e.g., Black, 1998, Green, Greenough, and Schlumpf, 1983; Ramachandran, 1995). Thus, the brain is primed for learning at any point during the lifetime, not just at highly constrained periods during early development. Again, relative plasticity across the lifespan is a common theme in contemporary theories of development (Lerner, 1998).

Another look at readiness. Given the spirited arguments that have been used by neuroscientists to support or deny the importance of early experiences for the development of numerous skills, one could be excused for thinking that neural maturation plays the dominant role in behavioral development. As we have seen already, this is certainly not the case even though early accounts of the inability to profit from practice were tied to nervous system maturation. McGraw (1935), based on her observation that Johnny did not appear to benefit from early exposure to tricycling, and Gesell and Thompson (1929), based on their observations that one twin did not benefit from early practice in stair climbing, made compelling arguments against early exposure, suggesting that skill development will not respond to practice before adequate "neural readiness." The readiness concept forms the basis from which the strongest argument can be mounted against early exposure to sport skill learning; however, readiness applies to all of the subsystems that contribute to the organization of behavior, not only the nervous system. As McGraw noted from Johnny's frustration at his futile attempts to master tricycling, the child can suffer considerably if learning is initiated before adequate readiness. Scott (1962) has also suggested that any attempt to teach too early may result in learning bad habits or simply learning "not to learn."

In a multidimensional view of development, numerous constraints can act as rate limiters to the emergence of new skills. This view does not deny the importance of neural maturation; quite the contrary, nervous system maturation is thought to play a vital role in development. It was noted earlier that some researchers would argue that the stabilization of synapse production at puberty signals readiness for higher-level learning (Goldman-Rakic et al., 1997). Another neurological event that is associated with readiness for learning is myelination (Almli and Finger, 1987). Myelination is the process by which neurons are insulated with a fatty protective coating to increase the rate at which nerve impulses can be transmitted. Myelination of the corpus callosum (a structure in the brain that separates the left from the right hemisphere), which is not completed until about the age of 10 (Yakolev and Lecours, 1967), has been implicated in the refinement of bimanual coordination, that is, coordination between limbs on opposite sides of the body. It has been suggested that tasks reliant on bimanual coordination will be performed more effectively once myelination completes the maturation of interhemispheric cooperation (Fagard, 1990). Here is another assertion that might support McGraw's and Gesell and Thompson's view on the importance of neural readiness before the initiation of practice on certain skills. However, whether or not the assertion is true remains to be determined.

In addition to neural maturation, a case can be made for delaying the initiation of learning a sport skill because any of the child's systems have not grown or matured sufficiently. For instance, Newell (1984, 1986) argues that body scale is an important component of the skill acquisition capability of developing children. Changes in the absolute and relative size of body parts to each other and to environmental features lead to changes in the biomechanical constraints on the motor control system. Changes in body part size need to be accompanied by nonproportional changes in strength for the child to effectively coordinate body parts to perform a skill. This characteristic means that differences in body scale might explain why the coordination required for a specific skill can be achieved by some children but not others. Most importantly, a child who successfully performed a skill at one age might have difficulty controlling the same skill at a later age because of changes in body scale.

McGraw (1935) provided an excellent example of the impact of body scale changes on the maintenance of skill improvements associated with early practice. Johnny was exposed to rollerskating when he was 12 months old. He proceeded to master the skill quickly and was quite adept at skating by the end of the training period. However, in follow up observations on the twins at age 3, McGraw (1939) noted that the skating pattern had become very disorganized and Johnny had a strong tendency to lose balance and tumble. She attributed this regression in performance to Johnny's growth, namely to the increase in the position of his center of gravity, which made it very difficult for Johnny to stand upright and balance on the skates. Similarly, Johnny had become quite adept at climbing slides, as had Jimmy, but both boys showed a regression in performance when observed at age 3 because they had great difficulty managing their longer legs. The longer legs made it difficult for the boys to keep the pelvis and therefore the center of gravity close to the slide.

In sports such as gymnastics, where a small body is advantageous, rapid changes in body size can be disastrous. This point has been reinforced recently in the failures of some gymnasts to continue competing at an international level. For example, Kristie Philips began gymnastics training at four years of age and won a world championship at age 14. However, she failed to make the U.S. Olympic team one year later because, according to many, she was unable to regain her level of skill after gaining 20 pounds following the onset of puberty. A similar story is told about another well-known American gymnast and Olympic medallist, Shannon Miller. The destabilization of movement competence following rapid growth has been substantiated in a recent empirical study (Heffernan and Thomson, 1999). In the study, boys who showed the most rapid changes in growth during the adolescent growth spurt also showed the most marked deterioration in their ability to judge their own movement capabilities. This finding suggests that growth might destabilize coordination patterns by itself but that the inability to quickly recalibrate perceptual processes following growth is likely also to make a contribution to the stability of coordination. Again, early practice might be wasted if the child must continually adapt patterns of coordination to changing body dimensions.

Bad habits associated with growth and maturation. Another potentially damaging effect of exposing a child to a skill before the child is physically big enough or mature enough is the development of bad habits. Bad habits can represent the child's attempt to compensate for missing prerequisites. Earlier, we noted that Tiger Woods might actually have benefited from not having the prerequisite size or strength to smash a golf ball great distances. Lack of strength forced him to develop other important aspects of his golf game. More often than not, though, the child is likely to be disadvantaged by inadequate size and strength. For example, Ward and Groppel (1980) have observed that success in learning and performing skills that utilize implements depends partly on the child's ability to accelerate and decelerate the implement. Large implements are likely to pose a problem for the child and the size of the equipment relative to the child might be the major determinant of when a child is ready to learn a sport skill.

Ward and Groppel (1980) have shown that when children are forced to learn tennis with an adult-sized racquet their pattern of coordination is less efficient than that of an adult learning the skill. Children tend to lean their trunk away from the ball and adduct their striking arm in an attempt to manipulate the racquet to hit the ball. I am convinced that two-handed groundstrokes in tennis emerged because children were given racquets at an age when it was next to impossible for them to manipulate the racquet with one hand. The compensation is effective for those players who can move around the court quickly and further compensate for the restricted reach that is afforded by a two-handed versus a one-handed grip. However, it is likely that slower players will have to change grips at some point in their careers if they are to remain competitive. Changing a stable grip pattern might be much more difficult to accomplish than learning the grip from the beginning (e.g., Bernstein, 1996).

Sometimes it is possible to accommodate body scale characteristics by adjusting the size of equipment with which the child interacts, such as changing ball sizes or the heights of basketball hoops or volleyball nets (Haywood, 1993; Ulrich, 1987). While this strategy can be a very useful one, it can also be problematic for at least three reasons. First, one size does not fit all. As Ulrich (1987) has noted, to maximize performance, children of different sizes and skill levels are likely to need different equipment and providing all children with the most appropriate equipment might be logistically impossible. Second, some type of recalibration of the pattern of coordination and the perceptual processes supporting that pattern will be required when the child transitions to the regulation equipment. Halverson (1966) has shown that young children regress from a relatively mature form of striking with a light implement to a less mature movement pattern with a heavier implement. Deciding on the appropriate time to make the transition to regulation equipment is, of course, another logistical problem. Finally, equipment is often scaled proportionately. What this means is that a basketball hoop is not only lowered to the ground but the hoop is also smaller, providing a more difficult target. Also, balls are made lighter in part by making them smaller, again presenting a smaller target. Small objects might be of benefit in some activities such as throwing but might be detrimental in other activities like catching or striking. From the speed-accuracy trade off (Fitts, 1954), which is a well-established phenomenon in the movement sciences, we know that movement time increases as the distance to a target increases or the size of the target decreases. Smaller targets increase the index of difficulty associated with aiming tasks.

Bad habits associated with perceptual processes. The developmental status of perceptual processes is also important to consider relative to the establishment of bad habits. In a previous section, we saw that Woollacott and her colleagues had observed a regression in postural control between the ages of 4 and 6 (e.g., Woollacott et al., 1987). It was suggested that the regression could reflect the beginning of intersensory integration whereby the child moves from primarily visual control of movement to an ability to integrate visual, vestibular, and somatosensory information for movement control. According to Woollacott, pressure to specialize in one motor skill or pressure to perform to a criterion before or during this age period could compromise the intersensory integration process. For example, if a child is forced to perform to a criterion of success that child might rely on only one source of information to control the movement. If the task were to kick a ball to a target with a particular degree of accuracy, the child might overly rely on vision to control the motion of the kicking limb and the placement of the foot on the ball.

Assuming that vision is required also to localize the position of the ball, the child could be at a disadvantage later when attempting to kick a moving ball in a game situation because visual attention is limited. If visual attention is devoted to guiding the kicking limb, then less visual attention is available to attend to the environment, including the ball, the boundaries, and other players. This example is very speculative and we know that visual dominance followed by an ability to use other sources of perceptual information is common during the learning of many skills (e.g., Bower, 1976; Fleishman and Rich, 1963). Therefore, one could argue that the transition speculated to occur during the development of postural control is not age-related but, instead, is related to a particular phase during the learning of postural control. Furthermore, it may be more than coincidental that the most rapid changes in the body's distribution of mass about its three primary axes of rotation occur between the ages of 4 and 7 (Jensen, 1981). Nevertheless, the suggestion by Woollacott et al. (1987) that early learning should be very playful and exploratory in nature with exposure to a wide range of activities under many different environmental and sensory conditions is a sound one.

Bad habits associated with cognitive processes. Cognitive immaturity is closely related to perceptual immaturity when considering the establishment of bad habits. A good example to describe this link was provided by McGraw's (1939) discussion of Johnny and Jimmy's inappropriate application of an earlier movement strategy used to solve the problem of obtaining a lure that was suspended from the ceiling. Both boys were ultimately able to solve the problem by manipulating pedestals of differing heights into an arrangement that permitted climbing to retrieve the lure. However, when tested at a later age, both boys used too many pedestals to solve the problem in comparison to age-matched children who had not practiced the task previously. According to McGraw, the inefficient strategy was a residual of earlier practice when the boys were less discriminating and probably immature in terms of their understanding of spatial relations. Johnny's inability to benefit from early exposure to tricycling could also be interpreted as an indication of cognitive immaturity as, many years after the study, McGraw (1985) hypothesized that by tying Johnny's feet to the pedals he was confronted with the task of solving the problem all at once or not at all. Had she not tied his feet to the pedals, Johnny probably would have discovered by trial-and-error the relationship between pushing on the pedals and moving the tricycle. As it was, he did not have the wherewithal to solve the problem all at once when practice was initiated.

The importance of prerequisites revisited. In the case for early exposure, an argument was made against the notion that skill learning is dependent on prerequisite learning. The argument was based largely on the failure to predict performance and learning on the basis of capacities or sub-skills thought to underlie the skill in question (e.g., Ericsson et al., 1993; Howe et al., 1999) and the inability to predict later performance from early performance—a fact that has been established for both adults (Magill, 2001) and children (Haubenstricker and Seefeldt, 1986). Yet, it is widely known that physical maturation has a significant impact on motor performance (Malina and Bouchard, 1991), suggesting that at least some basic capabilities, such as strength, provide the building blocks for skill development. Why, then, has it been so difficult to predict performance and learning from test batteries? Despite the intuitive importance of physical maturation and sub-skill development to skill learning, are these factors really unimportant? The answer to this question is an unequivocal, *no*. To understand why the answer is no we will turn again to systems theory.

From a systems perspective, later forms of behavior are built from earlier forms. However, here is the crux—the system's organization at one phase in development is not reducible to the organization at an earlier phase (e.g., Tucker and Hirsli-Pasek, 1993). Similarly, a particular skill is not reducible to the component systems from which the skill was assembled. In more familiar terms, the whole is more than the sum of its parts, just as a cake is more than the sum of its ingredients. The cake analogy is a useful one for understanding the implications of this idea. Quality ingredients (in sufficient quantity) increase the likelihood that the cake will be a quality product. However, the quality of the final product is impossible to predict from the quality and quantity of the ingredients. The same ingredients in the hands of two different cooks can result in two very different cakes, just as the same physical capacities and sub-skills can lead individuals to demonstrate very different levels of competence in a particular skill. Much of the learning process is actually dedicated to assembling the prerequisites into an organization that is both effective and efficient for solving the motor problem at hand (Arend, 1980) and the ease with which this task is accomplished stems from the amount of experience that the individual has had in solving other movement problems. (The implications of this idea will be elaborated upon in the final section of the chapter.) Thus, a systems perspective does not predict strong correlations between a particular skill and the abilities thought to comprise the skill and the correlations between the skill and its presumed sub-skills and capacities are likely to diminish as learning proceeds. So, basic prerequisite sub-skills such as throwing, as well as basic prerequisite capacities such as strength, are appropriately viewed as necessary but not sufficient characteristics for development of the more specific skills, such as pitching, that are involved in sports.

Why the Focus on Age of Exposure?

Many Factors Influence the Rate of Learning

To this point we have been preoccupied with trying to determine the appropriate age of exposure to sport skill learning. Yet, such a focus downplays the importance of numerous factors (independent of age) that influence the learning process. Furthermore, we could criticize the focus on those factors that are age dependent, such as neurological maturation and physical growth, because without reference to environmental factors, psychological development, and sociocultural concerns, a narrow focus on a few organismic constraints is hardly likely to provide thorough understanding of when sport skill learning is likely to proceed most effectively and efficiently. According to Howe et al. (1999), differences between people in the ease with which skills are acquired may result from any one of a number of factors including: (a) relevant prior knowledge and skills, (b) attentiveness, concentration, and distractibility, (c) interests and acquired preferences, (d) motivation and competitiveness, (e) self-confidence and optimism, (f) other aspects of temperament and personality, (g) enthusiasm and energy level, and (h) fatigue and anxiety. To these factors we could add many others, not the least of which might be the quality of instruction and the effectiveness of the practice strategy (see Magill, 2001 for a comprehensive treatment of factors that influence motor learning).

The type of practice might be far more important than the age at which practice is initiated and, if timing is important, it is likely to be the timing of a particular type of practice in relation to the phases of the learning process. For example, in their extensive research on international-level performers in athletic, artistic, and academic fields, Bloom and his colleagues (e.g., Bloom, 1985) have suggested that there are three distinct phases through which the successful learner progresses. The first phase is characterized by play and romance with the activity. The learner's interest and involvement is stimulated, there is freedom to have fun and explore, and the learner is given abundant encouragement, support, attention, and praise. At the end of the first phase, the learner begins to take lessons in the activity and parents help the learner to acquire regular habits by pointing out the value of the activity and noticing improvements in performance. This phase is considered important to establishing a long-term commitment to learning, though, as Sozniak (1985b) points out, maintaining a commitment later in the learning process relies on factors that are quite different from those needed to establish the commitment in the first place. The second phase culminates in full-time commitment to the activity. Daily amounts of practice are increased and more advanced teachers and training facilities are sought out. In the final phase, the learner makes a full-time commitment to improvement and practice is supervised by master teachers who have either reached exceptional levels of performance themselves or have guided others to that level of performance. The final phase culminates with the performer either making a living in the field as a professional or terminating engagement in the activity altogether.

Most importantly, the age of inception into the activity varies widely. For example, Olympic swimmers in Bloom's study were first exposed to the water between one and seven years of age (Kalinowski, 1985) and professional tennis players were introduced to tennis between three and eleven years of age (Monsaas, 1985). Furthermore, the passage of time spent in each of the phases also showed enormous variation. On the basis of these findings, as well as observation of learning phases that had gone awry and had to be corrected for improvement to continue, Sozniak (1985a) concluded that the "sequence of phases may be pedagogically important, although not psychologically or biologically determined" (p. 433). Hence, the most important variable was not when learning was initiated but the specific types of practice that were engaged in at a particular phase of the learning process. Overall, what appeared to be most important to the learner's success was the establishment of an attitude or motivation to work hard at the activity. This finding is especially pertinent given the conclusions reached by Ericsson and his colleagues (e.g., Ericsson et al., 1993) that to become an expert in any field, including sports and athletics, an individual must engage in hours of daily, *deliberate practice* for at least 10 years. More to the point, deliberate practice is not an inherently enjoyable or motivating activity.

Motivation is an extremely important constraint. The importance of establishing the appropriate motivation for learning cannot be underestimated. For example, many people are familiar with the Suzuki method for learning the violin. In support of the method, Gardner (1983) noted that many children who began the program of instruction without any previous signs of musical talent attained levels comparable to music prodigies of earlier times and gained access to some of the best music teachers in the world. (Though we should also acknowledge that an unknown number of individuals who were exposed to the Suzuki method did not become successful musicians.) Most importantly, Suzuki (1981) argued that any child could be highly educated if given the proper training and he blamed earlier failures on training methods that failed to induce enthusiasm and motivation.

Earlier we learned of the controversy surrounding the critical period concept in language acquisition. Much of the evidence for critical periods in language development is based on the ease (or lack thereof) with which a second language can be learned. However, Moyer (1999) has recently challenged the critical period concept by showing that highly motivated English speaking graduate students in a German program were able to obtain a high degree of authenticity in their pronunciation of German provided they were immersed in the learning of the language (the case characterizing first language learning). While age of first exposure to the language was highly correlated with success, professional motivation accounted for 41% of the variance in performance. Moyer concluded that cognitive and affective factors could compensate for whatever biological disadvantages might be associated with a late start in learning a second language. We will see in the next section that this suggestion is highly relevant to our consideration of the utility of the critical period concept for sport skill learning because it implies that higher-level psychological competencies can, in many ways, overcome anatomical or physiological constraints.

We should also keep in mind here the importance of considering the bidirectional relationship between motivation and learning. As Ausubel (1968) has stated, "the causal relationship between motivation and learning is typically reciprocal rather than unidirectional" (p. 365). Motivation is needed to want to participate in an activity initially but motivation can also be developed after exposure to the activity. With regard to the latter point, it is relevant to remember that the sweet taste of success is a very powerful motivator. This point has even greater significance when one considers a claim by Ericsson and Lehmann (1996) that whatever motivational factors predispose children and adults to engage in deliberate practice are likely to predict the ultimate level of expertise an individual can attain.

Behavioral development is highly flexible. The idea of compensation was addressed earlier with reference to the potential development of bad habits, but it is appropriate to readdress it here in the context of developmental plasticity. With respect to plasticity, compensation is associated with two terms that are familiar to developmentalists, *equipotentiality* and *equifinality*. Both terms mean that the same developmental outcomes can be achieved from many different initial conditions and through many different pathways (e.g., Gottlieb, Wahlsten, and Lickliter, 1998). Thus, individuals with many different capabilities, who start learning at very different ages, and who follow very different developmental trajectories can achieve the same level of proficiency in a given skill. Furthermore, there are many compelling stories of individuals who have overcome tremendous adversity to eventually triumph in sport. The gold medal winner in hammer throwing at the Melbourne Olympics was born with a paralyzed left arm and had to devise his own training techniques to overcome the disability (Jokl, 1958). Wilma Rudolph, who was the first female to win three gold medals in the same Olympic games, lost the use of her left leg at the age of 4 and was only able to walk without braces and reinforced shoes at age 11 (Ladd, 1988). Several athletes have overcome severe injuries or disabilities to win Olympic medals (Jokl, 1964).

Compensation is not only confined to the development of skill but also to its maintenance. A good example is the ability of older skilled typists to maintain typing speeds equivalent to younger skilled typists, despite slowed movement and reaction time, by previewing further ahead in the text that is being typed (Salthouse, 1984). Similarly, older chess experts are able to compete with younger participants at the same skill level through more extensive knowledge of the game (Charness, 1981). With respect to our remarkable ability to compensate for age-related declines in perceptual-motor capabilities, some researchers have even suggested that studies of aging shouldn't focus on why older people are poor at tasks, but should instead focus on how older people preserve such relatively good performance in spite of growing disability (e.g., Rabbitt, 1977).

Tying the discussion on compensation back to the critical period concept, it is pertinent to note here that nearly every demonstration of a critical period in animal behavioral development has been followed by a demonstration of some behavioral recovery from the effects of critical period exposure or deprivation (Bornstein, 1989; Colombo, 1982). Though, it should also be noted that while reports of behavioral recovery are abundant, findings of clear anatomical or physiological recovery are not (Colombo, 1982). These paradoxical observations provide strong support for the flexibility of behavioral development and our amazing ability to overcome what can appear to be major impediments to our potential for skill development.

Is rate of skill acquisition the most important variable? In the motor learning literature it is well known that the rate of skill acquisition is a rather nebulous index of learning. What is important is the extent to which a skill is maintained or retained over a period of time. That is, learning is characterized by the relative permanence of the behavioral changes that were induced by practice and not by the rate at which improvement occurred while practicing. There are a large number of variables that facilitate the rate of skill acquisition only to depress learning as measured by tests of retention (Magill, 2001). One might even conclude that the majority of variables that facilitate the rate of skill acquisition actually depress learning. We do not know whether the same holds true over developmental time, that is, whether skills that were acquired rapidly at an earlier age will be maintained at a later age. However, McGraw (1935, 1939) certainly was aware of the possibility and referred to the relative permanence of a skill acquired under one set of conditions, once those conditions were removed, as the *level of fixity* of the skill. We have seen already that there are numerous factors that could cause deterioration in performance once practice has discontinued, including changes in body scale and other changes associated with physical and psychological maturation. We know also that continued practice is necessary for continued improvement and, as such, the importance of establishing appropriate motivation to learn a skill becomes patently obvious again.

Do we have a paradox here as a result of what we know about learning and motivation? On the surface it would appear so. Learning is often facilitated by factors that tend to depress the rate of performance improvement during practice, while success, as determined by performance improvement, makes a major contribution to motivation to continue learning. In other words, we learn from our mistakes but are motivated by our success. This representation of the relationship between learning and motivation is far too simple, nevertheless, it does give us pause for thought. The finding that early success is a poor predictor of later success further complicates the situation as does Sozniak's (1985b) observation that being very good in one phase of learning may not have a high relationship to being good at a later phase, primarily because the motivation to learn in the early phases is quite different from that required to learn in the more complex and difficult phases.

The lack of congruence between early and later success has tremendous implications for parents, coaches, and teachers who make selection decisions in sport as well as those who subscribe to the notion of early talent identification. We must ask ourselves how many children have been cut or driven from sports because they did not show "promise" early in the skill acquisition process. The situation becomes even more concerning when one considers the relationship between physical maturation and motor performance as well as the variability that is apparent in the timing of maturation. During early and middle adolescence (from ages 9 to approximately 15) is when the greatest maturity associated variation in size is apparent (Malina and Bouchard, 1991). The variation is particularly pronounced in samples of 12 year-old girls and 14 year-old boys, where one boy at this chronological age might have a maturational age closer to an 11 year-old and another might have a maturational age closer to a 17 year-old. It is well known that boys who mature earlier tend to excel in sports that require strength and speed, although quite the opposite is often apparent for girls, where late maturers are the ones who tend to excel in sports (Malina and Bouchard, 1991). It is also well documented that teams who win competitions such as the Little League World Series are filled with players who are maturationally 2 to 3 years older than their chronological age. This means that some children are likely to have a performance advantage simply because of their maturational status and these are the children who are likely to be motivated by success and encouraged to stay in sports. Ultimately, the early maturers are more likely to gain access to the resources needed to achieve later success.

However, there is an infrequently cited longitudinal study showing that the performance advantage enjoyed by early maturing boys on a number of tests of motor performance is actually reversed in favor of later maturing boys when those boys are retested at age 30 (Lefevre, Beunen, Steens, Claessens, and Renson, 1990). The later maturing boys not only caught up to the early maturers but surpassed them on tests of functional strength and explosive strength. The implications are readily apparent when one considers that peak performance in many sports occurs during the twenties and early thirties (Schulz and Curnow, 1988), in many cases about 10 years after physical maturation has been completed. How many potentially great athletes have been driven away from sports because they were late maturers? For example, it is well known that Michael Jordan, who is considered to be the greatest basketball player of all time, was a victim of being physically less mature than his peers when he was cut from his high school varsity basketball team as a sophomore. Fortunately, for Jordan, the humiliation of being cut from the team motivated him to improve his game, however, an athlete with a different temperament or personality might have simply quit the sport. A similar story is told about the basketball star David Robinson, who was cut from his junior high school basketball team, and there are many other stories of professional athletes who have faced similar situations. Each of these stories further highlights the inadvisability of focusing on the rate of skill acquisition as a basis for predicting who has the potential to be successful in sports.

Summary and Implications

With such a bewildering array of findings in the literature on critical periods and readiness, can any clear implications be drawn for participation in youth sports? The answer to this question is definitely, yes. Perhaps the clearest implication that can be drawn from the arguments presented in this chapter is that there is no way to determine unequivocally an optimum age at which to expose a child to sport skill learning. The reason, quite simply, is that too many factors influence the rate at which motor skills are acquired and the degree to which they are retained. Furthermore, every child is different and differences extend along multiple dimensions. Each child grows and matures at his or her own rate and differences in the overall rate of growth and maturation are magnified by individual differences in the rate of change in different body parts and systems. Each child is exposed to a multitude of different experiences leading to unique interests as well as unique psychological and perceptual-motor capabilities. Even if we could standardize the experiences to which children were exposed, we should not expect that each child would react the same way to those same experiences.

The critical period concept appears to have little utility for an understanding of when to initiate and how to facilitate children's sport skill learning. Some have even questioned the utility of the critical period concept altogether. For example, it is not known whether critical period effects are replicable and it is not known for how many facets of development critical periods actually exist. With reference to the first question, studies have shown that previously documented critical periods evaporate when minor variations are introduced into the experimental context (Bateson, 1979). With reference to the second question, some researchers have suggested that there might be as many critical periods as there are combinations of dependent and independent variables (Denenberg, 1962), rendering the concept essentially meaningless.

The limited evidence that does exist to support critical periods in human development suggests that they are restricted to the normal functioning of basic perceptual processes in early development. Additionally, they are periods in which expected experience (such as exposure to patterns of light and sound) must be present for normal development. They are *not* periods in which augmented experience is beneficial for subsequent development. As such, the primary implication is that young children with congenital perceptual deficits should be identified early and should have their problems corrected as early as possible to permit normal perceptual functioning in later life. However, we would do well to remember that behavioral development is highly plastic across the lifespan, despite a potential lack of plasticity in specific anatomical or physiological systems.

The phenomenon in behavioral development that most closely resembles a critical period is the ease with which young children can acquire language and absolute pitch. Here, augmented experience appears beneficial for subsequent development of skill in language and music. Yet, there is considerable evidence that appropriately motivated individuals can acquire language and absolute pitch outside of the critical periods. Furthermore, many musicians actually question the value of absolute pitch for the development of musical skill. Some see it as more of a hindrance than a benefit.

There is no evidence that critical periods exist for the learning of sport skills nor that early exposure to a particular skill is critical to ultimate success. In addition, our discussion of the readiness concept suggests that there is no compelling reason for a child to specialize in a particular sport at a young age. Any advantage associated with an early start could well be offset by the disadvantage of having to continuously recalibrate the skill following changes in growth and maturation or to adapt the movement strategy following cognitive and perceptual development. On this point, we should keep in mind that the difficulty learning language and absolute pitch at later ages is thought to stem from interference associated with perceptual and motor habits developed at earlier ages. This idea is important because, although we saw examples where lack of prerequisites might have facilitated the learning of certain skills, lack of basic prerequisites (such as strength) is more likely to lead to the development of bad habits. Given that systems become increasingly stable over time, any habits developed at one age will be very difficult to break at later ages when missing prerequisites become available. Here is another reason why focus on variables other than the age of initiation into a sport, such as the quality of instruction or supervision, is extremely important.

The only sports in which specialization at a young age is necessary are those in which individual's performances peak before puberty. Gymnastics is an example of such a sport. Larger and heavier limbs and bodies are simply not conducive to the optimal production of movements that involve spinning and turning rapidly and maintaining stability on small bases of support. One could also make a case for early specialization in sports and performing arts where extreme anatomical and physiological adaptations are required to be competitive at elite levels. However, even here, research suggests that such adaptations are most readily accomplished when the appropriate stresses overlap with puberty. Thus specialization could be delayed until the onset of puberty. Even so, we should keep in mind that athleticism must not be confused with skill.

Throughout our discussion, it has been apparent that the relationship between prerequisites and performance is difficult to describe with certainty. Any scout for a professional sports team knows that tests of physical proficiency are poor predictors of who will ultimately succeed in the sport. Test batteries, in general, are poor predictors of performance. The reason, as we have seen, is that performance cannot be reduced to the constituents from which behavior is assembled. Furthermore, skill is much, much more than the sum of basic capabilities or sub-skills and skill becomes increasingly specialized as practice continues. Skill is the ability to consistently solve motor problems under a wide range of conditions and with an economy of effort (Bernstein, 1967, 1996; Gentile, 1972; Guthrie, 1935; Higgins, 1991). What differentiates the skilled from the less skilled individual is not an ability to control a movement pattern but an ability to creatively solve the movement problem under a myriad of different conditions (Higgins, 1991). The skilled individual achieves the objective despite the difficulty associated with the prevailing conditions. This view of skill has important implications for an understanding of how to facilitate motor skill development in children. If skill is viewed as a form of problem solving, then the way to promote the development of skill is quite simple—expose children to the most diverse range of problem solving opportunities possible!

Aside from arguments that can be based on critical periods and readiness, childhood is the most appropriate time for learning motor skills because it represents a period in life when the individual has the time to engage in such learning. Children require exposure to a wide variety of different motor skills under a wide variety of different task and environmental conditions. In other words, children should be exposed to many different movement-related goals (including those in which sensory processes are challenged) and those goals should be presented with many variations in the features of objects, surfaces, and other people that are central to the task. Furthermore, it is important for children to have freedom to select their own goals as well as their own criteria for success. Selecting goals and success criteria has been shown to facilitate interest and motivation in the process of performing and learning motor skills (Burton and Davis, 1996), an indispensable aspect of an environment that is conducive to learning, particularly given our earlier discussion of the frustration associated with the learning process as well as the considerable time and effort required to achieve skill in sport.

Following this point, I would argue that parents, teachers, and coaches should err on the side of creating a learning environment that is geared toward success, even though it is well-established that "we learn from our mistakes." This suggestion is another reflection of the importance of establishing motivation to continue participating in and learning sports and motor activities. Perceptions of self-confidence and self-esteem that result from success are primary determinants of enjoyment in sports and enjoyment (fun) is one of the primary reasons that children cite for participating in the first place (Weiss, 2000)! Furthermore, self-confidence results in a willingness to accept new motor challenges. With this point in mind, it is appropriate to finish this chapter by returning to Myrtle McGraw's conclusions about the effects of training on Johnny and Jimmy. McGraw (1935, 1939) maintained that one of the most enduring changes stemming from Johnny's exposure to a wide variety of challenging activities was in his attitude. Not only was Johnny more willing than Jimmy to take tackle new motor problems but he showed a higher degree of competence and skill in solving those problems. And, as noted earlier, attitude might be the best predictor available of those who are likely to succeed in sports.

References

Abernethy, B. (1991). Visual search strategies and decision-making in sport. *International Journal of Sport Psychology, 22,* 189–210.

Abernethy, B., and Russell, D. G. (1987). Expert-novice differences in an applied selective attention task, *Journal of Sport Psychology, 9,* 326–345.

Adolph, K. E. (1997). Learning in the development of infant locomotion. *Monographs of the Society for Research in Child Development, 62,* (Serial No. 251, 1–140).

Adolph, K. E. (2000). Specificity of learning: Why infants fall over a veritable cliff. *Psychological* Science, *11,* 290–295.

Almli, C. R., and Finger, S. (1987). Neural insult and critical period concepts. In M. H. Bornstein (Ed.), *Sensitive periods in development: Interdisciplinary perspectives* (pp. 123–143). Hillsdale, NJ: Erlbaum.

Anderson, D. I. (2000). Complex motor skill acquisition and the one-trial-learning phenomenon. *Journal of Human Movement* Studies, *38,* 23–56.

Arend, S. (1980). Developing the substrates of skillful movement. *Motor Skills: Theory into Practice, 4,* 3–10.

Ausubel, D. P. (1968). *Educational psychology: A cognitive view.* New York: Holt, Rinehart, and Winston.

Banks, M. S., Aslin, R. N., and Letson, R. D. (1975). Sensitive period for the development of human binocular vision. *Science, 190,* 675–677.

Bateson, P. (1979). How do sensitive periods arise and what are they for? *Animal Behaviour, 27,* 470–486.

Bernstein, N. A. (1967). *The coordination and regulation of movement.* London: Pergamon Press.

Bernstein, N. A. (1996). On dexterity and its development. In M. L. Latash and M. T. Turvey (Eds.), *Dexterity and its development* (pp. 3–244). Mahwah, NJ: Lawrence Erlbaum.

Bertalanffy, L. von (1968). *General system theory: Foundations, development, applications.* New York: Braziller.

Black, J. E. (1998). How a child builds its brain: Some lessons from animal studies of neural plasticity. *Preventive Medicine, 27,* 168–171.

Bloom, B. S. (1985). *Developing talent in young people*. New York: Ballantine Books.

Bornstein, M. H. (1989). Sensitive periods in development: Structural characteristics and causal interpretations. *Psychological* Bulletin, *105*, 179–197.

Bower, T. G. R. (1976). Repetitive processes in child development. *Scientific American, 235*, 38–47.

Brady, P. T. (1970). Fixed-scale mechanism of absolute pitch. *Journal of the Acoustical Society of America 48*, 883–887.

Bruer, J. T. (1998a). The brain and child development: Time for some critical thinking. *Public Health Reports, 113,* 388–397.

Bruer, J. T. (1998b). Brain science, brain fiction. *Educational Leadership, 56,* 14–18.

Bruer, J. T. (1999). *The myth of the first three years: a new understanding of early brain development and lifelong learning*. New York: Free Press.

Burton, A. W., and Davis, W. E. (1996). Ecological task analysis: Utilizing intrinsic measures in research and practice. *Human Movement Science, 15,* 285–314.

Campos, J. J., Anderson, D. I., Barbu-Roth, M. A., Hubbard, E. M., Hertenstein, M. J., and Witherington, D. (2000). Travel broadens the mind. *Infancy, 1*, 149–219.

Carnegie Corporation of New York (1994). *Starting points: Meeting the needs of our youngest children*. New York: Carnegie Corporation of New York.

Charness, N. (1981). Search in chess: Age and skill differences. *Journal of Experimental Psychology: Human Perception and Performance, 7*, 467–476.

Chase, W. G., and Simon, H. A. (1973). The mind's eye in chess. In W. G. Chase (Ed.), *Visual information processing* (pp. 215–281). New York: Academic Press.

Chugani, H. T. (1998). A critical period of brain development: Studies of cerebral glucose utilization with PET. *Preventive Medicine, 27,* 184–188.

Clark, J. E. (1995). On becoming skillful: Patterns and constraints. *Research Quarterly for Exercise and Sport, 66,* 173–183.

Clark, J. E., and Whitall, J. (1989). What is motor development? The lessons of history. *Quest, 41*, 183–202.

Colombo, J. (1982). The critical period concept: Research, methodology, and theoretical issues. *Psychological Bulletin, 91*, 260–275.

Daw, N. W. (1995). *Visual development*. New York: Plenum.

DiTullio, M., Wilczek, L., Paulus, D., Kiriakatis, A., Pollack, M., and Eisenhardt, J. (1989). Comparison of hip rotation in female classical ballet dancers versus female nondancers. *Medical Problems in Performing Artists, 4*, 154–158.

Elbert, T., Pantev, C., Wienbruch, C., Rockstroh, B., and Taub, E. (1995). Increased cortical representation of the fingers of the left hand in string players. *Science, 270,* 305–307.

Elkind, D. (1990). Academic pressures—too much, too soon: The demise of play. In E. Klugman and S. Smilansky (Eds.), *Children's play and learning: Perspectives and policy implications* (pp. 3–17). New York: Teachers College Press.

Ericsson, K. A., and Charness, N. (1994). Expert performance: Its structure and acquisition. *American Psychologist, 49,* 725–747.

Ericsson, K. A., Krampe, R. T., and Tesch-Römer, C. (1993). The role of deliberate practice in the acquisition of expert performance. *Psychological Review, 100,* 363–406.

Ericsson, K. A., and Lehmann, A. C. (1996). Expert and exceptional performance: Evidence of maximal adaptation to task constraints. *Annual Review of Psychology, 47,* 273–305.

Fagard, J. (1990). The development of bimanual coordination. In C. Bard, M. Fleury, and L. Hay (Eds.), *Development of eye-hand coordination across the life span* (pp. 262–282). Columbia, SC: University of South Carolina Press.

Fitts, P. M. (1954). The information capacity of the human motor system in controlling the amplitude of movement. *Journal of Experimental Psychology, 47,* 381–391.

Fleishman, E. A., and Rich, S. (1963). Role of kinesthetic and spatial-visual abilities in perceptual-motor learning. *Journal of Experimental Psychology, 66,* 6–11.

Fox, M. W. (1971). Overview and critique of stages and periods in canine development. *Developmental Psychobiology, 4,* 37–54.

Freud, S. (1910). *Three contributions to the sexual theory,* New York: Journal of Nervous and Mental Diseases Publishing Company.

Gabbard, C. (1998). Windows of opportunity for early brain and motor development. *Journal of Physical Education, Recreation, and Dance, 69,* 54–55, 61.

Gagné, R. M. (1968). Contributions of learning to human development. *Psychological Review, 75,* 177–191.

Gagné, R. M. (1970). *The conditions of learning* (2nd ed.). New York: Holt, Rinehart, and Winston.

Gallahue, D. L., and Ozman, J. C. (1995). *Understanding motor development: Infants, children, adolescents, adults* (3d ed.). Madison, WI: WCB Brown and Benchmark.

Gardner, H. (1983). *Frames of mind: The theory of multiple intelligences.* New York: Basic Books.

Gentile, A. M. (1972). A working model of skill acquisition with application to teaching. *Quest,* Monograph, *17,* 3–23.

Gesell, A. (1954). The ontogenesis of infant behavior. In L. Carmichael (Ed.), *Manual of child psychology* (2nd ed.) (pp. 335–373). New York: John Wiley and Sons.

Gesell, A., and Thompson, H. (1929). Learning and growth in identical infant twins: An experimental study by the method of co-twin control. *Genetic Psychology Monographs, 6,* 1–124.

Goldman-Rakic, P. S., Bourgeois, J. P., Rakic, P. (1997). Synaptic substrate of cognitive development: synaptogenesis in the prefrontal cortex of the nonhuman primate. In N. A. Krasnegor, G. R. Lyon, and P. S. Goldman-Rakic (Eds.), *Development of the prefrontal cortex: evolution, neurobiology, and behavior (pp. 27–47). Baltimore, MD: Paul H. Brooks Publishing.

Goodale, M. A. (1988). Modularity in visuomotor control: From input to output. In Z. Pylyshyn (Ed.), *Computational processes in human vision: An interdisciplinary perspective* (pp. 262–285). Norwood, NJ: Ablex.

Goodgame, D. (2000). The game of risk: How the best golfer in the world got even better. *Time, 156* (7), 56–62.

Gottlieb, G., Wahlsten, D., and Lickliter, R. (1998). The significance of biology for human development: A developmental psychobiological systems view. In Lerner, R. M. (Ed.), Theoretical models of human development (vol. 1, pp. 233–273). In W. Damon (Editor-in-chief), *Handbook of child psychology (5th ed)*. New York: John Wiley and Sons.

Green, E. J., Greenough, W. T., and Schlumpf, B. E. (1983). Effects of complex or isolated environments on cortical dendrites of middle-aged rats. *Brain Research, 264,* 233–240.

Greenough, W. T., Black, J. E., and Wallace, C. S. (1987). Experience and brain development. *Child Development, 58*, 539–559

Guthrie, E. R. (1935). *The psychology of learning*. New York: Harper.

Halverson, L. (1966). Development of motor patterns in young children. *Quest, 6,* 44–53.

Haubenstricker, J., and Seefeldt, V. (1986). Acquisition of motor skills during childhood. In V. Seefeldt (Ed.), *Physical activity and well-being* (pp. 41–102). Reston, VA: AAHPERD.

Haywood, K. M. (1993). *Life span motor development* (2nd ed.). Champaign, IL: Human Kinetics.

Hebb, D. O. (1949). *The organization of behaviour*. London: John Wiley.

Heffernan, D., and Thomson, J. A. (1999). Gone fishin': Perceiving what is reachable with rods during a period of rapid growth. In M. A. Grealy and J. A. Thomson (Eds.), *Studies in perception and action V.* Mahwah, NJ: Lawrence Erlbaum.

Henry, F. M. (1968). Specificity vs. generality in learning motor skill. In R. C. Brown and G. S. Kenyon (Eds.), *Classical studies on physical activity* (pp. 328–331). Englewood Cliffs, NJ: Prentice Hall. (Original work published 1958).

Hess, E. H. (1973). *Imprinting.* New York: Van Nostrand Reinhold.

Higgins, J. R. (1977). *Human movement: An integrated approach.* St. Louis: C. V. Mosby.

Higgins, S. (1991). Motor skill acquisition. *Physical Therapy, 71*, 48–64.

Hilgard, J. R. (1932). Learning and maturation in preschool children. *Journal of Genetic Psychology, 41,* 36–56.

Howe, M. J. A., Davidson, J. W., and Sloboda, J. A. (1999). Innate talents: Reality or myth? In S. J. Ceci and W. M. Williams (Eds.), *The nature-nurture debate: The essential readings* (pp. 258–289). Malden, MA: Blackwell.

Huttenlocher, P. R. (1979). Synaptic density in human frontal cortex—Developmental changes and effects of aging. *Brain Research, 163,* 195–205.

Huttenlocher, P. R. (1990). Morphometric study of human cerebral cortex development. *Neuropsychologia, 28,* 517–527.

Huttenlocher, P. R. (1992). Neural plasticity. In A. K. Astbury, G. N. McKhann, and W. I. McDonald (Eds.), *Diseases of the nervous system: Clinical neurobiology* (2nd ed., pp. 63–71). Philadelphia: WB Saunders.

Huttenlocher, P. R. (1994). Synaptogenesis, synapse elimination, and neural plasticity in human cerebral cortex. In C. A. Nelson (Ed.), *Threats to optimal development: Integrating biological, psychological* and *social risk factors* (pp. 35–54). Hillsdale, NJ: Erlbaum.

Inglis, F. M., Zuckerman, K. E., and Kalb, R. G. (2000). Experience-dependent development of spinal motor neurons. *Neuron, 26,* 299–305.

Jensen, R. K. (1981). The effect of a 12-month growth period on the body moments of inertia of children. *Medicine and Science* in *Sports and Exercise, 13,* 238–242.

Johnson, J. S., and Newport, E. L. (1989). Critical period effects in second language learning: The influence of maturational state on the acquisition of English as a second language. *Cognitive Psychology, 21,* 60–99.

Jokl, E. (1958). *The clinical physiology of physical fitness and rehabilitation.* Springfield, IL: Charles C. Thomas.

Jokl, E. (1964). *The scope of exercise in rehabilitation.* Springfield, IL: Charles C. Thomas.

Kakizawa, S., Yamasaki, M., Watanabe, M., and Kano, M. (2000). Critical period for activity-dependent synapse elimination in developing cerebellum. *The Journal of Neuroscience, 20,* 4954–4961.

Kalinowski, A. G. (1985). The development of Olympic swimmers. In B. S. Bloom (Ed.), *Developing talent in young people* (pp. 139–192). New York: Ballantine Books.

Kelso, J. A. S. (1995). *Dynamic patterns: The self-organization of brain and behavior.* Cambridge, MA: MIT Press.

Kelso, J. A. S., Southard, D. L., and Goodman, D. (1979). On the coordination of two-handed movements. *Journal of Experimental Psychology: Human Perception and Performance, 5,* 229–238.

Klemp, P., and Charlton, D. (1989). Articular mobility in ballet dancers: A follow-tip study after four years. *The American Journal of Sports Medicine, 17,* 72–75.

Kugler, P. N., Kelso, J. A. S., and Turvey, M. T. (1980). On the concept of coordinative structures as dissipative structures: I. Theoretical lines of convergence. In G. E. Stelmach and J. Requin (Eds.), *Tutorials in motor behavior* (pp. 3–47). Amsterdam: North-Holland.

Kugler, P. N., Kelso, J. A. S., and Turvey, M. T. (1982). On the control and coordination of naturally developing systems. In J. A. S. Kelso and J. E. Clark (Eds.), *The development of movement control and coordination.* New York: Wiley.

Ladd, T. (1988). Rudolph, Wilma Glodean. In D. L. Porter (Ed.), *Biographical dictionary of American sports: Outdoor Sports* (pp. 525–526). New York: Greenwood Press.

Lefevre, J., Beunen, G., Steens, G., Claessens, A., and Renson, R. (1990). Motor performance during adolescence and age thirty as related to age at peak height velocity. *Annals of Human Biology, 17,* 423–435.

Lenneberg, E. H. (1967). *Biological foundations of language.* New York: Wiley.

Lerner, R. M. (1998). Theories of human development: Contemporary perspectives. In R. M. Lerner (Ed.), Theoretical models of human development (vol. 1, pp. 1–24). In W. Damon (Editor-in-chief), *Handbook of child psychology* (5th ed). New York: John Wiley and Sons.

Lindsey, G. (1998–99). Brain research and implications for early childhood education. *Childhood Education, 75,* 97–100.

Long, M. (1990). Maturational constraints on language development. *Studies in Second Language Acquisition, 12,* 251–285.

MacGillivary, W. W. (1980). Perceptual style, critical viewing time, and catching skill. *International Journal of Sport Psychology, 11,* 22–33.

Magill, R. A. (2001). *Motor learning: Concepts and applications* (6th ed.). New York: McGraw-Hill.

Magill, R. A., and Anderson, D. I. (1996). Critical periods as optimal readiness for learning sport skills. In F. L. Smoll and R. E. Smith (Eds.), *Children and youth in sport: A biopsychosocial perspective* (pp. 57–72). Indianapolis: Brown and Benchmark.

Malina, R. M., and Bouchard, C. (1991). *Growth, maturation, and physical activity.* Champaign, IL: Human Kinetics.

Masters, R. S. W. (1992). Knowledge, nerves and know-how: The role of explicit versus implicit knowledge in the breakdown of a complex motor skill under pressure. *British Journal of Psychology, 83,* 343–358.

McGraw, M. B. (1935). *Growth: A study of Johnny and Jimmy.* New York: Appleton-Century.

McGraw, M. B. (1939). Later development of children specially trained during infancy: Johnny and Jimmy at school age. *Child Development, 10,* 1–19.

McGraw, M. B. (1946). Maturation of behavior. In L. Carmichael (Ed.), *Manual of child psychology* (pp. 332–369). New York: Wiley.

McGraw, M. B. (1985). Professional and personal blunders in child development research. *The Psychological Record, 35* 165–170.

Milner, A. D., and Goodale, M. A. (1995). *The visual brain in action.* New York: Oxford University Press.

Moltz, H. (1973). Some implications of the critical period hypothesis. *Annals of the New York Academy of Sciences, 223,* 144–146.

Monsaas, J. A. (1985). Learning to be a world-class tennis player. In B. S. Bloom (Ed.), *Developing talent in young people* (pp. 211–269). New York: Ballantine Books.

Moyer, A. (1999). Ultimate attainment in L2 phonology: The critical factors of age, motivation, and instruction. *Studies in Second Language Acquisition, 21,* 81–108.

Nelson, C. A., and Bloom, F. E. (1997). Child development and neuroscience. *Child Development,* 68, 970–987.

Newell, K. M. (1984). Physical constraints to development of motor skills. In J. R. Thomas (Ed.), *Motor development during childhood and adolescence* (pp. 105–120). Minneapolis, NM: Burgess.

Newell, K. M. (1986). Constraints on the development of coordination. In H. T. A. Whiting and M. G. Wade (Eds.), *Motor development in children: Aspects of coordination and control* (pp. 341–360). Dordrecht: Martinus Nijhoff.

Piaget, J. (1952). *The origins of intelligence in children.* New York: International Universities Press.

Piaget, J. (1954). *The construction of reality in the child.* New York: Basic Books.

Pollack, R. H. (1969). Some implications of ontogenetic changes in perception. In D. Elkind and J. H. Flavell (Eds.), *Studies in cognitive development* (pp. 365–407). New York: Oxford University Press.

Poppleton, W. L., and Salmoni, A. W. (1991). Talent identification in swimming. *Journal of Human Movement Studies, 20,* 85–100

Provins, K. A. (1997a). Handedness and speech: A critical reappraisal of the role of genetic and environmental factors in the cerebral lateralization of function. *Psychological Review, 104,* 554–571.

Provins, K. A. (1997b). The specificity of motor skill and manual asymmetry: A review of the evidence and its implications. *Journal of Motor Behavior, 29,* 183–192.

Rabbitt, P. M. A. (1977). Changes in problem-solving ability in old age. In J. E. Birren and K. W. Schaie (Eds.), *Handbook of the psychology of aging* (pp. 606–625). New York: Vail Nostrand Reinhold.

Rakic, P., Bourgeois, J. P., and Goldman-Rakic, P. S. (1994). Synaptic development of the cerebral cortex: Implications for learning, memory, and mental illness. In J. van Pelt, M. A. Corner, H. B. M. Uylings and F. H. Lopes da Silva (Eds.), *Progress in brain research, 102,* 227–243.

Ramachandran, V. S. (1995). Plasticity in the adult human brain: Is there reason for optimism? In B. Julesz and I. Kovacs (Eds.), *Maturational windows and adult cortical plasticity* (pp. 179–197). Reading, MA: Addison-Wesley.

Rochat, P., and Bullinger, A. (1995). Posture and functional action in infancy. In A. Vyt, H. Bloch, and M. Bronstein (Eds.), *Early child development in the French tradition* (pp. 15–34). Hillsdale, NJ: Erlbaum.

Salthouse, T. A. (1984). Effects of age and skill in typing. *Journal of Experimental Psychology: General, 113,* 345–371.

Schlaug, G., Jäncke, L., Huang, Y., and Steinmetz, H. (1995). In vivo evidence of structural brain asymmetry in musicians. *Science, 267,* 699–701.

Schmidt, R. A., and Lee, T. D. (1999). *Motor control and learning: A behavioral emphasis* (3rd ed.). Champaign, IL: Human Kinetics.

Schneider, W. (1993). Acquiring expertise: determinants of exceptional perform-ance. In K. A. Heller, F. J. Mönks, and A. H. Passow (Eds.), *International handbook of research and development of giftedness and talent*. New York: Pergamon.

Schulz, R., and Curnow, C. (1988). Peak performance and age among superath-letes: Track and field, swimming, baseball, tennis, and golf. *Journal of Gerontology: Psychological Sciences, 43*, 113–120.

Scott, J. P. (1962). Critical periods in behavioral development. *Science, 138*, 949–958.

Scott, J. P., and Marston, M. V. (1950). Critical periods affecting the development of normal and maladjustive social behavior in puppies. *Journal of Genetic Psychol-ogy, 77*, 25–60

Scott, J. P., Stewart, J. M., and De Ghett, V. J. (1974). Critical periods in the organization of systems. *Developmental Psychobiology, 7*, 489–513.

Shore, R. (1997). *Rethinking the brain: New insights into early development*. New York: Families and Work Institute.

Sozniak, L. A. (1985a). Phases of learning. In B. S. Bloom (Ed.), *Developing talent in voting people* (pp. 409–438). New York: Ballantine Books.

Sozniak, L. A. (1985b). A long-term commitment to learning. In B. S. Bloom (Ed.), *Developing talent in young people* (pp. 477–506). New York: Ballantine Books.

Spemann, H. (1938). *Embryonic development and induction*. New Haven: Yale University.

Starkes, J. L. (1987). Skill in field hockey: The nature of the cognitive advantage. *Journal of Sport Psychology, 9*, 146–160.

Starkes, J. L., and Deakin, J. M. (1985). Perception in sport: A cognitive approach to skilled performance. In W. F. Straub and J. M. Williams (Eds.), *Cognitive sport psychology* (pp. 115–128). Lansing, NY: Sports Science Associates.

Stockard, C. R. (1921). Developmental rate and structural expression: An experi-mental study of twins, 'double monsters' and single deformities, and the interaction among embryonic organs during their origin and development. *American Journal of Anatomy, 28*, 115–275.

Stoffregen, T. A., and Riccio, G. E. (1988). An ecological theory of orientation and the vestibular system. *Psychological Review, 95*, 3–14.

Stoffregen, T. A., Pagulayan, R. J., Bardy, B. B., Hettinger, L. J. (2000). Modu-lating postural control to facilitate visual performance. *Human Movement Science, 19*, 203–220.

Suzuki, S. (1981). Every child can become rich in musical sense. In E. Hermann (Ed.), *Shinichi Suzuki: The man and his philosophy* (pp. 136–141). Athens, OH: Ability Development Associates. (Originally presented in 1963).

Takeuchi, A. H., and Hulse, S. H. (1993). Absolute pitch. *Psychological Bulletin, 113*, 345–361.

Terhardt, E. (1974). Pitch, consonance, and harmony. *Journal of the Acoustical Society of America, 55*, 1061–1069.

Thelen, E. (1983). Learning to walk is still an "old" problem: A reply to Zelazo. *Journal of Motor Behavior, 15,* 139–161.

Thelen, E. (1995). Motor development: A new synthesis. *American Psychologist, 50,* 79–95.

Thelen, E., and Smith, L. B. (1994). *A dynamic systems approach to the development of cognition and action.* Cambridge, MA: MIT Press.

Thelen, E., and Smith, L. B. (1998). Dynamic systems theories. In R. M. Lerner (Ed.), Theoretical models of human development (vol. 1, pp. 563–634). In W. Damon (Editor-in-chief), *Handbook of child psychology* (5th ed). New York: John Wiley and Sons.

Thelen, E., and Ulrich, B. D. (1991). Hidden skills: A dynamical systems analysis of treadmill stepping during the first year. *Monographs of the Society for Research in Child Development, 56* (Serial No. 223).

Touwen, B. (1976). *Neurological development in infancy.* London: Spastics International Medical Publishers.

Tucker, M., and Hirsh-Pasek, K. (1993). Systems and language: Implications for acquisition. In L. B. Smith and E. Thelen (Eds.), *A dynamic systems approach to development: Applications* (pp. 359–384). Cambridge, MA: MIT Press.

Turvey, M. T., and Fitzpatrick, P. (1993). Commentary: Development of perception-action systems and general principles of pattern formation. *Child Development, 64,* 1175–1190.

Ulrich, B. D. (1987). Developmental perspectives of motor skill performance in children. In D. Gould and M. R. Weiss (Eds.), *Advances in pediatric sport sciences: Behavioral issues* (Vol. 2, pp. 167–186). Champaign, IL: Human Kinetics.

Ward, T., and Groppel, J. (1980). Sport implement selection: Can it be based upon anthropometric indicators? *Motor Skills: Theory into Practice, 2,* 103–110.

Watkins, A., Woodhull-McNeal, A. P., Clarkson, P. M., and Ebbeling, C. (1989). Lower extremity alignment and injury in young, preprofessional, college, and professional ballet dancers. Part I. Turnout and knee-foot alignment. *Medical Problems in Performing Artists, 4,* 148–153.

Weiss, M. R. (2000). Motivating kids in physical activity. *Research Digest: President's Council on Physical Fitness and Sports, 3,* 1–8.

Wiesel, T. N., and Hubel, D. H. (1963). Single-cell responses in striate cortex of kittens deprived of vision in one eye. *Journal of Neurophysiology, 20,* 1003–1017.

Woollacott, M. H., Debû, B., and Shumway-Cook, A. (1987). Children's development of posture and balance control: Changes in motor coordination and sensory integration. In D. Gould and M. R. Weiss (Eds.), *Advances in pediatric sport sciences: Behavioral issues* (Vol. 2, pp. 211–233). Champaign, IL: Human Kinetics.

Woollacott, M. H., and Shumway-Cook, A. (1990). Changes in postural control across the life span—A systems approach. *Physical Therapy, 70,* 53–61.

Wynder, E. L. (1998). Introduction to the report on the conference on the "critical" period of brain development. *Preventive Medicine, 27,* 166–167.

Yakolev, P. I., and Lecours, A. R. (1967). The myelogenetic cycles of regional maturation of the brain. In A. Minkowski (Ed.), *Regional development of the brain in early life* (pp. 3–70). Philadelphia, PA: Davis.

Yamada, J. (1991). The discrimination learning of the liquids /r/ and /l/ by Japanese speakers. *Journal of Psycholinguistic Research, 20*, 31–46.

Zanone, P. G., and Kelso, J. A. S. (1992). Evolution of behavioral attractors with learning: Nonequilibrium phase transitions. *Journal of Experimental Psychology: Human Perception and Performance, 18*, 403–421.

Acknowledgements

Preparation of this chapter was supported by a "Research Infrastructure in Minority Institutions" award from the National Center for Research Resources with funding from the Office of Research on Minority Health, National Institutes of Health #5 P20 RR11805. Sincere thanks are extended to my colleagues who gave helpful suggestions on how to improve earlier drafts of the chapter and to Trese Biagini and Sandra Larios for help in locating articles and checking references.

Part Three

Social

Processes

The antecedents and consequences of sport involvement, as well as sport participation itself, generally occur within a social context. As a result, the developing child's entry into the world of physical activity and sport is influenced not only by processes of biological and psychological maturation, but also by the social context in which he or she develops. Once the child is involved in sports, the social environment of sport continues to exert a strong influence on developmental processes that occur as a result of participation. The four chapters in this part of the book focus on the familial and social influences that help to determine initial involvement in sports, continued participation, and the psychosocial effects of the sport environment on the child.

The role of the family and gender-based influences in sport socialization of boys and girls is a timely and important topic of research in the field of sport sociology. In a penetrating analysis of this research, Susan L. Greendorfer, John H. Lewko, and Karl S. Rosengren address a paradoxical question: How can we reconcile the dramatically increasing involvement of girls in sports with a lack of research evidence for corresponding changes in sex-typing socialization practices that seem to encourage participation by boys and discourage "masculine" behavior on the part of girls? Their approach to understanding gender differences in sport participation and experiences takes into account the dominant role of ideological beliefs and cultural values in determining socialization practices. The chapter begins with coverage of family influences and gender-role stereotyping and includes an overview of studies pertaining to toy selection and preferences, parental interactions in early childhood play, and gender differences in activity levels as well as in early motor skill development. Research shows that despite increasing participation by girls, they continue to value and experience sport participation quite differently than do boys from early childhood on, and they also continue to receive different behavioral messages from parents and the culture at large as to what is to be valued and pursued. These findings are partly explained by recent studies that focus specifically on maternal employment and the changing role of fathers. In view of the changing structure of the family, the authors offer a comprehensive theoretical model of sport socialization influences that accords cultural ideologies a central role. The second section of the chapter reviews recent literature on sport socialization, using chronological age as a developmental framework. Beginning with the early years and moving to preadolescence, adolescence and the notion of continuity, which extends into adulthood, the authors observe that findings from sport socialization research have remained relatively unchanged for the past 30 years. Summary statements are then presented, forming a heuristic profile of sport socialization. The next section addresses two major limitations of sport socialization research—the lack of systematic research and the absence of an adequate theory of sport participation. The authors conclude the chapter by issuing some specific challenges to future researchers.

Three important classes of significant others influence children's psychosocial development in sport. Parents, coaches, and peers all can exert strong influences on the child's desire and choice to participate, degree of enjoyment while participating, decision to terminate sport involvement, and on personality and social development that occurs as a result of sport participation. In Chapter 8, Robert J. Brustad and Julie A. Partridge direct special attention to the roles of parents and peers in affecting psychosocial outcomes for youth sport participants. In explicating the nature of each form of influence, the authors maintain a developmental perspective from which they examine the impact of parents and peers at various developmental phases. For a number of reasons, adults (particularly parents) have relatively greater influence than do peers on children's psychosocial development during early and middle childhood. However, peer influence increases during later childhood and early adolescence and the peer group may supplant parents as the primary frame of reference for young athletes at later phases of youth sport involvement. With regard to parental influence, the chapter focuses on parents' roles in shaping children's self-perception characteristics through sport. In addition, children's affective experiences in sport are discussed in relation to parental roles in fostering positive emotional experiences in sport, specifically enjoyment, as well as in contributing to negative affective outcomes, such as competitive stress and trait anxiety, and burnout. With regard to peer influence, four areas are discussed. First, the impact of peer acceptance and rejection upon youngsters in sport is addressed. Second, the role of friendships and friendship quality upon youngsters' psychosocial development through sport is considered. Third, the topic of peer victimization is discussed as a potentially important area for knowledge development. Finally, peer influence on children's self-concept development is examined. Brustad and Partridge conclude their discussion of parental and peer influence with suggestions for future research and knowledge development.

Coaches, the third class of significant others, are the focus of the chapter by Frank L. Smoll and Ronald E. Smith. In Chapter 9, the authors present evidence that specific coaching behaviors can have a great impact on the psychosocial outcomes of participation, particularly for children who are low in self-esteem. The chapter begins with an overview of the theoretical model and basic research underlying the development of a coach-training program. The intervention is designed to assist coaches in relating more effectively to young athletes, thereby increasing the likelihood that they will have positive sport experiences. Consideration is then given to the content of the program and didactic procedures for its implementation. The chapter concludes with a discussion of applied research assessing the efficacy of the intervention. Experimental studies indicate that the training program has significant positive effects on young athletes' enjoyment of their sport experience, their attitudes toward the coach, and their degree of liking for teammates. Youngsters who play for trained coaches also show significant increases in self-esteem, reduction in sport performance anxiety, and a greatly lowered likelihood of dropping out of sport. Thus, coaches join parents and peers as important figures in the youth sport environment.

As violence continues to escalate in our society, increasing concern has focused on sport as a possible influence on the learning and promotion of aggressive behavior. In the final chapter of this part, Norman N. Morra and Michael D. Smith examine the social learning of aggressive and violent behaviors in ice hockey. They begin by critiquing the argument that frustration leads to aggression, justifying tactics such as fighting, slashing, and hitting from behind. Their interview and observational studies clearly illustrate the roles that parents, coaches, professional hockey players, administrators, and the mass media play in the learning and encouragement of illegal aggression. Such aggression is not merely tolerated; it is actively promoted and has become such an important part of the game's fabric that it may be difficult to eradicate. In this regard, the National Hockey League is castigated for routinely promoting rough play and fighting as beneficial to hockey both as a sport and a business. There are clear indications that through participation and exposure to professional hockey, young athletes become more accepting of illegal aggression and more likely to engage in such behaviors. Morra and Smith's chapter thus shows how sport participation can produce negative as well as positive outcomes for children and youth. (See also the chapter by Shields, Bredemeier, and Power in Part 5, which addresses moral development in greater detail.) Another, and arguably more serious issue, relates to the problem of sexual abuse of minor-league players by their coaches. The authors examine this largely ignored side of hockey violence, pointing out that such criminal behavior represents a breach of ethics by both coaches and reputable, longstanding organizations.

CHAPTER 7

Family and Gender-Based Influences in Sport Socialization of Children and Adolescents

Susan L. Greendorfer, University of Illinois
John H. Lewko, Laurentian University
Karl S. Rosengren, University of Illinois

Socialization is a complex learning process that involves social development, cognitive processes and cultural beliefs, values and practices. The process occurs when we interact with others, become acquainted with the social world in which we live, and learn about culturally agreed upon beliefs and values. Through socialization we actively formulate ideas about who we are and what is important in our lives (Coakley, 2001). In sum, socialization represents a complex and dynamic assimilation of social, cultural and cognitive processes through which we interact with others, synthesize information and actively participate in the social world around us.

Psychologists, sociologists and anthropologists have linked this important social process to play, games, physical activity and sport, maintaining that such activities represent a primary medium for teaching children fundamental concepts, ideas, norms, rules and expectations of society (Mead, 1934; Piaget, 1965; Roberts and Sutton-Smith, 1962). For the past 30 years researchers in sociology and psychology of sport have expanded upon the foundations proposed by these scholars. Numerous studies suggest that the process of socialization begins at an early age and strongly influences whether or not children will become involved in sport and physical activity and whether or not they will maintain interest in these activities as adolescents and adults.

In earlier overviews we used a general socialization framework to summarize findings on children's sport socialization, paying particular attention to influence of family, peers, school, parent versus sibling influence and father influence (Lewko and Greendorfer, 1978, 1982, 1988). In our last review, however, we attempted to expand our framework in order to include cultural influences (Greendorfer, Lewko, and Rosengren, 1996). This broadened perspective allows us to shift emphasis to cultural meanings, the value and importance of sports in specific cultural environments, the integration of sport into everyday life, and ideological meanings attached to children's motor skill development (Coakley, 2001; Greendorfer, in press). While the consideration of cultural influences would add significantly to our understanding of the sport socialization process, unfortunately, our search through the most recent literature revealed that very few researchers adopted such a perspective. Of those who have, sport socialization has been viewed from a macro perspective. That is, sport has been interpreted as symbolically and integrally connected to male identity and the meanings of masculinity, and perceptions of gender have been viewed as culturally rooted in physical activity participation and sport performance (Burstyn, 1999; Messner, 1996; Whitson, 1990). This perspective takes a holistic view, one in which motor skills and sport are believed to be a means of teaching boys how to play their gender roles. In a similar vein, some feminists have adopted a critical cultural studies perspective to examine the meaning of sport and of "woman" (Lenskyj, 1999; Theberge, 2000).

As previously indicated, we believe such considerations would greatly enhance our understanding of the complexities of sport socialization. However, we discovered that it would be virtually impossible for us to integrate these broad cultural perspectives with the more narrow social psychological traditions or to explain sport socialization in a framework other than that used in original research (Coakley, 2001). Despite this limitation, we have attempted to frame this overview with developmental, cultural and ideological orientations in mind. Our attention is directed toward themes or issues that could be assimilated into a reasonably coherent body of knowledge.

To begin, we agree with those who maintain that we are products of cultural values and ideas. We further agree that these beliefs and values overshadow our adult behavior in child rearing and form the basis of what we do when we socialize our children. Consequently, we perpetuate or *reproduce cultural ideology* through our own child rearing practices (Beal, 1994). Although sometimes treated as a separate issue, we concur with those researchers who maintain that ideological beliefs about gender are central to the general socialization process (Messner, 1996; Messner, Hunt, and Dunbar, 1999; Whitson, 1990). Hence, notions about gender influence us as parents to place greater emphasis on differences between the sexes rather than on similarities, and we form judgments about what is appropriate and inappropriate for each sex. This cultural dynamic, a product of ideological beliefs, is subtly interwoven into socialization practices, and as a result, we treat sons differently than we treat daughters.

Whenever we hold notions of appropriateness or inappropriateness based on biological sex, we are engaged in *gender role stereotyping,* a process in which a child's biological sex frequently determines which activities s/he will and will not be exposed to as well as the way (or manner) in which s/he will experience those activities. Consequently, interest and involvement in physical activities are not chance occurrences that depend simply upon a child's innate skill or motor talent. Rather, they are products of a cultural belief system that values certain activities or skills for one sex but not for the other. As such, they are integrally related to the type and nature of early childhood socialization practices.

Based on these premises and assumptions, we have organized this overview into several sections that loosely adhere to developmental life cycle periods. Our first section reviews past and current literature related to a variety of interrelated family influences. We begin this section with a discussion of gender-role stereotyping but also include an overview of studies pertaining to toy selection and preferences, parental interactions in early childhood play, and gender differences in motor skill development. In the following section we consider recent studies related to the changing structure of the family. In the third section, we consider research trends in sport socialization. We begin this section with some general statements, then offer a recent literature review that uses chronological age as a developmental framework. Unlike our previous reviews, in which we considered three time frames of early years, pre-adolescence and adolescence, we expand our overview to include the notion of continuity, which extends into adulthood. Our three remaining sections contain various summary statements. We begin with a heuristic profile of research findings pertaining to socialization influences, then consider limitations of the existing research and finally conclude by renewing our call for a more theoretically rich perspective that incorporates cultural influences.

Family Influence: Sex Typing, Toys, and Motor Skill Development

In developing this section we discovered that the majority of recent research has not yet overcome various limitations found in earlier studies. Most researchers still do not make associations between gender ideology, sex-typing, and early childhood socialization, let alone view these processes as precursors to play and physical activity involvement. Of greater concern, we found most research to be descriptive and atheoretical, the majority not organized into any type of developmental socialization framework. In addition, we were struck by the fact that family socialization practices have remained relatively stable over the past 30 years and that gender differences found in play styles of infants, toddlers and older children continue to be quite similar to those found during earlier periods (Colley, Eglinton, and Elliott, 1992; Fisher-Thompson, 1990; Huston and Alvarez, 1990; Ignico, 1990).

Our earlier reviews suggested that inconspicuous cultural practices underlie the socialization process and that the process of gender role socialization begins in early infancy, most notably through toy and play activities. This learning is shaped by ideological beliefs pertaining to gender—namely, those that clearly distinguish what males are, do and should be from what females are, do and should be. Evidence of such beliefs can be found in the delivery room if not earlier, and studies demonstrate that cultural values have not changed very much, particularly parental perceptions and expectations of sons and daughters. In a replication of the classic study of parents' descriptions of newborn sons and daughters by Rubin, Provenzano, and Luria (1974), Stern and Karraker (1989) found that parents still describe daughters as smaller, softer, cuter, and more delicate than sons, regardless of the child's actual physical attributes. In both of these studies sons were described as stronger, more coordinated and more alert than daughters. More recently, Karraker, Vogel, and Lake (1996) found that parents continue to describe their newborn infants in gender-stereotyped terms, rating newborn girls as finer featured, less strong, more delicate and more feminine than newborn boys.

Several studies of differential perceptions and expectations for boys and girls have been replicated over a twenty-year period (Ruben, et al., 1974; Block, 1983; Brooks-Gunn, 1986; Karraker et al., 1996; Stern and Karraker, 1989; Turner and Gervais, 1995). Consistent with findings from the original study by Rubin, et al., (1974), fathers more strongly tend to differentiate boys and girls, encourage more gender-appropriate behavior than mothers throughout childhood, and also put more pressure on boys to achieve than girls (Gervais, Turner, and Hinds, 1995; Lytton and Romney, 1991). In contrast to these findings, however, Karraker et al. (1996) found that fathers did not show greater gender stereotyping than mothers, suggesting that *gender stereotyped perceptions of newborns may have declined somewhat, although they have not disappeared.* For example, Carson, Burks, and Parke (1992) reported little change in the behaviors fathers engage in with their children. Fathers have more physical contact with infant sons than with infant daughters and engage in more rough-and-tumble play with their sons than with their daughters. In accordance with the literature on gender role stereotyping, fathers are more likely to cuddle their infant daughters than sons.

While dominant themes in the early gender role socialization literature suggest that little change has occurred in parents' perceptions and behaviors towards their sons and daughters, a few minor shifts have been observed over the past 10 years, making it difficult to assess the nature of change in the "ideological culture of social development." As we discuss in the section on family structure, the role of fathers in the family may presage a slight ideological shift (Tamis-Lemonda and Cabrera, 1999), and we may eventually see some substantial changes in differential perceptions and conceptions in the near future.

Gender-typed Choices

In contrast to the literature on parental perceptions only a few studies exist on gender-typed choices towards children, and our review suggests that little has changed since the 1970s. An inventory of the contents and structure of children's bedrooms offer one indication of differences in how boys and girls are socialized. Specifically, two sets of researchers examined the toys, decorations, and furniture contained in the bedrooms of boys and girls between 1 month and 6 years (Pomerleau, Bolduc, Malcuit, and Cossette, 1990; Rheinghold and Cook, 1975). In both studies, boys' rooms were more sports and action oriented than girls' rooms, while girls' rooms were more family oriented than boys' rooms. In these studies boys' rooms were found to contain more vehicles, machines, and sports equipment than girls' rooms, while more dolls and patterned decorations were found in girls' rooms. These practices reproduce cultural meanings that convey messages about gender, definitions of masculinity and femininity, images of gender superiority and inferiority, and gender appropriateness of activities.

Toys and Gender Role Stereotyping

Toys represent a potent mechanism of socialization, and the selection of boys' and girls' toys have been related to gender-typed beliefs. While the outcomes of these overt aspects of sex typing are clearly observable at early ages, the way this cultural dynamic of differential treatment inculcates values remains virtually invisible. For example, toy availability not only influences play experiences but also results in preferences and predispositions toward specific activities (McBride-Chang and Jacklin, 1993). We believe that it is this subtle reciprocal interaction that foreshadows how or whether children are socialized into physical activity and sport. Precursors of this process begin in early infancy, and regardless of how subtly the process operates, the ultimate socialization outcomes are clear: males are consciously encouraged relative to physical activity involvement, while females are nonconsciously directed away from physical activity (Lewko and Greendorfer, 1978, 1982, 1988).

Toy, play and sport behavior are *learned* activities. They are explicit outcomes of differential treatment—a discriminatory socialization practice—that begins when we give infant males balls, bats and blue items and infant females dolls, stuffed toys and pink items. Similar to our review of related topics, findings from recent studies indicate that little has changed relative to toy preferences. For example, Etaugh and Liss (1992) found that preferences for gender typical toys are still quite strong in children in kindergarten through 8th grade and that girls had a greater preference for masculine toys than boys had for feminine toys. With increasing age, children showed an increasing preference for masculine toys. In her study of toy selection and preference, Fisher-Thompson (1993) found that although adults/parents purchase toys according to traditional gender role categories, they are more likely to purchase non-sex-typed toys for their own children than for other children. She concluded, however, that her data support previous research that adults encourage sex-appropriate play in young children by purchasing toys according to traditional stereotypes and by purchasing for children the sex-typed toys that they request.

Other studies also demonstrate this consistency in findings. For example, Pennell (1999) found a strong pattern of gender-typing in children's toy requests, especially for boys. Boys asked for male-typed or neutral toys almost exclusively. In contrast, although girls' preferences were also gender-typed, their pattern peaked at age 5. After this age girls also included boy toys on their list. We find it difficult to assess whether or not this peak in preference patterns for girls represents a cultural shift, as Pennell also found that Santa's toy suggestions to boys and girls were equally gender-typed. In yet another recent study of toy preferences Servin, Bohlin and Berlin (1999) found that girls and boys chose different toys as early as 1 year of age. Although sex differences persisted over time (at ages 3 and 5 years), in contradiction to earlier studies, the authors found that feminine toys became less interesting for both girls and boys with increasing age.

Three recent studies examined parent-children's interactions in play activities. Pellet and Ignico (1993) found that boys were more stereotypical in perceptions of physical activities, that kindergarten and second grade children were more stereotypical than fourth and sixth grade children, and that parents were less stereotypical in their beliefs about gender-typed physical activities. In a cross-cultural study of similar activities, Leaper (2000) found gender-related differences in parents' interactive play with their children and concluded that role modeling in activity settings influenced the social construction of gender as well as socialization. Haight, Parke, and Black (1997) also found sex differences in parent interactions with their children during play activities. Finally, in one of the few studies of sibling influence on childhood and adolescent play preferences, Colley, Griffiths, Hugh, Landers, and Jaggli (1996) found more sex-stereotyped preferences among children who had same-sex siblings, while fewer such preferences were found among those with opposite sex siblings.

This relative stability of parental/adult toy selection and children's preferences suggests that despite a few behavioral shifts, cultural values relative to gender-role stereotyping have remained virtually unchanged. While we acknowledge some indication of a slight decline in differential treatment and stereotyping, we also note that these patterns have not disappeared. Given the invisible nature of cultural ideology, we cannot assess the degree to which these patterns have been weakened or whether or not observed shifts will have an effect on socialization practices.

Gender Differences in Activity Level and Early Motor Skills

While differential treatment may be considered a "natural," and hence, harmless practice, ultimately, this disparity results in some form of inequality. A major consequence of this inequality is disadvantage, which may not show itself until middle childhood. Nevertheless, such outcomes may have lifelong effects in how we culturally accord power or privilege to one sex over the other.

According to the literature, differential parental treatment may place females at a disadvantage during early childhood. In their meta-analytic study of sex differences in activity level of infants, Campbell and Eaton (1999) summarized 46 infancy studies (published from 1984–1998) comprising 78 male-female motor activity comparisons. Results demonstrated that male infants and children were more active than females. The authors argued that this early sex difference in activity level is biologically based. However, they believed socialization processes, such as gender-differentiated expectations and experiences, in conjunction with further sex-differentiated biological developments, amplify this early difference to produce the larger gender differences in activity found during childhood.

Yet, the suggestion that differential parental treatment places females at a disadvantage (Campbell and Eaton, 1999) runs counter to cultural ideology. A common belief held by both parents and researchers is that girls are more motorically and cognitively advanced during infancy and early childhood compared to boys. The empirical literature on this topic, however, is not clear. Some studies report that girls reach motor milestones generally ahead of boys, while other studies find few differences between boys and girls on motor skill performance prior to age 4 (Haywood and Getchell, 2001). If a gender difference is found in young children, it typically favors girls over boys for both fine and gross motor skills (Schneider, 1993; Sovik, 1993; but see Anastasia, 1981). Girls, for example, have been reported to exhibit better balance, agility, accuracy of movements, and greater overall coordination of skills than boys prior to age 5 (Schneider, 1993). Additionally, in skills such as galloping and skipping, girls perform at consistently higher levels than boys (Clark and Whitall, 1989). In early to middle childhood boys begin to gain an advantage in most activities involving gross motor skill and this advantage increases through adolescence (Thomas and French, 1985). While the source of these gender differences is not entirely clear, Thomas and French (1985) suggested that socialization practices may play a significant role. In their meta-analytic study, they found that the only skill where boys *appear* to have some sort of biological advantage is in throwing. More relevant to our point about cultural influence, Thomas and French found that any early motor competence or advantage favoring girls does not carry over to later athletic performance. Around the age of puberty gender ideology, rather than biological factors, seems to interact with socialization influences, and girls' interest and motor skill advantages in sport decline.

To briefly summarize our overview of family influences, we suggest the literature may be reflecting a slight decline rather than the disappearance of gender stereotyping during infancy and early childhood. Although little change has been observed in parent-infant/toddler-childhood play interactions or toy selection/preferences, some slight shifts suggest that gender stereotyping by parents may not be quite as strong as indicated in the earlier studies. Keeping this trend in mind, we now examine whether the changing family structure has influenced the sport socialization process.

Changing Family Structure and Sport Socialization

While the overwhelming evidence suggests that not much has changed in general family socialization practices since our last review (Greendorfer et al., 1996), there have been some significant shifts in the family system. We noted some of these trends in our last review; namely, increasing levels of maternal employment and greater father involvement in child rearing. We suggested that this shift in family structure *may lead to changes* in basic socialization practices, which in turn could affect how parents socialize children into physical activity and sport. On the other hand, the steady divorce rate and increase in single parenting could lead to greater barriers to sports involvement because greater economic pressures and time demands on a single parent, regardless of whether they are male or female, may make it difficult for the family to afford participation in certain organized sports programs. In addition single parenting may make it difficult if not impossible for a parent to juggle her/his own schedule around their children's sporting events. In this section, we examine how two factors, maternal employment and increase in father involvement, might affect the sport socialization process.

Influence of Maternal Employment

One of the major trends in the family system over the last 40 years has been the increase in working mothers. Seventy-one percent of mothers in two-parent families work outside the home (Hoffman, 1989), and most adolescents have a mother who works at least part time out of the home (Huston and Alvarez, 1990). Although the impact of maternal employment on sports participation has not been directly examined, maternal employment does seem to have an important effect on gender-role development and children's attitudes toward basic gender roles (Hoffman, 1989). We can infer from these findings that maternal employment may also have an indirect effect on sports.

Throughout childhood, children of working mothers are found to have less stereotyped views of female roles; they also have more positive attitudes towards non-traditional female roles (Chandler, Sawicki, and Stryffeler, 1981; Huston, 1983). Working women, generally, have higher educational and career aspirations for their daughters than women who do not work outside of the home (Huston and Alvarez, 1990). The influences of maternal employment are typically found to be strongest and most beneficial for daughters rather than sons (Hoffman, 1984, 1986). Regardless of the sex of the child, however, children of employed women compared to children of non-employed mothers have been found to reject many aspects of traditional gender roles (Hoffman, 1989). In addition, working mothers are more likely than non-working mothers to regard their daughters in very positive terms. Children of working mothers are also more likely to view women as competent members of society (Hoffman, 1989). Thus, maternal employment does seem to alter the socialization process in ways that are particularly beneficial for girls.

Huston and Alvarez (1990) suggest that maternal employment influences the development of sex-typed concepts through three basic avenues. First, maternal employment provides a model of the "competent woman." Second, maternal employment leads to changes in the basic household roles and activities of family members. Clearly, if both parents are working outside the home it becomes very difficult for the woman to perform all of the traditional female chores in the home without some help. To some extent, less is accomplished on the home front, but even the most pessimistic studies suggest that fathers pick up a bit of the slack (see the following section). Finally, and perhaps most significantly for socialization into values challenging gender ideology, maternal employment leads to increases in maternal power in the family. As a result, the working mother becomes an even stronger role model. How these influences come to play in sports participation has not yet been investigated. We suggest that children of working mothers are more likely to receive less gender stereotypic sport socialization influences; therefore, such children might make significantly different sport involvement choices than children of non-working mothers.

Changing Role of Fathers

While there is some evidence to suggest that the same-sex parent is the most influential member of the family with regard to their child's sport involvement (Greendorfer, in press; Lewko and Greendorfer, 1978), other research has found that fathers appear to play the primary role in influencing both boys and girls to participate in sports (Lewko and Greendorfer, 1978). Furthermore, fathers have often been reported to be the primary socialization agent for gender role development (Langlois and Downs, 1980; Fisher-Thompson, 1990). As mothers gain a larger role in the work place and play a greater role in providing income for the family, the role of the father as sole breadwinner and primary source of power in the family has finally begun to change (Tamis-LeMonda and Cabrera, 1999). It appears that current reality is beginning to match dominant popular beliefs (cultural ideology) about fathers that have existed for the last 15 years. Although popular belief has held that fathers are more nurturant and more involved in caregiving (Lamb, 1997), only recently have fathers begun to take on these roles to any significant degree. In this section we cite some of the evidence supporting this view of the father and offer some suggested consequences that this change in role might have for sport socialization.

The view of the father as a caring, nurturant, active participant in the family, especially with respect to childbearing, began to emerge in the 1970s. This new role was believed to be replacing earlier versions where the father was seen primarily as a moral teacher, breadwinner, or strong masculine role model (Lamb, 1997). Although research over the past decade has suggested that fathers have become more involved in childbearing, this increase in involvement has been modest (Lamb, 1997). Yet, it is possible that this increase can be attributed in part to changes in maternal employment, as in families where the mother works, fathers have been found to play a greater role in caregiving (Gottfried, Gottfried, and Bathurst, 1988).

While the public perception of the active father has gained ground, the actual degree of male involvement with their children has lagged far behind that of women (see Lamb, 1997, for a review). As previously indicated, however, in recent years the degree of father involvement has increased substantially. Part of this increase can be attributed to a broadening of the definition of "father" which is not restricted to individuals who are biologically related, but which also includes men who are part of recombined, blended and cohabitating of families. Thus, the current definition of fathers includes men who are "biologically," "socially," "legally" and "non-legally" connected to a family (Tamis-LeMonda and Caberera, 1999). The role of father has also shifted away from the instrumental role of primary breadwinner in response to shifts in family structure brought about by divorce, remarriage and cohabitation (Greene, Hearn, and Emig, 1996). Fathers now appear to be taking on more of the caregiving responsibilities, leading some researchers to argue that the emerging "ideal" role of the father is one of a "coparent" (Pleck and Pleck, 1997). In contrast, however, given the levels of workaholism prevalent in our society, clearly not all fathers are becoming involved. Nevertheless, the current data on father involvement suggest that more and more fathers are taking greater responsibility for caring for young children. Moreover, Tamis-LeMonda and Cabrera (1999) indicate that this trend is expected to continue.

A number of trends in society appear to be related to increases in father involvement, beginning with the continuing increase in working women. In 1950 only 12% of married women with young children worked outside of the home; in 1983 that figure had jumped to approximately 50%. As of 1997, 66% of married women with young children worked outside the home (Bureau of Labor Statistics, 1997). This rise in working women, coupled with a lack of affordable and accessible child care, has led to an increase in fathers serving as primary caregivers. In 1993, over 1.6 million young children were cared for by their fathers while their mothers were at work (Casper, 1997; Casper and O'Connell, 1998). Fathers are more likely to care for the children if the overall family income is low and if the work schedules of the mother and father do not overlap (Casper and O'Connell, 1998).

Changes in the perceptions of fathers, mothers, the courts, and society have also led to greater acceptance of the ideological belief that fathers can be effective caregivers. For example, the number of single fathers caring for their children increased by 25% between 1995 and 1998, and as of 1998, there were approximately 2.1 million single fathers (about 1/6th of all single parent families) (Bureau of Census, 1998).

Even though the shift in fathers' participation in childrearing appear to be significant, a larger percentage of mothers continues to provide the majority of basic caregiving needs of children (Lamb, 1997). Lamb also has indicated that even though the media have been trumpeting the virtues of the nurturant, active father for the last 10–15 years, many individuals continue to hold more traditional views of the role of fathers. As noted in our last review (Greendorfer, et al., 1996), perhaps the real change in the role of fathers in our society has been the creation of new options or a more diverse parental role for fathers rather than increased participation in child rearing. In other words, fathers now have the option to play the nurturant care-giver, but at the same time in many families most of the responsibility for feeding, clothing, and maintaining the health of the children remains primarily the mother's job. To some extent cultural beliefs may have presented a more favorable view of fathers in that they are receiving more credit and have a wider variety of parenting options available to them, while the workload for mothers has actually increased—a fact made invisible by this shift in cultural meanings. Consequently, due to the images created, we may be misinterpreting the degree of change that actually has occurred, and we may be ignoring the relatively unchanging nature of the underlying gender ideology.

Therefore, given only modest gains in father involvement in child rearing over the last decade or two, we wonder how increased father involvement in child rearing might impact on their children's orientations to or involvement in sport. The first question that must be addressed is whether fathers can be competent caregivers; if they cannot, we might expect negative outcomes in situations where fathers play the primary caregiving role. Studies indicate that fathers can be entirely competent as caregivers, which suggests that parenting skills seem to be learned "on the job" (Hipgrave, 1982; Levine, 1976; Russell, 1982, 1983) and not "in the genes." A second question is whether involved fathers act differently with their children than non-involved fathers. Research suggests that greater time spent in childcare leads to greater parental sensitivity to the needs of their children. Involved fathers tend to be more sensitive and responsive to their children than uninvolved fathers.

Regardless of the extent of father involvement, however, fathers tend to play more with their children and provide less caregiving than mothers (Lamb, 1997). Of the time they spend with their children, fathers spend approximately 4 times as much time engaged in play than engaged in caregiving (Hetherington and Parke, 1993; Parke, 1990). Even when fathers are very involved in caregiving they engage in more physically stimulating activities (rough and tumble) and play more with their children than mothers (Field, 1978). Children seem to like these activities, reacting more positively towards father play than mother play (Field, 1990). In one study by Clarke-Stewart (1978), 18-month-olds chose fathers rather than mothers as the preferred play partner. Thus, both fathers and children seem to enjoy playing together, and play continues to be an integral part of father-child relationships. Recent research has demonstrated that fathers' encouragement of rough and tumble play and degree of arousal during play with their 18-month-old children is significantly related to the children's rough and tumble play in 1st grade (McBride-Chang and Jacklin, 1993). These researchers also found that choice of more feminine toys was negatively related to the amount of rough and tumble play in boys and girls.

Based on these findings, regardless of the degree of father involvement, we might expect to find no differences in the extent to which involved or non-involved fathers may be primary socializers of their children's sport involvement. Unfortunately, this issue has yet to be studied. On the other hand, greater father involvement and greater warmth and closeness between father and child have been found to be related to better child well-being, social competence, and cognitive development (Lamb, 1997; Mac-Donald and Parke, 1984; Marsiglio, et al., 1998; Radin, 1982) and less traditional views of gender roles (Lamb, 1997; Radin and Sagi, 1982; Sagi, 1982). Combined with the earlier findings regarding play, these results suggest that involved fathers may raise children with less traditional views of appropriate behavior for boys and girls. Although the effect of father involvement in caregiving on children's choice of sports and the amount of sport participation has not yet been investigated, this line of research offers a potential rupture in the traditional "culture" of socialization by introducing some degree of modification in gender value orientations.

We might ask, given the public perception of greater father involvement, why fathers haven't become more involved. As previously suggested, while overall levels of father involvement in child rearing have increased, these increases have not pervaded our culture as a whole. For example, the division of labor and the nature of parenting roles in dual wage families seem to have changed over the last 15 years; however, in single wage families the family structure has remained fairly constant (Hoffman, 1989). Mothers have also been somewhat reluctant to give up some of the child rearing roles they have traditionally played (Beitel and Parke, 1990). This reluctance might seem justified if we consider that child rearing is one of the few domains in which women have had more power and control than men. Allowing men to take over some of these responsibilities not only reduces women's roles but also reduces any power potential they might have in the family structure.

The model of father as breadwinner remains quite strong, especially in some sectors of society. For example, in blue collar families where both parents work, the father is still expected to be the primary breadwinner. To the extent the mother works and earns as much or more income as the father and the father's income is viewed as inadequate to support the family, the father is viewed as a failure (Hood, 1986). Furthermore, there also continue to be many obstacles in the workplace for fathers' involvement with their children, with few if any opportunities for paternity leave or flexible work schedules. Probably the clearest message that little has changed in the workplace is the $100,000 fine to David Williams, a lineman on the Tennessee Titans football team, who chose to participate in his child's birth rather than play a professional football game.

Summarizing the literature on the changing role of fathers, we note that during the past few years society has shifted in the way it views fathers in our society. In part due to changing social, economic and political events, there has been a shift away from the traditional view of fathers primarily as breadwinners toward a view of fathers more as coparents. Although not all fathers have taken on increased caregiving responsibility, in those situations where fathers do take a more active role in childrearing, some slight shifts in gender role attitudes have been observed. Children in families with more involved fathers tend to have less stereotypical gender role attitudes than those in families where the father is uninvolved. While, this change in parental role has not yet influenced any changes in toddler-infant-childhood play styles, game, and toy selection or gender labeling of physical activities, since fathers remain primary playmates for their children, we would expect that their influence would continue to be a strong (if not the strongest) on sport socialization.

Given the contingencies on the changing family structure, then, we offer Figure 7.1 as a partial "model of influences," which offers the *potential for change* in sport

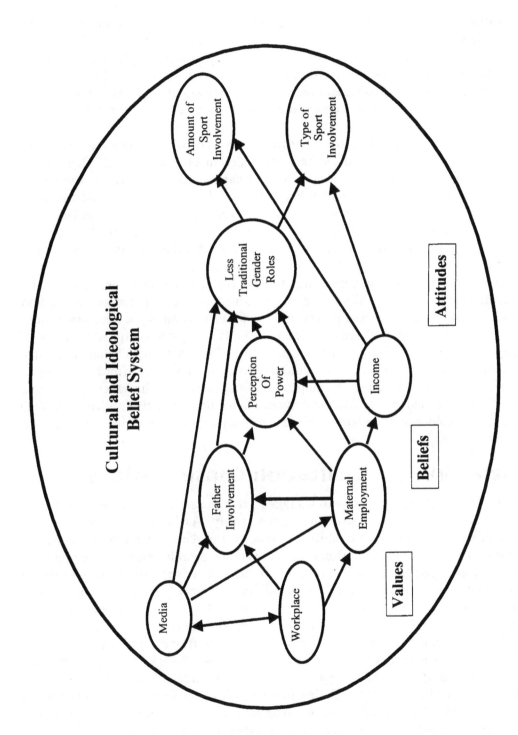

Figure 7.1. Model of Influences.

socialization influences. We view this diagram as complex, dynamic and multidirectional in flow. The larger oval can be interpreted as the pervasive cultural system of values, beliefs, attitudes and behaviors that creates the underlying ideological belief system that influences sport socialization practices. We see such influences as the mass media and workplace as impacting on father involvement, maternal employment and family values—all of which could have implications for gender stereotypes and sport socialization.

For example, positive portrayals/images of fathers as care givers may lead to increasing options for both fathers and mothers. Attitudes in the workplace, influenced by changing media images, could impose or remove barriers for both parents. The impact of these influences could affect availability or lack of flexible work time and could add to or relieve economic pressures to work overtime, thereby changing the cultural ideology that permits fathers to place work above family. On the other hand, economic constraints and desires to maintain a particular lifestyle (such as one that their parents enjoyed) seem to require two wage earners in the family. Consequently, an increasing number of working mothers has lead to increases in father involvement with children. The presence of a working mother not only offers opportunity of increased family income but also may lead to a perception of increased power in the family. This modified perception alone could result in less traditional gender roles, which ultimately could expand the range of "appropriate" sport activities for both boys and girls. These potential changes accompanied by an increase in "family access" could lead to greater ability to afford fees, lessons and perhaps more specialized sport equipment. In our opinion such changes must occur at the cultural level and then be filtered through a dynamic, interactive exchange through the media, workplace and the family in order to truly bring about changes in the sport socialization process.

General Sport Socialization Considerations

Thus far, our overview of research suggests that not much has changed in family socialization practices or the structure of the family. As indicated in the previous section, however, some apparent shifts are noteworthy. Unfortunately, the same can not be said for the sport socialization research. While research findings have remained relatively unchanged since our last review, we did notice increased research interest in continued sport participation of young adults and older populations. In order to examine progress that may have been made since our last review, we retained age as an organizing principle. To accommodate the lifespan extension in sport participation, we again consolidated material to encompass three time frames: the early years (ages 0–8), pre-adolescence (ages 9–12), and adolescence (ages 14–18). Noting the number of studies on adult sport socialization, however, we added a fourth time frame: adulthood (20–65+), but only included those studies that focused on continuity of activity from childhood or adolescence. Although the age ranges in various studies sometimes blur distinctions between these divisions, they do capture the basic age clusters. As in our previous reviews, given the absence of some type of conceptual developmental framework that guided most of the empirical studies, we question how much additional insight or understanding we have gained.

The Early Years

Few studies have directed attention to sport socialization before eight years of age. However, the developmental literature on sex-typing indicates this process begins in the family and is comprised of subtle social interactions through which parents simply do not make conscious efforts to provide basic motor skill instruction for daughters (Carson et al., 1993; Etaugh and Liss, 1992; Lewko and Greendorfer, 1988). As a result girls receive fewer rewards than boys for developing motor skills and are discouraged to participate in vigorous play/physical activity (Campbell and Eaton, 1999).

Three studies focus on parental treatment and gender differences at very early ages (Bloch, 1987; Eccles and Harold, 1991; Moore et al., 1991). Although their conceptual orientations differed significantly and they placed very little emphasis on explaining physical activity or sport involvement in the early years, these studies provide limited insight. Bloch's (1987) study is noteworthy because it examined sex differences in the social context of young children from birth through the pre-school years (ages 0–6 years). She found more gender similarities than differences in activities (no differences in gross motor play, construction activities, rough and tumble play, and art), observing that all children spent large amounts of time with family. More specifically, she observed that 90% of the adults in these activity settings were immediate family members and that time/presence of fathers and mothers was equal in both boys' and girls' settings. Unfortunately, in-depth interactions within family constellations were not obtained; nor was any attention given to value orientations of families or other cultural beliefs that might influence the observed behavior.

Moore et al., (1991) applied a pediatric research perspective to early childhood determinants of physical activity and later health status. Although they did not apply a particular theoretical framework, Moore and colleagues observed a strong, direct relationship between activity levels of parents and their 4–7 year old children. Using direct activity monitoring, Moore et al., (1991) observed that active fathers had a greater impact on their children than active mothers. Moreover, the greatest impact occurred when both parents were active, resulting in nearly a sixfold increase in the likelihood of the child being active. Parental activity appeared to impact more strongly on boys than on girls: if both parents were active, sons were 7.2 times and daughters 4.5 times more likely to be active. Although the authors suggested a number of mechanisms that might account for these findings, ranging from role-modeling to genetic predisposition, their focus was primarily on observable behaviors. They offered virtually no analysis of the socialization process and totally ignored the broad cultural context that provides the conditions, "climate," and setting for the proposed mechanisms.

The most theoretically advanced work was reflected in the study by Eccles and Harold (1991), who applied a *value expectancy model* to their 3-year longitudinal investigation of gender differences in sport involvement of children (ages 5, 6 and 8 years of age). In agreement with findings from studies of 30 years ago, they observed that not only are gender differences evident by Grade 1, but these differences persist over time on ratings of sport ability, how important it is to do well, enjoyment, and usefulness of what was learned. Girls see themselves as less able in sport, indicate that doing well in math and reading is more important than doing well in sport, and see sport as the least useful domain when ranked among math and reading. Despite the consistency of patterns, however, the researchers offer little insight as to why females gravitate toward some activities or ways in which preferences may be related to gender perceptions of superiority and inferiority. To date, researchers have ignored any examination of the relationship between cultural ideology and male development of motor skills, and explanations of findings fail to consider whether motor skill development (e.g., sport socialization) represents another domain for reproducing male power and privilege (Messner et al., 1999; Whitson, 1990).

The Eccles and Harold (1991) study also sheds some light on the social influence that parents exert on their children. More specifically, they found that children attended to the importance they believed parents attached to their doing well and to their participation in sport activities. Both boys' and girls' perceptions of the importance that parents attribute to doing well in sports were related to ratings of ability in sports. Gender differences also were found, as males reported higher perceptions of skill than females. Not only do these findings emphasize the importance of understanding ways in which family dynamics influence perceptions and choices of physical activity, but they also underscore the significance of more subtle social influences such as value structure and family culture.

Further support for parental influence was found in a comparative study that included parents as well as 5–10 year-old children (Jambor, 1999). Parents whose children participated in soccer demonstrated significantly different behaviors and attitudes about sport participation than did parents whose children did not participate. In addition, parents of participants cited reasons for their child's participation that were similar to reasons for participation given by their children. Finally, parents of participants indicated more benefits to sport participation than parents of nonparticipants.

Although some of the most recent research on young children's play interactions has included race and gender as factors, these studies have not theoretically analyzed sport socialization influences. They ignore cultural ideology, fail to consider the possibility that racial, ethnic or class influences could be linked to gender, and make no attempt to explain ways in which peers, gender and race influence physical activity participation. Research findings tend to be descriptive and, similar to earlier traditions, fail to offer insight into ways that racial as well as gender contexts affect children's play. For example, in their study age groups' elementary school playground interactions (1st and 2nd graders and 5th and 6th), Lewis and Phillipsen (1998) found that mixed-race interactions included more children than same-race interactions, that mixed-gender interaction was more likely to be mixed-race rather than same-race interaction, and that mixed-gender interaction was much more likely to include more than one race than all girls' or all boys' interactions. Girls and boys were equally likely to play in same- and mixed-race groupings, and older children played in same-gender and larger groups more than younger children did. In their study of child, family and contextual variables of 3rd and 5th grade African American and White children, Posner and Vandell (1999) found that girls were more likely to engage in academic and social activities, whereas boys were more likely to play in coached sports.

Preadolescence

By far the largest number of research studies on sport socialization focused on the middle years of childhood. In general, findings from these studies are consistent with trends reported in previous reviews, particularly those pertaining to parental influence and gender differences (Lewko and Greendorfer, 1988). Studies of parental influences provided only limited advances in our understanding of how children either become involved or remain involved in physical activities. While the gender difference studies seemed to reinforce earlier understandings that males and females experience sport differently, none examined the cultural conditions or underlying reasons for these differential experiences.

The studies by Colley et al. (1992) and Dempsey, Kimiecik, and Horn (1993) focused on children at approximately 9 years of age. Colley et al. adopted a social learning perspective to sport socialization and indicated that parental participation (as reported by the child) accounted for a negligible amount of variance in reported sport participation of the child. In their examination of parental influence, Dempsey et al. adapted the Eccles' expectancy-value model and found no relationships between parents' (self-reported) and children's (self-reported) moderate to vigorous physical activity participation (MVPA). These findings conflict with those of Moore et al. (1991) who used actual activity measurements with parents and younger (0–6 years) children. Dempsey et al. did, however, find that parents' beliefs about their children's MVPA competence accounted for a small amount of variance (6%) in their children's MVPA. The authors concluded that ". . . the relationship between parent and child belief systems about MVPA is probably more complex than the unidirectional one presented in this study" (Dempsey et al., 1993, p. 165). Although these findings suggest indirectly that ideological beliefs and values are significant aspects in sport socialization, unfortunately the authors did not extend their discussion beyond a social psychological framework.

In a study attempting to identify influences on children's attraction to physical activity, Brustad (1993) took the Eccles model (referred to in "The Early Years") one step further by obtaining data directly from parents as well as their 10-year old children. Despite some methodological constraints, Brustad found that parents who experienced high levels of enjoyment of physical activity encouraged their children's involvement in physical activity more so than parents who experienced less enjoyment in physical activity. Parents also differentiated between sons and daughters by providing sons with more encouragement to be physically active. Brustad also found that parental encouragement impacted on development of their children's perceived competence.

A study by DiLorenzo, Stucky-Ropp, Vander Wal, and Gotham (1998) applied social learning theory to their exploration of children's exercise and the longitudinal predictive value of such determinants. Collecting data from both parents and children in 111 families, the researchers found that *physical activity habits tend to persist over time* and that enjoyment of physical activity was a consistent predictor of physical activity among children in the 5th and 6th grades. For girls in the 8th and 9th grades, childhood exercise knowledge, mother's physical activity and child and mother's modeling/support emerged as predictors of involvement. For boys, child's self-efficacy for physical activity, exercise knowledge, parental modeling, and interest in sports media were important. The authors concluded that socialization in the family unit exerts a tremendous influence on health-related behaviors such as exercise, that the relative importance of determinants differs for girls and for boys, and that the pattern of these determinants appears to change over time.

Despite the proliferation of research on parent-child interaction on the sport socialization process, we have learned very little that is new, and our understanding of the process remains as circumscribed as it was 30 years ago. Unfortunately, those theoretical frameworks applied to research investigations have been limited to social psychological perspectives, and findings appear as decontextualized "variable knowledge" which has resulted in a fragmented and unfocused literature. One of the greatest difficulties in using social psychological paradigms is their failure to offer explanations of how dynamics of culture interact with or affect sport socialization influences. More powerful explanatory notions are needed if we are to understand the complex interactions that broad cultural influences have on behavior and orientations (Whitson, 1984). For example, we know that parental child rearing practices are mediated by race, ethnicity and social class, and that such practices typically include value climate and orientations integrally embedded in the cultural milieu (Greendorfer and Ewing, 1981). Yet, we have virtually no understanding of the complexities or the manner in which parental child rearing practices interact with cultural influences and how this dynamic affects childhood sport socialization.

Gender Differences

Because the topic of gender differences represents the largest focus of the sport socialization research across the four time frames, we have selected several studies in the pre-adolescent period for discussion. Although these studies vary in both their focus as well as their methodological sophistication, they do reflect a breadth of inquiry that is being pursued from the perspective of *gender differences.*

Colley et al. (1992) explored the impact of sex-typing of activities with a sample of nine-year-olds. Consistent with previous research on gender differences in play, the authors reported that boys appeared to be more rigidly sex-typed than girls: no boys played female sports whereas 20% of the females played male sports. Ignicio (1990) also examined sex-typing in a sample of 7 to 13 year olds who were involved in a university-based activity program. Males were reportedly more stereotyped in their labeling of physical activities than were the females. In a study focusing on gender stereotyping and presence of siblings, Colley, Griffiths, Hugh, Landers, and Jaggli (1996) found that interactions with same- and opposite-sex siblings was associated with activity preferences for both sexes. Specifically, more gender-stereotyped preferences were given by those with same-sex siblings and fewer were given by those with opposite sex siblings.

Pellett and Ignico (1993) examined age and gender differences in perceptions of gender-typed physical activities and whether a relationship existed between children's and parents' perceptions. In their longitudinal study of children in Grades K, 2, 4, and 6, as well as their parents, the authors found that boys were more stereotypical in perceptions than girls and that younger children (Grades K and 2) were more stereotypical in perceptions than those in Grades 4 and 6. Interestingly, all parent age groups were less stereotypical in their beliefs than all student groups, suggesting that influences in addition to parents also affect elementary school-aged children. Unfortunately, authors of these studies offer us only descriptive findings, citing facts or patterns without presenting conceptual explanations or noting whether subtle cultural shifts may have occurred in family socialization practices.

We are encouraged by a recent study that attempts to utilize the robust concept of *hegemony* (a lived system of meanings and values which when experienced as practice becomes reciprocally confirming; rather than being forced upon subordinate groups, hegemonic practices are accepted by consensus as "natural" or commonsense). Not only is it one of the few analyses of peer interactions, but this study also focuses on how children negotiate gender boundaries in middle childhood play (McGuffey and Rich, 1999). Over a nine-week period children were observed creating, defining and altering gender codes. When girls and boys disregarded pre-described boundaries, they entered an area referred to as the "gender transgression zone." This area of activity was one in which boys and girls could expand gender boundaries in "child culture." The authors found that high status boys used hegemonic masculinity to regulate both girls' and boys' boundaries by resisting gender transgressions. In addition, race and class had no influence on the boys' status system, although these factors were salient for girls' homosocial organization and behavior. Studies such as this could enrich our understanding of complex dynamics involved in the process of socialization, because they suggest ways in which power and ideology are culturally reproduced through interactional processes. We would hope to find more studies like this in the future.

Adolescence

Although adolescent sport socialization has been less researched than the childhood and pre-adolescent periods, several recent studies demonstrate that more attention is being given to this life cycle stage. Unlike our previous reviews, which leaned primarily on non-sport journals, this overview of adolescence relies mainly on sport journals. In these studies we found that researcher attention was directed primarily toward social influences on participation during adolescence and on *continuity* of participation during the transition to adulthood. Although studies assumed a social psychological emphasis, we were particularly struck by the absence of conceptual or theoretical frameworks.

We believe two studies of general adolescent activities are worthy of mention. Rekers, Sanders, Rasbury, Strauss, and Morey (1990) described a wide array of activity patterns of adolescents between 11 and 18 years of age. Of the 37 activities where significant gender differences emerged, only four were clearly sport-based: football, watching football on TV, member of a sports team, and gymnastics. Factor analyses revealed clear-cut gender differences on the first two factors: adolescent males involved themselves more in outdoor, aggressive activities, while adolescent females involved themselves in indoor, feminine activities. Particularly noteworthy, the Rekers et al., study underscored the important discovery that physical/sport activities do not dominate the life experiences of adolescents.

In a second study describing adolescent activity patterns, Kirshnit, Ham, and Richards (1989) obtained information from adolescent females and males in grades 5 through 9. Similar to Rekers et al., the authors found that only a very-small portion (6%) of the adolescents' total waking time was spent in sports. Of this time, a majority (69.9%) was involved primarily in informal sports. However, sport emerged as one of the most positive activities associated with higher levels of motivation, positive affect and arousal. Not surprisingly, gender differences also emerged, with girls spending less time overall in sports, particularly in informal sport participation.

In an in-depth interview study which examined the dynamics of decision-making about sport participation, Coakley and White (1992) noted that sport represents one of many activities that could impact on adolescents' transition to adulthood. The authors also identified a number of factors that influenced sport socialization. Similar to research emanating from the expectancy-value model (Brustad, 1993; Eccles and Harold, 1991), Coakley and White found that participation in sport activities was more likely if it offered the opportunity to enhance one's perceived competence. In addition, parental constraints emerged as a factor limiting participation of females. Specifically, the monitoring of activity settings, the composition of groups and the setting of time constraints appeared to limit the opportunities for freedom of choice. Interviewees expanded the notion of encouragement to include the provision of money and transportation, items that are rarely addressed in research delving into the construct of parental support and encouragement. Finally, but not unexpectedly, parental support and encouragement emerged as a key factor influencing sport participation.

A study by Hoyle and Leff (1997) focused on the role of childhood influences on adolescent participation in sport. Male and female tennis players provided information about the role their parents played in their tennis game, as well as their own view of their game. Similar to several of the studies previously mentioned, parental support was significantly associated with enjoyment and with the importance players ascribed to their tennis game. Players reporting a high level of parental support tended to report greater enjoyment of tennis and viewed tennis as a more important part of their lives. In a study examining correlates of physical activity among Icelandic adolescents, Vilhjalmsson and Thorlindsson (1998) found that in addition to perceived importance of sport, father, friends and older brothers were significant predictors of high levels of male sport involvement. This was one of the few studies not finding gender differences, as the authors reported that influences from significant others appeared to affect males and females in the same way.

We mentioned earlier that several recent studies utilized the concept of *continuity,* a theoretical proposition that individuals are predisposed to preserve and maintain longstanding patterns of thought and behavior throughout their life (Langley and Knight, 1999), specifically applying the notion to leisure activity as well as sport. Those studies included in this section focus on constancy of participation between childhood and adolescence, whereas those focusing on the transition between adolescence and adulthood are discussed in the following section.

In their descriptive study of predictors of participation in school-based athletics in high school, Antshel and Anderman (2000) found that students were more likely to participate in sports if they were male, came from a higher socioeconomic status, engaged in outdoor activities, admired an athlete and perceived participation as being socially desirable. One of the strongest predictors of sport participation among 10th grade students was whether they had participated in sport activities in earlier grades. The authors also noted that ethnicity was not a significant predictor of participation.

Examining involvement of youth from a different perspective, Telama and Yang (2000) analyzed age-related declines in physical activity among Finnish adolescents (at ages 9, 12, 15, and 18). Their data demonstrated a significant decline in frequency of physical activity and sport participation after the age of 12. Although the boys were more active than girls in the younger age groups, the decline of activity was steeper among males than females. After age 15, the female subjects participated in physical activity more frequently than male subjects. While the underlying theme of this study represents another dimension to be understood relative to sport socialization, we note that the authors not only failed to examine reasons for decline in activity, but they pursued none of the topics related to the disengagement/sport withdrawal literature (Greendorfer, in press).

Although pleased with the increased interest in adolescent sport socialization, we are disappointed in the caliber and direction of recent research. Even with the expanded consideration of "continuity" the absence of conceptual or theoretical frameworks severely limits potential for explanation or understanding of the process. In short, we question the degree of progress this recent research truly represents.

Continuity: Young Adulthood and Older Ages

Those studies examining continuity of sport involvement focused predominantly on participation influences during earlier life stages. If conceptual rationales were applied to the notion of continuity, they were very loose, at best. A recent study using retrospective information examined the extent to which childhood play activities predicted future sport participation of women (Giuliano, Popp, and Knight, 2000). Comparisons were made of adult sport and childhood play experiences between male and female athletes and nonathletes from Division III colleges. The authors found that playing with "masculine" (rather than "feminine") toys and games, playing in pre-dominantly male or mixed gender groups, and being considered a tomboy distin-guished between women who had become college athletes and those who did not. While this study offers little theoretical insight, it is one of the few to suggest that childhood play activities should be considered along with significant others and agents of socialization in predicting future sport participation of females.

Exploring continuity between adolescent and adult activities, Raymore, Barber, Eccles, and Godbey (1999) examined changes in leisure behavior patterns over a 3-year period during the transition from adolescence to young adulthood (mean age was 18 years at the start of the study). They found a durability in leisure activity patterns, observing stability as the most common pathway into young adulthood. Although the nature of the changes that occurred differed to some degree for males and females, the authors did not elaborate or fully explain these differences. Rather, they focused on similarities that were found in patterns and transitions. In their study of the relationship between high school sport participation and involvement in sport as adults, Curtis, McTeer, and White (1999) surveyed a representative national sample of adult Canadians. The authors found high school sport involvement to be a strong predictor of adult sport involvement, and the effect of this involvement persisted after controlling for social background factors. Moreover, the effects of school sport experiences held across age and gender. Although diminished in temporal distance from the high school years, the effects of high school sport involvement extended to subjects aged 40–59 for both sexes.

Continuity of life-span physical activity was also examined by Hirvensalo, Lin-tunen, and Rantanen (2000), who found that past physical activity was strongly related to high levels of physical activity in old age. For both women and men, competitive sport participation from ages as young as 10–19 years of age was a significant predictor for maintaining activity in older ages (65–84 years of age). In one of the few studies applying a conceptual framework to the notion of continuity, Langley and

Knight (1999) examined the integration of sport into the life course. The researchers found that successful competitive sport experiences were a significant factor in predicting general propensity for lifelong physical activity. They concluded that successful sport experiences were a significant mediator of past patterns and continuing activity involvement in sport.

What Have We Learned?

In order to help the reader reach some form of closure, we have expanded the profile of research findings included in our last review (Greendorfer et al., 1996). Although this profile summarizes our general understanding of socialization influences up to this point in time, we have taken some liberties in both the use of particular studies and in the selection of findings. The reader should therefore treat this profile as more heuristic than factual. We propose that our profile of sport socialization emerges from a developmental progression:

- In infancy and the early years children spend large amounts of time with close family, including time in physical activities;
- Some significant shifts in the family system have appeared, particularly with respect to the role of the father;
- Fathers appear to be taking on more caregiving responsibilities and emerging as coparents;
- Maternal employment is associated with less rigorous sex typing;
- Limited evidence on the family suggests that differential treatment and sex typing may not be as strong as in the past; however, these practices have not disappeared;
- Parental selection of infant and young children's toys continues to be sex typed, but degree of sex typing may be declining;
- Parents treat infant sons differently than infant daughters and this differential treatment is reflected in parental interactions in play activities with infants;
- Activities during the early years are more gender similar than gender differentiated;
- Active parents have active children, with boys being more active than girls;
- Parents who enjoy physical activity also encourage their children's involvement in physical activities;
- By grade 1, children hold sport-based perceptions about their ability, enjoyment and usefulness of sport that carry over time;
- By grade 1, gender differences in sport ability, enjoyment and perceived usefulness are evident;
- By grade 1, children are monitoring their parents' behavior for cues that reveal the importance that parents attach to participating and doing well in sports;
- During middle childhood, parental participation seems to lose its impact as an influence on children's participation;

- Perceptions of competence that children have are related to perceptions of the child's competence that are held by the parents;
- Lower parental pressure and lower maternal control in parenting are related to higher enjoyment in sport;
- Parents and children may hold different explanations for skill in sport that could influence further interaction;
- Boys continue to demonstrate greater rigidity in sex-typing of physical activities than do girls;
- In middle childhood, time spent in sports is affected by one's ability self-concept and the value attached to sport competence, with girls most negatively affected;
- Parents encourage sons more than daughters to be physically active, and parental encouragement affects children's own perceptions of competence:
- Parental support and encouragement take on various forms, from verbal feedback to monetary support to transportation;
- Adolescents spend very little of their waking time in sports, even though sports is one of the most positive activities they experience;
- Adolescent activities continue to be highly gender stereotyped;
- Parental support and involvement in physical activity influence adolescent participation and enjoyment of sport and physical activity;
- Childhood enjoyment in play and involvement in physical activity are strong predictors of adolescent and adult involvement in sport and physical activity;
- Sport and leisure activity patterns remain stable over time and are evident in the transition from adolescence to adulthood;
- Sport involvement during the high school years contributes to later adult involvement in sport.

Limitations of Current Research

One of the limitations mentioned in our previous reviews was the lack of systematic research on sport socialization. It was disappointing for us to discover that this limitation is as pervasive in the current research as it has been in the past. Despite the wide array of issues encompassed in recent sport socialization research, we note that the literature on socialization influences is replete with empirical findings that have not been organized into a coherent or focused body of knowledge. The most serious consequence of this limitation has been the manner in which research findings are presented. It was most disappointing to discover that the majority of researchers do not theoretically frame their findings; rather, findings are offered as fragmented, isolated variable knowledge with little, if any, explanation. The recitation of decontextualized findings adds little to our insight or understanding and exacerbates the realization that findings from recent research do not differ significantly from patterns obtained in the past (see Giuliano et al., 2000; Haight et al., 1997; Hirvensalo et al., 2000; Pennell, 1999; Servin et al., 1999). The fact that researchers have made few efforts to reconcile their findings with those from previous decades suggests to us that little progress has occurred either in our thinking or in the way we are pursuing sport socialization topics. We also note that any shifts in recent patterns are *rarely acknowledged as substantive findings;* researchers simply ignore opportunities to offer any type of explanation, conceptual or otherwise, for finding no gender, racial or class differences (Antshel and Anderson, 2000; Curtis et al., 1999; Hoyle and Leff, 1997; Lewis and Phillipsen, 1998).

In earlier studies considering significant other influences, researchers focused primarily on parents. Although we noticed a broadening of research designs to include parents' as well as children's perceptions (see DiLorenzo et al., 1998; Jambor, 1999; Pellett and Ignico, 1993), we were amazed by how few considered sibling or peer influences (Colley et al., 1996; McGuffey and Rich, 1999; Vilhjalmsson and Thorlindsson, 1998; Weiss and Barber, 1995). Moreover, we found a majority of these studies to be based on self-reports rather than observations of behavior in naturalistic settings.

A second limitation still encountered in recent research was the absence of an adequate theory of sport participation. Not only do a majority of researchers fail to apply a conceptual rationale to their empirical studies, but relatively few make any attempt to explain their findings from a theoretical or developmental perspective. Although we could assume some type of social psychological perspective in earlier studies, we found that several current researchers failed to make any reference whatsoever to a social psychological framework.

One promising exception is research based on the Eccles *expectancy-value model,* which provides substantial examination of the relationship between parental expectations of their child's ability in physical activities and the child's own perceptions of ability. Several recent studies have been based on this model which ". . . focuses attention on the role significant others play in shaping children's self-perceptions in two primary ways: (a) as interpreters of experience, and (b) as providers of experience" (Eccles and Harold, 1991, p. 13). Despite the popularity of this model, the insight gained relative to the development of children's perceptions as influenced by dynamic interactions with significant others has been relatively limited. Perhaps this line of inquiry would be better served if researchers adopted alternative methodologies. In the past we suggested a qualitative approach that respects the social-cognitive development of children.

Another alternative has been suggested in recent years. Specifically, Coakley (2001), advocating the use of critical and interactionist theories, suggested the use of in-depth interviews and field observations that would focus on how people actively make decisions about their sport participation and how they derive meaning from sports participation. As described by Coakley, the goal of such approaches is to obtain detailed descriptions of sport experiences as they occur in people's lives and to connect meanings with the larger cultural context in which sports and sport participation exist (p. 84). Consistent with Coakley's suggested alternatives, we would argue that any theoretical conceptualization of social-cognitive developmental aspects of the sport socialization process would be incomplete if they did not encompass a broader conceptual framework. The time has come for researchers to acknowledge that significant insight could be gained if research paradigms included notions about the cultural reproduction of dominant belief systems, particularly notions of how meanings about sport are formulated in culture and are reproduced in sport socialization practices. Obviously, such considerations of cultural contexts and meanings would have major implications for methodology.

Conclusions

We had two purposes for our updated review. One was to further integrate broad cultural perspectives with more narrow social psychological approaches to socialization research in general and sport socialization in particular. Our second purpose was to reconcile current research findings with those from studies of previous decades. It became apparent from the beginning of our overview, however, that we would have difficulty realizing either objective. While the absence of theory in most empirical studies was an impediment to our attempts at synthesis, the inconclusive findings related to shifts in the family structure and subsequent effects of such shifts in socialization practices imposed an overwhelming challenge if we attempted to integrate past and current research findings.

On the one hand, we found a few researchers who observed changes within the family structure, which indirectly suggests that adaptations in family socialization practices may be on the horizon. On the other, we had difficulty identifying a sufficient number of specific studies demonstrating that change has indeed occurred. For example, some researchers acknowledge a trend toward fathers becoming more involved as caretakers. Although we recognize that children in families with more involved fathers tend to have less stereotypical gender role attitudes, to date, we have not yet seen evidence that this change in parental role has influenced any changes in toddler-infant-childhood play styles, game, and toy selection or gender labeling of physical activities. Although we have identified a few studies that demonstrate a slight decline in differential treatment and stereotyping, dominant themes in the early gender role socialization literature suggest that evidence is lacking relative to changes in parents' perceptions and behaviors towards their sons and daughters. While slight shifts observed in parent-infant/toddler-childhood play interactions, toy selection and preferences suggest gender stereotyping by parents may not be quite as strong as in the past, we cannot ignore the fact that such practices have not disappeared. At best, all we can say is these shifts in family structure *may have implications for changes in family influence.*

Relative to direct family sport socialization influences, findings from studies have remained relatively unchanged since our last review. The challenge for researchers, then, is to more critically determine how to view social change. We advise the reader to keep three underlying questions in mind: (a) what constitutes social and cultural change, (b) what is the nature of change if indeed it has occurred, and (c) what is the relationship between ideological change and structural or behavioral change?

Realizing that our concluding comments have been very critical of the existent research, we would be remiss if we did not mention two positive developments that have potential for advancing our understanding of the sport socialization process. The inclusion of race, ethnicity and social class in some recent studies offers a refreshing addition to the research, and we urge scholars to recognize the importance of these factors within the broader context of culture. The dynamic intersections between each of these influences should be included in future research on the process of socialization. Also, while we believe the notion of continuity adds a dimension that has been missing in earlier sport socialization research, its potential to advance our knowledge and understanding has not yet been realized. Theories of continuity, absent from current sport socialization studies, could be easily integrated with socialization theory and invigorate conceptual explanations. Finally, more attention needs to be given to ways in which the mass media influence the sport socialization process. Although some recent studies have considered mass media influence as part of gender socialization (see DiLorenzo et al., 1998; Messner et al., 1999), this important component has been virtually ignored in socialization research and needs to be more meaningfully incorporated in future studies.

As mentioned earlier, we attempted to frame this overview on development and socialization with cultural and ideological orientations in mind. Moreover, we made every effort to include notions pertaining to cultural reproduction of ideological beliefs, values and orientations when appropriate. We believe this broadened perspective would allow us to view (sport) socialization as a negotiated reality that takes place within a more broadly defined social context than previously considered. It appears that some researchers are moving in this direction and are conceptualizing the process as fluid rather than fixed and as a cultural dynamic in which structured sets of pre-established interaction patterns and relationships are balanced with notions that allow for a range of differentiated interactions and exchanges that are negotiable and subject to interpretation (Coakley, 2001, pp. 83–88).

Recognizing that such a reconceptualization would critically change the nature of research topics in several ways, we believe that such a conceptual shift would allow us to better understand (sport) socialization. Approaches using a cultural framework attempt to capture the lived meanings and experience of sport in the lives of people, thereby making accommodations for a complex process with multiple levels of dynamic interactions and intersections. We would be unable to achieve such an objective if we were to remain within the constraints of the narrow psycho-social-behavioral paradigms that have dominated a majority of the sport socialization research. This alternative approach offers potential for understanding the persistence of gender difference and sex-typing that invisibly pervade so many aspects of culture as well as the socialization process. This alternative also could advance our understanding of cultural practices—the types as well as the nature of resistance to ideological challenges—particularly with respect to issues of gender (also race, ethnicity and class).

We argue for this approach because the status of sport socialization research has improved only slightly over the past 30 years, and those research efforts limited to variable factors of influence have imposed severe limitations on our understanding. In our opinion, the more promising future direction would be to expand theoretical considerations as previously described. We trust that researchers of the next generation accept our challenge and that future overviews of the sport socialization process offer the reader more than a reiteration of descriptive findings from studies that have pursued the same questions using the same methods for far too long.

References

Anastasia, A. (1981). Sex differences: Historical perspectives and methodological implications. *Developmental Review, 1*, 186–206.

Antshel, K., and Anderman, E. (2000). Social influences on sports participation during adolescence. *Journal of Research and Development in Education, 33*, 85–94.

Beal, C. (1994). *Boys and girls: The development of gender roles.* NY: McGraw-Hill.

Beitel, A., and Parke, R. D. (1990). *The role of maternal gatekeeping in father involvement.* Unpublished paper, University of Illinois, Urbana.

Block, J. (1983). Differential premises arising from differential socialization of the sexes: Some conjectures. *Child Development, 54, 1335–1354.*

Bloch, M. N. (1987). The development of sex differences in young children's activities at home: The effect of the social context. *Sex Roles, 16(5/6)*, 279–301.

Brooks-Gunn, J. (1986). The relationship of maternal beliefs about sex typing to maternal and young children's behavior. *Sex Roles, 14*, 21–35.

Brustad, R. (1993). Who will go out and play? Parental and psychological influences on children's attraction to physical activity. *Pediatric Exercise Science, 5*, 210–223.

Bureau of Census (1998). *Household and family characteristics: March 1998* (update). Report P20–515, Tables PPL-101. Unpublished tables. Washington, DC: Bureau of Census Population Division.

Bureau of Labor Statistics. (1997). *Marital and family characteristics of the labor force from the March 1997 Current Population Survey.* Unpublished statistics. Washington, DC: U.S. Department of Labor.

Burstyn, V. (1999). *The rites of men: Manhood, politics, and the culture of sport.* Toronto: University of Toronto Press.

Campbell, D., and Eaton, W. (1999). Sex differences in the activity level of infants. *Infant and Child Development, 8*, 1–17.

Carson, J., Burks, V., and Parke, R. (1993). Parent-child physical play: Determinants and consequences. In K. B. MacDonald (Ed.), *Parent-child play* (pp. 197–220). Albany, NY: SUNY Press.

Casper, L. (1997). My daddy takes care of me! Fathers as care providers. *Current Population Reports*, 50–59.

Casper, L., and O'Connell, M. (1998). Work, income, the economy, and married fathers as child care providers. *Demography, 35*, 243–250.

Chandler, T. A., Sawicki, R. F., and Stryffeler, J. M. (1981). Relationship between adolescent sexual stereotypes and working mothers. *Journal of Early Adolescence, 1*, 72–83.

Clark, J. E., and Whitall, J. (1989). Changing patterns of locomotion: From walking to skipping. In M. H. Woollacoft and A. Shumway-Cook (Eds.), *The development of posture and gait across the life span.* (pp. 129–151). Columbia, South Carolina: University of South Carolina Press.

Clarke-Stewart, K. A. (1978). And daddy makes three: The fathers' impact on mother and young child. *Child Development, 49*, 466–478.

Coakley, J. (2001). *Sport in society: Issues and controversies* (Seventh ed.). McGraw-Hill: Boston.

Coakley, J., and White, A. (1992). Making decisions: Gender and sport participation among British adolescents. *Sociology of Sport Journal, 9*, 20–35.

Colley, A., Eglinton, E., and Elliott, E. (1992). Sport participation in middle childhood: Association with styles of play and parental participation. *International Journal of Sport Psychology, 23*, 193–206.

Colley, A., Griffiths, D., Hugh, M., Landers, K. and Jaggli, N. (1996). Childhood play and adolescent leisure preferences: Associations with gender typing and the presence of siblings. *Sex Roles, 35(3–4)*, 233–245.

Curtis, J., McTeer, W., and White, P. (1999). Exploring effects of school sport experiences on sport participation in later life. *Sociology of Sport Journal, 16*, 348–365.

Dempsey, J. M., Kimiecik, J. C., and Horn, T. S. (1993). Parental influence on children's moderate to vigorous physical activity participation: An expectancy-value approach. *Pediatric Exercise Science, 5*, 151–167.

DiLorenzo, T., Stucky-Ropp, R., Vander Wal, J., and Gotham, H. (1998). Determinants of exercise among children, II: A longitudinal analysis. *Preventive Medicine, 27*, 470–477.

Eccles, J. S., and Harold, R. D. (1991). Gender differences in sport involvement: Applying the Eccles' expectancy-value model. *Journal of Applied Sport Psychology, 3*, 7–35.

Etaugh, C., and Liss, M. B. (1992). Home, school, and playroom: Training grounds for adult gender roles. *Sex Roles, 26*, 129–147.

Field, T. M. (1978). Interaction behaviors of primary versus secondary caretaker fathers, *Developmental Psychology, 14*, 183–184.

Field, T. M. (1990). *Infancy*. Cambridge, MA: Harvard University Press.

Fisher-Thompson, D. (1990). Adult gender typing of children's toys. *Sex Roles, 23*, 291–303.

Fisher-Thompson, D. (1993). Adult toy purchases for children: Factors affecting sex-typed toy selection. *Journal of Applied Developmental Psychology, 14*, 385–406.

Gervai, J., Turner, P., and Hinde, R. (1995). Gender-related behavior, attitudes, and personality in parents of young children in England and Hungary. *International Journal of Behavioral Development, 18,* 105–126.

Gottfried, A. E., Gottfried, A. W., and Bathurst, K. (1988). Maternal employment, family environment, and children's development: Infancy through the school years. In A. E. Gottfried and A. W. Gottfried (Eds.), *Maternal employment and children's development: Longitudinal research* (pp. 11–58). New York: Plenum.

Greendorfer, S. L. (in press). Sport socialization. In T. Horn (Ed.), *Advances in Sport Psychology* (2nd ed). Champaign, IL: Human Kinetics.

Greendorfer, S. L., and Ewing, M. E. (1981). Race and gender differences in children's socialization into sport. *Research Quarterly for Exercise and Sport, 52,* 301–310.

Greendorfer, S. L., Lewko, J. H., and Rosengren, K. S. (1996). Family influence in sport socialization: Sociocultural perspectives. In F. L. Smoll and R. E. Smith (Eds.), *Children and youth in sport* (pp. 89–111). Dubuque, IA: Brown and Benchmark.

Greene, A. D., Hearn, G., and Emig, C. (1996). *Developmental, ethnographic, and demographic perspectives on fatherhood: Summary of report of the conference.* Paper prepared for the NICHD Family and Child Well-Being Research Network.

Guiliano, T., Popp, K., and Knight, J. (2000). Footballs versus Barbies: Childhood play activities as predictors of sport participation by women. *Sex Roles, 42(34),* 159–181.

Haight, W., Parke, R., and Black, J. (1997). Mothers' and fathers' beliefs about and spontaneous participation in their toddlers' pretend play. *Merrill-Palmer Quarterly, 43*, 271–290.

Haywood, K. M., and Getchell, N. (2001). *Life span motor development* (3rd edition). Champaign, IL: Human Kinetics.

Hetherington, E. M., and Parke, R. D. (1993). *Child psychology: A contemporary view*. New York: McGraw-Hill.

Hipgrave, T. (1982). Childrearing by lone families. In R. Chester, P. Diggory, and M. Sutherland (Eds.), *Changing patterns of child bearing and child rearing*. London: Academic Press.

Hirvensalo, M., Lintunen, T., and Rantanen, T. (2000). The continuity of physical activity—A retrospective and prospective study among older people. *Scandinavian Journal of Medicine and Science in Sports, 10*, 37–41.

Hoffman, L. W. (1984). Maternal employment and the young child. In M. Perlmutter (Ed.), Parent-child interaction and parent-child relations in child development. *The Minnesota Symposia on Child Psychology*, (Vol. 7, pp. 223–282). Hillsdale, N.J.: Erlbaum.

Hoffman, L. W. (1986). Work, family, and the child. In M.S. Pallak and R. O. Perloff (Eds.), *Psychology and work: Productivity, change and employment* (pp. 173–220). Washington, D.C. American Psychological Association.

Hoffman, L. W. (1989). Effects of maternal employment in the two-parent family. *American Psychologist, 44,* 283–292.

Hood, J. C. (1986). The provider role: Its meaning and measurement. *Journal of Marriage and Family, 48,* 349–359.

Hoyle, R., and Leff, S. (1997). The role of parental involvement in youth sport participation and performance. *Adolescence, 32,* 233–243.

Huston, A. C. (1983). Sex-typing. In E. M. Hetherington (Ed.), P. H. Mussen (Series Ed.), *Handbook of child psychology, Vol 4. Socialization, personality, and social development* (pp. 387–468). New York: John Wiley.

Huston, A. C. and Alvarez, M. M. (1990). The socialization context of gender role development in early adolescence. In R. Montemayor, G. R. Adams, and T. P. Gullotta (Eds.), *From childhood to adolescence: A transitional period?* (pp. 156–179). London: Sage Publications.

Ignico, A. (1990). The influence of gender-role perception on activity preferences of children. *Play and Culture, 3,* 302–310.

Jambor, E. (1999). Parents as children's socializing agents in youth soccer. *Journal of Sport Behavior, 22,* 350–359.

Karraker, K., Vogel, D., and Lake, M. (1995). Parents' gender-stereotyped perceptions of newborns: The eye of the beholder revisited. *Sex Roles, 33(9–10),* 687–701.

Kirshnit, C. E., Ham, M., and Richards, M. H. (1989). The sporting life: Athletic activities during early adolescence. *Journal of Youth and Adolescence, 18(6),* 601–615.

Lamb, M. (1997). *The role of father in child development.* New York: Wiley.

Langlois, J. H., and Downs, A. C. (1980). Mothers, fathers, and peers as socialization agents of gender-typed play behaviors in young children. *Child Development, 51,* 1237–1247.

Langley, D., and Knight, S. (1999). Continuity in sport participation as an adaptive strategy in the aging process: A lifespan narrative. *Journal of Aging and Physical Activity, 7,* 32–54.

Leaper, C. (2000). Gender, affiliation, assertion and the interactive context of parent-child play. *Developmental Psychology, 36,* 381–393.

Lenskyj, H. (1999). Women, sport and sexualities: Breaking the silences. In P. White and K. Young (Eds.), *Sport and gender in Canada* (pp. 170–181). Toronto: Women's Press.

Levine, J. A. (1976). *And who will raise the children? New options for fathers (and mothers).* Philadelphia: Lippincott.

Lewis, T., and Phillipsen, L. (1998). Interactions on an elementary school playground: Variations by age, gender, race, group size and playground area. *Child Study Journal, 28*, 309–320.

Lewko, J. H. and Greendorfer, S. L.(1978). Family influence and sex differences in children's socialization into sport: A review. In D. M. Landers and R. W. Christina (Eds.) *Psychology of motor behavior and sport—1977,* (pp. 434–447). Champaign, IL: Human Kinetics Publishers.

Lewko, J. H. and Greendorfer, S. L.(1982). Family influence and sex differences in children's socialization into sport: A review. In F. L. Smoll, R. A. Magill and M. J. Ash (Eds.), *Children in sport* (2nd ed.), (pp. 279–293). Champaign, IL: Human Kinetics.

Lewko, J. H., and Greendorfer, S. L. (1988). Family influences in sport socialization of children and adolescents. In F. L. Smoll, R. A. Magill, and M. J. Ash (Eds.), *Children in Sport* (3rd ed.), (pp. 287–300). Champaign, IL: Human Kinetics.

Lytton, H., and Romney, M. (1991). Parents' sex-related differential socialization of boys and girls: a meta-analysis. *Psychological Bulletin, 109*, 267–296.

MacDonald, K., and Parke, R. (1984). Bridging the gap: Parent-child play interactions and peer competence. *Child Development, 55,* 1265–1277.

Marsiglio, W., Day, R., Braver, S., Evans, J., Lamb, M., and Peters, E. (1998). Report on the working group on conceptualizing male parenting. In Federal Interagency Forum on Child and Family Statistics, *Nurturing fatherhood: Improving data and research on male fertility, family formation and fatherhood* (pp. 101–174). Washington, DC: US Government Printing Office.

McBride-Chang, C., and Jacklin, C. N. (1993). Early play arousal, sex-typed play, and activity level as precursors to later rough-and-tumble play. *Early Education and Development*, 99–108.

McGuffey, C., and Rich, B. (1999). Playing in the gender transgression zone: Race, class and hegemonic masculinity in middle childhood. *Gender and Society, 13*, 608–627.

Mead, G. H. (1934). *Mind, self, and society.* Chicago.

Messner, M. (1996). Studying up on sex. *Sociology of Sport Journal, 13*, 221–237.

Messner, M., Hunt, D., and Dunbar, M. (1999). *Boys to men: Sports media messages about masculinity*, Oakland, CA: Children Now.

Miller, J., and Levy, G. (1996). Gender role conflict, gender-typed characteristics, self-concepts, and sport socialization in female athletes and nonathletes. *Sex Roles, 35 (1–2),* 111–122.

Moore, L. L., Lombardi, D. A., White, M. J., Campbell, J. L., Oliveria, S. A., and Ellison, R. C. (1991). Influence of parents' physical activity levels on activity levels of young children. *The Journal* of *Pediatrics, 118(2)*, 215–219.

Parke, R. D. (1990). In search of fathers: A narrative of an empirical journey. In I. Sigel and G. Brody (Eds.), *Methods of family research* (Vol. 1, pp. 153–188). Hillsdale, NJ: Erlbaum.

Pellett, T., and Ignico, A. (1993). Relationship between children's and parents' stereotyping of physical activities. *Perceptual and Motor Skills, 77 (3 Pt 2)*, 1283–1289.

Pennell, G. (1999). Doing gender with Santa: Gender-typing in children's toy preferences. *Dissertation Abstracts International: Section B: the Science and Engineering, Vol 59(8–B)*, 4541.

Piaget, J. (1965). *The moral judgment of the child.* New York: The Free Press. Pleck, E. H., and Pleck, J. H., (1997). Fatherhood ideals in the United States: Historical dimensions. In M. E. Lamb (Ed.), *The role of the father in child development* (3rd edition, pp. 33–48). New York: Wiley.

Pomerleau, A., Bolduc, D., Malcuit, G., and Cossette, L. (1990). Pink or blue: Environmental gender stereotypes in the first two years of life. *Sex Roles, 22*, 359–367.

Posner, J., and Vandell, D. (1999). After school activities and the development of low-income urban children: A longitudinal study. *Developmental Psychology, 35*, 868–879.

Radin, N. (1982). Primary-caregiving and role sharing fathers. In M. Lamb (Ed.), *Nontraditional families: Parenting and child development* (pp. 173–204). Hillsdale, NJ: Lawrence Erlbaum.

Radin, N., and Sagi, A. (1982) Childrearing fathers in intact families in Israel and the U.S.A. *Merrill-Palmer Quarterly, 28*, 111–136.

Raymore, L., Barber, B., Eccles, J., and Godbey, G. (1999). Leisure behavior pattern stability during the transition from adolescence to young adulthood. *Journal of Youth and Adolescence, 28*, 79–103.

Rekers, G. A, Sanders, J. A., Rasbury, W. C., Strauss, C. C., and Morey, S. M. (1988). Differentiation of adolescent activity participation. *Journal of Genetic Psychology, 150(3)*, 323–335.

Rheinghold, H. L., and Cook, K. V. (1975). The content of boys' and girls' rooms as an index of parent behavior. *Child Development, 46*, 459–463.

Roberts, J. M., and Sutton-Smith, B. (1962). Child training and game involvement. *Ethnology, 1*, 166–185.

Rubin, J. Z., Provenzano, F. J., and Luria, A. (1974). The eye of the beholder: Parent's views on the sex of newborns. *American Journal of Orthopsychiatry, 43*, 720–731.

Russell, G. (1982). Shared-caregiving families: An Australian study in M. E. Lamb (Ed.), *Nontraditional families: Parenting and child development.* Hillsdale, NJ: Erlbaum.

Russell, G. (1983). *The changing roles of fathers?* St. Lucia, Queensland: University of Queensland Press.

Sagi, A. (1982). Antecedents and consequences of various degrees of paternal involvement in child rearing: the Israeli project, In M. E. Lamb (Ed.), *Nontraditional families: Parenting and child development*, Hillsdale, NJ: Erlbaum.

Servin, A., Bohlin, G., and Berlin, L. (1999). Sex differences in 1-, 3-, and 5-year olds' toy-choice in a structured play-session. *Scandinavian Journal of Psychology, 40*, 43–48.

Schneider, W. (1993). The longitudinal study of motor development: methodological issues. In A. F. Kalverboer, B. Hopkins, and R. Geuze (Eds.), *Motor development in early and later childhood: longitudinal approaches*, (pp. 325–328). Cambridge: Cambridge University press.

Sovik, N. (1993). Development of children's writing performance: some educational implications. In A. F. Kalverboer, B. Hopkins, and R. Geuze (Eds.). *Motor development in early and later childhood: longitudinal approaches*, pp. 243–244. Cambridge: Cambridge University press.

Stern, M., and Karraker, K. H. (1989). Sex stereotyping of infants: A review of gender labeling studies. *Sex Roles, 20*, 501–522.

Tamis-LeMonda, C., and Cabrera, N. (1999). Perspectives on father involvement: Research and policy. *Social Policy Report, 13*, Society for Research in Child Development.

Telama, R., and Yang, X. (2000). Decline of physical activity from youth to young adulthood in Finland. *Medicine and Science in Sports and Exercise 32*, 1617–1622.

Theberge, N. (2000). *Higher goals: Women's ice hockey and the politics of gender*. Albany, NY: SUNY Press.

Thomas, J. R. and French, K. E. (1985). Gender differences across age in motor performance: A meta-analysis. *Psychological Bulletin, 98*, 260–282.

Turner, P., and Gervai, J. (1995). A multi-dimensional study of gender typing in preschool children and their parents: Personality, attitudes, preferences, behavior and cultural differences. *Developmental Psychology, 31*, 759–772.

Vilhjalmsson, R., and Thorlindsson, T. (1998). Factors related to physical activity: A study of adolescents. *Social Science and Medicine, 47*, 665–675.

Whitson, D. (1984). Sport and hegemony: On the construction of the dominant culture. *Sport Sociology Journal, 1*, 64–78.

Whitson, D. (1990). Sport in the social construction of masculinity. In M.A. Messner and D. F. Sabo (Eds.), *Sport, men and the gender order* (pp. 19–29). Champaign, IL: Human Kinetics.

Parental and Peer Influence on Children's Psychosocial Development Through Sport

Robert J. Brustad, University of Northern Colorado
Julie A. Partridge, University of Northern Colorado

Millions of youngsters participate in organized sport programs each year. Many of these young participants are extensively involved in sport during the childhood and adolescent years, and have opportunities to participate nearly year-round in competitive leagues and sport camps. The widespread involvement of youngsters in sport, in combination with the fairly intensive nature of this involvement for some, has raised long-standing concerns about the effects of sport involvement on developmental outcomes for children (e.g., Martens, 1978; Wiggins, this volume).

Concern about the developmental outcomes of sport participation for youngsters is fueled further by issues surrounding parental involvement in children's sport. Casual observation makes it evident that parents are heavily involved in youth sport roles as coaches, spectators, and administrators. The impact of this involvement on children's psychosocial development has been an issue that has generated a growing amount of research. More recently, there has been increasing attention devoted to the influence of peers in sport contexts. This research has enabled us to gain a broader, and more balanced, perspective on social influence in youth sport. The role of both parents and peers takes on added importance given evidence that indicates that North American youngsters appear to be starting their sport participation at increasingly earlier ages (Ewing and Seefeldt, 1996), and thus at earlier phases of their psychological and social development.

Our concern in this chapter will be for the influence of parents and peers on children's psychological, emotional, and social development. Development refers to the process of qualitative change in functioning that occurs as a consequence of maturation and experience. With regard to psychological development, primary attention will be devoted to social forms of influence upon the formation and refinement of children's self-concept through sport involvement. Concerns about emotional development will center upon the affective experiences that children may experience in sport, specifically stress and anxiety outcomes, enjoyment experiences, and tendencies toward burnout. In relation to social developmental concerns, our focus will be upon children's peer relations, particularly peer acceptance and rejection outcomes, friendship benefits, and peer victimization experiences. An additional, highly important area of study relates to the effects of organized sport participation on children's moral and ethical development; however, since this topic is directly addressed in the chapter by Shields, Bredemeier, and Power, we will not review this issue further here.

Parents and peers each have important roles in shaping developmental outcomes for young sport participants. However, it should be mentioned at the outset of this discussion that the nature and extent of each form of social influence varies in relation to the age and developmental status of the youngster. Although parents can strongly influence their child's psychosocial development throughout childhood and adolescence, this influence is strongest during early and middle childhood, lessens during later childhood and then is generally supplanted by peer forms of influence during adolescence. Parental influence on children's psychological development during earlier developmental phases is quite strong for at least three reasons. First, a relatively large proportion of the child's time during early childhood is spent within the context of the family. Second, prior to the age of about 8 years, children have generally not developed the necessary social skills, particularly role-taking abilities, to establish a solid network of social relations outside the family (Selman, 1976). Third, as a consequence of their cognitive developmental status, children younger than 8 years of age typically rely heavily on the feedback of parents and other adults in assessing personal competency (Horn and Hasbrook, 1986, 1987; Horn and Weiss, 1991; Stipek and McIver, 1989). Consequently, children's early sport interest, their initial participatory involvement, and many of the psychological outcomes of this involvement are strongly linked to parenting practices (Brustad, 1992; Brustad, Babkes, and Smith, 2001).

With age, children spend relatively more time in the company of their peers and peer forms of influence become increasingly influential in shaping children's psychosocial development. At about eight years of age, children begin to place increasing importance on peer informational sources, such as social comparison information and peer feedback, to form judgments about their capacities across various areas of achievement (Horn and Hasbrook, 1987; Horn and Weiss, 1991; Ruble, 1983). Furthermore, with increasing maturity, youngsters are able to use socially-based information more effectively and thus are able to make more accurate appraisals of their capacities than are younger children (Ruble, 1983; Veroff, 1969). To the extent that sport ability and participation are highly valued within one's peer group, peers will have even greater influence upon the psychological and social consequences of involvement

During later childhood and early adolescence, two salient social developmental goals emerge. On the one hand, youngsters desire to establish favorable social connections and to feel a strong sense of connectedness or belonging to a group. On the other hand, there is a strong desire toward individuation, or the need to be recognized as a unique individual with particular values and characteristics that distinguish one from others (Damon, 1983; Ruble and Goodnow, 1998). The simultaneous concern for individuality and social acceptance constitute important dimensions of psychosocial development during later childhood and adolescence. Issues related to peer influence in sport will be further discussed but we first turn our attention to understanding parental forms of influence.

Parental Influences on Children's Psychosocial Development

This section focuses on parental influences, with particular attention devoted to assessing the role of parents in shaping children's self-concept and affective experiences in sport.

Conceptual Approaches to Understanding Parental Influence

Given parents' extensive involvement in the organized sport experiences of their children, we would certainly anticipate that there would be consequences of this involvement upon children's participatory, motivational, and psychosocial outcomes in sport. Research conducted to date clearly supports this belief and will be discussed in much more detail later in the chapter. However, understanding *how* parents are likely to exert an influence is particularly important to gaining an appreciation of parental roles in sport and for directing our attention to the most appropriate intervention strategies.

Recent theoretical approaches to the understanding of parental socialization influence on children's sport involvement have relied upon multidimensional approaches that address the behavior, beliefs, and perceptions of both parents and their children. The two theoretical approaches that have been most commonly used in the youth sport literature are Harter's (1978, 1981) competence motivation theory and Eccles' expectancy-value model (Eccles and Harold, 1991; Eccles, Wigfield, and Schiefele, 1998). Each of these models is quite appropriate for our purposes because each addresses the dynamic interaction between parents and children in socialization contexts. Furthermore, each places primary interest on the psychological dimensions of the socialization experience, including beliefs, values, and perceptions that are integral to the psychosocial context of children's achievement behavior.

Harter's model starts with the fundamental premise that children have an inherent desire to feel competent in various realms of achievement. In order to experience feelings of competence, children will engage in mastery efforts in various domains of achievement. As children initiate efforts toward mastery, parental feedback and reinforcement become critical forms of socialization influence. If parents respond to children's independent mastery efforts with approval and encouragement, this will enhance children's beliefs about the importance of self-initiated efforts and result in the internalization of an intrinsic reward system. Furthermore, according to Harter, children will experience a more favorable sense of competence, a stronger internal sense of control, and have more enjoyment and less anxiety while engaged in efforts toward mastery. Conversely, children who fail to receive encouragement from their parents for their independent mastery efforts, or who only receive parental support when they achieve successful outcomes, are more likely to become dependent upon external forms of approval on achievement tasks. In turn, they will tend to have more external control perceptions and lower perceived competence and be more likely to have unfavorable affective experiences (higher anxiety, lower enjoyment) in similar achievement contexts. This profile will logically contribute to a lessened participatory interest on similar types of tasks.

From a developmental standpoint, Harter's model has been important because it focuses attention on the role of parental socialization processes upon the developmental course of youngsters' perceptions of competence and control, as well as upon their intrinsic or extrinsic motivational orientations. Harter's conceptual approach has been used in the sport domain to understand children's participatory involvement patterns (Klint and Weiss, 1987), the affective characteristics of children's sport participation (Brustad, 1988; Brustad and Weiss, 1987) and children's self-perceptions in sport (Weiss, Ebbeck, and Horn, 1997; Williams, 1994), among other topics. Relevant research that has addressed parental influence upon psychosocial outcomes for children in sport will be addressed later.

Eccles' expectancy-value socialization model (Eccles, 1998; Eccles and Harold, 1991) represents a second theoretical perspective from which to understand the influence of parents upon children's psychosocial outcomes in sport. Eccles' theory is specifically directed toward understanding parental influence upon children's involvement in various achievement areas in relation to the expectancies and values that parents maintain regarding their child's involvement. Central to the model are the constructs of parental value, which refers to parents' beliefs about the relative importance of various domains of achievement (e.g., sport, music, mathematics) and parental expectancies, which are parents' beliefs about children's abilities, interests, and natural aptitudes in varying achievement areas. In accordance with parental value orientations, parents are believed to provide greater exposure and more extensive opportunities for their children in those domains that the parents highly value. From this perspective, parents who highly value sport participation will likely introduce their child to sport at an earlier age, will provide more encouragement during the child's initial engagement, will make available the necessary equipment, and will facilitate the child's access for current and future involvement. In such circumstances, the child has a "head start" toward success in this area.

Whereas the value construct represents a general personal orientation toward the perceived merits of particular achievement domains, the construct of parental expectancy refers to the specific beliefs that parents hold about the likelihood that a child will experience success in a given domain of achievement, such as sport. According to Eccles' perspective, parents evaluate each child's interests and abilities in relation to their perceptions of the likelihood that the child will attain success in particular achievement areas. In the interest of enabling their child to experience success, parents will provide the youngster with greater encouragement in some domains than in others. Furthermore, parents have an important role in interpreting achievement-related information for the child. For example, under circumstances of success by high-expectancy children, the parent may communicate that this outcome was expected because of the child's natural ability whereas, given less successful outcomes, the parent may communicate that the result was attributable to a lack of effort. In either case, the parental feedback provided is likely to foster the child's belief that they have natural aptitude in this area of achievement. Parental expectancies are communicated in a variety of manners and are also specific to each child, which can help to explain individual differences in children's interests within the same family. It should be noted that a fundamental component of Eccles' model relates to potential gender-related effects. Parents may value certain domains more for boys or for girls (e.g., sport, mathematics) and they may hold stereotypical views about boys' and girls' natural interests and abilities across various domains of achievement.

In Eccles' theory, parental values and expectancies have a profound socialization influence in that parental beliefs are theorized to shape children's own cognitions and self-perceptions. Eccles proposes that children typically internalize the achievement-related beliefs of their parents and their subsequent appraisal of achievement situations, and motivational characteristics in these contexts, are affected by personally-held values and expectations. Thus, if children come to value an activity, and anticipate that they will have success at the activity, they are more likely to participate in the activity, will hold more favorable self-perceptions of ability, will be more goal-directed, will have more beneficial attributional processes, and will persist longer in the activity than would a child with a less favorable belief system. Eccles' theory represents a comprehensive theoretical framework from which to understand the influence of parental socialization patterns upon psychological and motivational outcomes for children in sport. Having addressed major theoretical perspectives on parental socialization influence on the psychological dimensions of children's sport participation, attention will be directed toward two specific areas of study: children's self-concept development and the affective characteristics of children's sport experiences.

Parental Influences on Children's Self-Concept Development

The formation and refinement of the self-concept is an important dimension of psychological development during childhood and adolescence. A growing body of research in developmental psychology and education has identified self-concept variables, particularly perceived competence and perceived control, as key influences upon children's achievement behaviors (e.g., Harter, 1999; Skinner, 1995; Schunk,

1991). Furthermore, self-perceptions such as perceived competence and self-efficacy have a fundamental role in the most prominent motivational theories in sport (Bandura, 1986; Harter, 1978; Nicholls, 1984). Consequently, understanding the processes under which children form beliefs about themselves and their personal capacities is an essential area of pursuit for youth sport researchers.

Theoreticians and researchers (Fox, 1997; Harter, 1999; Marsh and Peart, 1988) consider the self-concept to have a multidimensional structure. Multidimensionality refers to the idea that the overall self-concept is comprised of a number of distinct, domain-specific self-perceptions. Self-perceptions of competence (one's domain-specific perceptions of ability) have been the most widely studied self-perception characteristic in sport. Much less research interest has been devoted to understanding children's perceptions of control, or the amount of control or influence that one believes they possess over outcomes in a particular achievement domain.

With regard to perceived competence, it is important to note that the number and nature of competence dimensions varies in accordance with the developmental status of the child (Harter, 1983, 1999). For example, during the middle to late childhood years, children generally differentiate among five areas of self-evaluation relative to scholastic competence, athletic competence, peer acceptance, physical appearance, and behavioral conduct. During adolescence, youngsters maintain these five dimensions and generally develop additional categories of self-appraisal relative to job competence, capacity for close friendships, and ability in romantic relationships (Harter, 1999). At younger ages, children do not necessarily have very accurate self-perceptions of ability. However, children become increasingly capable of assessing their abilities with age and development (Harter, 1983, 1999; Horn and Harris, this volume). During the middle childhood years, children also begin to develop an overall sense of self-worth, or self-esteem, that is representative of global feelings of worth or value as a person.

Research also indicates that children ascribe unequal importance to the various dimensions of the self and self-evaluations on those dimensions that are most important to the youngster have the greatest impact on the person's overall self-concept (Harter, 1998). Gender differences may also exist in this regard as research exists to suggest that athletic ability is more highly valued by males than by females during later childhood and adolescence (Adler, Kless, and Adler, 1992; Chase and Dummer, 1992).

In relation to parental socialization influence, social psychological theory has long held that the self-concept is shaped through social interaction (Cooley, 1902/1956; Mead, 1934). Cooley originally proposed the image of the "looking glass self" through which individuals come to adopt views of themselves as they are reflected through the appraisals and behaviors of significant others. The image of the "looking glass self" is useful for this discussion of self-concept development because it highlights the role of social influence in shaping children's self-concepts.

There is no doubt that significant others have a major influence in shaping the self-evaluations of young sport participants because the public nature of sport provides extensive opportunities for social evaluation and immediate feedback from parents and peers (Scanlan, this volume). As a consequence of children's reliance on adult sources of information in judging competence during early and middle childhood, in combination with parents' typically high levels of involvement in their children's athletic competitions, we would anticipate that parental behaviors and feedback significantly impact children's self-concept development, particularly during the initial years of sport participation.

Research in the athletic domain indicates that children are likely to adopt their parents' appraisals of their physical ability and to hold similar expectations for their own future achievement. For instance, Felson and Reed (1986) found a significant relationship between parental judgments of their child's physical abilities and the child's self-appraisals of ability, even when actual levels of physical ability were statistically controlled. Similarly, McCullagh, Matzkanin, Shaw, and Maldonado (1993) found a correspondence between parent and child appraisals of the child's competence.

From their theoretically-based perspective, Eccles and Harold (1991) conducted a three-year longitudinal study of the relationship between parental beliefs and children's self-perceptions and activity choices across various domains, including sport. Specifically, the researchers assessed parental perceptions of their child's competence (expectancy) and parental beliefs about the importance and usefulness of each activity area (value). Their findings indicated that parental expectancies and values were significant predictors of children's own competence perceptions and achievement-related value beliefs which, in turn, helped to explain why children chose to participate in the free-choice activities in which they engaged. In additional tests of Eccles' theory, Brustad (1993, 1996) found that children's perceptions of physical competence were significantly related to the amount of parental encouragement that they received to be physically active. These findings were consistent with Eccles' theoretical belief that parents more strongly encourage their child to participate in those domains in which the parents hold more favorable beliefs about the child's competency (and in domains of achievement which parents more highly value) and that children develop more favorable self-perceptions in those areas in which they receive greater encouragement and more opportunities. In their study of youth soccer participants, Green and Chalip (1997) also found that high parental expectation levels for their child in sport were significantly related to higher levels of perceived soccer competence by the child.

Parental reinforcement patterns and affective responses to children's sport involvement may constitute additional vehicles through which parents convey important competence-related information to children. Research by Scanlan and Lewthwaite (1984) revealed that young wrestlers who perceived greater parental (and coach) satisfaction with their performance had higher personal expectations for their future performance. In a more recent study, Babkes and Weiss (1999) found that youth soccer players who perceived that their parents held more favorable beliefs about their ability, and who reported that they received a greater frequency of positive and contingent responses from their parents regarding their athletic performance, had more favorable perceptions of soccer competence, as well as higher levels of intrinsic motivation, than did their peers who reported less favorable interactions with their parents in the sport context. These sport-related findings are strengthened by a similar pattern of findings in academic settings (e.g., Parsons, Adler, and Kaczala, 1982; Phillips, 1987). For example, Phillips (1987) found that highly academically competent children (as assessed through objective achievement tests) who underestimated their ability generally had parents who also held low perceptions of the child's ability.

The nature and extent of parental influence upon children's self-perceptions should vary substantially according to developmental status since children utilize parental evaluation sources much more extensively during childhood than during adolescence. Furthermore, the nature of parental influence likely changes with the child's development as parental achievement expectations also change in relation to the age of the child. For example, Felson (1990) found in the academic context that parental achievement standards tend to become more demanding as children move from childhood into adolescence. Felson commented that this reflected a general tendency for parents to move from an orientation toward "unconditional, positive regard" (citing Rogers, 1951) during the childhood years to a more demanding, achievement-related orientation as children age. Furthermore, mothers and fathers may have unequal forms of influence in relation to the child's stage of development. Specifically, Felson found that mothers had a stronger influence upon children's self-appraisals of ability during the elementary school years but that fathers' appraisals became more influential during the middle school years. Thus, understanding the specifics of how children's self-perceptions of competence are shaped by parents should include a consideration of the developmental status of the child, changes in achievement expectation standards of parents in relation to the age of the child, and the relative roles of mothers and fathers in the process.

Whereas the study of parental influence upon children's self-perceptions of competence has received extensive attention in the youth sport literature, research on how parents influence children's sport-related control perceptions and children's self-esteem development has received much less attention. With regard to perceptions of control, academic research (Skinner, 1995; Skinner, Wellborn, and Connell, 1990) has found that parenting practices influence children's perceptions of control in academic settings and, in turn, their subsequent motivational and achievement outcomes. In sport, interest on this topic has not been extensive and research has been complicated by measurement problems (Brustad, 1998). Clearly, more research is needed to understand parental socialization influence upon children's perceptions of control.

Parental influence on children's self-esteem development through sport is also a worthy topic for investigation, but one that has yet to receive much research attention. In part, this is as expected, since self-esteem is a construct representing an individual's global sense of worth or value as a person, and thus is a much broader construct than is perceived competence. Harter's (1988) research indicates that high self-esteem children can be distinguished from low self-esteem children on the basis of the support they receive from significant others. Specifically, high self-esteem children report that parents (and peers) "accept them, support them, and hold them in high regard" (p. 69). In sport, parents have numerous opportunities to demonstrate acceptance and to provide or withhold support, thereby influencing children's self-esteem development. Therefore, there is potential benefit in examining parental influences on children's self-esteem development as it is affected by athletic involvement, particularly since research indicates that other adults, namely coaches, have a considerable effect on young athletes' self-perceptions and self-esteem characteristics (Black and Weiss, 1992; Smith, Smoll, and Curtis, 1979).

Parental Influence on Affective Outcomes for Children in Sport

One of the major areas for study in children's sport has been focused on understanding the effects of competitive sport involvement upon emotional outcomes for young participants. Given the extensive involvement of parents in youth sport, a large proportion of this research has assessed parental roles and forms of influence. Initially, concern was directed primarily toward identifying the causes and consequences of negative affective experiences for youngsters in sport, particularly stress and anxiety outcomes. However, in the evolution of youth sport research, attention to these possible negative outcomes has been counterbalanced by more recent interest on the contributors to, and correlates of, positive emotional experiences such as enjoyment outcomes for youth sport participants (Babkes and Weiss, 1999; Leff and Hoyle, 1995). The importance of understanding children's emotional responses to sport participation is underscored by the role of affect in prominent theoretical perspectives on motivation in sport (e.g., Harter, 1978, 1981; Scanlan and Simons, 1992).

Initial efforts at understanding the effects of sport participation on children and adolescents frequently resulted in the conclusion that organized sport involvement was highly stressful for many youngsters (Brower, 1978; Smilkstein, 1980) and that the competitive focus of youth sport programs was responsible for many youngsters dropping out of sport (Orlick 1974). However, subsequent research has painted a somewhat different picture regarding the nature and effects of children's emotional experiences in sport. As Passer (1988) and Smith, Smoll, and Passer (this volume) have argued, sport participation is not inherently stressful for all youngsters, but substantial individual differences appear to exist with regard to children's emotional responses to sport involvement. Parenting practices are widely considered to be important determinants of both positive and negative emotional consequences in sport.

A body of research has been conducted on the correlates of competitive state and trait anxiety and the nature of parental influence upon these outcomes. Competitive state anxiety represents a transitory and situation-specific form of anxiety, whereas competitive trait anxiety is conceptualized as the general tendency to view competition as threatening and to respond with correspondingly higher levels of state anxiety (Martens, 1977). Studies have found a relationship between parenting practices and children's precompetition state anxiety levels. In their research with young wrestlers, Scanlan and Lewthwaite (1984) found that youngsters who reported higher levels of parental pressure and who worried more frequently about meeting parental (and coach) expectations experienced higher state anxiety prior to competiton. Similarly, Gould, Eklund, Petlichkoff, Peterson, and Bump (1991) found that prematch state anxiety for youth wrestlers was significantly related to parental pressure to wrestle. Finally, in their study of young male gymnasts, Weiss, Weise, and Klint (1989) found that the top two precompetition worries for these youngsters were about "what my parents will think" and "letting my parents down." Thus, this line of research indicates that children who experience higher levels of precompetition anxiety do so, at least in part, because of concerns about how their performance outcomes will be evaluated by their parents.

Parenting practices have similarly been linked to competitive trait anxiety (CTA) levels for young athletes engaged in sport. Since competitive trait anxiety represents a general personal tendency to appraise competitive situations as threatening, high-CTA children are of particular concern because they may experience enduring stress throughout their sport participation and, consequently, may be more likely to discontinue sport because of less favorable emotional experiences in this context. Researchers have found that high-CTA children are characterized, in part, by the tendency to worry more frequently about receiving negative evaluations from others (Brustad, 1988: Lewthwaite and Scanlan, 1989; Passer, 1983). These research findings on anxiety in youth sport parallel those in the educational literature that also indicate that concern about negative evaluation from parents is a major source of test anxiety for youngsters (Wigfield and Eccles, 1990).

Whereas initial interest on affective outcomes for children in sport centered primarily on understanding sources of state and trait anxiety, more recent interest has been directed to the topic of burnout. Sport burnout has been conceptualized as a negative, long-term emotional state characterized by physical and emotional exhaustion and a reduced sense of personal accomplishment (Raedeke, 1997). Understanding the causes and consequences of sport burnout takes on added importance given increasing concerns about the quantity and intensity of some youngsters' sport participation, as well as concerns about tendencies toward increasing sport specialization in North American youth sport (Wiersma, 2000).

Coakley (1992) found that burnout among adolescent athletes was most common among highly accomplished youngsters whose parents invested considerable time and resources in their child's sport. Moreover, these young athletes typically felt that they had little input into the decisions that shaped their sport participation and this lack of a sense of personal control likely diminished their interest in maintaining involvement. Raedeke (1997) studied sport burnout among adolescent swimmers and hypothesized that burnout would most commonly occur when feelings of entrapment in the athletic role outweighed feelings of attraction to the sport. In general, these expectations were supported as swimmers who reported stronger feelings of role entrapment had higher burnout levels than those who reported greater sport attraction.

The experience of burnout is much more likely to occur during adolescence, as opposed to childhood, as the intensity and time demands of sport involvement increase. Developmental influences can also contribute to the burnout experience. Thoits (1983) described the tendency for adolescents to acknowledge a greater complexity to their sense of self as they move through the adolescent developmental phase. As Coakley (1992) argued, a narrow or constricted adolescent identity that can emanate from prolonged and intense sport involvement runs contrary to this adolescent developmental tendency toward increasing differentiation and complexity of the self-concept and can foster a negative emotional state. Further empirical work is needed on the causes of sport burnout in young athletes but this is clearly an important issue for youth sport researchers that should be addressed in relation to both parental and developmental forms of influence.

Increasing research attention has been devoted to understanding the nature of parental influence upon favorable affective outcomes for youngsters in sport. This line of investigation has focused primarily upon youngsters' enjoyment experiences in sport. Enjoyment has typically been operationalized as the amount of fun youngsters experience in the sport over the course of the season. In their study of young male wrestlers, Scanlan and Lewthwaite (1986) found that high levels of enjoyment were predicted by high parental satisfaction with performance, favorable adult interactions and involvement patterns, and a low frequency of negative maternal interactions regarding participation. Similarly, Brustad (1988) found that high enjoyment was associated with low perceived parental pressure for young male and female basketball players. Interestingly, team win-loss records and actual levels of ability (as estimated by each player's coach) were not related to these youngsters' enjoyment experiences in this study. Former elite figure skaters reported that bringing pleasure or pride to their family was an important dimension of their sport enjoyment (Scanlan, Stein, and Ravizza, 1989). In research conducted with adolescent Norwegian soccer players, Ommundsen and Vaglum (1991) found that the positive emotional involvement of parents (and coaches) was significantly related to enjoyment for these young athletes. Leff and Hoyle (1995) reported that children's perceptions of parental support, which was described as parental facilitation of children's involvement in athletics, was significantly related to higher levels of enjoyment for both male and female tennis players. Research by Babkes and Weiss (1999) found that talented youth soccer players reported higher levels of enjoyment when they perceived that their fathers were involved in their sport but did not exert high levels of pressure upon them.

A relatively clear picture emerges with regard to the influence of parents upon children's emotional experiences in sport. In general, the research suggests that parental involvement *per se* is neither a positive nor a negative influence in itself. However, the nature of this involvement can have a profound effect upon youngsters' emotional experiences. When children perceive that their parents provide appropriate encouragement and are facilitative of their sport involvement, it is much more likely that the child will experience enjoyment, as opposed to anxiety. Conversely, when young athletes are concerned about incurring negative evaluations following their performance, feel "pressured" by their parents to participate and do well in sport, and feel that adults provide them with little input or control over the decisions that shape their sport experiences, it is much more likely that the youngster will experience anxiety or burnout during the experience. Parental influence is certainly important in this regard and the nature of this influence also needs to be considered in relation to youngsters' developmental status.

Peer Influences on Children's Psychosocial Development

The knowledge base on peer influence on children's psychological and social development through sport has grown considerably in recent years. Historically, research on peers has not received the same level of attention as has research focused on parental and coach influence. Recently, however, there has been much greater recognition that peers, and not just adults, are essential contributors to the youth sport environment and are highly influential in shaping psychological and social outcomes for children in sport contexts. Furthermore, youth sport researchers have increasingly incorporated theoretical perspectives and empirical research findings on peer influence from other areas of study, most notably developmental and educational psychology, and have used knowledge and theory to chart an appropriate course for research in sport.

Knowledge about the role of peers in sport is particularly important given that peer influence can extend across a variety of social and psychological dimensions. We will discuss peer influence in relation to peer acceptance and rejection outcomes, friendship experiences, and peer victimization consequences. In addition, we will discuss peer influence in relation to children's self-concept development. For at least three reasons, the peer group should constitute an important form of influence in sport contexts. First, sport achievement is highly valued by children and adolescents in our culture (Chase and Dummer, 1992) and youngsters should be affected both psychologically and socially by their involvement in the sport setting. Second, the participation motivation research clearly indicates that affiliation with others and the development of positive social relations are major motives underlying children's interest in sport involvement and the quality of their experiences while engaged (Weiss and Petlichkoff, 1989). Third, the peak years of sport involvement for youngsters coincide with the developmentally-related tendency for youngsters to rely on peer informational sources in assessing personal competence (Horn and Hasbrook, 1986, 1987; Veroff, 1969; Horn and Weiss, 1991). For this reason, the reflected appraisals of peers are particularly instrumental in shaping children's self-perceptions in sport. We will turn our attention first to social developmental outcomes for children in sport; specifically, peer acceptance or rejection, the benefits of friendships, and peer victimization effects and, subsequently, address self-concept development.

Peer Acceptance and Rejection

Peer acceptance is defined as one's status within, or liking by, the peer group (Bukowski and Hoza, 1989). Conversely, an absence of status or liking is considered to constitute peer rejection. Acceptance or rejection is integral to the psychological and social development of children because of its impact on children's social interaction opportunities, their ability to make friends, the favorability of their self-concepts, and their affective reactions to achievement outcomes in sport contexts (Brustad, et al., 2001; Smith, 1999). For children who are repeatedly picked last to participate in playground "pick-up" games, the message that may be relayed (either explicitly or implicitly) is that these children have low ability levels, or some other undesirable characteristic that makes other children unwilling to include them. If this message is given to a child regarding some activity that is perceived to be of low importance within the peer group, the child may experience little negative reaction to such an evaluation. However, if the child receives negative feedback regarding their abilities in a high status activity, this can have much more detrimental effects upon the child's psychological and social development (Smith, 1999).

Although there are many achievement domains through which children and adolescents can gain peer acceptance via achievement and success, sport is one of the most important areas for children to possess ability. The relationship between physical ability and peer acceptance has been one of the more popular topics in peer sport research and this line of research supports the hypothesized relationship between physical prowess and status attainment within the peer group. In their study of 8- to 13-year-old males and females enrolled in a summer sport program, Weiss and Duncan (1992) found that children who were higher in both actual and perceived physical competence had higher levels of peer acceptance. Related studies have also found that the relationship between peer acceptance and physical skill is influenced by gender (Adler et al., 1992; Chase and Dummer, 1992). This research indicates that boys overwhelmingly identify athletic ability as the most important social status determinant during late childhood (ages 10–12 years). However, the relative importance of sport ability within girls' peer groups appears to be much less than for boys. Thus, we may conclude that sport ability influences levels of acceptance and rejection by peers, but the extent of this influence is moderated by gender.

Reviews of the youth sport participation motivation literature have also concluded that for both boys and girls, affiliative motives are at least as strong as achievement motives in influencing children's interest in becoming involved in sport (Weiss and Chaumeton, 1992; Weiss and Petlichkoff, 1989). This interest in affiliation with others further reflects the extent to which youngsters view sport as a viable means of developing social relations and of gaining acceptance from others. Peer acceptance also seems to result in favorable achievement-related outcomes for children. Harter (1988) found that children who reported higher perceptions of social support from peers (and parents) had higher self-esteem, higher intrinsic motivation, and more positive affect in achievement situations such as sport. Conversely, a perception of peer rejection (i.e., lack of status among a peer group) may result in increased feelings of social isolation. Friendships may be the component of peer relations that is most important as a protection for children and adolescents against feelings of isolation and loneliness.

Friendships

Friendship refers to a close, affective bond that develops between two individuals (Ladd, Kochenderfer, and Coleman, 1997). Friendships are closely related to Sullivan's (1953) concept of "chumships," and have been found to act as a buffer against some of the negative consequences of peer rejection by providing children and adolescents with a dependable, external form of validation of their self-worth. Although peer acceptance and friendships are both favorable forms of peer influence, it is important to make the distinction between the two because it is possible for children to have high levels of peer acceptance while lacking quality friendships. It is also possible for a child to experience general peer rejection but if the child can forge quality friendships, these friendships can still have a positive impact on his or her psychosocial development and reduce some of the detrimental effects of peer rejection (Parker and Asher, 1993). A further distinction is that peer acceptance refers to levels of acceptance or regard by "generalized others" whereas friendships refer specifically to the approval and emotional support provided by a "specific other."

In sport, friendships may develop because individuals share similar interests, or because others fulfill sport-specific friendship expectations. Two general, basic psychosocial goals for children and adolescents can be met through peer group activities: connectedness and individuation (Damon, 1983; Zarbatany, Ghesquiere, and Mohr, 1992; Rubin, Bukowski, and Parker, 1998). Feelings of connectedness can be supported through conversations with friends and through watching television or listening to music with a friend. Individuation needs can be reinforced through sports and games by providing youngsters with the opportunity to demonstrate their unique abilities and capacities. Friendships provide different types of benefits in relation to each of these goals. Feelings of connectedness can be enhanced by sharing and discussing life experiences with friends whereas individuation needs can be bolstered by friends through the provision of esteem support in achievement contexts.

In their study, Zarbatany et al. (1992) used interviews with 10- to 12-year-olds (38 girls, 29 boys) to better understand the friendship expectations that children have for both their same-sex and opposite-sex friends across five different peer activities. The children in their study were asked to imagine that they were taking part in the activity with another person (e.g., a boy who was their friend), and what they would like the other person to say or do. Results indicated that children hold different expectations for their friends in different activities; however, these expectations did not differ in relation to gender. For academic activities, friends were expected to provide helping behaviors, while noncompetitive activities were expected to elicit inclusion and acceptance behaviors from friends. In activities such as sports and games, Zarbatany and colleagues found that friends were expected to demonstrate behaviors meant to enhance positive self-evaluations (i.e., ego reinforcement and preferential treatment). This was believed to be due to the competitive public nature of these activities and the importance of maintaining a positive self-image by being successful in them.

Building upon findings that children hold different expectations for friendships in different domains, Weiss and Smith (1999) began to expand the friendship expectation knowledge base in sport. They developed a friendship quality scale based upon specific expectations that children have for their sport-related friendships. Their instrument, the Sport Friendship Quality Scale (SFQS), was adapted from the Friendship Quality Questionnaire (FQQ) of Parker and Asher (1993) and items from the previous measure were modified for use in a sport-specific context. Factor analysis of the SFQS revealed six different dimensions of friendship: self-esteem and supportiveness, loyalty and intimacy, things in common, conflict resolution, companionship and pleasant play, and conflict. While the SFQS is still a relatively new instrument in the field of sport psychology, it represents an important step toward understanding the nature and influence of peer relationships in the sport context. Much future research remains for the purpose of assessing the influence of specific friendship characteristics and overall friendship quality upon psychological and social outcomes for youngsters in sport.

Peer Victimization

Although peer research to date has been focused primarily in the areas of peer acceptance/rejection and friendship components, developmental and educational research has indicated that a third important element of peer influence should also be considered. Peer victimization refers to a group of behaviors that can be considered to be physically and/or verbally threatening to an individual (Ladd et al., 1997). This concept is different than that of peer rejection, which is merely considered to be the absence of status or liking within the peer group. Victimization is a more direct form of peer influence in which the recipient of the negative behaviors not only fails to gain acceptance by peer group members, but is subject to a variety of undesirable outcomes (Ladd et al., 1997). Such outcomes may include general victimization, such as being picked on, physical victimization (being hit or kicked), direct verbal victimization (having kids say mean things to them), or indirect verbal victimization (having bad things said about them to other kids). The impact of peer victimization has been documented within the educational psychology literature: however, little work has been conducted to understand the frequency and nature of such victimization behaviors within sport. Given the nature of sport, it is possible that physical forms of victimization would be more prevalent than in other settings. Furthermore, it is important to know if gender may be a mediating variable in victimization, with boys preferring more overt, physical forms of bullying, and girls preferring more covert forms of victimization (e.g., mean-spirited gossip). Research is needed in this area of peer influence to better understand what impact victimization behaviors may have on youth sport participants and how victimization episodes may influence sport participation motivation for participants and nonparticipants alike.

Self-Concept Development

The imagery of the "looking-glass self" (Cooley, 1902/1956) is particularly useful for understanding the nature of peer group influence on youngsters' sense of self in later childhood and early adolescence. Whereas the reflected appraisals of parents are very important during early and middle childhood, the mirror of self provided by peers takes on increasing strength and clarity during later childhood and through adolescence. This "transfer of loyalty to the peer group" (McCabe, Roberts, and Morris, 1991, p. 95) is attributable to the tendency for children to spend relatively more time in the company of their peers as they move through this developmental phase, and is also due to the fact that cognitive developmental changes occur in youngsters' preferences for peer-based informational sources in assessing personal competencies. During the late childhood and early adolescent years that correspond with peak sport participatory involvement, youngsters' self-concepts are generally comprised of five dimensions (Harter, 1983, 1999). These dimensions include scholastic competence, athletic competence, peer acceptance, physical appearance, and behavioral conduct. Thus, the salience of the peer group during this developmental era makes children's perceptions of athletic competence and peer acceptance particularly likely to be influenced by peer evaluation sources. In contrast with the extensive research that has examined the correspondence between parental and child judgments of children's abilities during childhood (e.g., Eccles and Harold, 1991; Phillips, 1987), researchers have only recently begun to examine the influence of peer judgments on children's self-perceptions. In one of the only studies to pursue this line of research, Weiss, Smith, and Theebom (1996) examined this issue in relation to youngsters' self-esteem. These researchers found that self-esteem enhancement was identified as an important characteristic of friendship quality for youngsters in sport contexts. Specifically, self-esteem enhancement was considered to consist of friends' provision of positive reinforcement, their willingness to accept mistakes, and their tendency to say nice things. Clearly, a greater amount of research attention is needed to understand the nature and strength of peer influence on children's self-perceptions, particularly because of the established link between youngsters' self-perception characteristics and motivational patterns in sport (Weiss, 1993). The relationship that has been established between physical ability and peer acceptance during childhood and adolescence (Weiss and Duncan, 1992) further points to the influence of peers in shaping self-concept.

Recommendations for Future Research

The body of knowledge on parental and peer influence on children's psychosocial development through sport has continued to grow at a rapid rate. It has been particularly encouraging to see the increasing attention dedicated to the role of peers in sport. Even since the publication of the previous edition of this book, considerably more empirical research attention has been directed to peers and we are just beginning to recognize the nature and extent of peer influence. However, there remains a great deal to be known about the role of peers in sport across virtually all aspects of children's psychological and social development.

The continued development of research on peer influence has the potential to be used for the design and implementation of intervention strategies that can facilitate peer relations in sport. Such intervention efforts may prove to be highly beneficial in contributing to a more favorable participatory climate for youngsters in sport, and in reducing the incidence of sport attrition, particularly during the onset of adolescence, a developmental epoch that corresponds with high levels of sport attrition. Furthermore, we would anticipate that research-based peer interventions could yield benefits for many additional dimensions of youngsters' psychosocial development in sport (perceived competence, feelings of peer acceptance, friendship development, etc.).

Although the nature of parental influence in youth sport has been more extensively studied than has peer influence, there still remains a great deal to be known in this area as well. Most research to date has examined parental influence without reference to the developmental status of the child. Since research (Felson, 1990) indicates that parental socialization practices and expectations change in relation to the age of the child, it would be very helpful to examine the nature of parental influence with regard to the child's age, developmental status, and even level of sport participation. Similarly, we do not understand very well the relative influence of fathers and mothers in the sport socialization process nor how the influence of each may vary over time. In addition, youth sport researchers interested in parental socialization influence upon children's self-concept formation could dedicate attention to the role of parents in shaping youngsters' self-esteem and perceptions of control through sport involvement. Finally, given the effectiveness of intervention approaches with coaches in enhancing sport outcomes for children (e.g., Barnett, Smoll, and Smith, 1992), a highly appropriate fine of research would investigate the efficacy of parent-based intervention approaches on resultant psychological and social outcomes for children.

At the present time, we have an appreciation for the role of social influences in shaping immediate psychosocial outcomes in sport but we do not yet have a strong sense for how sport participation influences children's long-term psychological or social development (Weiss, 1993). To gain this understanding, it will be necessary to focus on aspects of individual change rather than to rely solely on cross-sectional data. Using longitudinal, and perhaps qualitative, approaches may help us to gain a better understanding of individual development through sport over time. Overall, we anticipate that through continued interest on the topic of parental and peer influence in sport, that researchers will contribute to enhancing sport experiences for young athletes.

References

Adler, P.A., Kless, S. J., and Adler, P. (1992). Socialization to gender roles: Popularity among elementary school boys and girls. *Sociology of Education, 65,* 169–187.

Babkes, M. L., and Weiss, M. R. (1999). Parental influence on children's cognitive and affective responses to competitive soccer participation. *Pediatric Exercise Science, 11,* 44–62.

Bandura, A. (1986). *Social foundations of thought and action: A social cognitive theory.* Englewood Cliffs, NJ: Prentice-Hall.

Barnett. N. P., Smoll, F. L., and Smith, R. E. (1992). Effects of enhancing coach-athlete relationships on youth sport attrition. *The Sport Psychologist, 6,* 111–127.

Black, S. J., and Weiss, M. R. (1992). The relationship among perceived coaching behaviors, perceptions of ability, and motivation in competitive age-group swimmers. *Journal of Sport and Exercise Psychology, 14,* 309–325.

Brower, J. J. (1978). Little league baseballism: Adult dominance in a "child's game." In R. Martens (Ed.), *Joy and sadness in children's sport* (pp. 39–49). Champaign, IL: Human Kinetics.

Brustad, R. J. (1988). Affective outcomes in competitive youth sport: The influence of intrapersonal and socialization factors. *Journal of Sport and Exercise Psychology, 10,* 307–321.

Brustad, R. J. (1992). Integrating socialization influences into the study of children's motivation in sport. *Journal of Sport and Exercise Psychology, 14,* 59–77.

Brustad, R. J. (1993). Who will go out and play? Parental and psychological influences on children's attraction to physical activity. *Pediatric Exercise Science, 5,* 210–223.

Brustad, R. J. (1996). Attraction to physical activity in urban schoolchildren: Parental socialization and gender influences. *Research Quarterly for Exercise and Sport, 67*, 316–323.

Brustad, R. J. (1998). Developmental considerations in sport and exercise psychology measurement. In J. L. Duda (Ed.), *Advances in sport and exercise psychology measurement* (pp. 461–470). Morgantown, WV: Fitness Information Technology.

Brustad, R. J., Babkes, M. L., and Smith, A. L. (2001). Youth in sport: Psychological considerations. In R.N. Singer, H. A. Hausenblas, and C. M. Janelle (Eds.), *Handbook of sport psychology* (2nd Ed., pp. 604–635). New York: John Wiley and Sons.

Brustad, R. J., and Weiss, M. R. (1987). Competence perceptions and sources of worry in high, medium, and low competitive trait-anxious young athletes. *Journal of Sport Psychology, 9*, 97–105.

Bukowski, W. M., and Hoza, B. (1989). Popularity and friendship: Issues in theory, measurement, and outcome. In T. J. Berndt and G. W. Ladd (Eds.), *Peer relationships in child development* (pp. 15–45). New York: Wiley.

Chase, M. A., and Dummer, G. M. (1992). The role of sports as a social status determinant for children. *Research Quarterly for Exercise and Sport, 63*, 418–424.

Coakley, J. (1992). Burnout among adolescent athletes: A personal failure or social problem? *Sociology of Sport Journal, 9*, 271–285.

Cooley, C. H. (1902/1956). *Human nature and the social* order. Glencoe, IL: Free Press.

Damon, W. (1983). *Social and personality development*. New York: Norton.

Eccles, J., and Harold, R. (1991). Gender differences in sport involvement: Applying the Eccles' expectancy-value model. *Journal of Applied Sport Psychology, 3*, 7–35.

Eccles, J. S., Wigfield, A., and Schiefele, U. (1998). Motivation to succeed. In W. Damon (Series Ed.) and N. Eisenberg (Vol. Ed.), *Handbook of Child Psychology: Vol. 3. Social, emotional, and personality development* (5th Ed., pp. 1017–1095). New York: Wiley.

Ewing, M. E., and Seefeldt, V. (1996). Patterns of participation and attrition in American agency-sponsored youth sports. In F. L. Smoll and R. E. Smith (Eds.), *Children and youth in sport: A biopsychosocial perspective* (pp. 31–45). Dubuque, IA: Brown and Benchmark.

Felson, R. B. (1990). Comparison processes in parents' and children's appraisals of academic performance. *Social Psychology Quarterly, 53*, 264–273.

Felson, R. B., and Reed, M. (1986). The effect of parents on the self-appraisals of children. *Social Psychology Quarterly, 49*, 302–308.

Fox, K. R. (1997). *The physical self: From motivation to well-being*. Champaign, IL: Human Kinetics.

Gould. D., Eklund, R., Petlichkoff, L., Peterson, K., and Bump, L. (1991). Psychological predictors of state anxiety and performance in age-group wrestlers, *Pediatric Exercise Science, 3*, 198–208.

Green, B.C. and Chalip, L. (1997). Enduring involvement in youth soccer: The socialization of parent and child. *Journal of Leisure Research, 29*, 61–77.

Harter, S. (1978). Effectance motivation reconsidered. *Human Development, 21*, 34–64.

Harter, S. (1981). A model of intrinsic mastery motivation in children: Individual differences and developmental change. In W. A. Collins (Ed.), *Minnesota symposium on child psychology: Vol. 14* (pp. 215–255). Hillsdale, NJ: Lawrence Erlbaum Associates.

Harter, S. (1983). Developmental perspectives on the self-system. In E. M. Hetherington (Ed.), *Handbook of child psychology: Socialization, personality, and social development* (pp. 275– 385). New York: John Wiley and Sons.

Harter, S. (1988). Causes, correlates and the functional role of global self-worth: A life-span perspective. In J. Kolligan and R. Sternberg (Eds.), *Perceptions of competence and incompetence across the life-span* (pp. 67–98). New Haven, CT: Yale University.

Harter, S. (1998). The developmental of self-representations. In W. Damon (Series Ed.) and N. Eisenberg (Vol. Ed.), *Handbook of Child Psychology: Vol. 3. Social, emotional, and personality development* (5th Ed., pp. 553–617). New York: Wiley.

Harter, S. (1999). *The construction of the self: A developmental perspective*. New York: The Guilford Press.

Horn, T. S., and Harris, A. (2002). Perceived competence in young athletes: Research findings and recommendations for coaches and parents. In F. L. Smoll and R. E. Smith (Eds). *Children and youth in sport: A biopsychosocial perspective* (2nd Ed., pp. 435–464). Dubuque, IA: Kendall/Hunt.

Horn, T. S., and Hasbrook, C. A. (1986). Informational components influencing children's perceptions of their physical competence. In M. R. Weiss and D. Gould (Eds.), *Sport for children and youths* (pp. 81–88). Champaign, IL: Human Kinetics.

Horn, T. S., and Hasbrook, C. A. (1987). Psychological characteristics and the criteria children use for self-evaluation. *Journal of Sport and Exercise Psychology, 9*, 208–221.

Horn, T. S., and Weiss, M. R. (1991). A developmental analysis of children's self-ability judgments in the physical domain. *Pediatric Exercise Science, 3*, 310–326.

Klint, K. A., and Weiss, M. R. (1987). Perceived competence and motives for participating in youth sports: A test of Harter's competence motivation theory. *Journal of Sport Psychology, 9*, 55–65.

Ladd, G. W., Kochenderfer, B. J., and Coleman, C. C. (1997). Classroom peer acceptance, friendship, and victimization: Distinct relational systems that contribute uniquely to children's school adjustment? *Child Development, 68(6)*, 1181–1197.

Leff, S. S., and Hoyle, R. H. (1995). Young athletes' perceptions of parental support and pressure. *Journal of Youth and Adolescence, 24*, 187–203

Marsh, H. W., and Peart, N.D. (1988). Competitive and cooperative physical fitness training programs for girls: Effects on physical fitness and multidimensional self-concepts. *Journal of Sport and Exercise Psychology, 10*, 390–407.

Martens, R. (1977). *Sport competition anxiety test.* Champaign, IL: Human Kinetics.

Martens, R. (1978). *Joy and sadness in children's sport.* Champaign, IL: Human Kinetics.

McCabe, A. E., Roberts, B. T., and Morris, T. E. (1991). Athletic activity, body image, and adolescent identity. In L. Diamant (Ed.), *Mind-body maturity* (pp. 91–103). New York: Hemisphere.

McCullagh, P., Matzkanin, K., Shaw, S.D., and Maldonado, M. (1993). Motivation for participation in physical activity: A comparison of parent-child perceived competence and participation motives. *Pediatric Exercise Science, 5*, 224–233.

Mead, G. H. (1934). *Mind, self, and society.* Chicago: University of Chicago Press.

Nicholls, J. G. (1984). Conceptions of ability and achievement motivation. In R. Ames and C. Ames (Eds.), *Research on motivation in education: Vol. 1. Student motivation* (pp. 39–73). New York: Academic Press.

Ommundsen, Y., and Vaglum, P. (1991). Soccer competition anxiety and enjoyment in young boy players: The influence of perceived competence and significant others' emotional involvement. *International Journal of Sport Psychology, 22*, 35–49

Orlick, T. D. (1974, November/December). The athletic dropout: A high price for inefficiency. *Canadian Association for Health, Physical Education and Recreation Journal*, 21–27.

Parker, J. G., and Asher, S. R. (1993). Friendship and friendship quality in middle childhood: Links with peer group acceptance and feelings of loneliness and dissatisfaction *Developmental Psychology, 29*, 611–621.

Parsons, J. E., Adler, T. F., and Kaczala, C. M. (1982). Socialization of achievement attitudes and beliefs: Parental influences. *Child Development, 53*, 310–321.

Passer, M. W. (1983). Fear of failure, fear of evaluation, perceived competence and self-esteem in competitive trait-anxious children. *Journal of Sport Psychology, 5*, 172–188.

Passer, M. W. (1988). Determinants and consequences of children's competitive stress. In F. L. Smoll, R. A. Magill, and M. J. Ash (Eds.), *Children in Sport* (3rd Ed., pp. 203–228). Champaign, IL: Human Kinetics.

Phillips, D. (1987). Socialization of perceived academic competence among highly competent children. *Child Development, 58*, 1308–1320.

Raedeke, T. D. (1997). Is athlete burnout more than just stress? A sport commitment perspective. *Journal of Sport and Exercise Psychology, 19*, 396–417.

Rogers, C. R. (1951). *Client-centered therapy.* Boston: Houghton-Mifflin.

Rubin, R. H., Bukowski, B. H., and Parker, J. G. (1998). Peer interactions, relationships, and groups. In W. Damon (Series Ed.) and N. Eisenberg (Vol. Ed.), *Handbook of Child Psychology: Vol. 3. Social, emotional, and personality development* (5th Ed., pp. 619–700). New York: Wiley.

Ruble, D. N. (1983). The role of social comparison processes in achievement-related self-socialization. In E. T. Higgins, D. N. Ruble, and W. W. Hartup (Eds.), *Social cognitions and social development: A sociocultural perspective* (pp. 134–157). New York: Cambridge University,

Ruble, D. N., and Goodnow, J. J. (1998). Social development in childhood and adulthood. In D. T. Gilbert, S. T. Fiske, and G. Lindzey (Eds.), *The handbook of social psychology* (4th Ed., pp. 741–787). New York: Oxford University Press.

Scanlan, T. K. (2002). Social evaluation and the competition process: A developmental perspective. In F. L. Smoll and R. E. Smith (Eds.), *Children and youth in sport: A biopsychosocial perspective* (2nd Ed., pp. 393–407). Dubuque, IA: Kendall/Hunt

Scanlan, T. K., and Lewthwaite, R. (1984). Social psychological aspects of competition for male youth sport participants: I. Predictors of competitive stress. *Journal of Sport Psychology, 6*, 208–226.

Scanlan, T. K., and Lewthwaite, R. (1986). Social psychological aspects of competition for male youth sport participants: IV. Predictors of enjoyment. *Journal of Sport Psychology, 8*, 25–35

Scanlan, T. K., and Simons, J. P. (1992). The construct of sport enjoyment. In G. Roberts (Ed.), *Motivation in sport and exercise* (pp. 199–215). Champaign, IL: Human Kinetics.

Scanlan, T. K., Stein, G. L., and Ravizza, K. (1989). An in-depth study of former elite figure skaters: II. Sources of enjoyment. *Journal of Sport and Exercise Psychology, 11*, 65–83.

Schunk, D. H. (1991). Self-efficacy and academic motivation. *Educational Psychologist, 26*, 207–231.

Selman, R. L. (1976). Social-cognitive understanding: A guide to educational and clinical practice. In T. Lickona (Ed.), *Moral development and behavior* (pp. 299–316). New York: Holt, Rinehart, and Winston.

Skinner, E. A. (1995). *Perceived control, motivation, and coping*. Thousand Oaks, CA: Sage.

Skinner, E. A., Wellborn, J. G., and Connell, J. P. (1990). What it takes to do well in school and whether I've got it: A process model of perceived control and children's engagement and achievement in school. *Journal of Educational Psychology, 82*, 22–32.

Smilkstein, G. (1980). Psychological trauma in children and youth in competitive sport. *The Journal of Family Practice, 10*, 737–739.

Smith, A. L. (1999). Perceptions of peer relationships and physical activity participation in early adolescence. *Journal of Sport and Exercise Psychology, 21*, 321–350.

Smith, R. E., Smoll, F. L., and Curtis, B. (1979). Coach effectiveness training: A cognitive behavioral approach to enhancing relationship skills in youth sport coaches. *Journal of Sport Psychology, 1*, 59–75.

Smith, R. E., Smoll, F. L., and Passer, M. W. (2002). Sport performance anxiety in young athletes. In F. L. Smoll and R. E. Smith (Eds.), *Children and youth in sport: A biopsychosocial perspective* (2nd Ed., pp. 501–536). Dubuque, IA: Kendall/Hunt.

Stipek, D., and McIver, D. (1989). Developmental change in children's assessment of intellectual competence. *Child Development, 60*, 521–538.

Sullivan, H. S. (1953). *The interpersonal theory of psychiatry*. New York: Norton.

Thoits, P.A. (1983). Multiple identities and psychological well-being: A reformulation and test of the social isolation hypothesis. *American Sociological Review, 48*, 174–187.

Veroff, J. (1969). Social comparison and the development of achievement motivation. In C. P. Smith (Ed.), *Achievement-related motives in children* (pp. 46–101). New York: Russell Sage Foundation.

Weiss, M. R. (1993). Psychological effects of intensive sport participation on children and youth: Self-esteem and motivation. In B. Cahill and A. Pearl (Eds.), *Perspectives on intensive participation in youth sports* (pp. 39–69). Champaign, IL: Human Kinetics.

Weiss, M. R., and Chaumeton, N. (1992). Motivational orientations in sport. In T. S. Horn (Ed.), *Advances in sport psychology* (pp. 61–99). Champaign, IL: Human Kinetics.

Weiss, M. R., and Duncan, S.C. (1992). The relationship between physical competence and peer acceptance in the context of children's sports participation. *Journal of Sport and Exercise Psychology, 14*, 177–191.

Weiss, M. R., Ebbeck, V., and Horn, T. S. (1997). Children's self-perceptions and sources of competence information: A cluster analysis. *Journal of Sport and Exercise Psychology, 19*, 52–70.

Weiss, M. R., and Petlichkoff, L. M. (1989). Children's motivation for participation in and withdrawal from sport: Identifying the missing links. *Pediatric Exercise Science, 1*, 195–211

Weiss, M. R., and Smith, A. L. (1999). Quality of youth sport friendships: Measurement development and validation. *Journal of Sport and Exercise Psychology, 21*, 145–166.

Weiss, M. R., Smith, A. L., and Theebom, M. (1996). "That's what friends are for": Children's and teenagers' perceptions of peer relationships in the sport domain. *Journal of Sport and Exercise Psychology, 18*, 347–379.

Weiss, M. R., Wiese, D. M., and Klint, K. A. (1989). Head over heels with success: The relationship between self-efficacy and performance in competitive youth gymnastics. *Journal of Sport and Exercise Psychology, 11*, 444–451.

Wiersma, L. D. (2000). Risks and benefits of youth sport specialization: Perspectives and recommendations. *Pediatric Exercise Science, 12*, 13–22.

Wiggins, D. K. (2002). A history of highly competitive sport for American children. In F. L. Smoll and R. E. Smith (Eds.), *Children and youth in sport: A biopsychosocial perspective* (2nd Ed., pp. 19–37). Dubuque, IA: Kendall/Hunt.

Wigfield, A., and Eccles, J. S. (1990). Test anxiety in elementary and secondary school students. *Educational Psychologist, 24*, 159–183.

Williams, L. (1994). Goal orientations and athletes' preferences for competence information. *Journal of Sport and Exercise Psychology, 16*, 416–430.

Zarbatany, L., Ghesquiere, K., and Mohr, K. (1992). A context perspective on early adolescents' friendship expectations. *Journal of Early Adolescence, 12*, 111–126.

CHAPTER 9

Coaching Behavior Research and Intervention in Youth Sports

Frank L. Smoll, University of Washington
Ronald E. Smith, University of Washington

Youth sports are a firmly established part of contemporary Western society, and they directly touch the lives of many people (Berryman, this volume; Wiggins, this volume). In the Unites States alone, an estimated 41 million youngsters participate in nonschool sports, and approximately 6 to 7 million 14- to 18-year-olds take part in interscholastic athletics (Seefeldt, Ewing, and Walk, 1992). There has been continued growth over the past several decades, which has been accompanied by a greater degree of adult involvement as well (Martens, 1988, Weiss and Hayashi, 1996). Consequently, these programs have become extremely complex social systems that have attracted the attention of researchers interested in studying the impact of competition on psychosocial development (see Brown and Branta, 1988; Brustad, 1993; Cahill and Pearl, 1993; Gould and Weiss, 1987; Malina, 1988; Malina and Clark, 2001; Weiss, 2001; Weiss and Gould, 1986).

Much of the controversy that surrounds youth sports concerns the roles that adults play in the process. There is, however, general agreement that an important determinant of the effects of participation lies in the relationship between coach and athlete (Martens, 1997; Seefeldt and Brown, 1996; Smith and Smoll, 2002; Smoll and Smith, 1989). Coaches influence the effects that sport participation has on children through the interpersonal behaviors they engage in, the values and attitudes they transmit both verbally and through example, and the goal priorities they establish (for example, winning versus equal participation and fun). Coaches not only occupy a critical position in the athletic setting, but their influence can extend into other areas of the child's life as well. For example, because of the high frequency of single-parent families, coaches often find themselves occupying the role of a substitute parent.

Most athletes have their first sport experiences in programs staffed by volunteer coaches. These individuals typically know their sport and the skills involved quite well, but they rarely have had any formal training in creating a healthy psychological environment for young athletes. Educational programs have thus been developed for the purpose of positively affecting coaching practices and thereby increasing the likelihood that youngsters will have favorable sport experiences. For example, national coaching associations of many countries have programs that provide training in sport psychology as well as other areas, such as sport pedagogy, exercise physiology, and sports medicine (cf. Australia [Oldenhove, 1996]; Canada [Wankel and Mummery, 1996]; Finland [Laakso, Telama, and Yang, 1996]; Portugal [Goncalves, 1996]; and the United States [Weiss and Hayashi, 1996]).

In a research program that has spanned two decades, we have focused on interactions between coaches and young athletes. The major thrust of our collaborative efforts has been to discover how specific coaching behaviors affect children's reactions to their athletic experience, and to use this information to develop an intervention designed to assist coaches in relating more effectively to young athletes. The ultimate objective is for positive coach-athlete interactions to contribute in a desirable way to youngsters' personal, social, and athletic development. This chapter presents overviews of (a) the theoretical model and basic research underlying the development of our coach-training program, (b) the content of the program and procedures for its implementation, and (c) applied research assessing the efficacy of the intervention.

Developing a Coach-Training Program

A crucial first step in developing a training program is to determine what is to be presented. In this regard, our work was guided by a fundamental assumption that a training program should be based on scientific evidence rather than on intuition and/or what we "know" on the basis of informal observation. An empirical foundation for coaching guidelines not only enhances the validity and potential value of the program, but it also increases its credibility in the eyes of consumers (Smith and Smoll, 1997). We now describe our approach to generating an empirical data base for our coach-training program.

Theoretical Model and Research Paradigm

Recognition of the potential impact of coaches on athletes' psychological welfare prompted several questions that served as an impetus for our preliminary work. For example, what do coaches do, and how frequently do they engage in such behaviors as encouragement, punishment, instruction, and organization? What are the psychological dimensions that underlie such behaviors? And, finally, how are observable coaching behaviors related to children's reactions to their organized athletic experiences? Answers to such questions are not only a first step in describing the behavioral ecology of one aspect of the youth sport setting, but they also provide an empirical basis for the development of psychologically-oriented intervention programs.

To begin to answer such questions, we carried out a systematic program of research over a period of several years. Our approach was guided by a mediational model of coach-athlete interactions, the basic elements of which are represented as follows:

Coach's Behaviors → Athletes' Perceptions and Recall → Athletes' Evaluative Reactions

This model stipulates that the ultimate effects of coaching behaviors are mediated by the athletes' recall and the meaning they attribute to the coach's actions. In other words, what athletes remember about their coach's behaviors and how they interpret these actions affects the way athletes evaluate their sport experiences. Furthermore, a complex of cognitive and affective processes are involved at this mediational level. These processes are likely to be affected not only by the coach's behaviors, but also by other factors, such as the athlete's age, what he or she expects of coaches (normative beliefs and expectations), and certain personality variables, such as self-esteem and anxiety. The basic three-element model was thus expanded to reflect these factors (Smoll and Smith, 1989). The more comprehensive model, which is presented in Figure 9.1, specifies a number of situational as well as coach and athlete individual difference variables that are expected to influence coach behaviors and the perceptions and reactions of athletes to them.

In accordance with the model, we have sought to determine how observed coaching behaviors, athletes' perception and recall of the coach's behaviors, and athlete attitudes are interrelated. We have also explored the manner in which athlete and coach individual difference variables might serve as moderator variables and influence the basic behavior-attitude relations.

Measurement of Coaching Behaviors

Because coaches play such a vital role in influencing both skill development and psychosocial outcomes, they are a natural focus of behavioral assessment measures (see Smith, Smoll, and Christensen, 1996). To measure leadership behaviors, we developed the Coaching Behavior Assessment System (CBAS) to permit the direct observation and coding of coaches' actions during practices and games (Smith, Smoll, and Hunt, 1977). The behavioral categories were derived from content analyses of numerous audiotaped "play-by-play" reports of coaches' actions during practices and games. Both the measurement approach and some of the categories derive from a social-behavioral orientation, and the categories incorporate behaviors that have been shown to affect both children and adults in a variety of nonathletic settings (Bales and Slater, 1955; Komaki, 1986; White, 1975).

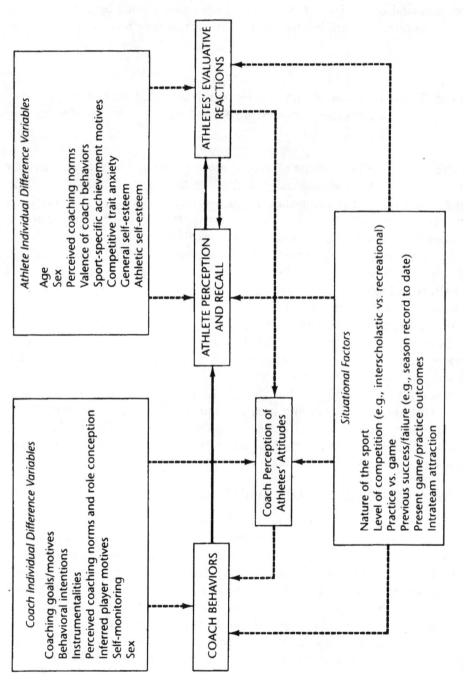

Figure 9.1. A theoretical model of coaching behaviors, their antecedents, and their effects on athletes, with hypothesized relations among situational, cognitive, behavioral, and individual difference variables. Reprinted with permission from Journal of Applied Social Psychology, Vol. 18, No. 18, pp. 1522–1551. © V. W. Winston & Son, Inc., 360 South Ocean Boulevard, Palm Beach, FL 33480. All rights reserved.

The 12 CBAS categories are divided into two major classes of behaviors. *Reactive* (elicited) behaviors are responses to immediately preceding athlete or team behaviors, whereas *spontaneous* (emitted) behaviors are initiated by the coach and are not a response to a discernible preceding event. As shown in Table 9.1, reactive behaviors are responses to either desirable performance or effort, mistakes and errors, or misbehaviors on the part of athletes. The spontaneous class is subdivided into game-related and game-irrelevant behaviors. The system thus involves basic interactions between the situation and the coach's behavior. Use of the CBAS in observing and coding coaching behaviors in a variety of sports indicates that the scoring system is sufficiently comprehensive to incorporate the vast majority of overt leader behaviors, that high interrater reliability can be obtained, and that individual differences in behavioral patterns can be discerned (Chaumeton and Duda, 1988; Cruz et al., 1987; Horn, 1984, 1985; Jones, Housman, and Kornspan, 1997; Krane, Eklund, and McDermott, 1991; Rejeski, Darracott, and Hutslar, 1979; Sherman and Hassan, 1986; Wandzilak, Ansorge, and Potter, 1988).

Basic Research Relating Coaching Behaviors to Children's Evaluative Reactions

Following development of the CBAS, field studies were conducted to assess relations between coaching behaviors and athlete variables specified in the conceptual model (Curtis, Smith, and Smoll, 1979; Smith and Smoll, 1990; Smith, Smoll, and Curtis, 1978; Smith, Zane, Smoll, and Coppel, 1983; Smoll, Smith, Curtis, and Hunt, 1978). In the largest study (Smith et al., 1978), 51 male Little League Baseball coaches were observed by trained coders during 202 complete games. A total of 57,213 individual coaching behaviors were coded into the 12 categories, and a behavioral profile based on an average of 1,122 behaviors was computed for each coach.

Several self-report measures were developed to assess coaches' beliefs, attitudes, and perceptions. These were combined into a questionnaire that the coaches completed at the end of the season. Coaches' self-perception of their behaviors was of primary importance. This was assessed by describing and giving examples of the 12 CBAS behaviors and asking coaches to indicate on a 7-point scale how often they engaged in the behaviors in the situations described.

Data from 542 players were collected after the season during individual interviews and questionnaire administrations carried out in the children's homes. Included were measures of their recall and perception of the coach's behaviors (on the same scales as the coaches had rated their own behavior), their liking for the coach and their teammates, the degree of enjoyment they experienced during the season, and their general self-esteem.

Table 9.1 Response Categories of the Coaching Behavior Assessment System

Response Category	Behavioral Description
Class I. Reactive Behaviors	
Responses to Desirable Performance	
Reinforcement (R)	a positive, rewarding reaction (verbal or non-verbal) to a good play or good effort
Nonreinforcement (NR)	failure to respond to a good performance
Responses to Mistakes	
Mistake-Contingent Encouragement (EM)	encouragement given to a player following a mistake
Mistake-Contingent Technical Instruction (TIM)	instructing or demonstrating to a player how to correct a mistake he/she has made
Punishment (P)	a negative reaction, verbal or nonverbal, following a mistake
Punitive Technical Instruction (TIM + P)	technical instruction following a mistake which is given in a punitive or hostile manner
Ignoring Mistakes (IM)	failure to respond to a player mistake
Response to Misbehavior	
Keeping Control (KC)	reactions intended to restore or maintain order among team members
Class II. Spontaneous Behaviors	
Game-Related	
General Technical Instruction (TIG)	spontaneous instruction in the techniques and strategies of the sport (not following a mistake)
General Encouragement (EG)	spontaneous encouragment which does not follow a mistake
Organization (O)	administrative behavior which sets the stage for play by assigning duties, responsibilities, positions, etc.
Game-Irrelevant	
General Communication (GC)	interactions with players unrelated to the game

Coaching behaviors, children's attitudes, and winning. At the level of overt behavior, three independent behavioral dimensions were identified through factor analysis—supportiveness (comprised of reinforcement and mistake-contingent encouragement), instructiveness (general technical instruction and mistake-contingent technical instruction *versus* general communication and general encouragement), and punitiveness (punishment and punitive technical instruction *versus* organizational behaviors). The first two dimensions correspond closely to the classic leadership styles of relationship orientation and task orientation emphasized in leadership theories such as Fiedler's (1967) Contingency Model, Situational Leadership (Hersey and Blanchard, 1977), and the Vertical Dyad Linkage model of Graen and Schiermann (1978) and identified in other research on leadership behavior (e.g., Stogdill, 1959).

Relations between coaches' scores on these behavioral dimensions and player measures provided clear evidence for the crucial role of the coach. The most positive outcomes occurred when children played for coaches who engaged in high levels of reinforcement (for both desirable performance and effort) and who responded to mistakes with encouragement and technical instruction. Not only did the children who had such coaches like their coaches more and have more fun, but they also liked their teammates more.

There were some interesting surprises in the data. First, punitive and hostile actions occurred less frequently but had more devastating effects than we had anticipated. Although only about 3% of the coded behaviors were punitive and critical in nature, they correlated more strongly (and negatively) than any other behavior with children's attitudes. Second, general encouragement bore a curvilinear relation to children's attitudes; either very low or very high levels were linked to negative attitudes toward the coach. Third, the team's won-lost record was essentially unrelated to how well the players liked the coach and how much they wanted to play for the coach in the future. On the other hand, players on winning teams felt that their parents liked the coach more and that the coach liked them more than did players on losing teams. Apparently, winning made little difference to the children, but they knew that it was important to the adults. It is worth noting, however, that winning assumed greater importance beyond age 12, although it continued to be a less important attitudinal determinant than coach behaviors.

Coach and athlete perceptions. Another important issue concerns the degree of accuracy with which coaches perceive their own behaviors. Correlations between CBAS observed behaviors and coaches' ratings of how frequently they performed the behaviors were generally low and nonsignificant. The only actions on their self-report measure that correlated significantly (around .50) with the observational measures were the punitive behaviors. Overall we found that children's ratings on the same perceived behavior scales correlated much more highly with CBAS measures than did the coaches' own reports! It thus appears that coaches were, for the most part, blissfully unaware of how they behaved and that athletes were more accurate perceivers of actual coach behaviors. Because behavior change requires an awareness of how one is currently behaving, this finding clearly indicated the need to increase coaches' self-awareness when developing an intervention program.

Coaching behaviors and athletes' self-esteem. Because of our interest in self-esteem as a moderator variable that might influence responses to coaches' behaviors, we tested a self-enhancement model of self-esteem development (Shrauger, 1975; Swann, 1996; Tesser, 1988) against the consistency model (e.g., Rogers, 1951). The self-enhancement model posits that most people have a strong need to enhance their self-evaluations and to feel positively about themselves. People who are low in self-esteem are thought to have particularly strong self-enhancement needs. Therefore, they should value positive feedback and respond very favorably to people with whom they have self-enhancing interactions. A different prediction is derived from the consistency model, which suggests that people with low self-esteem may actually be more comfortable with someone who provides negative feedback that is congruent with their negative self-image, thereby satisfying needs for cognitive consistency.

To test the models, we examined the reactions of children who scored either low, moderate, or high on a measure of general self-esteem to coaches who were either quite high or quite low on the supportiveness behavioral dimension (i.e., the tendency of the coach to reinforce desirable performance and effort and to respond to mistakes with encouragement). Attraction responses toward the coaches revealed a significant interaction between coach supportiveness and athletes' level of self-esteem. As shown in Figure 9.2, children with low self-esteem were more responsive than other children to variations in supportiveness, and the pattern of their responses favors the self-enhancement model. Rather than liking the nonsupportive coaches, these children reacted especially negatively to them, presumably because the coaches fustrated their self-enhancement needs by being nonsupportive (Smith and Smoll, 1990). This finding extends to a naturalistic setting a body of results derived from laboratory studies which, collectively, suggest that self-enhancement motivation causes people who are low in self-esteem to be especially responsive to variations in supportiveness (Brown, Collins, and Schmidt, 1988; Dittes, 1959; Swann, Griffin, Predmore, and Gaines, 1987; Tesser and Campbell, 1983).

The Coach-Training Program

Data from the basic research indicated clear relations between coaching behaviors and the reactions of youngsters to their athletic experience. These relations provided a solid foundation for developing a set of coaching guidelines that constitute the core of our program, which is known as Coach Effectiveness Training (CET). The data-based guidelines serve two other functions: (a) they allow us to structure CET as an information-sharing rather than speculative enterprise, and (b) the scientific origin of the guidelines increases their credibility with coaches. An overview of CET content and procedures for its implementation is now presented. A more comprehensive

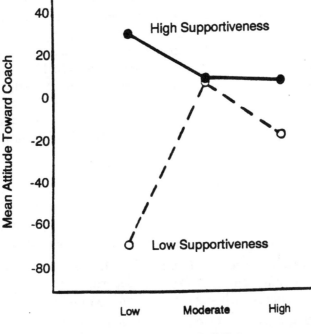

Figure 9.2. Mean evaluations of coaches by athletes as a function of athletes' self-esteem and supportiveness of the coach (data from Smith & Smoll, 1990).

discussion of cognitive-behavioral principles and techniques used in conducting psychologically oriented coach-training programs appears elsewhere (Smoll and Smith, 2001).

Coach-Training Principles

CET was conceptualized and designed within a cognitive-behavioral framework (Bandura, 1986). The empirically derived behavioral guidelines (i.e., coaching *do's* and *don'ts*) are based primarily on social influence techniques that involve principles of positive control rather than aversive control, and the conception of success or "winning" as consisting of giving maximum effort. The behavioral guidelines, which are summarized in Appendix A, emphasize the desirability of *increasing* four specific target behaviors: reinforcement (for effort as well as for good performance); mistake-contingent encouragement; corrective instruction (given in an encouraging and supportive fashion); and technical instruction (spontaneous instruction in the techniques and strategies of the sport). Coaches are also urged to *decrease* nonreinforcement, punishment, and punitive instruction, as well as to avoid having to use regimenting behaviors (keeping control) by establishing team rules early and reinforcing compliance with them. The guidelines are placed in a goal context of increasing positive coach-athlete and athlete-athlete interactions, developing team cohesion, and developing in athletes a positive desire to achieve rather than a fear of failure.

As far as winning is concerned, CET urges coaches to focus on athletes' effort and enjoyment rather than on success as measured by statistics or scoreboards. Coaches are thus encouraged to emphasize "doing your best," "getting better," and "having fun" as opposed to a "win at all costs" orientation. More specifically, a four-part philosophy of winning is taught in CET (Smith and Smoll, 2002):

1. *Winning isn't everything, nor is it the only thing.* Young athletes cannot get the most out of sports if they think that the only objective is to beat their opponents. Although winning is an important goal, it is *not* the most important objective.

2. *Failure is not the same thing as losing.* It is important that athletes do not view losing as a sign of failure or as a threat to their personal value.

3. *Success is not equivalent to winning.* Neither success nor failure need depend on the outcome of a contest or on a won-lost record. Winning and losing pertain to the outcome of a contest, whereas success and failure do not.

4. *Athletes should be taught that success is found in striving for victory (i.e., success is related to comitment and effort).* Athletes should be taught that they are never "losers" if they give maximum effort.

This philosophy is designed to maximize young athletes' enjoyment of sport and their chances of deriving the benefits of participation, partly as a result of reducing competitive anxiety. In what ways does this philosophy combat stress? With respect to Point 1, given that sport is heavily achievement-oriented, seeking victory is encouraged. However, the philosophy attempts to reduce the ultimate importance of winning relative to other prized participation motives (e.g., skill development and affiliation with teammates). Most notably, in recognition of the inverse relation between enjoyment and competitive anxiety, *fun* is highlighted as the paramount objective (Scanlan and Lewthwaite, 1984; Scanlan and Passer, 1978, 1979).

Points 2 and 3 of the philosophy are designed to promote separation of the athlete's feelings of self-worth from the game outcome. This orientation is supported by Gallwey and Kriegel (1977), who emphasized that "the key to overcoming fear of failure is breaking one's attachment to results" (p. 85). Adults can help children develop healthy attitudes about competition by showing that winning and losing does not change their value and affection for them as individuals.

Finally, in Point 4, young athletes are encouraged to attribute their failures to an unstable, controllable factor (i.e., lack of effort) instead of lack of ability (a stable, less controllable factor). There is considerable evidence that such an approach benefits children's motivation, performance, and feelings about themselves. For example,

Dweck's (1975) highly successful attributional retraining program with low-achieving children involved nothing more complicated than explicitly attributing failure to a lack of effort and encouraging subjects to try harder. Children who received direct instruction in how to interpret the causes of their failures showed improved performance (in a math problem-solving task) and were better able to cope with failure. Within the realm of sport, one might expect this approach to lessen the effects of failure, thereby reducing stress for athletes.

Didactic Procedures

In a CET workshop, which lasts approximately 2.5 hours, behavioral guidelines are presented both verbally and in written materials (a printed outline and a 24-page manual) given to the coaches. The manual (Smoll and Smith, 1997) supplements the guidelines with concrete suggestions for communicating effectively with young athletes, gaining their respect, and relating effectively to their parents. The importance of sensitivity and being responsive to individual differences among athletes is also emphasized. The written materials serve to (a) help keep the workshop organized, (b) facilitate coaches' understanding of the information, (c) eliminate the need for coaches to take notes, and (d) give coaches a tangible resource to refer to in the future. Also, visual aids (content slides and cartoons illustrating important points) are used to facilitate ease of comprehension and retention as well as to add to the organizational quality of the session.

We strongly believe in the importance of establishing an empirical foundation for training guidelines, but we also feel that the ability to present supportive data increases the credibility of the guidelines for the coaches. A CET workshop therefore includes a description of the development and testing of the program. As a prelude to presenting behavioral guidelines, the CBAS is described, using lay terms and avoiding scientific jargon. This provides coaches with a set of perceptual categories for organizing their own experiences and self-perceptions. After establishing a familiarity with potential behaviors, coaches are informed of how the various behaviors affect young athletes, and this, in turn, sets the stage for the presentation of coaching guidelines.

In introducing coaching guidelines, we emphasize that they should not be viewed as a "magic formula," nor that mere knowledge of the principles is sufficient. We stress that the challenge is not so much in learning the principles; they are relatively simple. Rather, the challenge is for the coach to integrate the guidelines into his or her own coaching style. When coaches believe that adoption of the guidelines is a result of their own dedication and effort, they are more likely to attribute behavioral changes to themselves rather than to the trainer. This approach is supported by evidence that self-attributed behavioral changes are more enduring than those attributed to some outside causal agent (Deci and Ryan, 1987).

The most basic objectives of CET are to communicate coaching principles in a manner that is easily comprehended, and to maximize the likelihood that coaches will adopt the information. As part of our approach to creating a positive learning environment, coaches are encouraged to share their own experiences and associated practical knowledge with the group. CET workshops are thus conducted with an interactive format in which coaches are treated as an integral part of the session rather than a mere audience. The open atmosphere for exchange promotes active versus passive learning, and the dialogue serves to enhance the participants' interest and involvement in the learning process.

The instructional procedures described above contain many verbal modeling cues that essentially tell coaches what to do. To supplement the didactic verbal and written materials, coaching guidelines are transmitted via behavioral modeling cues (i.e., actual demonstrations showing coaches how to behave in desirable ways). In CET, such cues are presented by a live model (the trainer) and by symbolic models (coach cartoons), as many forms of modeling have been shown to be highly effective in changing behavior (Bandura, 1986; Perry and Furukawa, 1986). In addition, modeling is frequently used in conjunction with later role playing of positive behaviors (e.g., Edelstein and Eisler, 1976; Nay, 1975). Coaches are kept actively involved in the training process by presenting critical situations and asking them to role play appropriate ways of responding. This form of behavioral rehearsal has great promise in enhancing acquisition of desired behaviors, in providing the opportunity to practice the behaviors, and in establishing an increased level of participant involvement during the workshops.

One of the striking findings from our basic research was that coaches had very limited awareness of how often they behaved in various ways (Smith et al., 1978). Thus, an important goal of CET is to increase coaches' awareness of what they are doing, for no change is likely to occur without it. CET coaches are taught the use of two proven behavioral-change techniques, namely, behavioral feedback (Edelstein and Eisler, 1976; McFall and Twentyman, 1973) and self-monitoring (Kanfer and Gaelick-Buys, 1991; Kazdin, 1974; McFall, 1977). To obtain feedback, coaches are encouraged to work with their assistants as a team and share descriptions of each others' behaviors. Other potential feedback procedures include coaches soliciting input from athletes and provision of feedback by a league committee.

Self-monitoring (observing and recording one's own behavior) is another behavioral-change technique that has potential for increasing coaches' awareness of their own behavioral patterns and encouraging their compliance with the guidelines. CET coaches are given a brief self-monitoring form that they are encouraged to complete immediately after practices and games (see Smoll and Smith, 2001, pp. 396–397). On the form, they indicate approximately what percentage of the time they engaged in the recommended behaviors in relevant situations. For example, coaches are asked, "Approximately what percentage of the times they occurred did you respond to mistakes/errors with encouragement?" Self-monitoring is restricted to desired behaviors in light of evidence that tracking of undesired behaviors can be detrimental to effective self-regulation (Cavior and Maribotto, 1976; Gottman and McFall, 1972;

Kirschenbaum and Karoly, 1977). Coaches are encouraged to engage in self-monitoring on a regular basis in order to achieve optimal results.

CET also includes discussion of coach-parent relationships and provides instructions on how to organize and conduct a sport orientation meeting with parents. Some purposes of the meeting are to inform parents about their responsibilities for contributing to the success of the sport program and to guide them toward working cooperatively and productively with the coach (see Smoll, 2001).

Applied Research Assessing the Efficacy of CET

Three national coaching education programs are currently available in the United States that include curricular components designed to assist coaches in creating a positive and enjoyable athletic environment—the American Coaching Effectiveness Program (ACEP), the National Youth Sport Coaches Association program (NYSCA), and the Program for Athletic Coaches' Education (PACE). Weiss and Hayashi (1996) noted that ACEP, NYSCA, and PACE "have provided coaching workshops to thousands of individuals involved in community-based and school-sponsored sports, but evaluation research is essential to determine the effectiveness of these training programs on increasing sport science knowledge and applications" (p. 53). In commenting on the importance of evaluation research, Lipsey and Cordray (2000) stated that "the overarching goal of the program evaluation enterprise is to contribute to the improvement of social conditions by providing scientifically credible information and balanced judgment to legitimate social agents about the effectiveness of interventions intended to produce social benefits" (p. 346). In this regard, recently reported results suggest that participation in PACE had a modest positive effect on the beliefs of coaches in their capacity to effect the learning and performance of their athletes (Malete and Feltz, 2000). The investigators labeled these results as "statistically significant findings, but not practically significant when applied to the origical scale" (p. 417). Whether enhancement of perceived coaching efficacy causes desirable changes in coaching practices and athlete outcome measures is an important topic for future research. At this time, however, CET is the only program that has been subjected to systematic evaluation to determine its influence on coaches' behaviors and the effects of such behaviors on youngsters' psychosocial development.

We have focused on five important outcome questions in our program evaluation studies. First, does the CET program affect the behaviors of the trained coaches in a manner consistent with the behavioral guidelines? Second, the program is designed to help coaches create an environment that would be expected to increase children's positive reactions to coach, teammates, and their sport experience. How does the program affect children's reactions to their athletic experience? Third, does exposure to a positive interpersonal environment created by trained coaches result in an increase in general self-esteem, particularly among low self-esteem children? Fourth, does CET training help reduce performance anxiety among young athletes? And, finally, do positive changes in the first four outcomes increase the likelihood that the young athletes will choose to return to the sport program? The remainder of this chapter summarizes our program evaluation research.

Experimental Field Research

In an initial field experiment (Smith, Smoll, and Curtis, 1979), 31 Little League Baseball coaches were randomly assigned to an experimental (training) or to a no-treatment control group. During a preseason CET workshop, behavioral guidelines were presented and modeled by the trainers. In addition to the information-modeling portion of the program, behavioral feedback and self-monitoring procedures were employed in an attempt to increase the coaches' self-awareness of their behaviors and to encourage them to comply with the coaching guidelines. To provide behavioral feedback, observers trained in the use of the CBAS observed experimental group coaches for two complete games. Behavioral profiles for each coach were derived from these observations and were then mailed to the coaches so that they were able to see the distribution of their own behaviors. Also, trained coaches were given brief self-monitoring forms that they completed immediately after the first 10 games of the season.

To assess the effects of the experimental program, CBAS data were collected throughout the season and behavioral profiles were generated for each coach in the experimental and control groups. Postseason outcome measures were obtained from 325 children in individual data collection sessions in their homes. On both observed behavior and player perception measures, the trained coaches differed from the controls in a manner consistent with the coaching guidelines. The trained coaches gave more reinforcement in response to good performance and effort, and they responded to mistakes with more encouragement and technical instruction and with fewer punitive responses. These behavioral differences were, in turn, reflected in their players' attitudes. The average won-lost percentages of the two groups of coaches did not differ. Nevertheless, the trained coaches were better liked and were rated as better teachers. Additionally, players on their teams liked one another more and enjoyed their sport experience more. These results seemingly reflect the more socially supportive environment created by the trained coaches. Perhaps most encouraging was the fact that children who played for the trained coaches exhibited a significant increase on a measure of general self-esteem as compared with scores obtained a year earlier, while those who played for the untrained coaches showed no significant change.

Replication and Extension Studies

Replication of our research on the efficacy of CET has been conducted, with the inclusion of several additional outcome measures. The subjects were 18 coaches and 152 children who participated in three Little League Baseball programs. Utilizing a quasi-experimental design, one league (8 teams) was designated the experimental group. The control group included 10 teams from two other leagues. Prior to the season, the experimental group coaches participated in CET. The control coaches participated in a technical skills training workshop conducted by the Seattle Mariners baseball team. To assess the effects of CET, preseason and postseason data were collected for 62 and 90 children in the experimental and control groups, respectively.

The study yielded four major results. First, we found that the CET intervention resulted in player-perceived behavioral differences between trained and untrained coaches that were in accordance with the behavioral guidelines. Thus, as in previous research (Smith et al., 1979), the experimental manipulation was successful in promoting a more desirable pattern of coaching behaviors. Second, the behavioral differences resulting from the CET program were accompanied by player evaluative responses that favored the trained coaches. The trained coaches were better liked and were rated as better teachers by their players. Moreover, their players reported that they had more fun playing baseball, and a higher level of attraction among teammates was again found despite the fact that their teams did not differ from controls in won-lost records. Third, consistent with a self-esteem enhancement model and with our previous findings (Smith and Smoll, 1990), children with low self-esteem who played for the trained coaches exhibited a significant increase in general self-esteem; low-esteem youngsters in the control group did not (Smoll, Smith, Barnett, and Everett, 1993). Fourth, the children who played for the CET coaches decreased in sport performance anxiety over the course of the season, whereas those who played for the control coaches did not change (Smith, Smoll, and Barnett, 1995).

An extension of the above study was completed one year following the CET intervention (Barnett, Smoll, and Smith, 1992). At the beginning of the next baseball season, dropout rates were assessed for youngsters who had played for the two groups of coaches. If a child was not playing baseball, a brief home interview was scheduled. During this session, the children completed a questionnaire designed to assess their reasons for discontinuing participation. The results revealed a 26% dropout rate among the control group children, a figure that is quite consistent with previous reports of 22% to 59% annual attrition rates in youth sport programs (Gould, 1987). In contrast, only 5% of the children who had played for the CET-trained coaches failed to return to the sport program the next season. There was no difference in won-lost percentages between dropouts and returning players; thus the attrition was not a consequence of a lack of team success. Moreover, evidence suggested that the withdrawal was a function of the players' sport experience rather than something that occurred during the 9-month interim. Finally, the questionnaire responses revealed that dropouts in the control group more often reported reasons for withdrawing that were associated with having a negative reaction to their sport experience the previous year.

In summary, CET has proven to be an economical and effective program that alters coaching behaviors in a desirable fashion and thereby has positive psychosocial effects on the children who play for trained coaches. Five classes of outcome variables have been significantly influenced by the training program—coaching behaviors, children's attitudes, self-esteem, performance anxiety, and attrition. We attribute the consistently positive results derived from our relatively brief intervention to the fact that our basic research helped to identify a set of core principles that are relatively easy for coaches to learn and that have a strong impact on young athletes.

In concluding this chapter, it is appropriate to restate our firm belief that extended efforts to improve the quality and value of coach-training programs are best achieved via well-conceived and properly conducted evaluation research. Future research will not only serve to advance understanding of the effects of competition, but will also provide for enriched opportunities for children and youth in sport.

References

Bales, R. F., and Slater, P. (1955). Role differentiation in small decision-making groups. In P. Parson and R. F. Bales (Eds.), *Family, socialization, and interaction process* (pp. 259–306). Glencoe, IL: Free Press.

Bandura, A. (1986). *Social foundations of thought and action: A social cognitive theory*. Englewood Cliffs, NJ: Prentice-Hall.

Barnett, N. P., Smoll, F. L., and Smith, R. E. (1992). Effects of enhancing coach-athlete relationships on youth sport attrition. *The Sport Psychologist, 6,* 111–127.

Berryman, J. W. (2002). The rise of boys' sports in the United States, 1900 to 1970. In F. L. Smoll and R. E. Smith (Eds.), *Children and youth in sport: A biopsychosocial perspective* (2nd ed., pp. 5–17). Dubuque, IA: Kendall/Hunt.

Brown, E. W., and Branta, C. F. (Eds.). (1988). *Competitive sports for children and youth: An overview of research and issues*. Champaign, IL: Human Kinetics.

Brown, J. D., Collins, R. L., and Schmidt, G. W. (1988). Self-esteem and direct versus indirect forms of self-enhancement. *Journal of Personality and Social Psychology, 55,* 445–453.

Brustad, R. J. (1993). Youth in sport: Psychological considerations. In R. N. Singer, M. Murphey, L. K. Tennant (Eds.), *Handbook of research on sport psychology* (pp. 695–717). New York: Macmillan.

Cahill, B. R., and Pearl, A. J. (Eds.). (1993). *Intensive participation in children's sports*. Champaign, IL: Human Kinetics.

Cavior, N., and Marabotto, C. M. (1976). Monitoring verbal behaviors in a dyadic interaction. *Journal of Consulting and Clinical Psychology, 44,* 68–76.

Chaumeton, N. R., and Duda, J. L. (1988). Is it how you play the game or whether you win or lose?: The effect of competitive level and situation on coaching behaviors. *Journal of Sport Behavior, 11,* 157–173.

Cruz, J., Bou, A., Fernandez, J. M., Martin, M., Monras, J., Monfort, N., and Ruiz, A. (1987). Avaluacio conductual de les interaccions entre entrenadors i jugadors de basquet escolar. *Apunts Medicina de L'esport, 24*, 89–98.

Curtis, B., Smith, R. E., and Smoll, F. L. (1979). Scrutinizing the skipper: A study of leadership behaviors in the dugout. *Journal of Applied Psychology, 64*, 391–400.

Deci, E. L., and Ryan, R. M. (1987). The support of autonomy and the control of behavior. *Journal of Personality and Social Psychology, 53*, 1024–1037.

Dittes, J. (1959). Attractiveness of a group as a function of self-esteem and acceptance by group. *Journal of Abnormal and Social Psychology, 59*, 77–82.

Dweck, C. S. (1975). The role of expectations and attributions in the alleviation of learned helplessness. *Journal of Personality and Social Psychology, 31*, 674–685.

Edelstein, B. A., and Eisler, R. M. (1976). Effects of modeling and modeling with instructions and feedback on the behavioral components of social skills. *Behavior Therapy, 7*, 382–389.

Ewing, M. E., and Seefeldt, V. (2002). Patterns of participation in American agency-sponsored youth sports. In F. L. Smoll and R. E. Smith (Eds.), *Children and youth in sports: A biopsychosocial perspective* (2nd ed., pp. 39–56).

Fiedler, F. E. (1967). *A theory of leadership effectiveness*. New York: McGraw-Hill.

Gallwey, W. R., and Kriegel, R. (1977, November). Fear of skiing. *Psychology Today*, pp. 78–85.

Goncalves, C. (1996). Portugal. In P. De Knop, L-M. Engstrom, B. Skirstad, and M. R. Weiss (Eds.), *Worldwide trends in youth sport* (pp. 193–203). Champaign, IL: Human Kinetics.

Gottman, J. M., and McFall, R. M. (1972). Self-monitoring effects in a program for potential high school dropouts: A time series analysis. *Journal of Consulting and Clinical Psychology, 39*, 273–281.

Gould, D. (1987). Understanding attrition in children's sport. In D. Gould and M. R. Weiss (Eds.), *Advances in pediatric sport sciences* (pp. 61–85). Champaign, IL: Human Kinetics.

Gould, D., and Weiss, M. R. (Eds.). (1987). *Advances in pediatric sport sciences: Vol. 2. Behavioral issues*. Champaign, IL: Human Kinetics.

Graen, G., and Schiemann, W. (1978). Leader member agreement: A vertical dyad linkage approach. *Journal of Applied Psychology, 63*, 206–212.

Hersey, P., and Blanchard, K. H. (1977). *Management of organizational behavior* (3rd ed.). Englewood Cliffs, NJ: Prentice-Hall.

Horn, T. S. (1984). Expectancy effects in the interscholastic athletic setting: Methodological considerations. *Journal of Sport Psychology, 6*, 60–76.

Horn, T. S. (1985). Coaches' feedback and changes in children's perceptions of their physical competence. *Journal of Educational Psychology, 77*, 174–186.

Jones, D. F., Housner, L. D., and Kornspan, A. S. (1997). Interactive decision making and behavior of experienced and inexperienced basketball coaches during practices. *Journal of Teaching in Physical Education, 16*, 454–468.

Kanfer, F. H., and Gaelick-Buys, L. (1991). Self-management methods. In F. H. Kanfer and A. P. Goldstein (Eds.), *Helping people change: A textbook of methods* (4th ed., pp. 305–360). New York: Pergamon.

Kazdin, A. E. (1974). Self-monitoring and behavior change. In M. J. Mahoney and C. E. Thoresen (Eds.), *Self-control: Power to the person* (pp. 218–246). Monterey, CA: Brooks/Cole.

Kirschenbaum, D. S., and Karoly, P. (1977). When self-regulation fails: Tests of some preliminary hypotheses. *Journal of Consulting and Clinical Psychology, 45*, 1116–1125.

Komaki, J. L. (1986). Toward effective supervision: An operant analysis and comparison of managers at work. *Journal of Applied Psychology, 71*, 270–279.

Krane, V., Eklund, R., and McDermott, M. (1991). Collaborative action research and behavioral coaching intervention: A case study. In W. K. Simpson, A. LeUnes, and J. S. Picou (Eds.), *The applied research in coaching and athletics annual 1991* (pp. 119–147). Boston, MA: American Press.

Laakso, L., Telama, R., and Yang, X. (1996). Finland. In P. De Knop, L-M. Engstrom, B. Skirstad, and M. R. Weiss (Eds.), *Worldwide trends in youth sport* (pp. 126–138). Champaign, IL: Human Kinetics.

Lipsey, M. W., and Cordray, D. S. (2000). Evaluation methods for social intervention. *Annual Review of Psychology, 51*, 345–375.

Malete, L., and Feltz, D. L. (2000). The effect of a coaching education program on coaching efficacy. *The Sport Psychologist, 14*, 410–417.

Malina, R. M. (Ed.). (1988). *Young athletes: Biological, psychological, and educational perspectives*. Champaign, IL: Human Kinetics.

Malina, R. M., and Clark, M. A. (Eds.). (2001). *Organized sport in the lives of children and adolescents*. Champaign, IL: Sagamore.

Martens, R. (1988). Youth sport in the USA. In F. L. Smoll, R. A. Magill, and M. J. Ash (Eds.), *Children in sport* (3rd ed., pp. 17–23). Champaign, IL: Human Kinetics.

Martens, R. (1997). *Successful coaching* (2nd ed.). Champaign, IL: Human Kinetics.

McFall, R. M. (1977). Parameters of self-monitoring. In R. B. Stuart (Ed.), *Behavioral self-management: Strategies, techniques and outcomes* (pp. 196–214). New York: Brunner/Mazel.

McFall, R. M., and Twentyman, C. T. (1973). Four experiments on the relative contributions of rehearsal, modeling, and coaching to assertion training. *Journal of Abnormal Psychology, 81*, 199–218.

Nay, W. R. (1975). A systematic comparison of instructional techniques for parents. *Behavior Therapy, 6*, 14–21.

Oldenhove, H. (1996). Australia. In P. De Knop, L-M. Engstrom, B. Skirstad, and M. R. Weiss (Eds.), *Worldwide trends in youth sport* (pp. 245–259). Champaign, IL: Human Kinetics.

Perry, M. A., and Furukawa, M. J. (1986). Modeling methods. In F. H. Kanfer and A. P. Goldstein (Eds.), *Helping people change: A textbook of methods* (3rd ed., pp. 66–110). New York: Pergamon.

Rejeski, W., Darracott, C., and Hutslar, S. (1979). Pygmalion in youth sport: A field study. *Journal of Sport Psychology, 1*, 311–319.

Rogers, C. R. (1951). *Client-centered therapy*. Boston: Houghton Mifflin.

Scanlan, T. K., and Lewthwaite, R. (1984) Social psychological aspects of competition for male youth sport participants: I. Predictors of competitive stress. *Journal of Sport Psychology, 6*, 208–226.

Scanlan, T. K., and Passer, M. W. (1978). Factors related to competitive stress among male youth sports participants. *Medicine and Science in Sports, 10*, 103–108.

Scanlan, T. K., and Passer, M. W. (1979). Sources of competitive stress in young female athletes. *Journal of Sport Psychology, 1*, 151–159.

Seefeldt, V., and Brown, E. W. (Eds.). (1996). *Program for athletic coaches' education: Reference manual*. Carmel, IN: Cooper.

Sherman, M. A., and Hassan, J. S. (1986). Behavioral studies of youth sport coaches. In M. Pieron and G. Graham (Eds.), *The 1984 Olympic Scientific Congress proceedings: Vol. 6. Sport pedagogy* (pp. 103–108). Champaign, IL: Human Kinetics.

Shrauger, J. S. (1975). Responses to evaluation as a function of initial self-perceptions. *Psychological Bulletin, 82*, 581–596.

Smith, R. E., and Smoll, F. L. (1990). Self-esteem and children's reactions to youth sport coaching behaviors: A field study of self-enhancement processes. *Developmental Psychology, 26*, 987–993.

Smith, R. E., and Smoll, F. L. (1997). Coaching the coaches: Youth sports as a scientific and applied behavioral setting. *Current Directions in Psychological Science, 6*, 16–21.

Smith, R. E., and Smoll, F. L. (2002). *Way to go, coach! A scientifically-proven approach to coaching effectiveness* (2nd ed.). Portola Valley, CA: Warde.

Smith, R. E., Smoll, F. L., and Barnett, N. P. (1995). Reduction of children's sport performance anxiety through social support and stress-reduction training for coaches. *Journal of Applied Developmental Psychology, 16*, 125–142.

Smith, R. E., Smoll, F. L., and Christensen, D. S. (1996). Behavioral assessment and interventions in youth sports. *Behavior Modification, 20*, 3–44.

Smith, R. E., Smoll, F. L., and Curtis, B. (1978). Coaching behaviors in little league baseball. In F. L. Smoll and R. E. Smith (Eds.), *Psychological perspectives in youth sports* (pp. 173–201). Washington, DC: Hemisphere.

Smith, R. E., Smoll, F. L., and Curtis, B. (1979). Coach Effectiveness Training: A cognitive-behavioral approach to enhancing relationship skills in youth sport coaches. *Journal of Sport Psychology, 1*, 59–75.

Smith, R. E., Smoll, F. L., and Hunt, E. B. (1977). A system for the behavioral assessment of athletic coaches. *Research Quarterly, 48*, 401–407.

Smith, R. E., Zane, N. W. S., Smoll, F. L., and Coppel, D. B. (1983). Behavioral assessment in youth sports: Coaching behaviors and children's attitudes. *Medicine and Science in Sports and Exercise, 15*, 208–214.

Smoll, F. L. (2001). Coach-parent relationships in youth sports: Increasing harmony and minimizing hassle. In J. M. Williams (Ed.), *Applied sport psychology: Personal growth to peak performance* (4th ed., pp. 150–161). Mountain View, CA: Mayfield.

Smoll, F. L., and Smith, R. E. (1989). Leadership behaviors in sport: A theoretical model and research paradigm. *Journal of Applied Social Psychology, 19*, 1522–1551.

Smoll, F. L., and Smith, R. E. (1997). *Coaches who never lose: Making sure athletes win, no matter what the score.* Portola Valley, CA: Warde.

Smoll, F. L., and Smith, R. E. (2001). Conducting sport psychology training programs for coaches: Cognitive-behavioral principles and techniques. In J. M. Williams (Ed.), *Applied sport psychology: Personal growth to peak performance* (4th ed., pp. 378–400). Mountain View, CA: Mayfield.

Smoll, F. L., Smith, R. E., Barnett, N. P., and Everett, J. J. (1993). Enhancement of children's self-esteem through social support training for youth sport coaches. *Journal of Applied Psychology, 78*, 602–610.

Smoll, F. L., Smith, R. E., Curtis, B., and Hunt, E. (1978). Toward a mediational model of coach-player relationships. *Research Quarterly, 49*, 528–541.

Stogdill, R. M. (1959). *Individual behavior and group achievement.* New York: Oxford University Press.

Swann, W. B. (1996). *Self-traps: The elusive quest for higher self-esteem.* San Francisco: Freeman.

Swann, W. B., Jr., Griffin, J. J., Predmore, S. C., and Gaines, B. (1987). The cognitive-affective crossfire: When self-consistency confronts self-enhancement. *Journal of Personality and Social Psychology, 52*, 881–889.

Tesser, A. (1988). Toward a self-evaluative maintenance model of social behavior. In L. Berkowitz (Ed.), *Advances in experimental social psychology* (Vol. 21, pp. 69–92). Orlando, FL: Academic Press.

Tesser, A., and Campbell, J. (1983). Self-definition and self-evaluation maintenance. In J. Suls and A. G. Greenwald (Eds.), *Psychological perspectives on the self* (Vol. 2, pp. 1–32). Hillsdale, NJ: Erlbaum.

Wandzilak, T., Ansorge, C. J., and Potter, G. (1988). Comparison between selected practice and game behaviors of youth soccer coaches. *Journal of Sport Behavior, 11*, 78–88.

Wankel, L. M., and Mummery, W. K. (1996). Canada. In P. De Knop, L-M. Engstrom, B. Skirstad, and M. R. Weiss (Eds.), *Worldwide trends in youth sport* (pp. 27–42). Champaign, IL: Human Kinetics.

Weiss, M. R. (2001). *Developmental sport and exercise psychology: A lifespan perspective*. Morgantown, WV: Fitness Information Technology.

Weiss, M. R., and Gould, D. (Eds.). (1986). *Sport for children and youths*. Champaign, IL: Human Kinetics.

Weiss, M. R., and Hayashi, C. T. (1996). The United States. In P. De Knop, L-M. Engstrom, B. Skirstad, and M. R. Weiss (Eds.), *Worldwide trends in youth sport* (pp. 43–57). Champaign, IL: Human Kinetics.

White, M. A. (1975). Natural rates of teacher approval and disapproval in the classroom. *Journal of Applied Behavior Analysis, 8*, 367–372.

Wiggins, D. K. (2002). A history of highly competitive sport for American children. In F. L. Smoll and R. E. Smith (Eds.), *Children and youth in sport: A biopsychosocial perspective* (2nd ed., pp. 19–37). Dubuque, IA: Kendall/Hunt.

Appendix A

Summary of Coaching Guidelines

I.   Reacting to Athlete Behaviors and Game Situations

    A.   Good plays

Do: Provide *reinforcement*! Do so immediately. Let the athletes know that you appreciate and value their efforts. Reinforce effort as much as you do results. Look for positive things, reinforce them, and you will see them increase. Remember, whether athletes show it or not, the positive things you say and do remain with them.

Don't: Take their efforts for granted.

    B.   Mistakes

Do: Give *encouragement* immediately after mistakes. That's when the youngster needs your support the most. If you are sure the athlete knows how to correct the mistake, then encouragement alone is sufficient. When appropriate, give *corrective instruction*, but always do so in an encouraging manner. Do this by emphasizing not the bad things that just happened, but the good things that will happen if the athlete follows your instruction (the "why" of it). This will make the athlete positively self-motivated to correct the mistakes rather than negatively motivated to avoid failure and your disapproval.

Don't: *Punish* when things are going wrong! Punishment isn't just yelling. It can be tone of voice, action, or any indication of disapproval. Athletes respond much better to a positive approach. Fear of failure is reduced if you work to reduce fear of punishment. Indications of displeasure should be limited to clear cases of lack of effort; but, even then, criticize the lack of effort rather that the athlete as a person.

Don't: Give corrective instruction in a hostile, demeaning, or harsh manner. That is, avoid *punitive instruction*. This is more likely to increase frustration and create resentment than to improve performance. Don't let your good intentions in giving instruction be self-defeating.

    C.   Misbehaviors, lack of attention

Do: Maintain order by establishing clear expectations. Emphasize that during a game all members of the team are part of the activity, even those on the bench. Use reinforcement to strengthen team participation. In other words, try to prevent misbehaviors by using the positive approach to strengthen their opposites.

Don't: Get into the position of having to constantly nag or threaten athletes in order to prevent chaos. Don't be a drill sergeant. If an athlete refuses to cooperate, deprive him or her of something valued. Don't use physical measures, such as running laps. The idea here is that if you establish clear behavioral guidelines early and work to build team spirit in achieving them, you can avoid having to repeatedly *keep control*. Youngsters want clear guidelines and expectations, but they don't want to be regimented. Try to achieve a healthy balance.

II. Getting Positive Things to Happen and Creating a Good Learning Atmosphere

Do: Give *technical instruction*. Establish your role as a caring and competent teacher. Try to structure participation as a learning experience in which you are going to help the athletes develop their abilities. Always give instruction in a positive fashion. Satisfy your athletes' desire to improve their skills. Give instruction in a clear, concise manner and, if possible, demonstrate how to do skills correctly.

Do: Give encouragement. Encourage effort, don't demand results. Use encouragement selectively so that it is meaningful. Be supportive without acting like a cheerleader.

Do: Concentrate on the activity. Be "in the game" with the athletes. Set a good example for team unity.

Don't: Give either instruction or encouragement in a sarcastic or degrading manner. Make a point, then leave it. Don't let "encouragement" become irritating to the athletes.

Note. These guidelines were excerpted from the manual that is given to CET workshop participants (Smoll and Smith, 1997, pp. 7–15).

CHAPTER 10

Interpersonal Sources of Violence in Hockey: The Influence of the Media, Parents, Coaches, and Game Officials

Norman N. Morra, York University
Michael D. Smith, York University

"Within the last thirty years, I watched many pro games and seldom did they end without fights. I think this was a sort of a ritual . . . arranged almost deliberately. Fights desecrate hockey. They distort the essence of the sport as a noble competition in ingenuity, speed, skills, and shrewdness" (Tarasov, 1997, pp. 32–33).

Prior research on sports violence has shown that parents and coaches strongly influence youths who play minor hockey (Smith, 1979, 1983, 1987; Vaz, 1982). These studies and others showed how coaches and parents, along with professional hockey players, instill highly aggressive attitudes in young men. The closer a youth advances to the professional ranks the more likely he will use tactics such as fighting and illegal stick-work to play the sport (Colburn, 1985; 1986). Besides parents and coaches, we maintain that game officials and media members contribute indirectly to violence in minor hockey. Bandura (1986) affirms that children vicariously learn violence by emulating the macho behavior of their video idols. The media molds former athletes such as bodybuilder Arnold Schwarzenegger and martial arts black belt Jean Claude Van Damme into violent heroes for children. Likewise, in a less explicit way, professional hockey enforcers such as Tie Domi and Donald Brashear earn enormous salaries and serve as negative role models for younger players.

Method and Data

The understanding of any sociological problem requires some knowledge of its past. C. Wright Mills (1961) argued that social science helps to unravel complex issues by examining three intersecting elements—history, biography, and society. We have chosen Mills' method for two reasons: (a) It allows us to look at the interpersonal relationships pertinent to hockey violence; (b) it forces us to question society's role in the matter.

The historical part of this study extends from the 1950s until the present. Within this time span, we will outline some salient incidents of violence in the National Hockey League (NHL). We include biographical descriptions of persons who helped formulate this history. Next, we will show how particular individuals within the media benefit through the promotion of fighting. Before updating the interpersonal processes of these groups, we will examine earlier significant studies that have dealt with the sources of violence in hockey. Finally, we describe how some parents, coaches, and game officials influence the behavior of young hockey players at present.

Our research incorporates select data from previous studies in the 1970s and 1980s that addressed the issue of hockey violence. We also observed current professional matches on television and many minor league games at arenas within metropolitan Toronto. The children and youths we focused on were between the ages of 7 and 18 years. Besides parents, coaches, and referees, we interviewed arena managers and equipment handlers: individuals on the periphery of minor hockey. These adults gave us relatively unbiased accounts of hockey violence. Further discussions, with two noted Canadian journalists, helped us to clarify the nuances of violence in the sport. Interviews with two administrators in the Canadian Amateur Hockey Association (CAHA) made us aware of the difficulty in trying to eliminate this problem. Additional data came from sources such as videotapes, magazine articles, TV documentaries and newspaper reports.

Frustration-Aggression: A Rationale for Violence

Most sports, including basketball, football, soccer, international and collegiate hockey, eject and often suspend players for fighting. Contrary to the zero tolerance approach of these sports, professional hockey's executives, managers and coaches laud fighting as multifunctional and necessary to the sport's survival. They credit fighting as a "safety valve," reducing the intensity of competition, a way to protect star players, and a source of fan entertainment. Gruneau (1993) critically links the concept of a safety valve to "the catharsis hypothesis" whereby "fighting in sports provides controlled and symbolic outlets for aggression" (p. 177). Such thinking stems from the Freudian-based frustration-aggression theory of Dollard, Doob, Miller, Mower, and Sears (1939) and underpins the violence that the public, including parents of young players, interprets as justifiable in hockey. Frustration-aggression theory evolved out of the 1930s Great Depression when North American morale was at its lowest point. Dollard and his colleagues concluded that after enduring repeated frustration, and resisting the impulse to retaliate, people *invariably* attack whoever frustrates them. Hobsbawm (1996) argues that the horrendous economic slump of 1938–39 generated a "pessimism" which steered Americans toward accepting simple answers for both their economic woes and the escalating world violence. The frustration-aggression thesis justified a nation's bitterness over poverty and the extreme social turbulence arising from the Second World War.

The Violent Past of Professional Hockey

Hockey has been an integral part of Canadian culture for nearly a century. Its violent aspect, however, is traceable to one source: the NHL. Traditionally, the NHL has served as the model for hockey in North America and abroad (Tarasov, 1969; Tretiak, 1987). Although many of our young men dream of someday playing in the NHL, the sport is no longer exclusively Canadian. With the increasing numbers of American, European and Scandinavian players in the NHL today, children from other countries also share this dream.

Today's star players, such as Mike Modano and Paul Kariya, have suffered injuries due to the cross-checks and slashes from their opponents' sticks. These two athletes serve as hockey's ambassadors and as exemplars for younger players. Nowadays these top athletes, as well as former great players, Wayne Gretzky and Mario Lemieux, rarely fought[1], but this has not always been the case. Professional hockey players during the 1950s and early 1960s considered it their duty to fight when others challenged them. Hockey players, whatever their status, viewed fighting as crucial for maintaining their honor. Failure to respond to an opponent's provocation was inexcusable. Those who backed down from a fight disgraced themselves and their teammates; it was conduct unbecoming a professional hockey player. Pundits of the sport maintained that fighting was a way to blow off steam, thus preventing serious injuries attributable to illegal stick-work (Colburn, 1986).

Fights, whether premeditated or not, followed a set of procedures. The primary rule required each player to drop his stick and gloves before exchanging blows (Colburn, 1985). Players who violated this code with such disreputable acts as "sucker punching" or spearing became the targets of a swift retribution by the other team. One administrator with the CAHA mentioned that young men in the Western Junior "A" Hockey League, for example, still act out this ritual. Because protective head and face gear is now mandatory in minor hockey, some players see this as a drawback to an even fight. For those combatants insistent on keeping fights fair, it is obligatory to remove their helmets before fighting. We observed this custom take place during a Juvenile game in a Toronto house league.

---

1. Lemieux, part owner of the Pittsburgh Penguins, returned to play for Pittsburgh on December 27, 2000.

Superstars of the 1950s, such as Maurice Richard[2] and Gordie Howe, seldom backed away from a challenge. Detroit's Howe, among the game's finest players, commanded respect from his opponents. His career spanned four decades; he played, although with less and less intensity, until the age of 52. Howe also holds, besides his longevity, the distinction of being the only man to play a contact sport with his two adult sons. Howe's ability to fight, and the illegal use of his elbows and stick, are legendary in hockey lore. Today's players, regardless of their age, are familiar with the exploits of Gordie Howe.

Other talented but nonviolent superstars of the fifties, such as Montreal's Jean Beliveau and New York Rangers' Andy Bathgate, were consummate professionals. Although these athletes were positive role models for the youth of their time, neither received their full measure of respect. Bathgate, because of his outspoken criticism of hockey violence, met with ridicule of team owners, the media, and his peers. The NHL, in fact, ruled that Bathgate's decrying of hockey violence in print was detrimental to the sport and fined him $500 (Dunnell, 1959).

Beliveau did earn the acclaim of fans and players but intimidation was never a part of his game. The phlegmatic Beliveau, however, failed to receive the same adulation as his teammate, Maurice (Rocket) Richard. Richard was the first NHL player to score 50 goals in as many games. Followers of the sport remember him equally for his volatile temper and unbridled hatred of the opposition. His charisma excited the Montreal fans who cheered any act of violence by Richard. In spite of his talent, Richard was responsible for one particularly abhorrent deed. In March 1955, irked by the close checking of Boston's Hal Laycoe, he slammed his stick across Laycoe's face. The blow shattered Laycoe's glasses and he fell to the ice where Richard hit him several more times with his stick. The NHL suspended Richard for the balance of the season and the following playoffs. In the aftermath of this incident, on St. Patrick's day, the infamous Rocket Richard riot took place. Irate fans smashed windows and looted stores in the downtown section of Montreal (Frayne, 1973).

Once the league expanded into the lucrative U.S. sports market in 1967, team owners and managers realized how senseless it was to let star players fight. Hockey's superstars attracted the customers, and it was ludicrous to have them inactive due to injuries or suspensions incurred through fights. Chicago's Bobby Hull was the prime example of this dilemma. Hull, with his introduction of the slapshot and the curved blade, helped to revolutionize the game. Despite being a productive and spectacular scorer, Hull had difficulty in fending off his rougher opponents. To protect the league's superstars management devised a systematic division of labor. Owners hired players with marginal skills but fighting ability to protect their teams' top players. In

---

2. Richard passed away in 2000. The media praised his charisma and achievements while downplaying the violent side of his hockey career.

the case of Hull, Chicago promoted a minor league tough guy, Reg Fleming, specifically for the job of enforcer.

Other teams recognized the benefit of this tactic and quickly adopted its format. Whenever an enforcer was unable to carry out his task, it became the responsibility of any player to assist his team's star. The Philadephia Flyers of the 1970s were masters of this strategy. They stocked their club with several fighters to intimidate other teams and enable their top playmaker, Bobby Clarke,[3] to execute his fiercely competitive game with impunity. Sports writers labeled them "The Broad Street Bullies," and the Flyers asserted themselves as the most fearsome team of the seventies. Ontario's Attorney General, Roy McMurtry, laid criminal charges against several Flyers after a particularly violent game in Toronto duringthe 1974–75 season. The Flyers were, according to McMurtry, "a very bad example for young kids who ape the professionals" (Schultz, 1981, p. 136).

With the increase in bench-clearing brawls and retaliatory acts with the stick, referees were unable to prevent games from getting out of control. Much of this violence predicated itself on players' loyalty to one another. The NHL tried to curtail the rise in brawling with the "third man in" rule. The rule said that any player attempting to help a teammate already in a fight would face eviction from the game. In addition, that same player would later receive a fine and suspension. Although this rule helped to prevent team brawls, it did not eradicate fighting. It reinforced instead the longstanding ritual of two men engaging in hand-to-hand combat. In brief, owners made token efforts to eliminate brawling, but managed to preserve fighting as part of the game.

In spite of the NHL's rule changes and the increase in fines and suspensions, the demand for tougher enforcers persists. Some believe hockey is less violent today and that the time of the enforcer has passed. Nonetheless, teams still use specialty players to fill this role. For example, the Winnipeg Jets (1993) obtained the rambunctious but highly popular, Tie Domi, from the New York Rangers. The Jets gave up a skilled player and guaranteed Domi a substantial salary to protect their team's sensational rookie, Finnish import Teemu Selanne. Domi's presence allowed Selanne to score at his record shattering clip (Burman and Lee, 1993). For the 2000–01 season, Domi earns close to $1.7 million U.S. playing for the Toronto Maple Leafs; Selanne is a member of the Anaheim Mighty Ducks.[4]

---

3. Clarke, presently General Manager of the Philadelphia Flyers, applies the same toughness in dealing with his own players. The most notable case involves Eric Lindros, his concussions and trade demands.
4. NHL Players' Association Website (www.nhlpa.com).

Selling Hockey Violence: TV, Videos, Magazines

Although fighting and dirty play has existed in professional hockey since it began in 1908, we think its continuance depends significantly on television. It is difficult to contest that television, from its inception, has affected entire segments of viewers (McLuhan and Fiore, 1967). TV and video are technological tools and represent the essential seductive force in our consumer culture (Baudrillard, 1983). Rarely do we dispute what we see on television. We have witnessed violence such as the Gulf War, strife in Bosnia, the beatings of Rodney King and Reginald Denny. These images document the reality of our present-day existence (Murphy and Choi, 1993). With continuous sports channels such as ESPN in the U.S. and TSN in Canada, the violence of football, hockey, and boxing is instantly available for viewers at any time of the day.

Television shows us how professionals use intimidation as an expedient way to nullify an opponent's effectiveness. Violence, however, existed as a feature of the sport long before the introduction of television. TV simply brought it to countless viewers. Young boys avidly watch professional hockey on TV and simulate the good and bad actions of their sports heroes. Although the Canadian Federal Government's Fair Play Commission and other agencies try to stop foul play, purveyors of fight videos, for example, are negating their efforts. Television, along with other media, are businesses in pursuit of financial gain. Their success relies heavily upon the cooperation of certain NHL players who are willing to play along with the condoning of violence. This complicity by players, perhaps unwitting, manifests itself in their discourse with certain sports journalists. The foremost example of an individual who capitalizes on the promotion of violence is former Boston Bruins coach, Don Cherry. For over a decade, the ubiquitous Cherry has enjoyed the status of a Canadian celebrity. We cannot estimate the extent of his wealth, but Cherry's financial success is undeniable. He is the host of his own TV show and appears as a guest on various radio programs. He does commercials for automotive parts, trust companies, department stores, lotteries, colognes and a slew of other products. Much of his prosperity is attributable to his tireless advocating for the retention of fighting in hockey.

The forum for most of Cherry's diatribe is the intermission segment "Coach's Corner" during telecasts of NHL games aired on CBC's "Hockey Night in Canada" (Harrison, 1993). For millions of Canadian viewers the ritual of watching this program is akin to the fervor many Americans have for "Monday Night Football" on ABC. With his entertaining, uninhibited speech style, and right-wing utterances. Cherry amuses some but antagonizes others. As his ratings soar the public anticipates his outbursts. Because of Cherry's immense popularity, the CBC grants him considerable leeway to voice his contentious opinions.

Cherry especially harangues foreign players for taking NHL jobs away from Canadians. He singles out Soviets for their lack of fortitude and blames them for the dirty stick-work prevalent in today's hockey. His list of undesirables also includes Scandinavians, some Americans, and French-Canadians. He uses his TV and radio programs as outlets for others who share his conviction that slashing and spearing is a result of safety gear such as face masks. Cherry believes minor hockey regulations overprotect youngsters. As a result, they feel immune to injury and resort to illicit stick-work to control others. This argument contains some truth but to call for the removal of protective equipment such as visors would surely jeopardize the welfare of young players. Many of his TV guests are current and past enforcers who delight in Cherry's showing film clips of their more savage battles. The TV studio audience reacts to these fights with howls of approval. Cherry has also compiled twelve editions of hockey's most brutal fight videos entitled "Rock Em Sock Em." These products are available in stores everywhere and continue to sell steadily.

Although Cherry profits in the propagandizing of hockey violence, he is not alone in capitalizing on its promotion. Distributors in Minnesota, for instance, market a series of videotapes called *Sports Pages* (Combined Artists, 1992). "Killer Hockey" was the subtitle of the video that we analyzed. The cover of this videotape shows two players fighting. The blurb on the reverse side of the box advertises 30 minutes of "broken bones, the bloody gashes and the damage caused by flying pucks—and fists." It also lures young viewers with the names of their favorite NHL players who fail to appear in the video. The message this product delivers is that hockey is a brutal sport meant only for tough men.

The May 1993 edition of the magazine *Hockey Heroes* features fighting as its theme. In the top corner of its front cover is the caption "Blood On Ice!" The cover's photograph shows a bleeding Bob Probert[5] of the Detroit Red Wings staving off a relentless Tie Domi. One article by Stan Fischler asserts "fighting is as much a part of the woof and warp of hockey as a stick and a puck" (p. 11). Fischler argues that fighting is entertainment and must remain in the sport. He insists that without violence Americans will show little interest in hockey and stop attending games. Perhaps this is correct, but it is equally true that children, as well as adults, purchase these videos and magazines.

Previous Research on the Influence of Parents, Coaches, and Teammates

Parents

Data from a survey of Toronto hockey players conducted in the late 1970s reveal the extent to which hockey parents approve of violence (Smith, 1979). Six hundred and four players were asked if they thought their father and mother would approve of a minor hockey league player punching another player in four situations: (a) if ridiculed, (b) if threatened, (c) if shoved, or (d) if punched by the other player. Indexes

---

5. Probert earned $1.8 million U.S. as a member of the 2000 Chicago Black Hawks (NHL Players' Association Website: www.nhlpa.com).

of Parents' Approval of Hockey Fighting were constructed by summing the *yes* responses to these items. Table 10.1 shows variations in players' scores on these indexes by age and level of competition (house league or recreational versus competitive).

Table 10.1 Hockey Players' Perceptions of Their Parents' Approval of Hockey Fighting by Age and Level of Competition (in Percent)[1]

	Fathers' Approval			Mothers' Approval		
	Low	Medium	High[2]	Low	Medium	High
Age						
12–13 *(N = 166)*	77	20	3	89	8	3
14–15 *(N = 196)*	66	25	9	85	8	3
16–17 *(N = 130)*	47	31	22	81	14	5
18–21 *(N = 112)*	40	19	41	75	18	7
Level of Competition						
House League *(N = 330)*	76	18	6	94	6	0
Competitive *(N = 274)*	41	31	29	71	21	8
All players *(N = 604)*	60	24	16	83	13	4

[1]Adapted from Smith (1979, p. 113).

[2]Low = approval in no situations; medium = approval in one or two situations; high = approval in three or four situations.

The majority of fathers (60%) rank low on the Fathers' Approval Index, which is to say these fathers would not, in the eyes of their offspring, approve of a player punching another player in any of the situations presented. But approval increases sharply with age and level of competition. In the older older age and competitive rows, the majority of fathers fall into the medium-approval (one or two situations) and high-approval (three or four situations) categories. Of the 18- to 21-year-olds, 41% felt their parents would approve of fighting in at least three of the situations, compared with only 3% of the 12- to 13-year-olds; 29% of the fathers of competitive-level players were seen as high approvers, compared with 6% of the house-league fathers. Mothers consistently were perceived as less approving than fathers; still, 25% and 29% in the 18- to 21-year-old and competitive rows are in the medium- and high-approval categories combined.

Coaches

How extensive is hockey coaches' approval of rough play? Almost all of 83 high school players interviewed by Smith (1975) stated that their coaches would approve (most of them "strongly") of "hard but legal body-checking." Over half of the more than 1,900 boys surveyed by Vaz (1982) reported that their coaches regularly emphasized "playing rough and being aggressive." When asked "What are three most important qualities a coach looks for in selecting players for all-star teams?" 62% of the oldest boys (aged 15 and 16) included, out of nine possible response choices, "being aggressive at all times"; 56% included "physical size and strength"; 25% included "guts and courage." (More than half of these boys were house-leaguers, and their responses probably pulled these percentages down.)

Such findings are not surprising; much of what is called aggressive play is sanctioned by the official rules of the game. What of officially legal violence? Table 10.2 reveals that Toronto minor hockey players see coaches as somewhat more approving of violence than fathers, yet only 21% of all coaches come under the high-approval heading. Again, this overall figure obscures differences in age and level of competition. Over 50% of the 18- to 21-year-olds and 36% of the competitive-level players saw their coaches as high approvers.

Table 10.2   Hockey Players' Perceptions of Their Coaches Approval of Hockey Fighting by Age and Level of Competition (in Percent)[1]

| | Coaches' Approval | | |
	Low	Medium	High[2]
Age			
12–13 (N = 166)	74	17	9
14–15 (N = 196)	59	30	11
16–17 (N = 130)	39	36	25
18–21 (N = 112)	25	23	52
Level of Competition			
House league (N = 330)	70	22	8
Competitive (N = 274)	32	32	36
All players (N = 604)	53	26	11

[1]Adapted from Smith (1979, p. 113)

[2]Low = approval in no situations; medium = approval in one or two situations; high = approval in three or four situations.

Players' perceptions of coaches' sanctions for assaultive play do seem to have an impact on players' attitudes and conduct at all levels of hockey. Vaz (1982) reported statistically significant associations in all age divisions between players' perceptions of how much their coaches emphasized "playing rough and being aggressive" and players' approval of "taking out an opposing player any way you can to save a goal even though you risk injuring the opposing player." Smith (1979) has demonstrated statistically that the more coaches approve of fighting, the more players fight, and the more penalties they receive.

Teammates

The importance of peer approval of understanding violence in gangs, prisons, violent subcultures of all sorts, and among boys and men in general has long been recognized. Respect is what counts. You get it by demonstrating physical courage, gameness, recklessness sometimes, disdain for injury, and a willingness to fight if necessary. You lose it by revealing a lack of "heart" or "guts," by "chickening out."

Quantitative data on hockey players' violence approval—their own and the perceptions of their teammates—are shown in Table 10.3. These data indicate that amateur hockey players perceive their teammates as considerably more approving of fighting than their coaches and parents. Sixty-four percent of the respondents viewed other team members as approving of fighting in at least three of the four situations presented. Comparisons with players' own attitudes, however, reveals an anomaly described by Matza (1964) in his research on delinquency. It is apparent in Table 10.3 that individual violence approval is extensive, but not as extensive as that which individuals attribute to teammates collectively. It seems what individuals say and do about violence in the presence of peers is one thing, but their private attitudes are another. This results in a shared misunderstanding in which individuals think others value violence more than they actually do.

To what extent would players privately *prefer* less fighting and other sorts of illegal rough play? The foregoing players were asked "Would you like to see more, about the same, or less fistfighting in your games?" Forty-five percent said less. When asked "Would you like to see more, about the same, or less illegal stick-work in your games?" 82% said less. How many players quit hockey because of the violence? This question has yet to be adequately answered, but more than a few have done so, one suspects.

Closer inspection of the data in Table 10.3 shows that the gap in violence approval between individuals and teammates closes with age, as does the gap between house-league and competitive-level players. Probably selection and socialization processes jointly account for this. As the less pro-violent get older, they quit hockey at increasingly faster rates than the more pro-violent. In fact, the general dropout rate is precipitous after age 12. Further, as the less pro-violent who stay in hockey are socialized into the culture of the game with age, and in competitive-level as opposed to house-league competition, they bring their attitudes increasingly into line with the attitudes they impute to their peers.

Table 10.3 Hockey Players' Perceptions of Hockey Fighting and Perceptions of Teammates' Approval of Hockey Fighting by Age and Level of Competition (in Percent)[1]

	Players' Approval			Teammates' Approval		
	Low	Medium	High[2]	Low	Medium	High
Age						
12–13 *(N = 166)*	54	25	21	23	23	54
14–15 *(N = 196)*	37	39	24	11	27	61
16–17 *(N = 130)*	13	49	38	4	26	70
18–21 *(N = 112)*	17	24	59	9	13	78
Level of Competition						
House League *(N = 330)*	48	28	24	16	25	59
Competitive *(N = 274)*	15	42	43	8	21	71
All players *(N = 604)*	33	34	33	13	23	64

[1]Adapted from Smith (1979, p. 113).

[2]Low = approval in no situations; medium = approval in one or two situations; high = approval in three or four situations

Hockey players approve of violence, it seems, to the extent that it brings respect and works as a game tactic and career booster. Separable analytically, these uses merge empirically, each reinforcing the other. Though the latter becomes increasingly salient as players learn the occupational culture, the former remains important. Professional hockey players—grown men—cling to rituals of fighting (even when it is counterproductive in terms of winning) that most males leave behind in the schoolyard.

Recent Evidence of Violence in Hockey

Talent, Excitement, Macho Identity

Due to the speed, rise in stick-work and ever-increasing size of its players, professional hockey has become a lethal sport. Fans often enjoy immediate and sustained periods of excitement without the delays in baseball, football, basketball and soccer. Barring an icing call, offside, or penalty, the action continues until the first team scores a goal. Unlike other sports, player substitution or "changing on the fly" occurs while the play continues. This blend of fan excitement, speed and sustained action provides a formula for a superior brand of entertainment. Ironically, these same qualities, when coupled with the players' passion and skill, trigger much of the tripping, slashing, spearing, high-sticking, elbowing, and hitting from behind. Although elite scorers such as Anaheim's Paul Kariya, Pittsburgh's Jaromir Jagr and Dallas' Mike Modano entertain hockey viewers, they remain the targets for "enforcers" and less talented players. These enforcers vie for top salaries while offering spectators—regardless of gender—the vicarious enjoyment of watching combat in the arena (Bryant, 1989; Bryant, Comisky, and Zillman, 1981).

Because hockey has traditionally fostered macho values, some superstars defend their honor and fight opponents who challenge them. Coaches, however, often discourage their top players from fighting and losing their services through penalties or injuries. But the dilemma is solvable because most teams, since the 1960s, employ at least one "enforcer" or "goon" to protect their best players. Although this division of labor continues, one team, the current Toronto Maple Leafs, combines a designated fighter, Tie Domi, with talented but hyper-aggressive veterans Shayne Corson and Gary Roberts. Corson especially characterizes the typical hockey player with his roughness, dedication to teammates and stoic approach to the game. Despite consistently ranking among the NHL's top penalty leaders, Corson projects an ambiguous and possibly self-serving image to young viewers. Appearing articulate and amiable, the rugged Corson acknowledges that he has always "played on the edge and pushed things to the limit [since] it's hard to know what is going to get called" (Campbell, 2000).

The NHL arbitrarily decides what constitutes a rule infraction and applies swift punishment during a game by segregating the offenders in a penalty box for short periods of time. These penalties vary according to their severity, ranging from two minutes for tripping to five for fighting, and ejection for "game misconduct." The concept of intent or *mens rea*, difficult to establish in a court of law, is highly problematic in hockey where body contact is essential to the game.

Brutal Body Contact: Violence or Skill?

Players learn effective ways of "taking out" opponents from as early as bantam (age 13–14) and perfect their technique as they advance through the more rugged junior and professional ranks. They also understand the importance of keeping their heads up and staying aware of their approaching opponent. This occurs in football when receivers run their routes to catch a pass, and in hockey, when players skate out of their own zone. The most devastating collisions occur in the transitional areas of mid-field in football and center-ice in hockey. For example, consider the crunching shoulder check that New Jersey defender Scott Stevens laid against Philadelphia Flyers' premier forward Eric Lindros during the 2000 Stanley Cup semifinals. Stevens aimed his thumping but legal check against Lindros' head as he advanced toward the New Jersey zone while looking down at the puck. Mindful of how his hit might impact Lindros' health and career, Stevens said "I'm very well aware of the concussion problem, so I always try to be careful [but] with the medical advice he's received, I have to assume Eric knows the risks" (Woolsey, 2000). Did Stevens intend to remove Eric Lindros from the game or did Lindros, who had suffered several recent concussions, return prematurely to compete in the playoffs? Stevens' hit may have eliminated Lindros but it also helped the New Jersey captain earn the most valuable player award for the 2000 Stanley Cup playoffs. Ultimately, New Jersey won the Stanley Cup by using superior defense and a highly aggressive style of play against Dallas.

Hockey on Trial: The McSorley-Brashear Incident

On February 21, 2000, Boston Bruins' aging enforcer Marty McSorley—the third most penalized player in NHL history—slashed the right temple of his younger Vancouver Canuck counterpart, Donald Brashear. Following his coaches' instructions to avenge the loss in an earlier fight with the Vancouver forward, McSorley skated alongside Brashear, raised his stick above his shoulders, and delivered his slash. Dislodging Brashear's helmet, the blow knocked him backward forcing his head to hit the ice surface. Brashear received a severe grade-three concussion, facial cuts and lapsed in and out of consciousness (Girard, 2000). Despite his injuries, Brashear recuperated and returned to play before the end of the regular schedule. League president Gary Bettman suspended McSorley indefinitely and the Vancouver police laid a charge of "assault with a weapon" against the Bruin enforcer.

The trial took place in Vancouver, British Columbia and lasted from September 25 until October 6, 2000 when Judge Bill Kitchen issued a guilty verdict against McSorley. Both Kitchen and the media confirmed that both McSorley and professional hockey bore full responsibility for the attack. The televised replays of the incident confirmed that the intent to injure was foremost in McSorley's mind. Kitchen spared McSorley a criminal record by placing him on probation for 18 months and forbidding him to play against Brashear during that time. Although McSorley's guilt or innocence of the charge was his first concern, Judge Kitchen maintained that the incident should "prompt a healthy discussion of hockey and the role of violence in the sport" (Hume, 2000). Ultimately, Bettman suspended McSorley from the NHL for a full year from the date of his stick attack.

Considering the several potentially career-ending injuries that players received during the 1999–2000 season, it seems logical to ask this question: Do some NHL players value winning over the respect and welfare of their peers? Also, do these players understand the example they set for the youth and some adults that emulate their aggressive behavior? Eitzen (1993) refers to unrestrained aggressive play as either a taken-for-granted "normative" brand of violence or as extreme and "deviant." For instance, one could easily classify boxer Mike Tyson's biting of Evander Holyfield's ear during a title bout as deviant violence. Considering the degree to which younger players learn from their NHL models, a restructuring of the rules is necessary to save hockey from the barbarism that Dallas forward Brett Hull has bitterly termed "rodeo on ice" (Klein and Reif, 1998). League officials, administrators and referees should prohibitively sanction coaches and players who use tactics such as high-sticking and hitting from behind. Perhaps the rule-makers should reevaluate legal maneuvers, such as Scott Stevens shoulder check on Lindros' head, as a definite rule violation.

Parents Investing for Success

To understand fully how parents contribute to hockey violence we must first consider their own involvement in their sons' hockey careers. The economic factor plays a significant part in parents attaching such importance to their sons' success in minor hockey. As the interest in competitive hockey rises so too does the expense of playing the sport. Parents today often feel an obligation to give their children the best equipment and training available.

In Canada, the cost to outfit a 16-year-old is approximately $800. This amount includes the basic equipment: skates, pads, pants, skates, helmets, and sticks. High-quality goaltender equipment costs more than $2000. To provide a minor league hockey career for their children, parents must be financially secure. Children from single parent homes seldom have the opportunity to pursue the sport. This financial commitment to minor hockey can undermine some parents' ability to cover their own auto and mortgage payments. Due to the prohibitive costs associated with minor hockey, many parents find it difficult to meet their own expenses along with sustaining their boys' hockey careers. Once the best players advance to the Junior "A" level at the age of 18, parents no longer pay for their equipment and other expenses related to hockey. Young men in this division often play in cities away from home and receive modest salaries.

Lower-income parents are unable to subsidize necessary extras such as hockey schools and attendance at out-of-town tournaments. This excessive financial worry places a strain on the lives of family members. The daily routines of hockey families tend to revolve around tryouts, practices and games. With this commitment to the boy's success in hockey, some parents sacrifice their own limited leisure time. Inevitably, these parents gauge their success as parents in relation to how well their sons perform in hockey. At this stage certain parents become obsessive with their boys' achievements in hockey. One minor-league coach told us that some parents reimburse their sons for scoring goals and winning fights.

Our field observations showed that a son's hockey game implicates the entire family. As a rule, hockey families arrive at the arena an hour before the game. Parents move around the lobby and chatter while nervously awaiting the opening face-off. Family members often sport their child's team colors and wear jackets emblematic of his club. Once the game begins parents demarcate their territories by sitting directly behind their boy's team bench. Immersion in the game is total and attuned to principally their own offspring. Booing and catcalls are directed at times at the referee and certain opposing players. From the stands, parents urge their children to book, hold, slash, and use any illegal device to prevent the other team from scoring. The closer a team comes to scoring the louder the parents shout and the more vicious the play becomes. It is around the goaltender's net where much of the high-sticking and hitting from behind takes place.

Some parents lose their composure and resort to abusive language. After a recent Bantam game (13-year-olds) at a North Toronto arena, one particularly irate father from a visiting Ottawa team berated the referee. His son's team had lost to an older more experienced Midget team (15-year-olds). Since this was an invitational tournament, the age discrepancy was irrelevant. If anything, the younger players may have welcomed this as a learning experience. This father, however, blamed the referee for the defeat of his son's team. "You really blew this one, jerk," he shouted down at the referee. The players on the ice who were shaking hands noticed this father's display of temper as they exited to their respective dressing rooms. The referee shook his head in disbelief, but the angry father persisted by challenging the referee to meet him in the parking for a fight.

At times parents do resort to actual violence such as hitting other adults. A CBC documentary "The Spirit of the Game" (Burman and Lee, 1993) showed how some parents react when their children are hurt. A part of the documentary showed what happened to a 12-year-old Winnipeg boy during a Peewee game. An opponent rammed the boy heavily into the boards from behind causing fractures to his left arm and shoulder. After the boy left for the hospital, the game turned into a free-for-all and resembled more a battle than a sport. The referee wisely terminated the game and brought a halt to the violence. One father from the injured boy's team approached the opposing coach, spat in his face, and shoved him. When an interviewer inquired about this parent's conduct, he replied that seeing the injured boy sprawling on the ice filled him with frustration and he lashed out at the coach.

Parental behavior such as this occurs in minor hockey to a certain extent. In its attempt to eliminate such irresponsible conduct the CAHA (1992) has created a videotape entitled "Hockey Parents Make The Difference." It simulates how some parents misbehave when they come to the arena to watch their sons' play. The CAHA believes that this video can teach parents how to behave while attending their sons' games. The message this video imparts is clear: Abusive parents should stay away from the arena.

Coaches: In Search of the Right Stuff

Hockey coaches frequently encourage aggressive behavior. NHL teams seek out this quality when hunting for players who will advance to the professional ranks. Coaches are responsible for developing gameness and character in their players. These attributes lack importance if players are incapable of defending themselves against other more intimidating competitors. Scouts for NHL teams regard the combination of penalty minutes with high point totals as indicative of a junior player's ability to compete professionally. Coaches who foster these traits in their players also improve their chances of obtaining professional coaching jobs.

Unquestionably, combativeness can lead to success in hockey. Gaining possession of the puck, on offense and defense, is elementary to the game. For this reason coaches tend to select bigger, stronger boys who can outmuscle their rivals for the puck. Coaches will of course pick smaller talented players who display "guts." But if they must choose between a bigger and smaller player of equal ability, they invariably take the larger boy. This is true in minor and professional hockey. Youths with size, ability and heart are the ones most likely to make it in major league hockey.

If players are reluctant to play an aggressive brand of hockey, a coach may set the initiative himself. He does this as a way to motivate his players. How professional coaches behave in emotionally charged situations may also serve as a model for their minor-league counterparts. During the 1993 NHL playoffs, the Toronto coach took exception to the way that several Los Angeles Kings players manhandled his smaller star forward. The Toronto coach appeared furious and rushed toward the Los Angeles bench while shouting at the opposing coach. This type of display is meant to wake up a team's more lethargic players. The Maple Leafs won this particular game because their coach's ploy worked. In cases where referees overlook other team's fouls, coaches expect their players to retaliate and administer their own justice.

Any boy who fails to execute this highly aggressive brand of play can expect a reprimand from his coach. If the same boy allows an opponent to skate around him or does not defend his goaltender in a scuffle, the coach invariably benches him. Furthermore, should a young man continue to show a lack of desire in the following week's practice, the coach restricts his playing time in the next game. Although many coaches in minor hockey prefer that boys abide by the rules, they still demand a show of physical and mental toughness on the part of their players. The problem for inexperienced players is how to differentiate between assertive and violent behavior.

Lethal Effects of Sexual Abuse

Although most research in sport violence addresses physical brutality, sexual abuse equally hurts children and youth. The pain and stigma of abuse inflicted during a youth's career can extend into adulthood and prove emotionally devastating. Both the media and parents, extolling dreams of success in the NHL, provide *disreputable* coaches with the bait to entrap impressionable young athletes. Sheldon Kennedy and Martin Kruze are two such victims. Kennedy experienced a brief, unsuccessful NHL career marred by drugs and alcohol; Martin Kruze committed suicide in 1997. As adults, both underwent exhaustive therapy to ease the emotional and psychological pain caused by their minor league coaches, Graham James and Gordon Stuckless, respectively.

Kennedy's abuse started as a promising 14-year-old player in Winnipeg, Manitoba where James pursued him to play for his team and to live in his apartment. According to Kennedy, during his first night at the apartment, James had brandished a gun at him before attempting sexual advances (Robinson, 1998). The abuse lasted from 1984 until Kennedy entered his turbulent 7-year NHL career in 1989.[6] Acting as a quasi-mentor, James had emotionally manipulated Kennedy so that he depended on him for aiding his hockey career and fostering his fragile self-esteem. Kennedy asserted that "Graham knew I needed a father-figure . . . because it was brutal at home and he preys on that. He knows exactly what he is doing" (Robinson, 1998, p. 178).

For decades the NHL iced only six teams, and two Canadian arenas, Toronto's Maple Leaf Gardens and the Montreal Forum, were centers of hockey culture and pride. They housed two of the most lucrative franchises in sport. Since 1931 until the early 1970s the Toronto Maple Leaf organization held down players' salaries by having a farm system that fed the parent team with an abundance of competitive young players. Younger players were eager to play for the status of wearing the "blue and white sweater" of the Maple Leafs and accepted less money (Dowbiggen, 1993). One such aspiring youth was Martin Kruze—a victim of sexual abuse by two Maple Leaf Gardens' equipment managers, George Hannah and Gordon Stuckless, between 1975 through 1982. Both men lured the impressionable Kruze, and other children, into sexual acts with the promise of meals, hockey and concert tickets. Aware of Kruze's shame, these adults used the "unspoken threat of discovery" to continuously violate the boy with impunity throughout his adolescence (Reilly, 1997)

After years of drug abuse, eating disorders, and several suicide attempts, 35-year-old Martin Kruze jumped to his death from a bridge 100 feet above Toronto's Don Valley Parkway. While struggling to affirm his self-respect, Kruze spoke openly about his abuse and encouraged other victims to deal openly with their trauma. Three days prior to his suicide a Toronto judge sentenced Stuckless to 2 years in jail for 22 counts of indecent assault and two counts of sexual assault.[7] Both Stuckless and Hannah, who died earlier, robbed Kruze of his dignity and exploited the coach-athlete relationship for their own pathological reasons.

Officials: The New Breed

The trend in hockey today is toward the elimination of fouls such as high-sticking and hitting from behind. The CAHA has guidelines for players to follow to ensure a balance between fun and the development of a child's skill in the sport. To counter unsportsmanlike attitudes, the Canadian Federal Government's Department of Fitness and Amateur Sport has created a commission to encourage fair play among youths (Smith, 1987). Referees try to implement the commission's polices by mediating

---

6. Kennedy estimates over 300 incidents of sexual abuse.
7. Kruze's next to last suicide attempt was a few days prior to his fatal jump. His family blames the provincial health care system for releasing him prematurely from a Toronto hospital's psychiatric ward (Pasqualloto, 1997).

disputes with players and coaches in a sensible manner. The more recent introduction of women referees in minor hockey has also helped to modify the violent behavior of certain players. One coach informed us that a particular woman referee in the Metropolitan Toronto Hockey League (MTHL) was more proficient at officiating than any of her male peers. This referee could skate faster and understood the rules better than many of the men.

Game officials must now meet with team captains and coaches prior to the start of each match. Granted, this approach has been in effect in baseball and football for some time but is new to minor hockey. In the past, referees governed the sport with an iron fist and seldom tolerated any dialogue with the players. Referees frequently issued misconduct penalties to those players seeking clarification on a particular ruling. The policy in minor hockey now places much of the onus for responsible behavior squarely on the players and coaches. A player who commits an infraction such as butt-ending with his stick receives a match penalty and a suspension for three games. Many referees, however, officiate minor hockey games as a way to supplement their incomes. Several of the ones that we saw were overweight and struggled to keep pace with the speedier youths. As a result, these referees tended to find themselves out of position and unable to make proper calls on plays at the opposite end of the rink. Once players are beyond the referee's field of vision they have the opportunity to engage in vicious stick-work.

Referees can also be inconsistent in their interpretation of the rules and in assessing penalties to each team. Although most sports allow their officials discretion in making their judgement calls, coaches and players still complain that referees seldom judge any recurring infraction in exactly the same way. Consequently, some players feel that the referee will not penalize an opponent for committing a foul against them—so they retaliate. In attempting to maintain the flow of the game, referees tend to overlook the initial violation and catch the obvious act of retaliation.

Summary and Conclusion

The problem of violence persists in minor hockey. We addressed previous important research dealing with the influence parents, coaches, and teammates had in contributing to how players learn violence as a way to succeed in the sport. In utilizing this research as our base we have added to the understanding of this problem in three ways. First, by giving a historical account of violence in the NHL we showed how past and present players have encouraged violence by acting as negative role models for young players. Second, our examination of game officials has pointed out the necessity for a more rigorous set of standards to upgrade their conditioning and knowledge of the rules. League officials must also recognize that certain women are equally capable of being referees and integrate them into minor hockey. Finally, we addressed the question of the media, television especially, and how it profits by keeping violence alive throughout all of hockey.

This chapter has also concerned itself with the attitudes children and youth learn to succeed as adults in North American society. The larger social order stresses the importance of individualism and competitiveness as prime attributes for the achievement of success. We have tried to show that competition is basic to hockey but it must divorce itself from violence in the pursuit of cultural rewards such as money and fame. Before all else, our society has to acknowledge that the priorities of amateur sport for young people are fun, sportsmanship and the development of physical skills. It is the responsibility of adults to reinforce these values and to ensure that children freely enjoy sports without fear for their safety. Parents, coaches, and referees must ally themselves with those who accentuate fair play. Clearly, administrators and referees must enforce more stringent penalties for the illegal use of hockey sticks as weapons. Hockey is one of the world's most electrifying sports and can thrive without violence. Hopefully, the media and professional hockey will eventually alter their approach to the game by stressing its more skillful aspects.

Finally, parents and league officials need to implement policies to eliminate deviant coaches, who might sexually exploit children. If society fails to protect children by offering them a secure environment to enjoy sport and to associate with adults, then our culture surely demands a more critical scrutiny of its values.

References

Bandura, A. (1986). *Social foundations of thought and action: A social cognitive theory*. Englewood Cliffs, NJ: Prentice-Hall.

Baudrillard, J. (1983). *Simulations*. New York: Semiotext(e).

Bryant, J. (1989). Viewers' enjoyment of televised sports. In L. Wenner (Ed.), *Media, sports, and society* (pp. 270–289). Newbury Park, CA: Sage.

Bryant, J., Comisky, P., and Zillman, D. (1981). The appeal of rough-and-tumble play in televised professional football. *Communication Quarterly, 29*, 256–262.

Burman, T. (Producer), and Lee, M. (Reporter), (1993). *The spirit of the game* [Videotape]. Toronto: Canadian Broadcasting Corporation.

Campbell, K. (2000, October 13). Leafs' Corson running afoul of the law: Winger piles up penalty minutes under crackdown. *The Toronto Star*, p. F2.

Canadian Amateur Hockey Association (Producer). (1992). *Parents make the difference* [Videotape]. Calgary, Alberta: Hockey Canada.

Colburn, K., Jr. (1985). Honor, ritual and violence in ice hockey. *Canadian Journal of Sociology, 10*, 153–170.

Colburn, K., Jr. (1986). Deviance and legitimacy in ice hockey: A microstructural theory of violence. *Sociological Quarterly, 27*, 63–74.

Combined Artists (Producer). (1992). *Sports pages: Killer hockey* [Videotape]. Plymouth, MN: Sitmar Entertainment.

Dollard, J., Doob, L., Miller, N., Mower, O., and Sears, R. (1939). *Frustration and aggression*. New Haven, CT: Yale University Press.

Dowbiggen, B. (1993). *The defense never rests*. Toronto: Harper Collins.

Dunnell, M. (1959, December 9). Jungle Law in NHL—Bathgate. *The Toronto Star*, pp. 1; 17.

Eitzen, S. (1993). Ethical dilemmas in sport. In S. Eitzen (Ed.), In *Sport in contemporary society: An anthology* (pp. 109–122). New York: St. Martin's Press.

Fischler, S. (1993, May). Fighting belongs in hockey. *Hockey Heroes*, pp. 10–13.

Frayne, T. (1973). *Famous hockey players*. New York: Dodd, Mead and Company.

Girard, D. (2000, October 7). McSorley found guilty of stick assault. *The Toronto Star*, p. F2.

Gruneau, R., and Whitson, D. (1993). *Hockey night in Canada: Sports, identities, and cultural politics*. Toronto: Garamond Press.

Harrison, R. (Producer). (1993). *Hockey night in Canada* [Videotape]. Toronto: Molstar.

Hobsbawm, E. (1996). *The age of extremes: A history of the world, 1914–1991*. New York: Random House.

Hume, M. (2000, October 7). McSorley guilty of assault: NHL's player's verdict in slashing case sparks debate about violence in hockey. *National Post*, pp. A1; A19.

Klein, J., and Reif, K. (1998). *The death of hockey*. Toronto: Macmillan Canada.

Matza, D. (1964). *Delinquency and drift*. New York: Wiley.

McLuhan, M., and Fiore, Q. (1967). *The medium is the massage: An inventory of effects*. New York: Bantam Books.

Mills, C. W. (1961). *The sociological imagination*. New York: Grove Press.

Murphy J. W., and Choi, J. M. (1993). Imagocentrism and the Rodney King affair. *ETC: A Review of General Semantics, 49*, 478–484.

National Hockey League Players' Website (NHLPA, 2000). [On-line], Available: www.nhlpa.com.

Pasqualloto, S. (1997, November 3). Kruze family says public health system failed. *Newsworld* [On-line], Available: www.newsworld.cbc.ca/archive.

Reilley, R. (1997, November 4). Who pushed Martin Kruze? *Sports Illustrated* [On-line], Available: www.cnnsi.com.

Robinson, L. (1998). *Crossing the line: Violence and sexual assault in Canada's national sport*. Toronto: McLelland and Stewart.

Schultz, D. (1981). *The hammer: Confessions of a hockey enforcer*. Toronto: Collins.

Smith, M. D. (1979). Towards an explanation of hockey violence: A reference other approach. *Canadian Journal of Sociology, 4*, 105–124.

Smith, M. D. (1983). *Violence and sport*. Toronto: Butterworths.

Smith, M. D. (1987). *Violence in Canadian amateur sport: A review of literature*. Ottawa: Ministry for Fitness and Amateur Sport, Government of Canada.

Tarasov, A. (1969). *Road to Olympus*. Toronto: Griffin House.

Tarasov, A. (1997). *Tarasov: Hockey's rise to international prominence through the eyes of a coaching legend* (pp. 32–33). S. Kokhanovskaya (Trans.). Glendale, CA: Griffin Publishing.

Tretiak, V. (1987). *Tretiak: The legend.* S. and M. Budman (Trans.). Edmonton, Alberta: Plains Publishing.

Vaz, E. W. (1982). *The professionalization of young hockey players.* Lincoln, NE: University of Nebraska Press.

Woolsey, G. (2000, December 5). Stevens' hit on Lindros just a matter of timing. *The Toronto Star*, p. C8.

Part Four

Anatomical and Physiological Concerns

The rise of youth sports at both national and international levels has been accompanied by the application of advanced training techniques. The training programs are designed to create stresses on the body systems through emphasis on extreme intensity and duration of activity. They are geared to specialization in a single sport, and they involve year-round participation. Because gaps exist in our understanding of the effects of exercise stress on children and youth, training programs for young athletes are often formulated on the basis of research conducted with adults. In spite of this practice, the general assumption that youngsters thrive on adult training regimes must be questioned.

There is little doubt that a certain minimum of physical activity is necessary to support normal growth and that vigorous activity is essential for promoting optimal physical fitness. However, some physicians, educators, community leaders, and parents have opposed youth sports on the grounds that highly intense sport training may cause excessive physical stress and might be hazardous for youngsters. More specifically, many important questions have been raised. What are the biophysical characteristics of young athletes, and what are the effects of strenuous physical activity on their growth and biological maturation? Do the stresses imposed by endurance-type training regimes make excessive demands on the cardiovascular systems of children and youth? How do male-female morphological and physiological characteristics affect sex differences in sport performance during childhood and adolescence? What are the effects of physical training on menstrual functioning? What are the effects of anabolic steroids on muscle strength and size, and what are the adverse effects of steroid use? What is the nature of overuse injuries in youth sports, and what is known about risk factors for their occurrence? The chapters that follow address these questions as well as other salient issues.

In Chapter 11, Robert M. Malina presents a comprehensive survey of the biological growth and maturation of young male and female athletes. Distinctions are initially drawn between *growth, maturation,* and *development.* Although these terms are often used synonymously, they refer to separate processes that occur at the same time. Moreover, their dynamic interaction has tremendous implications for youngsters' success in athletics. Malina explicates the complex interrelations among body size, physique, body composition, and biological maturity status in children and adolescents. Next, a summary is presented of the growth and maturity characteristics of young athletes in several sports. The coverage includes the topic of age at menarche, and an in-depth analysis is provided of the manner in which biological and cultural factors interact to affect sport socialization. In this context, a two-part (biocultural) hypothesis is offered as a plausible explanation for the later mean ages at menarche reported in athletes in many sports. Does regular training for sports affect growth and maturity? In addressing this frequently asked question, Malina reviews evidence concerning the potentially negative influences of intensive training on growth (height and weight) and biological maturity (timing and tempo of progress to the mature state). In the final section of the chapter, several issues are highlighted that merit further study and evaluation: risk of injury, psychological stress, maturity matching to equalize competition, talent identification and selection, and manipulation of young athletes. Clearly, an understanding of the above is vital if adults are to make informed decisions that impact the physical, social, and emotional well-being of young athletes.

Cardiovascular functioning is a major concern within the domain of exercise physiology. Donald A. Bailey approaches this topic in Chapter 12 by considering the cardiorespiratory differences between children and adults. Emphasizing that children are not simply miniature adults, the author cites important adult-child differences in aerobic and anaerobic responses to strenuous physical exercise. The question of whether or not functional changes resulting from early sport training persist into adult years is addressed, along with an examination of problems inherent in investigating training effects in children. Next, Bailey explains why children are less efficient than adults with respect to temperature regulation. He points out that such differences have precautionary implications for children's sport programs conducted in climatic extremes of heat or cold. Attention is then given to recent studies of the effect of childhood activity on bone mineral acquisition. A strong case is presented for the contention that bone mineral accumulation in children can be enhanced by mechanical loading factors associated with sport and physical training. This has considerable significance for the prevention of skeletal fragility and osteoporosis in older adults. The chapter concludes with a discussion of physiological and philosophical perspectives concerning the early identification and development of athletic potential.

The next chapter describes the biophysical characteristics of the postmenarcheal female athlete (14 to 16 years of age), who is emerging into full adulthood. In addition to examining real morphological sex differences that affect athletic performance, Lynda B. Ransdell debunks several common myths, such as those associated with sex differences in pelvic width and the body's center of gravity. For example, only about 50% of women have a gynecoid pelvis; and, in reality, it is difficult to tell a male pelvis from a female pelvis. Consideration is also given to sex differences in various physiological parameters, including systemic oxygen transport, lactate threshold, and maximal oxygen uptake, which is the best single measure of cardiorespiratory efficiency. Sex differences in strength, swimming, and running performance are then analyzed relative to these biophysical differences. In so doing, the author points out that women's world records provide evidence that elite women athletes are capable of superior physical performances. Indeed, the performance differences that once separated men and women have lessened significantly over the past two decades. The final parts of the chapter are devoted to athletes' menstrual function. The three phases of the menstrual cycle are described, and the effects of the phases on sport performance are discussed. Conversely, the effects of intense athletic training are examined relative to risk factors, potential harm, and reversibility of menstrual cycle dysfunction. In this regard, it is noted that although athletic menstrual dysfunction poses no known danger to future reproductive function, it constitutes an important risk factor for long-term bone health. The chapter concludes with a call for prevention and early identification as the best approaches for dealing with athletic menstrual dysfunction.

Anabolic steroids are synthetic derivatives of the male sex hormone, testosterone. They are administered orally or as injectable agents, and they are used by adolescent athletes to improve performance, improve physical appearance, and meet peer approval. In Chapter 14, Mimi D. Johnson and David A. Van de Loo provide information concerning the physiologic effects, potential benefits, and complications of steroid use. In this regard, it is noted that anabolic steroid use results in an increase in muscle strength and size in some individuals who use them under specific conditions. However, these individuals are at risk for numerous harmful consequences, such as sexual and reproductive disorders, heart disease, liver and kidney damage, and premature epiphyseal closure resulting in stunted growth. After detailing the adverse physical effects of steroids, the authors describe untoward psychological effects, including increased aggressive behavior, mood swings, and irritability. The chapter includes consideration of the prevalence, dose, and manner of steroid use by adolescent athletes, and black market sources of these drugs. In addition to the importance of early identification of steroid users, emphasis is given to various forms of intervention, the goals of which are to induce complete abstinence, to restore physical and psychological health, and to prevent relapse. The final part of the chapter is devoted to prevention of steroid use via drug testing, law enforcement, and multifaceted educational approaches aimed at children and young adolescents.

The last chapter of this part focuses on the topic of overuse injuries, which are occurring with greater frequency in youth sports. These injuries result from repeated mictotrauma to areas of the body over a prolonged period of time—a typical scenario in the training regimens for many sports. In an authoritative review, Lyle J. Micheli and Peter A. Salob present information pertaining to overuse injury of bone, that is, stress fracture. In describing the nature of this medical malady, the authors identify the types of stress fractures and distinguish between child and adult body sites for their occurrence; they also discuss the types of stress fractures sustained in specific sports. Next, several risk factors that contribute to the occurrence of such injuries are analyzed, including those associated with (a) physical training (e.g., volume of training, rate of progression of training), (b) intrinsic mechanical factors (e.g., muscle tendon imbalance, anatomical malalignment), (c) nutritional factors, (d) hormonal factors, and (e) extrinsic mechanical factors (e.g., playing surfaces, athletic footwear). Salob and Micheli then discuss the etiology of stress fractures that commonly occur at various body sites: low back, upper extremity, pelvis and hip, and ankle and foot. The chapter concludes with brief consideration of how understanding of risk factors aids in the prevention of stress fractures in young athletes.

The Young Athlete: Biological Growth and Maturation in a Biocultural Context

Robert M. Malina, Michigan State University

Children and youth participate in sport at many levels ranging from free play and local leagues through national and international elite competitions. The social sanction given to youth sports and the necessary skills for successful participation gives sport a significant position not only in the youngster's world but also in the broader cultural complex within which the individual lives.

The popularity of sports programs for children and adolescents, both agency-sponsored and interscholastic, and the national and international success of youth in several sports at relatively young ages are not without problems. Some issues relate to equality of access to sport, readiness of children for sport, specialization at an early age, talent identification and selection, parental pressures, and so on. Others relate to risks associated with intensive training and competition, and other demands of sport, especially high performance sports. These include potential for compromised growth and maturity, injury and psychological stress, among others.

Society, specifically the electronic and print media, often analyzes and evaluates sport and sport figures (i.e., elite athletes) in incredible detail. Such national and international preoccupation with sport may add to stresses experienced on young athletes. And, under occasional and unfortunate conditions, the treatment of young athletes and some of the techniques of training for high performance sports may fall within the bounds of child abuse.

Youth sports thus span the local through international landscapes. The success of youth sports programs and of youth in sport generates much discussion, pro and con, concerning the physical, social, and emotional well-being of young athletes. It is in this context that several issues related to organized sport for children and adolescents are addressed: (a) the growth and maturity characteristics of young athletes, (b) interactions of biological and cultural factors in sport, (c) the effects of regular training for sport on indicators of growth and maturity, and (d) several issues in youth sports that merit further study and evaluation.

Growth, Maturation, and Development

As children and adolescents progress from birth to adulthood, they experience three interacting processes. They *grow*, *mature*, and *develop*. Although these terms are often treated as having the same meaning, they refer to three distinct tasks in the daily lives of children and adolescents for approximately the first two decades of life.

Growth

Growth refers to the increase in the size of the body as a whole and of its parts. As children grow, they become taller and heavier, they increase in lean and fat tissues, their organs increase in size, and so on. Heart volume and mass follow a growth pattern like that for body weight, while the lungs and lung functions grow proportionally to height. Different parts of the body grow at different rates and different times, resulting in changes in body proportions. The legs grow faster than the trunk during childhood; hence, the child becomes relatively longer-legged for his/her height.

Maturation

Maturation refers to progress towards maturity—the biologically mature state. The mature state varies with body system. All tissues, organs, and systems of the body mature. When working with children and adolescents, maturity must be viewed in two contexts—timing and tempo. Timing refers to when specific maturational events occur, for example, age at the beginning of changes in breast morphology in girls, the age at the appearance of pubic hair in boys and girls, or the age at peak height velocity or maximum growth during the adolescent growth spurt. Tempo refers to the rate at which maturation progresses, for example, how quickly or slowly the youngster passes through the adolescent growth spurt or passes from initial changes to the mature state of breast morphology. Timing and tempo are highly individual characteristics and vary considerably among individuals.

Development

Development refers to the acquisition of behavioral competence—the learning of appropriate behaviors expected by society. As children experience life at home, school, church, sports, recreation, and other community activities, they develop cognitively, socially, emotionally, morally, and so on. They are learning to behave in a culturally appropriate manner. Motor development—the development of competence in motor behaviors—is an important aspect of behavioral competence related to sport. Proficiency in motor skills and in sport specific skills is central to performance and is related to body size and maturity, especially in late childhood and adolescence. The term *development* is occasionally used in the context of biological maturity (e.g., development of secondary sex characteristics), but the view of development in the context of behavioral competence within a given culture sets it apart from the biological context.

Interactions

The three processes—growth, maturation, and development—occur at the same time and interact. They interact to influence the child's self-concept, self-esteem, body image, and perceived competence. Parents, teachers, coaches and other adults should be aware of these interactions. How a youngster is coping with his/her sexual maturity or adolescent growth spurt may influence his/her behaviors, including peer relationships and sport-related behaviors and performance. A mismatch between the demands of a sport and those of normal growth and maturity may be a source of stress among young athletes which may potentially influence behavior and performance.

Interrelationships of Growth and Maturation

Details of the assessment of growth and maturity, and of changes that occur during childhood and adolescence are described in Malina, Bouchard, and Bar-Or (in press). As noted, growth refers to an increase in the size of the body or its parts, including body composition, physique, and specific systems. Biological maturation refers to the tempo and timing of progress to the mature state. Commonly used indicators of biological maturity include skeletal age (bone age), secondary sex characteristics (breasts, genitals, pubic hair, menarche), and age at peak height velocity (maximum rate of growth during the adolescent spurt).

Participants in youth sports are ordinarily grouped on the basis of chronological age, the age of the child based on his/her date of birth and the calendar. Quite often, whole year categories are used, that is, 10 years of age includes those between 10.0 and 10.99 years. Thus, two children whose ages are, respectively, 10.0 and 10.9, are classified as 10 years of age although almost one year separates them. And, there is considerable variation in size, body composition, strength and motor skill among children of the same chronological age.

Individual differences in growth and maturation are additonal factors. Children of the same chronological age who differ in maturity status also differ in size, physique and body composition, and in muscular strength and motor performance. The differences are especially marked just before and during the adolescent growth spurt and puberty, about 9 to 14 in girls and 11 to 16 in boys. Boys who are advanced in maturity status (i.e., skeletal age is advanced relative to chronological age by a year or more; early sexual maturity for chronological age) are generally taller and heavier, have more weight-for-height, are more mesomorphic, are stronger, and perform motor tasks requiring speed and power better than boys who are later in biological maturity status (i.e., skeletal age lags behind chronological age by a year or more; sexual maturity occurs at a later chronological age). Later maturing boys tend to be more linear in build than early maturing boys. Later in adolescence (i.e., about 17 to 19 years of age) the size, strength and performance differences between boys of contrast-ing maturity status are reduced or disappear. It is important to note that the differences between boys of contrasting maturity status are most apparent at the time when participation in sports is perhaps most important in the culture of youth (i.e., 11–14 years), and it is the early maturing boy who often has the advantage in many sports at these ages.

Girls advanced in biological maturity (i.e., advanced skeletal age relative to chronological age; early menarche) also are taller and heavier, and they have more weight-for-height than later maturing girls (skeletal age lags behind chronological age; later menarche) of the same chronological age. Early maturing girls are somewhat endomorphic, whereas late maturing girls are more linear (ectomorphic) in build. Early maturing girls are also somewhat stronger early in puberty, but by 13 to 14 years of age the differences virtually disappear compared to late maturing girls. Motor performances of adolescent girls are not as strongly related to maturity status as in boys, and it is often later maturing girls who attain better performances as adolescence progresses.

The preceding has compared children of the same chronological age who are early and late in the tempo and timing of biological maturation. However, the majority of children fall between the extremes and are classified as average or "on time" in biological maturity. They have skeletal ages that fall within one year plus or minus of their chronological ages, and they attain sexual and somatic maturity within one year plus or minus of the population average. Their growth, strength and performance characteristics generally fall between the extreme groups and there is considerable overlap.

Who Is an Athlete?

The young athlete is different from his/her peers in that he/she is successful in sport. Young athletes are usually defined in terms of success on agency or interscho-lastic teams and in age-group or select competitions for individual sports. Young athletes are thus a select group, usually based on skill but sometimes on size and physique. The issue of selection is discussed later in the chapter. Most of the available data on the growth and maturity of young athletes are based on samples that can be classified as select, elite, junior national, or international caliber (Malina, 1994, 1998a). Corresponding information for athletes at the local level are not extensive.

Growth and Maturity Characteristics of Young Athletes

The following is extracted from more comprehensive reviews (Malina, 1994, 1998a; Malina et al., in press), which include the primary references. In order to appropriately evaluate the growth and maturity characteristics of young athletes, it is important to be familiar with the selective or exclusive nature of many sports. Some sports selectively choose or exclude youth on the basis of body size during childhood. A primary example in this context is artistic gymnastics, which often attempts to identify potential athletes at 5 to 6 years of age (Malina, 1999). Body size plays a more important role in other sports later in childhood and during the transition into adolescence. At this time, size is closely related to individual differences in the timing and tempo of the adolescent growth spurt and sexual maturation. This section summarizes current information on trends in height and weight, physique, body composition, and biological maturity status of young athletes.

Size Attained

Average heights of athletes in different sports are expressed relative to percentiles of United States growth charts (Hamill, Drizd, Johnson, Reed, and Roche, 1977) in Table 11.1. Although new growth charts have been recently made available for American youth (Kuczmarski et al., 2000), available data for young athletes pre-date the new charts so that the earlier reference values are appropriate. Further, secular change in the height of American youth is negligible.

Table 11.1   Heights and Weights of Young Athletes Relative to Percentiles (P) of United States Reference Data

Sport	Males Height	Males Weight	Females Height	Females Weight
Basketball	P 50 – >P90	P 50 – >P90	P 75 – >P90	P 50 – P 75
Soccer	P 50±	P 50±	P 50	P 50
Volleyball			P 75	P 50 – P 75
Ice hockey	P 50±	P 50		
Distance runs	P 50±	•P 50	•P 50	<P 50
Sprints	•P 50	•P 50	•P 50	•P 50
Swimming	P 50 – P 90	> P 50 – P 75	P 50 – P 90	P 50 – P 75
Diving	<P 50	•P 50	•P 50	P 50
Gymnastics	•P 10 – P 25	•P 10 – P 25	•P 10 – <P 50	P 10 – <P 50
Tennis	P 50±	•P 50	>P 50	P 50±
Figure skating	P 10 – P 25	P 10 – P 25	P 10 – <P 50	P 10 – <P 50
Ballet	<P 50	P 10 – P 50	•P 50	P 10 – <P 50

Adapted from Malina (1994, 1998a) which contain the references for individual studies. The U.S. reference data of Hamill et al. (1977) were used in making the comparisons.

The trends indicated in Table 11.1 should be interpreted as follows. Male athletes in many sports have heights that, on average, fluctuate just above and below the reference medians; this is indicated in the table as ±P 50. If average heights are consistently above the median, this is indicated as >P 50, and if average heights of athletes in a sport are consistently below the median, this is indicated as <P 50.

Athletes of both sexes and in most sports have, on average, heights that equal or exceed the reference medians. Gymnastics is the only sport that consistently presents a profile of short height in both sexes. Average heights for most samples of gymnasts are near P10 (see also Beunen, Malina, and Thomis, 1999; Malina, 1999). Figure skaters of both sexes also present shorter heights, on average, though data are less extensive than for gymnasts. These trends are based on group means. Given the range of normal variation among individuals and variation associated with individual differences in pubertal timing and tempo, there are individual exceptions to the trends suggested in the tables.

Body weight presents a similar pattern. Young athletes in most sports tend to have body weights that, on average, equal or exceed the reference medians. Gymnasts, figure skaters and ballet dancers of both sexes consistently show lighter body weights. Gymnasts and figure skaters have appropriate weight-for-height, while ballet dancers have low weight-for-height. A similar trend is suggested for female distance runners.

Physique

Physique refers to the configuration of the body as a whole. It is most often viewed in the context of somatotype, which summarizes an individual's physique in terms of the varying contributions of endomorphy (relative fatness, laterality), mesomorphy (relative muscularity and skeletal robustness), and ectomorphy (relative linearity). Although there is some variation during adolescence due to individual differences in the timing and intensity of the adolescent growth spurt, an individual's somatotype is relatively stable during growth. It is also not significantly influenced by intensive training, except for local changes associated with heavy resistance training which may not be sufficient to markedly alter an individual's somatotype (see Malina et al., in press).

Physique is a selective factor in many sports, that is, youngsters are selected in part on the basis of their body build. It is also a limiting factor in that certain physiques are simply not suitable for some sports, and young athletes in a some sports often have somatotypes similar to those of successful adult athletes in the respective sports. This is especially apparent among gymnasts (Carter and Brallier, 1988; Claessens, 1999), divers (Geithner and Malina,1993), and athletes in several winter sports (Orvanova, 1987). Carter and Heath (1990) provide a comprehensive overview of the somatotype characteristics of athletes in a variety of sports and at several competitive levels.

Body Composition of Young Athletes

Child and adolescent athletes have less relative fatness (percentage body fat) than non-athletes of the same age and sex. Male athletes and non-athletes both show a decline in percentage body fat during adolescence, but athletes generally have less relative fatness. Female athletes also have a lower percentage body fat than non-athletes, especially during adolescence, and it appears that the differences between female athletes and non-athletes are greater than the corresponding differences in males. Relative fatness does not increase much with age during adolescence in female athletes, while it does in non-athletes (Malina et al., in press). As expected, there is variation among athletes and among athletes in different sports.

Maturity Status of Male Athletes

With few exceptions, young male athletes in a variety of sports tend to be average (on time) or advanced (early) in biological maturity (Malina, 1994, 1998a). Other than gymnasts, who show, on average, skeletal ages that lag behind chronological age, there is a lack of late maturing boys who are successful in sport during early- and mid-adolescence (about 12 to 15 years). In some sports, advanced maturity is more apparent in adolescence. For example, among youth soccer and ice hockey players, a broad range of skeletal maturity is represented among participants 10 to 12 years of age. That is, boys with delayed (late), "on time" (average) and advanced (early) skeletal ages are almost equally represented. Among players 13 to 16 years of age, on the other hand, late maturing boys (skeletal age behind chronological age by more than one year) are minimally represented. Thus, with advancing chronological age and experience, and the tendency for the sports to become more selective or exclusive, boys advanced in biological maturity are more common among elite adolescent players in soccer and ice hockey (Malina, 2000). This may reflect selection or exclusion (self, coach, sport system, or some combination), differential success of boys advanced in maturity, the changing nature of the games (more physical contact may be permitted in older age groups with an advantage for larger, stronger, more mature boys), or some combination of these factors.

In contrast, late maturing boys are often successful in some sports in later adolescence (16 to 18 years), e.g., track and basketball (Malina, Beunen, Wellens, and Claessens, 1986). This is associated with catch-up in biological maturity and late adolescent growth. All youth eventually reach maturity, and maturity-associated differences in body size are reduced and have less significance for performance in late adolescent boys.

Maturity Status of Female Athletes

Most discussions of biological maturity of female athletes focus on age at menarche. Mean ages at menarche in North American and European girls vary, in general, between 12.5 and 13.5 years, but the age range within which menarche may normally occur is 9 through 17 years. Menarche is a late event during puberty and occurs, on average, about one year after peak height velocity or the time of maximum growth rate in height during the adolescent spurt.

This indicator of biological maturity in girls is important in discussions of youth sports for several reasons. First, menarche has significant value judgments associated with its attainment in many cultures, and the psychological importance of menarche in the development of adolescent girls has no counterpart in the sexual maturation process of boys. Second, there are several methods of estimating the age when menarche occurs, and they differ in their accuracy and in the information provided. And third, a good deal of the sport science and popular literature focus on later ages at menarche commonly observed in athletes with the inference that training "causes" the lateness.

Later mean ages at menarche are often reported in athletes in many, but not all, sports (Malina, 1983, 1998a, 1998b; Beunen and Malina, 1996). When the distribution of recalled ages at menarche in large samples of athletes and non-athletes of the same chronological age and from similar social backgrounds are considered, there is considerable overlap between samples. The distribution for athletes is simply shifted to the right, or later ages, by about one year or so. There are both early- and late-maturing athletes and non-athletes; it is just that there are more later maturing athletes than non-athletes.

Information on the age at menarche in adolescent athletes (i.e., teen-age athletes in contrast to young adult and adult athletes) is actually rather limited. Reliable information for young athletes is derived from longitudinal studies and status quo surveys. The *prospective method* is used in longitudinal studies in which girls are examined at close intervals during adolescence, usually every three months or so. The girl (or her mother) is interviewed as to whether menarche has occurred and when. Given that the interval between examinations is relatively short, age at menarche can be reliably estimated for individual girls. Sample sizes in longitudinal studies are ordinarily not large enough to derive population estimates and may not reflect the normal range of variation. The *status quo method* is used to estimate age at menarche in a sample of girls. A large representative sample of girls which covers the age range in which menarche normally occurs, about 9 to 17 years, is surveyed. Two bits of information are required: first, the exact age of each girl, and second, whether or not she has attained menarche, that is, simply yes or no. The percentage of girls in each age class who attained menarche is calculated, probits for each percentage are plotted for each age group, and a straight line is then fitted to the points. The point at which the line intersects 50% is the estimated median age at menarche for the sample. The resulting estimated median age at menarche (and 95% confidence intervals) applies only to the population and does not apply to individual girls.

The *retrospective method* requires the individual to recall the age at which menarche occurred. If the interview is done at close intervals as in longitudinal studies, the method is reasonably accurate. If it is done some time after menarche as in the case of university level and other adult athletes, it is affected by error in recall. However, with careful interview procedures, for example, attempting to place the event in the context of a season or event of the school year or holiday, reasonably accurate estimates of the age at menarche can be obtained from most late adolescents (17 to 19 years) and adults. Use of the retrospective or recall method with younger adolescent athletes excludes those who have not yet attained menarche and thus biases the mean age for the sample.

Presently available data from status quo and longitudinal studies of adolescent athletes are summarized in Table 11.2. Retrospective data for athletes in a variety of sports are reported elsewhere (Malina, 1983, 1996, 1998b; Beunen and Malina, 1996). If an average of 13.0 years and a standard deviation of 1.0 year is accepted for North American and European girls, about 95% of girls will attain menarche between 11.0 and 15.0 years. Most samples of adolescent athletes have mean ages at menarche within the range of normal variation. Only several samples of gymnasts and ballet dancers have mean ages at menarche older than 15.0 years. Both of these activities have extremely selective criteria which tend to favor the late maturing girls.

Table 11.2 Ages at Menarche (years) in Samples of Adolescent Athletes Based on Prospective and Status Quo Studies

Prospective Studies[1]		Status Quo Studies[1]	
Gymnastics, Poland	15.1±0.9	Gymnastics, World[3]	15.6±2.1
Gymnastics, Switzerland	14.5±1.2	Gymnastics, Hungarian	15.0±0.6
Gymnastics, Sweden	14.5±1.4	Figure skating, U.S., Canada	14.2±0.5
Gymnastics, United Kingdom[2]	14.3±1.4	Swimming, age group, U.S.	13.1±1.1
Swimming, United Kingdom	13.3±1.1	Swimming, age group, U.S.	12.7±1.1
Tennis, United Kingdom	13.2±1.4	Diving, Junior Olympic, U.S.	13.6±1.1
Track, Poland	12.3±1.1	Ballet, Yugoslavia	13.6
Rowing, Poland	12.7±0.9	Ballet, Yugoslavia	14.1
Elite ballet, U.S.	15.4±1.9	Track, Hungary	12.6
		Soccer, age group, U.S.	12.9±1.1
		Several team sports, Hungary	12.7

Adapted from Malina (1998a) which includes the references for specific studies, with the exception of figure skaters (Vadocz, Siegel, and Malina, in press).

[1]Prospective data report means, while status quo data report medians.

[2]Among the British athletes, 13% had not yet attained menarche so that the estimated mean ages will be somewhat later. Small numbers of Swiss and Swedish gymnasts and ballet dancers also had not reached menarche at the time of the respective studies.

[3]This sample is from the 1987 world championships in Rotterdam. It did not include girls under 13 years of age so that the estimate may be biased towards an older age.

Sample sizes in studies of adolescent athletes are generally small, and studies in which the athletes are followed from prepuberty through puberty are limited to small, select samples. A potentially confounding issue in such studies is selective attrition. Do earlier maturing girls selectively drop out of gymnastics or figure skating? Or, do sports like gymnastics, figure skating and ballet systematically select for late maturing girls, or systematically exclude early maturing girls?

Biocultural Interactions

The preceding has focused on the growth and maturity characteristics of young athletes in a variety of sports, many of whom can be classified as select, elite, junior national, or international caliber. Growth (size attained) and maturity (skeletal age, age at menarche) are outcomes of underlying biological processes. In healthy, adequately nourished children, growth and maturation are genotypically regulated (Malina et al., in press). However, growth and maturity cannot be treated in isolation from the cultural or social conditions into which an individual is born and under which he/she is reared. The processes underlying growth and maturation are responsive to these environments including, for example, socioeconomic status, family size, diet, rearing styles, emotional states, health status, physical activity and training, and others. The individual's genotype can influence how he/she responds to specific environmental stresses, including the stress of systematic training (Bouchard, Malina, and Perusse, 1997). In other words, not everyone responds to the same environmental stress in the same manner. Some of these issues will become more apparent when the training for sport is evaluated as a possible factor influencing the growth and maturation of young athletes (see below).

The sociocultural environment into which an individual is born and in which he/she is reared is of primary importance in sport. It is the matrix within which opportunity for sport is made available and in which talent for sport is realized. Thus, it is important to recognize that any discussion of sport for youth from the local to international levels can be done neither in a purely biological manner nor in a purely social or cultural manner. Biology and culture must be viewed in concert, in a biocultural perspective. Sport is a cultural phenomenon (i.e., culturally sanctioned). However, individuals physically-biologically perform the demands of a sport within a particular cultural context. The term *biocultural* is preferred to *biosocial* because culture encompasses more than social relationships and psychosocial interactions. Several examples of biocultural interactions in youth sports are subsequently discussed.

Social Circumstances

Social circumstances may either interact with or vary with a youngster's growth and maturity, and in turn, influence his/her opportunities and experiences in sport. Many individuals have the potential to succeed in sport, but not all have the opportunity or the environment in which to realize this potential. Outstanding young athletes are thus not a random sample and are not ordinarily representative of the general population of children and youth.

Parental encouragement and support often influence a youngster's early experiences in sport. Parental attitudes, in turn, are probably affected by their own early experiences in sport, and many youth have one or both parents who themselves were involved in organized youth sports.

In some sports, such as gymnastics, figure skating, swimming, diving, and tennis, socioeconomic factors play a significant role. These sports are commonly associated with clubs and have special facility needs that are often expensive (e.g., ice time, gym time, swimming and diving facilities).

Given opportunity and encouragement, those most suited to the demands of a sport and capable of adapting to them physically, emotionally and psychologically presumably will experience a degree of success, persist in the sport and perhaps attain elite status. On the other hand, a child with the requisites to be an outstanding figure skater or swimmer, but who does not have access to skating and swimming facilities, good coaches, and so on, will likely not have the opportunity to reach his/her potential, or may be diverted to a sport for which he/she is not suited. For example, how many elite gymnastic, swimming, diving, tennis or figure skating programs have their facilities located in inner cities? In other words, how many potentially elite gymnasts, swimmers, divers, skaters or tennis players are being overlooked due to lack of opportunity?

Physical Characteristics and Opportunity

The physical characteristics (e.g., skill and size) of a youngster are important factors affecting performance and early success in sport. This success may provide other advantages, for example, being noticed and early access to expert coaching, that builds upon the youngster's talent. This is an example of an individual's physical characteristics interacting with social circumstances to secure access to expert coaching, and in turn improved performance, further success, heightened motivation, and so on, all of which may lead to persistence in sport. In a retrospective study of Olympic swimmers, Bloom (1982) emphasized the importance of physical characteristics in providing early competitive advantages:

> Natural physical characteristics that give an individual some initial advantage over his or her age mates are likely to function to motivate the individual to enter and compete in a sport. They also help him or her secure the teaching and training needed to convert an individual with small initial advantages into a world-class athletes. (p. 515)

Biological Maturity and Sport Socialization

Growth and maturity do not occur in a social vacuum. Changing relationships with peers, parents and coaches accompany the adolescent growth spurt and sexual maturity. Individual variation in the timing and tempo of the growth spurt and sexual maturity, including changes in size, body composition, strength, performance and behavior, are the backdrop against which youth evaluate and interpret their status among peers. Participation and perhaps success in sport are important components of this evaluative process.

Such an interaction between biological maturity and social circumstances regarding sport may occur among adolescent girls. As indicated earlier, there is considerable overlap in the distribution of recalled ages at menarche in large samples of athletes and non-athletes of the same chronological age and from similar social backgrounds. The distribution for athletes is simply shifted to the right, or later ages, by about one year or so. There are both early- and late-maturing athletes and non-athletes; it is just that there are more later maturing athletes than non-athletes. A two-part hypothesis, a biocultural interpretation, for the later menarche observed in athletes has been suggested (Malina, 1983).

First, the physique characteristics associated with later maturity, especially the tendency towards linearity, lower weight for stature, less fatness, relatively longer legs, and relatively narrow hips compared to shoulder (Malina et al., in press), are generally more suitable for success in athletic performance. Later maturers also tend to perform better on many motor tasks, and the differences between contrasting maturity groups of girls are more apparent in later adolescence, about 16 to 18 years of age (Beunen et al., 1978). Conversely, the physique characteristics associated with earlier maturity, a lateral build, greater weight for stature, higher fatness, relatively shorter legs, and relatively broad hips, may be less ideal for successful athletic performance, especially in tasks in which the body must be rapidly moved or projected (e.g., runs and jumps). The preceding does not preclude the fact that some early-maturing girls will have a physique suitable for athletic performance and perform well. However, on average, late-maturing girls more often have such characteristics.

Second, the process of socialization into or away from sport may interact with the girl's biological maturity status. Specifically, it has been suggested that early-maturing girls are perhaps socialized away from sport while late-maturing girls are socialized into sport (Malina, 1983). Among girls, as in boys, earlier maturation may represent a performance advantage in some sports in early adolescence, 9 to 11 years. The larger body size of early maturers may be an advantage in sports that place a premium on size and strength; however, the larger body size may be a disadvantage in sports such as gymnastics, diving and figure skating. And, with the attainment of menarche, the early-maturing girl (menarche before 12 years of age) experiences new social roles and changing interests which may contribute to the process of being socialized away from sport. The structure of the sport system may be a contributory factor; that is, the status of a young teenager in her social group is linked to her femininity, and until quite recently, sport was not considered feminine in some quarters of society.

A related factor may be self-esteem. It is reasonably well documented that self-worth or self-esteem declines in girls during the transition into puberty, and early-maturing girls do not fare well compared to girls average ("on time") and late in maturation (Brooks-Gunn and Peterson, 1983; Simmons and Blyth, 1987). There is also ethnic variation. Global self-worth declines in American White girls but is stable in American Black girls from 9 to 14 years, and adjusting for stage of sexual maturation, body mass index (BMI) and household income does not alter the trends. Further, as the BMI increases, scores for global self-worth, physical appearance and social acceptance decrease, but the decreases in physical appearance and social acceptance scores with an increase in the BMI are less in Black than in White girls (Brown et al., 1998). Implications of these results for participation in youth sports need to be systematically addressed. Nevertheless, early maturing girls often have decreased self-esteem and are at a disadvantage socially compared to later maturing peers.

On the other hand, the late-maturing girl may be socialized into sport partly because of her lateness, that is, through her physical characteristics and skill. She has the opportunity to continue in athletics and thus more time to learn the skills, experience success in sport, and adapted to the multiple demands of a sport attaining menarche. Since late-maturing girls are older chronologically when they attain menarche (usually after the 14th birthday), they perhaps have not experienced the social pressures about athletics for girls and/or are more able to cope with the pressures. In contrast to early maturers, late-maturing girls generally have an elevated sense of self-esteem. Late-maturing girls may thus have heightened motivational levels due in part to success in athletics, and this success may carry over into social interactions.

Late-maturing girls are also more "in phase" in a biological and developmental sense with early- and average-maturing boys of the same chronological age; late-maturing girls thus may have a more favored position in the adolescent social setting. This is illustrated in Table 11.3. A late-maturing girl who attains menarche at 14 years of age is biologically closer to early- and average-maturing boys, who are more often good athletes (see above). Early-maturing girls, on the other hand, are out of phase in a biological and developmental sense with female and male chronological age peers. An early-maturing girl who attains menarche before 12 years of age is 3 to 4 years advanced biologically relative to most of her male chronological age peers. Such differences in biological maturity and in turn developmental status are considerable in the world of youth in the transition into or in the midst of adolescence. Early maturing girls thus commonly seek out associations with older age groups. In this way, biological earliness or lateness may influence socialization away from or into sport within a given chronological age group (see H. E. Jones, 1949a).

Table 11.3   Timing of Peak Height Velocity (PHV) and Menarche

	Ages (yrs) at Attaining Maturity Indicators		
	Early	**Average**	**Late**
Girls			
PHV	<11	**11–13**	**>13**
Menarche	<12	**12–14**	**>14**
Boys			
PHV	**<13**	**13–15**	>15

Based on composite data for North American and European youth (Malina et al., in press). Approximate mean ages of PHV in girls and boys are, respectively, 12.0 and 14.0 years, and approximate mean age of menarche is 13.0 years, with standard deviations of about one year. Values in bold print indicate similarity in maturational time (developmentally in phase) of average ("on time") and late-maturing girls with early and average ("on time") maturing boys.

This two-part hypothesis (Malina, 1983) has been modified by Hata and Aoki (1990) to include a significant role for physique. Based on observations on Japanese athletes, these authors propose first, that the increasing age at menarche associated with advancement in level of athletic competition is a result of selection ". . . in the socialization process into (or away from) sports participation . . .," and second, that the variation in mean ages at menarche by sport at a given competitive level is ". . . mainly a reflection of the diversity of suitable physiques by sport" (p. 181).

In contrast to girls, it is the late-maturing boy who is less likely to experience success in youth sport. Adolescent boys who have their growth spurts after 15 years of age (see Table 11.3), or who have skeletal ages that lag behind their chronological ages by more than one year, are biologically and developmentally out of phase or synchrony with the majority of adolescents. They tend to be shorter and lighter than average and deficient in muscular strength and power. They also do not perform as well as adolescent boys who are early and average in maturity status (Malina et al., in press), and they differ behaviorally. Early maturity is associated with enhanced popularity and social status among adolescent boys (H. E. Jones, 1949b; M. C. Jones and Bayley, 1950; Mussen and Jones, 1957). And, most sports emphasized for young males place a premium on size, strength, power and speed, and the late maturing boy is at a distinct disadvantage. Thus, late maturity is probably an integral component of the sport socialization process in boys, but it has not received systematic study.

Talent Identification

A popular term in discussions of youth sports, especially high performance sports, is *talent identification*, that is, the identification of individuals who have the physical, behavioral, and psychological requisites for success in a given sport. It is obviously a biocultural process. How identification and its corollary selection are carried out, however, varies with the objectives of sports programs.

The majority of youth sport programs emphasize mass participation. Age and willingness to participate are the criteria, and probably involve a parent-child decision. The primary motivations for children in such youth sport programs are to have fun, to be with friends and to make new friends, to learn skills, to be physically fit, and to compete and win (Smoll and Smith, 1999). The only selection here is parental selection of a program, which is potentially important because at this level the majority of coaches are volunteers with variable backgrounds and experiences in working with children in the context of sport. However, as some programs become competitive and specialized, identification and selection of talented youngsters systematically occurs both informally (e.g., observing youngsters in game situations, noting those who are more skilled and inviting them for a specific team) and formally (e.g., regular tryouts).

In contrast, high performance programs that emphasize the elite have as their objective the identification, selection, and training of individuals with potential for success in the regional, national, and international arenas (see Regnier, Salmela, and Russell, 1993). A good deal of the information presented earlier on the growth and maturity of young athletes is derived from samples that can be classified as select, elite, junior national, or international caliber. Many of them have probably come through formal or informal talent identification programs.

Much discussion about the identification and selection of young athletes has focused on the success of sport systems in several countries of the former Eastern European bloc, which was based in part on systematic identification and selection at relatively young ages (Bompa, 1985; Brane and Leskosek, 1990; Hartley, 1988; Karacsony, 1988). Many of these practices have been extended, with modification, to some sports in Western countries (Bajin, 1987; Feigley, 1987; Jiang, 1993; Poppleton and Salmoni, 1991), and have been incorporated into those of other countries, with China, perhaps, presently the most visible example (Ho, 1987; Lawrence, 1992; Reilly, 1988). The objective of such selection programs is quite clear:

> Priority is given to selection of those children and young people thought most likely to benefit from intensive sports training and to produce top-class results in national and international competition. (Hartley, 1988, p. 50)

Although there is variation by sport, the general pattern of identification and selection refined in many Eastern European countries includes initial evaluation of physical (physique, anthropometric, and motor) and behavioral characteristics, often as early as 3 to 8 years for some sports (e.g., gymnastics, diving, swimming, and figure skating). Secondary evaluations vary with sport. For example, in Romania secondary selections were made at 9 to 10 years for gymnastics, figure skating and swimming, and at 10 to 15 years for girls and 10 to 17 years for boys in other sports (Bompa, 1985). Potential rowers, basketball players and weight lifters were not selected until after puberty in the former Soviet Union and German Democratic Republic (Hartley, 1988). Ballet, though considered primarily as an art form, also has rather rigorous, selective anatomical criteria that rival those of some sports (Hamilton, 1986). Emphasis is commonly on extreme linearity and thinness.

Obviously the physical, motor, and behavioral requisites vary among sports, and the process of selection is ongoing. Selection is based on the assumption that the requisites for a given sport can be identified at a young age and subsequently perfected through specific training. In a perhaps simplistic view, the equation has two parts, the demands of a sport and the characteristics of the performer deemed suitable for the sport. The former are ordinarily described in technical manuals and can be summarized into three components: objectives, tasks (skills and tactics) and rules. The latter are more difficult to describe but may be operationally defined as ability, the biocultural matrix that includes the growth, maturity, and developmental characteristics of the individual. The preceding has been related to the concept of readiness for sport (Malina, 1988, 1993). That is, readiness occurs when a child's ability is commensurate with or exceeds the demands of a sport; unreadiness occurs when the child's ability is exceeded by the demands of a sport.

Thus, success or failure in sport, or of a talent identification and selection program, can be viewed as dependent upon the balance between the individual's ability and the demands of a sport. The latter are relatively constant (i.e., high-level performance). Ability is dynamic, changing as the child grows, matures, and develops. The ultimate caveat for the success of talent identification and selection programs, of course, is "Wait and see!"

Does Training for Sport Influence Growth and Maturity?

Although regular physical activity, including training for sport, is often viewed as necessary to support normal growth and maturation (Malina et al., in press), in the past decade or so, concern has been expressed on a more or less regular basis for potential negative influences of intensive training for sport on growth (i.e., size attained) and maturity (i.e., timing and tempo of progress to the mature state), especially in young female athletes. It has been suggested, for example, that intensive training during childhood and adolescence may stunt growth and delay the sexual maturation of girls (American Medical Association and American Dietetic Association, 1991; Tofler, Stryer, Micheli, and Herman, 1996). On the other hand, potential negative influences of training for sport on the growth and maturation of boys is rarely expressed, most often in the context of young wrestlers who may drastically modify their diets to meet specific body weight criteria for the sport. How can the available data for young athletes in a variety of sports be interpreted? Does training for sport affect size attained (growth) and skeletal, sexual, and somatic maturity? The following discussion is based on Malina (1994, 1998a, 1998b, 1999, 2000; Malina et al., in press), which includes the primary references. It is limited to height, weight, and indices of biological maturity.

What Is Training?

Training refers to systematic, specialized practice for a specific sport or sport discipline for most of the year. It also may refer to specific short-term experimental programs. Physical activity is not the same as regular training. Training programs are ordinarily specific (e.g., endurance running, strength training, sport skill training) and vary in intensity and duration. Training is often quantified as hours per week. What is important is the duration and intensity of specific activities performed during this time. Training in gymnastics and figure skating includes stretching, light weights, choreography and formal instruction by coaches, in addition to numerous repetitions of specific stunts and routines. Soccer training includes stretching, endurance- and strength-related activities, skill instruction and drills, and game situations. Thus, not all "training" time is spent in intensive physical activity. The quantification and specification of training programs by sport needs closer attention in order to evaluate potential effects on growth and maturity.

Training and Growth in Height and Weight

Sport participation and training for sport have no apparent effect on growth in height and the rate of growth in height in healthy, adequately nourished children and adolescents. The heights of young athletes probably reflect the size demands of specific sports. The smaller size of athletes in gymnastics and figure skating is evident long before systematic training was initiated. Athletes in these two sports also have parents who are shorter than average, suggesting a familial contribution to their smaller size. Both sports also tend to selectively favor shorter participants. Short term longitudinal studies of athletes in several sports indicate rates of growth in height that are well within the range of normally expected variation among children and adolescents.

In contrast to height, body weight can be influenced by regular training for sport, resulting in changes in body composition. Training is associated with a decrease in fatness in both sexes and occasionally with an increase in fat-free mass, especially in boys. Changes in fatness depend on continued, regular activity or training (or caloric restriction, which often occurs in sports like gymnastics, ballet, figure skating and diving in girls and wrestling in boys) for their maintenance. When training is significantly reduced, fatness tends to accumulate. It is difficult to separate specific effects of training on fat-free mass from expected changes that occur with normal growth and sexual maturation during adolescence. This is especially so in boys who almost double their estimated fat-free mass during adolescence.

Training and Biological Maturity

The timing and tempo of biological maturation are highly individual characteristics. This individuality, which has a significant genotypic component, needs to be considered in evaluating potentially positive or negative influences attributed to regular training for sport.

Regular training for sport does not influence the skeletal maturity of the hand and wrist. Short term longitudinal studies of male and female athletes in several sports and non-athletes indicate similar gains in skeletal age and chronological age.

Regular training for sport does not influence age at peak height velocity and the rate of growth in height during the spurt in boys and girls. It has been suggested that intensive training may delay the timing of the growth spurt and stunt the growth spurt in female gymnasts (Theintz, Howald, Weiss, and Sizonenko, 1993). The data upon which this conclusion is based are not sufficiently longitudinal to warrant such a conclusion, and many potentially confounding factors were not considered, especially the rigorous selection criteria for gymnastics, marginal diets, and so on. Female gymnasts as a group show the growth and maturity characteristics of short normal, slow maturing children with short parents (Malina, 1999).

Longitudinal data on the sexual maturation of either girls or boys who are regularly active in and/or training for sport are not extensive. The limited longitudinal data indicate no effect of regular physical activity or training on the timing and progress of breast and pubic hair development in girls, and genital and pubic hair development in boys.

Discussions of the potential influence of training on sexual maturity focus most often on later average ages at menarche which, as noted earlier, are often observed in athletes in many but not in all sports. Training for sport is commonly indicated as the factor which is responsible for the later ages at menarche among athletes, with the inference that training "delays" this late pubertal landmark. Unfortunately, studies of athletes do not consider factors which are known to influence menarche. Diet is an obvious factor and athletes in sports with characteristically late ages at menarche (gymnastics and ballet) often show energy intakes that are consistently lower than their energy expenditures (i.e., a chronic energy deficit). There is a familial tendency for later maturity in athletes. Mothers of ballet dancers, gymnasts, figure skaters, and athletes in several other sports attain menarche later than mothers of non-athletes, and sisters of athletes attain menarche later than average (Brooks-Gunn and Warren, 1988; Malina, Ryan, and Bonci, 1994; Vadocz, Siegel, and Malina, in press; Stager and

Hatler, 1988). The number of siblings in the family is also related to age at menarche in both non-athletes and athletes (Malina, Katzmarzyk, Bonci, Ryan, and Wellens, 1997). The complexity of factors related to the timing of menarche is highlighted in the conclusions of two comprehensive discussions of exercise and reproductive health of adolescent girls and women: ". . . although menarche occurs later in athletes than in nonathletes, it has yet to be shown that exercise delays menarche in anyone" (Loucks et al., 1992, p. S288), and ". . . the general consensus is that while menarche occurs later in athletes than in nonathletes, the relationship is not causal and is confounded by other factors" (Clapp and Little, 1995, pp. 2–3).

The literature on training and menarche is confused in part by altered menstrual function, which is common in athletes. Menarche refers only to the first menstrual period. Cessation of menstrual cycles after menarche has occurred (secondary amenorrhea) or infrequent cycles (oligomenorrhea) is a different issue beyond the scope of this discussion (see Malina, 1998b). But in the context of normal puberty, menstrual cycles immediately following menarche tend to be anovulatory and often irregular (Malina et al., in press). The development of more or less regular menstrual cycles takes place over several years after menarche. Hence, some of the menstrual irregularities observed in adolescent athletes may in fact reflect the normal process of sexual maturation involved in the establishment of regular menstrual cycles.

The effects of training on the sexual maturation of boys does not receive the same attention as that given to girls. This is not surprising since early and average maturity are characteristic of the majority of adolescent male athletes, and late maturers are represented in only several sports. It is somewhat puzzling, however, why one would expect training to influence the sexes differently. The underlying neuroendocrine processes that mediate sexual maturation are similar in both sexes, and other environmental stresses related to sport, such as anxiety and sleep problems, undoubtedly affect boys as well as girls. However, with the exception of wrestling, emphasis on extreme weight regulation is not characteristic of sports for boys.

Overview of Potential Training Effects

Intensive training for sport does not appear to have a negative influence on growth and maturity. In adequately nourished children and adolescents, growth in height and biological maturity are under genotypic regulation (Malina et al., in press). Regular training for sport has the potential to favorably influence body composition by increasing bone mineral and skeletal muscle, and decreasing fatness. In the few athletes who may present problems related to growth and maturity, factors other than training must be more closely evaluated before attributing the observations to regular training for sport (Malina, 1998a). In many cases of short stature, the shortness has a familial component, that is, short children tend to have short parents. Shortness may also be related to late maturity, which may also be familial. Linearity of physique is associated with later maturation in both sexes, and some sports select for this characteristic of physique (Malina et al., in press).

In some sports, the growth and maturity of young athletes may be compromised by chronically marginal or poor nutritional status, and occasionally by disordered eating. Dietary practices associated with an emphasis on thinness, an optimal weight for performance, or specific weight categories for competition may possibly influence growth and maturity, especially if they involve energy deficits for prolonged periods. Disordered eating behaviors are related factors in these contexts. The energetic demands of intensive training may also compete with the energy and nutrients requirements of the growth and maturational processes in rapidly growing children and adolescents. Psychological and emotional stresses associated with training and competition are additional concerns, especially high levels of stress associated with coach-athlete or parent-athlete interactions. Thus, if intensive training for sport influences growth and maturity, it most likely interacts with, or is confounded by, other factors so that a specific effect of training per se may be impossible to extract.

Allowing for the wide range of individual variation in normal growth and maturity (Malina et al., in press) and in responsiveness to training (Bouchard et al., 1997), why would all children and adolescents be expected to respond to training in a similar manner? Rather, can we identify the young athlete who might be at risk for potentially compromised growth and maturation? If so, how can the sport environment be modified to eliminate the risk? A unique feature of the sport environment of young athletes is adult control—coaches, parents, sport administrators, judges and other officials. Presumably, these adults have the health, safety, and best interests of child and adolescent athletes at heart!

Issues in Youth Sports Related to Growth and Maturation

Participation in sport has associated risks. Concern for compromised growth and maturity has already been discussed. Risk of injury and psychological stress are two other major concerns. Related issues in organized sports include maturity matching to equalize competition and reduce the risk of injury, exclusion and cutting, and manipulation. These issues are subsequently addressed.

Risk of Injury

Risk of injury is real in sport and many other activities of childhood and adolescence (see Micheli and Salob, this volume). Data on the prevalence and incidence of injuries among child and adolescent athletes are limited by the lack of suitable exposure data for practices and competitions to accurately estimate rates. The definition of an injury, which varies considerably among studies, is a confounding factor. The National Athletic Trainers Association has conducted a high school injury surveillance project for the 1995–1997 academic years. The study permits comparison of five sports in males and five sports in females, and also permits comparison of similar (baseball/softball) or the same (basketball, soccer) sports in males and females. A unique feature of this study is that all injuries were reported by certified athletic trainers (Powell and Barber-Foss, 1999, 2000). Corresponding data for youth sports, especially at the local level, are extremely limited. Injury data for youth athletes below the high school level are often limited to those who present to clinics and emergency rooms, or who are included insurance company statistics. Individuals who are injured, but who are not presented to medical and/or insurance personnel, are not represented in the statistical base. Such surveys probably underestimate the true incidence of injuries in youth sport, since it is likely that many minor injuries are unreported or self-treated.

The injury-related literature in youth sports often focuses on risk factors related to the young athlete (internal) and to the sport environment (external) (Caine and Lindner, 1990; Micheli, 1983, 1985; Stanitski, 1988). Needless to say, interactions between the athlete and the sport environment are important considerations in the risk of injury.

Potential risk factors related to the young athlete include a variety of characteristics that are related to size, physique, maturity status, performance and/or physical fitness. These change with age and are interrelated. Commonly indicated as risk factors related to the young athlete include: (a) physique—body build unsuitable for a specific sport, (b) problems in structural alignment, (c) lack of flexibility, (d) lack of muscular strength or a strength imbalance, (e) marginal and/or poor skill development, (f) behavioral factors, including risk taking and inability to cope with stress, (g) previous injury and specifically inadequate rehabilitation from prior injury, (h) the adolescent growth spurt—individual differences in timing and tempo, strength imbalance, reduction in flexibility, adolescent awkwardness, and (i) maturity-associated variation—maturity mismatches in size and strength, late maturation.

Discussions of risk factors related to the young athlete are often descriptive and speculative. The specific contribution of the specific risk factors of young sports participants to injuries sustained in the context of sport is not known with certainty (Malina, 2001). There is a need for information on the unique aspects of risk factors for injury. For example, how do age, experience, growth and maturity interact in the context of sport injuries? Given the association among age, experience, growth, and maturity, is age per se a risk factor? Is lack of skill a risk factor? Are the more skilled more able to avoid the risk of injury, or are the less skilled less likely to avoid the risk of injury? What is it about the growth spurt that places the adolescent athlete at risk?

Psychological Stress

Discussions of potential psychological risks in sports for children and youth are usually set in the context of competitive stress (see Smith, Smoll, and Passer, this volume). Stress may be accentuated in individual sports such as gymnastics, figures skating, diving, and distance running, sports in which athletes compete and perform as individuals. An additional factor in aesthetic sports is the presence of adults in the capacity as officials who evaluate the performances. In contrast, team sports involve a greater number of particpants interacting at one time. The larger number of athletes and the highly interactive nature of activities in team sports tend to diffuse responsibility so that the performance of an individual athlete may be less conspicuous and performance evaluation may be less of a threat. In other words, team sports have the buffer of team members which may alleviate stress associated with performance, errors, and losing.

Potential consequences of competitive stress, and specifically negative outcomes associated with it, include low self-esteem, elevated anxiety, aggressive behavior, possibly increased risk for injury, and burnout. The latter term, which is commonly used in the context of high performance sports, refers to withdrawal from sport related to chronic stress associated with the demands of training and competition. Signs of chronic stress include behavioral alterations such as agitation, sleep disturbances, and loss of interest in practice and in the sport. Other manifestations include depression, lack of energy, skin rashes and nausea, and frequent illness (Weinberg and Gould, 1999). Unfortunately, data on the prevalence or incidence of such conditions among elite young athletes or among youth sport participants are not available; a good deal of the information is anecdotal and is limited to individual sports such as tennis and swimming.

Many factors are involved in competitive stress and burnout. Two especially important factors are negative performance evaluations and inconsistent feedback from coaches and officials. Negative evaluations are usually critical rather than supportive, whereas inconsistent feedback often translates into mixed messages for the young athlete. Other contributing factors are the athlete's perception of not being able to meet expectations imposed by self and/or others (coaches, parents), a training environment that is not supportive, and the stress of intensive competition per se. Overprotection by coaches, trainers, parents and sport officials is an additional factor. It tends to limit the exposure of young athletes to new situations and in turn opportunities to develop coping mechanisms. These sport-related stresses are superimposed on and interact with the normal stresses of adolescence, that is, school, peer pressures, social relationships (boy friends, girl friends), economic independence, and so on.

Among growing, maturing, and developing young athletes there is also the need to be a child or adolescent. All too often, some young athletes find themselves in the microcosm of a sport organized and operated by and for the satisfaction of adults. It thus should come as no surprise that a factor in stress and burnout may be conflicting demands between sport and the universal tasks of childhood and adolescence—growth, maturation, and development.

Maturity Matching

The issue of maturity matching in youth sports is ordinarily set in the context of two related issues: (a) grouping children for a sport—by ability, grade, or maturity status, and (b) "playing up" or "moving up"—children moving up in grade to participate. "Moving up" may occur in some small communities where there may not be enough children to constitute a team, or may occur because an individual is skilled and wants to play at a higher level of competition. These are legitimate questions for which there is not a simple solution. They occur most often among children of middle-school age, about 11 to 15 years of age (see Malina and Beunen, 1996 for a more detailed discussion of issues in maturity matching).

Size, strength, and skill mismatches are common in many youth sports in spite of efforts to group participants for competition by age and skill. Matching participants by body size and biological maturity is often suggested as a means to equalize competition for the purpose of reducing the risk of injury and increasing the chance for success. Results of presently available studies of the relationship between maturity status and risk of injury in young athletes are limited (Malina, 2001). There is a need for systematic study of variation in maturity status, and of variation in size, strength and power associated with individual differences in maturity, as potential risk factors for injury in sport. The issue of enhanced success in youth sport associated with matching has apparently not been addressed, perhaps because the process of maturity matching is complex.

Matching in youth sports is largely done on the basis of chronological age and sex, and to some extent level of skill. Body size (most often body weight) and biological maturity (almost exclusively sexual maturity) are used less often. As noted earlier, skill, strength, size, and maturity are interrelated. Sex differences in pubertal timing and in size, strength and skill, which become especially apparent about 10 to 14 years of age, are also important.

Although matching may equalize competition and reduce the risk of injury, it generally does not take into consideration individual differences in behaviors (i.e., social, emotional, and cognitive). A child's level of behavioral development does not necessarily proceed in concert with his/her physical growth and maturity. A late maturing 13-year-old boy may resent participating with 11-year-old boys of similar maturity status. Similarly, an early maturing 11-year-old girl may not want to participate with equally mature, but older and more experienced 13-year-old girls. Matching may thus have potential behavioral consequences which can influence self-concept and self-esteem.

The consequences of matching for sport need further study. What is the effect of maturity matching on behavioral development when, for example, on older child is biologically more suited to compete with younger children, or a younger child is biologically more suited to compete with older children? Younger, early maturing boys may be threatened by having to participate and compete with chronologically older boys of the same maturity status. Conversely, older boys may not want to participate with younger boys of the same maturity status due largely to social concerns. For example, there may be less recognition in successfully competing versus less mature individuals. The peer group is a major force during middle childhood and early adolescence, and the team is a significant peer group. Although children and youth have several peer groups, matching by size, skill and maturity status often alters peer group structure and in turn may influence social relationships and development.

Most discussions of maturity matching and equating for sports competition focus on youth. It is also important to reverse the question. That is, how can sports be modified to meet the characteristics and needs of their youthful participants? How can tasks and rules of a sport be adjusted to meet the changing needs of growing, maturing and developing youth? Eliminating body checking in youth ice hockey, for example, significantly reduces the number of injuries. On the other hand, the demands of sports such as artistic gymnastics and figure skating have seemingly been altered by administrators, judges and coaches (i.e., adults) so that "women's" competitions in these sports at elite levels are often competitions among "prepubertal girls." It is imperative that those involved with youth sports programs, or with elite young athletes, should be encouraged to seriously consider how the respective sports can be matched to the needs and characteristics of children and adolescents—the youthful participants!

Issues in Talent Identification and Selection

Talent identification and selection practices have been discussed earlier. Issues related to decision making, elimination or cutting, and manipulation, among others, need more consideration. Does the child have a voice in the selection process? Are parents involved? Accounts in the electronic and print media often highlight parents who are seemingly more interested in their child's success than is the child. Are decisions made independently by coaches or other sports authorities? What kind of guidance is available for the child, or parents, when he/she is selected? What are the implications of being labeled "talented" for individual and parental expectations?

Selection initially involves elimination of many individuals and subsequently cutting of others as competition becomes more specialized and rigorous. The merit of selection programs is usually cast in the context of the number of successful athletes (gold medals). Little, if anything, is ever indicated about the individuals who do not make it through the process, and they are the vast majority. What is the influence of "not being selected" or "being cut" on subsequent participation in sport or in physical activity?

The growth and maturity characteristics of young athletes may influence the processes of exclusion and inclusion involved in talent identification. That is, some youth will be excluded from participation in a sport and others will be included on the basis of their growth and maturity status. Processes vary among sports, sport organizations, and countries. Nevertheless, two important questions for young athletes need more detailed study: (a) What influence do the processes of inclusion and exclusion have on maximizing the possibility that a youngster with the greatest potential for success at the highest levels of competition will still be participating in the sport and be available for selection to high level teams in their late adolescent and early adult years?, and (b) What influence do the processes of inclusion and exclusion have on the likelihood that most youth will continue to participate in a sport and receive the health-related benefits of this form of physical activity throughout adolescence and into adulthood?

The first question is related to the identification of a select few participants who might bring national recognition through the success of its highest level teams. In contrast, the second question is related to a philosophy of well-being associated with health benefits that may be received by the general populace through participation in sports.

At first, it might seem that solutions to these vastly different questions must be different. The desire to win often drives the participatory process in sport. Many coaches, even at local levels of competition, experience pressures to win. These pressures may result in a tendency for coaches, parents, and program administrators to directly or indirectly select skilled (i.e., "talented" early maturing players, who can help youth teams win now) and exclude later maturing youngsters, who might have the potential to become national caliber performers when they reach full physical maturity.

Youth players, who are not chosen for an advanced or select team or club, and the associated special coaching, quickly get the message that they will "not make it" or "do not have what it takes." They probably drop out of the sport and pursue other activities. In many instances, decisions as to who will be selected to play, and the converse, who will be excluded, are often placed in the hands of individuals with little or no background in understanding the growth, maturation and development of youth and their potential influences on the selection/exclusion process and performance. This is probably the case in youth programs operated by volunteer administrators and coaches, and in programs looking for immediate success or gratification.

The processes used to select athletes in a sport should be changed. They should be directed at providing the best possible training throughout childhood and adolescence to all individuals interested in participating in a sport and to encourage them to continue to play, irrespective of how successful they might be during their childhood years. This approach will lead to a broader base of individuals participating in a sport through adolescence into adulthood, thus fulfilling the health-related benefits of sport and providing a larger pool of individuals which may include a greater number who potentially could be the best athletes.

Manipulation of Young Athletes

The term *manipulate* has several meanings, but two come to mind when discussing manipulation in the context of sport: to manage or utilize skillfully, and to change so as to meet one's own goal. There is a fine line between the two. Coaching is to a large extent a form of manipulation, that is, managing youngsters carefully and skillfully so that they will learn and work cooperatively to attain their goals or to achieve their potential. Many coaches manage young athletes quite skillfully to bring about talented performances of individuals and teams. On the other hand, some coaches and others involved with young athletes (parents and sport organizations) may use manipulative strategies with young athletes to meet their own purposes.

Manipulation of young athletes can take several forms—*social, sexual, nutritional, chemical*, and *commercial*. These categories are somewhat arbitrary and are not mutually exclusive.

Social manipulation, specifically in the context of selection for sport, is obvious. Talent identification and selection are themselves forms of social manipulation which occur at relatively young ages in some sports (see above). Identifying and selecting the potentially talented athlete at an early age is the first step in a relatively long term process, which involves several forms of social manipulation (preferential treatment, differential access to resources, etc.).

Overdependence of elite young athletes on coaches and sport organizations is another form of social manipulation. It is easy to see the strong control that a coach or organization can exert over young athletes, particularly when they are impressionable and may not fully comprehend their success in sport. Such control may strain relationships between the athlete and parents to the extent that some coaches may not, or perhaps do not, differentiate where coaching stops and the life of the youngster begins.

Another form of social manipulation, usually by parents in concert with a football coach, is to hold a boy back in school for one grade. This presumably permits the boy an "extra" year of growth compared to his age/grade peers so that he will be considerably larger than his classmates the next year.

Sexual abuse of young athletes is another form of manipulation. As noted above, elite sport often fosters excessive dependence of young athletes upon their coaches, sport officials and sport organizations. In many cases, young athletes, and often their parents, place blind trust in coaches. An unfortunate byproduct of such circumstances is sexual abuse, which is occasionally highlighted in the media (see Morra and Smith, this volume). Coaches exert some degree of power over their athletes and coach-athlete relationships are important in sport. Unfortunately, some coaches have abused this power and overstepped the bounds of ethical and professional behavior. Parents and other adults involved with youth in the context of sport must be aware and vigilant. It is sad, however, that some parents and athletes are willing to tolerate such coaches if they produce results!

Nutritional manipulation of young athletes is most apparent in those sports which emphasize weight control in order to maintain an aesthetic and/or slender build (gymnastics, figure skating, ballet, distance running) or defined weight categories for competition (wrestling). Caloric restriction is common among young athletes in these sports, often at the direct suggestion of coaches, parents and judges (in gymnastics and figure skating), and very often as a result of off-hand comments on body weight, shape, or fatness.

Young athletes are often encouraged to maintain weight or to lose weight for the sake of optimizing performance in the eyes of the coach or sport officials. Coaching practices, such as weekly or daily "weigh-ins" and consistent negative feedback about body appearance, are in fact a form of nutritional manipulation. Young athletes are often required to maintain a coach-prescribed body weight when the natural course of growth in teenage youth is to gain weight. These practices may lead young athletes to perceive themselves as fat (when they in fact are not) and to believe that they must stop eating. Such unrealistic demands on the young athletes and corresponding concerns with body weight may lead to problems of disordered eating.

Chemical manipulation can take several forms—diuretics to lose weight; anabolic steroids to build muscle mass and strength; various drugs to suppress maturation; and perhaps others. Some unscrupulous coaches may utilize diuretics with young athletes for the purpose of weight loss in order to meet league prescribed weight limits. Other practices associated with making weight limits include vomiting and laxatives as well as extreme caloric restriction.

The use of anabolic steroids is a major concern among athletes at any level. The potential risks of steroid use are well documented (see Johnson and Van de Loo, this volume). If administered to children, anabolic steroids may alter the normal pattern of maturation (accelerate sexual and skeletal maturity) and growth (stunting in adult height). Use of steroids over an extended period have harmful side effects, both short-term (acne, insomnia, headaches) and long-term (elevated cholesterol levels, abnormal liver function).

A more recent potential form of chemical manipulation to enhance success in sport is the use of synthetic growth hormone to increase the stature of normal children to enhance success in sport. In addition to ethical concerns, metabolic risks and long term benefits of growth hormone in normal children are not known with certainty. Among normal short children treated with synthetic growth hormone, the gain in final height is quite small.

The use of various drugs to suppress the sexual maturation of female gymnasts has been alleged. But this practice has not been documented with certainty.

Commercial manipulation of young athletes is increasingly more common. Sports merchandising is commonplace. What is often overlooked is the fact that elite young athletes are sometimes the merchandise! Another form of commercial manipulation involves the formation of corporations to underwrite the cost of elite training programs, with the understanding that the future earnings of the budding young athletes will be shared by all investors. It is clear that talented athletes in a variety of sports are constantly being sought at very young ages. In a sense, the talented youngster is viewed primarily as a property with large earning potential by parents, coaches, and sport organizations.

In summary, the modern "sports system" with its emphasis on high level performance may be a major manipulator of young athletes. Some children and adolescents are being exploited by the institution of big time sports. Their health, well-being and education may be sacrificed for the sake of success in sport. What is the cost of athletic excellence for the child and adolescent? Activities and practices related to sport should have as their goal the benefit and well-being of the young athletes. If not, they have no place in youth sports. Such issues need to be considered from the perspective of the young athlete and not from that of involved adults.

References

American Medical Association/American Dietetic Association. (1991). *Targets for adolescent health: Nutrition and physical fitness*. Chicago: American Medical Association.

Bajin, B. (1987). Talent identification program for Canadian female gymnasts. In B. Petiot, J. H. Salmela and T. B. Hoshizaki (Eds.), *World identification for gymnastic talent* (pp. 34–44). Montreal: Sports Psyche Editions.

Beunen, G., de Beul, G., Ostyn, M., Renson, R., Simons, J., and Van Gerven, D. (1978). Age at menarche and motor performance in girls aged 11 through 18. In J. Borms and M. Hebbelinck (Eds.), *Pediatric work physiology* (pp. 118–123). Basel: Karger.

Beunen, G., and Malina, R. M. (1996). Growth and biological maturation: Relevance to athletic performance. In O. Bar-Or (Ed.), *The encyclopedia of sports medicine: The child and adolescent athlete* (pp. 3–24). Oxford: Blackwell Scientific Publications.

Beunen, G., Malina, R. M., and Thomis, M. (1999). Physical growth and maturation of female gymnasts. In F. E. Johnston, B. Zemel, and P. B. Eveleth (Eds.), *Human growth in context* (pp. 281–289). London: Smith-Gordon.

Bloom, B. S. (1982). The role of gifts and markers in the development of talent. *Exceptional Children, 48*, 510–522.

Bompa, T. O. (1985). Talent identification. In *Sports: Science periodical on research and technology in sport, physical testing*, GN-1. Ottawa: Coaching Association of Canada.

Bouchard, C., Malina, R. M., and Perusse, L. (1997). *Genetics of fitness and physical performance*. Champaign, IL: Human Kinetics.

Brane, D., and Leskosek, B. (1990). Racunalnisko podprt sistem iskanja visokih in motoricno sposobnih in njihova usmer janje v kocarko (computer aided system for identifying tall and motor-capable children and their direction into basketball). In *Sport Mladih (Sport and the Young, Proceedings of IV Congress of Sports Pedagogues of Yugoslavia and I International Symposium)* (pp. 623–628). Ljubljana-Bled: University of Ljubljana.

Brooks-Gunn, J., and Peterson, A. (1983). *Girls at puberty: Biological and psychosocial perspectives*. New York: Plenum.

Brooks-Gunn, J., and Warren, W. P. (1988). Mother-daughter differences in menarcheal age in adolescent girls attending national dance company schools and non-dancers. *Annals of Human Biology, 15*, 35–43.

Brown, K. M., McMahon, R. P., Biro, F. M., Crawford, P., Schreiber, G. B., Similo, S. L., Waclawiw, W., and Striegel-Moore, R. (1998). Changes in self-esteem in Black and White girls between the ages of 9 and 14 years: The NHLBI Growth and Health Study. *Journal of Adolescent Health, 23*, 7–19.

Caine, D. J., and Lindner, K. (1990). Preventing injury to young athletes. Part 1: Predisposing factors. *Canadian Association for Health, Physical Education, and Recreation Journal, 56*, 30–35.

Carter, J. E. L. (1988). Somatotypes of children in sports. In R. M. Malina (Ed.), *Young athletes: Biological, psychological, and educational perspectives* (pp. 153–165). Champaign, IL: Human Kinetics.

Carter, J. E. L., and Brallier, R. M. (1988). Physiques of specially selected young female gymnasts. In R. M. Malina (Ed.), *Young athletes: Biological, psychological, and educational perspectives* (pp. 167–175). Champaign, IL: Human Kinetics.

Carter, J. E. L., and Heath, B. H. (1990). *Somatotyping—Development and applications*. Cambirdge: Cambridge University Press.

Claessens, A. L. (1999). Elite female gymnasts: A kinanthropometric overview. In F. E. Johnston, B. Zemel, and P. B. Eveleth (Eds.), *Human growth in context* (pp. 273–280). London: Smith-Gordon.

Clapp, J. F., and Little, L. K. (1995). The interaction between regular exercise and selected aspects of women's health. *America Journal of Obstetric Gynecology, 173*, 2–9.

Feigley, D. S. (1987). Characteristics of young elite gymnasts. In B. Petiot, J. H. Salmela and T. B. Hoshizaki (Eds.), *World identification for gymnastic talent* (pp. 94–112). Montreal: Sports Psyche Editions.

Geithner, C. A., Malina, R. M. (1993). Somatotypes of Junior Olympic divers. In R. M. Malina and J. Gabriel (Eds.), *Proceedings of the 1993 United States diving sports science seminar* (pp. 36–40). Fort Lauderdale, FL: U.S. Diving.

Hamill, P. V. V., Drizd, R. A., Johnson, C. L., Reed, R. D., and Roche, A. F. (1977). NCHS growth charts for children, birth–18 years, United States. *Vital and Health Statistics*, Series 11, No. 165.

Hamilton, W. G. (1986). Physical prerequisites for ballet dancers: Selectivity that can enhance (or nullify) a career. *Journal of Musculoskeletal Medicine, 3*, 61–66.

Hartley, G. (1988). A comparative view of talent selection for sport in two socialist states—the USSR and the GDR—with particular reference to gymnastics. In *The growing child in competitive sport* (pp. 50–56). Leeds: The National Coaching Foundation.

Hata, E., and Aoki, K. (1990). Age at menarche and selected menstrual characteristics in young Japanese athletes. *Research Quarterly for Exercise and Sport, 61*, 178–183.

Ho, R. (1987). Talent identification in China. In B. Petiot, J. H. Salmela, and T. B. Hoshizaki (Eds.), *World identification for gymnastic talent* (pp. 14–200). Montreal: Sports Psyche Editions.

Jiang, J. (1993). How to select potential Olympic swimmers. *American Swimming Magazine* Feb/March, 14–19.

Johnson, M. D., and Van de Loo, D. A. (2002). Anabolic steroid use in adolescent athletes. In F. L. Smoll and R. E. Smith (Eds.), *Children and youth in sport: A biopsychosocial perspective* (2nd ed., pp. 339–365). Dubuque, IA: Kendall/Hunt.

Jones, H. E. (1949a). Adolescence in our society. In *The family in a democratic society, Anniversary papers of the Community Service Society of New York* (pp. 70–84). New York: Columbia University Press.

Jones, H. E. (1949b). *Motor performance and growth.* Berkeley: University of California Press.

Jones, M. C., and Bayley, N. (1950). Physical maturing among boys as related to behavior. *Journal of Educational Psychology, 41*, 129–148.

Karacsony, I. (1988). The discovery and selection of talented athletes and talent management in Hungary. In *The growing child in competitive sport* (pp. 34–49). Leeds: The National Coaching Foundation.

Kuczmarski, R. J., Ogden, C. L., Grummer-Strawn, L. M., Flegal, K. M., Guo, S. S., Wei, R., Mei, Z., Curtin, L. R., Roche, A. F., and Johnson, C. L. (2000). CDC growth charts: United States. *Advance Data from Vital and Health Statistics*, No. 314. Hyattsville, MD: National Center for Health Statistics.

Lawrence, S. V. (1992, February 17). China's sporting dreams. *U.S. News and World Report, 112,* 59.

Loucks, A. B., Vaitukaitis, J., Cameron, J. L., Rogol, A. D., Skrinar, G., Warren, M. P., Kendrick, J., Limacher, M. C. (1992). The reproductive system and exercise in women. *Medicine and Science in Sports and Exercise, 24* (6, supp.), S288–S293.

Malina, R. M. (1983). Menarche in athletes: A synthesis and hypothesis. *Annals of Human Biology, 10*, 1–24.

Malina, R. M. (1988). Readiness for competitive sports. In *The growing child in competitive sport* (pp. 67–77). Leeds: The National Coaching Foundation.

Malina, R. M, (1993). Youth sports: Readiness, selection and trainability. In J. W. Duquet and J. A. P. Day (Eds.), *Kinanthropometry IV* (pp. 285–301). London: E. and F. N. Spon.

Malina, R. M. (1994). Physical growth and biological maturation of young athletes. *Exercise and Sport Science Reviews, 22*, 389–433.

Malina, R. M. (1998a). Growth and maturation of young athletes—Is training for sport a factor? In K. M. Chan and L. J. Micheli (Eds.), *Sports and children* (pp. 133–161). Hong Kong: Williams and Wilkins Asia Pacific.

Malina, R. M. (1998b). Physical activity, sport, social status and Darwinian fitness. In S. S. Strickland and P. S. Shetty (Eds.), *Human biology and social inequality* (pp. 165–192). Cambridge: Cambridge University Press.

Malina, R. M. (1999). Growth and maturation of elite female gymnasts: Is training a factor? In F. E. Johnston, B. Zemel, and P. B. Eveleth (Eds.), *Human growth in context* (pp. 291–301). London: Smith-Gordon.

Malina, R. M. (2000). Growth and maturation: Do regular physical activity and training for sport have a significant influence? In N. Armstrong and W. van Mechelen (Eds.), *Oxford textbook of paediatric exercise science and medicine* (pp. 95–106). Oxford: Oxford University Press.

Malina, R. M. (2001). Injuries in organized sports for children and adolescents. In J. Frost (Ed.), *Children and injuries* (pp. 199–248). Tucson, AZ: Lawyers and Judges Publishing.

Malina, R. M., and Beunen, G. (1996). Matching of opponents in youth sports. In O. Bar-Or (ed.), *The encyclopedia of sports medicine: The child and adolescent athlete* (pp. 202–213). Oxford: Blackwell Scientific Publications.

Malina, R. M., Beunen, G., Wellens, R., and Claessens, A. (1986). Skeletal maturity and body size of teenage Belgian track and field athletes. *Annals of Human Biology, 13*, 331–339.

Malina, R. M., Bouchard, C., and Bar-Or, O. (in press). *Growth, maturation, and physical activity* (2nd ed.). Champaign, IL: Human Kinetics.

Malina, R. M., Katzmarzyk, P. T., Bonci, C. M., Ryan, R. C., and Wellens, R. E. (1997). Family size and age at menarche in athletes. *Medicine and Science in Sports and Exercise, 29*, 99–106.

Malina, R. M., Ryan, R. C., and Bonci, C. M. (1994). Age at menarche in athletes and their mothers and sisters. *Annals of Human Biology, 21*, 417–422.

Micheli, L. J. (1983). Overuse injuries in children's sports: The growth factor. *Orthopedic Clinics of North America, 14*, 337–360.

Micheli, L. J. (1985). Preventing youth sports injuries. *Journal of Physical Education, Recreation, and Dance, 56*, 52–54.

Micheli, L. J., and Salob, P. A. (2002). Overuse injuries in young athletes. In F. L. Smoll and R. E. Smith (Eds.), *Children and youth in sport: A biopsychosocial perspective* (2nd ed., pp. 367–391). Dubuque, IA: Kendall/Hunt.

Morra, N. N., and Smith, M. D. (2002). Interpersonal sources of violence in hockey: The influence of the media, parents, coaches, and game officials. In F. L. Smoll and R. E. Smith (Eds.), *Children and youth in sport: A biopsychosocial perspective* (2nd ed., pp. 235–255). Dubuque, IA: Kendall/Hunt.

Mussen, P. H., and Jones, M. C. (1957). Self-conceptions, motivations, and interpersonal attitudes of late- and early-maturing boys. *Child Development, 28*, 243–256.

Orvanova, E. (1987). Physical structure of winter sports athletes. *Journal of Sport Sciences, 5*, 197–248.

Poppleton, W. L., and Salmoni, A. W. (1991). Talent identification in swimming. *Journal of Human Movement Studies, 20*, 85–95.

Powell, J. W., and Barber-Foss, K. D. (1999). Injury patterns in selected high school sports: A review of the 1995–1997 seasons. *Journal of Athletic Training, 34,* 277–284.

Powell, J. W., and Barber-Foss, K. D. (2000). Sex-related injury patterns among selected high school sports. *American Journal of Sports Medicine, 28,* 385–391.

Regnier, G., Salmela, J., and Russell, S. J. (1993) Talent detection and development in sport. In R. N. Singer, M. Murphey and L. K. Tennant (Eds.), *Handbook of research on sport psychology* (pp. 290–313). New York: Macmillan.

Reilly, R. (1988, August 15). Here no one is spared. *Sports Illustrated, 69,* 70–77.

Simmons, R. G., and Blyth, D. A. (1987). *Moving into adolescence: The impact of pubertal change and social context.* New York: Aldine de Gruyter.

Smith, R. E., Smoll, F. L., and Passer, M. W. (2002). Sport performance anxiety in young athletes. In F. L. Smoll and R. E. Smith (Eds.), *Children and youth in sport: A biopsychosocial perspective* (2nd ed., pp. 501–536). Dubuque, IA: Kendall/Hunt.

Smoll, F. L., and Smith, R. E. (1999). *Sports and your child: A 50-minute guide for parents.* Portola Valley, CA: Warde.

Stager, J. M., and Hatler, L. K. (1988). Menarche in athletes: The influence of genetics and prepubertal training. *Medicine and Science in Sports and Exercise, 20,* 369–373.

Stanitski, C. L. (1988). Management of sports injuries in children and adolescents. *Orthopedic Clinics of North America, 19,* 689–697.

Theintz, G. E., Howald, H., Weiss, U., and Sizonenko, P. C. (1993). Evidence for a reduction of growth potential in adolescent female gymnasts. *Journal of Pediatrics, 122,* 306–313.

Tofler, I. R., Stryer, B. K., Micheli, L. J., and Herman, L. R. (1996). Physical and emotional problems of elite female gymnasts. *New England Journal of Medicine, 335,* 281–283.

Vadocz, E. A., Siegel, S. R., and Malina, R. M. (in press). Age at menarche in competitive figure skaters: Variation by level and discipline. *Journal of Sport Sciences.*

Weinberg, R. S., and Gould, D. (1999). *Foundations of sport and exercise psychology* (2nd ed.). Champaign, IL: Human Kinetics.

CHAPTER 12

Sport and the Child: Physiological and Skeletal Considerations

Donald A. Bailey, University of Saskatchewan
and University of Queensland

During the growing years, physical activity is an important contributing factor if normal development of the child is to be maintained and encouraged (Malina and Bouchard, 1991). This fact is now well accepted. However, in recent years a debate has arisen regarding the potential benefits or risks of excessive physical training on the physical growth and development of children. With the increasing national and international prestige attached to athletic success, we are seeing more and more training and sport programs being developed for progressively younger children. There is ample evidence that the number of highly skilled young athletes involved in rigorous training programs is increasing (Rowland, 1993; Trost, Levin, and Pate, 2000). This is particularly true in sports like swimming, gymnastics, figure skating, and tennis. Some of the training programs for specific sports are of extreme intensity and duration. Indeed, some young children today are involved in training programs that are more intense than would have been believed possible even for adults 30 years ago. Do these programs have an effect on the dynamics of human growth? When are children ready for the rigors of intense sport training and competition? Are there critical times during which a training stimulus may be more important in eliciting increases in functional or skeletal capacity? These and many more questions are waiting for answers. But answers are not easy to come by for a variety of reasons, including the difficulty in isolating the training stimulus from the multiplicity of other factors that affect the growing organism. Recognizing that there are gaps in our knowledge about the physiological responses of children to extreme exercise, there are certain things we do know about the effects of sport training on physiological and skeletal development in growing children. It is the purpose of this chapter to review some of the issues related to this topic.

Perspective

From a physiological point of view, concern has been voiced from some quarters that the stresses imposed by certain competitive sport-training regimes, particularly those of an endurance nature, may make excessive demands on the cardiovascular systems of children or early adolescents. In healthy children there is little evidence to substantiate this concern. Under certain circumstances heavy exercise can have deleterious effects on a child's health, but these negative effects can usually be attributed to sport injuries (Garrett, 1993) or overuse syndromes (Kibler, 1993; Caine, Caine, and Lindner, 1996; Micheli and Salob, this volume).

It is true that there have been cases of sudden death or cardiac arrest in young athletes during or immediately following games or practices, but, invariably, underlying pathology has been identified as the cause of death. Even in young cardiac patients sudden death during exertion is not as high as might be expected. Lambert, Menon, Wagner, and Vlad (1974) examined pooled data from nine countries on cardiac deaths in girls under age 21. Only 10% died while engaged in sport, 32% while playing, and 58% during sleep or rest. The investigators concluded that catastrophe was not prevented by the avoidance of physical exertion in young cardiac patients. For this age group at least, the contention that exercise never caused death in a normal heart is probably correct (Jokl and McClellan, 1971). Moreover, Epstein and Maron (1986) report that the chances of a young athlete, with previously unrecognized heart disease, dying during training or competition is small, in the range of 1 per 200,000 participants. Clearly, the chance of sudden death in children during exercise from undetected heart disease is exceedingly small. Even children with diagnosed congenital heart disease are nowadays encouraged to participate in recreational sport activities because of the beneficial effects to be derived from participation (Reybrouck and Gewillig, 2000).

Similarly, there is little reason to believe that the physical demands of sport have deleterious effects on physiological function in the young athlete. Numerous studies have verified that in the absence of injury or disease, the growth and development of the cardiorespiratory and metabolic capacities of children do not seem to be adversely affected by athletic training or sport participation. To the contrary, young athletes or highly active children generally attain a high functional efficiency (Cunningham and Paterson, 1988; Rowland, 1993). In studying the physiological characteristics of children during the adolescent period, the wide variability in the onset, magnitude and duration of the adolescent growth spurt impose severe problems. A comprehensive review of the growth and maturity characteristics of young athletes is beyond the scope of this chapter but appears elsewhere (see Armstrong and van Mechelen, 2000; Armstrong and Welsman, 1997; Malina, this volume). In general, it can be said with some assurance that in terms of functional physiological and skeletal characteristics, young athletes of both sexes develop as well as non-athletes. The experience of athletic competition and training is probably beneficial to the development of the functional capacity.

There are, however, a number of areas of concern having to do with the child and sport participation that are currently receiving considerable attention. One has to do with musculo-skeletal damage associated with intensive athletic training. Because of the dissociation between linear growth and bone mineral accrual during adolescence (Bailey, Martin, McKay, Whiting, and Mirwald, 2000), there is a transient period of relative skeletal fragility resulting in a temporary increase in fracture risk. The relationship between fracture incidence in children and the timing of the adolescent growth spurt has been well documented, with fracture rates increasing dramatically during the circum-pubertal years (Bailey, Wedge, McCulloch, Martin, and Bernhardson, 1989). In addition to traumatic fractures, overuse injuries also have potential long term consequences. As suggested by Caine, Caine, and Lindner (1996), there is concern that the tolerance limits of the growth plate in growing children might be exceeded by the mechanical stresses imposed by contact (shear forces) or repetitive loading sports. This could lead to a disturbance in bone growth. At risk are the lower extremities of young athletes who participate in contact sports such as tackle football, or the upper extremities and spine of young competitive gymnasts who may experience chronic growth plate injuries (Caine, 1990). Studies suggest, however, that occurrences like this are rare and that in most cases child and youth sports are relatively safe with most injuries being mild and self-limiting (Baxter-Jones, Maffulli, and Helms, 1993; Micheli and Klein, 1991).

Another area of concern has to do with the skeletal integrity of extremely active young female women experiencing menstrual dysfunction. It is well established that anorexia nervosa, for which amenorrhea is one of the essential diagnostic criteria, is associated with reduced levels of bone mineral density (Bachrach, Katzman, and Litt, 1991). Further to this, many reports document irregular or absent menses and reduced bone mineral density in girls who train intensely for sports requiring leanness for elite performance. Estimates as to the extent of menstrual dysfunction in elite athletic women range from 2% to 51% depending on the activity in which they are engaged, as compared to 2% to 5% in control subjects (Snow-Harter, 1994). It has now been well established that a persistent negative energy balance resulting from a reduced caloric intake coupled with a high energy expenditure is involved in menstrual dysfunction (Ransdell, this volume). This situation has lead to a concern that bone loss, secondary to an estrogen deficit which accompanies amenorrhea, is a potential cause of stress fractures in the short term and osteoporosis in later years.

For the present, however, it can be said that healthy children have few adverse physiological responses to normal levels of physical activity; on those rare occasions when they do occur, they are usually reversible and can be minimized with proper precautions. The body of a youngster is a wonderful machine with sophisticated built-in controls and instinctive limit-defining sensors. In the absence of externally created pressure or stress, a young body functions very effectively. However, it must be remembered that children are not miniature adults, and there are a number of basic physiological differences between children and adults that affect the ability to perform. Recognition and consideration of this fact are basic to any acceptable sport program involving growing children.

Children Are Not Scaled-Down Adults

The ability to sustain physical performance while competing in or training for a sport activity depends to a large degree on the ability of the organism to transfer oxygen from the atmosphere to the working tissues. Maximal aerobic power or maximal oxygen uptake (VO_2 max) represents the greatest volume of oxygen that can be utilized per unit of time under conditions of maximal exertion. To this end, maximal aerobic power is considered to be one of the best measures of cardiorespiratory efficiency because it is dependent on the interrelationships of all the body systems concerned with oxygen transport and is independent of motivation.

Maximal aerobic power in children can be significantly increased in response to sport training programs (Mahon, 2000). This response is similar to changes seen in adults as a result of intensive training (Krahenbuhl, Skinner, and Kohrt, 1985). Values for relative maximal aerobic power expressed per kilogram of body weight (VO_2 max/kg) are quite high in children who are involved in athletics (Hakkinen, Mere, and Kauhanen, 1989; Armstrong and Welsman, 1997). However, if one looks at metabolic reserve—that is, the difference between maximal oxygen uptake and oxygen uptake needed for a given task—children are shown to be at a disadvantage (Rowland, 1990). The relative oxygen cost of walking or running is higher in children (Rowland, and Green, 1988). It has been suggested that the higher oxygen cost in young children in performing a given task is probably the result of mechanical inefficiency (Daniels, Oldridge, Nagle, and White, 1978). In addition, it has been shown that there is a continuum of improved running economy with growth during both childhood and adolescence (Bar-Or, 1983). For example, an 8-year-old child running at a pace of 180 meters per minute is operating at 90% of maximal aerobic power, while a 16-year-old running at the same speed is operating at only 75% of maximum. Thus, in comparison to an adult, the child is not as aerobically efficient as might be expected from looking at the high relative maximal aerobic power values (MacDougall, Roche, Bar-Or, and Moroz, 1979).

Curiously, in spite of the above consideration, children grade physical effort lower than adolescents, and adolescents perceive the same effort as being less strenuous than do adults. Bar-Or (1977) conducted a study on over 1,000 male subjects, ranging in age from 7 to 68 years, who performed an identical cycle ergometry test. The younger the individual, the lower the subjective perceived effort, although the relative intensity of effort demonstrated by heart and circulatory reactions was equally great. These data suggest that a given physiologic strain is perceived to be less by children than by older individuals. The reasons for this are discussed at length elsewhere

(Bar-Or and Ward, 1989). These results raise an interesting question: Is it possible that young children under external pressure may be pushed too far?

There are also differences between children and adults with respect to the anaerobic energy system. This is the energy system that is utilized by the working muscles in the absence of oxygen. Work that results from anaerobic reactions can only be sustained for short periods of time, in contrast to aerobic work, which can be carried on for many minutes, even hours. Accumulating evidence supports the contention that the ability to derive energy from the anaerobic lactate pathway is not as well developed in children as is in the adult (Eriksson, 1980; Inbar and Bar-Or, 1986; Reybrouck, 1989). Children's energy metabolism appears to be directed more to the aerobic rather than the anaerobic provision of energy (Armstrong and Welsman, 1997). In addition, gains in anaerobic capacity in growing children do not appear to be closely related to increasing size or increasing aerobic power, indicating a wide range of variation in the development of this pathway (Paterson, Cunningham, and Bumstead, 1986).

Detailed discussions of other child-adult differences with respect to other metabolic pathways have been provided elsewhere (Armstrong and van Mechelen, 2000; Armstrong and Welsman, 1997; Rippe, 1999). It is sufficient here to refer back to Astrand and Rodahl (1986). In discussing children's work performance they concluded that when dimensional differences between children and adults are taken into consideration, children are clearly not yet mature working machines.

Physiological Adaptations of Children to a Training Stimulus

Sport competition and training subjects the developing organism to a variety of stresses that may give rise to any number of significant responses. Whether adapting to repeated training sessions or to a single game situation, the growing child undergoes changes. The magnitude of these changes varies with the timing, duration, and intensity of the training stimulus. It should be noted that the physical exertion associated with sport training is only one of many factors that may affect the growing child. Thus, our knowledge of children's adaptation to exercise is difficult to define and not completely understood. Notwithstanding, when the literature is critically analyzed, some facts are apparent.

In studying the physiological response of the oxygen transport system to sport training, another dimension is added beyond simple quantitative change. Qualitative changes may occur in children during growth and/or training with or without quantitative alteration. Qualitative changes at the cellular level are not easily observed or measured; therefore major gaps exist in our understanding of the processes involved in the physiological response to exercise. The traditional approach to studying the influence of sport training and physical activity on functional growth of the oxygen transport system has been to compare athletes with nonathletes. Most of these studies have been of short duration, involving pre-test and post-test measurement and many have failed to control for maturational differences. Taking into consideration all the constraints and limitations inherent in studying training-mediated responses in growing children, what conclusions can be drawn?

A number of early studies suggested that sport training or high activity prior to adolescence had a small or limited effect on maximal aerobic power (Ilmarinen and Rutenfranz, 1980; Mirwald, Bailey, Cameron, and Rasmussen, 1981; Weber, Kartodihardjo, and Klissouras, 1976). However, as the intensity of training programs for young children has increased, it has become apparent that maximal aerobic power can be significantly improved in response to an intense training stimulus (Mahon, 2000). This response in children does not appear to be much different from that seen in adults (Krahenbuhl, Skinner, and Kohrt, 1985; Rowland 1993). Because most of the sporting tasks at this age are performed at less than maximal work rates, it has been suggested that the use of maximal aerobic power as a measure for evaluating the oxygen transport system in prepubescent children may be misleading (Stewart and Gutin, 1976). Sport training or a high level of physical activity has been shown to lead to improvements in submaximal efficiency that are independent of changes at maximal effort (Lussier and Buskirk, 1977; Mirwald and Bailey, 1984).

In adolescence it has been suggested that the effectiveness of aerobic training may be greatest at or around the time of peak height velocity in boys (Kobayashi et al., 1978; Mirwald, Bailey, Cameron, and Rasmussen, 1981). Biologically, this would seem reasonable in view of the marked changes taking place in endocrine function during this stage of development. Research is needed to confirm this hypothesis.

What happens when training ceases in growing children? Here again studies are needed, but it appears that, as in adults, adaptations to short-term training are not permanent (Michael, Evert, and Jeffers, 1972). Similarly, the aerobic response to long term training in children appears to be lost in adult years with the cessation of training (Eriksson, 1976).

A major consideration in studies looking at the effects of sport training in children is the role of heredity. Early data from twin studies suggested that the principle determinant of variability in maximal aerobic power among individuals who lived under similar environmental conditions was genetic (Howald, 1976; Komi, Klissouras, and Karvinen, 1973; Weber et al., 1976). While there is no doubt that genetically acquired characteristics contribute greatly to physiological capacity, other studies are more cautious in their interpretation of the interaction between the environment and heredity. Estimates of the contribution of genetic effects to maximal aerobic power range from 30% to 50% (Bouchard, 1986; Malina and Bouchard, 1991).

Why is our understanding of the growing child's response to sport training still so fragmentary in spite of the surge of interest in the child as an elite young athlete? The gaps in our understanding are primarily attributable to an inherent methodological constraint that has been and continues to be a major challenge for investigators working in this area. As Bar-Or (1983) states:

In adults, changes in function between pre- and post-intervention can be attributed with fair certainty to the conditioning program, not so with children or adolescents. Here, changes due to growth, development, and maturation often outweigh and mask those induced by the intervention. It is intriguing that many of the physiological changes that result from conditioning and training also take place in the natural process of growth and maturation. (p. 38)

Thermodynamics and Children

Not all sporting events or training sessions are held under ideal climatic conditions. In many regions of the world, climate can play a crucial role in terms of an individual's ability to perform. Climate is an especially important consideration in regard to sport programs for children, where many activities are performed outside, sometimes under less than ideal weather conditions. In general, it can be said that children are not as efficient as adults in terms of temperature regulation, especially under conditions of extreme heat or cold (Bar-Or, 1983; Falk, 2000; Rowland, 1993).

A child has a smaller absolute surface area than an adult. However, when surface area is expressed per unit of body mass, the situation is reversed. Because heat loss is related to surface area and heat production to body mass, children should, theoretically, be at a disadvantage in a cold climate and favored in a warm one. However, there are other considerations that place children at a disadvantage in a hot climate as well, in spite of their relatively large surface area. Children have a lower sweating rate than adults; consequently, their evaporative capacity is deficient (Davies, 1981; Inbar, Bar-Or, Dotan, and Gutin, 1981). The effect of a deficient evaporative capacity is to raise skin temperature and create a less favorable temperature gradient between the body core and the periphery. This, in turn, inhibits heat transfer by convection. The lower sweating rate in children is apparent both in absolute terms and when normalized per unit of body surface area (Bar-Or, 1983) and results from a lower output per sweat gland rather than a reduced number of glands. Sweat excretion per gland is 2.5 times greater in the adult compared to the child (Bar-Or, 1980). In summary, although low sweat production conserves water in the exercising child, it inhibits heat transfer in a hot climate.

Another age-related difference in adaptation to exercise in heat is the rate of acclimatization. The process of adaptation to heat takes considerably longer in children than in adults (Inbar et al., 1981). Further, children do not instinctively drink enough fluids to replenish fluid loss. Bar-Or (1983) reports that children exercising in dry heat will voluntarily become dehydrated even if allowed to drink ad libitum.

The implications of climatic conditions for the exercising child are clear. All leaders involved in sport programs for children should be made aware that in climatic extremes of heat or cold, children are less efficient in terms of temperature regulation than adults and that precautions are warranted.

Skeletal Adaptations of Children to a Training Stimulus

Until recently, it was felt that regular sport training had no apparent effect on linear growth variables (e.g. stature) in children and youth (Malina and Bouchard, 1991). However, the issue was reopened by a report indicating a reduction of growth potential in elite adolescent female gymnasts who trained an average of 22 hours per week (Theintz, Howald, Weiss, and Sizonenko, 1993). This study supported an earlier report by Ziemilska (1985) on girls and boys involved in intensive gymnastic training. Thus, the issue of the effect of intensive training for sports like gymnastics on the growth of children has re-emerged. It has been suggested that further investigation into this issue is warranted (Mansfield and Emans, 1993). However, when the literature is critically evaluated taking into consideration the importance of controlling for maturational status in evaluating growing children it is difficult not to conclude that regular sport training has no apparent effect on stature or growth in adequately nourished children (Malina, 2000).

The potential of weight-bearing sports and physical activity to positively influence bone mineral acquisition during the growing years is a subject of increasing interest. Two recent reviews provide a detailed discussion of this topic (Bailey, Faulkner, and McKay, 1996; Barr and McKay, 1998). Although there was some degree of inconsistency in the results of the studies reviewed, the available evidence was still strongly supportive, suggesting a significant and positive relationship between physical activity and bone mineral accrual. The reviewers noted the need for more carefully controlled prospective studies to confirm the degree of relationship. They attributed some of the inconsistent results to limitations in study design. These include small numbers of subjects, short duration of intervention, the difficulty in accurately assessing normal physical activity patterns in children and adolescents, and the failure to control for the wide range in maturational status for children of the same chronological age (Bailey et al., 1996).

Since the publication of these reviews, additional studies have appeared in the literature which provide further evidence as to the importance of sport and physical activity in terms of bone mineral accrual during the growing years. Strong evidence comes from two recent preferred limb studies, one on adults who were active as children (Kannus et al., 1995) and one on children exposed to altered bilateral loading patterns (Bailey, Faulkner, Kimber, Dzus, and Yong-Hing, 1997). Preferred limb studies provide a unique experimental model for studying the effect of mechanical loading on bone mineral acquisition. Because both limbs share genetic, endocrine and nutritional influences, any bilateral disparity in bone mineral accumulation can safely be attributed to differences in mechanical usage.

One such study from Finland provides an excellent insight into the effect of childhood activity on bone mineral acquisition (Kannus et al., 1995). Bone mineral content of the playing and non-playing arms was measured in 105 nationally ranked adult female racquet-sport players and 50 healthy women of similar age, height, and weight who served as controls. The young adult athletes who began playing and training for their sport at or before menarche had bilateral differences in bone mineral content (BMC) of 17 to 24% compared to those who began training after menarche (8 to 14%). In the control group the difference in BMC between limbs was 4%. Clearly, the greater bone mineral in the playing arm can be attributed to the greater strain imposed on this limb by the sport. The starting age appears to be an important consideration, further emphasizing the greater adaptive response to loading of immature bone over mature bone (Forwood and Burr, 1993).

Even the small amount of additional loading placed through the dominant arm in early life appears to be related to an augmentation of bone mineral in children (Faulkner et al., 1993). The reported bilateral differences of 4% to 6% between the dominant and non-dominant arms in normally growing children ages 8 to 16 would be difficult to mimic with intervention in later life.

In another preferred limb study, bone mineral density (BMD) was measured by dual energy x-ray absorptiometry (DXA) in regions of the involved and non-involved proximal femur in 17 children (aged 7 to 14) with unilateral Legg Calvé Perthes disease (Bailey et al., 1997). Children with this condition have an altered weight-bearing pattern whereby there is increased mechanical loading on the non-involved normal hip and reduced loading on the involved painful hip. Thus, these children provide a unique opportunity to study the impact of differential loading on bone mineral acquisition during the growing years while controlling for genetic and other factors. A significantly higher BMD was found for regions of the proximal femur on the non-involved side over the involved side (4% to 15%). More importantly, regions on the non-involved side were significantly greater than either chronological or skeletal age-based normative standards. The results of this study provide further support for the concept that mechanical loading of the skeleton during the growing years is an important factor in terms of bone mineral acquisition.

Recent circum- and post-pubertal studies have provided further evidence to indicate that sport and physical activity during youth is associated with a higher bone mineral accumulation (Cassell, Benedict, and Speaker, 1996; Gunnes and Lehmann, 1997). In the prepubertal skeleton, two recent exercise intervention trials have utilized a mixed program of additional hours of physical activity (30 minutes, 3 times) per week. These programs were successful in stimulating increased bone mineral accrual in the intervention groups at the proximal femur and lumbar spine in both girls (Morris, Naughton, Gibbs, Carlson, and Wark, 1997) and boys (Bradney et al., 1998)

In a longitudinal observational study of normal children, 53 girls and 60 boys were measured annually over a 6-year period. Bone mineral accrual rates at the lumbar spine, femoral neck, and total body were found to be significantly related to sport and physical activity patterns as measured by multiple questionnaire assessments each year (Bailey, McKay, Mirwald, Crocker, and Faulkner, 1999). To control for the well documented maturational differences between children of the same chronological age, comparisons between children in different activity groups were made at similar developmental ages (age of peak accrual ± 1-year) as opposed to chronological age comparisons. To control for size differences, height and weight were entered as co-variates in the statistical analyses. After controlling for maturational and size differences between activity groups, the active boys and girls accumulated significantly more bone mineral in the 2-year period around peak than their inactive peers (699 ± 90 grams versus 582 ± 80 grams). These findings in favor of the active children were consistent and statistically significant across all sites. This study is unique in demonstrating that bone mineral accrual rates across the adolescent years are dependent on the level of normal everyday sport and physical activity.

Studies that have investigated the response of growing bone to differential loading in young animals have also been the subject of a comprehensive review (Forwood and Burr, 1993). This review concluded that the animal studies provide incontrovertible evidence that growing bone has a greater capacity to add new bone to the skeleton in response to mechanical loading factors than mature bone. The consistency of the animal evidence suggests that these investigations have relevance for humans. Considered as a whole, the studies noted above and the animal and human review papers make a strong case for the contention that bone mineral accumulation in children can be enhanced by loading factors associated with sport and physical training. Because the prevention of skeletal fragility and osteoporosis in older adults depends in part on the maximization of bone mineral accrual during the growing years, this has major clinical significance (see Ransdell, this volume).

Is Earlier Better?

On the theory that if some training is good, vast amounts must be better, we are seeing youngsters at increasingly earlier ages being subjected to intensive training regimes, in the hopes of developing world champions. In some countries of the world, exceptional talent is identified at an early age, and children are put through intensive programs, on the speculation that they will eventually arrive at the top. We are not told what happens to the youngsters who do not make it.

The theory that the younger we start a child, the better the chances of his or her becoming an adult champion deserves close scrutiny. Some studies have suggested that early success offers no promise of the same later on. Clarke (1971), for example, found that outstanding elementary school athletes may not be outstanding in junior or senior high school and visa versa. Could it be that intensive participation and competition in the under-11 age group is not the great spawning ground it is purported to be? True, there are examples of child athletes who later set world records, but the examples are not nearly as numerous as we may have been led to believe.

Many world class runners, for instance, were not acclaimed internationally as juniors. Scores of names come to mind of Olympic medalists who were not outstanding child athletes. In fact, an argument can be put forward that too much success too early makes future success less certain. Of the all-time top junior men's 100 meter performers, only one went on to win a world championship or an Olympic medal as a senior (Matthews, 1993). In this example, early success was no guarantee of future stardom. As in all human endeavors, there are exceptions to this observation, but the exceptions are rare enough not to discredit the hypothesis. The point that needs to be made is that all that can safely be said with confidence about fast young runners is that they are fast young runners.

Swimming is often cited as another example of what can be accomplished if training is started at an early age. Shane Gould, the famous Australian swimmer, for example, was only 15 when she held every world freestyle record from 100 to 1500 meters, an unparalleled achievement. At the Sydney Olympics in 2000, 16-year-old Megan Quann of the U.S.A. edged out 15-year-old Leisel Jones of Australia for the gold medal in the 100 meter breast stroke. But swimmers not only start early, they also tend to quit early. Dara Torres, an Olympic medalist at 33, is a rare exception to this observation. The assistant United States swimming coach at the Montreal Olympics in 1976 is quoted as saying, "In some ways, the age-group program is backfiring. Sure it gets young kids into swimming, but it also burns them out before they are even close to their potential peak" (Kirshenbaum, 1977, p. 49). It is certainly reasonable to speculate that more success would be achieved if the people involved in the sport stayed with it longer. In many sports, children "dropping out" is a major concern.

A number of years ago, Dr. Gabe Mirkin, who was then medical editor for *Runner's World* magazine and author of a number of books on sports medicine, documented the case of his young running son. As a 9-year-old, the boy ran the mile in under 5 minutes and he held 12 age-class world records before he was 10. At age 10 he quit running. Mirkin's (1984) observation as a sports medicine physician and as a former advocate of running training at an early age is still pertinent to the discussion today:

> Kids burn out. They don't get injured. Of the hundreds of kids who came through, I didn't see a single long term injury. Some of these kids were running 70 or 80 miles a week, hard. You'd see a few injuries then—but, boy, the drop-out rate was frightening. Too much too soon. (p. 24)

Even granting the opposite point of view—that is, to get a world-beater of tomorrow we must train and crown young champions at an early age (an unverified premise)—and further assuming that it is possible to identify and select potential champions at an early age (a dubious assumption)—the primary mandate of people working in children's sport programs should still be to respond to the long-term activity needs of all children. If athletic potential can be identified at an early age, it is logical to assume that a lack of potential should be just as easy to identify. If this is the case, should we not devote more time to the unskilled youngsters who have no motivation or encouragement toward physical activity? Perhaps what is needed in programs for the very young is to pay less attention to the selection of athletes and provide more encouragement to all youngsters to participate in sports and vigorous physical activities. If this occurs, every child will have a chance to realize his or her potential, and the talent pool will be enlarged.

In North America a significant number of children who are late maturing and following a slower-than-average developmental timetable are denied a chance to even try to participate in sport because most competitions for youngsters and adolescents are based on chronological age. Because size is an important determinant in many activities, youngsters who are small for their age are often discriminated against or discouraged though they may have potential and may eventually be of average or even above-average adult size. Somehow we need to organize physical activity and sport programs so that more children can experience the feeling of success that comes from someone saying, "Well done."

Conclusion

Only selected aspects of the physiological and skeletal response of the child to the rigors imposed by sport training and competition have been considered in this chapter. Other areas of research are undoubtedly relevant and important. For instance, there is a need for a more detailed examination of hormonal responses to sport training, especially as they relate to bone mineral content in young female endurance athletes (see Ransdell, this volume). Further studies are obviously necessary, as there are still many gaps in our knowledge of the underlying biological processes involved in the response of the growing child to sport participation. From a physiological perspective, the following quotation, drawn from a position statement prepared by the Canadian Association of Sports Sciences, summarizes material presented in this chapter and still represents an appropriate guideline for adults involved in sport programming for children (Hughson, 1986).

> From a physiological and medical point of view, it should be recognized that each child is different in his/her response and tolerance to exercise, due to a great range of variability in growth rates, anthropometric indices, gender, and state of health, even in children of a similar chronological age. Younger pre-pubertal children should be encouraged to participate in a wide variety of motor skills, whereas, older post-pubertal children can become more specialized in their training and sport participation. A child's performance and adaptation to training should not be directly compared to an adult's, as significant differences exist, especially during the years of accelerated growth. Environmental exercise tolerance is also more limited in children than adults. (p. 162)

Are young children ready for sport? Perhaps the question should be rephrased. Are adults, represented by parents, coaches, teachers, and spectators, ready to be involved in children's sport? While sport participation can be healthy for children, it is unfortunately not always the case. Adults involved in sport programs for children, be they local recreational leagues or elite championship venues, have a responsibility to ensure that a child's happy participation is not jeopardized by unrealistic adult expectations. It is imperative that adults make the distinction between encouraging children to gain satisfaction from doing their best and pushing children beyond their capabilities and levels of interest. At this age, the burden is on the leadership. Adults should have a thorough understanding of structural and functional differences that exist between children and adults. Sport programs for children should be designed accordingly.

References

Armstrong, N., and van Mechelen, W. (Eds.). (2000). *Pediatric exercise science and medicine*. Oxford: Oxford University Press.

Armstrong, N., and Welsman, J. (1997). *Young people and physical activity*. Oxford: Oxford University Press.

Astrand, P. O., and Rodahl, K. (1986). *Textbook of work physiology* (3rd ed.). New York: McGraw-Hill.

Bacharach, L. K., Katzman, D. K., and Litt, I. F. (1991). Recovery from osteopenia in adolescent girls with anorexia nervosa. *Journal of Clinical Endocrinology and Metabolism, 72*, 602–606.

Bailey, D. A., Wedge, J. H., McCulloch, R. G., Martin, A. D., and Bernhardson, S. C. (1989). Epidemiology of fractures of the distal end of the radius in children associated with growth. *Journal of Bone and Joint Surgery, 71A*, 1225–1231.

Bailey, D. A., Faulkner, R. A., and McKay, H. A. (1996). Growth, physical activity and bone mineral acquisition. *Exercise and Sport Sciences Reviews, 24*, 122–166.

Bailey, D. A., Faulkner, R. A., Kimber, K., Dzus, A., and Yong-Hing, K. (1997). Altered loading patterns and femoral bone mineral density in children with unilateral Legg-Calvé-Perthes disease. *Medicine and Science in Sports and Exercise, 29*, 1395–1399.

Bailey, D. A., McKay, H. A., Mirwald, R. M., Crocker, P. E., Faulkner, R. A. (1999) The University of Saskatchewan Bone Mineral Accrual Study: A six year longitudinal study of the relationship of physical activity to bone mineral accrual in growing children. *Journal of Bone and Mineral Research, 14*, 1672–1679.

Bailey, D. A., Martin, A. D., McKay, H. A., Whiting, S., and Mirwald, R. L. (2000). Calcium accretion in girls and boys during puberty: A longitudinal analysis. *Journal of Bone and Mineral Research, 15*, 2245–2250.

Barr, S. I., and McKay, H. A. (1998). Nutrition, exercise and bone status in youth. *International Journal of Sport Nutrition, 8,* 124–142.

Bar-Or, O. (1977). Age-related changes in exercise perception. In G. Berg (Ed.), *Physical work and effort* (pp. 255–266). Oxford: Pergamon Press.

Bar-Or, O. (1980) Climate and the exercising child—A review. *International Journal of Sports Medicine, 1,* 53–65.

Bar-Or, O. (1983). *Pediatric sports medicine for the practitioner.* New York: Springer-Verlag.

Bar-Or, O., and Ward, D. S. (1989). Rating of perceived exertion in children. In O. Bar-Or (Ed.), *Advances in pediatric sport sciences* (pp. 151–168). Champaign, IL: Human Kinetics.

Baxter-Jones, A., Maffulli, N., and Helms, P. (1993). Low injury rates in elite athletes. *Archives of Disease in Childhood, 68,* 130–132.

Bouchard, C. (1986). Genetics of aerobic power and capacity. In R. M. Malina and C. Bouchard (Eds.), *Sport and human genetics* (pp. 55–98). Champaign, IL: Human Kinetics.

Bradney, M., Pearce, G., Sullivan, C., Bass, S., Beck, T., Carlson, J., and Seeman, E. (1998). Moderate exercise during growth in prepubertal boys: Changes in bone mass, size, volumetric density and bone strength: A controlled study. *Journal of Bone Mineral Research, 13,* 12–23.

Caine, D. J. (1990). Growth plate injury and bone growth: An update. *Pediatric Exercise Science, 2,* 209–229.

Caine, D. J., Caine, C. G., and Lindner, K. J. (1996). *Epidemiology of sports injuries.* Champaign, IL: Human Kinetics.

Cassell, C., Benedict, M., and Specker, B. (1996). Bone mineral density in elite 7 to 9 yr old female gymnasts and swimmers. *Medicine and Science in Sports and Exercise, 28,* 1243–1246.

Clarke, H. H. (1971). *Physical and motor tests in the Medford Boys' Growth Study.* Englewood Cliffs, NJ: Prentice-Hall.

Cunningham, D. A., and Paterson, D.H. (1988). Physiological characteristics of young active boys. In E. W. Brown and C. F. Branta (Eds.), *Competitive sports for children and youth* (pp. 159–169). Champaign, IL: Human Kinetics.

Cunningham, D. A., Paterson, D. H., Blimkie, C. J., and Donner, A. P. (1984). Development of cardiorespiratory function in circumpubertal boys: A longitudinal study. *Journal of Applied Physiology, 56,* 302–307.

Daniels, J., Oldrige, N., Nagle, F., and White, B. (1978). Differences and changes in VO2 among young runners 10 to 18 years of age. *Medicine and Science in Sports, 10,* 200–203.

Davies, C. T. M. (1981). Thermal responses to exercise in children. *Ergonomics, 24,* 55–61.

Epstein, S. E., and Maron, B. J. (1986). Sudden death and the competitive athlete: Perspectives on preparticipation screening studies. *Journal of the American College of Cardiology, 7*, 220–230.

Eriksson, B. O. (1976). The child in sport and physical activity—Medical aspects. In J. G. Albinson and G. M. Andrews (Eds.), *Child in sport and physical activity* (pp. 43–65). Baltimore: University Park Press.

Eriksson, B. O. (1980). Muscle metabolism in children—A review. *Acta Paediatrica Scandinavica, 283* (Suppl.), 20–27.

Falk, B. (2000). Temperature regulation. In N. Armstrong and W. van Mechelen (Eds.), *Pediatric exercise science and medicine* (pp. 223–239). Oxford: Oxford University Press.

Faulkner, R. A., Houston, C. S., Bailey, D. A., Drinkwater, D. T., McKay, H. A., and Wilkinson, A. A. (1993). Comparison of bone mineral content and bone mineral density between dominant and non-dominant limbs in children 8–16 years of age. *American Journal of Human Biology, 5*, 491–499.

Forwood, M., and Burr, D. (1993). Physical activity and bone mass: Exercise in futility? *Bone Mineral, 21*, 89–112.

Garrett, W. E. (1993). Clinical/pathological perspectives. In B. R. Cahill and A. J. Pearl (Eds.), *Intensive participation in children's sports* (pp. 195–201). Champaign, IL: Human Kinetics.

Gunnes, M., and Lehmann, E. H. (1996). Physical activity and dietary constituents as predictors of forearm cortical and trabecular bone gain in healthy children and adolescents: A prospective study. *Acta Paediatrica, 85*, 19–25.

Hakkinen, K., Mero, A., and Kauhanen, H. (1989). Specificity of endurance, sprint, and strength training on physical performance capacity in young athletes. *Journal of Sports Medicine, 29*, 7–35.

Howald, H. (1976). Ultrastructure and biochemical function of skeletal muscle in twins. *Annals of Human Biology, 3*, 80.

Hughson, R. (1986). Children in competitive sports—A multidisciplinary approach. *Canadian Journal of Applied Sport Sciences, 11*, 162–172.

Ilmarinen, J., and Rutenfranz, J. (1980). Longitudinal studies of the changes in habitual physical activity of schoolchildren and working adolescents. In K. Berg and B. O. Eriksson (Eds.), *Children and exercise IX.* (pp. 149–159). Baltimore, University Park Press.

Inbar, O., and Bar-Or, O. (1986). Anaerobic characteristics in male children and adolescents. *Medicine and Science in Sports and Exercise, 18*, 264–269.

Inbar, O., Bar-Or, O., Dotan, R., and Gutin, B. (1981). Conditioning versus exercise in heat as methods for acclimatizing 8- to 10-year-old boys to dry heat. *Journal of Applied Physiology: Respiratory, Environmental and Exercise Physiology, 50*, 406–411.

Jokl, E., and McClellan, J. (1971). *Exercise and cardiac death*. Baltimore: University Park Press.

Kannus, P. H., Haapasalo, H., Sankelo, M., Sievanen, H., Pasanen, M., Heinonen, A., Oja, P., and Vuori, I. (1995). Effect of starting age of physical activity on bone mass in the dominant arm of tennis and squash players. *Annals of Internal Medicine, 123*, 27–31, 1995.

Kibler, W. B. (1993). Musculoskeletal adaptations and injuries associated with intense participation in youth sports. In B.R. Cahill and A. J. Pearl (Eds.), *Intensive participation in children's sports* (pp. 203–216). Champaign, IL: Human Kinetics.

Kirshenbaum, J. (1977, April 25). Gimmicks, gadgets, goodby records. *Sports Illustrated*, pp. 40–49.

Kobayashi, K., Kitamura, K., Miura, M., Sodeyama, H., Murase, Y., Miyashita, M., and Matusi, H. (1978). Aerobic power as related to growth and training in Japanese boys: A longitudinal study. *Journal of Applied Physiology, 44*, 666–672.

Komi, P. V., Klissouras, V., Karvinen, E. (1973). Genetic variation in neuromuscular performance. *Internationale Zeitschrift fur Angewandte Physiologie, 31*, 289–304.

Krahenbuhl, G. S., Skinner, J. S., and Kohrt, W. M. (1985). Developmental aspects of maximal aerobic power in children. *Exercise and Sport Sciences Reviews, 13*, 503–538.

Lambert, E. C., Menon, V. A., Wagner, H. A., and Vlad, P. (1974). Sudden unexpected death from cardiovascular disease in children. *American Journal of Cardiology, 34*, 89–96.

Lussier, L., and Buskirk, E. R. (1977). Effects of an endurance training regimen on assessment of work capacity in pre-pubertal children. *Annals of the New York Academy of Sciences, 301*, 734–747.

MacDougall, J. D., Roche, P. D., Bar-Or, O., and Moroz, J. R. (1979). Oxygen cost of running in children of different ages: Maximal aerobic power of Canadian school-children [Abstract]. *Canadian Journal of Applied Sport Science, 4*, 237.

Mahon, A. D. (2000). Exercise training. In N. Armstrong and W. van Mechelen (Eds.), *Pediatric exercise science and medicine* (pp. 201–222). Oxford: Oxford University Press.

Malina, R. M. (2000). Growth and maturation: Do regular physical activity and training for sport have a significant influence? In N. Armstrong and W. van Mechelen (Eds.), *Pediatric exercise science and medicine* (pp. 95–106). Oxford: Oxford University Press.

Malina, R. M. (2002). The young athlete: Biological growth and maturation in a biocultural context. In F. L. Smoll and R. E. Smith (Eds.), *Children and youth in sport: Biopsychosocial perspectives* (2nd ed., pp. 261–292). Dubuque, IA: Kendall/Hunt.

Malina, R. M., and Bouchard, C. (1991). *Growth, maturation and physical activity*. Champaign, IL: Human Kinetics.

Mansfield, M. J., and Emans, S. J. (1993). Growth in female gymnasts: Should training decrease during puberty? *Journal of Pediatrics, 122*, 237–240.

Matthews, P. (Ed.). (1993). *Athletics 1993: The international track and field annual*. Windsor, UK: Harmsworth Active.

Michael, E., Evert, J., and Jeffers, K. (1972). Physiological changes of teenage girls during 5 months of detraining. *Medicine and Science in Sports, 4*, 214–218.

Micheli, L. J., and Klein, J. D. (1991). Sports injuries in children and adolescents. *British Journal of Sports Medicine, 25*, 6–9.

Micheli, L. J., and Salob, P. A. (2002). Overuse injuries in young athletes. In F. L. Smoll and R. E. Smith (Eds.), *Children and youth in sport: Biopsychosocial perspectives* (2nd ed., pp. 367–391). Dubuque, IA: Kendall/Hunt.

Mirkin, G. (1984, December). A conversation with Gabe Mirkin. *Runner's World*, p. 24.

Mirwald, R. L., and Bailey, D. A. (1984). Longitudinal comparison of aerobic power and heart rate responses at submaximal and maximal workloads in active and inactive boys aged 8 to 16 years. In J. Borms, R. Hauspie, A. Sand, C. Susanne, and M. Hebbelinck (Eds.), *III International congress of auxology: Human growth and development* (pp. 561–570). New York: Plenum Press.

Mirwald, R. L., Bailey, D. A., Cameron, N., and Rasmussen, R. L. (1981). Longitudinal comparison of aerobic power on active and inactive boys aged 7.0 to 17.0 years. *Annals of Human Biology, 8*, 405–414.

Morris, F. L., Naughton, G. A., Gibbs, J. L., Carlson, J. S., and Wark, J. D. (1997). Prospective 10-month exercise intervention in premenarcheal girls: Positive effects on bone and lean mass. *Journal of Bone Mineral Research, 12*, 1453–1462.

Paterson, D. H., Cunningham, D. A., and Bumstead, L.A. (1986). Recovery O_2 and blood lactate acid: Longitudinal analysis in boys aged 11 to 15 years. *European Journal of Applied Physiology and Occupational Physiology, 55*, 93–99.

Ransdell, L. B. (2002). The maturing young female athlete: Biophysical considerations. In F. L. Smoll and R. E. Smith (Eds.), *Children and youth in sport: Biopsychosocial perspectives* (2nd ed., pp. 311–338). Dubuque, IA: Kendall/Hunt.

Reybrouck, T. M. (1989). The use of anaerobic threshold in pediatric exercise testing. In O. Bar-Or (Ed.), *Advances in pediatric sport sciences* (pp. 131–149). Champaign, IL: Human Kinetics.

Reybrouck, T. M., and Gewillig, M. (2000). Exercise testing and daily physical activity in children with congenital heart disease. In N. Armstrong and W. van Mechelen (Eds.), *Pediatric exercise science and medicine* (pp. 313–321). Oxford: Oxford University Press.

Rippe, J. M. (Ed). (1999). *Lifestyle medicine*. Malden, MA: Blackwell Science.

Rowland, T. W. (1990). *Exercise and children's health*. Champaign, IL: Human Kinetics.

Rowland, T. W. (1993). The physiological impact of intensive training on the prepubertal athlete. In B. R. Cahill and A. J. Pearl (Eds.), *Intensive participation in children's sports* (pp. 167–193). Champaign, IL: Human Kinetics.

Rowland, T. W., and Green, G. M. (1988). Physiological response to treadmill exercise in females: Adult-child differences. *Medicine and Science in Sports and Exercise, 20*, 474–478.

Snow-Harter, C. M. (1994). Bone health and prevention of osteoporosis in active and athletic women. *The Athletic Woman, 13*, 389–404.

Stewart, K. J., and Gutin, B. (1976). Effects of physical training of cardiorespiratory fitness in children. *Research Quarterly, 47*, 110–120.

Theintz, G. E., Howald, H., Weiss, U., and Sizonenko, P. C. (1993). Evidence for a reduction of growth potential in adolescent female gymnasts. *Journal of Pediatrics, 122*, 306–313.

Trost, S. G., Levin, S., and Pate, R. R. (2000). Sport, physical activity and other health behaviors in children and adolescents. In N. Armstrong and W. van Mechelen (Eds.), *Pediatric exercise science and medicine* (pp. 295–304). Oxford: Oxford University Press.

Weber, G., Kartodihardjo, W., and Klissouras, V. (1976). Growth and physical training with reference to heredity. *Journal of Applied Physiology, 40*, 211–215.

Ziemilska, A. (1985). Effects of intensive gymnastic training on growth and maturation of children. *Biology of Sport, 2*, 279–294.

CHAPTER 13

The Maturing Young Female Athlete: Biophysical Considerations

Lynda B. Ransdell, University of Utah

The child athlete does not forever remain preadolescent. In the case of the young girl, puberty begins mysteriously; menarche occurs, and the young girl becomes a woman. This chapter will discuss the characteristics of this period—the morphological and physiological changes, and the hormonal demands of a maturing reproductive system—and how serious athletic training affects these biophysical functions. But, where to begin? Pubescence is a period of rapid change. Is the female teenage athlete still a girl? A postadolescent "young woman?" Or a fully reproductive adult woman? Is her appropriate counterpart a prepubertal boy? A postadolescent young man? Or a fully grown reproductive adult male?

The first section of this chapter describes the emerging young female athlete with emphasis on how her morphological and physiological characteristics differ from a similarly aged male. Second, the effect of these characteristics on performance is considered. Additional sections describe how the menstrual cycle affects the young female athlete's performance and how athletic training may affect her menstrual cycle.

The Postmenarcheal Female Athlete

This chapter focuses on the postmenarcheal female athlete who is 14 to 16 years of age. She has experienced peak height velocity and menarche (initiation of the menstrual cycle) and will grow in height only slightly more. She has had two to three years of "menstrual cycles," although she has most likely not had many fully ovulatory cycles until recently in her life. Most bony dimensions of her body—sitting height, arm length, leg length, shoulder and hip widths, foot and hand size—are very near full adult size, but her estrogen sensitive body tissues will continue to mature for several years.

Only a select proportion of girls train *seriously* to become athletes. Many enjoy sports and play on recreational teams at school, church, or a youth agency. Some participate on club teams. Some girls experience early maturation, develop breasts and "womanly" hips early in puberty, become "socialized out of sport," develop "other interests," and no longer pursue sport in earnest. A few taste athletic success, are fortunate to display early talent, and thrive in competitive settings. Some of these girls experience late maturation, which may help them achieve relatively tall height, long limbs, slim hips, low body fat, good muscular definition, and an efficient cardiovascular system. (See Malina [this volume] for a discussion of the later menarche commonly observed in talented athletes.) With few exceptions, this chapter is about athletic girls—those with exceptional talent, an unusual genetic disposition, or the driving will to succeed.

Morphological Characteristics

Some prepubescent and early adolescent girls are very successful in sport at the national and international levels. In activities such as gymnastics, ballet, figure skating, and swimming, it is not unusual for adolescent girls to participate in international competitions and win top awards, including Olympic medals and World Championships. Most likely these sports are begun very early in life, and by the time the young girl has reached such skill levels, she is a seasoned competitor. It is also likely that, depending on the particular sport, she would be morphologically described as very lean and compact and as displaying few secondary sex characteristics. Very likely, too, she will have a late age at menarche (Malina, 1994, this volume). These girls, contrary to popular opinion, do not suddenly blossom into voluptuous women and drop out of sport. Rather, they are morphologically well suited to their sports, and while they mature (develop breasts and hips as other girls do) their bodies remain well suited to their sports.

A more common scenario is that the young female athlete develops her skills and trains for team sports during junior high and high school. She excels in high school and perhaps wins an athletic scholarship to college. For most sports, further physical maturation is an advantage because it allows the athlete to build more strength, develop more coordination and grace, and garner the experience needed for team play. Of course, as her body becomes more mature, some of the nymphlike qualities are lost. This is most often attributed to attainment of the *gynecoid* pelvis. So many misunderstandings accompany this notion that some explanation is in order. The true female pelvis has a round and roomy birth canal that, theoretically, allows for an easy delivery and, so the myth goes, gives women wider hips than men. This is the pelvis typically pictured in anatomy books for comparison with a typical male pelvis (the *android* pelvis). However, only about 50% of women have a gynecoid pelvis. In reality, there are many perfectly normal pelvic shapes, and it is difficult to tell a male pelvis from a female pelvis. With respect to *absolute* anthropometric dimensions, the typical man has a slightly wider pelvis (greater breadth across the iliac crests) than a typical woman. Additionally, in terms of *proportional* dimensions, a man has a wider pelvis, relative to his height, leg length, or thigh length. The typical woman, however, has broader hips relative to her shoulders (greater ratio of bicristal to biacromial breadth) (Roche and Malina, 1983; Malina, Bouchard, and Bar-Or, in press). This proportional sex difference may be the actual root of the myth that women have wider hips than men.

During the postmenarcheal period of life, other myths arise in regard to male and female morphological differences relative to sport and athletic performance. One such myth is related to the *center of gravity* (or center of mass), a balance point of the body located at the intersection of the three primary planes: the sagittal, frontal, and transverse. Many sport technique books, and even sports medicine textbooks, state that a woman's center of gravity is significantly lower than a man's. It is further implied that she is less skilled in jumping, changing directions quickly, and running. Atwater (1990) reviewed the literature and reported a difference of about 1% in the average height of the center of gravity for men and women. Her biomechanical analysis led her to conclude that one's center of gravity is determined more by relative leg length (i.e., ratio of leg length to height), absolute height, and body type than it is by sex.

In addition to the mythological difference in pelvis size and center of gravity, there are very real morphological differences. One such difference is the *Q-angle*. Despite continued debate on this topic, recent research suggests that on average, women tend to have larger Q-angles than men (Dibrezzo and Oliver, 2000; Livingston, 1998). The notion here is that the females' wider pelvis and her shorter femur result in a smaller angle between the neck of the femur and the shaft of the femur. This is called the *femoral angle*. A smaller femoral angle may cause the shaft of the femur to slope more inward (medially). If the femur slopes inward, the Q-angle, which is "the intersection of two lines in the midpatellar region, one drawn down the femur in the direction of the quadriceps pull and other drawn up the tibia from the tibial tuberosity," will increase (Wells, 1991, p. 11). A Q-angle larger than 15 degrees (which leads to "knock-kneed" positioning of the legs) is thought to cause the patella to track laterally in the patellofemoral groove (Francis, 1988; Hunter, 1988) and, consequently, predispose women to knee problems in sport (Cox 1985). The Q-angle is also thought to cause a lateral shift of the pelvis during running. Despite the wealth of hypotheses on the relationship between the Q-angle and knee injuries, few prospective research studies exist (Dibrezzo and Oliver, 2000). However, several researchers maintain that the Q-angle is an important biomechanical determinant of patellofemoral dysfunction, or knee pain associated with patellofemoral articulation (Atwater, 1990; Cross and Crichton, 1987; Swenson, Hough, and McKeag, 1987).

Other morphological differences in women, compared to men, include a smaller intercondylar notch (the notch at the head of the femur where the anterior cruciate ligament is attached), increased joint laxity, and strength imbalances between the hamstrings and quadriceps. Additionally, differences in foot alignment and tibial rotation may also appear (Christiansen, 2001; Crussemeyer and Dufek, 2000; Dibrezzo and Oliver, 2000; Moeller and Lamb, 1997). These sex differences may contribute to a higher risk of injury in the female athlete, particularly at the knee (Dibrezzo and Oliver, 2000; Goldberg, 1989; Hutchinson and Ireland, 1995).

Although the young female will continue to develop some lean body mass, particularly if she utilizes weight or resistance training, she will likely never develop the muscle mass that the postpubertal male is capable of developing. Small sex differences in body size and muscle mass are evident during the childhood years, and they become accentuated with the onset of puberty. Any advantage that the prepubertal girl had relative to the more slowly developing prepubertal boy is lost rather quickly. Although sex differences in motor performance are not extensive prior to puberty, at the onset of puberty, the male secondary school athlete will run faster, throw farther and more powerfully, jump farther and higher, and be capable of greater feats of strength than the female secondary school athlete (Haubenstricken and Seefeldt, 1986; Haywood and Getchell, 2001; Smoll and Schutz, 1985, 1990; Thomas and French, 1985). The secondary sex characteristics typical of the "raging hormones" of adolescence are now evident. In the girl, this is characterized by stages 3, 4, and 5 breast development and stages 3, 4, and 5 pubic and axillary hair development (Rogol, 1988). In the boy, this is characterized by corresponding stages of penis and testes development, of axillary and pubic hair development, a deepening voice, and a receding hair line.

Changes in body composition are often rather extreme during this period of life. Young boys who exercise lose their "baby fat" and become slim, muscular, and well toned. Their leg, arm, and chest musculature takes on a much heavier quality, and chest and facial hair may appear. On the contrary, young girls may deposit considerable thigh and gluteal subcutaneous fat. The gyneoid body fat distribution pattern develops in those who are genetically predisposed. Even in those not destined to have thigh-gluteal fat distribution, the lesser muscle mass and the "softer" appearance of the typical female body is obvious (Malina and Bouchard, 1988; Malina et al., in press; Malina and Roche, 1983).

In a variety of studies with trained and untrained 14- to 16-year-old females and males, a wide range of percent body fat is reported. Published studies with untrained females report between 18% and 23% body fat, while studies with female athletes report 12% to 23% body fat (Wells and Ransdell, 1996). Published studies with untrained males report between 11% and 13% body fat, while male athletes report 4.5% to 12% body fat (Wells and Ransdell, 1996). Percent body fat varies considerably among athletes, but among female adolescent athletes, the leanest typically participate in appearance or endurance oriented sports (e.g., gymnastics, figure skating, cross-country running). There are no specific trends for the sports with the "leanest" athletes among the males. For both genders, athletes, compared to untrained subjects, have less body fat and higher lean mass relative to their fat mass (lean:fat). Female adolescent athletes have higher relative fat (percent body fat) and less lean body mass than their male counterparts, as is true of fully mature athletes.

One area that has not been adequately studied is the extent to which *changes* in body composition affect performance level. Although weight loss is widely practiced in a variety of sports, rapid weight loss typically does not have beneficial effects and may have adverse effects on strength, anaerobic power, and endurance (Kohrt, 2000). Additionally, there is not much data on the effects of *gradual* weight loss on physiological function in women athletes who are already lean. Although one would expect that a longer weight loss period would be more beneficial for biochemical adaptations, women athletes who lose weight—even gradually—may lose 26% to 58% of their lean body mass (Kohrt, 2000).

Physiological Characteristics

Until pubertal development, there is little sex difference in maximal oxygen uptake (VO_{2max}), the best single measure of cardiorespiratory efficiency or maximal aerobic power (Armstrong and Welsman, 2000). With her lesser development of muscle mass and her large deposition of adipose tissue, the postmenarcheal female's rate of improvement in VO_{2max} usually declines, whereas the male's continues to increase. Thus, sex differences are not often seen before age 10, but consistent differences are evident by age 14 (Armstrong and Welsman, 2000).

Studies examining aerobic capacity in trained and untrained 14- to 16-year-old females and males report a wide range of values. Untrained adolescent females have VO_{2max} values of approximately 38 $ml \cdot kg^{-1} min^{-1}$, while adolescent female athletes report VO_{2max} values between 41 and 63 $ml \cdot kg^{-1} min^{-1}$ (Wells and Ransdell, 1996). Untrained adolescent males have VO_{2max} values of 50–56 $ml \cdot kg^{-1} min^{-1}$, while adolescent male athletes report VO_{2max} values between 60 and 75 $ml \cdot kg^{-1} min^{-1}$ (Wells and Ransdell, 1996). For both genders, athletes, compared to untrained subjects, have higher aerobic capacity (VO_{2max}). Female athletes generally have lower aerobic capacity compared to their male counterparts. Interestingly, VO_{2max} values of adolescent athletes are comparable to those of adult athletes, particularly in sports not highly dependent on oxidative capacity. In sports where success is highly dependent on high VO_{2max} (e.g., middle- and long-distance running and cross-country skiing), adolescent athletes have somewhat lower values than elite adult athletes. Apparently a long period of training is necessary to develop world-class levels of VO_{2max} for endurance sports.

Puberty affects several factors important to cardiorespiratory efficiency. Changing proportions of muscle mass and fat mass directly affect the metabolically active tissue mass, which directly affects VO_{2max}. As muscle mass increases in postpubertal males, so does the metabolically active tissue mass; consequently, VO_{2max} will most likely increase, even without training. Contrary to what happens in comparably aged boys, in girls, muscle mass remains relatively constant and adipose tissue mass increases; consequently, the relative proportion of metabolically active tissue mass will not increase significantly. Fat weight is essentially "dead weight" that contributes to the workload, but not to the work effort. At full adult stature, the male is about 25 pounds heavier and has about 10% less body fat than the female. This accounts for a major portion of the sex difference in VO_{2max}.

Another factor important to VO_{2max} is systemic oxygen transport. This involves at least two variables: maximal cardiac output and oxygen-carrying capacity. Both factors are altered by pubertal development. Maximal cardiac output (Q) is a function of heart rate (HR) and stroke volume (SV). Both Q, the quantity of blood pumped by the heart per minute, and SV, the quantity of blood pumped per heart beat, are partially limited by heart size. Following pubertal development, the female's heart is smaller than the male's—mostly as a result of her generally smaller body size. The woman's heart rate will attempt to compensate for its smaller volume by beating more rapidly at submaximal cardiac output. This compensatory increase in heart rate does not occur at maximal workloads.

The maximum oxygen-carrying capacity of the blood is determined primarily by hemoglobin (Hb), an iron-containing molecule in the red blood cells. Men have approximately 6% more red blood cells than women, and 10% to 15% more Hb per 100 milliliters of blood than women (Astrand and Rodahl, 1977; DeVries, 1980). Although it is usually assumed that these differences develop partly as a result of smaller body size and partly as a result of the monthly menstrual blood loss experienced by the female following menarche, when these differences first develop is not entirely clear.

Interestingly, the role of hemoglobin in determining VO_{2max} has been recently questioned. Weight, Alexander, Elliot, and Jacobs (1992) found higher concentrations of 2,3-diphosphoglycerate (a phosphate compound that enhances the release of oxygen to the tissues) in women may compensate for the lower hemoglobin levels in women.

In addition to the sex differences in hemoglobin and 2,3-diphosphoglycerate that may affect oxygen carrying capacity, another factor that may affect it is pulmonary capillary volume (Dempsey, 1985). Because women have smaller lungs than men, their pulmonary capillary volume may be less, which may affect their ability to transport oxygen throughout the system.

Taken together, these differences generally mean that if all other factors remain equal, the postmenarcheal female will stabilize in VO_{2max} while her male counterpart will continue to increase in VO_{2max}, even without training. Mittleman and Zacker (2000) have proposed that the VO_{2max} of an adult woman is typically 10% to 15% lower than that of an adult man. Unless considerable training to increase skeletal muscle oxidative capacity and cardiac output is coupled with little (if any) gain in adipose tissue, the average postmenarcheal girl will not experience gains in VO_{2max}.

Other physiological sex differences that may affect performance include anaerobic power, lactate threshold, and performance (running) economy. However, these variables have not been systematically studied in pre- or postpubertal athletes. Most assume that because postmenarcheal females have less muscle mass than males, their corresponding anaerobic power will be less. This appears to be true, based on normative data presented by Bar-Or (1983, p. 313). His data indicate that, compared to females, males typically have higher peak power output during the Wingate Anaerobic Power Test. Additional data summarized by Wells and Ransdell (1996) support the findings of Bar-Or. Peak power reported by moderately active and endurance trained girls ranged from 437.5 to 617.3 while that of moderately active and endurance trained boys ranged from 483.0 to 833.0.

Lactate threshold (LT) refers to the level of exercise at which blood lactate rises above 4mM. It is usually expressed as a percentage of VO_{2max}. One's LT is typically related to aerobic enzyme activity (Mittleman and Zacker, 2000). No sex differences in the percentage of VO_{2max} at which lactate threshold is reached have been noted in adults (Kohrt, O'Connor, and Skinner, 1989; Weyland, Cureton, Conley, Sloniger, and Liu, 1994). However, LT is usually reached at a lower absolute power output (running pace or ergometer power output) by women (Van Praagh, 2000). This means that at a given absolute workload, a larger anaerobic component may be required of the postpubertal female athlete compared to that of the male. However, when exercise power outputs are expressed in terms of percent VO_{2max}, the relative aerobic-anaerobic metabolic contributions are similar.

Performance economy (most often referred to as running economy, cycling economy, or swimming economy) is the oxygen uptake required to perform a submaximal exercise bout. Of the measures of performance economy, running economy has been studied the most. Most researchers have reported that running economy in adult athletes does not differ between the sexes if subjects are equally trained or performance matched (Billat, Beillot, Jan, Rochcongar, and Carre, 1996; Joyner, 1993; Speechley, Taylor, and Rogers, 1996; Wells, 1991); however, some have reported better running economy for men (Daniels and Daniels, 1992) or women (Weyland et al., 1994). It seems likely that considerable variation in performance economy occurs during periods of rapid growth and/or rapid motor development, but presumably those periods have passed by age 14 and are not a factor of sexual dimorphism in postpubertal athletes. Clearly, this area needs further research at all levels of performance.

Performance Differences

Sex differences in performance have lessened significantly throughout the past two decades. Women's world records in most sporting events provide evidence that elite women athletes are capable of superior physical performances. At almost any distance (5k to 42k), the first woman will cross the finish line before 80% of the men (Christensen, 2001). Clearly, the differences that once separated performances of men and women are now significantly lessened. As more individuals participate in athletics and more rewards are used to entice athletes to perform, it is more likely that athletes with the unique combination of genes for top level athletic performance will be identified early (Schechter, 2000).

In addition to a larger pool of athletes, another factor that has contributed to the lessening of the performance gap between men and women is the advancement of scientific and technical knowledge (e.g., equipment, coaching, nutrition, biomechanical studies, and training techniques). The sections that follow contain information about sex differences in strength training, swimming, and running performance. Potential explanations for these differences are also included.

Differences in Strength Performance

Table 13.1 presents sex differences in world powerlifting records for the teenage division in measures of upper (bench press) and lower (squat) body strength. Previous research with drug-free adult populations has concluded that the sex differences in strength are greatest for the heaviest weight classes (Ransdell and Wells, 1999). For adolescent strength athletes, although the largest percentage differences are in the 82.5 kg weight class, in other weight divisions, no clear trends for sex differences can be established. For example, the sex difference in lower body strength (13 to 15 age group) for the 56.0 kg weight class is 36%, while that for the heavier 67.5 kg weight class is only 19%. Similarly, the sex difference in upper body strength (16 to 17 age group) for the 56.0 kg weight class is 44%, while that for the heavier 67.5 kg weight class is only 17%.

When *average* performance difference (weight classes combined) between the sexes is considered, 13- to 15-year-olds report a 35% difference in squat performance and a 38% difference in bench press performance. Sex differences between lower and upper body strength are surprisingly similar for this younger age group (e.g., 35% vs. 38%). Sex differences for 16-to 17-year-olds are slightly higher at 36% for squat performance and 46% for bench press performance. With increasing age and maturity, performance differences in both upper and lower body strength will probably continue to increase.

Previous research has also concluded that compared to men, women are proportionately stronger in the lower body than in the upper body. This conclusion was reached because in untrained populations, the sex difference in upper body strength (56%) was significantly higher than in lower body strength (39%) (e.g., approximately 17%) (Ransdell and Wells, 1999). In trained populations, the sex difference in upper body strength (43%) was also higher than in lower body strength (27%) (e.g., approximately 16%) (Ransdell and Wells, 1999). Data from Table 13.1, using highly trained powerlifters, indicate that sex differences in upper and lower body strength are much lower than has been previously reported. When the average difference in upper body strength was subtracted from the average difference in lower body strength, percentage differences between upper and lower body strength for this population were between 1% and 8%.

Table 13.1   Sex Differences in World Powerlifting Records, Men's and Women's Teenage Divisions (as of 4/23/01)

Weight Class (kg) and Event	Weight Lifted 13–15 y Men (kg)	Weight Lifted 13–15 y Women (kg)	Percentage Difference 13–15 y	Weight Lifted 16–17 y Men (kg)	Weight Lifted 16–17 y Women (kg)	Percentage Difference 16–17 y
52.0						
Squat	149.5	118	21	187.5	127.5	32
Bench	93	56	40	100	82.5	18
56.0						
Squat	165	105.5	36	172.5	115	33
Bench	88	57.5	35	120	67.5	44
60.0						
Squat	185	131.5	29	220	122.5	44
Bench	97.5	70.5	28	123	60	51
67.5						
Squat	187.5	151.5	19	237.5	175	26
Bench	102.5	72.5	29	132.5	110	17
75.0						
Squat	250	140	44	260	157.5	39
Bench	130	70	46	160	85	47
82.5						
Squat	260	97.5	63	249.5	140	44
Bench	150	77	49	165	77.5	53

Notes:

*Women's records for the 44 and 48 kg weight classes are not included because comparable weight classes are not available in the men's division.

$$**\text{Percentage Difference} = \frac{\text{Men's Record} - \text{Women's Record}}{\text{Men's Record}} \times 100$$

***Source: *http://www.home.xnet.com/~frantz/MENSTEENAGEWPC.htm*

Why do these sex differences in strength performance exist? First, subtle cultural biases may prevent women from training hard to obtain world class powerlifting status. Women powerlifters may have trouble securing sponsorships, thus competing full time may be less likely for a woman than for a man. Additionally, several physiological mechanisms may explain the aforementioned sex differences in performance. The sex differences in strength that occur with maturation probably occur because of testosterone. Testosterone typically affects body composition and increases muscular development and lean body mass in the male. The muscle fiber and total cross-sectional area of muscle in women is approximately 60% to 85% of that in men. Because women typically have smaller muscle mass than men, fewer enzymes are available for anaerobic power generation (Christensen, 2001). Interestingly, previous research suggested that size and strength gains in women following resistance training were minimal (e.g., 50% of the hypertrophy of men). More recent studies using sophisticated measurements of muscle cross section have demonstrated that compared to men, women respond with similar hypertrophy; however, the mechanisms may be slightly different (Cureton, Collins, Hill, and McElhannon, 1988; Hickson, Hidaka, and Foster, 1994; Staron et al., 1994).

Although sex differences in strength still exist, they have lessened considerably. It is probable that with increased intensity and specificity of strength training, women will continue to improve in strength and lessen the current performance gap.

Differences in Swimming Performance

Table 13.2 presents current U.S. national records and percentage differences in the freestyle event for 14- to 15- and 16- to 17-year-old age group swimmers. The table reveals very small sex differences in swimming performance (3% to 12%) during adolescence, with slightly smaller percentage differences than fully mature swimmers (Ransdell and Wells, 1999). Also, there is a trend toward smaller sex differences as performance distance increases. The percentage difference for the 50 freestyle is around 10% while the difference for the 1650 freestyle is only 3% to 6%.

The greater height and longer arms and legs of the adolescent male provide a morphological advantage by providing more projection over the water at the start and a longer reach at the finish of a race. The male's larger muscle mass also provides more explosive power off the starting blocks.

Differences in Running Performance

U.S. national age-group records (13 to 16 age group) for a full range of running events are provided in Table 13.3. For 13- to 14-year-old performers, sex differences in running performance are inconsistent across distance. Runners who compete at the shortest (100 m) and longest (3,000 m) distances demonstrate a 6–8% difference in performance, while runners at the middle distance (400 m) demonstrate a 12% performance difference. For 15- to 16-year-old performers, the sex differences in performance are smaller at the sprint distances (100–200 m) than at longer distances (1,500–3,000 m). In all running events, the male's larger muscle mass, lesser percentage of body fat, and higher VO_{2max} provide him with greater driving force and higher oxidative capacity than the female of comparable age.

Table 13.2   Sex Differences in U.S. Swimming Records, Freestyle Event (as of 4/23/01)

Event	Time 14–15 y Men	Time 14–15 y Women	Percentage Difference 14–15 y	Time 16–17 y Men	Time 16–17 y Women	Percentage Difference 16–17 y
50 Freestyle	:20.79	:22.96	9.54	:20.20	:22.54	10.48
$m \cdot sec^{-1}$	2.41	2.18		2.48	2.22	
100 Freestyle	:45.49	:49.53	8.18	:44.43	:50.24	11.56
$m \cdot sec^{-1}$	2.20	2.02		2.25	1.99	
200 Freestyle	1:43.80	1:49.75	5.70	1:37.70	1:48.66	10.24
$m \cdot sec^{-1}$	1.93	1.82		2.05	1.84	
500 Freestyle	4:34.89	4:51.43	5.49	4:20.18	4:44.78	8.33
$m \cdot sec^{-1}$	1.82	1.72		1.92	1.76	
1000 Freestyle	9:30.84	9:51.41	3.43	9:02	9:45.69	7.57
$m \cdot sec^{-1}$	1.75	1.69		1.85	1.71	
1650 Freestyle	15:54.76	16:23.13	2.89	15:25.41	16:19.71	5.62
$m \cdot sec^{-1}$	1.73	1.68		1.78	1.68	

Notes:

$$\text{*Percentage Difference} = \frac{\text{Men's Speed (m} \cdot \text{s}^{-1}\text{)} - \text{Women's Speed (m} \cdot \text{s}^{-1}\text{)}}{\text{Men's Speed (m} \cdot \text{s}^{-1}\text{)}} \times 100$$

**Source: *http://www.usswim.org/*

Table 13.3   Sex Differences in U.S. Track and Field Records (as of 4/23/01)

Event	Time 13–14 y Men	Time 13–14 y Women	Percentage Difference 13–14 y	Time 15–16 y Men	Time 15–16 y Women	Percentage Difference 15–16 y
100 meter	10.94	11.61	5.80	10.54	11.53	8.64
m·sec^{-1}	9.14	8.61		9.49	8.67	
200 meter	21.91	23.63	7.34	21.10	23.26	9.28
m·sec^{-1}	9.13	8.46		9.48	8.60	
400 meter	47.16	53.43	11.67	45.99	53.63	14.25
m·sec^{-1}	8.48	7.49		8.70	7.46	
800 meter	1:57.01	2:09.0	9.36	1:53.37	2:09.69	12.61
m·sec^{-1}	6.84	6.20		7.06	6.17	
1500 meter	3:56.00	4:36.9	14.78	3:56.84	4:25.57	10.74
m·sec^{-1}	6.36	5.42		6.33	5.65	
3000 meter	9:08.86	9:57.16	8.22	8:27.0	10:00.2	15.54
m·sec^{-1}	5.47	5.02		5.92	5.00	

Notes:

*Women's records for the 44 and 48 kg weight classes are not included because comparable weight classes are not available in the men's division;

**Percentage Difference $= \dfrac{\text{Men's Record} - \text{Women's Record}}{\text{Men's Record}} \times 100$

***Source: http://www.usatf.org/statistics/youth/recordsboys.shtml and http://www.usatf.org/statistics/youth/recordsgirls.shtml

Although sex differences in the performances of adolescents who compete in ultra distance races or marathons are not reviewed in this chapter, sex differences in adult runners are *smaller* at longer distances than shorter distances. Bam, Noakes, Juritz, and Dennis (1997) graphed sex differences in adult running performance. They concluded that at distances greater than 42 km, sex differences were negligible, with women potentially outperforming men at distances greater than 70 km. Similar findings were reported by Speechly et al. (1996), who found that women outperformed men at distances greater than 90 km. Most of the reasons for the supposed sex advantage for women who run ultra distances are related to estrogen. Although the results are tentative, estrogen may be beneficial in the following ways:

- Glycogen uptake and storage in the liver and muscle increases with estrogen (Hackney, 1990; Ramamani, Aruldhas, and Govindarajulu, 1999).
- Lipid synthesis and lipolysis are enhanced in muscle and adipose tissue with estrogen (Nicklas, Hackney, and Sharp, 1989; Bonen et al., 1983).
- Water retention is enhanced with estrogen (Stachenfeld et al., 1999).
- Less free radical damage occurs with higher estrogen levels (Tidus and Bombadier, 1999).

Because estrogen levels are fluctuating and regular menstrual cycles are not well-established in 14- to 16-year-old girls, it makes sense that sex differences in this population are less well established, such that a consistent trend is not demonstrated.

Despite these age- and sex-related differences in performances at a variety of distances, the differences are relatively quite small. These outstanding performances by both sexes illustrate that biological differences between the sexes do not result in large performance differences either in adolescence or at full maturity.

Effects of the Menstrual Cycle on Athletic Performance

The menstrual cycle is the single most unique function of the human female. It is the only function that is completely unmatched by the male. The maturation of the reproductive system and the onset of the menstrual cycle is surely the most significant physiological event of puberty. From just before menarche (the first menstrual period) through menopause (the last menstrual period), the woman's hormonal environment is characterized by cyclic fluctuations that result in numerous and significant changes in various target organs and tissues. During this time a woman is capable of maintaining a pregnancy should fertilization of an ovum occur. This section briefly describes how the three phases of the menstrual cycle differ from one another and, further, examines how these different phases affect athletic performance. Specifically, consideration will be given to (a) the effect of the menstrual cycle on various physiological variables related to performance, and (b) the effect of the menstrual cycle on performance.

The Menstrual Cycle

The menstrual cycle, which lasts approximately 28 days (but may vary from 20 to 38 days), is divided into three distinct phases. *Menses*, which occurs from days 1 through 4 to 7, is menstrual bleeding. There is no need to provide a rich environment for growth of a fetus (e.g., the ovum is not fertilized), so the endometrial lining is shed. This phase is characterized by low levels of steroid hormones (e.g., estrogen and progesterone) from the ovary. The *follicular phase* occurs from approximately day 5 until ovulation occurs on approximately day 14 or 15. This phase is characterized by the proliferation of tissues lining the endometrium (the beginning of the uterine cycle) and by maturation of a primary follicle in the ovary (the ovarian cycle).

The follicular phase occurs under the direct influence of the gonadotropins (e.g., follicle stimulating hormone (FSH) and luteinizing hormone (LH)) from the pituitary gland. As the follicle develops, it secretes increasing amounts of estrogen, which eventually stimulates the LH surge resulting in ovulation. The *luteal phase* begins following ovulation and lasts until menstrual flow begins (approximately days 15 through 28). During this phase, there is continued growth and development of the endometrial layer in preparation for the implantation of a fertilized ovum. This includes the development of secretory glands and the storage of glycogen in the endometrial lining. The ruptured follicle becomes the corpus luteum, which secretes progesterone, the dominant hormone of this phase. If fertilization does not occur, the corpus luteum regresses and hormone secretion plummets. Without hormonal support, the rich endometrial lining can no longer be supported. It gradually collapses, which results in menstrual bleeding, and the cycle begins over again. Table 13.4 and Figure 13.1 illustrate the plasma hormone concentrations and endometrial and ovarian changes characteristic of each menstrual phase.

Table 13.4   Characteristics of the Menstrual Cycle Phases

Phase of Cycle	Events	Hormonal Environment
Menses (Days 1 through 4–7)	*Uterus* Menstrual bleeding Shedding of endometrial lining *Ovary* Disintegration of corpus luteum	Low estrogen Low progesterone Low luteinizing hormone (LH) Low follicle stimulating hormone (FSH)
Follicular Phase (Days 4 through ovulation on approximately days 14–16)	*Uterus* Proliferation of endometrial lining *Ovary* Development of mature follicle Secretion of increasing amounts of estrogen Ovulation	Rising FSH Rising estrogen levels LH surge (sharp rise just prior to ovulation)
Luteal Phase (From ovulation until 1st day of flow, approximately days 15 to 28)	*Uterus* Development of secretory glands in endometrium *Ovary* Formation of corpus luteum	High progesterone High estrogen (until final days)

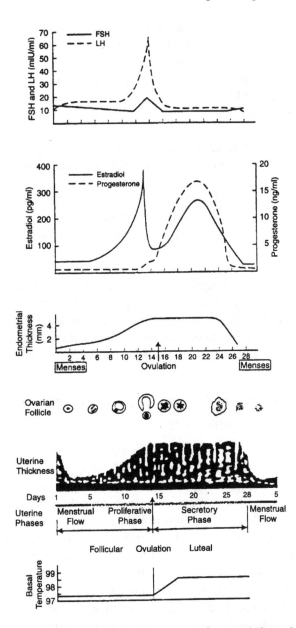

Figure 13.1. Plasma hormoe concentrations, endometrial and ovarian changes, and basal body temperatures characteristic of each menstrual phase.

Sources: "Menstruation" by M. M. Shangold, in *Women and Exercise: Physiology and Sports Medicine* (p. 132) by M. M. Shangold and G. Mirkin (Eds.), 1988, Philadelphia: F. A. Davis; *Human Physiology: The Mechanisms of Body Function* (4th ed., p. 572) by A. J. Vander, J. H. Sherman, and D. S. Luciano, 1985, New York: McGraw-Hill; *Women, Sport & Performance: A Physiological Perspective* (2nd ed., p. 65) by C. L. Wells, 1991, Champaign, IL: Human Kinetics Publishers.

Many biological variables show a regularly repeating pattern or periodicity. Most biological rhythms show a 24-hour or circadian rhythm, but some, besides those already described, show a circalunar or 28-day variability in accordance with the menstrual cycle. The variable which shows the most consistent circalunar rhythm is basal body temperature, which is elevated during the luteal phase. Other variables that may show a circalunar periodicity include the following:

- Weight gain late in the luteal phase
- Hyperemia of the breast with a corresponding increase in breast volume late in the luteal phase
- Increased capillary and red blood cell fragility, and decreased hemoglobin concentration and red blood cell count during menses
- Increased resting respiratory minute volume (V_E) in the luteal phase

However, the 14- to 16-year-old female athlete may not experience many, if any, of these periodic variations because her menstrual cycle may still be irregular in occurrence and anovulatory. The periodicity described exists only when there are distinct hormonal differences among phases, and particularly when there is high plasma progesterone in the luteal phase. Anovulatory menstrual cycles do not display distinct hormonal fluctuations. No data are available on phase periodicity in the adolescent girl.

Effect of the Menstrual Cycle on Physiological Variables Important to Athletic Performance

The bulk of information about menstrual cycle periodicity and variables that are important to athletic performance has been gleaned from the study of fully adult women. Many of these studies have failed to adequately establish phase of the menstrual cycle and small samples of untrained subjects were used to establish relationships (Lebrun, 2000). The relation between the menstrual cycle and performance has not been adequately studied in the younger female athlete. However, it is likely that fluctuations in hormonal status that are common in the adolescent girl can have multiple consequences for the cardiovascular, respiratory, and metabolic systems. The section that follows will summarize what is known about the relation between the menstrual cycle and performance, using information from adult women, and when available, from adolescent girls. (For a comprehensive review of this issue, see Lebrun [2000].)

Basal body temperature and responses to heat stress. The elevation in basal body temperature during the luteal phase is thought to reflect a higher hypothalamic "set point" and cause a delay in the sweating response in women exposed to high environmental temperatures during their luteal phase. However, numerous studies have failed to show menstrual phase differences in body core or mean skin temperatures, body heat content, sweating rate, evaporative heat loss, oxygen uptake, ventilation volume, or oxygen pulse (oxygen uptake per heart beat) during exercise (Horvath and Drinkwater, 1982; Wells, 1977; Wells and Horvath, 1973, 1974). In addition, no differences were found, either before or after heat acclimation, in amenorrheic women (absent menstrual cycles) or women with normal menstrual cycles (Frye, Kamon, and Webb, 1982). Thus, no grounds exist to believe that the menstrual cycle affects temperature regulation during exercise in postmenarcheal athletes.

Respiratory ventilation (V_E). Progesterone stimulates ventilatory drive and elevates V_E during pregnancy and the luteal phase of the menstrual cycle. In normally menstruating trained and sedentary subjects, exercise ventilation was elevated in the luteal phase, when estrogen and progesterone were elevated (Regenstedner et al., 1989, 1990; Schoene, Robertson, Pierson, and Paterson, 1981). In highly trained young athletes, V_E was elevated during the luteal phase at 55% and 80% of maximal performance (Williams and Krahenbuhl, 1997). Other studies have failed to show a difference in V_E with menstrual phase (Hall-Jurkowski, Jones, Toews, and Sutton, 1981: Stephenson, Kolka, and Wilkerson, 1982).

Maximal aerobic power and performance economy. Two investigations of maximal aerobic power (VO_{2max}) relative to menstrual cycle phase have been conducted, one in college athletes (Allsen, Parson, and Bryce, 1977) and the other in amenorrheic and regularly menstruating athletes (Schoene et al., 1981). Neither reported cyclic differences in VO_{2max} with menstrual phase. In addition, performance economy ($VO_{2submax}$) at various menstrual phases has been examined during bicycle ergometry and running. No cyclic differences were found (Lamont, 1986: Schoene et al., 1981; Williams and Krahenbuhl, 1997).

Effect of the Menstrual Cycle on Athletic Performance

Considering the interest in physiological variability occurring with the menstrual cycle, it is surprising so few objective investigations of athletic performance have been done. Of those that have been done, anecdotal and retrospective evidence suggests that performances are "best" in the intermenstrual, postovulatory, or postmenstrual phase and "worst" during the premenstrual phase (Formin, Pivovarova, and Voronova, 1989; Lebrun, 1993, 1994, 2000). Moller-Nielson and Hammar (1989) suggested that in women soccer players, more injuries occurred during the premenstrual and menstrual phases—especially in women who reported significant premenstrual symptoms.

Brooks-Gunn, Gargiulo, and Warren (1986) conducted the only well-controlled study on performance in adolescent athletes (mean age 16 ± 1.4 years). They timed six menstruating national-level swimmers in 100-yard freestyle and their 100-yard "best event" twice a week for 12 weeks. Average performance times were calculated for the entire menstrual cycle, the follicular phase (a 10-day period after flow stopped), the luteal phase (a 4-day period before onset of flow), and menses. For four of the swimmers, fastest times occurred during menses, and slowest times occurred during the luteal phase. Basal body temperature (BBT) was obtained to verify menstrual phase. For two girls, BBT did not show the characteristic rise during the luteal phase indicating that their cycles were anovulatory.

Other investigators have reported no periodic differences in objectively measured performance in menstruating athletes. In highly trained college swimmers, Quadagno, Faquin, Lim, Kuminka, and Moffatt, (1991) reported no menstrual phase differences in repeated time trials for 100-meter and 200-meter freestyle. Schoene and colleagues (1981) reported no differences in time to exhaustion on a bicycle ergometer with menstrual phase in trained young adult women.

Lebrun (2000) discussed the relation between strength and the menstrual cycle. She described several studies that examined handgrip strength, strength and endurance of knee flexion and extension, and leg press and bench press strength throughout the menstrual cycle (Dibrezzo, Fort, and Brown, 1991; Higgs and Robertson, 1981; Quadagno et al., 1991). It was concluded that most studies, including a well-designed prospective study that used hormonal verification (Lebrun, 1995), did not show a relationship between menstrual cycle phase and strength. However, Lebrun (2000) was quick to add that most findings should be interpreted with caution because they were conducted without hormonal verification.

Many women claim that with variations in the menstrual phase, they experience variations in body weight, breast tenderness, bloating, psychological mood and motivation, food cravings, ability to concentrate and make decisions, and incidence of headaches and backache. In most instances, these "subjective complaints" are not verified by statistically significant findings when studied "objectively." In nearly all instances, between-subject variance exceeds within-subject variance, resulting in nonsignificant findings. The few athletes who truly experience cyclic variations in either their physical or mental well-being, particularly those who experience dysmenorrhea (painful menses) or premenstrual syndrome (weight gain, bloating, headache, mood shifts, etc. late in the luteal phase), should consult a specialist in sport gynecology or endocrinology. Typically, there is little need to adjust training or competition schedules because of the menstrual cycle.

Effects of Physical Training on Menstrual Function

Considerable documentation supports the notion that highly trained women athletes have a higher prevalence of menstrual dysfunction than the nonathletic population (American College of Sports Medicine, 1997; Drinkwater, Bruemner, and Chestnut, 1990: Loucks et al., 1992; Wells, 1991). Although the prevalence of menstrual dysfunction in young adolescent athletes is unknown, these athletes are considered particularly vulnerable because their reproduction systems have not fully matured. In many instances, menarche may occur later in this population than in the nonathletic population (see Malina, this volume). Thus, the athletes described here may have a lower gynecological age (years between menarche and menopause) than their nonathletic counterparts.

No doubt exists that heavy exercise stresses the hypothalamic-pituitary-ovarian (and adrenal) axes sufficiently to influence circulating levels of gonadotropic and ovarian hormones. Various menstrual irrregularities such as luteal phase deficiency, anovulatory cycles, oligomenorrhea (irregular menses), and full-blown amenorrhea (menses less than three times per year) may result. Full descriptions of these menstrual dysfunctions are beyond the scope of this chapter but can be found in the position statement of the American College of Sports Medicine (1997), or chapters by Wells (1991) or Shangold (1988).

Who Is at Risk for Athletic Menstrual Dysfunction?

Although the basic cause of athletic menstrual dysfunction is unknown, several associated factors are well documented. These include low gynecological and chronological age, a strenuous training regimen, and nutritional insufficiency (low caloric intake with/without low protein intake). The latter two factors were originally coupled into a general model often referred to as "energy drain," which relates to excessive energy expenditure relative to energy intake (Warren, 1983; Wells and Gilman, 1990). An adolescent driven to excel in a demanding sport may be at particular risk for developing poor nutritional habits leading to disordered eating. At this age, major morphological changes may take place very rapidly. Many adolescent athletes are faced with rapid weight gain and increases in breast volume and gluteal-thigh subcutaneous fat characteristic of adult maturity. These athletes' relatively undeveloped bodies suddenly become cumbersome. Some respond by adopting severe dietary practices, including disordered eating behaviors such as anorexia nervosa and bulimia. (See Beals [2000] for a complete discussion of the identification, consequences, prevention, and treatment of disordered eating in athletes.) Athletes who participate in sports in which a lean physique and low body fat are considered advantageous (gymnastics, ballet, figure skating, distance running) appear to be at highest risk. Pathogenic weight-control behaviors have been reported in 15% to 62% of young female athletes (Dummer, Rosen, Heusner, Roberts, and Counsilman, 1987; Rosen, McKeag, Hough, and Curley, 1986), and nutritional deficiencies are not uncommon (Loosli and Benson, 1990). Athletes with menstrual dysfunction often have a very low percentage of body fat, but this characteristic should be considered one symptom of many that may contribute to the problem.

Is Athletic Menstrual Dysfunction Harmful?

Athletes who train excessively, eat minimally, and become amenorrheic are at risk of developing the female athlete triad. The female athlete triad consists of disordered eating (a spectrum of disorders including anorexia nervosa and bulimia nervosa), amenorrhea (absence of menses), and osteoporosis (low bone mineral density). These components of the triad are related in etiology, pathogenesis, and consequences (American College of Sports Medicine, 1997).

All forms of athletic menstrual dysfunction, especially amenorrhea, are characterized by low levels of estrogen (hypoestrogenemia). Normal levels of estrogen are essential for the normal deposition of bone mineral in the bone matrix. From puberty on, inadequate estrogen exposure is followed by a net loss of bone mineral (osteopenia) and a thinning of bone tissue (Chestnut, 1984; Dhuper, Warren, Brooks-Gunn, and Fox, 1990; Drinkwater et al., 1990; Emans et al., 1990; Warner and Shaw, 2000). This puts athletes with menstrual dysfunction at increased risk for low bone mineral content of both trabecular (cancellous bone of the spine and ends of long bones) and cortical bone (compact bone of the appendicular skeleton) (Myburgh, Bachrach, Lewis, Kent, and Marcus, 1993). In addition, there is evidence that peak bone mineral density, a factor thought to be highly predictive of osteoporosis, occurs at a much earlier age than previously thought and may correspond with cessation of longitudinal growth and epiphyseal closure (Gilsanz et al., 1988). Thus the most important complications of athletic menstrual dysfunction are: poor development of peak bone mineral density, loss of bone mineral mass, and early postmenopausal osteoporosis. Several studies have verified that with return of menses, bone mineral density improves but remains below mean age-group levels (Drinkwater, Nilson, Ott, and Chestnut, 1986; Jonnavithula, Warren, Fox, and Lazaro, 1993; Lindberg, Powell, Hunt, Ducey, and Wade, 1987); thus amenorrheic athletes may have compromised bone mineral density throughout the remainder of their lives.

In addition to bone mineral problems, athletes with low estrogen and amenorrhea may have more musculoskeletal injuries than athletes with regular menses (Lloyd et al., 1986). Warren and colleagues (1986, 1990) reported that young amenorrheic ballerinas had an exceptionally high prevalence of scoliosis and stress fractures and described femoral head collapse in a 20-year-old with an eating disorder and hypoestrogenism dating from age 13. Femur fractures have been described in hypoestrogenic athletes of varying ages (Dugowson, Drinkwater, and Clark, 1991; Kadel, Teitz, and Kronmal, 1992; Leinberry, McShane, Stewart, and Hume, 1992).

Fortunately, athletic menstrual dysfunction appears to have no lasting effect on future reproductive function. With reduction or discontinuation of training, menstruation usually resumes in two months or less, and anecdotal evidence suggests that formerly amenorrheic athletes are fully capable of bearing children. Thus, athletic menstrual dysfunction does not appear to be harmful to reproductive function.

Clearly, amenorrhea is a serious health problem. But, why does it occur? Disordered eating is thought to be a primary contributor. It is dangerous because it can lead to dehydration, a loss of fat-free mass, a failure to replace depleted glycogen after training, and ultimately, a decrease in performance (American College of Sports Medicine, 1997). Failure to eat an adequate number of calories may cause changes in the musculoskeletal, cardiovascular, endocrine, thermoregulatory, and other systems (American College of Sports Medicine, 1997) which can lead to the cessation of menstruation. A position statement by the American College of Sports Medicine (1997) concluded that it is not hard training alone that is causing problems with the female athlete triad. The most problematic cases occur when hard training is combined with restricted or sub-optimal energy intake.

In addition to the aforementioned mechanisms of poor nutrition and excessive training, Warren and Stiehl (1999) provide an eloquent summary of other hypothesized mechanisms that may help explain the occurrence of amenorrhea. First, it is suggested that the beta-endorphins which commonly accumulate with exercise, may suppress luteinizing hormone (LH) pulses. Low levels of LH may in turn cause a decrease in the levels of estradiol and progesterone. Another hypothesis suggested by Warren and Stiehl (1999) is that with reduced caloric intake and low body weight, leptin, a regulator of eating behavior and a vital component of the hypothalamic-pituitary-endocrine feedback loop, may be lower than normal. Low levels of leptin may be related to hypogonadotropism. Other reasons thought to underlie amenorrhea include low body weight or body fat and stress (Warren and Stiehl, 1999).

No matter what causes the triad, the key issue for athletes, coaches, and medical personnel is that the triad is often unrecognized as a problem. Female athletes who become amenorrheic are often happy that they do not have to deal with the inconvenience of having a regular menstrual cycle. What they don't realize is that this loss of the menstrual cycle is often related to a loss of estrogen which can lead to abnormally low bone mineral density and higher than average rates of injury (Cann, Martin, Genant, and Jaffe, 1984; Drinkwater et al., 1984; Marcus et al., 1985; Warner and Shaw, 2000).

In view of the above, practitioners working with female athletes at risk for the triad should ensure that individuals with even one aspect of the triad are screened, and if necessary treated. Amenorrhea is not normal or desirable. It is a symptom of an underlying problem that should be medically evaluated within the first 3 months of occurrence (American College of Sports Medicine, 1997). Given that amenorrhea is the easiest component of the triad to recognize, individuals who work with female athletes must recognize the connection between inadequate dietary intake, the high stress of intensive training, menstrual dysfunction, and musculoskeletal injury. Prevention and early identification are the best treatments for athletic menstrual dysfunction. Once identified, a multidisciplinary network of professionals should be utilized to plan and implement treatment (Nattiv, 1994).

Clearly, the participation of adolescent females in physical activity and sport is desirable. However, identification of athletes at risk for components of the triad is essential to ensure safe participation. The ultimate goal is to have every athlete continue to participate in healthy levels of activity for a lifetime.

References

Allsen, P. E., Parsons, P., and Bryce, G. R. (1977). Effect of the menstrual cycle on maximum oxygen uptake. *The Physician and Sportsmedicine, 5,* 53–55.

American College of Sports Medicine (1997). The female athlete triad. *Medicine and Science in Sports and Exercise, 29,* i-ix.

Armstrong, N., and Welsman, J. R. (2000). Development of aerobic fitness during childhood and adolescence. *Pediatric Exercise Science, 12,* 128–149.

Astrand, P.-O., and Rodahl, K. (1977). *Texbook of work physiology* (2nd ed.). New York: McGraw-Hill.

Atwater, A. E. (1990). Gender differences in distance running. In P. Cavanagh (Ed.), *Biomechanics of distance running* (pp. 321–361). Champaign, IL: Human Kinetics.

Bam, J., Noakes, T. D., Juritz, J., and Dennis, S. C. (1997). Could women outrun men in ultramarathon races? *Medicine and Science in Sport and Exercise, 29,* 244–247.

Bar-Or. O. (1983). *Pediatric sports medicine for the practitioner.* New York: Springer-Verlag.

Beals, K. A. (2000). Subclinical eating disorders in female athletes. *Journal of Physical Education, Recreation, and Dance, 71,* 23–29.

Billat, V., Beillot, J., Jan, J., Rochcongar, P., and Carre, F. (1996). Gender effect on the relationship of time limit at 100% VO_{2max} with other bioenergetic characteristics. *Medicine and Science in Sports and Exercise, 28,* 1049–1055.

Bonen, A., Haynes, F. J., Watson-Wright, W., Sopper, M. M., Pierce, G. N., Low, M. P., and Graham, T. E. (1983). Effects of menstrual cycle on metabolic responses to exercise. *Journal of Applied Physiology, 55,* 1506–1513.

Brooks-Gunn, J., Gargiulo, J. M., and Warren, M. P. (1986). The effect of cycle phase on the performance of adolescent swimmers. *The Physician and Sportsmedicine, 14,* 182–192.

Cann, C. E., Martin, M. C., Genant, H. K., and Jaffe, R. B. (1984). Decreased spinal mineral content in amenorrheic women. *Journal of the American Medical Association, 251,* 626–629.

Chestnut, C. H., III. (1984). Treatment of postmenopausal osteoporosis. *Comprehensive Therapy, 10,* 41–47.

Christensen, C. (2001). Women's physiology and exercise: Influences and effects. In: G.L. Cohen (Ed.), *Women in Sport: Issues and Controversies* (2nd ed., pp. 179–198). AAHPERD Publications: Reston, VA.

Cox, J. S. (1985). Patellofemoral problems in runners. *Clinics in Sports Medicine, 4*, 699–707.

Cross, M. J., and Crichton, K. J. (1987). *Clinical examination of the injured knee.* Baltimore: Wilkins and Wilkins.

Crussenmeyer, J. A., and Dufek, J. S. (2000). Biomechanics. In B. Drinkwater (Ed.), *Women in sport.* (pp. 93–107). Malden, MA: Blackwell Science.

Cureton, K. J., Collins, M. A., Hill, D. W., and McElhannon, Jr., F.M. (1988). Muscle hypertrophy in men and women. *Medicine and Science in Sports and Exercise, 20*, 338–344.

Daniels, J. and Daniels, N. (1992). Running economy of elite male and elite female runners. *Medicine and Science in Sports and Exercise, 24*, 483–489.

Dempsey, J. A. (1985). Is the lung built for exercise? *Medicine and Science in Sports and Exercise, 18*, 143–155.

DeVries, H. (1980). *Physiology of exercise for physical education and athletics* (3rd ed.). Dubuque, IA: Wm. C. Brown.

Dhuper, S., Warren, M. P., Brooks-Gunn, J., and Fox, R. (1990). Effects of hormonal status on bone density in adolescent girls. *Journal of Clinical Endocrinology and Metabolism, 71*, 1083–1088.

Dibrezzo, R., Fort, I. L., and Brown, B. (1991). Relationships among strength, endurance, weight, and body fat during three phases of the menstrual cycle. *Journal of Sports Medicine and Physical Fitness, 31*, 89–94.

Dibrezzo, R., and Oliver, G. (2000). ACL injuries in active girls and women. *Journal of Physical Education, Recreation, and Dance, 71*, 24–27.

Drinkwater, B. L., Bruemner, B., and Chestnut, C. H., III. (1990). Menstrual history as a determinant of current bone density in young athletes. *Journal of the American Medical Association, 263*, 545–548.

Drinkwater, B. L., Nilson, K., Chestnut, C. H., III, Bruemner, W. J., Shainholtz, S., and Southworth, M. B. (1984). Bone mineral content of amenorrheic and eumenorrheic athletes. *New England Journal of Medicine, 311*, 277–281.

Drinkwater, B. L., Nilson, K., Ott, S., and Chestnut, C. H., III. (1986). Bone mineral density after resumption of menses in amenorrheic athletes. *Journal of the American Medical Association, 256*, 380–382.

Dugowson, C. E., Drinkwater, B. L., and Clark, J. M. (1991). Nontraumatic femur fracture in an obligomenorrheic athlete. *Medicine and Science in Sports and Exercise, 23*, 1323–1325.

Dummer, G. M., Rosen, L. W., Heusener, W. W., Roberts, P. J., and Counsilman, J. E. (1987). Pathogenic weight-control behaviors of young competitive swimmers. *The Physician and Sportmedicine 15*, 75–84.

Emans, S. J., Grace, E., Hoffer, F. A., Gundberg, C., Ravnikar, V., and Woods, E. R. (1990). Estrogen deficiency in adolescents and young adults: Impact on bone mineral content and effects of estrogen replacement therapy. *Obstetrics and Gynecology, 76*, 585–592.

Formin, S. K., Pivovarova, V. I., and Voronova, V. I. (1989). Changes in the special working capacity and mental stability of well-trained women skiers at various phases of the biological cycle. *Sports Training Medicine and Rehabilitation, 1*, 89–92.

Francis, P. R. (1988). Injury prevention through biomechanical screening: Implications for female athletes. In J. L. Puhl, C. H. Brown, and R. O. Voy (Eds.), *Sport science perspectives for women* (pp. 97–110). Champaign, IL: Human Kinetics.

Frye, A. L., Kamon, E., and Webb, M. (1982). Responses of menstrual women, amenorrheal women, and men to exercise in a hot, dry environment. *European Journal of Applied Physiology, 48*, 279–288.

Gilsanz, V., Gibbens, D. T., Carlson, M., Boechat, M. I., Cann, C. E., and Schulz, E. E. (1988). Peak trabecular vertebral density: A comparison of adolescent and adult females. *Calcified Tissue International, 43*, 260–262.

Goldberg, V. (1989, November 29). Women warned of possible injury if early workouts are too intense. *NCAA News, 41*, 8.

Hackney, A. C. (1990). Effects of menstrual cycle on resting muscle glycogen content. *Hormone and Metabolic Research, 22*, 647.

Hall-Jurkowski, J. E., Jones, N. L., Toews, C. J., and Sutton, J. R. (1981). Effects of the menstrual cycle on blood lactate, oxygen delivery and performance during exercise. *Journal of Applied Physiology: Respiratory, Environmental and Exercise Physiology, 51*, 1493–1499.

Haubenstricker, J. L., and Seefeldt, V. (1986). Acquisition of motor skills during childhood. In V. Seefeldt (Ed.), *Physical activity and well-being* (pp. 41–102). Reston, VA: American Alliance for Health, Physical Education, Recreation and Dance.

Haywood, K. M., and Getchell, N. (2001). *Life span motor development* (3rd ed.). Champaign, IL: Human Kinetics.

Hickson, R. C., Hidaka, K., and Foster, C. (1994). Skeletal muscle fibre type, resistance training, and strength related performance. *Medicine and Science in Sports and Exercise, 26*, 593–598.

Higgs, S. L., and Robertson, L. A. (1981). Cyclic variations in perceived exertion and physical work capacity in females. *Canadian Journal of Applied Sport Sciences, 6*, 191–196.

Horvath, S. M., and Drinkwater, B. L. (1982). Thermoregulation and the menstrual cycle. *Aviation, Space, and Environmental Medicine, 53*, 790–794.

Hunter, L. Y. (1988). The frequency of injuries in women's sports. In J. L. Puhl, C. H. Brown, and R. O. Voy (Eds.), *Sport science perspectives for women* (pp. 49–58). Champaign, IL: Human Kinetics.

Hutchinson, M. R., and Ireland, M. L. (1995). Knee injuries in female athletes. *Sports Medicine, 19*, 288–302.

Jonnavithula, S., Warren, M. P., Fox, R. P., and Lazaro, M. I. (1993). Bone density is compromised in amenorrheic women despite return of menses: A 2-year study. *Obstetrics and Gynecology, 81*, 669–674.

Joyner, M. J. (1993). Physiological limiting factors and distance running: Influence of gender and age in record performance. *Exercise and Sport Sciences Reviews, 21*, 103–133.

Kadel, N. J., Teitz, C. C., and Kronmal, R. A. (1992). Stress fractures in ballet dancers. *The American Journal of Sports Medicine, 20*, 445–449.

Kohrt, W. (2000). Body composition. In B. Drinkwater (Ed.), *Women in Sport.* (pp. 353–363). Malden, MA: Blackwell Science.

Kohrt, W., O'Connor, J. S., and Skinner, J. S. (1989). Longitudinal assessment of responses by triathletes to swimming, cycling, and running. *Medicine and Science in Sports and Exercise, 21*, 569–575.

Lamont, L. S. (1986). Lack of influence of the menstrual cycle on blood lactate. *The Physician and Sportsmedicine, 14*, 159–163.

Lebrun, C. M. (1993). Effect of the different phases of the menstrual cycle and oral contraceptives on athletic performance. *Sports Medicine, 16*, 400–430.

Lebrun, C. M. (1994). The effect of the phase of the menstrual cycle and the birth control pill on athletic performance. *Clinics in Sports Medicine, 13*, 419–441.

Lebrun, C. M. (1995). Effects of menstrual cycle phase on athletic performance. *Medicine and Science in Sports and Exercise, 27*, 437–444.

Lebrun, C. M. (2000). Effects of the menstrual cycle and oral contraceptives on sport performance. In B. Drinkwater (Ed.), *Women in Sport* (pp. 37–61). Malden, MA: Blackwell Science.

Leinberry, C. F., McShane, R. B., Stewart, W. G., and Hume, E. L. (1992). A displaced subtrochanteric stress fracture in a young amenorrheic athlete. *The American Journal of Sports Medicine, 20*, 485–487.

Lindberg, J. S., Powell, M. R., Hunt, M. M., Ducey, D. E., and Wade, C. E. (1987). Increased vertebral bone mineral in response to reduced exercise in amenorrheic runners. *Western Journal of Medicine, 146*, 39–42.

Livingston, L.A. (1998). The quadriceps angle: A review of the literature. *Journal of Orthopedic and Sports Physical Therapy, 28*, 105–109.

Lloyd, T., Triantafyllou, S. J., Baker, E. R., Houts, P. S., Whiteside, J. A., Kalenak, A., and Stumpf, P.G. (1986). Women athletes with menstrual irregularity have increased musculoskeletal injuries. *Medicine and Science in Sports and Exercise, 18*, 374–379.

Loosli, A. R., and Benson, J. (1990). Nutritional intake in adolescent athletes. *Pediatric Clinics of North America, 37*, 1143–1163.

Loucks, A. B., Vaitukaitis, J., Cameron, J. L., Rogol, A. D., Skrinar, G., Warren, M. P., Kendrick, J., and Limacher, M. C. (1992). The reproductive system and exercise in women. *Medicine and Science in Sports and Exercise, 24*, S288–S293.

Malina, R. M. (1994). Physical growth and biological maturation of young athletes. *Exercise and Sport Sciences Reviews, 22*, 389–433.

Malina, R. M. (2002). The young athlete: Biological growth and maturation in a biocultural context. In F. L. Smoll and R. E. Smith (Eds.), *Children and youth in sport: A biopsychosocial perspective* (2nd ed., pp. 261–292). Dubuque, IA: Kendall/Hunt.

Malina, R. M., and Bouchard, C. (1988). Subcutaneous fat distribution during growth. In C. Bouchard and F. E. Johnston (Eds.), *Fat distribution during growth and later health outcomes* (pp. 63–84). New York: Liss.

Malina, R. M., Bouchard, C., and Bar-Or, O. (in press). *Growth, maturation, and physical activity* (2nd ed.). Champaign, IL: Human Kinetics.

Malina, R. M., and Roche, A. F. (1983). *Manual of physical status in childhood: Vol. 2. Physical performance.* New York: Plenum.

Marcus, R., Cann, C., Madvig, P., Minkoff, J., Goddard, M., Bayer, M., Martin, M., Gaudiani, L., Haskell, W., and Genant, J. (1985). Menstrual function and bone mass in elite women distance runners. *Annals of Internal Medicine, 102*, 158–163.

Mittleman, K. D., and Zacker, C. M. (2000). Factors influencing endurance performance, strength, flexibility, and coordination. In B. Drinkwater (Ed.), *Women in sport.* (pp. 23–36). Malden, MA: Blackwell Science.

Moeller, J. L., and Lamb, M. M. (1997). Anterior cruciate ligament injuries in female athletes: Why are women more susceptible? *The Physician and Sportsmedicine, 25*, 31–48.

Moller-Nielson, J., and Hammar, M. (1989). Women's soccer injuries in relation to the menstrual cycle and oral contraceptive use. *Medicine and Science in Sports and Exercise, 21*, 126–129.

Myburgh, K. H., Bachrach, L. K., Lewis, B., Kent, K., and Marcus, R. (1993). Low bone mineral density at axial and appendicular sites in amenorrheic athletes. *Medicine and Science in Sports and Exercise, 25*, 1197–1202.

Nattiv, A. (1994). The female athlete triad. *The Physician and Sportsmedicine, 22*, 60–68.

Nicklas, B. J., Hackney, A. C., and Sharp, R. L. (1989). The menstrual cycle and exercise: Performance, muscle glycogen and substrate responses. *International Journal of Sports Medicine, 10*, 264–269.

Quadagno, D., Faquin, L., Lim, G. N., Kuminka, W., and Moffatt, R. (1991). The menstrual cycle: Does it affect athletic performance? *The Physician and Sportsmedicine, 19*, 121–124.

Ramamani, A., Aruldhas, M. M., and Govindarajulu, P. (1999). Differential response of rat skeletal muscle glycogen metabolism to testosterone and estradiol. *Canadian Journal of Physiology and Pharmacology, 77*, 300–304.

Ransdell, L. B., and Wells, C. L. (1999). Sex differences in physical performance. *Women in Sport and Physical Activity Journal, 8*, 55–81.

Regensteiner, J. G., McCullough, R. G., McCullough, R. E., Pickett, C. K., and Moore, L. G. (1990). Combined effects of female hormones and exercise on hypoxic ventilatory response. *Respiratory Physiology, 82*, 107–114.

Regensteiner, J. G., Woodward, W. D., Hagerman, D. W., Weil, J. V., Pickett, C. K., Bender, P. R., and Moore, L. G. (1989). Combined effects of female hormones and metabolic rate on ventilatory drives in women. *Journal of Applied Physiology, 66*, 808–813.

Roche, A. F., and Malina, R. M. (1983). *Manual of physical status and performance in childhood: Vol. 1. Physical status.* New York: Plenum.

Rogol, A. D. (1988). Pubertal development in endurance-trained female athletes. In E. W. Brown and C. F. Branta (Eds.), *Competitive sports for children and youth* (pp. 173–193). Champaign, IL: Human Kinetics.

Rosen, L. W., McKeag, D. B., Hough, D. O., and Curley, V. (1986). Pathogenic weight-control behavior in female athletes. *The Physician and Sportsmedicine, 14,* 79–86.

Schechter, B. (2000). How much higher? How much faster? *Scientific American, 11,* 10–13.

Schoene, R. B., Robertson, H. T., Pierson, D. J., and Peterson, A. P. (1981). Respiratory drives and exercise in menstrual cycles of athletic and nonathletic women. *Journal of Applied Physiology: Respiratory, Environmental, and Exercise Physiology, 50,* 1300–1305.

Shangold, M M. (1988). Menstruation. In M. M. Shangold and G. Mirkin (Eds.), *Women and exercise: Physiology and sports medicine* (pp. 129–144). Philadelphia: F. A. Davis.

Smoll, F. L., and Schutz, R. W. (1985). Physical fitness differences between athletes and nonathletes: Do changes occur as a function of age and sex? *Human Movement Science, 4,* 189–202.

Smoll, F. L., and Schutz, R. W. (1990). Quantifying gender differences in physical performance: A developmental perspective. *Developmental Psychology, 26,* 360–369.

Speechly, D. P., Taylor, S. R., and Rogers, G. C. (1996). Differences in ultra-endurance exercise in performance-matched male and female runners. *Medicine and Science in Sport and Exercise, 28,* 359–365.

Stachenfeld, N. S., DiPietro, L., Kokoszka, C. A., Silva, C., Keefe, D. L., and Nadel, E. R. (1999). Physiological variability of fluid regulation hormones in young women. *Journal of Applied Physiology, 86,* 1092–1096.

Staron, R. S., Karapondo, D. L., Kraemer, W. J. Fry, A. C., Gordon, S. E., Falkel, J. E., Hagerman, F. C., and Hikida, R. S. (1994). Skeletal muscle adaptations during early phase of heavy-resistance training in men and women. *Journal of Applied Physiology, 76,* 1247–1255.

Stephenson, L. A., Kolka, M. A., and Wilkerson, J. E. (1982). Metabolic and thermoregulatory responses to exercise during the human menstrual cycle. *Medicine and Science in Sports and Exercise, 14,* 270–275.

Swenson, E. J., Hough, D. O., and McKeag, D. B. (1987). Patellofemoral dysfunction. *Postgraduate Medicine, 82,* 125–141.

Thomas, J. R., and French, K. E. (1985). Gender differences across age in motor performance: A meta-analysis. *Psychological Bulletin, 98,* 260–282.

Tiidus, P.M., and Bombardier, E. (1999). Oestrogen attenuates post-exercise myeloperoxidase activity in skeletal muscle of male rats. *Acta Physiologica Scandinavica, 166,* 85–90.

Van Praagh, E. (2000). Development of anaerobic function during childhood and adolescence. *Pediatric Exercise Science, 12*, 150–173.

Warner, S. E., and Shaw, J. (2000). Estrogen, physical activity, and bone health. *Journal of Physical Education, Recreation, and Dance, 71*, 19–23, 27–28.

Warren, M. P. (1983). The effects of undernutrition on reproductive function in the human. *Endocrinology Reviews, 4*, 363–377.

Warren, M. P., Brooks-Gunn, J., Hamilton, L. H., Warren, L F. and Hamilton, W. G. (1986). Scoliosis and fractures in young ballet dancers. *New England Journal of Medicine, 314*, 1348–1356.

Warren, M. P., Shane, E., Lee, M. J., Lindsay, R., Dempster, D. W., Warren, L. F., and Hamilton, W. G. (1990). Femoral head collapse associated with anorexia nervosa in a 20-year-old ballet dancer. *Clinical Orthopaedics and Related Research, 251*, 171–176.

Warren, M. P., and Stiehl, A. L. (1999). Exercise and female adolescents: Effects on the reproductive and skeletal systems. *Journal of the American Women's Medical Association, 54*, 115–120.

Weight, L.M., Alexander, D., Elliot, T., and Jacobs, P. (1992). Erythropoietic adaptations to endurance training. *European Journal of Applied Physiology, 64*, 444–448.

Wells, C. L. (1977). Sexual differences in heat stress response. *The Physician and Sportsmedicine, 5*, 78–90.

Wells, C. L. (1991). *Women, sport, and performance: A physiological perspective* (2nd ed.). Champaign, IL: Human Kinetics.

Wells, C. L., and Gilman, M. (1990). An ecological approach to training. *American Academy of Physical Education Papers, 24*, 15–29.

Wells, C. L., and Horvath, S. M. (1973). Heat stress responses related to the menstrual cycle. *Journal of Applied Physiology, 35*, 1–5.

Wells, C. L., and Horvath, S. M. (1974). Responses to exercise in a hot environment as related to the menstrual cycle. *Journal of Applied Physiology, 36*, 299–302.

Wells, C. L., and Ransdell, L. B. (1996). The maturing young female athlete: Biophysical considerations. In F. L. Smoll and R. E. Smith (Eds.), Children and youth in sport: A biopsychosocial perspective (pp. 200–225). Dubuque, IA: Brown and Benchmark.

Weyland, P. G., Cureton, K. J., Conley, D. S., Sloniger, M. A., and Liu, Y. L. (1994). Peak oxygen deficit predicts sprint and middle-distance track performance. *Medicine and Science in Sports and Exercise, 26*, 1174–1180.

Williams, T. J. and Krahenbuhl, G.S. (1997). Menstrual cycle phase and running economy. *Medicine and Science in Sports and Exercise, 29*, 1609–1618.

CHAPTER 14

Anabolic Steroid Use in Adolescent Athletes

Mimi D. Johnson, University of Washington
David A. Van de Loo, Midelfort Clinic

More than 40 years ago, elite athletes began using anabolic steroids in an attempt to improve athletic performance in sports that require great strength and size (Lamb, 1984). Since that time, the use of anabolic steroids has spread to professional, college, and high school athletics (Corder, Dezelsky, Toohey, and DiVito, 1975; Lamb, 1984). Up to 65% of high school anabolic steroid users participate in school-sponsored sports (Buckley et al., 1988). We who are involved with young athletes should understand the physiologic effects and potential adverse effects of steroids, how and why adolescents use steroids, and the role we can play in identifying and preventing steroid use.

Anabolic and Androgenic Effects of Steroids

Anabolic steroids are synthetic derivatives of the natural male sex steroid hormone, testosterone. Testosterone is synthesized in normal male testes and is the major hormone responsible for the androgenic and anabolic effects noted during male adolescence and adulthood. The androgenic and anabolic effects of testosterone cannot be totally separated as they are due to the same action of the hormone in different tissues, not to different actions of the hormone (Kruskemper, 1968; Wilson and Griffin, 1980). Although synthetic steroids are usually referred to as anabolic steroids, they have both anabolic and androgenic properties.

Testosterone's androgenic properties influence the growth of the male reproductive tract and the development of secondary sexual characteristics. In the pubertal male, androgenic effects include the increase in length and diameter of the penis; appearance of pubic, axillary, and facial hair; and the development of the prostate gland and scrotum (Rogol, 1985).

Testosterone's anabolic properties affect the nonreproductive tract tissues. Anabolic effects include the stimulation of long bone growth with subsequent induction of epiphyseal closure at puberty, the enlargement of the larynx and thickening of the

339

vocal cords, an increase of skeletal muscle mass and strength, an increase in protein synthesis, a decrease in body fat, and the development of libido and sexual potential (Rogol, 1985).

Developers of synthetic steroids have modified the testosterone molecule in an attempt to minimize its unwanted androgenic effects. Nevertheless, all synthetic steroids have androgenic effects and are properly referred to as anabolic-androgenic steroids (Kruskemper, 1968; Wilson and Griffin, 1980).

Effects of Steroids on Muscle Strength and Size

Many factors, including heredity, intensity of training, diet, and the status of the psyche (Wright, 1980), contribute to the development of muscle strength. Studies that have attempted to determine the effects of anabolic steroids on muscle strength in humans have yielded conflicting results, most likely due to methodological and interpretive inconsistencies (American College of Sports Medicine, 1984; Haupt and Rovere, 1994). However, it is apparent that improvements in muscle strength and size may result from steroid use in individuals who (a) intensively train in weight lifting immediately before using anabolic steroids and continue intensive weight lifting during the steroid regimen, (b) maintain a high-protein, high-calorie diet, and (c) measure their strength improvement using the same single repetition, maximal weight technique (i.e., bench press) they used in training (American College of Sports Medicine, 1984; Haupt and Rovere, 1984). The frequency, duration, and intensity of training needed to achieve these improvements have not been documented. There may also be a threshold of response of body composition to anabolic steroids, as well as a variation in the response to different types of steroids (Friedl, Dettori, and Hannan, 1991).

In addition to their anabolic effects in athletes, anabolic-androgenic steroids have both anticatabolic and motivational effects. Anabolic steroids may increase muscle strength and size through one or more of the following proposed mechanisms:

1. Anabolic steroids may antagonize the increased protein breakdown that usually occurs during the muscular stress of athletic training. Intense weight training can lead to a catabolic state or negative nitrogen balance (Haupt and Rovere, 1984). Steroids convert a negative nitrogen balance to a positive one by improving the use of ingested protein and increasing nitrogen retention (Kruskemper, 1968).

2. Anabolic steroids may have the ability to induce protein synthesis in skeletal muscle cells (Murad and Haynes, 1985). This effect continues indefinitely during steroid treatment and occurs in both the healthy and the catabolic state (Haupt and Rovere, 1984).

3. Anabolic steroids may block the glucocorticosteroid-induced depression of protein synthesis that occurs during stressful events such as training. Glucocorticosteroids, which have a catabolic effect, are released during training. Anabolic

steroids compete for glucocorticosteroid receptor sites and may reverse the catabolic effect (Haupt and Rovere, 1984; Kruskemper, 1968).

4. Anabolic steroids may affect an athlete's training habits. Athletes using steroids claim to experience a state of euphoria, increased aggressive behavior, and diminished fatigue, all of which can have a positive effect on weight training (Wilson and Griffin, 1980). Athletes also report the ability to train more frequently and intensively while using the drugs and to recover more rapidly from workouts (Crawshaw, 1985). Whether this perception has a psychological basis (placebo effect) or a physiological basis is not clear.

In 1972 Ariel and Saville reported that athletes who took a placebo thinking that it was an anabolic steroid increased their strength over what would have been expected in the absence of an anabolic steroid. Rozenek et al. (1990) reported a lower plasma lactate concentration following exercise in steroid users than in nonusers. If a difference in lactate concentration exists, it may explain the subjective feelings of faster recovery in individuals taking anabolic steroids.

5. Finally, an increase in growth hormone may accentuate the anabolic effect of steroids (Alen, Rahkila, Reinilla, and Vihko, 1987). In growing adolescents, exogenous testosterone has been shown to promote an increase in the frequency and magnitude of growth hormone secretory bursts (Cowart, 1989). A 5- to 60-fold increase in serum growth hormone concentration has been seen in some power athletes who use steroids, but this has not been a consistent finding (Alen et al., 1987).

How Anabolic Steroids Are Used

Anabolic steroids are available as oral and injectable agents. Testosterone undergoes rapid degradation following both oral and parenteral (injectable) administration. Therefore, molecular changes have been made to increase the oral bioavailability and the half-life of the synthetic drugs (Murad and Haynes, 1985). Molecular changes have also been made in an attempt to decrease the unwanted androgenic effects of the drugs (Murad and Haynes, 1985). Anabolic steroids have legitimate medical uses, but athletes use them because of their potential anabolic effects. Athletes have developed several patterns of use, and even young athletes have found these drugs easy to obtain.

Most of the orally administered anabolic steroids are alkylated at the 17-alpha position, rapidly absorbed, and associated with an increased risk of hepatotoxicity (Kruskemper, 1968). The parenteral (injectable) steroids, which include the testosterone esters and the 19-nortestosterone derivatives, are injected intramuscularly and are slowly absorbed. Modification of some synthetic steroids has resulted in a partial dissociation between the androgenic and anabolic actions of the drugs, but complete separation of these activities has never been fully achieved. All synthetic steroids have some androgenic effects (Kruskemper, 1968; Wilson, 1988). The testosterone esters have the highest androgenic potency (androgenic:anabolic ratio of 1:1), whereas many of the 19-nortestosterone esters and the oral steroids have decreased androgenicity (Gribbin and Matts, 1976). Some of the commonly used anabolic steroids are listed in Table 14.1.

Table 14.1   Anabolic Steroids Used by Athletes

ORAL ANABOLIC STEROIDS		INJECTABLE ANABOLIC STEROIDS	
Generic name	**Trade name**	**Generic name**	**Trade name**
Oxymetholone*	Anadrol	Nandrolone decanoate**	Deca-Durabolin
Oxandrolone*	Anavar	Nandrolone phenpropionate**	Durabolin
Methandrostenolone*	Dianabol	Testosterone cypionate[+]	Depo-testosterone
Ethylestrenol*	Maxibolin	Testosterone enanthate[+]	Delatestryl
Stanozolol*	Winstrol	Testosterone propionate[+]	Oreton
Fluoxymesterone*	Halotestin	Methenolone enanthate	Primobolan depot
Norethandrolone	Nilevar	Boldenone undecyclenate	Equipoise
Methenolone acetate	Primobolan	Trenbolone acetate[++]	Finajet
Mesterolone	Proviron	Trenbolone[++]	Parabolan
Testosterone undecanoate		Stanozolol	Winstrol V

*17-alpha alkylated steroids

**19-nortestosterone esters

[+]estosterone esters

[++]European veterinary steroids, reported in underground handbooks.

M. D. Johnson, Anabolic Steroid Use in Adolescent Athletes. In A. C. Hergenroeder, J. G. Garrick (Eds.), *Sports Medicine. The Pediatric Clinics of North America.* Philadelphia: W. B. Saunders, Vol. 37:6, 1990.

Synthetic steroids are employed in the treatment of several medical conditions at dosages that typically approximate physiologic replacement levels. Anabolic steroids are used as hormone replacement therapy in boys and men whose testes fail to secrete androgens normally. They are also used to stimulate pubertal development in some young men with marked developmental delay (Rogol, 1985) and to treat short stature in individuals with Turner syndrome (Moore, 1988). Synthetic steroids have also been used to treat osteoporosis in women, hereditary angioneurotic edema, and late stages of breast cancer.

The dosage of anabolic steroids used by athletes depends on the particular needs and sport of the athlete. Endurance athletes may use steroids for their alleged anticatabolic effects, and use dosages approximating physiologic replacement levels, or approximately 7 mg/day of testosterone. Sprinters who desire increased strength and power may use 1.5 to 2 times replacement levels (Yesalis and Bahrke, 1995). Athletes in strength sports, wanting to "bulk up," often take doses that are two to more than 100 times greater than replacement levels (Lamb, 1984; Shikles, 1989, Yesalis and Bahrke, 1995).

Steroid users have developed several patterns of use in an attempt to maximize the anabolic effects of steroids and minimize the side effects. Athletes will use more than one steroid at a time, referred to as *stacking*. The stack or "array" of drugs often includes at least one oral and one injectable agent. Some individuals begin using steroids at low doses, increase them gradually, and then taper them (sometimes called *pyramiding*) (Duchaine, 1989; Frankle, Cicero, and Payne, 1984). Users decide to stop, add, change, or increase the dose of a drug when increases in strength and size are no longer being attained through weight lifting (sometimes called a *plateau*). Although some users take the drugs year-round, most users cycle the steroids by taking them for 6 to 12 weeks, then undergo a drug-free period that averages 2 to 3 months. An example of a steroid cycle is shown in Table 14.2.

Athletes report that anabolic steroids are easy to obtain (Terney and McLain, 1990). Friends, other athletes, coaches, doctors, pharmacists, veterinarians, dealers, mail-order sites, and gyms have been reported as sources for anabolic steroids (Buckley et al., 1988; Office of Inspector General, 1990; Whitehead, Chillag, and Elliot, 1992). The majority of anabolic steroid users obtain the drugs from black market sources (Buckley et al., 1988; Windsor and Dumitru, 1989; Yesalis and Bahrke, 1995). Officials believe that the source of black market steroids is evenly divided between clandestinely manufactured goods, smuggled products, and diverted legally manufactured products (Shikles, 1989). Some of the drugs are manufactured in the United States, but the majority are smuggled into the country from Mexico or Europe (Kenney, 1994; Shikles, 1989).

Table 14.2   An Example of a Steroid Cycle

Week	Testosterone cypionate 200 mg/cc injection	Testosterone enanthate 200 mg/cc injection	Oxandrolone 2.5 mg/tab
1	2 cc/wk	2 cc/wk	10 tab/day
2	2 cc/wk	2 cc/wk	9 tab/day
3	1 1/2 cc/wk	1 1/2 cc/wk	8 tab/day
4	1 1/2 cc/wk	1 1/2 cc/wk	7 tab/day
5	1 cc/wk	1 cc/wk	6 tab/day
6	1 cc/wk	1 cc/wk	5 tab/day
7	1/2 cc/wk	1/2 cc/wk	4 tab/day
8	1/2 cc/wk	1/2 cc/wk	3 tab/day
9	1/4 cc/wk	1/4 cc/wk	2 tab/day
10	1/4 cc/wk	1/4 cc/wk	1 tab/day

Therapeutic doses of testosterone cypionate and enanthate range from 50-400 mg every 2-4 weeks (Murad and Haynes, 1985). The therapeutic dose of oxandrolone is 5-10 mg/day (Murad and Haynes, 1985).

M. D. Johnson, Steroids. In P. G. Dyment (Ed.), *Sports and the Adolescent. Adolescent Medicine: State of the Art Reviews*. Philadelphia: Hanley and Belfus, Vol. 2:1, 1991.

"Counterfeit" steroids make up a significant proportion of anabolic steroids on the black market. Counterfeited drugs include mislabeled drugs, drugs that are subpotent or adulterated with other substances, and bogus drugs that contain none of the substances they purport to contain. In 1989, it was reported that the Department of Justice and the FDA had uncovered more than 35 different counterfeit steroid products and more than 85 different labels used in their distribution (Shikles, 1989). The safety of these drugs is questionable, since they are often manufactured in underground labs (*Anabolic Reference Guide*, 1989; Duchaine, 1989). Steroid users may attempt to counter the side effects of steroids by using other drugs available on the black market such as human chorionic gonadotropin (HCG) to stimulate natural testosterone production, antiestrogenic agents (tamoxifen) to decrease gynecomastia (Duchaine, 1989; Taylor, 1987), diuretics, and antiacne medications (Yesalis and Bahrke, 1995).

Adverse Effects of Steroid Use

The adverse effects that one might experience from using steroids depend on the age, sex, and health of the user, the particular drugs and doses being used; and the frequency of use (Wilson and Griffin, 1980). Many of the short-term side effects of anabolic steroids appear to be reversible once they are discontinued. However, long-term adverse effects have not been well studied and most of the information comes from reports of individuals who have taken anabolic steroids in therapeutic doses (Shikles, 1989). Chronic anabolic steroid use has the potential to lead to deleterious long-term effects. Presently, there are very few life-threatening effects of steroid use, and these have been rarely seen. Potential complications of anabolic steroid use are summarized in Table 14.3 and discussed in the following section.

Endocrine Effects

Anabolic steroids affect the endocrine and reproductive system of both male and female users. Decreased spermatogenesis (Mauss et al., 1975), gynecomastia (development of male breast tissue) (Friedl and Yesalis, 1989), prostatic hypertrophy and priapism (prolonged painful erections) (Rogol, 1985), and carcinoma of the prostate (Roberts, 1986) have been reported in association with anabolic steroid use by males. In females, excess androgens may result in irreversible signs of masculinization and menstrual irregularities (Kruskemper, 1968). Some of these effects might prove to be more serious in prepubertal and pubertal users because of their developing endocrine and reproductive systems. Problems with glucose tolerance (Cohen and Hickman, 1987) and thyroid hormone disturbances (Kruskemper, 1968) have also been reported in association with anabolic steroid use.

In the male, excessive amounts of exogenous androgens in the serum result in negative feedback to the hypothalamus and anterior pituitary gland, causing a decrease in the secretion of follicle-stimulating hormone (FSH) and luteinizing hormone (LH). The decrease of these hormones results in decreased testosterone production, testicular atrophy, and a decrease in spermatogenesis. Although these changes appear to be reversible, abnormal sperm and decreased numbers of sperm have been noted for up to six months following discontinuation of steroids (Mauss et al., 1975).

Gynecomastia, the occurrence of mammary tissue in the male, is generally a sign of estrogen androgen imbalance. As many as half of all boys exhibit some degree of transient breast swelling during normal pubertal development. In steroid users, gynecomastia may result from the conversion (aromatization) of exogenous androgens (i.e., the testosterone esters) to estradiol (Friedl and Yesalis, 1989). Gynecomastia may be even more pronounced in persons with altered hepatic (liver) function because of decreased clearance of the parent steroid or estrogenic metabolites by the liver (Kley, Strohmeyer, and Kruskemper, 1979). In steroid users, the breast tissue may become less prominent and less painful once steroids are stopped, but the problem may worsen with further steroid use and may not disappear entirely even with complete cessation of steroids (Friedl and Yesalis, 1989).

Table 14.3   Potential Complications of Anabolic Steroid Use

Endocrine
  Male
    Decreased reproductive hormones
    Testicular atrophy
    Oligospermia/azospermia
    Gynecomastia
    Prostatic hypertrophy
    Prostatic carcinoma*
    Priapism
  Female
    Masculinization
    Hirsutism*
    Deepening of voice*
    Clitoral hypertrophy*
    Menstrual irregularities
  Adolescent
    Accelerated maturation*
  Altered glucose tolerance
Renal
  Elevated BUN, creatinine
  Wilms' tumor*
Musculoskeletal
  Adolescent:
    Premature epiphyseal closure*
  Increased risk of musculotendinous injury
Dermatologic
  Acne
  Alopecia*
  Temporal hair recession*
Cardiovascular
  Decreased HDL cholesterol
  Increased LDL cholesterol
  Hypertension
  Clotting abnormalities

Hepatic
  Elevated liver function test values
  Cholestatic jaundice
  Tumor formation*
  Peliosis hepatitis*
Psychological
  Aggressive behavior
  Mood swings
  Increased or decreased libido
  Dependency
  Acute psychosis
  Manic and/or depressive episodes
Subjective Effects**
  Edema
  Muscle spasm
  Nervous tension
  Increased urine output
  Headache
  Dizziness
  Nausea
  Euphoria
  Skin rash
  Urethritis
  Scrotal pain
  Irritability

Table adapted from Johnson MD: Pediatr Clin North Am 37:1111-1123, 1990.
*Considered irreversible.
**Adapted from Haupt HA, Rovere GD: Anabolic steroids: A review of the literature. *Am J Sports Med* 12:477,1984.
Johnson MD: Steroids. in P. G. Dyment (Ed.), *Sports and the Adolescent. Adolescent Medicine: State of the Art Reviews.* Philadelphia: Hanley and Belfus, Vol. 2:1, 1991.

In females, signs of excess androgens include hirsutism (excessive body and facial hair) and deepening of the voice (Wilson and Griffin, 1980). As with other anabolic steroid effects, considerable variation occurs in the frequency and the degree to which these signs develop. If the use of anabolic steroids is discontinued as soon as these adverse effects are noted, they may slowly subside; but with prolonged steroid use, these effects may worsen and become irreversible. Clitoral hypertrophy, which is irreversible, has been reported (Wilson and Griffin, 1980). Amenorrhea and other menstrual irregularities have also been associated with anabolic steroid use (Kruskemper, 1968).

In prepubertal or pubertal males, steroid use accelerates maturation, with the premature development of secondary sexual characteristics and changes in physique (Kruskemper, 1968). Wilson and Griffin (1980) have stated that "florid virilization" may occur in children even when anabolic steroids are used in small amounts and for relatively limited periods of time. Some of these effects that are felt to be inconsequential or reversible in adults may affect biologically immature males differently.

Cohen and Hickman (1987) have reported increased insulin resistance with altered glucose tolerance in athletes using anabolic steroids. A decrease in serum concentrations of thyroxine (T4), triiodothyronine (T3), free thyroxine (FT4), and thyroid-stimulating hormone (TSH) have also been observed (Alen et al., 1987; Kruskemper, 1968). Alen et al. (1987) suggested that decreased concentrations of these hormones may be due to a decrease in thyroid-binding globulin (TBG). Thyroid hormone is apparently available at the cellular level, and clinical thyroid function is normal (Alen et al., 1987).

Cardiovascular Effects

Anabolic steroid use may affect myocardial structure and function. Urbausen, Holpes, and Kindermann (1989) reported increased left ventricular wall thickness and impaired diastolic function in steroid-using body builders. Sachtleben et al. (1993) found that myocardial thickness in steroid users was greater than that in nonusers. A significant increase in myocardial thickness also occurred in steroid users on-cycle as compared with users who were off-cycle. No evidence exists to suggest that steroids improve aerobic capacity. Sachtleben et al. (1993) reported decreased maximum oxygen consumption in users as compared with nonusers and suggested that cardiac contractility may decrease as a result of chronic steroid use.

Anabolic steroid use results in a decrease in the HDL cholesterol level and may result in an increase in the LDL cholesterol level (Hurley et al., 1984). The resulting increased LDL/HDL cholesterol ratio may signify an increased risk for coronary artery disease (Strauss, 1993). Cholesterol levels appear to return to baseline once steroid use is discontinued (Cohen, Noakes, and Benade. 1988). No occurrences of accelerated arteriosclerosis have been reported in anabolic steroid-using athletes, but two cases of myocardial infarction (heart attack) have been reported in young steroid users (Bowman, 1990; McNutt, Ferenchick, Kirlin, and Hamlin, 1988).

Anabolic steroids may increase red blood cell mass, therefore elevating the hemoglobin and hematocrit in users (Murad and Haynes, 1985). Normally, adult males have higher hematocrits than females as a result of the positive effect of testosterone on red blood cell production. Administration of androgens to women increases red cell production. Long-term androgen therapy, as in treatment for breast cancer, has resulted in polycythemia (an increase of red blood cells above normal) (Wilson and Griffin, 1980), but significant polycythemia has not been reported in athlete steroid users.

Other adverse cardiovascular effects reported in association with anabolic steroid use include: edema (swelling) due to the retention of fluid and sodium (Kruskemper, 1968); reversible hypertension (Messerli and Frohlich, 1979); and a decrease in clotting factors, increase in fibrinolytic activity, and enhanced platelet aggregation in association with the use of specific steroids (Ferenchick, 1990). Cerebrovascular accidents (strokes) in young steroid users have been reported (Frankle, Eichberg, and Zachariah, 1988; Mochiniki and Richter, 1988; Yesalis and Bahrke, 1995). In addition, some steroid users use diuretics to lose excess fluid and increase muscle definition. This may cause abnormal levels of serum potassium and place the individuals at greater risk for cardiac arrythmias.

Hepatic Effects

Hepatotoxicity is most commonly associated with the 17-alpha alkylated steroids, which are taken orally (Kruskemper, 1968). Use of these steroids may result in an elevation of liver function test values (Wilson and Griffin, 1980), indicating liver damage. The muscle damage incurred by weight lifting alone may cause an elevation in serum aspartate aminotransferase (AST) and alanine aminotransferase (ALT) (Strauss, Wright, Finerman, and Catlin, 1983), but more specific measurements of liver function, including alkaline phosphatase, conjugated bilirubin, and liver isoenzymes of lactate dehydrogenase, have been elevated in some steroid users (Haupt and Rovere, 1984). Lamb (1984) reported that abnormally elevated liver function tests typically revert to normal following cessation of steroid use but that continued administration of steroids could result in obstruction of the bile canals (cholestasis) and jaundice. Steroid-induced cholestatic jaundice typically resolves within several months of discontinuing the drugs (Kruskemper, 1968).

Both benign and malignant liver tumors (Johnson et al., 1972; Sweeney and Evans, 1976) and peliosis hepatitis, a rare disease causing blood-filled sacs in the liver (Bagheri and Boyer, 1974), have been associated with steroid use. Athletes with histories of extensive steroid use have died of hepatocellular carcinoma (Goldman, 1985; Overly, Dankoff, Wang, and Singh, 1984). One steroid-using bodybuilder developed hepatocellular carcinoma and died of uncontrolled bleeding following hepatic rupture (Creagh, Rubin, and Evans, 1988).

Renal Effects

Although an increase in serum creatinine may be seen in steroid-free weight lifters due to the increase in skeletal muscle mass (Strauss et al., 1983), steroid use may cause an increase in serum BUN, creatinine, and uric acid (Crawshaw, 1985). Elevation of these values in steroid users indicates that the drugs may have a negative effect on kidney function, although the abnormal values typically return to normal once the drugs are discontinued.

Fatal kidney tumors (Wilms' tumors), which are uncommon in adults, have been reported in adult athletes using steroids (Prat, Gray, Stolley, and Coleman, 1977; Strauss et al., 1983). Determining whether these tumors were related to steroid use or occurred coincidentally is not possible (Strauss et al., 1983). Nevertheless, evidence suggests that steroids may be weak carcinogens and capable of initiating tumor growth or promoting tumor growth in the presence of other carcinogens (Lamb, 1994).

Musculoskeletal Effects

The prepubertal or pubertal adolescent using excessive amounts of steroids for a prolonged period of time may experience premature epiphyseal closure with resulting stunted growth (Murad and Haynes, 1985). Children with poorly controlled diseases of androgen excess are initially taller than their peers but become relatively short adults (Rogol, 1985). This can result from accelerated advancement of bone age relative to acceleration in height velocity and from early onset of puberty with premature closure of the epiphyses (Moore, 1988). However, premature growth cessation has not been systematically studied in the adolescent using anabolic steroids (Yesalis and Bahrke, 1995).

Anabolic steroid use may result in an increased risk of musculotendinous injuries. McKillop, Ballantyne, Borland, and Ballantyne (1989) reported that creatine phosphokinase, the most sensitive enzyme index of muscle damage, was abnormally elevated in steroid users. Michna and Stang-Voss (1983) noted degenerative changes in the tendon fibers of female mice following administration of anabolic steroids. Cases of atypical spontaneous tendon ruptures in bodybuilders using steroids have also been reported (Hill, Suker, Sachs, and Brigham, 1983; Kramhoft and Solgaard, 1986).

Dermatologic Effects

Acne is a commonly reported side effect of anabolic steroid use. The prevalence of acne at puberty is related to the growth and secretory activity of the sebaceous glands (Murad and Haynes, 1985). Sebaceous glands are very sensitive to androgenic stimulation (Kruskemper, 1968). The high doses of testosterone and anabolic steroids that are self-administered by athletes can increase the amount of sebum excretion from sebaceous glands (Kiraly, Alen, Rahkila, and Horsmanheimo, 1987). Furthermore acne lesions resulting from steroid use, commonly on the chest and back, do not always respond to routine treatment. The use of tetracycline or isotretinoin for treatment of refractory acne could have additional adverse consequences in steroid users who have decreased hepatic clearance.

Other cutaneous manifestations associated with steroid use include: alopecia (hair loss), folliculitis (inflammation of hair follicles), hirsutism (presence of excessive body and facial hair, especially in women), and striae (stretch marks) (Scott, M. J., Jr., and Scott, M. J., III, 1989). Temporal hair recession and alopecia may be seen in men and women using steroids for a prolonged period of time (Houssay, 1976). In females, the scalp alopecia is usually not total, but considerable sparseness of hair is readily visible and may be permanent (Scott, M. J., Jr., and Scott, M. J., III, 1989).

Infections and Immune Response

Steroid users who share needles increase their risk of transmitting infections such as hepatitis B and acquired immune deficiency syndrome (AIDS). According to DuRant, Rickert, Ashworth, Newman, and Slavens (1993), 25% of adolescent anabolic steroid users shared needles to inject drugs during the previous 30 days. Adolescent steroid users may not perceive themselves as being at risk for infections; however, the human immunodeficiency virus (HIV) sero-status of individuals who inject steroids is not known. There have been cases of AIDS reported in steroid users who shared needles with HIV-infected cohorts (Scott, M. J., and Scott, M. J., Jr., 1989; Sklarek, Mantovani, Erens, Heisler, and Niederman, 1984).

Steroid users may also be at risk for other bacterial and viral infections. Skin or systemic infections could be caused by impure drugs or by contaminated vials, syringes, or needles. In addition, reduced serum immunoglobulins could lead to a reduced resistance to infection. A decrease in immunoglobulins, particularly IgA, has been reported in steroid-using bodybuilders (Calabrese et al., 1989).

Psychological Effects

Numerous psychological changes have been associated with anabolic steroid use. In most steroid users, psychological changes are minor, but in some steroid users, psychological changes may be severe and sufficient to cause significant morbidity and even mortality (Perry, Yates, and Anderson, 1990; Pope and Katz, 1992). Whether or not anabolic steroid users develop dependency remains controversial (Brower, 1992). Unfortunately, adolescents may be at an increased risk for development of the psychological effects associated with steroid use (Windsor and Dumitru, 1989; Yesalis et al., 1989).

Anabolic steroid use has been associated with increased aggressive behavior, mood swings, and irritability (Pope and Katz, 1988; Strauss et al., 1983). Other psychological changes that may result from steroid use include somatization (Perry, Yates, and Anderson, 1990), distractibility, forgetfulness and confusion (Su et al., 1993), and increased self-esteem, and changes in libido (Strauss et al., 1983). Taylor

(1987) reported a study in which 90% of health club athletes with a history of steroid use experienced episodes of overaggressiveness, and violent behavior ("roid rage") that they believed were induced by steroids. Su et al. (1993) noted significant, albeit subtle, increases in irritability, mood swings, violent feelings, anger, and hostility following the administration of steroids to individuals with no previous steroid use or history of psychiatric problems in a placebo-controlled prospective study. Yates et al. (1990), who found that the steroid users in their study displayed increased antisocial traits, suggested that antisocial traits may in themselves contribute to the aggressive behavior noted in steroid users. However, the discovery of neuronal androgen receptors in the brain (Sheridan, 1983) suggests there may be a neurochemical basis for aggressive behavior associated with steroid use and that individuals with antisocial traits may be especially sensitive to the effects of anabolic steroids.

Overt psychotic symptoms and manic or depressive episodes have been reported during steroid use in persons who were symptom-free prior to initiating steroids (Pope and Katz, 1988). Su et al. (1993) reported one case of mania, one case of hypomania, and one case of major depression following administration of relatively small doses of steroids to individuals in their prospective study. Indeed, the psychologic effects seen in individuals who use supraphysiologic doses may be markedly greater than those observed in many studies where only physiologic doses have been administered. Several legal cases have involved previously nonviolent persons who committed violent acts, including murder, while using steroids (Pope and Katz, 1990). Steroid use has also been associated with suicide (Brower, Blow, Eliopulos, and Beresford, 1989; Elofson and Elofson, 1990; Pope and Katz, 1992).

Evidence suggests that anabolic steroid use may result in dependency (Brower, Blow, Beresford, and Fuelling, 1989; Brower, Eliopulos, Blow, Catlin, and Beresford, 1990). Some steroid users fulfill the *Diagnostic and Statistical Manual*, 3rd edition, revised criteria for psychoactive substance dependence (Brower, Blow, Beresford, and Fuelling, 1989; Brower, Blow, Young, and Hill, 1991; Brower, Eliopulos, Blow, Catlin, and Beresford, 1990). Steroid users report that they have difficulty discontinuing the drugs and have a strong desire to reinitiate use once they have discontinued (Brower, Blow, Young, and Hill, 1991; Brower, Eliopulos, Blow, Catlin, and Beresford, 1990; Office of Inspector General, 1990). Users report continued steroid use despite adverse consequences (Brower, Blow, Beresford, and Fuelling, 1989).

Following cessation of steroids, users may experience fatigue, depression, anorexia, dissatisfaction with body image (Brower, Eliopulos, Blow, Catlin, and Beresford, 1990), decreased self-esteem (Hays, Littleton, and Stillner, 1990), restlessness, insomnia, decreased libido, headaches, and suicidal thoughts (Brower, Blow, Young, and Hill, 1991). Tennant, Black, and Voy (1988) reported a case in which physical withdrawal symptoms, such as those seen in opiate withdrawal, occurred upon cessation of extremely high doses of steroids. Some individuals may be psychologically dependent on steroids because of its muscle building effects and the resulting social reinforcement (Brower, 1992). Others who quit may resume steroid use to self-treat their withdrawal depression. It has not been established that anabolic steroid dependence results from a psychoactive or neurochemical effect on the brain (Brower, 1992).

The psychological effects of steroids on adolescents may be the most concerning of all the potential side effects. The developing nervous system of the teen may be especially vulnerable to these effects. The adolescent may lack the maturity to handle drug-induced mood changes. In addition, the development of the appropriate social skills and controls necessary to deal with pubertal changes may be made more difficult when the changes are occurring more rapidly than usual. Yesalis, Kennedy, Kopstein, and Bahrke (1993) reported that the strong association between steroid use and aggressive acts or crimes against property was most pronounced in the 12- through 17-year-old age group. Indeed, Burnett and Kleiman (1994) found that adolescent steroid users on a cycle reported significantly higher levels of depression, anger, vigor, and total mood disturbance as compared with users not on a cycle.

In addition, adolescents may be at greater risk for addiction. Those who take larger than therapeutic doses over longer periods of time appear more likely to become addicted (Brower, 1992). Signs of steroid habituation have been noted in adolescents (Yesalis et al., 1989). Yesalis et al. (1989) reported that, despite knowledge of possible dire health consequences, one-quarter of adolescent steroid users in their study were unwilling to discontinue steroid use, even if everyone else did. These "heavy users" were characterized by initiation of steroid use at a younger age than most, completion of a greater number and length of steroid cycles, having used multiple anabolic steroid drugs simultaneously, and having used injectable anabolic steroids (Yesalis et al., 1989).

Overall, the psychological effects of anabolic steroids are variable and transient upon discontinuation of the drugs. With estimates of 1 million or more past or current users in the U.S., a relatively small percentage of individuals appear to experience mental disturbances severe enough to require treatment (Yesalis and Bahrke, 1995). And in those individuals, the role of previous mental status, genetic susceptibility to addiction, environmental and peer influences, concurrent illegal drug use, and individual expectations is unclear and unknown.

Adolescent Anabolic Steroid Use

Corder et al. first reported the use of anabolic steroids by adolescent athletes in 1975, although it has been rumored that high school athletes have been using them since 1959. Since 1988, numerous local and state surveys have revealed that between 3% and 12% of male high school students (Buckley et al., 1988; Johnson, Jay, Shoup, and Rickert, 1989; Terney and McLain, 1990; Windsor and Dumitru, 1989; Komoroski and Rickert, 1992; Blessing, Heath, and Escobeda, 1993) and between .5% and 2.5% of female high school students have used anabolic steroids (Johnson et al., 1989; Terney and McLain, 1990; Windsor and Dumitru, 1989). The 1997 Youth Risk and Behavior Surveillance System data revealed that of ninth to twelfth graders in public and private high schools in the U.S., 4.1% of males and 2.0% of females have used anabolic steroids at least once in their lifetime (Hewitt, Smith-Akin, and Higgins, 1997).

The relative risk of anabolic steroid use is approximately 2 to 3 times greater for male adolescents as compared with female adolescents. There is a broad age range associated with anabolic steroid use, with some users as young as 10 years of age (Bahrke, Yesalis, Kopstein, and Stephens, 2000). There has been no clear-cut relation between race or ethnicity and anabolic steroid use (Bahrke et al., 2000; Blessing et al., 1993; Buckley et al., 1988; DuRant et al, 1993; Komoroski and Rickert, 1992). And there has been no significant association found between socioeconomic status and anabolic steroid use (Bahrke et al., 2000; Komoroski and Rickert, 1992; Windsor and Dumitru, 1989). Whitehead, Chillag, and Eliott (1992) reported that the rate of steroid use did not vary significantly based on high school enrollment or city size. They stated that schools with fewer than 100 students and towns of fewer than 2,000 people had similar use rates when compared with earlier studies of major metropolitan areas. There have been disparate findings on the relation between academic performance and anabolic steroid use, with some reporting lower grades among steroid users and others reporting no significant association (Bahrke et al., 2000; DuRant, Escobedo, and Heath, 1995).

Anabolic steroid users are significantly more likely to participate in school-sponsored athletics than are nonusers (Bahrke et al., 2000; Buckley et al., 1988; Johnson et al., 1989; Terney and McLain, 1990; Whitehead et al., 1992), and many reported using steroids to improve athletic performance. Sports with the highest prevalence of steroid use are football, wrestling, and track and field (Bahrke et al., 2000; Buckley et al., 1988; Terney and McLain, 1990), but steroid use has been reported in all sports (Terney and McLain, 1990). It is likely that the values and behaviors demonstrated by elite athlete role models who have used steroids reinforce similar values and behaviors in young athletes. The pressure to win that parents, coaches, and peers place on athletes may motivate some to look for an advantage in their sport. Some young athletes may perceive that their only chance to compete with steroid-using peers is to use steroids themselves.

Other investigators have reported that anabolic steroid use was not significantly associated with school-sponsored athletics. According to Buckley et al. (1988), 35% of adolescent steroid users were not involved in organized sport activities. Many of these adolescents were using steroids to improve appearance. Whitehead et al. (1992) also reported that the predominant reason for steroid use was to improve appearance, indicating that adolescent insecurity with body image may be a major factor in those individuals who use anabolic steroids to improve appearance. This is not surprising when one considers the importance society places on appearance, in addition to the adolescent's heightened concern about body image. As male adolescents become increasingly aware of their bodies and compare themselves with others, they may become impatient with the normal rate of muscle development. Their concern about appearance may motivate them to pursue a shortcut toward increased size. The experience of being "big" seems to carry special significance in making some adolescents feel good about themselves. In this way, use of anabolic steroids may become a method of improving self-esteem. This underlying agenda may be prevalent in many adolescent steroid users, even those involved in sports.

Knowing other steroid users has been reported to be associated with anabolic steroid use. Some teens use steroids because friends use them (Buckley et al., 1988; Johnson et al., 1989; Komoroski and Rickert, 1992). Achieving independence from parents and adopting peer codes and lifestyles are normal developmental tasks during adolescence. Peer pressure is known to be a strong force in illicit drug and alcohol use (Robinson et al., 1987). Goldberg et al (1996a) have postulated that anabolic steroid use is reinforced, or discouraged, by peers, family, media, coaches, sports figures, and perceived positive effects of use. Other potential risk factors include a "win-at-all-costs" attitude, overestimates of steroid use among peers, lack of information about the adverse effects of steroids, belief in media messages that promote steroid use, belief in personal invulnerability to unwanted effects, impulsive and hostile behaviors, reduced ability to "resist" a drug offer, perceived lower personal athletic ability, poor body image, and lack of antianabolic steroid attitudes (Goldberg et al., 1996a).

Anabolic steroid use by adolescents has been found to be associated with other high-risk behaviors. Studies reveal a significant relation between steroid use and the use of cocaine, marijuana, smokeless tobacco, cigarettes, alcohol, and shared needles (DuRant et al., 1993, 1995; Whitehead et al., 1992; Yesalis et al., 1993). Moreover, Middleman and DuRant (1996) reported that the following were associated with anabolic steroid use: driving after drinking, carrying a gun, number of sexual partners in the last 3 months, not using a condom, history of sexually transmitted diseases, not wearing a helmet on a motorcycle, not wearing a seat belt, injury sustained in a physical fight requiring medical attention, and suicide attempts requiring medical attention.

Identifying Adolescent Steroid Users

Many sport organizations consider steroid use unethical and illegal. For this reason, it is unusual for an adolescent to volunteer information regarding personal steroid use. Coaches, trainers, educators, parents, nurses, and physicians must become aware of the level of steroid use, maintain a high index of suspicion, and look for subtle side effects to detect anabolic steroid use in adolescent athletes. Early identification of an adolescent who displays the more common but less severe side effects may allow for evaluation and intervention before the individual places himself or herself at significant risk for side effects that are less common but more severe and potentially fatal. If steroid use is suspected or confirmed. the adolescent should be referred to a knowledgeable, nonjudgmental physician for an appropriate history, physical examination, and laboratory evaluation to detect evidence of complications.

Recognizable adverse effects due to anabolic steroid use may include: rapid weight gain, especially if lean body mass has increased; a disproportionate development of the upper torso; marked muscular growth; premature maturation in prepubertal males; yellow coloring of the eyes or skin; puffy face or extremities; mood changes; increased aggressiveness; needle marks in large muscle groups; increased growth of body or facial hair in females; and a deepened or raspy voice in females. Breast enlargement in males and severe acne can be normal occurrences during puberty but also are possible signs of steroid use. Steroid use might also be suspected in a male who complains of urinary dribbling or pain with urination.

It is important to be knowledgeable, yet nonjudgmental, when inquiring about steroid use. Suspicion of steroid use might prompt one to ask the adolescent if he or she is involved in weight training. The adolescent may then be asked about legal performance aids such as protein powders or amino acid supplements. One may then inquire whether the individual knows anyone who uses or has used steroids; then ask whether he or she has ever thought about using them or has tried them. Confirmation of anabolic steroid use by the adolescent should prompt a referral for appropriate evaluation and intervention.

Intervention

Intervention may include monitoring of steroid users, encouraging them to pursue alternatives to steroid use, and supporting treatment for those who are dependent on steroid use. Some physicians feel that by monitoring steroid use, one is supporting it. Others feel that monitoring steroid users for potential side effects is no different from monitoring alcoholics for cirrhosis. Some professionals claim that the athlete will use steroids anyway and that testing periodically for serious effects is preferred to no testing at all. One might even use monitoring as a step in persuading the user to discontinue steroid use. For example, one could obtain a panel of laboratory tests, gain the steroid user's confidence, then persuade the individual to take a "drug holiday." One could then repeat the laboratory tests during the drug holiday and review the improved laboratory results with the steroid user (Strauss, 1993).

A nonjudgmental inquiry of the reasons for an adolescent's steroid use will allow the physician or other professional to assess the adolescent's fund of knowledge regarding steroids and correct any false information about physiologic effects or complications. Both the potential risks and the merits of anabolic steroid use must be presented to adolescents. It is not helpful to attempt to talk a teenager out of using steroids by saying they do not work or by exaggerating the potential adverse effects. That approach will decrease the credibility of the professional and potentially alienate the adolescent. Instead, the teen can be encouraged to think of alternatives to steroid use, including appropriate nutrition, strength training, and development of talents or attributes that might improve self-esteem.

The adolescent who is addicted to steroids may not be able to stop using in response to education. Treatment for these individuals may include detoxification, rehabilitation, and relapse prevention. Initial goals of treatment are to provide relief for withdrawal symptoms; to prevent complications such as suicide; to restore the function of the hypothalamic-pituitary-gonadal axis, which may have been suppressed during steroid use; and to foster a therapeutic alliance (Brower, 1992). Both supportive therapy and pharmacotherapy may be used. Rehabilitation goals are to induce complete abstinence from anabolic steroids, to restore health and psychosocial functioning, and to prevent relapse. A combination of individual counseling, peer-group supportive therapy and family therapy may be effective. Relapse prevention is complicated by the user's strong internal and external urges to resume use (Brower, Blow, Young, and Hill, 1991). These urges must be addressed through individual counseling around issues of self-esteem. In addition, alternatives to steroid use must be encouraged and facilitated. Finally, relapse prevention techniques must help the individual predict risky situations and develop avoidance strategies.

Prevention

Drug testing and law enforcement may impact the use of anabolic steroids by adolescent athletes. However, education by informed, nonjudgmental professionals may have a greater impact on young adolescents' decisions regarding personal use of anabolic steroids. Well-informed parents, coaches, and educators may aid in the prevention of inappropriate anabolic steroid use by adolescents.

Testing

Scheduled drug testing for anabolic steroids is not effective because the advance warning allows athletes to cycle off the drugs prior to the testing date (Strauss, 1993), but random short-notice testing in which athletes have only a few hours' notice before they provide a sample may be a more effective deterrent (Strauss, 1993). Numerous collegiate and professional organizations test for anabolic steroid use (Shikles, 1989). Unfortunately, drug testing is prohibitively expensive at the high school level, and few laboratories have the equipment to perform accurate testing. Testing of individuals by physicians for the purpose of proving use may only alienate the adolescent and make anticipatory guidance difficult, but if testing is performed, it should be done with a reputable lab.

Testing is initiated with a urine screen for anabolic steroids using radioimmunoassay (Hatton and Catlin, 1987). The testosterone to epitestosterone ratio is used to screen for exogenous testosterone use. This ratio is normally 1:1 and considered positive for steroid use at 6:1. If screening is positive, the drug or its metabolites are identified by performing gas chromatography with mass spectrometry (Hatton and

Catlin, 1987). Oral steroids are usually detectable for several weeks after discontinuation (Hatton and Catlin, 1987). Parenteral agents are usually detected for up to three months after they are discontinued, but Hatton and Catlin have reported detection six months following discontinuation of their use.

Enforcement

In 1990, the U.S. Congress passed legislation to regulate anabolic steroids as controlled substances (Anabolic Steroids Control Act of 1990). However, the inability to control the import, distribution, and sale of other illicit substances regulated at the national level indicates that law enforcement alone may not be effective in preventing further steroid use. Enforcement must also involve schools, coaches, and parents to be successful. An enforced school policy for adolescent athletes and their parents that outlines consequences for steroid use may impact on adolescents' use of steroids. Yet until genuine penalties for steroid use are implemented, especially for college, professional, and Olympic athletes who serve as role models for adolescents, there may be little deterrence to steroid use in the adolescent age group.

Education

Some educational strategies directed toward adolescents have been assessed for effectiveness in altering adolescents' potential for using anabolic steroids. An effective program must include the education of coaches, parents, trainers, and educators, as well as adolescents.

In one study that assessed the effectiveness of educational intervention, Bents et al. (1990) reported that athletes who participated in a program that provided information about anabolic steroid use, nutrition principles, and strength-training techniques were less likely to use steroids than athletes who had not participated in the program. However, Goldberg, Bents, Bosworth, Trevisan, and Elliot (1991) reported that young athletes' attitudes toward anabolic steroid use were not altered following educational intervention, and Bents et al. (1989) reported that high school athletes showed a higher potential for steroid use after educational intervention using a lecture/handout format. Informational approaches to education on illicit drugs and alcohol have failed to decrease their use (Comerci and Macdonald, 1990). Programs that use these approaches assume that teenagers use drugs and alcohol because they are not aware of the side effects and social consequences of such use; they do not address the reasons for teenage drug use (Comerci and Macdonald, 1990).

Several investigators have concluded that educational intervention may be more effective if it is aimed at young adolescents before they begin use, and while they are at the experimental-use phase (Buckley et al., 1988; Moore, 1988; Yesalis et al., 1990). Elliot and Goldberg (1996) reiterate that the focus of a prevention program should be not on the users or those who have never considered use under any circumstances, but on those with an intent to try steroids. They describe a multidimensional peer-taught team-based prevention program called The Adolescent Training and Learning to Avoid Steroids Prevention Program (ATLAS), which has been shown to be effective in reducing anabolic steroid use (Goldberg et al., 1996a). The ATLAS program consists of classroom sessions with education on anabolic steroids, refusal skills, media messages, sports nutrition (energy and protein requirements) and supplements, and a 7- or 8-week weight room intervention where students are instructed in types of weight training and different weight-lifting techniques. There is also one parent-education session. The investigators report that this intervention has been associated with the following outcomes: significant reduction in adolescent intent to use steroids, greater knowledge of anabolic steroids and other drug effects, greater belief in personal vulnerability to the harmful effects of steroid use, more negative attitudes about steroid users, reduced impulsivity, improved feelings of athletic abilities, higher self-esteem, stronger belief that coaches and parents were against steroid use, more competent drug refusal skills, less belief in media messages, and improved nutrition and exercise behaviors (Goldberg et al., 1996a, 1996b).

Educational programs must also be provided for parents, educators, trainers and coaches who serve as positive role models for adolescents. In one study, 26% of the inquiries for steroid use were made by parents for their sons (Salva and Bacon, 1991). From this study, it is evident that some athletes must cope with parental as well as personal and societal pressures. Parents should be informed of the potential adverse effects of steroid use and encouraged to support fair play in their teenagers' sport activities. Educators and coaches are in daily contact with adolescent athletes and could play an important part in effective prevention programs. Educators could provide factual information and promote increased self-esteem by guiding adolescents toward realistic goals. Coaches and trainers could channel individuals into sports that are suited to their projected adult body sizes and strength. This may remove the temptation to use steroids in an attempt to attain size or strength incompatible with genetic potential. Society places tremendous importance on values that influence anabolic steroid use in today's adolescents—winning and appearance. Concerted efforts of educators, coaches, parents, and adolescents to deemphasize these values and reinforce a healthy steroid-free lifestyle could potentially curb the use of anabolic steroids by adolescents.

Summary

Evidence confirms that anabolic steroids used under certain circumstances can enhance size and strength in some individuals. Short-term adverse effects of anabolic steroid use have been studied in adults but have not been well studied in adolescents. The risk of long-term consequences of steroid use is unknown. In a society where athletes are so heavily rewarded for winning, eliminating steroid use will be difficult. A multifaceted approach to educate children at a younger age with broad-based programs that address the reasons for steroid use and emphasize alternatives to drug use such as proper nutrition and strength training may impact adolescent's use of these agents.

Further research is needed to determine potential benefits of steroid use, risks of steroid use by adolescents, and effectiveness of educational programs. Unfortunately, the illicit status and potential adverse effects of steroids impede the development of well-controlled, prospective studies regarding potential benefits and risks of these drugs used by adolescents at supraphysiologic doses. Until we can follow steroid-using athletes over a long period, determine precisely what steroids were taken, and how much for how long, many of our questions will remain unanswered.

References

Alen, M., Rahkila, P., Reinila, M., and Vihko, R. (1987). Androgenic-anabolic steroid effects on serum thyroid, pituitary and steroid hormones in athletes. *The American Journal of Sports Medicine, 15*, 357–361.

American College of Sports Medicine. (1984). Position stand on the use of anabolic-androgenic steroids in sports. *Sports Medicine Bulletin, 19*, 13–18.

Anabolic Reference Guide (4th ed.). (1989). Golden, CO: Mile High Publishing.

Anabolic Steroids Control Act of 1990 (P. L. 101–647, Sec. 1901–1907) (1990). United States Code Congressional and Administrative News (Vol. 4, pp. 104 STAT. 4851–104 STAT. 4854). St. Paul: West Publishing.

Ariel, G., and Saville, W. (1972). Anabolic steroids: The physiological effects of placebos. *Medicine and Science in Sports and Exercise, 4*, 124–126.

Bagheri, S. A., and Boyer, J. L. (1974). Peliosis hepatitis associated with androgenic-anabolic steroid therapy. *Annals of Internal Medicine, 81*, 610–618.

Bahrke, M. S., Yesalis, C. E., Kopstein, A. N., and Stephens, J. A. (2000). Risk factors associated with anabolic-androgenic steroid use among adolescents. *Sports Medicine, 29*, 397–405.

Bents, R., Trevisan, L., Bosworth, E., Boyea, S., Elliot, D., and Goldberg, L. (1989). The effect of teaching interventions on knowledge and attitudes of anabolic steroids among high school athletes. *Medicine and Science in Sports and Exercise, 21* (Suppl.), S26. (Abstract No. 152)

Bents, R., Young, J., Bosworth, E., Boyea, S., Elliot, D., and Goldberg, L. (1990). An effective educational program alters attitudes toward anabolic steroid use among adolescent athletes. *Medicine and Science in Sports and Exercise, 22* (Suppl.), S64. (Abstract No. 382)

Blessing, D. L., Heath, G. W., and Escobeda, L. (1993). Prevalence of anabolic steroid use among American adolescents. *Medicine and Science in Sports and Exercise, 25* (Suppl.), S128. (Abstract No. 707)

Bowman, S. (1990). Anabolic steroids and infarction [Letter to the editor]. *British Medical Journal, 300*, 750.

Brower, K. J. (1992). Clinical assessment and treatment of anabolic steroid users. *Psychiatric Annals, 22*, 35–40.

Brower, K. J., Blow, F. C., Beresford, T. P., and Fuelling, C. (1989). Anabolic androgenic steroid dependence. *The Journal of Clinical Psychiatry, 50*, 31–33.

Brower, K. J., Blow, F. C., Eliopulos, G. A., and Beresford, T. P. (1989). Anabolic androgenic steroids and suicide [Letter to the editor]. *American Journal of Psychiatry, 146*, 1075.

Brower, K. J., Blow, F. C., Young, J. P., and Hill, E. M. (1991). Symptoms and correlates of anabolic androgenic steroid dependence. *British Journal of Addiction, 86*, 759–768.

Brower, K. J., Eliopulos, G. A., Blow, F. C., Catlin, D. H., and Beresford, T. P. (1990). Evidence for physical and psychological dependence on anabolic androgenic steroids in eight weight lifters. *American Journal of Psychiatry, 147*, 510–512.

Buckley, W. E., Yesalis, C. E., III, Friedl, K. E., Anderson, W. A., Streit, A. L., and Wright, J. E. (1988). Estimated prevalence of anabolic steroid use among male high school seniors. *Journal of the American Medical Association, 260*, 3441–3445.

Burnett, K. F., and Kleiman, M. E. (1994). Psychological characteristics of adolescent steroid users. *Adolescence, 29*, 81–88.

Calabrese, L. H., Kleiner, S. M., Barna, B. P., Skibinski, C. I., Kirkendall, D. T., Lahita, R. G., and Lombardo, J. A. (1989). The effects of anabolic steroids and strength training on the human immune response. *Medicine and Science in Sports and Exercise, 21*, 386–392.

Cohen, J. C., and Hickman, R. (1987). Insulin resistance and diminished glucose tolerance in powerlifters ingesting anabolic steroids. *Journal of Clinical Endocrinology and Metabolism, 64*, 960–963.

Cohen, J. C., Noakes, T. D., and Benade, A. J. S. (1988). Hypercholesterolemia in male power lifters using anabolic-androgenic steroids. *The Physician and Sportsmedicine, 16*, 49–56.

Comerci, G. D., and Macdonald, D. I. (1990). Prevention of substance abuse in children and adolescents. In V. C. Strasburger and D. E. Greydanus (Eds.), *Adolescent medicine: State of the art reviews* (Vol. 1, pp. 127–143). Philadelphia: Hanley and Belfus.

Corder, B. W., Dezelsky, T. L., Toohey, J. V., and DiVito, C. L. (1975). Trends in drug use behavior at ten central Arizona high schools. *Arizona Journal of Health, Physical Education, and Recreation, 18*, 10–11.

Cowart, V. S. (1989). If youngsters overdose with anabolic steroids, what's the cost anatomically and otherwise? *Journal of the American Medical Association, 261*, 1856–1857.

Crawshaw, J. P. (1985). [Interview with John A. Lombardo, Christopher Longcope, and Robert O. Voy]. Recognizing anabolic steroid abuse. *Patient Care, 19*, 28–47.

Creagh, T. M., Rubin, A., and Evans, D. J. (1988). Hepatic tumours induced by anabolic steroids in an athlete. *Journal of Clinical Pathology, 41*, 441–443.

Duchaine, D. (1989). *Underground steroid handbook II.* Venice, CA: HLR Technical Books.

DuRant, R. H., Escobedo, L. G., and Heath, G. W. (1995). Anabolic-steroid use, strength training, and multiple drug use among adolescents in the United States. *Pediatrics, 96*, 23–28.

DuRant, R. H., Rickert, V. I., Ashworth, C. S., Newman, C., and Slavens, G. (1993). Use of multiple drugs among adolescents who use anabolic steroids. *The New England Journal of Medicine, 328*, 922–926.

Elliot, D., and Goldberg, L. (1996). Intervention and prevention of steroid use in adolescents. *The American Journal of Sports Medicine, 24*, S-46—S-47.

Elofson, G., and Elofson, S. (1990). Steroids claimed our son's life. *The Physician and Sportsmedicine, 18*, 15–16.

Ferenchick, G. S. (1990). Are androgenic steroids thrombogenic? [Letter to the editor]. *The New England Journal of Medicine, 322*, 476.

Frankle, M. A., Cicero, G. J., and Payne, J. (1984). Use of anabolic androgenic steroids by athletes [Letter to the editor]. *Journal of the American Medical Association, 252*, 482.

Frankle, M. A., Eichberg, R., and Zachariah, S. B. (1988). Anabolic androgenic steroids and a stroke in an athlete: Case report. *Archives of Physical Medicine and Rehabilitation, 69*, 632–633.

Friedl, K., Dettori, J., and Hannan, C. (1991). Comparison of the effects of high dose testosterone and 19-nortestosterone to a replacement dose of testosterone on strength and body composition in normal men. *Journal of Steroid Biochemistry and Molecular Biology, 40*, 607–612.

Friedl, K. E., and Yesalis, C. E. (1989). Self-treatment of gynecomastia in bodybuilders who use anabolic steroids. *The Physician and Sportsmedicine, 17*, 67–79.

Goldberg, L., Bents, R., Bosworth, E., Trevisan, L., and Elliot, D. L. (1991). Anabolic steroid education and adolescents: Do scare tactics work? *Pediatrics, 87*, 283–286.

Goldberg, L., Elliot, D. L., Clarke, G. N., Mackinnon, D. P., Zoref, L., Moe, E., Green, C., and Wolf, S. L. (1996a). The Adolescents Training and Learning to Avoid Steroids (ATLAS) Prevention Program. *Archives of Pediatric and Adolescent Medicine, 150*, 713–721.

Goldberg, L., Elliot, D. L., Clarke, G. N., Mackinnon, D. P., Moe, E., Zoref, L., Green, C., Wolf, S. L., Greffrath, E., Miller, D. J., and Lapin, A. (1996b). Effects of a multidimensional anabolic steroid prevention intervention. *Journal of the American Medical Association, 276*, 1555–1562.

Goldman, B. (1985). Liver carcinoma in an athlete taking anabolic steroids [Letter to the editor]. *Journal of the American Osteopathic Association, 85*, 56.

Gribbin, H. R., and Matts, S. G. (1976). Mode of action and use of anabolic steroids. *The British Journal of Clinical Practice, 30*, 3–9.

Hatton, C. K., and Catlin, D. H. (1987). Detection of anabolic androgenic steroids in urine. *Clinics in Laboratory Medicine, 7*, 655–668.

Haupt, H. E., and Rovere, G. D. (1984). Anabolic steroids: A review of the literature. *The American Journal of Sports Medicine, 12*, 469–484.

Hays, L. R., Littleton, S., and Stillner, V. (1990). Anabolic steroid dependence [Letter to the editor]. *American Journal of Psychiatry, 147*, 122.

Hewitt, S. M., Smith-Akin, C. K., and Higgins, M. M. (1997). Youth risk behavior surveillance: United States 1997. In Center for Disease Control, *Surveillance Summaries*, 47, p. 61.

Hill, J. A., Suker, J. R., Sachs, K., and Brigham, C. (1983). The athletic polydrug abuse phenomenon: A case report. *The American Journal of Sports Medicine, 11*, 269–271.

Houssay, A. B. (1976). Effect of anabolic-androgenic steroids on the skin, including hair and sebaceous glands. In C. D. Kochakian (Ed.), *Anabolic-androgenic steroids* (pp. 155–190). New York: Springer-Verlag.

Hurley, B. F., Seals, D. R., Hagberg, J. M., Goldberg, A. C., Ostrove, S. M., Holloszy, J. O., Wiest, W. G., and Goldberg, A. P., (1984). High-density-lipoprotein cholesterol in bodybuilders vs. powerlifters. *Journal of the American Medical Association, 252*, 507–513.

Johnson, F. L., Lerner, K. G., Siegel, M., Feagler, J. R., Majerus, P. W., Hartmann, J. R., and Thomas, E. D. (1972). Association of androgenic-anabolic steroid therapy with development of hepatocellular carcinoma. *Lancet, 2*, 1273–1276.

Johnson, M. D. (1990). Anabolic steroid use in adolescent athletes. In A. C. Hergenroeder and J. G. Garrick (Eds.), *The pediatric clinics of North America* (Vol. 37, pp. 1111–1123). Philadelphia: W. B. Saunders.

Johnson, M. D. (1991). Steroids. In P. G. Dyment (Ed.), *Adolescent medicine: State of the art reviews* (Vol. 2, pp. 79–92). Philadelphia: Hanley and Belfus.

Johnson, M. D., Jay, M. S., Shoup, B., and Rickert, V. I. (1989). Anabolic steroid use by male adolescents. *Pediatrics, 83*, 921–924.

Kenney, J. (1994). *Extent and nature of illicit trafficking in anabolic steroids: Report of the international conference on the abuse and trafficking of anabolic steroids.* (Drug Enforcement Administration Conference Report, 34–35).

Kiraly, C. L., Alen, M., Rahkila, P., and Horsmanheimo, M. (1987). Effect of androgenic and anabolic steroids on the sebaceous gland in power athletes. *Acta Dermato-Venereologica (Stockh), 67*, 36–40.

Kley, H. K., Strohmeyer, G., and Kruskemper, H. L. (1979). Effect of testosterone application on hormone concentrations of androgens and estrogens in male patients with cirrhosis of the liver. *Gastroenterology, 76*, 235–241.

Komoroski, E. M., and Rickert, V. I. (1992). Adolescent body image and attitudes to anabolic steroid use. *American Journal of Diseases of Children, 146*, 823–828.

Kramhoft, M., and Solgaard, S. (1986). Spontaneous rupture of the extensor pollicis longus tendon after anabolic steroids. *Journal of Hand Surgery, 11*, 87.

Kruskemper, H. L. (1968). *Anabolic steroids* (C. H. Doering, Trans.). New York: Academic Press.

Lamb, D. R. (1984). Anabolic steroids in athletics: How well do they work and how dangerous are they? *The American Journal of Sports Medicine, 12*, 31–38.

Mauss, J., Borsch, G., Bormacher, K., Richter, E., Leyendecker, G., and Nocke, W. (1975). Effect of long-term testosterone oenanthate administration on male reproductive function: Clinical evaluation, serum FSH, LH, testosterone, and seminal fluid analyses in normal men. *Acta Endocrinologica, 78*, 373–384.

McKillop, G., Ballantyne, F. C., Borland, W., and Ballantyne, D. (1989). Acute metabolic effects of exercise in bodybuilders using anabolic steroids. *British Journal of Sports Medicine, 23*, 186–187.

McNutt, R. A., Ferenchick, G. S., Kirlin, P. C., and Hamlin, N. J. (1988). Acute myocardial infarction in a 22-year-old world class weight lifter using anabolic steroids. *The American Journal of Cardiology, 62*, 164.

Messerli, F. H., and Frolich, E. D. (1979). High blood pressure: A side effect of drugs, poisons and food. *Archives of Internal Medicine, 139*, 682–687.

Michna, H., and Stang-Voss, C. (1983). The predisposition to tendon rupture after doping with anabolic steroids. *International Journal of Sports Medicine, 4*, 59. (Abstract)

Middleman, A. B., and DuRant, R. H. (1996). Anabolic steroid use and associated health risk behaviors. *Sports Medicine, 21*, 251–255.

Mochizuki, R. M., and Richter, K. J. (1988). Cardiomyopathy and cerebrovascular accident associated with anabolic-androgenic steroid use. *The Physician and Sportsmedicine, 16*, 109–114.

Moore, W. V. (1988). Anabolic steroid use in adolescence. *Journal of the American Medical Association, 260*, 3484–3486.

Murad, F., and Haynes, R. C. (1985). Androgens. In A. G. Gilman, L. S. Goodman, T. W. Rall and F. Murad (Eds.), *The pharmacological basis of therapeutics* (7th ed., pp. 1440–1458). New York: Macmillan.

Office of Inspector General, Office of Evaluation and Inspections. (1990). *Adolescents and steroids: A user perspective* (DHHS Publication No. OEI-06-90-01081). Washington, DC: U. S. Government Printing Office.

Overly, W. L., Dankoff, J. A., Wang, B. K., and Singh, U. D. (1984). Androgens and hepatocellular carcinoma in an athlete [Letter to the editor]. *Annals of Internal Medicine, 100*, 158–159.

Perry, P. J., Yates, W. R., and Anderson, K. H. (1990). Psychiatric symptoms associated with anabolic steroids: A controlled, retrospective study. *Annals of Clinical Psychiatry, 2*, 11–17.

Pope, H. G., Jr., and Katz, D. L. (1988). Affective and psychotic symptoms associated with anabolic steroid use. *American Journal of Psychiatry, 145*, 487–490.

Pope, H. G., Jr., and Katz, D. L. (1990). Homicide and near-homicide by anabolic steroid users. *The Journal of Clinical Psychiatry, 51*, 28–31.

Pope, H. G., Jr., and Katz, D. L. (1992). Psychiatric effects of anabolic steroids. *Psychiatric Annals, 22*, 24–34.

Prat, J., Gray, G. F., Stolley, P. D., and Coleman, J. W. (1977). Wilms tumor in an adult associated with androgen abuse. *Journal of the American Medical Association, 237*, 2322–2323.

Roberts, J. T. (1986). Adenocarcinoma of prostate in 40-year-old body-builder [Letter to the editor]. *The Lancet, 2*, 742.

Robinson, T. N., Killen, J. D., Taylor, C. B., Telch, M. J., Bryson, S. W., Saylor, K. E., Maron, D. J., Maccoby, N., and Farquhar, J. W. (1987). Perspectives on adolescent substance use: A defined population study. *Journal of the American Medical Association, 258*, 2072–2076.

Rogol, A. D. (1985). Drugs to enhance athletic performance in the adolescent. *Seminars in Adolescent Medicine, 1*, 317–324.

Rozenek, R., Rahe, C. H., Kohl, H. H., Marple, D. N., Wilson, G. D., and Stone, M. H. (1990). Physiological responses to resistence-exercise in athletes self-administering anabolic steroids. *The Journal of Sports Medicine and Physical Fitness, 30*, 354–360.

Sachtleben, T. R., Berg, K. E., Elias, B. A., Cheatam, J. P., Felix, G. L., and Hofschire, P. J. (1993). The effects of anabolic steroids on myocardial structure and cardiovascular fitness. *Medicine and Science in Sports and Exercise, 25*, 1240–1245.

Salva, P. S., and Bacon, G. E. (1991). Anabolic steroids: Interest among parents and nonathletes. *Southern Medical Journal, 84*, 552–556.

Scott, M. J., and Scott, M. J., Jr. (1989). HIV infection associated with injections of anabolic steroids [Letter to the editor]. *Journal of the American Medical Association, 262*, 207–208.

Scott, M. J., Jr., and Scott, M. J., III (1989). Dermatologists and anabolic-androgenic drug abuse. *Cutis, 44*, 30–35.

Sheridan, P. J. (1983). Androgen receptors in the brain: What are we measuring? *Endocrine Reviews, 4*, 171–178.

Shikles, J. L. (1989). *Drug misuse: Anabolic steroids and human growth hormone* (GAO/HRD-89-109). Washington, DC: United States General Accounting Office.

Sklarek, H. M., Mantovani, R. P., Erens, E., Heisler, D., Niederman, M. S., and Fein, A. M. (1984). AIDS in bodybuilders using anabolic steroids [Letter to the editor]. *The New England Journal of Medicine, 311*, 1701.

Strauss, R. H. (1993). [Interview with Don Catlin, Jim Wright, Harrison Pope, Jr., and Mariah Liggett]. Assessing the threat of anabolic steroids. *The Physician and Sports Medicine, 21*, 37–44.

Strauss, R. H., Wright, J. E., Finerman, G. A. M., and Catlin, D. H. (1983). Side effects of anabolic steroids in weight-trained men. *The Physician and Sportsmedicine, 11*, 87–96.

Su, T., Pagliaro, M., Schmidt, P. J., Pickar, D., Wolkowitz, O., and Rubinow, D. R. (1993). Neuropsychiatric effects of anabolic steroids in male normal volunteers. *Journal of the American Medical Association, 269*, 2760–2764.

Sweeney, E. C., and Evans, D. J. (1976). Hepatic lesions in patients treated with synthetic anabolic steroids. *Journal of Clinical Pathology, 29*, 626–633.

Taylor, W. N. (1987). Synthetic anabolic-androgenic steroids: A plea for controlled substance status. *The Physician and Sports Medicine, 15*, 140–150.

Tennant, F., Black, D. L., and Voy, R. O. (1988). Anabolic steroid dependence with opioid-type features [Letter to the editor]. *The New England Journal of Medicine, 319*, 578.

Terney, R., and McLain, L. G. (1990). The use of anabolic steroids in high school students. *American Journal of Diseases of Children, 144*, 99–103.

Urhausen, A., Holpes, R., and Kindermann, W. (1989). One- and two-dimensional echocardiography in bodybuilders using anabolic steroids. *European Journal of Applied Physiology, 58*, 633–640.

Whitehead, R., Chillag, S., and Elliott, D. (1992). Anabolic steroid use among adolescents in a rural state. *The Journal of Family Practice, 35*, 401–405.

Wilson, J. D. (1988). Androgen abuse by athletes. *Endocrine Reviews, 9*, 181–199.

Wilson, J. D., and Griffin, J. E. (1980). The use and misuse of androgens. *Metabolism, 29*, 1278–1295.

Windsor, R., and Dumitru, D. (1989). Prevalence of anabolic steroid use by male and female adolescents. *Medicine and Science in Sports and Exercise, 21*, 494–497.

Wright, J. E. (1980). Anabolic steroids and athletics. *Exercise and Sport Sciences Reviews, 8*, 149–202.

Yates, W. R., Perry, P. J., and Anderson, K. H. (1990). Illicit anabolic steroid use: A controlled personality study. *Acta Psychiatrica Scandinavica, 81*, 548–550.

Yesalis, C. E., and Bahrke, M. S. (1995). Anabolic-androgenic steroids. *Sports Medicine, 19*, 326–340.

Yesalis, C. E., Kennedy, N. J., Kopstein, A. N., and Bahrke, M. S. (1993). Anabolic-androgenic steroid use in the United States. *Journal of the American Medical Association, 270*, 1217–1221.

Yesalis, C. E., Streit, A. L., Vicary, J. R., Friedl, K. E., Brannon, D., and Buckley, W. (1989). Anabolic steroid use: Indications of habituation among adolescents. *Journal of Drug Education, 19*, 103–116.

Yesalis, C. E., Vicary, J. R., Buckley, W. E., Streit, A. L., Datz, D. L., and Wright, J. E. (1990). Educational strategies for combating anabolic steroid use. *NIDA Research Monograph, 102*, 196–214.

chapter 15

Overuse Injuries in Young Athletes

Lyle J. Micheli, Children's Hospital Boston
and Harvard Medical School
Peter A. Salob, Children's Hospital Boston

The participation of children and adolescents in sports has been growing steadily. With the increased hours spent in training and performance, the number of overuse injuries has also increased. For example, in a recent national figure skating tournament, one-third of the top skaters were unable to compete because of overuse-type stress fractures.

Overuse injuries have received a good deal of attention both in the media and in research laboratories. As a result, much more is now known about their causes, risk factors, and prevention than was previously described. With the use of X-rays, magnetic resonance imaging (MRI), single photon emission computerized tomography (SPECT) bone scans, and computerized tomography (CT) scans, the diagnosis of overuse injuries is more readily made. Early detection has allowed the physician to confirm the diagnosis at a younger age and earlier stage, thus minimizing the long-term complications of chronic overuse injuries. Once a proper diagnosis is made, treatment and retraining aimed at preventing recurrence is possible. This chapter reviews what is presently known about overuse injury of bone (stress fracture), including risk factors for its occurrence, and typical sites of stress fractures in young athletes.

Overuse Injuries: An Overview

Sport-related injuries occur from two different mechanisms or combinations thereof. Acute macrotraumatic injuries are those which occur as a result of a single application of major force to an area of the body, such as a twisting injury of the ankle from a jump in basketball or a blow to the side of the leg in a football game. The second mechanism of injury, repetitive microtrauma, results in so-called overuse injuries which reflect repetitive microstress to areas of the body over a prolonged period of time, as is typically seen in the training regimen for sports.

In recent years, more knowledge has been gained of the risk factors responsible for the occurrence of overuse injuries, particularly in young athletes. Overuse injuries in this age group are being seen with greater frequency in sports medicine clinics. There are undoubtedly a variety of reasons for this, including (a) the increased participation in highly-competitive sports by children and adolescents, (b) the growing emphasis on increased duration and complexity of training at younger ages, particularly in individual sports such as gymnastics, figure skating, and swimming, and (c) the inclination of young athletes to specialize in a specific sport at an early age, rather than participating in whatever sport is in season (O'Neill and Micheli, 1988).

Overuse injuries may occur in a variety of tissues in the young athlete, including cartilage (Osteochondritis dissecans, Osgood-Schlatter disease, and epiphyseal growth plate arrest), bone (stress fractures), muscle-tendon units (tendonitis), and fascia (compartment syndrome). They have in common a history of repetitive training or cyclic low-level forces applied to an anatomical structure, with the probable association of certain anatomical or physiological susceptibilities in the affected individuals.

A noteworthy trend in sports medicine is the assignment of paramount emphasis on the prevention of injuries. In the past, the great majority of physician attention in sports medicine was directed toward a proper diagnosis and appropriate treatment. This remains extremely important, but contemporary practitioners must also assume responsibility for determining risk factors for the occurrence of injury, particularly training-related overuse injuries, as a first step in injury prevention. It is of little benefit to an athlete to have a stress fracture identified and resolved with treatment if the injury recurs as a result of lack of training modification. The prevention of sport-related injuries deserves equal emphasis in the armamentarium of the sports medicine specialist.

Overuse Injuries: Stress Fractures

The overuse injury of bone (stress fracture) has attracted particular attention in medicine and, specifically, athletic medicine. The first report of a stress fracture in the medical literature was that of a German military surgeon, Breithaupt, in 1855; he noted the occurrence of these lesions in young military recruits (Breithaupt, 1855). The lesions were subsequently identified as "march fractures" because of their propensity for occurrence with military training, and later by a variety of terms including fatigue fracture, spontaneous fracture, pseudofracture, and insufficiency fracture. Numerous risk factors have recently been identified. These range from diet to training regimen, and have often been classified as intrinsic (inherent to the athlete him/herself) or extrinsic (produced by the environment in which the athlete competes or practices).

Types of Stress Fractures

Stress fractures can be divided into two general categories: (a) insufficiency fractures, and (b) fatigue fractures of bone. This division, first suggested by Pentecost, Murray, and Brindley, (1964), describes an insufficiency fracture as being produced by normal or physiological stresses applied to bone that has an abnormal or pathological ability to handle the stress because of deficient structural characteristics. An example is found in the female athlete with amenorrhea which has caused reduced bone density, leading to increased susceptibility to stress fractures. A fatigue fracture, on the other hand, occurs when excessive cyclic stress is applied to bone of normal structure. This is commonly found, for example, in the gymnast who repeatedly does lumbar hyperextension maneuvers, putting large repetitive loads on the lumbar region.

Stress Fractures in Children: Different Sites Than Adults

While traditionally based on an adult model, stress fractures have been categorized as those occurring in the metaphysis or diaphysis of bone (in particular, long bones), it is now appropriate, given new findings, to broaden the categories to include stress fractures occurring in the subchondral bone of the joint surface in children and adolescents, and at the physeal plate (Bruns and Maffulli, 2000). It is important to note that the response of the growing skeleton to repetitive training is quite different than that of the fully mature skeleton. Stress fractures in the child or growing adolescent occur in a different pattern of injury, involving different sites, both throughout the body and within the very structures of the bones involved. They also have a different clinical and radiographic presentation, as well as healing response (Devas, 1963; Engh, Robinson, and Milgram, 1970; Walker, Green, and Spindler, 1996; Walter and Wolf, 1977). In the lower extremity, the tibia appears to be much more commonly affected than the fibula or bones of the foot. In addition, fatigue fractures of the tibia in children tend to occur at the juncture of the diaphysis and metaphysis, while adult fractures are more commonly in the diaphysis, in particular the distal third of the diaphysis of the tibia (see Figure 15.1). Fibular fractures, which are much more common in adults, nonetheless may occur in the child. As opposed to tibial stress fractures, which are thought to be due to impact, fibular stress fractures may be related more to distraction and rotation forces occurring in the process of running or jumping.

Sports at Special Risk

There are trends between sports which reflect the different patterns of forces involved in these activities (Miller, 1999) (see Table 15.1). Running sports characteristically involve fatigue fractures of the lower extremity, in particular, of the tibia, fibula, and foot (Devas, 1958; Devas and Sweetnam, 1956; Matheson et al., 1987a, 1987b; McBryde, 1985; Norfray et al., 1980; Orava and Hulkko, 1984; Orava, Pura-

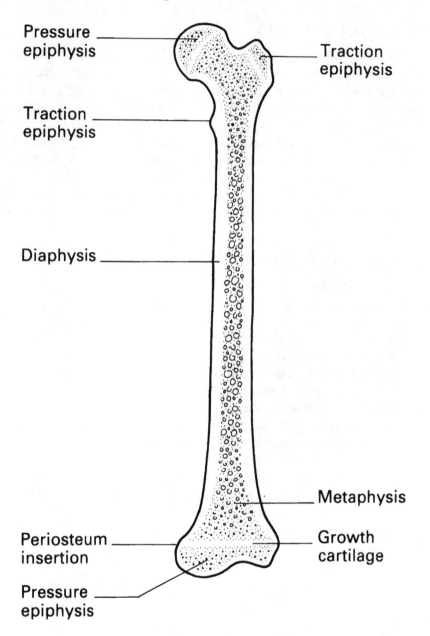

Figure 15.1. A schematic long bone of a child with epiphysis, metaphysis, and diaphysis noted. Redrawn from: "Clinical implications of youth participation in sports" by P. Renström and C. Roux, in *The Encyclopaedia of Sports Medicine, Vol. I: The Olympic Book of Sports Medicine* (p. 474) by A. Dirix, H. G. Knuttgen, and K. Tittel (Eds.), 1988, Oxford, England: Blackwell Scientific Publishers.

nen, and Ala-Ketole, 1978). Certainly, stress fractures of the femur and pelvis can occur in runners, but these are less common. By contrast, the jumping sports, such as basketball, demonstrate a relatively higher incidence of stress fractures of the distal femur, pelvis, and patella (Devas, 1960; Kaltsas, 1981). Overhand throwing and racquet sports are associated with stress fractures of the humerus, first rib, and elbow (Allen, 1974; Belkin, 1980; Lankenner and Micheli, 1985; Miller, 1960; Rettig, 1983; Rettig and Beltz, 1985). Recent reports have demonstrated repetitive overuse physeal stress fractures of the distal radius and ulna in gymnasts, and scaphoid stress fractures as well as articular surface osteochondral injuries of the elbow in gymnasts and throwers (Albanese et al., 1989; Carter, Aldridge, Fitzgerald, and Davies, 1988; Walker et al., 1996).

Table 15.1   Sport-Specific Stress Fractures

Sport	Location
Running	Tibia, navicular, fibula, hip/femur
Marching	Second metatarsal
Golfing	Ribs
Bowling	Ulna
Weight lifting	Ribs, clavicle
Gymnastics	Foot, acromion, distal radius, spine (pars interarticularis)
Baskeball	Fibula, foot (fifth metatarsal, navicular), proximal tibia
Football	Metatarsals
Dancing	Metatarsals, midshaft tibia
Rowing	Ribs

Differential Diagnosis

It is imperative for the sports physician dealing with a young athlete who presents with chronic pain always to include the possibility of stress fracture in the differential diagnosis. Diagnosis may be aided by the fact that clinical presentation in the child or adolescent with stress fracture is often more dramatic than that seen in the adult. In superficial bones there may be an area of swelling or very localized tenderness; and in radiographs healing callous formed in response to repetitive microfracture and subsequent partial healing at the site may be evident (Devas, 1963). This is less commonly true in the adult. A very careful history, taking into account the exact details of training, can help determine that, first of all, an overuse injury is present, and secondly, what type of overuse injury and which tissue of involvement is most suspect. It is important to remember, however, that infection or tumor may present in a chronic fashion in the child or adolescent athlete. As these entities are relatively more common in the musculoskeletal system of the child than in the adult, additional care must be taken to eliminate them. We have seen a fatigue fracture of the distal femur in a cross-country runner diagnosed unnecessarily late, initially confused with chronic patellofemoral stress syndrome, and treated with exercise and icing to the knee. We have also seen a young athlete with pain at the knee that was again diagnosed as patellofemoral stress syndrome and treated with icing and exercises when the etiology was actually a tumor of the distal femur. Exertional compartment syndrome has also been mistaken for a stress fracture (Boden and Osbahr, 2000). Athletes with this condition have pain, usually over the anterior tibia, that increases with activities and decreases with rest. Compartment syndrome is sometimes distinguished by neurological symptoms caused by increased pressures.

Risk Factors

As already indicated, it is useful when assessing the young athlete complaining of chronic or training-related pain of gradual onset to have in mind a specific set of risk factors for overuse. These factors are listed in Table 15.2. Often two or more such factors appear to contribute to the occurrence of a given overuse injury. For example, a young athlete rapidly increases the volume of training while wearing inadequately cushioned older shoes on a surface that has become hard due to lack of rain.

Physical training. Training error appropriately heads the list, as it is the most frequently encountered risk factor in the development of overuse injuries in young athletes. The most important components in this cause-effect relationship appear to be (a) increases in the total volume of training, and (b) the rate of progression of training (Bennell, Matheson, Meeuwisse, and Brukner, 1999; Mustajoki, Laapio, and Meurmann, 1983; Nilsson and Westlin, 1971; Swissa et al., 1989). We have learned empirically that most athletes should not increase their training more than 10% per week. A young runner, then, who is running 20 minutes a day, 5 days a week, can safely increase to 22 minutes a day, 5 days a week, the following week. We have seen a case of an elite distance runner at the college level who decreased his running from 90 miles a week to 60 miles a week during a 3-week exam period. When he quickly resumed his previous training regimen of 90 miles a week, he developed a stress fracture of the tibia.

Intensive summer sport camps specialized in only one sport often precipitate overuse injury through a rapid, narrowly-focused increase in training. For example, a youngster interested in soccer who is playing perhaps a total of 8 to 10 hours a week may suddenly be put in a summer camp situation in which he or she is training in soccer 6 hours a day, 5 days a week. This violation of a single risk factor may be sufficient to cause the onset of a tibial or fibular stress fracture. A study of ballet dancers who trained more than 5 hours per day showed a 16 times increase in the rate of stress fractures over peers who danced less than 5 hours per day (Kadel, Teitz, and Kronmal, 1992).

Table 15.2 Potential Risk Factors for Stress Fractures

Physical Training
   Volume of training
   Rate of progression of training
   Physical fitness
   Recovery periods
   Cultural deconditioning
Intrinsic Mechanical Factors
   Muscle tendon imbalance
   Muscular strength and endurance
   Anatomical alignment
   Bone mineral density
Nutrional Factors
   Calcium intake
   Caloric intake/eating disorders
   Nutrient deficiencies
Hormonal Factors
   Sex hormones
   Menarchal age
   Other hormones
Extrinsic Mechanical Factors
   Surface
   Footwear/insoles/orthotics
   External loading

Poor physical fitness prior to training has also been suggested to increase the risk of stress fracture. In one study, military recruits who had low levels of physical activity prior to basic training had 3 times as many stress fractures as physically active recruits (Shaffer, Brodine, Almeida, Williams, and Ronaghy, 1999). Lack of rest periods in a training regimen has also been shown to be a risk factor.

At the present time there is a good deal of debate regarding the level of fitness, or lack thereof, in children in industrialised nations, particularly the United States. It can be hypothesized that the child who is physically inactive suffers decreased levels of fitness in all body tissues, particularly in the musculoskeletal tissues. Conversely, the response of the musculoskeletal system to increased levels of physiological stress is to increase bone size, density, and strength. These improved physical characteristics should exert a protective effect on the child who begins progressive sport-specific athletic training, and decrease the potential for overuse injuries in general and stress fractures in particular. On the other hand, the relatively inactive and culturally deconditioned child who does an excessive amount of sitting at school, riding in automobiles, and watching of television not only has been demonstrated to have increased levels of obesity, but undoubtedly will demonstrate decreased levels of structural strength of the bones and joints.

Intrinsic mechanical factors. Muscle-tendon imbalance is perhaps the second most important risk factor for overuse injury in this age group. Growth generally, and the adolescent growth spurt in particular, may contribute to changes in the relative strength and flexibility of agonist or antagonist muscle groups across major joints (Micheli, 1983). Hence, a careful assessment of muscle-tendon characteristics should be included in any preparticipation screening of young athletic candidates. Four different characteristics of growth should be assessed: (a) decreases in flexibility in association with growth and, in particular, growth spurts; (b) strength increases with growth which may not be uniform, additionally contributing to imbalances about joints; (c) imbalances of muscle strength or flexibility which are related to the particular demands or training regimens of specific sports or activities; and (d) repetitive techniques, such as overhand throwing or swimming, which can result in joint contractures and secondary asymmetric stresses upon the bones and joints involved. This is particularly important with respect to the prevention of stress fractures. Matheson and his colleagues have proposed that muscle bulk and, in particular, the potential for muscle fatigue, may be important contributory factors to the etiology of stress fractures (Matheson et al., 1987b).

Anatomical malalignment, particularly of the spine and lower extremities, has been suggested as a contributory factor in the occurrence of overuse injuries in young athletes. The malalignments may include (a) discrepancies of leg length, (b) abnormalities of hip rotation, (c) coronal alignment of the femur and tibia, such as genu valgum or tibia vara, and (d) excessive flattening of the arch or pronation of the foot. Unfortunately, no specific studies of risk factors for stress fracture in young athletes have yet been done. However, studies of military recruits have suggested a number of potential risk factors (Giladi, Milgrom, Simkin, and Danon, 1991; Pester and Smith, 1992). Giladi et al. (1987), for example, found that excessive external rotation of the hip in military recruits increased the risk of lower extremity stress fracture two-fold compared with those having less hip turnout or internal rotation. Similarly, there have been a number of clinical observations that tibia vara may increase the potential for tibial stress fracture in running athletes, particularly among young women (Dickson and Kichline, 1987; Engber, 1977). Excessive pronation has been discussed as a risk factor for overload of the entire lower extremity, including the potential for stress fractures (Dickson and Kichline, 1987). High-arched cavus feet, with their apparent decreased ability to absorb impact, have also been implicated in overuse injuries about the foot and lower leg (Cornwell, 1984).

The contribution of bone mineral density as a risk factor has been controversial. Giladi et al. (1987) found no difference in tibial bone density in military recruits, while studies of female athletes showed a relation between stress fracture incidence and low bone mineral density at the femoral neck, lumbar spine, and tibia (Bennell et al., 1996; Myburgh, Hutchins, Fataar, Hough, and Noakes, 1990; Zeni, Street, Dempsey, and Staton, 2000).

Nutritional and hormonal factors. The combination of eating disorders, amenorrhea, and osteopenia has been referred to as the "female athlete triad." All of these factors contribute to the incidence of stress fracture in female athletes. Studies have shown significantly lower levels of bone mineral density in amenorrheic versus umenorrheic female athletes matched by age, weight, sport, and training regimen (Drinkwater et al., 1984; Warren, 1987; Warren, Brooks-Gund, Hamilton, Warren, and Hamilton, 1986). Barrow and Saha (1988) found a 2:1 ratio of occurrence of stress fractures in amenorrheic versus menstruating runners, while another study of female athletes at Penn State University found 24% of amenorrheic college athletes to have stress fractures, while the overall prevalence of stress fractures in female athletes was 9% (Brukner and Bennell, 1997; Cook et al., 1987).

Poor nutrition, as frequently seen in sports requiring low body weight such as gymnastics, ballet or distance running, has been shown to contribute to a higher incidence of stress fractures. Studies of college athletes have shown that eating disorders virtually double the likelihood for developing a stress fracture (Callahan, 2000, Kaiserauer, Snyder, Sleeper, and Zierath, 1989; Nattiv, Puffer, and Greet, 1997).

Extrinsic mechanical factors. Impact absorbing qualities and the mechanical stabilization potential of footwear used in sports, particularly the running sports, appear to be major components of overuse injury prevention. The importance of impact absorbing materials not only in the hindfoot and heel area but also in the forefoot of shoes has been noted (Cavanagh, 1980; Milgrom et al., 1985). A recent study of stress fractures of the foot in basketball players demonstrated this point (Cavanagh et al., 1990). Clinical observation for a number of years has implicated relative hardness of running or performing surfaces as a possible contributing factor in the occurrence of lower extremity stress fractures in distance runners and dancers (McMahon and Greene, 1979; Seals, 1983; Walter, Hart, McIntosh, and Sutton, 1989; Washington, 1978).

Overuse Injuries in the Growing Athlete

Growth is the defining characteristic of the child or adolescent. With physeal closure childhood ends, the adolescent approaches the adult stage of physical development, and, in turn, the characteristics of the musculoskeletal system changes dramatically. Growth cartilage has been demonstrated to be more susceptible to repetitive trauma than adult cartilage, whether at the physis, articular surface, or apophyseal sites of major muscle-tendon insertions. Repetitive microtrauma to the growth plate from athletic activities during childhood and adolescence has been suggested as an etiologic factor in adult-onset arthritis at both the hip and knee (Bright, Burstein, and Elmore, 1974; Murray and Duncan, 1971; Stulberg, Cordell, Harris, Ramsey, and MacEwen, 1975).

There is a growing body of evidence demonstrating that repetitive microtrauma, especially during floor work and vaulting activities, has resulted in a new overuse injury of the physeal plate in young gymnasts. The gymnast complaining of wrist pain with repetitive activities, particularly on hand impact, must be assessed very carefully for the possibility of either scaphoid stress fracture or distal radial physeal injury. This, in turn, can result in relative overgrowth of the ulna and progression of serious joint derangement at the wrist in this athletic age group.

The articular cartilage in the child is also undergoing endochondral ossification and is, in effect, a growth plate. Repetitive impact or shear stresses to the adult articular cartilage can result in mechanical disruption and the development of chondromalacia. In the child, the response to similar repetitive forces appears to result in a "stress fracture" of the subchondral bone. Osteochondritis dissecans of the capitellum in the child baseball pitcher or gymnast represents stress fractures of the subchondral bone in this age group (Patel and Nelson, 2000). Similarly, osteochondritic defects at the knee, ankle, and within the foot in runners, gymnasts, and field sport players, as well as young dancers, may reflect similar stress fractures at the joint surface (Conway, 1937).

Osgood-Schlatter disease of the tibial tubercle is the best known apophyseal stress fracture. The general class of overuse injuries, entitled "traction apophysitises," appears to be very similar in pattern of injury to stress fractures of long bone diaphysis and metaphysis (Micheli, 1987; Ogden and Southwick, 1976). Similar injuries occur at the heel (Sever's disease) and in the foot at the tarsal accessory navicular (Micheli and Ireland, 1987).

During periods of accelerated growth rate—especially those occurring in the summer and during the adolescent growth spurt, where primary sites of growth are within the long bones—a relative tightness of the muscle-tendon units spanning these bones and joints may occur. Periods of "growth spurt" may be followed by secondary transient increase in muscle-tendon tightness or imbalances of alignment, which may increase the chance of overuse injury in general and stress fracture in particular. During these periods of increased susceptibility, careful attention must be given to supplemental exercises to combat muscle imbalances, as well as programs which decrease the total volume of training.

Sites of Stress Fractures in Young Athletes

Low Back

Young athletes involved in sports with repetitive flexion or, in particular, repetitive extension maneuvers of the back may have onset of back pain which ultimately is found to be due to stress fracture through the pars intraarticularis of the lumbar spine. These injuries were once thought to be primarily genetic or congenital in origin, but this has been largely disproved. It is now widely recognized that these are acquired lesions which result from repetitive stress to the lumbar spine. In most cases, ultimate fatigue failure occurs through the pars intraarticularis, but on occasion, the pedicle or facet of the spine is involved.

The advent of diagnostic techniques, including single photon emmision computed tomography (SPECT) bone scan, have greatly aided our ability to make an early diagnosis of this injury, particularly before frank fracture has occurred through the pars (see Figure 15.2). However, the sports physician must be alert to the occurrence of this injury and have a very high index of suspicion for it based upon patient history and physical examination. In a young athlete who complains of insidious onset of pain and who, on physical examination, is found to have pain with provocative hyperextension testing, a posterior element failure of the stress type must be presumed until proven otherwise.

If these lesions are detected early, prior to skeletal maturity, before fibrous union or nonunion has occurred, there is a good potential for healing. Conservative treatment includes relative rest, possible immobilization in spinal orthotics, and physical therapy. Unfortunately, because the environment for fracture is that of distraction rather than compression, once frank bone lesions have occurred, particularly if bilateral in the posterior elements, ultimate union can be very difficult to achieve.

Upper Extremity

As noted above, stress fractures of the upper extremity in young athletes are relatively uncommon, but certainly are to be suspected in the throwing sports or in sports involving repetitive impacting of the upper extremity. Stress fractures of the humerus and forearm occurring in the throwing sports appear to be due to repetitive torsional stress of the upper extremity (Thomas and Blitz, 2000). In the child athlete with open growth plates, this stress may be localized at the physeal plate and has been dubbed "Little League shoulder" (Cahill, Tullos, and Fain, 1974). Frank rotational fractures through the humerus have occurred from throwing, and fractures of the forearm have also been reported in young athletes.

Repetitive impacting at the elbow in young athletes who have not yet reached full skeletal maturation can result in osteochondral lesions of the capitellum, or partial avulsion injuries at the medial epicondyle of the elbow, due to repetitive traction in secondary fatigue failure through the cartilage bone junction of the epicondyle.

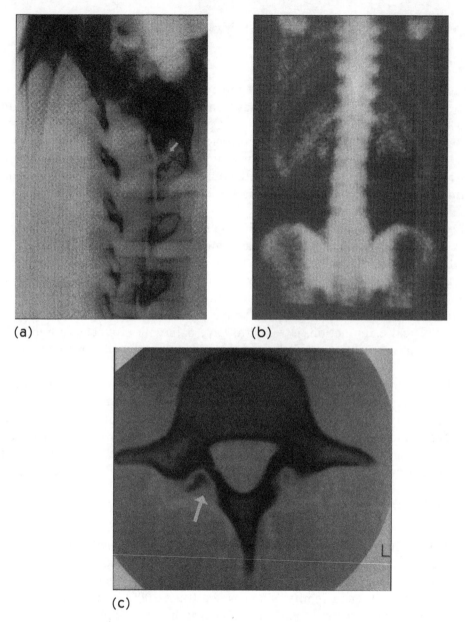

(a)

(b)

(c)

Figure 15.2. (a) Oblique radiographs of the lumbar spine demonstrating fracture at the pars intraarticularis of the fifth lumbar vertebra (spondylolysis). (b) Single photon emission computerized tomography (SPECT) bone scan demonstrating increased radionucleotide uptake at the site of bilateral spondylolysis of the fifth lumbar vertebra. (c) Computerized tomography (CT) scan image demonstrating a unilateral spondylolysis of the lumbar vertebra. Note the reactive hypertrophy of the opposite pars intraarticularis.

Fatigue fractures have also been reported across the olecranon from repetitive throwing in young athletes.

Fatigue fractures at the wrist have been reported as a result of repetitive impacting of the upper extremity in young athletes (Fulcher, Kiefhaber, and Stern, 1998). Most notable have been the reports of physeal injury of the distal radius and ulna in young gymnasts. Stress fractures of the carponavicular have also been reported in this population.

Pelvis and Hip

Stress fractures about the pelvis and hip in young athletes are relatively rare. These have been much more commonly reported in mature women runners or athletes involved in jumping sports. Nonetheless, iliac crest stress injuries have been reported in children and adolescents as a result of repetitive training. Much more commonly in this age group, stresses about the pelvis will result in frank apophyseal avulsions (Micheli, 1990) (see Figure 15.3).

Stress fractures of the femur in young athletes have certainly been reported (Walter and Wolf, 1977). Distal stress fractures of the femur are much more common than proximal stress fractures. Occasionally, however, hip pain in the young athlete will ultimately be found to be due to a fracture of the base of the neck of the femur.

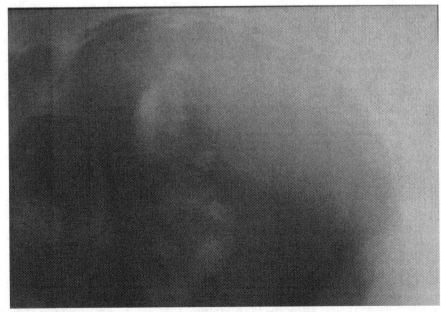

Figure 15.3 Stress fracture of the iliac crest apophysis in a young runner resulting in pain, tenderness, and limp.

These stress fractures have unfortunately often been confused with the reports of stress fractures of the hip in military recruits. In that population, these injuries have often been detected late, with frank displacement and therefore a poor prognosis. In the young athletes, however, these are often compression-type stress fractures at the base of the femur, and if detected early, healing can be expected with relative rest and limited weightbearing.

The stress fractures of the femur more commonly seen in this age group are those of the distal femur. These can be encountered in the jumping sports, but have also been seen in young runners. Very often the first complaint with this fracture is knee pain. The diagnosis may not be suspected early on. We have encountered cases of frank displacement of these fractures in this age group.

Ankle and Foot

Ankle pain in a young athlete undergoing repetitive training may also be due to stress fracture. The medial malleolus is particularly vulnerable to stress fracture and partial avulsions (Stanitski and Micheli, 1993). Stress fractures of the foot may also occur. While stress fractures of the body of the os calcis are relatively rare in this age group, apophyseal injuries, such as Sever's apophysitis at the heel and painful accessory navicular in the midfoot, have been reported (Micheli, 1987; Micheli and Ireland, 1987).

Two stress fractures of the foot in young athletes bear special mention. Stress fractures of the tarsal navicular (Figure 15.4) may present as low grade, aching midfoot pain. Too often, accurate diagnosis is not made sufficiently early, leading to frank fracture through the navicular. This appears to be due to the fact that these pains are frequently nonspecific, and plain radiographs are unremarkable early on. Early detection can, of course, be made with bone scan, and dissection of the frank fracture is often possible only with computerized tomography (CT) scanning. Delayed detection of this fracture is doubly unfortunate because this is a bone with a slow rate of healing and a relatively high rate of complications from this injury.

The second site of difficult stress fractures in the foot in young athletes is the base of the fifth metatarsal. Once again, these stress fractures are often detected late, after they have become fully established. This is a slow healing bone, and one which sometimes requires internal fixation to attain satisfactory union of stress fractures. Other special stress fractures that have been encountered in young athletes undergoing repetitive training include stress fractures of the proximal second metatarsal and, more commonly, the shaft of the metatarsal.

Prevention of Stress Fractures in Young Athletes

This discussion of stress fractures in young athletes has emphasized the recognition of risk factors in the hope that this will aid in early diagnosis and the prevention of later complications. In most cases of stress fracture, early diagnosis results in

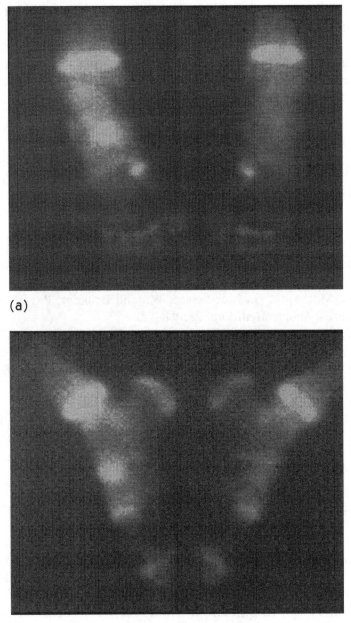

(a)

(b)

Figure 15.4. (**a**) Anteroposterior and (**b**) lateral views of single photon emission computerized tomography (SPECT) bone scan demonstrating increased radionucleotide uptake at the site of a right tarsal navicular stress fracture.

simpler treatment and promotes satisfactory union, with the ability to resume problem-free athletic training. In addition, as our understanding of risk factors for the occurrence of this serious overuse injury increases, it will hopefully be possible to detect individuals with a special propensity for stress fractures, so that steps may be taken to prevent the occurrence of these injuries through careful management of training regimens.

References

Albanese, S. A., Plamer, A. K., Kerr, D. R., Carpenter, C. W., Lisi, D., and Levinsohn, E. M. (1989). Wrist pain and distal growth plate closure of the radius in gymnasts. *Journal of Pediatric Orthopaedics, 9*, 23–28.

Allen, M. E. (1974). Stress fracture of the humerus: a case study. *American Journal of Sports Medicine, 12*, 244–245.

Barrow, G. W., and Saha, S. (1988). Menstrual irregularity and stress fractures in collegiate female distance runners. *American Journal of Sports Medicine, 16*, 209–216.

Bennell, K., Matheson, G., Meeuwisse, W., and Brukner, P. (1999). Risk factors for stress fractures. *Sports Medicine, 28*, 91–122.

Bennell, K. L., Malcom, S. A., Thomas, S. A., Reid, S., Brukner, P., Ebeling, P., and Wark, J. (1996). Risk factors for stress fractures in track and field athletes: A 12 month prospective study. *American Journal of Sports Medicine, 24*, 810–818.

Belkin, S. C. (1980). Stress fractures in athletes. *Orthopaedic Clinics of North America, 11*, 735–742.

Boden, B. P., and Osbahr, D. C. (2000). High-risk stress fractures: Evaluation and treatment. *Journal American Academy of Orthopaedic Surgery, 8*, 344–353.

Breithaupt, M. D. (1855). Zur pathologie des menschlichen Fusses. *Medizinische Zeitung, 24*, 169–171, 175–177.

Bright, R. W., Burstein, A. H., and Elmore, S. M. (1974). Epiphyseal plate—cartilage. A biomechanical and histological analysis and failure modes. *Journal of Bone and Joint Surgery, 56A*, 688–703.

Brukner, P., and Bennell, K. (1997). Stress fractures in female athletes. Diagnosis, management and rehabilitation. *Sports Medicine, 24*, 419–429.

Bruns, W., and Maffulli, N. (2000). Lower limb injuries in children in sports. *Clinics in Sports Medicine, 19*, 637–662.

Cahill, B. R., Tullos, H. S., Fain, R. H. (1974). Little League shoulder. *Journal of Sports Medicine, 2*, 150–153.

Carter, S. R., Aldridge, M. J., Fitzgerald, R., and Davies, A. (1988). Stress changes of the wrist in adolescent gymnasts. *British Journal of Radiology, 61*, 109–112.

Callahan, L. R. (2000). Stress fractures in women. *Clinics in Sports Medicine, 19*, 303–314.

Cavanagh, P. R. (1980). *The running shoe book*. Mountain View, CA: Anderson World.

Cavanagh, P. R., Robinson, J., McClay, I. S., Andriacchi, T., Edington, C., Frederick, E. C., Gross, E., Hass, S., Lake, M., Martin, P., Miller, T., Scott, N., Valiant, G., and Williams, K. R. (1990). A biomechanical perspective on stress fractures in professional basketball palyers. *Medicine and Science in Sports and Exercise, 22 (Suppl)*, S104.

Conway, F. M. (1937). Osteochondritis dissecans: Description of the stages of the condition and its probable traumatic etiology. *American Journal of Surgery, 38*, 691.

Cook, S. D, Harding, A. F., Thomas, K. A., Morgan, E. L., Schnurpfeil, K. M., and Haddad, R. J. (1987). Trabecular bone density and menstrual function in women runners. *American Journal of Sports Medicine, 15*, 503–507.

Cornwell, G. (1984). Sports medicine and the cavus foot. *British Columbia Medical Journal, 26*, 573–574.

Devas, M. B. (1958). Stress fractures of the tibia in athletes or "shin soreness." *Journal of Bone and Joint Surgery, 40B*, 227–239.

Devas, M. B. (1960). Stress fractures of the patella. *Journal of Bone and Joint Surgery, 42B*, 71–74.

Devas, M. B. (1963). Stress fractures in children. *Journal of Bone and Joint Surgery, 45B*, 528–541.

Devas, M. B., and Sweetnam, R. (1956). Stress fractures of the fibula: A review of 50 cases in athletes. *Journal of Bone and Joint Surgery, 38B*, 818–829.

Dickson, T. B., and Kichline, P. D. (1987). Functional management of stress fractures in female athletes using a pneumatic leg brace. *American Journal of Sports Medicine, 15*, 86–89.

Drinkwater, B. L., Nilson, K., Chestnut, C. M., III, Bruemner, W. J., Shainholtz, S., and Southworth, M. B. (1984). Bone mineral content of amenorrheic and umenorrheic athletes. *New England Journal of Medicine, 311*, 277–281.

Engber, W. D. (1977). Stress fractures of the medial tibial plateau. *Journal of Bone and Joint Surgery, 59A*, 767–769.

Engh, C. A., Robinson, R. A., and Milgram, J. (1970). Stress fractures in children. *Journal of Trauma, 10*, 532–541.

Fulcher, S., Kiefhaber, T., and Stern, P. (1998). Upper-extremity tendonitis and overuse syndromes in the athlete. *Clinics in Sports Medicine, 17*, 433–448.

Giladi, M., Milgrom C., Simkin A., and Danon, Y. (1991). Stress fractures: Identifiable risk factors. *American Journal of Sports Medicine, 19*, 647–652.

Giladi, M., Milgrom, C., Stein, M., Kashtan, H., Margulies, J., Chisin, R., Steinberg, R., Kedem, R., Aharonson, Z., and Simkin, A. (1987). External rotation of the hip. A predictor of risk for stress fractures. *Clinical Orthopaedics and Related Research, 216*, 131–134.

Kadel, N. J., Teitz, C. C., and Kronmal, R. A. (1992). Stress fractures in ballet dancers. *American Journal of Sports Medicine, 20*, 445–449.

Kaiserauer S., Snyder A. C., Sleeper M., and Zierath, J. (1989). Nutritional, physiological and menstrual status of distance runners. *Medicine and Science in Sports and Exercise, 21*, 120–125.

Kaltsas, D.-S. (1981). Stress fractures of the femoral neck in young adults. *Journal of Bone and Joint Surgery, 63B*, 33–37.

Lankenner, P. A., and Micheli, L. J. (1985). Stress fracture of the first rib. *Journal of Bone and Joint Surgery, 67A*, 159–160.

Matheson, G. O., Clement, D. B., McKenzie, D. C., Taunton, J. E., Lloyd-Smith, D. R., and MacIntyre, J. B. (1987a). Scintigraphic update of ^{99m}Tc at nonpainful sites in athletes with stress fractures: The concept of bone strength. *Sports Medicine, 4*, 65–75.

Matheson, G. O., Clement, D. B., McKenzie, D. C., Taunton, J. E., Lloyd-Smith, D. R., and MacIntyre, J. B. (1987b). Stress fractures in athletes: A study of 320 cases. *American Journal of Sports Medicine, 15*, 46–58.

McBryde, A. M. (1985). Stress fractures in runners. *Clinics in Sports Medicine, 4*, 737–752.

McMahon, T. A., and Greene, P. R. (1979). The influence of track compliance on running. *Journal of Biomechanics, 12*, 893–904.

Micheli, L. J. (1983). Overuse injuries in children's sports: The growth factor. *Orthopaedic Clinics of North America, 14*, 337–360.

Micheli, L. J. (1987). The traction apophysitises. *Clinics in Sports Medicine, 6*, 389–404.

Micheli, L. J. (1990). Injuries to the hip and pelvis. In J. A. Sullivan and W. A. Grana (Eds.), *The pediatric athlete* (pp. 167–172). Park Ridge, IL: American Academy of Orthopaedic Surgeons.

Micheli, L. J., and Ireland, M. L. (1987). Prevention and management of calcaneal apophysitis in children: An overuse syndrome. *Journal of Pediatric Orthopaedics, 7*, 34–38.

Milgrom, C., Giladi, M., Kashtan, H. Simkin, A., Chisin, R., Margulies, J., Steinberg, R., Aharonson, Z., and Stein, M. (1985). A prospective study of the effect of a shock absorbing orthotic device on the incidence of stress fractures in military recruits. *Foot and Ankle, 6*, 101–104.

Miller, J. E. (1960). Javeline thrower's elbow. *Journal of Bone and Joint Surgery, 42B*, 788–792.

Miller, M. (1999). The medical care of athletes. In J. Beaty (Ed.), *Orthopaedic knowledge update* (Vol. 6, pp. 119–120). Rosemont, IL: American Academy of Orthopaedic Surgeons.

Murray, R. O., and Duncan, C. (1971). Athletic activity in adolescence as an etiologic factor in degenerative hip disease. *Journal of Bone and Joint Surgery, 53B*, 406–419.

Mustajoki, P., Laapio, H., and Meurmann, K. (1983). Calcium metabolism, physical activity, and stress fractures. *Lancet, 2*, 797.

Myburgh, K. H., Hutchins, J., Fataar, A. B., Hough, S. F., Noakes, T. D. (1990). Low bone density is an etiologic factor for stress fractures in athletes. *Annals of Internal Medicine, 113*, 754–759.

Nattiv, A., Puffer, J. C., and Greet, G. A. (1997). Lifestyles and health risks of collegiate athletes: A multi-center study. *Clinical Journal of Sports Medicine, 7*, 262–272.

Nilsson, B. E., and Westlin, N. E. (1971). Bone density in athletes. *Clinical Orthopaedics and Related Research, 77*, 179–182.

Norfray, J. F., Schlacteri, L., Kernahan, W. T., Arenson, D. J., Smith, S. D., Roth, I. E., and Schlefman, B. S. (1980). Early confirmation of stress fractures in joggers. *Journal of the American Medical Association, 243*, 1647–1649.

O'Neill, D. B., and Micheli, L. J. (1988). Overuse injuries in the young athlete. *Clinics in Sports Medicine, 7*, 591–610.

Ogden, J. A., and Southwick, W. O. (1976). Osgood-Schlatter's disease and tibial tuberosity development. *Clinical Orthopaedics and Related Research, 116*, 180–189.

Orava, S., and Hulkko, A. (1984). Stress fracture of the mid-tibial shaft. *Acta Orthopaedica Scandinavica, 55*, 35–37.

Orava, S., Puranen, J., and Ala-Ketole, L. (1978). Stress fractures caused by physical exercise. *Acta Orthopaedica Scandinavica, 49*, 19–27.

Patel, D., and Nelson, T. (2000). Sports injuries in adolescents. *Medical Clinics of North America, 84*, 983–1007.

Pentecost, R. L., Murray, R. A., and Brindley, H. H. (1964). Fatigue, insufficiency, and pathological fractures. *Journal of the American Medical Association, 187*, 1001–1004.

Pester, S., and Smith, P. C. (1992). Stress fractures in the lower extremities of soldiers in basic training, *Orthopaedic Review, 21*, 297–303

Renström, P., and Roux, C. (1988). Clinical implications of youth participation in sports. In A. Dirix, H. G. Knuttgen, and K. Tittel (Eds.), *The Encyclopaedia of Sports Medicine, Vol. I: The Olympic Book of Sports Medicine* (p. 474). Oxford, England: Blackwell Scientific Publishers.

Rettig, A. C. (1983). Stress fracture of the ulna in an adolescent tournament tennis player. *American Journal of Sports Medicine, 11*, 103–109.

Rettig, A. C., and Beltz, M. F. (1985). Stress fracture in the humerus in an adolescent tournament tennis player. *American Journal of Sports Medicine, 13*, 55–58.

Seals, J. G. (1983). A study of dance surfaces. *Clinics in Sports Medicine, 2*, 557–561.

Shaffer, R., Brodine, S., Almeida, S., Williams, K., and Ronaghy, S. (1999). Use of measures of physical activity to predict stress fractures in young men undergoing a rigorous physical training program. *American Journal of Epidemiology, 149*, 236–242.

Stanitski, C. L., and Micheli, L. J. (1993). Observations on symptomatic medial malleolar ossification centers. *Journal of Pediatric Orthopaedics, 13*, 164–168.

Stulberg, S. D., Cordell, L. D., Harris, W. H., Ramsey, and MacEwen, G. D. (1975). Unrecognized childhood hip disease: A main course of idiopathic osteoarthritis of the hip. In *The Hip: Proceedings of the Third Open Scientific Meeting of the Hip Society, Vol. 13* (pp. 212–228). St. Louis: C. V. Mosby.

Swissa, A., Milgrom, C., Giladi, M., Kashtan, H., Stein, M., Margulies, J., Chisin, R., and Aharonson, Z. (1989). The effect of pretraining sports activity on the incidence of stress fractures among military recruits. A prospective study. *Clinical Orthopaedics and Related Research, 245*, 256–260.

Thomas, A., and Biltz, G. (2000). Preventing upper extremity overuse injuries in child and adolescent athletes. *Minnesota Medicine, 83*, 47–9.

Walker, R., Green, N., and Spindler, K., (1996). Stress fractures in skeletally immature patients. *Journal of Pediatric Orthopaedics, 16*, 578–84

Walter, N. E., and Wolf, M. D. (1977). Stress fractures in young athletes. *American Journal of Sports Medicine, 5*, 165–170.

Walter, S. D., Hart, L. D., McIntosh J. M., and Sutton, J. R. (1989). The Ontario cohort study of running-related injuries. *Archive of Internal Medicine, 149*, 2561–4.

Warren, M. P. (1987). Excessive dieting and exercise. The dangers for young athletes. *Journal of Musculoskeletal Medicine, 4*, 31–40.

Warren, M. P., Brooks-Gund, J., Hamilton L. M., Warren, L. F., and Hamilton, W. G. (1986). Scoliosis and fractures in young ballet dancers: Relation to delayed menarche and secondary amenorrhea. *New England Journal of Medicine, 314*, 1348–1353.

Washington, E. L. (1978). Musculoskeletal injuries in theatrical dancers: Site, frequency, and severity. *American Journal of Sports Medicine, 6*, 75–98.

Zeni, A. I., Street, C. C., Dempsey, R. L., and Staton, M. (2000). Stress injury to the bone among women athletes. *Physical Medicine and Rehabilitation Clinics of North America, 11*, 929–47.

Part Five

Psychological Issues

From both demographic and sociological perspectives, youth sports have become an important feature of cultures around the world. In ever-increasing numbers, youngsters spend significant amounts of time practicing or competing in athletics. In North America, young athletes typically participate about 11 hours per week, and they commonly play several sports throughout the year. How does this intense involvement, and the social environments in which it occurs, affect their psychological development? What psychological processes determine these effects? The chapters in this section address these and other questions concerning psychological development and functioning within youth sports.

Fot the most part, sports are conducted within a social context where participants are evaluated by others and develop internal standards for evaluating their own performance. In Chapter 16, Tara Scanlan addresses the important role of social evaluation in the competitive environment. She frames the impact and consequences of social evaluation using a conceptual model of competition that addresses relations between the objective sport environment, the youngster's appraisal and interpretations of that environment (subjective sport environment), the responses of the athlete to the subjective environment, and the evaluative consequences of these interacting factors. Athletic environments differ in their potential for evaluation by others.

Within these environments, children compare themselves (and are compared) with their peers, they infer through the feedback they receive how others evaluate their ability level and performance, and they actively seek feedback from others. Through these sources of information, participants draw conclusions about their strengths, weaknesses, and overall ability level. These evaluations help determine important motivational consequences, such as the development of performance anxiety and achievement motivation. The degree of perceived success or failure experienced in the sport environment affects both approach and avoidance motivation, as well as important aspects of the self-concept. Children may respond so as to maximize subsequent information about their abilities (as in choosing opponents of similar or slightly better ability), or they may avoid such feedback and the feared self-evaluations that would attend failure by choosing not to participate. The points raised in Scanlan's discussion of evaluation are amplified in subsequent chapters.

Motivational differences among athletes and their consequences on behavior are at the forefront of contemporary sport psychology research. In Chapter 17, Siobhain McArdle and Joan Duda describe a burgeoning area of research and theory development that focuses on the achievement-oriented implications of sport motivation and sport environments. Achievement goal theory addresses athletes' conceptions of success and perceptions of the athletic environment. Athletes can construe their competence and success in light of two goal orientations. In a task orientation, athletes define success in terms of task mastery, skill improvement, or giving best effort. In an ego orientation, success and competence are defined in terms of comparisons with and triumphs over others. This distinction can also be applied to the motivational climates that characterize sport environments, which can take the form of task or ego orientations. These motivational climates produce markedly different effects on athletes' enjoyment and intrinsic motivation, success standards and attributions, conceptions of sports' purpose, perceived competence, competitive anxiety, and self-esteem. In all of these areas, task-oriented motivational climates created by coaches and parents produce more salutary effects. The authors then review specific measures that can be taken to create a task-involving motivational climate.

Athletics are an achievement context and, as discussed earlier by Scanlan and by McArdle and Duda, a critical aspect of the developing child's self-concept is judgments of personal competence. Thelma Horn and Amy Harris describe the determinants and consequences of perceived sport competence from early childhood through adolescence. Research has shown that self-perceptions of athletic competence are linked not only to performance, but also to such psychological outcomes as emotional reactions, motivation, and persistence. Taking a developmental approach, Horn and Harris show how children's perceptions of competence are linked to emergent maturational changes in physical, cognitive, and emotional abilities. These personal changes are accompanied by changes that occur in the nature of the sport environment as children's age increases, illustrating important nature-nurture interactions. From the preschool to the adolescent years, as children's cognitive abilities increase, youngsters change markedly in the nature of the information they use to infer their competence and in the ways they process such information. An understanding of these processes allows Horn and Harris to provide age-linked guidelines for parents, teachers, and coaches to help them foster self-perceptions of competence in children. These research-based guidelines vividly illustrate how scientific understanding can inform intervention in the service of children's psychological well-being.

Many of the positive developmental consequences ascribed to the youth sport environment focus on its competitive nature. In a provocative counterpoint to this view, Terry Orlick focuses on the other side of the competition coin: the damaging effects that such an environment can have on the child's enjoyment of sport and on self-concept development (see also Chapter 10 on the learning of aggression in youth hockey and Chapter 22 on moral development in sport). Common complaints made by youth sport participants include too much pressure to win, not enough fun, and inadequate playing time for many children. An alternative to the competitive sport environment is provided by cooperative games, which remove the pressure of competing against others, include all athletes for the duration of the game, provide fun-filled interaction, and encourage consideration for others. Orlick is convinced that cooperative structures provide a more psychologically healthy environment for children than does the competitive environment. He also suggests that the sport environment can be used as a setting for learning psychological skills that can not only enhance sport performance, but also serve as general life skills. Such skills can facilitate adaptation in other life domains, such as academics and social interactions. Mental skills training has become commonplace in the training of elite athletes, but Orlick shows how such training can be done with children as well.

Previous chapters have addressed the factors that influence self-perceptions of sport competence. But what about the skills themselves? Becoming competent in athletics involves the acquisition of many different skills, some physical, some technical, and others strategic in nature. In Chapter 20, Jere D. Gallagher, Karen E. French, Katherine T. Thomas, and Jerry R. Thomas focus on mind-body interactions in skill development. What are the mental and physical processes that turn sport novices into experts? Gallagher et al. focus on the cognitive processes underlying the development of sport-specific knowledge structures: perception, memory, and decision-making. The authors show how the underlying knowledge base expands with age and experience. Attentional capacity and selectivity are important capabilities that increase with age and cognitive maturity. Labeling, rehearsal, and more complex organization of facts and procedures expand knowledge. Such knowledge has several aspects, namely, factual information, knowledge of procedures in executing the skills, and strategic knowledge. As in previous chapters, we see that an understanding of underlying psychological processes have definite practical implications. The authors end the chapter with specific recommendations for how practice and game situations can be structured to enhance the development of decision capabilities and technical skills. Quality, not quantity, of practice is the important thing, as is creating an enjoyable sport environment that will motivate children to refine their skills.

In Chapter 21, Ronald E. Smith, Frank L. Smoll, and Michael W. Passer analyze the nature of sport performance anxiety and what can be done to reduce it. The anxiety response can have adverse consequences on enjoyment of the sport experience, performance, physical well-being, and continuation in sport. The authors present a conceptual model of sport performance anxiety that specifies relations between stressful (demanding) situations, cognitive appraisal processes, physiological responses, and coping responses. The model helps organize empirical findings on the situational and interpersonal determinants of anxiety experienced by young athletes prior to, during, and after competition. The model also provides a framework for applying situational and athlete-directed interventions designed to reduce stress. Specifically, the authors describe guidelines and procedures that have proven effective in reducing situational sources of stress associated with the nature of the sport, coaching roles and relationships, and parent roles and responsibilities. Stress can also be reduced by intervening at the level of the athlete. The authors describe a stress management training program that has been used to teach young athletes cognitive and physiological coping skills to control or reduce the anxiety response itself. Finally, stress reduction at the behavioral level is discussed within the context of the athlete's level of physical skills. Such skills help reduce situational demands that can produce stress.

A major justification for youth sport participation is that sport helps "build character." Yet, we read on an almost daily basis examples of antisocial behavior performed within the sport environment. Are we building character, or characters? In a provocative finale to this part of the book, David Light Shields, Brenda Light Bredemeier, and F. Clark Power review the literature on sport participation and find that in some instances, sport participation is associated with lower levels of moral reasoning and a greater acceptance of immoral acts performed in the service of winning. To understand the factors that underly the impact of sport experiences on moral behavior, the authors adapt a theoretical model proposed by James Rest. This model specifies a set of four psychological competencies that increase the likelihood of behaving morally. The first, interpretation, causes participants to interpret the situation in terms of how one's actions affect the welfare of others. Moral judgment allows an athlete to formulate what a moral course of action would be. The third process, choice, causes the athlete to select from competing outcomes or ideals the one to act upon. Finally, the process of implementation allows one to carry out the chosen morally appropriate alternative. For each of these processes, the cognitive-affective and situational factors that affect the process are specified. These factors result in concrete suggestions for how the sport environment can be structured so as to encourage the development of moral values, empathy, and sportsmanship-related self-regulatory skills. The authors end by describing a "moral community" approach to structuring the sport experience to enhance character education. This approach strives to build a sense of community on sport teams that features shared norms for ethical behavior, together with the development of an achievement climate that emphasizes skill mastery over winning at all costs.

All the chapters in Part V serve as urgent reminders that those who structure and supervise youth sport programs, particularly coaches and parents, have a strong but often unrecognized responsibility for the impact of the athletic experience on the psychological development of young athletes. They also demonstrate the important practical applications that scientific research can have.

CHAPTER 16

Social Evaluation and the Competition Process: A Developmental Perspective

Tara K. Scanlan, University of California, Los Angeles

Almost half of our nation's children and youth spend a large amount of their time participating in an important achievement arena to them—sports. The significance of this achievement experience to the developing child needs to be determined, and the complex relationship between competition and social-psychological development requires understanding. This chapter takes a necessary first step in this regard by presenting a conceptualization of the competition process typically encountered by youngsters in the naturalistic sport environment. Of primary interest are children between the ages of 4 and 12 years. The focus is on the examination of *social evaluation* as a key element of the competition process because of its centrality, pervasiveness, and developmental importance. Related discussion concerns whether the social evaluation is actually perceived by participants and, if so, whether the evaluative information is actively sought. Finally, potential long-term, developmental consequences of the socially evaluative sport experience are considered.

Selecting a Viable Approach to Study Competition

To understand the complex competition process, it is necessary to determine a viable approach to serve as a starting point for its study. Two major approaches to the study of competition are the traditional reward approach and the formulation articulated in Martens in the mid-seventies (1975, 1976). The reward approach defines competition as a situation in which rewards are distributed unequally among participants based on their performance in an activity (Church, 1968). The problems with the reward approach that have limited its scientific viability have been enumerated extensively by Martens (1975, 1976) and will be reviewed only briefly.

The major limitation of the reward approach is that the competitive situation defined on a reward basis cannot be clearly operationalized. It is difficult to achieve "consensus on the criteria for the distribution of the rewards, on the subjective value of the rewards, and on the goal to be achieved" (Martens, 1975, p. 70). It is quite possible that the goals striven for and the rewards sought might be entirely different for each competitor involved in the competition. Therefore, use of the reward definition forces the experimenter to make critical assumptions and inferences about the individual's perceptions, responses, and response consequences regarding the competitive situation.

The more viable approach to the study of competition, conceptualized by Martens (1975, 1976), has overcome the major deficiencies of the reward definition and provides a more workable alternative for scientific inquiry. Hence, this approach will be used to provide the underlying framework for the ensuing discussion. Martens provides clear operational definitions and makes no assumptions regarding how the individual perceives the competitive situation, the response made to it, or the consequences of the response. Instead, these factors have been divided into stages to be examined systematically.

Martens (1975) has depicted competition as a process consisting of four interrelated stages that filter through the individual. The stages include the objective competitive situation, subjective competitive situation, response, and consequences.

The *objective competitive situation* (OCS) refers to those "real factors in the physical or social environment that are arbitrarily defined as constituting a competitive situation" (Martens, 1975, p. 69).

The OCS is based on social evaluation rather than on reward. It is defined as a situation in which the "comparison of an individual's performance is made with some standard in the presence of at least one other person who is aware of the criterion for comparison and can evaluate the comparison process" (Martens, 1975, p. 71). The comparison standard can be an individual's past performance level, an idealized performance level, or another individual's performance.

The second stage of the competition process is the *subjective competitive situation* (SCS) and involves how the individual perceives, appraises, and accepts the OCS. The SCS is very important because it reflects the manner in which the individual perceives reality. Therefore, it is from this base that the individual operates.

The resultant response emitted in stage three is a direct function of the SCS. Responses can be made on a psychological, physiological, or behavioral level. Possible responses include the decision to compete or to avoid competition, attempts to modify the objective competitive situation, and overt competitive behavior.

The fourth stage of the competition process involves the short- or long-term *consequences* arising from the comparison process, which can be perceived as positive, negative, or neutral. The perceived consequences provide important information that updates the SCS and affects future competitive responses.

Beginning with this framework, which identifies social evaluation as a key component of the competition process, it is now possible to detail the social evaluation potential in the naturalistic objective competitive situation encountered by children engaged in competitive youth sport. The subject competitive situation and response stages will be examined to determine if children perceive the social evaluation potential in the OCS and, if it is perceived, how children then respond in terms of information-seeking and self-protective behavior. The potential long-term consequences of the competition process will then briefly be discussed in terms of implications for social psychological development. Figure 16.1 provides a schematic overview of the ensuing discussion.

The Nature of Social Evaluation as It Occurs in the Naturalistic Objective Competitive Situation (OCS)

The naturalistic OCS typically encountered by children encompasses considerable social evaluation potential. *Social evaluation* is the appraisal of one's ability based on information received from other persons (Jones and Gerard, 1967). Children have been found to be active information seekers who derive information from both social and non-social sources (Horn and Harris, this volume; Jones and Gerard, 1967; Weiss, Ebbeck, and Horn, 1997; White, 1959). The developing child has little past experience upon which to draw and, consequently, is very dependent on significant adults and peers for information about reality, and the adequacy of his or her abilities for dealing with this reality (Harter, 1978; Horn and Hasbrook, 1984; Jones and Gerard, 1967). As depicted in Figure 16.1, the typical OCS includes at least three separate social evaluation processes, including comparative appraisal, reflected appraisal, and consultation.

The Comparative Appraisal Process

Comparative appraisal is the process of comparing with others to determine one's own relative standing on a specific ability (Jones and Gerard, 1967). Comparative appraisal occurs in the OCS when the comparison standard is another individual's performance rather than a past or idealized performance standard. The developmental findings clearly show that comparative appraisal becomes very important to children at approximately four to five years of age and intensifies through the elementary school years (Masters, 1972; Veroff, 1969). The following developmental progression indicates why this seems to occur.

Very young children do not compare or compete with others (Greenberg, 1932; Masters, 1972; Veroff, 1969). Instead, their time is spent autonomously accruing information about their own personal abilities. This is accomplished through exploration, solitary play, mastery attempts, and striving to attain autonomous achievement

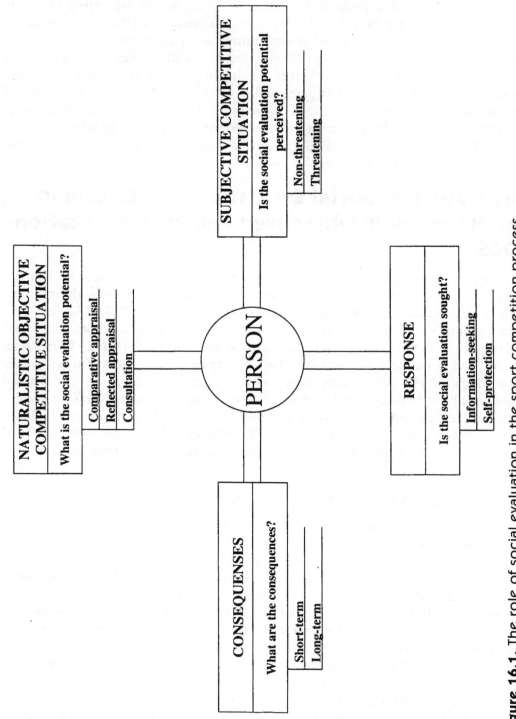

Figure 16.1. The role of social evaluation in the sport competition process.

goals and feedback from adults (Cook and Stingle, 1974; Harter, 1978; Veroff, 1969; Weiss and Ferrer-Caja, in press; White, 1959). Eventually, however, personal or absolute ability is placed into a larger relative framework through comparative appraisal to achieve an accurate, meaningful, and complete assessment of ability. Developmentally, the child appears to be ready to engage in this process around four or five years of age, when the first signs of comparative and competitive behavior are evidenced (Cook and Stingle, 1974; Horn and Hasbrook, 1984; Greenberg, 1932; Leuba, 1933; Masters, 1972; Ruble, Boggiano, Feldman, and Loebl, 1980; Veroff, 1969). Further, there is an increase in comparative and competitive behavior with age throughout the elementary school period, with the greatest intensity occurring around grades 4, 5, and 6 (Cook and Stingle, 1974; Kagan and Madsen, 1972; McClintock and Nuttin, 1969; Nelson, 1970; Nelson and Kagan, 1972; Veroff, 1969). It is during this important age span that many children are engaged in competitive youth sport activities, where much of the comparative appraisal occurs. Further, the focus of the appraisal is on motor ability. To excel motorically is one of the most prized and esteemed abilities of children at this age level. For example, personal perceptions of physical competence are positively related to self-esteem (e.g., Ebbeck and Stuart, 1993), sport enjoyment (e.g., Scanlan and Simons, 1993), motivation (e.g., Brustad, R.J., Babkes, M.L., and Smith, A.L., 2001); Weiss and Ferrer-Caja, in press), and peer relations (Brustad, 1993b; Evans and Roberts, 1987). Therefore, the comparative appraisal process involves a central ability, making the outcomes of this process potentially very important.

The Reflected Appraisal Process

Reflected appraisal is the second social evaluation process that can occur in the OCS. This is the process by which the child "derives an impression of his position on some attribute through the behavior of another person toward him" (Jones and Gerard, 1967, p. 321). Children can obtain extensive information about their motor abilities by attending to the overt or covert cues emitted by someone who is in the position to evaluate their abilities. Comparative and reflected appraisal are similar in that evaluative ability information is derived from a social source. However, the two processes differ in certain ways. First, in comparative appraisal, children evaluate their relative abilities by comparing with another person's ability, but do not make any reference to the other person's direct behavior toward them (Jones and Gerard, 1967). Reflected appraisal involves the evaluation being "mediated by the behavior of the other person toward the person himself" (Jones and Gerard, 1967, p. 324). In this sense, the evaluation is inferred from the emitted behavior. Second, comparative appraisal involves evaluation through comparison with social standards, whereas reflected appraisal includes comparison with either social or objective standards. For example, a coach might unintentionally transmit reflected appraisal cues to a child after the youngster has won or lost a wrestling match (where the comparison standard was social), or after the child has caught or missed a fly ball (where the comparison standard was objective rather than social).

A considerable amount of reflected appraisal exists in the OCS. First, most competitive situations are public so there are many people from whom to extract cues, including coaches, parents, teammates, opponents, and spectators. Second, evaluation from significant others—particularly parents, coaches, and peers—is more important and creates a greater impression on children than evaluation from persons of lesser status (Jones and Gerard, 1967). Third, evaluative cues may be unintentionally emitted, yet obvious to the child. Examples include subtle parental reactions reflecting pride and approval after a touchdown, and embarrassment and disapproval after a fumble. Other examples include the nonverbal signs of elation by coaches, teammates, and supporting fans when a player of superior ability steps up to bat with the bases loaded, or the chagrin revealed by these same individuals when an inferior player is placed in a similar situation. These latter examples also illustrate how reflected appraisal frequently represents an evaluation that is based on repeated observations rather than on a one-time occurrence—which only tends to increase the potency of reflected appraisal. Fourth, evaluative cues in the OCS are often overtly manifested. Spectators often cheer or jeer, teammates frequently offer praise or reproof, and opponents sometimes congratulate or ridicule.

The Consultation Process

Consultation, the third social evaluation process, involves children asking another person for an ability appraisal or receiving an evaluation without explicitly requesting one (Jones and Gerard, 1967). The evaluation is direct rather than inferred and, again, is typically received from significant others. For example, parents often place great value on their child's motor ability; consequently they have much to say about his or her performance. It is the coach's job to evaluate ability and they offer players extensive information during practices which speaks to strengths, progress, and areas requiring improvement. Frequently, coaches make overt evaluations that indicate their appraisal of a player's ability compared to other players. Selecting a team, choosing the starters, and picking all-star candidates are all examples of evaluations coaches make that reinforce important comparative appraisal information for the youth.

In sum, the OCS encompasses extensive social evaluation potential through the processes of comparative appraisal, reflected appraisal, and direct consultation. Therefore, much information is available to participants from which to establish accurate and complete ability assessments. Involvement in the competition process occurs during the age period when the social evaluation process is particularly intense and important. Furthermore, the specific ability being appraised—motor ability—is of central importance to the developing youth.

The Subjective Competitive Situation

The subjective competitive situation (SCS) requires examination to determine if the social evaluation in the OCS is actually perceived by the competitors (see Figure 16.1). Evidence of this perception would establish that social evaluation is a real and salient factor to the competition process.

The SCS is difficult to assess because it is a cognitive variable requiring inference. One indicant used to assess the social evaluation potential in the SCS has been the perception of threat to self-esteem. Potential threat to self-esteem generally increases when social evaluation potential is high, when success and failure are clearly defined, and when negative outcomes and evaluation can be incurred. This perceived threat can induce psychological stress as manifested by state anxiety. *State anxiety* is defined by Spielberger (1966) as "subjective consciously perceived feelings of apprehension and tension, accompanied by or associated with activation or arousal of the autonomic nervous system" (p. 17). State anxiety is a *right-now* reaction to the immediate situation and can be assessed by physiological measures of autonomic arousal, by observation, and by psychological inventories. Two psychological inventories commonly used to study youth are Spielberger's (1973) State Anxiety Inventory for Children (SAIC) and the Competitive State Anxiety Inventory for Children (CSAI-C) developed by Martens and his associates (Martens, Burton, Rivkin, and Simon, 1980). Studies from three related lines of research that provide insight into the SCS and the perception of threat are reviewed next.

The first line of research was initiated by the author with a laboratory experiment designed to assess threat in the SCS and to determine the factors that induce it (Scanlan, 1975, 1977). Specifically, the effects of competitive trait anxiety (A-trait) and success-failure on state anxiety (A-state) manifested prior to and after a highly socially evaluative competition were investigated. An overview of this experiment is provided because it was the first study to assess perceived threat resulting from high social evaluation potential in the OCS.

Competitive A-trait, assessed by the Sport Competition Anxiety Test (SCAT; Martens, 1977), is an important intrapersonal factor related to perceived threat. It is a "relatively stable personality disposition that describes a person's tendency to perceive competitive situations as threatening or non-threatening" and to respond with varying A-state levels (Martens and Gill, 1976, p. 699). Various findings in the general and test anxiety literature have shown consistently that high A-trait individuals exhibit greater A-state than low A-trait individuals when in evaluative or psychologically stressful situations (Hodges and Durham, 1972; Lamb, 1972; Phillips, Pitcher, Worsham, and Miller, 1980; Sarason, 1968; Wine, 1982). Therefore, it was hypothesized in this study that high competitive A-trait children would evidence higher A-state than low competitive trait children when facing a socially evaluative competitive situation.

The degree of success or failure experienced during competition, defined in terms of win-loss outcomes, is an important situational determinant of perceived threat to self. Individuals achieving successful outcomes should be less threatened by the information about their ability, should expect greater positive evaluation from others, and should be more confident in their ability to effect positive outcomes in similar future encounters than individuals incurring failure. Individuals attaining moderately successful outcomes receive little definitive evaluative information and should approximate their precompetitive perceptions. Results from the general anxiety literature have indicated consistently that A-state decreases with success and increases with failure (Hodges and Durham, 1972; Ishiguro, 1965). Therefore, it was hypothesized that children experiencing more successful competition outcomes would evidence lower postcompetition A-state than children experiencing fewer successful outcomes.

The experimental design was a Competitive A-trait X Success-Failure (2 x 3) factorial. The two levels of the first factor were high and low competitive A-trait. The Sport Competition Anxiety Test (SCAT) was administered to 306 boys between 10 and 12 years of age several weeks prior to the experimental phase of the study. The 41 high competitive A-trait boys and the 42 low competitive A-trait boys, representing the respective upper and lower quartiles on SCAT, were selected as participants. The three levels of success-failure were induced by manipulating win percentage on a complex motor maze task. The success group won 80% (W80), the moderate-success group won 50% (W50), and the failure group won only 20% (W20) of 20 contests. Both high and low A-trait boys were randomly assigned to success-failure conditions.

A-state was assessed by Spielberger's State Anxiety Inventory for Children (SAIC) at four different time periods. An initial basal measure was taken after a lengthy rest period. Assessments also were made just prior to competition, immediately after competition, and after a final debriefing session.

Providing support for the two hypotheses, the findings demonstrated that competitive A-trait and success-failure are important factors in the perception of threat. Competitive A-trait was found to be a significant predictor of precompetitive A-state. High competitive A-trait individuals indicated greater A-states than low competitive A-trait individuals. The results also indicated that postcompetition A-state levels significantly increased between successful (W80), moderately successful (W50), and failure (W20) outcome groups.

The results of this study have been shown to be internally and externally valid. They have been successfully replicated under similar laboratory conditions (Martens and Gill, 1976) and in the natural field setting of competitive youth sport (Scanlan and Lewthwaite, 1984; Scanlan and Passer, 1978, 1979). Extensive social evaluation potential existed in the objective competitive situation of each study, and the evidence suggests that this social evaluation is actually perceived. Moreover, it is perceived by participants of both genders and in individual as well as team sports.

Further evidence that the social evaluation in the OCS is perceived by young competitors has been supported by two additional lines of research. First, studies have indicated that even greater precompetition state anxiety is manifested in the particularly evaluative individual sport context than in the team sport domain (Griffin, 1972; Johnson, 1949; Simon and Martens, 1979; see Scanlan, 1984 for an elaboration of this issue). Second, it has been demonstrated that participants evidence concern about performance failure and negative social evaluation. These cognitions have been shown to be predictors of higher competitive trait anxiety (Gould, Horn, and Spreemann, 1983; Lewthwaite and Scanlan, 1989; Passer, 1983) and precompetition state anxiety levels (Scanlan and Lewthwaite, 1984). Brustad (1993a) provides a thorough review of perceived parental and coach evaluative reactions related to threat to self-esteem; and Scanlan, Stein, and Ravizza (1991) report similar appraisal factors related to threat in elite performers.

In sum, the findings of the three lines of research provide insight into threat in the subjective competitive situation. The evidence indicates that the social evaluation potential in the OCS is actually perceived and, therefore, is a salient factor in the competition process. The manner in which the subjective competitive situation is responded to in terms of seeking the available ability information and subsequent evaluation is examined next.

Response

It has been shown that children are very aware of and can feel threatened by the social evaluation potential in the objective competitive situation. Referring again to Figure 16.1, the next point of interest is determining how children respond to this social evaluation. Do they actively seek the ability information that emanates from evaluation, or do they avoid this information, when possible, to protect themselves? Answers to these questions are needed to further establish the importance and pervasiveness of social evaluation information.

A matter of particular relevance to this discussion is determining how children, under different levels of perceived threat, structure the competitive situation when given the opportunity to select their own future opponents. Do they structure the situation to maximize or minimize information about their abilities? Festinger's social comparison theory provides some insight into the issue.

Festinger (1954) developed a theory of social comparison based on the premise that human beings are motivated to obtain evaluative information about their abilities and, in the absence of objective standards, seek comparative appraisal. Further, comparison is made with similar-ability others to maximize information gain. The paradigm usually employed to assess this hypothesis has been structured in the following way. Participants are told that their score, representing performance on a positively or negatively valued attribute, has fallen at the median of a list of scores ordered by rank. They are then asked which score in the ranked list they would like to see. Typically, if the extreme scores have been established and the trait is positive, participants choose to see the score of a similar to slightly superior other in the rank order (Gruder, 1971; Hakmiller, 1966; Radloff, 1966; Singer and Shockley, 1965). This consistent finding indicates support for Festinger's information-seeking hypothesis.

However, several findings have demonstrated that when threat to self-esteem exists in social evaluation situations, self-protective behavior occurs. Further, such behavior increases as the probability of incurring threatening ability information increases. Results indicate that individuals reduce the probability of receiving this threatening information by comparing with individuals of lesser relative ability, thereby assuring successful comparative appraisal (Dreyer, 1954; Friend and Gilbert, 1973; Hakmiller, 1966).

The following hypotheses can be derived from the social comparison findings. First, successful, unthreatened participants structure the situation to maximize information gain by selecting opponents of equal or slightly greater relative ability. Conversely, unsuccessful, threatened participants minimize information gain by selecting opponents of lesser relative ability. In this way, they protect themselves from incurring further negative appraisal information.

Scanlan (1977) tested these two hypotheses in the competition laboratory experiment presented earlier. Opponent preference questions were administered during the postcompetition period immediately after postcompetition A-state was assessed. The results supported the first hypothesis but not the second. Children in all three success-failure groups (W80, W50, W20) indicated a strong preference for opponents who equaled their abilities. These findings indicate that children engage in maximum information-seeking behavior during competition, regardless of their level of perceived threat.

Consequences

The final stage of the competition process involves the short- and long-term consequences which can be positive, negative, or neutral (see Figure 16.1). Whenever social evaluation of ability occurs, positive or negative consequences can result during any given competition. The child might receive successful comparative appraisal information and positive reflected and/or consultation evaluation from significant others. Conversely, unsuccessful comparative appraisal and negative social evaluation might be incurred. It is probable that the consequences of any one *isolated* competitive experience will have minimal effect on social psychological development—unless, the consequences are particularly aversive. The important point is that many children engage in intense competition over extended periods of time with similar consequences potentially being repeated over and over again. This repetition makes developmental considerations, such as self-esteem development, relevant. Through this repetition the accrual of primarily successful or unsuccessful experiences, as perceived by the participant, can result. Also, through this repetition, success-failure experiences might somewhat balance out, leading to relatively neutral long-term consequences.

The second important point is that the consequences of the competition process must be kept within the perspective of the total socialization process. The extensive evaluative information available in the objective competitive situation can result in children establishing an accurate assessment of an ability that is very important to them. Whether this information, be it positive or negative, results in favorable, neutral, or adverse consequences is largely dependent upon the perspective provided by significant others. For example, children who continually receive negative comparative appraisal but gain support and guidance from their parents and coaches might significantly benefit from the competitive experience. The potential negative consequences might be neutralized or even supplanted with more positive outcomes. The children might learn to put comparative appraisal outcomes in perspective, learn to accept their capabilities and limitations within this particular achievement arena, and learn to define success and failure in terms of accomplishing realistic personal performance and effort goals. The potential negative impact of the consequences might be reduced further if the children can demonstrate other abilities, function competently in other evaluative achievement settings, and receive positive evaluation from significant others regarding their abilities.

In sum, the competition process must be placed within the larger socialization process to be adequately understood. Although competition is an important process, it cannot be isolated from the child's greater social context. The role of significant others and competence in other situations need to be considered as they influence the positive, negative, or neutral long-term consequences of competition.

References

Brustad, R. J. (1993a). Youth in sport: Psychological considerations. In R. N. Singer, M. M. Murphey, and L. K. Tennant (Eds.), *Handbook of sport psychology* (pp. 695–717). New York: MacMillan.

Brustad, R. J. (1993b). Who will go out and play? Parental and psychological influences on children's attraction to physical activity. *Pediatric Exercise Science, 5*, 210–223.

Brustad, R. J., Babkes, M. L., and Smith, A. L. (2001). Youth in sport: Psychological considerations. In R. N. Singer, H. A. Hausenblas, and C. M. Janelle (Eds.), *Handbook of sport psychology* (2nd ed., pp. 604–635). New York: John Wiley and Sons.

Church, R. M. (1968). Applications of behavior theory to social psychology: Imitation and competition. In E. C. Simmel, R. H. Hoppe, and G. A. Milton (Eds.), *Social facilitation and imitative behavior,* (pp. 135–168). Boston: Allyn and Bacon.

Cook, H., and Stingle, S. (1974). Cooperative behavior in children. *Psychological Bulletin, 81*, 918–933.

Dreyer, H. S. (1954). Aspiration behavior as influenced by expectation and group comparison. *Human Relations, 7*, 175–190.

Ebbeck, V., and Stuart, M. E. (1993). Who determines what's important? Perceptions of competence and importance as predictors of self-esteem in youth football players. *Pediatric Exercise Science, 5*, 253–262.

Evans, J., and Roberts, G. C. (1987). Physical competence and the development of children's peer relations. *Quest, 39*, 23–35.

Festinger, L. A. (1954). A theory of social comparison processes. *Human Relations, 7*, 117–140.

Friend, R. M., and Gilbert, J. (1973). Threat and fear of negative evaluation as determinants of locus of social comparison. *Journal of Personality, 41*, 328–340.

Gould, D., Horn, T., and Spreemann, J. (1983). Sources of stress in junior elite wrestlers. *Journal of Sport Psychology, 5*, 159–171.

Greenberg, P. J. (1932). Competition in children: An experimental study. *American Journal of Psychology, 44*, 221–248.

Griffin, M. R. (1972). An analysis of state and trait anxiety experienced in sports competition at different age levels. *Foil* (Spring), 58–64.

Gruder, C. L. (1971). Determinants of social comparison. *Journal of Experimental Social Psychology, 7*, 473–489.

Hakmiller, K. L. (1966). Threat as a determinant of downward comparison. *Journal of Experimental Social Psychology Supplement, 2*, 32–39.

Harter, S. (1978). Effectance motivation reconsidered. *Human Development, 21*, 34–64.

Hodges, W. F., and Durham, R. L. (1972). Anxiety, ability and digit span performance. *Journal of Personality and Social Psychology, 24*, 401–406.

Horn, T. S., and Harris, A. (2002). Perceived competence in young athletes: Research findings and recommendations for coaches and parents. In F. L. Smoll and R. E. Smith (Eds.), *Children and youth in sport: A biopsychological perspective* (2nd., pp. 435–464). Dubuque, IA: Brown and Benchmark.

Horn, T. S., and Hasbrook, C. (1984). Informational components influencing children's perceptions of their physical competence. In M. R. Weiss and D. Gould (Eds.), *Sport for children and youths* (pp. 81–88). Champaign, IL: Human Kinetics.

Ishiguro, S. (1965). Motivational instructions and GSR on memory, especially as related to manifest anxiety. *Psychological Reports, 16*, 786.

Johnson, W. R. (1949). A study of emotion revealed in two types of athletic contests. *Research Quarterly, 20*, 72–79.

Jones, E. E., and Gerard, H. B. (1967). *Foundations of social psychology.* New York: Wiley.

Kagan, S., and Madsen, M. C. (1972). Rivalry in Anglo-American and Mexican children of two ages. *Journal of Personality and Social Psychology, 24*, 214–220.

Lamb, D. H. (1972). Speech anxiety: Towards a theoretical conceptualization and preliminary scale development. *Speech Monographs, 39*, 62–67.

Leuba, C. (1933). An experimental study of rivalry in children. *Journal of Comparative Psychology, 16*, 367–378.

Lewthwaite, R., and Scanlan, T. K. (1989). Predictors of competitive trait anxiety in male youth sport participants. *Medicine and Science in Sports and Exercise, 21*, 221–229.

Martens, R. (1975). *Social psychology and physical activity.* New York: Harper and Row.

Martens, R. (1976). Competition: In need of a theory. In D. M. Landers (Ed.), *Social problems in athletics* (pp. 9–17). Urbana: University of Illinois Press.

Martens, R. (1977). *Sport Competition Anxiety Test.* Champaign, IL: Human Kinetics.

Martens, R., Burton, D., Rivkin, F., and Simon, J. (1980). Reliability and validity of the Competitive State Anxiety Inventory (CSAI). In C. H. Nadeau, W. R. Halliwell, K. M., Newell, and G. C. Roberts (Eds.), *Psychology of motor behavior and sport—1979* (pp. 91–99). Champaign, IL: Human Kinetics.

Martens, R., and Gill, D. (1976). State anxiety among successful and unsuccessful competitors who differ in competitive trait anxiety. *Research Quarterly, 47*, 698–708.

Masters, J. C. (1972). Social comparison by young children. In W. W. Hartup (Ed.), *The young child* (pp. 320–339). Washington, DC: National Association for Education of Young Children.

McClintock, C., and Nuttin, J. (1969). Development of competitive game behavior in children across two cultures. *Journal of Experimental Social Psychology, 5*, 203–218.

Nelson, L. L. (1970). *The development of cooperation and competition in children from ages five to ten years old: Effects of sex, situational determinants, and prior experiences.* Unpublished doctoral dissertation, University of California, Los Angeles.

Nelson, L. L., and Kagan, S. (1972). The star-spangled scramble. *Psychology Today, 6*, 53.

Passer, M. W. (1983). Fear of failure, fear of evaluation, perceived competence, and self-esteem in competitive trait anxious children. *Journal of Sport Psychology, 5*, 172–188.

Phillips, B. N., Pitcher, G. D., Worsham, M. E., and Miller, S. C. (1980). Test anxiety and the school environment. In I.G. Sarason (Ed.), *Test anxiety: Theory, research, and applications* (pp. 327–346). Hillsdale, NJ: Lawrence Erlbaum.

Radloff, R. (1966). Social comparison and ability evaluation. *Journal of Experimental Social Psychology Supplement, 2*, 6–26.

Ruble, D., Boggiano, A., Feldman, N., and Loebl, J. (1980). Developmental analysis of the role of social comparison in self-evaluation. *Developmental Psychology, 16*, 105–115.

Sarason, I. G. (1968). Verbal learning, modeling, and juvenile delinquency. *American Psychologist, 23*, 254–266.

Scanlan, T. K. (1975). *The effects of competition trait anxiety and success-failure on the perception of threat in a competitive situation.* Unpublished doctoral dissertation, University of Illinois, Urbana-Champaign.

Scanlan, T. K. (1977). The effects of success-failure on the perception of threat in a competitive situation. *Research Quarterly, 48*, 144–153.

Scanlan, T. K. (1984). Competitive stress and the child athlete. In J. M., Silva and R. S. Weinberg (Eds.), *Psychological foundations of sport* (pp. 118–129). Champaign, IL: Human Kinetics.

Scanlan, T. K. and Lewthwaite, R. (1984). Social psychological aspects of competition for male youth sport participants: I. Predictors of competitive stress. *Journal of Sport Psychology, 6*, 208–226.

Scanlan, T. K., and Passer, M. W. (1978). Factors related to competitive stress among male youth sports participants. *Medicine and Science in Sports, 10*, 103–108.

Scanlan, T. K., and Passer, M. W. (1979). Sources of competitive stress in young female athletes. *Journal of Sport Psychology, 1*, 151–159.

Scanlan, T. K., and Simons, J. P. (1993). The construct of sport enjoyment. In G. C. Roberts (Ed.), *Motivation in sport and exercise* (pp. 199–215). Champaign, IL: Human Kinetics.

Scanlan, T. K., Stein, G. L., and Ravizza, K. (1991). An in-depth study of former elite figure skaters: III. Sources of stress. *Journal of Sport and Exercise Psychology, 13*, 103–108.

Simon, J., and Martens, R. (1979). Children's anxiety in sport and nonsport evaluative activities. *Journal of Sport Psychology, 1*, 160–169.

Singer, J. E., and Shockley, V. L. (1965). Ability and affiliation. *Journal of Personality and Social Psychology, 1*, 95–100.

Spielberger, C. D. (1966). *Anxiety and behavior.* New York: Academic Press.

Spielberger, C. D. (1973). *Preliminary test manual for the State-Trait Anxiety Inventory for Children* ("How I Feel Questionnaire"). Palo Alto, CA: Consulting Psychologists Press.

Veroff, J. (1969). Social comparison and the development of achievement motivation. In C. P. Smith (Ed.), *Achievement-related motives in children* (pp. 46–101). New York: Russell Sage Foundation.

Weiss, M., and Chaumerton, N. (1993). Motivational orientations in sport. In T. S. Horn (Ed.), *Advances in sport psychology* (pp. 61–99). Champaign, IL: Human Kinetics.

Weiss, M., Ebbeck, H., and Horn, T. S. (1997). Children's self-perceptions and sources of competence information: A cluster analysis. *Journal of Sport and Exercise Psychology, 19*, 52–70.

Weiss, M., and Ferrer-Caja, E. (in press). Motivational orientations and sport. In T. S. Horn (Ed.), *Advances in sport psychology* (2nd ed.). Champaign, IL.: Human Kinetics.

White, R. W. (1959). Motivation reconsidered: The concept of competence. *Psychological Review, 66,* 297–334.

Wine, J. D. (1982). Evaluation anxiety. In H. W. Krohne and L. Laux (Eds.), *Achievement, stress and anxiety* (pp. 207–219). Washington, DC: Hemisphere.

CHAPTER 17

Implications of the Motivational Climate in Youth Sports

Siobhain McArdle, University of Birmingham
Joan K. Duda, University of Birmingham

The number of children from Western countries (such as the United States and Canada) who participate in youth sports is staggering. For the majority of these children, engagement in sport is a leisure-time endeavor. These youngsters do not possess the talent to be elite performers and "play" sport mostly because it is fun. However, this does not make their sport engagement trivial. The athletic setting still can be a salient achievement arena for the recreational participant in youth sport programs. In this case, athletics provides an opportunity for such boys and girls to develop their physical skills, foster their sense of efficacy in the physical domain, promote the adoption of an active lifestyle, and contribute to their current and future psychological and physical well-being. Moreover, sport involvement for the not exceptionally able child can be a forum that puts a smile on her or his face and a "glow" in her or his heart! It, too, can be a context in which young people learn to deal with disappointments, delayed gratifications, rules, and responsibilities in a constructive manner.

And then there are the gifted young athletes. What would we hope sport participation means in their case? Well, really what was listed above as aspirations for desirable and adaptive sport engagement apply to this subgroup of boys and girls as well! A further consideration, though, is what is necessary for such young people to maximize their talents and move on to excellence. For such a transition and transformation to be successful, child athletes need to grow into young adult participants and, depending on the sport in question, often adult athletes. They have to be able to endure and capitalize on more arduous training and competitive demands than those facing their recreational counterpart.

The overall "story" with respect to the impact of athletic involvement for all children (regardless of ability level) can be a happy tale or a sad, unfortunate, perhaps even grueling, chronicle. Relevant to sport scientists and sport practitioners is understanding what makes the youth sport experience per se and its outcomes positive and/or negative. In essence, there is a need to gain insight into the nature and determinants of young athletes' motivational processes. Only with such knowledge can we try and "set the stage" for an optimal encounter among all those youngsters who take the chance and give sport "a go."

Achievement Goal Theory

A viable platform for understanding variations in young people's interpretations of and responses to the youth sport setting is the achievement goal framework (Ames, 1992; Dweck, 1999; Nicholls, 1989). This framework holds that if we want to understand the motivation of the young athlete, it is necessary to understand the function and the meaning of his or her goal directed actions. The function and meaning of achievement activities such as sport are assumed to relate to how participants define success and how they judge whether or not they have demonstrated high ability. A key assumption of achievement goal theory is that developing and demonstrating competence is central to achievement environments.

Nicholls (1984, 1989) contends that there are two different ways of defining success and construing one's level of competence and these are labeled task involvement and ego involvement. When a young athlete is task-involved, subjective success and perceived competence are processed in a self-referenced manner. In this case, a youngster feels successful and competent when she or he has learned something new, witnessed skill improvement, mastered the task at hand, and/or gave a best effort. When interpreting sport in a task-involved way, the child or adolescent is concerned with what she or he is doing and how to do it better. Importantly, even if a young person perceives himself/herself to possess lower ability than others, he or she can still feel competent and successful if focused on task-involved criteria (Nicholls, 1989).

On the other hand, when young athletes are in a state of ego involvement, their definition of personal success and demonstrated competence are other-referenced. The focus here is to show that one is superior to relevant others. The child or youth can do this by outperforming their peers or doing similarly but not giving a concerted effort. When ego-involved, young athletes are preoccupied with how they are doing compared to others and whether or not their ability is (comparatively) adequate. Experiencing personal improvement or knowing that one did his or her "best" would not occasion subjective success and a sense of demonstrated competence for such a sport competitor. Indeed, knowing that one tried hard and "failed" would result in an ego-involved athlete feeling especially incompetent.

It is important to note that the development of an ego-involved conception of success and competence in children involves the capacity to differentiate between the concepts of effort and ability (Nicholls, 1984, 1989). Research in both education and sport illustrates that children go through stages in their understanding of hard work and ability and their interdependence (Fry and Duda, 1997; Nicholls and Miller,

1984). Specifically, for most youngsters prior to the age of 12, they either don't recognize the differences between trying hard and being able (i.e., very young children think that if one tries then one has high ability and vice versa) or they think that effort is the primary determinant of success or failure in sport (i.e., they think that people succeed or fail because they tried or did not exert effort, respectively). With maturity, children acquire an understanding of ability as current capacity. That is, by the time they are eleven or twelve years of age, most children can comprehend that outcomes are influenced by level of ability and how hard one works (as well as other factors). They understand that if someone can do very well and not give much effort, the individual in question must be very capable. Children, by the time they move into adolescence, also recognize the sobering reality that (in terms of achievement) effort can only get someone so far if she/he does not possess the requisite ability or talent. As a result of such differences in processing ability, effort, and their interplay, young athletes cannot be truly "ego-involved" until they possess a mature understanding of competence. Moreover, because of such cognitive developmental factors, younger children are inclined to be task-involved.

Achievement goal theory (Dweck, 1999; Nicholls, 1989) assumes that task- and ego-involved goals elicit qualitatively different motivational processes. Specifically, it is proposed that task involvement should foster adaptive achievement behaviors such as persisting in the face of failure, exerting effort, and selecting challenging goals (Roberts, Treasure and Kavussanu, 1997). This prediction regarding the positive motivational consequences of task involvement is not dependent on whether the young athlete thinks he or she is highly able or doubts his or her level of competence.

The ego-involved athlete is more concerned with his or her ability relative to others (Nicholls, 1984, 1989; Roberts, 1992). Superior ability for the ego-involved individual is demonstrated when the performance of others is exceeded. In the short-term, it is expected that positive achievement patterns will be associated with ego involvement but only when the athlete's confidence is high. Achievement goal theory (Nicholls, 1989) predicts, however, that perceptions of high competence are often at risk when ego goals prevail. This is because perceived ability is externally referenced and dependent on the performance of others. If the ego-involved young athlete starts to question his or her ability to adequately meet performance demands, he or she is more likely to reduce persistence and avoid the challenge at hand (Nicholls, 1989; Roberts, 1992).

Goal Orientations

As the childhood years start to wane, whether a youth sport participant is task- and/or ego-involved is largely influenced by individual differences in goal orientations and situational factors (Treasure et al., 2001). To this end, older children and adolescents will differ in which conception of ability they emphasize and in their personal criteria for "successful" sport achievement.

With respect to individual differences in goal orientations, Nicholls (1989) first proposed that people vary in the tendency to be task- and/or ego-involved in achievement settings. These dispositions are labeled task and ego orientation, respectively. Research from both the educational and sport domains supports the contention that these two goal orientations are not bipolar but rather orthogonal (Duda, 1996). That is, children can be high or low in both ego and task orientations as well as either high in one of the goal dimensions and low in the other. It is proposed that dispositional goal orientations are developed through childhood socialization processes and represent differential "interpretive lenses" by which individuals process and respond to achievement situations.

Motivational Climate

Besides individual differences in goal orientations, goal perspective theory suggests that other elements influence the individual's degree of and fluctuation in task or ego involvement. One important factor influencing goal involvement is the situation at hand (Nicholls, 1989). The achievement goal literature highlights the fact that student/athlete motivation occurs within a social context. How individuals give meaning to their experiences in a particular setting is largely dependent on both the expectations of the individual, their prior experience (Maehr, 1984), and the situational goals deemed to be emphasized by significant others in that context (Ames, 1992). With respect to the latter element, the social contexts or "motivational climates" surrounding young athletes can vary in the degree to which they are task- and/or ego-involving.

Research in the educational domain (Ames and Archer, 1988) indicates that a person is more likely to invest in and adopt adaptive achievement strategies in mastery-oriented or task-involving environments. These are situations in which the emphasis is on learning and developing new skills rather than interpersonal evaluation. On the other hand, maladaptive achievement strategies and motivational problems tend to mark predominantly performance-oriented or ego-involving climates. In these contexts, the criteria of success emphasized revolve around social comparison and normative feedback.

The link between task and ego-involving situational factors (i.e., variation in the motivational climate) to students' perceived causes of success and failure, perceptions of ability, reasons for participation, and indicators of the quality of experience has received considerable attention in the educational domain (e.g., Ames and Archer, 1988; Nicholls, Cheung, Lauer, and Patashnick, 1989). Research in the arena of sport has replicated and extended the findings from many of these classroom-based studies. The following section presents some of the results from this body of research and highlights what appear to be the implications of the motivational climate for the achievement striving and physical and mental health of young athletes.

Influence of significant others on motivational climate. Maehr (1983), an educational psychologist, emphasised the importance of studying contexts in which both the authority structure and reward system is adult-defined. Similarly, researchers in the sport domain have highlighted the relevance of considering the role of adult significant others (such as coaches and parents) when explaining the achievement behaviors of young sport participants (Brustad, 1992; Duda, 1987). In short, the domains of sport and education are environments in which evaluation, recognition, and organizational practices of adult figures and athletes'/students' motivation for learning and participation are often intertwined.

Reflecting the motivational significance of the motivational climate operating in sport, studies have shown a strong association between athletes' goal orientations and the situational goal structure created by his or her coach, physical education teacher, and parents (Duda and Hom, 1993; Papaioannou, 1994; Seifriz, Duda, and Chi, 1992; White, 1996). For example, in terms of potential parental influence, Ebbeck and Becker (1994) explored the extent to which perceived parental goal orientations predicted the goal orientations of youth sport participants ranging in age from 10 to 14 years. Results indicated that the task and ego orientations of the athletes were related to the degree to which they perceived their parents endorsed learning and effort or normative comparisons, respectively. Consistent with the results of Ebbeck and Becker (1994), White (1996) found that the goal orientations of young female athletes attending a volleyball training camp were linked to the underlying strategies the individual believed his or her parent used to judge ability and success. Specifically, girls who perceived their parents focused on learning/enjoyment tended to endorse task goals whereas young athletes who perceived their parents valued success without effort were more likely to exhibit stronger ego orientations. Other researchers have reported like findings in similarly aged sport participants (Duda and Hom, 1993; Duda, Bernadot, and Kim, in press).

Measurement of motivational climate. In any situation that could be potentially beneficial or detrimental to a child, the first question we should pose is "how does the child perceive this situation," and secondly, "are these perceptions facilitative or debilitative?" Ames and Archer (1988) were the first to address these questions and developed a measure which tapped into the perceived situational goal structures operating in the educational domain. Results provided evidence for the existence of two predominant motivational climates, specifically a mastery-oriented (or task-involving) environment and a performance-oriented (or ego-involving) environment.

Based on this initial work, Seifriz et al. (1992) developed the Perceived Motivational Climate in Sport Questionnaire (PMCSQ) designed to assess athletes' perceptions of the situational goal structures created by the coach in the sport environment. Similar to the work of Ames and Archer (1988), two major motivational climates were identified, namely a task-involving climate and an ego-involving climate. An ego-involving environment was characterized as one in which mistakes were punished, the better players received more encouragement and rewards, and there was support for intra-team rivalry. Conversely, perceptions of a task-involving climate stemmed from the view that each team member was a valuable contributor and that the coach placed emphasis on effort and improvement.

Based on Ames' (1992) contention that the motivational climate is a composite of several underlying dimensions, Newton, Duda, and Yin (2000) revised and extended the original PMCSQ and developed the Perceived Motivational Climate in Sport Questionnaire-2 (PMCSQ-2). This instrument comprises two over-riding perceived task and ego climate scales and several subscales tapping specific facets of a task-involving and ego-involving atmosphere. Conceptually similar to the climate dimensions proposed by Seifriz et al. (1992), the structures undergirding perceptions of task involvement in the PMCSQ-2 include the coach's recognition of effort/improvement and the view that each team member has a role to play on the team. Grounded in the literature linking cooperation and cohesion with an emphasis on task goals (Chambliss, 1989; Duda and Nicholls, 1992), items capturing the coach's encouragement of cooperation between teammates were also incorporated as measures of perceived task-involvement. Conversely, the subscales underlying the ego climate dimension consisted of Intra-Team Member Rivalry, Unequal Recognition and Punishment for Mistakes. Past research has provided evidence for the validity and reliability of the PMCSQ and the PMCSQ-2 (Duda and Whitehead, 1998: Newton et al., 2000).

In addition to teachers and coaches, primary caregivers also have the potential to influence the criteria used by young athletes to evaluate success and failure. By emphasizing certain cues and rewards, parents can create a motivational climate for their children that is either more or less task- and/or ego-involving. The Parent-Initiated Motivational Climate Questionnaire (PIMCQ) (White, Duda, and Hart 1992) was developed to assess young athletes' perceptions of the goal structures operating in their home environment. More specifically, the PIMCQ measures the child's perceptions of the value his/her parents' place on various processes and outcomes associated with learning a new physical skill (and, therefore, does not refer to the sporting context specifically). The two subscales of the PIMCQ assess the degree to which the athlete perceives the motivational environment created by their significant others as either task- or ego-involving. White and colleagues (1992) found that boys, more than girls, felt their parents were supportive of achieving success without effort (a facet of an ego-involving climate). Girls tended to believe that their parents valued and reinforced learning new skills (an aspect of a task-involving climate) more than boys. Further, girls, in contrast to boys, were less likely to view their parents as a presence that increased their concern over making mistakes (which is a dimension of an ego-involving environment). The PIMCQ was later revised to form the PIMCQ-2 (White, 1996). The newly revised measure includes items assessing whether the child perceived enjoying learning a physical activity as valued by his or her parents.

Motivational Climate and Indices of Motivation and Adjustment

Enjoyment/Intrinsic Motivation

Enjoyment has been identified as integral to motivation in youth sports (Scanlan, Carpenter, Lobel, and Simons, 1993). In earlier descriptive research, children identified "having fun" as a key reason for participation in sport whereas *lack of* enjoyment was linked to dropping out from athletic activities (Brustad, 1993; Weiss and Petlichkoff, 1989). When sport is viewed as enjoyable, it becomes valuable to the individual and promotes intrinsic interest for the task at hand (Roberts et al., 1997).

The sport literature, in general, has revealed a positive association between reported enjoyment and participants' degree of task orientation. (Duda, 1992; Duda and Hall, 2001). With respect to the correlates to the perceived motivational climate specifically, Seifriz and colleagues (1992) found high school male basketball players who perceived their coach to be creating a task-involving environment to express greater enjoyment of their sport. This association held regardless of the team's won-lost record. In a study by Newton and Duda (1999), perceptions of a task-involving climate (i.e., an emphasis on cooperative learning and effort/improvement, specifically) were positively linked to enjoyment and interest among a sample of 385 female volleyball players (*M* age = 15.2 years).

When a young athlete is intrinsically motivated, she participates in sport because she enjoys the sport and wants to be involved. It is purported by Ryan and Deci (2000) that "perhaps no single phenomena reflects the positive potential of human nature as much as intrinsic motivation" (p. 70). To be intrinsically motivated describes the individual who seeks out new experiences, challenges, and endeavors to learn and expand his or her current capabilities. In essence, intrinsic motivation is fundamental to positive and adaptive motivational striving.

Ryan and Deci (2000) suggest that the enhancement of intrinsic motivation requires certain supportive social and environmental factors. In their Self-Determination Theory (Deci and Ryan, 1985), they propose that conditions which meet the individual's fundamental needs for competence, autonomy, and relatedness lead to higher levels of intrinsic motivation. The reverse is assumed to be true for contextual factors that do not satisfy these three needs.

So, what are the expected links between meeting the needs for competence, autonomy, and relatedness and task and ego goals? Duda, Chi, Newton, Walling, and Catley (1995) pointed out that an emphasis on ego goals, which entail a normatively-defined criterion for success, means that perceptions of ability will inevitably be challenged. Perceived ability is held to be more resilient when the focus is on task goals. In terms of fostering feelings of autonomy, the criteria underlying success are more within the athlete's personal volition when he or she is task-involved. When one is ego-involved, a sense of satisfaction with achievement is dependent on what others do and how hard they tried and not primarily on one's own performance and exerted effort. It is difficult, if often not impossible, to control the behavior of other people! Finally, as mentioned above, past work has revealed an interdependence between task goals (whether dispositional or situationally-emphasized) and the salience of cooperation in sport (e.g., Duda and Nicholls, 1992). It is much easier to feel related to others in a cooperative environment. In contrast, when athletes are ego-involved, other people (whether teammates or opponents) are there as standards of comparison rather than sources of collaboration. Further, considering particular attributes of an ego-involving environment, it is hard to envision how a rivalrous and punitive setting that exacerbates ability differences between athletes can promote a sense of relatedness.

From an achievement goal perspective, then, it makes sense that task goals are expected to foster intrinsic interest whereas ego goals can undermine intrinsic motivation. As pointed out by Nicholls (1989), the activity can be considered an end in itself when athletes are task-involved. When someone is focused on ego goals, however, the athlete's goal directed behavior is viewed as simply a means to an end, namely the demonstration of superior ability (Nicholls, 1989).

Endemic to the self-determination framework (Deci and Ryan, 1985; Ryan and Deci, 2000) is the assumption that there are different types of motivations that vary along a self-determination continuum. At the least self-determined extreme of the continuum is a type of motivation identified as amotivation. This term describes athletes who believe their behaviors are the result of forces beyond their control. That is, they do not perceive contingencies between their actions and consequent outcomes. Children who are amotivated are probably the most likely to encounter motivational problems as they see no sense of purpose to their actions.

Next on the continuum are three types of extrinsic motivation, namely external regulation, introjected regulation, and identified regulation. External regulation refers to behaviors that are tied to external rewards and constraints. In sport, the classic example of an externally regulated young athlete is one who participates because he/she is enamoured with trophies, the recognition following success, etc. Introjected regulation refers to behaviors that are the result of self-imposed "shoulds." The young competitor who engages in sport because he thinks he "has to" and would feel guilty if he doesn't would exemplify this motivation type. Identified regulation occurs when the values of the athlete influence his or her behavior and the execution of an action is the result of choice. However, when motivated in this way, the athlete decides to engage in the activity but doesn't really enjoy the activity for its own sake. Lastly, the most self-determined type of motivation on the continuum is intrinsic motivation. In this instance, the athlete pursues sport based on his or her inherent interest in and love of the activity rather than on external rewards or other or self-imposed regulations and constraints.

Research in the physical domain suggests that the athlete/student is likely to feel more self-determined in contexts perceived as predominantly task-involving. For example, in their study of adolescent male basketball players, Seifriz and colleagues

(1992) found that perceptions of a task-involving atmosphere on the team corresponded to greater intrinsic motivation. In a physical education setting, Curry et al. (1996) assessed the influence of the motivational climate on the level of interest young girls expressed in physical education classes. Perceptions of a mastery climate were positively associated with intrinsic interest. In support of these findings, Digelidis and Papaioannou (1999) studied the interrelation between age, intrinsic motivation and perceived motivational climate in young students participating in Greek physical education classes. Results revealed that for the older students, viewing the physical education classes as less task-involving related to diminished intrinsic motivation.

Treasure, Standage, and Lochbaum (1999) examined the relation between the motivational climate and types of motivation (along the self-determination continuum) in elite male youth soccer players (M age = 16.3 years). Climates which were deemed high in their task-involving features and low in their ego-involving characteristics were positively associated with intrinsic motivation and identified regulation and negatively related to external regulation and amotivation. Climates that were seen to be highly ego-involving, however, were coupled with greater reported external regulation and amotivation by this sample of young athletes. These results support the tenets of achievement goal theory and self-determination theory and suggest that self-determination is more likely to germinate and grow when the child athlete perceives the atmosphere manifested by the coach as conducive to task involvement.

Beliefs about the Causes of Success

A substantial number of sport studies have revealed a logical interdependency between the emphasis placed on task and ego goals and athletes' views about what leads to success in sport. In terms of dispositional goals, specifically, task orientation has been positively associated with the beliefs that cooperation and hard work are integral to success, whereas ego orientation has been linked to the view that success is achieved through the possession of superior ability (Duda, Fox, Biddle, and Armstrong, 1992; Hom, Duda, and Miller, 1993; Treasure and Roberts, 1994). Similar patterns have been found between perceptions of the motivational climate and beliefs regarding the determinants of sport success (Seifriz et al., 1992; Treasure, 1997). For example, in a study examining the link between perceptions of the situational goal structure and beliefs about success in young female basketball players (M age = 14.01 years), Treasure and Roberts (1998) found a positive association between perceptions of a task-involving climate and the belief that effort is integral to success. In contrast, participants who perceived the climate as more ego-involving were more likely to endorse the beliefs that ability and deceptive tactics are viable antecedents to success.

Believing that possessing high ability is central to success does not necessarily precipitate motivational difficulties as long as the athlete believes he or she can demonstrate superior competence. For those young athletes who hold such a belief system, perform poorly, and perceive the climate as ego-involving, maladaptive motivational problems may ensue. For example, such children may try to avoid the demonstration of low ability by choosing tasks that are very easy (so success, although not especially meaningful and beneficial to skill development, is almost guaranteed) or much too difficult (so there is an "excuse" for failing), giving up on the task, or resorting to cheating behaviors or more external means to succeed (Dweck, 1986; Dweck and Leggett, 1988).

Beliefs about the Purposes of Sport

One of the perpetuating myths surrounding participation in sport is that sport builds "character" via the development of sportspersonship. To qualify this faulty assumption, one should ask, what type of "character" do we hope sport will develop in children? Achievement goal theory provides a starting point by which we can address this question. The literature suggests that achievement goals are associated with athletes' views on the wider purposes of sport engagement (Roberts et al., 1997). Research involving children and adolescent sport participants (Duda, 1989; Ommundsen and Roberts, 1999; Treasure and Roberts, 1994) indicates that task orientation is associated with the belief that the purpose of sport is to promote good citizenship and promote the merits of hard work and cooperation. Ego orientation is linked to the beliefs that the function of sport is to increase one's popularity, self-esteem, and competitive nature (Duda, 1989) as well as to teach deceptive tactics (Treasure and Roberts, in press).

This body of research suggests that the "character" development of the predominantly ego-oriented youngster may be distinctly different to that of the largely task-oriented child. The former young athlete appears to mostly adopt an "what's in it for me?" approach to physical activity participation (Duda, 1996), whereas the latter young sport participant seems likely to ask "how will participating in this physical activity develop my physical, mental, and social skills?"

Although only a paucity of studies have examined the relation between perceptions of the motivational climate and athletes' views about what sport should do, studies to date are consistent with the theoretical tenets of achievement goal theory (Nicholls, 1989) and earlier work on the correlates of goal orientations (Duda, 1989). Ommundsen, Roberts, and Kavussanu (1998), in their study of Norwegian university students participating in team sports, found perceptions of a task-involving situational goal structure to be associated with the belief that sport is important for the development of lifetime skills. In contrast, perceptions of an ego-involving climate were linked to viewing sport as a way of increasing social status. Similarly, in a study involving 148 student athletes, Ommundsen and Roberts (1999) found that perceiving the motivational climate as strongly ego-involving was negatively associated with the belief that sport should foster prosocial attitudes and behaviors (e.g., "sport helps me cooperate with others"). Athletes who viewed the environment created by the coach as both high in its task-involving features as well as high in ego-involving attributes were more likely to believe that sport should help to develop a sense of social responsibility and provide them with lifetime skills. When discussing the applied implications of these results, Ommundsen and Roberts (1999) state, "Although it may be difficult to intervene to change the dispositional goals of action of the athlete, the criteria of success and failure inherent in the sport context are firmly in the hands of the coach" (p. 396). All in all, the results to date suggest that by creating a climate that is task-involving, coaches can possibly contribute to characteristics and values among young athletes that are respected both in the domain of sport and in the wider society.

Perceived Competence

Perceived competence (Harter, 1978, 1981), *perceived ability* (Dweck, 1986, Nicholls, 1984, 1989), and *self-efficacy* (Bandura, 1977, 1986) are all terms which, loosely defined, refer to the individual's beliefs in his or her capabilities to successfully meet situational performance demands (McAuley, 1992). Contemporary research in the sport domain has linked the competence judgements of children with emotions such as enjoyment and anxiety, as well as motivation to adhere to physical activity (Weiss, Ebbeck, and Horn, 1997). Given the implications of a child's perceived competence for long-term involvement in sport and the quality of that experience, it is important to understand the processes by which a young athlete assesses his or her physical ability. Specifically, what are the cues or sources of information incorporated into the child's judgement of his or her ability in the physical domain?

Harter's (1978, 1981) competence motivation theory suggests that the child applies both internal and external evaluation processes to interpret goal directed behavior and its subsequent outcomes. Internal evaluation refers to self-referenced criteria, such as degree of effort exerted. External evaluation is reflected in the emphasis placed on feedback and reinforcement communicated by significant others (e.g., parents), normative comparisons with peers, and by objective performance feedback.

Perceptions of the motivational climate can enhance or contribute to decrements in perceptions of ability (Newton and Duda, 1999) via orienting athletes toward internal and/or external sources of competence information. As alluded to above, we would expect perceptions of a task-involving climate to be positively associated with perceived competence. Due to its comparative and more outcome-oriented nature, a perceived ego-involving motivational environment would be predicted to hold negative implications for perceptions of ability among young athletes.

Indirect support for these contentions was provided in a study by Weiss et al. (1997). Children involved in a sport camp were classified (via statistical analyses) into one of four profiles based on their self-perceptions and sources of physical competence information. Examination of the four profiles highlighted two of the profile groups as at-risk (defined as those with negative psychological characteristics). In one of the groups, pregame anxiety was rated the most consequential source of competence information, whereas parental evaluation was identified as a moderately important source of information. Not surprisingly, this group of children (ages 8 to 9 years) reported the highest levels of pre-game anxiety and expressed low perceived physical competence. The other "at risk" group of children were older (ages

10 to 13 years). For them, social comparison/evaluation (reflective of ego involvement) was judged the most significant source of competence information. This group of athletes scored high in competitive trait anxiety, low in self-esteem, and low in perceived physical competence. It is important to note that neither of these two profile groups rated self-referenced or more task-involved criteria (such as self-improvement and personal effort) as valuable sources of information when assessing their physical competence. Thus, based on achievement goal theory, we would expect that these children would be prone to questioning their competence and other motivational struggles.

More direct support for the expected relations between perceptions of the motivational climate and perceived ability was garnered by Treasure (1997) and Causgrove-Dunn (2000). In the latter investigation, the correspondence between ratings of the task- and ego-involving aspects of the sport environment and perceived competence was examined among 65 children with movement difficulties (M age = 11.01 years). Findings indicated that children reported higher perceptions of ability when the environment was deemed more task- rather than ego-involving. In his study of young children learning soccer skills, Treasure (1997) reported parallel results.

This line of research suggests that children who, because of the situationally-emphasized goal structures operating on their team, approach achievement settings with a view that success stems from outperforming others may eventually develop low perceptions of competence. The child who judges her ability on the basis of demonstrating superiority could be considered "ripe" for subsequent defeat and failure. In contrast, because it dims the spotlight on ability differences and allows for more and primarily internally-referenced sources of competence (and success) information, a task-involving environment should fuel a sense of adequate (and, hopefully, increasing) competence among children.

Negative Affect/Anxiety

The sport literature suggests that athletes are more likely to experience competitive anxiety when they perceive the demands of the activity surpass their abilities to meet those demands *and* the consequences of not meeting the demands is deemed consequential. In Smith and his colleagues' (1996, this volume) conceptual model of sport performance anxiety, individual differences are held to play a critical role in such appraisals. From an achievement goal perspective, it is argued that individual differences in goal orientations are relevant to athletes' interpretations of a competitive situation and his or her ensuing affective response (Duda and Hall, 2001). For example, Roberts (1986) argues that athletes predisposed to ego goal orientations are primarily concerned with social comparisons and the adequacy of their competence. As such, these individuals are more likely to experience negative affect and fear of failure if they are unable to demonstrate superior ability in a competitive situation. On the other hand, athletes who tend to endorse task goals are more likely to emphasize personal improvement and mastery. Athletes who view success in this manner are not as threatened by the prospect of normative comparisons and should be less prone to perceiving that the demands of the activity outweigh their abilities. Consequently, task-involved athletes should be less likely to experience debilitating anxiety in difficult competitive circumstances.

Smith et al.'s (1996, this volume) multidimensional model of anxiety proposes that along with individual difference factors, athletes' appraisal processes are also influenced by situational factors. The achievement goal literature suggests that one critical situational factor is the motivational environment seen to be operating on a sport team (Duda and Hall, 2001). Walling, Duda, and Chi (1993), in their study involving young adolescent athletes, examined the link between reported degree of worry while participating in sport and perceptions of the motivational climate created by the coach. Results indicated that perceptions of a task-involving atmosphere were negatively related to performance worry. The reverse was true for perceptions of an ego-involving climate.

The expectations and critical responses of coaches have previously been implicated in the literature as predictors of young athletes' stress responses (Scanlan and Lewthwaite, 1984). Achievement goal research elaborates on this process of social influence and reinforces the significance of coaches to athletes' affective responses in the sport milieu. Treasure and Roberts (1995) suggest that the motivational climate can potentially influence the meaning of success for the athlete so that interpersonal evaluation rather than personal mastery are fundamental to the individual's achievement goals. Other researchers (Covington, 1992; Gould, Petlichkoff, and Weinberg, 1984) support this view, proposing that irrespective of the athlete's dispositional goal orientation, pronounced environmental factors potentially can elicit a range of responses both facilitative and debilitative in nature. The potential overriding implications of the motivational climate for both positive and negative affect are highlighted by Ntoumanis and Biddle (1999) who suggest that situational factors may "lead (even) task-oriented people to experience less positive affect than would normally be expected" (p. 329).

Self-Esteem and Body Image

Self-esteem is defined as individuals' emotional self-evaluative approval or disapproval of the way in which they view themselves (Harter, 1993). Body image has been equated to individuals' personal perceptions of and satisfaction with their body shape and size (Wardle and Foley, 1989). From a developmental perspective, positive feelings about the self and one's body have been argued to promote behavioural adaptation (Kaplan, 1980), and psychological well-being and stability (Harter, 1993). When self-esteem and body image are negative, young athletes mental and physical health may be at risk.

Research by Duda and colleagues (Duda et al., in press) involving young gymnasts is probably one of the few existing studies to examine the relation between perceptions of motivational climate and both self-esteem and body image. Pre-elite gymnasts who were members of the U.S. Talent Opportunity Program (TOP) National Artistic

Gymnastics Team (9 to 11 years old) and gymnasts competing at the international level (*M* age = 15.5 years) participated in this investigation. Results indicated that self-esteem and body esteem were positively associated with a perceived task-involving atmosphere and negatively predicted by a perceived ego-involving goal structure in the gym. In a summer sports program operating for disadvantaged youths (age range 10 to 16 years), Walker, Roberts, and Harnisch (1998) found that children who perceived the climate as task-involving also reported higher levels of self-esteem. Conversely, perceptions of an ego-involving climate were coupled with lower self-esteem.

Altering the Motivational Climate

Despite research indicating the substantial influence of coaches/teachers and parents on the motivational processes of children, limited work in the sport domain has examined the effectiveness of altering the motivational climate they create. Epstein (1988, 1989) proposed the acronym *TARGET* to describe a variety of structural features in the achievement context relevant to the understanding of motivational processes. These structures include the *T*ask, *A*uthority, *R*eward, *G*rouping, *E*valuation, and *T*iming facets of the situation (for a definition of each structure, see Table 17.1). The TARGET framework provides a means of examining the implications of task design, use of authority, recognition, implementation of group structure, evaluation procedures, and performance timetables on a wide range of motivational processes. The framework also highlights the essential point that the environments created for students, athletes, and others are multi-dimensional. Extending the work of Epstein (1988, 1989), Ames (1992) proposed that the manipulation of the different (but most likely interrelated) structural "building blocks" influence the degree to which children perceive the environment surrounding them as more or less ego-or task-involving.

Early work in the educational domain successfully illustrated that the motivational climate could be manipulated in the classroom (Ames, 1992). Continuing this line of research in the sport domain, Theeboom, De Knop, and Weiss (1995) assigned children attending a summer sports program to one of two conditions (i.e., a task-involving climate versus an ego-involving climate). In creating the two divergent environments, Theeboom and colleagues drew upon the TARGET taxonomy. Effects of variations in the motivational climate on children's motivation, enjoyment, physical competence, and motor skill development were analyzed. The first promising finding of this investigation was the observation that the sport climate could be successfully modified. Further, consistent with achievement goal theory, participants in the task-involving program expressed greater enjoyment, and they demonstrated better motor skills than children assigned to the ego-involving condition. Although quantitative analysis did not show any significant difference between the groups with respect to perceived competence and intrinsic motivation, Theeboom et al. (1995) reported that their qualitative analyses of interviews taken at the end of each lesson revealed a higher level of intrinsic motivation in the task-involved group.

Table 17.1 An Overview of the TARGET Structures and Strategies for Fostering Task Involvement in Sport

TARGET Structure	Strategies	Example	Potential Outcomes
Task. What the child is asked to do. Encompasses the demands of the task and how meaningful it is for the child.	Provide varying, optimally challenging training programs and practice/competitive goals that are personally meaningful.	In gymnastics, the coach works with the athletes to set their own short-term performance goals for each apparatus. The coach has the athletes engage in drills that are challenging/fun.	Athlete will begin to understand the process involved in learning complex skills. It is thought that perceptions of skill development should positively influence the child's confidence in his or her ability.
Authority. The degree to which the child partici- pates in deci- sion making processes.	Allow the child to participate in decision-making concerning aims and regulations that affect his/her actions.	The gymnast is encouraged to maintain a training log. Decisions regarding strategies for improving performance are shared between coach and athlete.	Athletes' perceptions of competence and personal control should be maximized when they "have a say" in their sport participation.
Recognition. Rewards and incentives for progress and achieve- ment.	Recognition is given one-on-one for exerted effort, performance improvement and learning from mistakes.	After training, the coach privately speaks to the gymnast and recognizes her hard work in learning a difficult floor routine.	Recognition of progress foster feelings of intrinsic satisfaction and continued interest in participation. Rewards less likely to become extrinsic sources of motivation and social comparisons between athletes reduced.

Table 17.1 (cont.)

Grouping. The manner is which individuals are grouped during training.	Criteria for grouping include differences among athletes that may facilitate learning and cooperation.	Among gymnasts of varying skill levels, set training times are established in which the athletes work together in small groups of mixed ability. Cooperation is encouraged and some group goals set.	Athletes perceive greater cooperation amongst team-mates, potentially fostering greater enjoyment and persistence. Cohesion can be increased and social competence enhanced.
Evaluation. Nature of and criteria underlying assessment.	The athlete is evaluated by the coach on the basis of progress and exerted effort. The athlete is involved in his or her self-evaluation.	After performing his or her floor routine, the gymnast is asked to identify positive/negative aspects of the performance. Coach's evaluation standard stems from correct aspects of performance process and informational feedback given for incorrect aspects.	Evaluative systems that promote self-referenced evaluations facilitate task involvement and can enhance self-esteem, level of intrinsic interest and perceptions of ability.
Timing. The time limit placed on learning and performance outcomes.	Time allocations are flexible and accommodate the individual's own rate of skill development.	Two similarly aged gymnasts who are developing skills at different rates are given their own (different) short-term goals. In private, the coach works with each athlete in an individualized fashion.	Flexible rates of instruction based on differences in skill acquisition can improve the quality of the athlete's experience and foster perceptions of competence.

Based on the work of Ames (1990, 1992), Epstein, (1989), Grolnick and Ryan (1987), and Maehr (1984).

In a sample of young school children, Solomon (1996) created gender-specific juggling classes with either a task-involving or ego-involving goal structure. The results of the study showed that individuals in the task-involving lesson demonstrated greater persistence in learning difficult juggling tasks. Those children in the ego-involving class had less resolve on troublesome tasks and tended to attribute success to ability. In a similar manner, Papaioannou and Kouli (1999) instructed teachers of 10 physical education classes in junior high schools in Greece to change strategies employed while students engaged in volleyball drills. Results showed that students in the ego-involving physical education class reported greater somatic anxiety and less state self-confidence than in the task-involving climate. When compared to the task-involving class, the students in the ego-involving climate valued winning with minimum effort and perceived their classmates as more worried, less predisposed to learning, and more competitive. Furthermore, Papaioannou and Kouli (1999) found that perceptions of a task-involving climate were positively associated with dimensions of the flow state—namely, concentration, autotelic experience, and loss of self-consciousness (subscales from the Flow State Scale; Jackson and Marsh, 1996).

Results of these intervention studies suggest that through the use of a framework such as Epstein's (1988, 1989) TARGET taxonomy, it is possible for a coach or PE teacher to increase the saliency of certain goals and in doing so, create either a task-involving or ego-involving climate. The literature to date would suggest that developing an environment that promotes hard work, learning, and cooperation (i.e., is task-involving) is associated with adaptive achievement cognitions, affective responses, and behaviors. To this end, significant adults have the potential to positively impact the quantity and quality of the child's motivation in sport and other physical activity settings.

In Table 17.1, strategies for promoting a task-involving environment and specific examples of how such strategies might be employed in one exemplar sport (in this case, gymnastics) are provided. The potential outcomes of such manipulations of the different "building blocks" are also presented.

Future Directions

Although recent attention has been given to the efficacy of altering the motivational climate (Theeboom et al., 1995; Treasure and Roberts, 1995), in one respect, such work may be just ahead of itself. Duda (2001) has suggested that when considering interventions to modify the climate created by coaches (or physical education teachers), it is important to assess if the objective environment created by the coach corresponds with what children think their coaches/PE teachers are doing. Specifically, we need to ascertain the degree of congruency between the objective task- and ego-involving features of the climate with the perceived subjective task- and ego-involving situational cues. With this aim in mind, existing valid observational systems such as the Coaching Behavior Assessment System (Smith, Smoll, and Hunt, 1977) could be adapted to more carefully ascertain the task- and ego-involving behaviors of coaches (Chaumeton and Duda, 1988) and/or new observational assessment tools need to be developed.

Given that task and ego involvement can fluctuate throughout an activity, future research should also work towards developing a measurement of goal states for young athletes. In regard to the assessment of goal involvement, Duda and Whitehead (1998) suggest measuring a constellation of variables representative of task and ego processing and preoccupation. For example, goal states may be captured through the examination of variations in the child's focus of attention, concerns over his or her actions, self-awareness, perceived level of exertion and awareness of the presence of others while engaging in sport. Such a measure might prove beneficial to the prediction of youth sport participants' reactions to particular training sessions and competitive occasions.

More work is needed on the predicted interdependence between young athletes' goal orientations and their views of the motivational climate operating on their team (Dweck and Leggett, 1988; Newton and Duda, 1999; Treasure and Roberts, 1998). How do young athletes who are high and/or low in task and ego orientation respond to environments that are more or less task- and/or ego-involving?

Along these lines, we should also continue to explore the possible interactions between goal orientations and the subjective (and objective) motivational climate using cross-sectional as well as longitudinal research designs (Duda, 2001). We believe that in order to understand the "big picture" we need to get a sense of patterns of behavior such as persistence, effort, exertion, task choice, and performance outcomes *over time* (Duda, 2001). Endemic to achievement goal theory (Nicholls, 1989) is the quest for understanding long-term achievement striving rather than short-term successful performance outcomes. Moreover, as emphasized by Duda (2001), determining the influence of task and ego goals on young athletes' motivation would be limited if the influence of both goal orientations and the perceived motivational climate are not considered *and* there is no contemplation of indicators of well-being and moral functioning (i.e., we only take into account achievement outcomes).

Conclusion

We know that the saliency of the contextual goal structure can influence the way in which young children interpret situational cues. Perceptions of those situational cues will influence how young athletes approach achievement activities and the focus of their achievement-related concerns. Children who perceive the motivational climate as more task-involving than ego-involving appear more likely to hold adaptive beliefs about what causes success in sport and views about the purposes of sport as well as exhibit positive affective states, intrinsic motivation, and higher levels of self-esteem. In Table 17.2, these major findings are summarized and illustrative studies are cited. At the very least, this literature indicates how important adult "significant others" can be in the youth sport setting. The existing research grounded in achievement goal theory informs us that the goals significant others embrace do influence whether children's experiences in sport can be considered positive or negative. In other words, the youth sport setting (whether centered on the recreational participant or elite young athlete) is not inherently good or bad. The complexion of sport for young people seems to be dependent on psychological environment that is created.

Table 17.2   Children in Sport: Summary of Selected Studies on the Link Between Perceptions of the Motivational Climate and Achievement-Related Cognitions, Behaviors, and Affect Responses

Achievement patterns	When the climate is perceived as task involving...	When the climate is perceived as ego-involving...	Example Substantiating Research
Intrinsic Motivation	⇑ Emphasis is placed on improvement and working together enhancing intrinsic motivation.	⇓ Conducive to heightened tension, perceived pressure to outdo team mates linked to low levels of self determination.	Seifriz, Duda and Chi (1992)
Enjoyment in participation	⇑ Varying and challenging training programs increase enjoyment.	⇓ Pressures associated with social comparisons decrease enjoyment.	Theeboom, DeKnop and Weiss (1995)
Anxiety/worry	⇑ Not threatened by normative comparisons, less likely to experience worry.	⇓ Normative comparisons and concerns about ability increase anxiety.	Walling, Duda and Chi (1993)

Table 17.2 (cont.)

Satisfaction	⇑	Satisfaction derived from learning and mastery.	⇓ Satisfaction gained from out-performing others.	Treasure and Roberts (1998)
Self-Esteem	⇑	Perceptions of learning, mastery and adequate competence enhance self-esteem.	⇓ Contingent self worth. May result in deflated self-esteem.	Duda, Bernadot, and Kim (in press)
Beliefs about Success		Fosters the belief that hard work leads to success.	Fosters the belief that possessing ability leads to success.	Seifriz, Duda and Chi (1992)
Purposes of Sport Participation		Fosters the view that sport should develop social responsibility and life skills.	Fosters the view that sport should not promote co-operation with others.	Ommundsen and Roberts (1999)
Motor Skills	⇑	Promotes skill development.	⇓ Slower rate of skill development.	Theeboom, DeKnop and Weiss (1995)
Perceived Competence	⇑	Perceptions of ability self referenced.	⇓ Perceptions of ability based on normative comparisons.	Treasure (1997)
Flow	⇑	Facilitates concentration, autotelic experience and loss of self-consciousness.	Not linked to flow experiences.	Papaioannou and Kouli (1999)

Establishing and maintaining a task-involving climate may not be an easy feat. The amount of pressure placed on coaches from the athletes themselves, their parents, league administrators, the media, and communities/the society at large is widely recognized. Today words like *accountability* place coaches in a position where meeting certain performance criteria dictates funding (or whether they keep their jobs!) and consequent opportunities for the athletes. But, what about the coach's accountability regarding the welfare and development of young athletes? One compelling message of the achievement goal literature is that it is possible (and seemingly desirable) for coaches to create a micro-climate that counters the ego-involving messages that might be seen to smother a coach's best intentions regarding his or her athletes. Further, this line of work provides researchers and practitioners strategies for how we can foster the possible lifetime rewards that can be gained from participating in sport specifically and physical activity in general, among youngsters, regardless of their ability level.

References

Ames, C. (1992). Classrooms: Goals, structures, and student motivation. *Journal of Educational Psychology, 84*, 261–271.

Ames, C., and Archer, J. (1988). Achievement goals in the classroom: Students' learning strategies and motivation processes. *Journal of Educational Psychology, 80*, 260–267.

Bandura, A. (1977). Self-efficacy: Toward a unifying theory of behavioral change. *Psychological Review, 84*, 191–215.

Bandura, A. (1986). *Social foundations of thought and action: A social cognitive theory*. Englewood Cliffs, NJ: Prentice-Hall.

Brustad, R. J. (1992). Integrating socialization influences into the study of children's motivation in sport. *Journal of Sport and Exercise Psychology, 14*, 59–77.

Brustad, R. J. (1993). Youth in sport: Psychological considerations. In R. N. Singer, M. Murphy, and L. K. Tennant (Eds.), *Handbook of research on sport psychology* (pp. 695–717). New York: MacMillan.

Causgrove-Dunn, J. (2000). Goal orientations, perceptions of the motivational climate, and perceived competence of children with movement difficulties. *Applied Physical Activity Quarterly, 17*, 1–19.

Chambliss, D. (1989). The mundanity of excellence: An ethnographic report on stratification and Olympic swimmers. *Sociology Theory, 7*, 70–86.

Chaumeton, N. R., and Duda, J. L. (1988). Is it how you play the game or whether you win or lose?: The effect of competitive level and situation on coaching behaviors. *Journal of Sport Behavior, 11*, 157–173.

Covington, M. V. (1992). *Making the grade: A self-worth perspective on motivation and school reform*. Cambridge, UK: Cambridge University Press.

Curry, F., Biddle, S., Famose, J., Goudas, M., Sarrazin, P., and Durand, M. (1996). Personal and situational factors influencing intrinsic interest of adolescent girls in school physical education: A structural equation modelling analysis. *Educational Psychology, 16*, 305–315.

Deci, E. L., and Ryan, R. M. (1985). *Intrinsic motivation and self-determination in human behavior*. New York: Plenum.

Digelidis, A., and Papaioannou, A. (1999). Age-group differences in intrinsic motivation, goal orientations and perceptions of athletic competence, physical appearance and motivational climate in Greek physical education. *Scandinavian Journal of Medicine in Sports, 9*, 375–380.

Duda, J. L. (1987). Toward a developmental theory of children's motivation in sport. *Journal of Sport Psychology, 9*, 130–145.

Duda, J. L. (1989). The relationship between mastery and competitive orientation and the perceived purpose of sport among male and female high school athletes. *Journal of Sport and Exercise Psychology, 11*, 318–335.

Duda, J. L. (1992). Motivation in sport and exercise: Conceptual constraints and convergence. In G. C. Roberts (Ed.), *Motivation in sport and exercise* (pp. 57–91). Champaign, IL: Human Kinetics.

Duda, J. L. (1996). Maximizing motivation in sport and physical education among children and adolescents: The case for greater task involvement. *Quest, 48*, 290–302.

Duda, J. L. (2001). Achievement goal research in sport: Pushing the boundaries and clarifying some misunderstandings. In G. C. Roberts (Ed.), *Advances in Sport and Exercise Motivation* (pp. 129–182). Champaign, IL.: Human Kinetics.

Duda, J. L., Bernadot, D., and Kim, M-S. (in press). The relationship of the motivational climate to psychological and energy balance correlates of eating disorders in female gymnasts. *The Sport Psychologist*.

Duda, J. L., Chi, L., Newton, M., Walling, M. D., and Catley, D. (1995). Task and ego goal orientations and intrinsic motivation in sport. *International Journal of Sport Psychology, 26*, 40–63.

Duda, J. L., Fox, K. R., Biddle, S. J. H., and Armstrong, N. (1992). Children's achievement goals and beliefs about success in sport. *British Journal of Educational Psychology, 62*, 313–323.

Duda, J. L., and Hall, H. K. (2001). Achievement goal theory in sport: Recent extensions and future directions. In R. Singer, H. Hausenblas, and C. Janelle (Eds.), *Handbook of sport psychology* (2nd ed., pp. 417–443). New York: John Wiley and Sons.

Duda, J. L., and Hom, H. L. (1993). The interrelationships between children's and parent's goal orientations in sport. *Pediatric Exercise Science, 5*, 234–241.

Duda, J. L., and Nicholls, J. G. (1992). Dimensions of achievement motivation in schoolwork and sport. *Journal of Educational Psychology, 84*, 1–10.

Duda, J. L., and Whitehead, J. (1998). Measurement of goal perspectives in the physical domain. In J. L. Duda (Ed.), *Advances in sport and exercise psychology measurement* (pp. 21–48). Morgantown, WV: Fitness Information Technology, Inc.

Dweck, C. S. (1986). Motivational processes affecting learning. *American Psychologist, 41*, 1040–1048.

Dweck, C. S. (1999). *Self-theories and goals: Their role in motivation, personality, and development*. Philadelphia: Taylor and Francis.

Dweck, C. S., and Leggett, E. L. (1988). A social-cognitive approach to motivation and personality. *Psychological Review, 95*, 256–273.

Ebbeck, V., and Becker, S. L. (1994). Psychosocial predictors of goal orientations in youth soccer. *Research Quarterly for Exercise and Sport, 65*, 335–362.

Epstein, J. (1988). Effective schools or effective students? Dealing with diversity. In R. Haskins and B. MacRae (Eds.), *Policies for America's public schools* (pp. 89–126). Norwood, NJ: Ablex.

Epstein, J. (1989). Family structures and student's motivation: A developmental perspective. In C. Ames and R. Ames (Eds.), *Research on motivation in education* (Vol. 3, pp. 259–295). New York: Academic Press.

Fry, M. D., and Duda, J. L. (1997). A developmental examination of children's understanding of effort and ability in the physical and academic domains. *Research Quarterly for Exercise and Sport, 68*, 331–344.

Gould, D. R., Petlichkoff, L. M., and Weinberg, R. S. (1984). Antecedents of temporal changes in, and relationships between CSAI-2 components. *Journal of Sport Psychology, 6*, 289–304.

Harter, S. (1978). Effectance motivation reconsidered: Toward a developmental model. *Human Development, 21*, 34–64.

Harter, S. (1981). The development of competence motivation in the mastery of cognitive and physical skills: Is there a place for joy? In G. C. Roberts and D. M. Landers (Eds.), *Psychology of motor behavior and sport—1980* (pp. 3–29). Champaign, IL: Human Kinetics.

Harter, S. (1993). Causes and consequences of low self-esteem in children and adolescents. In R. F. Baumeister (Ed.), *Self-esteem: The puzzle of low self-regard*, (pp. 87–116). New York: Plenum.

Hom, H., Duda, J. L., and Miller, A. (1993). Correlates of goal orientations among young athletes. *Pediatric Exercise Science, 5*, 168–176.

Jackson, S. A., and Marsh, H. W. (1996). Development and validation of a scale to measure optimal experience: The Flow State Scale. *Journal of Sport and Exercise Psychology, 18*, 17–35.

Kaplan, H. (1980). *Deviant behavior in defense of self*. New York: Academic Press.

Maehr, M. L. (1983). On doing well in science. Why Johnny no longer excels; why Sarah never did. In S. G. Paris, G. M. Olson, and H. W. Stevenson (Eds.), *Learning and motivation in the classroom*. Hillsdale, NJ: Lawrence Erlbaum and Associates.

Maehr, M. L. (1984). Meaning and motivation: Toward a theory of personal investment. In R. Ames and C. Ames (Eds.), *Research on motivation in education: Student motivation* (Vol. 1, pp. 115–144). New York: Academic Press.

McAuley, E. (1992). Understanding exercise behavior: A self-efficacy perspective. In G. C. Roberts (Ed.), *Motivation in sport and exercise* (pp. 107–127). Champaign, IL: Human Kinetics.

Newton, M., and Duda, J. L. (1999). The interaction of motivational climate, dispositional goal orientations, and perceived ability in predicting indices of motivation. *International Journal of Sport Psychology, 30*, 63–82.

Newton, M., Duda, J. L., and Yin, Z. (2000). Examination of the psychometric properties of the Perceived Motivational Climate in Sport Questionnaire-2 in a sample of female athletes. *Journal of Sports Sciences, 18*, 1–16.

Nicholls, J. G. (1984). Achievement motivation: Conception of ability, subjective experience, mastery choice, and performance. *Psychological Review, 91*, 328–346.

Nicholls, J. G. (1989). *The competitive ethos and democratic education*. Cambidge, MA: Harvard University Press.

Nicholls, J. G., Cheung, P. C., Lauer, J., and Patashnick, M. (1988). Individual differences in academic motivation: Perceived ability, goals, beliefs and values. *Learning and Individual Differences, 1*, 63–84.

Nicholls, J. G., and Miller, A. T. (1984). Development and its discontents: The differentiation of the concept of ability. In J. Nicholls (Ed.), *Advances in motivation and achievement: Vol. 3. The development of achievement motivation* (pp. 185–218). Greenwich, CT: JAI Press.

Ntoumanis, N., and Biddle S. J. H. (1999). Affect and achievement goals in physical activity: A meta-analysis. *Scandinavian Journal of Medicine and Science in Sports, 6*, 46–56.

Ommundsen, Y., and Roberts, G. C. (1999). Effect of motivational climate profiles on motivational indices in team sport. *Scandinavian Journal of Medicine and Science in Sports, 9*, 389–397.

Ommundsen, Y., Roberts, G. C., and Kavussanu, M. (1998). Perceived motivational climate and cognitive and affective correlates among Norwegian athletes. *Journal of Sports Sciences, 16*, 153–164.

Papaioannou, A. (1994). The development of a questionnaire to measure achievement orientations in physical education. *Research Quarterly for Exercise and Sport, 65*, 11–20.

Papaioannou, A., and Kouli, O. (1999). The effect of task structure, perceived motivational climate and goal orientations on students' task involvement and anxiety. *Journal of Applied Sport Psychology, 11*, 51–71.

Roberts, G. C. (1986). The perception of stress: A potential source and its development. In M. R. Weiss and D. R. Gould (Eds.), *Sport for children and youths* (pp. 119–126). Champaign, IL: Human Kinetics.

Roberts, G. C. (1992). Motivation in sport and exercise: Conceptual constraints and convergence. In G. C. Roberts (Ed.), *Motivation in sport and exercise* (pp. 3–30). Champaign, IL: Human Kinetics.

Roberts, G. C., Treasure, D. C., and Kavussanu, M. (1997). Motivation in physical activity contexts: An achievement goal perspective. In M. L. Maehr and P. R. Pintrich (Eds.), *Advances in motivation and achievement (Vol. 10)* (pp. 413–447). Greenwich, CT: JAI.

Ryan, E. L., and Deci, R. M. (2000). Self-Determination Theory and the facilitation of intrinsic motivation, social development, and well-being. *American Psychologist, 55,* 68–78.

Seifriz, J. J., Duda, J. L., and Chi, L. (1992). The relationship of perceived motivational climate to intrinsic motivation and beliefs about success in basketball. *Journal of Sport and Exercise Psychology, 14,* 375–391.

Scanlan, T. K., Carpenter, P. J., Lobel, M., Simons, J. P. (1993). Sources of enjoyment for youth sport athletes. *Pediatric Exercise Science,* 275–285.

Scanlan, T. K., and Lewthwaite, R. (1984) Social psychological aspects of competition for male youth sport participants: I. Predictors of competitive stress. *Journal of Sport Psychology, 6,* 208–226.

Smith, R. E. (1996). Performance anxiety, cognitive interference, and concentration enhancement strategies in sports. In I. G. Sarason, G. R. Pierce, and B. R. Sarason (Eds.), *Cognitive interference: Theories, methods, and findings* (pp. 261–283). Mahwah, NJ: Erlbaum.

Smith, R. E., Smoll, F. L., and Hunt, E. B. (1977). A system for the behavioral assessment of athletic coaches. *Research Quarterly, 48,* 401–407.

Smith, R. E., Smoll, F. L., and Passer, M. W. (2002). Sport performance anxiety in young athletes. In F. L. Smoll and R. E. Smith (Eds.), *Children and youth in sport: A biopsychosocial perspective* (2nd ed., pp. 501–536). Dubuque, IA: Kendall/Hunt.

Solmon, M. A. (1996). Impact of motivational climate on students' behaviors and perceptions in a physical education setting. *Journal of Educational Psychology, 88,* 731–738.

Theeboom, M., De Knop, P., and Weiss, M. (1995). Motivational climate, psychological responses and motor skill development in children's sport: A field-based intervention study. *Journal of Sport and Exercise Psychology, 3,* 294–311.

Treasure, D. C. (1997). Perceptions of the motivational climate and elementary school children's cognitive and affective responses. *Journal of Sport and Exercise Psychology, 19,* 278–290.

Treasure, D. C., Duda, J. L., Hall, H. K., Roberts, G. C., Ames, C., and Maehr, M. L. (2001). Clarifying misconceptions and misrepresentations in achievement goal research in sport: A response to Harwood, Hardy, and Swain. *Journal of Sport and Exercise Psychology, 23,* 317–329.

Treasure, D. C., Standage, M., and Lochbaum, A. (1999, September). *Perceptions of the motivational climate and situational motivation in elite youth sport.* Paper presented at the annual meeting of the American Association of Applied Sport Psychology, Banff, Alberta, CA.

Treasure, D. C., and Roberts, G. C. (1994). Cognitive and affective concomitants of mastery and competitive goal orientations during the middle school years. *Journal of Sport and Exercise Psychology, 16*, 15–28.

Treasure, D. C., and Roberts, G. C. (1995). Applications of achievement goal theory to physical education: Implications for enhancing motivation. *Quest, 47*, 475–489.

Treasure, D. C., and Roberts, G. C. (1998). Relationship between adolescent females' achievement goal orientations, perceptions of the motivational climate, beliefs about success and sources of satisfaction in basketball. *International Journal of Sport Psychology, 29*, 211–230.

Treasure, D. C., and Roberts, G. C. (in press). Students' perceptions of the motivational climate, achievement beliefs and satisfaction in physical education. *Research Quarterly for Exercise and Sport.*

Walling, M. D., Duda, J. L., and Chi, L. (1993). The Perceived Motivational Climate in Sport Questionnaire: Construct and predictive validity. *Journal of Sport and Exercise Psychology, 15*, 172–183.

Wardle, J., and Foley, E. (1989). Body image: Stability and sensitivity of body satisfaction and body size estimation. *International Journal of Eating Disorders, 8*, 55–62.

Walker, B. W., Roberts, G. C., and Harnisch, D. (1998). Predicting self-esteem in a national sample of disadvantaged youths. *Journal of Sport and Exercise Psychology, S20.*

Weiss, M. R., and Petlichkoff, L. M. (1989). Children's motivation for participation in and withdrawal from sport: Identifying the missing links. *Pediatric Exercise Science, 1*, 195–211.

Weiss, M. R., Ebbeck, V., and Horn, T. S. (1997). Children's Self-Perceptions and Sources of Physical Competence Information: A cluster analysis. *Journal of Sport and Exercise Psychology, 19*, 52–70.

White, S. A. (1996). Goal orientation and perceptions of the motivational climate initiated by parents. *Pediatric Exercise Science, 8*, 122–129.

White, S. A., Duda, J. L., and Hart, S. (1992). An exploratory examination of the parent-initiated motivational climate questionnaire. *Perceptual and Motor Skills, 75*, 875–880.

CHAPTER 18

Perceived Competence in Young Athletes: Research Findings and Recommendations for Coaches and Parents

Thelma S. Horn, Miami University
Amy Harris, Lakota Public Schools

Imagine that you are watching a youth sport soccer practice. In particular, your attention is captured by two of the children, both of whom are very highly skilled. Not only do they appear to have a lot of general physical and motor ability, but they also are very competent in the basic soccer skills. After the practice, you talk to their coach, who verifies your positive evaluations of these two children. Specifically, the coach tells you that these two children have both been playing soccer for several years and have considerable talent for the game. As part of a project you are doing for a coaching theory class, you interview these two children. After extensive conversations with each of them separately, you find that they have quite different perceptions of their sport ability. One child tell you, somewhat matter-of-factly, "Yeah, I think I'm pretty good at soccer. Actually, I'm pretty good at most sports. Usually I'm one of the best players on the team." The other child is considerably more hesitant about her soccer and sport ability. She says, "Well, I don't think that I'm really all that good at soccer. There are a lot of skills I can't do, and I wish that I could be a lot better." It is obvious to you that these two children, who are very similar in their level of *actual* soccer ability, differ considerably in their *perceptions* of their own ability. One child has a very high perception of her soccer (and sport) ability, while the other child has a lower perception of her ability. Do these differences in perceived competence or perceived ability matter? Should we, as interested adults, be concerned about what children think about their ability in a sport or physical activity?

As the example in the previous paragraph suggests, perceived sport or physical competence can be defined as the child's belief concerning how competent or capable she or he is at a particular sport or physical activity. Perceived competence can be measured or assessed in relatively broad or general terms (i.e., "How good are you at sports?") or in regard to a more specific sport (i.e., "How good are you at baseball, or tennis, or gymnastics?") or even a more specific skill within a sport (i.e., "How good are you at receiving a serve in tennis or shooting a free throw in basketball?"). Researchers and practitioners alike are very much aware that considerable variability exists between children in their perceptions of sport competence. As the example in the first paragraph illustrates, even if two children appear (to the adult) to have the same level of sport competence, they may have quite different perceptions of their competence.

In recent years, researchers in the sport psychology area have found that children's perceptions of competence are very important because they are very much related to, and can even predict, children's performance and behavior in sport and other physical activity situations. Specifically, researchers have found that children who have high perceptions of their sport or physical competence are more apt than are children with lower perceptions of competence to experience positive affect in sport situations (e.g., more enjoyment, pride, satisfaction, and happiness) and less apt to experience negative affect (e.g., less boredom, anxiety, and anger) (Boyd and Yin, 1996; Ebbeck and Weiss, 1998; Ommundson and Vaglum, 1991; Scanlan and Lewthwaite, 1986). Similarly, high perceptions of competence are related to such other positive achievement cognitions as an internal locus of control, an internal, stable, and personally controllable attributional pattern, an intrinsic motivational orientation, and high self-esteem (Ebbeck and Weiss, 1998; Weiss, McAuley, Ebbeck, and Wiese, 1990; Weiss, Bredemeier and Shewchuk, 1986). Behaviorally, children with high perceptions of competence have been found to be more persistent after they experience failure at a physical task and to have higher expectancies for performance success than do children with low perceptions of competence (Rudisill, 1989). More recently, Smith (in press) and Kimiecik and his colleagues (Kimiecik, Horn, and Shurin, 1996) have shown that children's perceptions of their physical competence or physical self-worth are predictive of their level of physical activity. That is, children with higher perceptions of physical competence or physical self-worth were found to exhibit higher levels of daily physical activity than did children with lower perceptions of their physical abilities. Thus, the research to date clearly indicates that perceived competence is an important factor that affects children's performance and behavior in sport and daily life situations.

Given the important role that perceived competence plays in regard to children's sport performance and behavior, it would seem reasonable that we, as interested adults (e.g., parents, teachers, coaches, researchers) would want to facilitate positive perceptions of competence in all children. The issues we need to address, then, include: What can we do to help each child believe that he or she is competent? What techniques can we, as coaches, use in practices and games to help each child feel good about her or his sport performance? How should we, as parents, respond to a child who has just missed a crucial free throw in a basketball game in order to "protect" her or his perception of competence?

To identify answers to the preceding questions, we first need to understand how children form their perceptions of competence. That is, we need to know what processes they use to make judgments about their sport ability and/or what information they use to determine whether they are good or not so good at a particular sport or sport skill. Similarly, we need to know how information such as a missed free throw affects children's feelings about themselves and their basketball ability.

Over the last 15 years, researchers in the sport psychology area have conducted a considerable amount of research designed to examine perceptions of competence in children and adolescents (see recent reviews by Weiss and Ferrer-Caja, in press and Weiss and Ebbeck, 1996). The results of this research have provided important information concerning the correlates, consequences, and antecedents of perceived competence in children. A critical review of this research, however, clearly indicates that these results need to be examined and interpreted from a developmental perspective. That is, the available research and theory indicate that children's perceptions of their sport competence change both quantitatively and qualitatively over the childhood and adolescent years. These changes may certainly be (and probably to a large extent are) caused by the maturational changes that occur in regard to children's physical, cognitive, and emotional capabilities. As children grow and develop physically, cognitively, and emotionally from birth to age 18, it would be understandable that the processes they use to evaluate their sport competence would correspondingly change. However, it is also true that the sport environment (e.g., the program structure and philosophy, the coach's behavior, the training demands, the reward system) changes as the child's age increases. Thus, the changes that we see in regard to children's perceptions of sport competence may be due not only to maturation (i.e., age-related changes in children's physical, cognitive, and emotional capabilities) but also as a response to changes in the sport and/or broader social environment itself.

This chapter reviews and describes the developmental progressions that tell us how children of different ages form their perceptions of sport competence. Because of the interrelationships between maturational processes and the sport environment, these developmental progressions are examined within the context of the youth sport setting. Finally, this information is combined and synthesized to identify possible techniques that can be used to facilitate high perceptions of sport competence in all children.

Perceived Sport Competence: Developmental Patterns

Researchers who have studied perceived competence in children from a developmental perspective have basically asked three questions. First, does the level of children's perceived competence change with age (i.e., do younger children have higher or lower perceptions of competence than do older children)? Second, does the accuracy with which children judge their sport ability change with age (i.e., are older children better at estimating or judging their ability at a sport than are younger children)? Third, do the processes children use to judge their performance change with age (i.e., do younger children use different information or different processes to judge their performance and their ability at a sport than do older children)?

The simple answer to all three of these questions is yes. Children's perceptions of their competence do change in all of the preceding ways with age. In the next sections of this chapter, these developmental changes, and the corresponding socioenvironmental changes, are identified and discussed. For purposes of conceptual ease, the age-related changes in children's self-perceptual processes are somewhat arbitrarily broken up into three developmental stages: early childhood (ages three to six), middle and late childhood (ages seven to twelve), and adolescence (ages 13 to 18).

Early Childhood

Although relatively little research has been conducted in the physical or sport domain with children in this age group, comparable research in the developmental and educational psychology areas (e.g., Harter, 1990; Stipek and Mac Iver, 1989; Stipek, Recchia, and McClintic, 1992) indicate that children as young as two or three do engage in the self-evaluation process (i.e., they do evaluate or judge their performance at a task) and that by three or four they already have a rudimentary conception or perception of personal competence that can be measured at least to some degree by using interview and/or observational techniques. Harter's (1990) work with children at this age indicates, however, that their perceptions of competence in the various achievement domains (physical, cognitive, social) are not nearly as well delineated or differentiated from each other as they are in older children.

Researchers in the educational and developmental psychology literatures (e.g., Harter, 1990; Stipek and Mac Iver, 1989) have also found that young children's perceptions of competence are generally high and quite inaccurate. That is, children at this age tend to have very high perceptions of their ability as compared with measures of their actual ability. Thus, although there certainly are exceptions, most children in this age range tend to be eternal optimists in regard to their capabilities. As Stipek and Mac Iver (1989) caution, however, the positive bias young children show may be evident only when the assessments are made in regard to general competence (e.g., How good are you at sports? How smart are you?). When young children are asked to rate their competence in regard to specific skills (e.g., Can you catch a baseball? How good are you at batting? Can you count to 100?), they may be more realistic (and perhaps more accurate) in their self-assessments.

As noted earlier, relatively fewer research studies have been conducted by researchers in the sport or physical activity domain to examine the perceived competence of very young children. One exception to this is the work completed by Beverly Ulrich (1987; Ulrich and Ulrich, 1997). To measure perceived competence in young children, Ulrich has used an adapted version of a pictorial scale developed by Harter and her colleagues (Harter, Pike, Efron, Chao, and Bierer, 1983). This adapted scale consists of a series of line drawings showing children engaged in a variety of motor, sport, or play-oriented tasks. The researcher shows each child the set of drawings and asks the child to indicate how good he or she is at each task. These ratings are then used to calculate a score representing the child's perceived physical competence.

Ulrich's research with this scale (Ulrich, 1987; Ulrich and Ulrich, 1997) shows that children in kindergarten and first grade do have relatively high perceptions of their physical competence. Some gender differences in perceived competence were also found, but these differences varied somewhat depending on what kinds of skills were being assessed. Specifically, girls were higher than boys in perceived competence when the depicted skills were more play-oriented and primarily locomotor in nature (e.g., skipping, running, hopping). However, when children were asked to judge their competence in regard to fundamental motor skills (e.g., jumping, throwing, catching) or sport-specific skills (e.g., batting a baseball; dribbling a basketball; kicking a soccer ball), then the boys were higher than the girls in perceived competence. Thus, it appears that already in early childhood, gender differences occur in some aspects of children's self-assessments.

Although it is certainly important for us to know how high (or how low) children's perceptions of their competence are and/or how accurate they are in judging their sport and motor ability, it may be more valuable for us to know how they go about judging their performance. That is, what information do they use to judge whether they are good or not so good at a particular skill or activity? How do they explain or justify their judgments concerning their competence? Based on research and theory from the developmental and educational psychology literatures (Stipek and Mac Iver, 1989; Stipek et al., 1992), it appears as if young children's perceptions of competence (or their judgments concerning their performance) are based primarily on simple task accomplishment. Specifically, children in this age range are most apt to feel competent or successful when they complete a task that has a visually salient and intrinsically defined standard of success (e.g., completing a puzzle, stacking a set of blocks, running from one spot to another). Thus, if a preschooler who has stated that she is really good at jumping is asked how she knows she is so good at that skill, she might cite a particular jumping task she can do to justify her high self-competence rating (e.g., "I know I am good at jumping because I can jump across the creek that is behind my house."). This child is basing her perception of jumping ability on successful task accomplishment or completion (i.e., being able to jump across a creek) with no consideration for the objective difficulty of the task (how wide or narrow the creek is) or the subjective difficulty of it (i.e., whether or not most children her age can do the same thing).

Stipek et al. (1992) have demonstrated that children as young as three years may certainly be aware of and/or able to compare their performance with that of their peers (i.e., to know who came in first in a race or who stacked the most blocks). However, their affective reactions to their performance appear to be predominantly dictated by their ability to accomplish (or finish) the task rather than by whether or not their performance was better or worse than their peers. If, for example, a group of children in this age range are running a race, the child who is in the lead may actually stop to wait for her friends to catch up with her so that they can all cross the finish line together. When they do so, all of these children will then show joy with their performance simply because all of them accomplished the task (i.e., crossed the finish line). Stipek et al. did find that age has some impact on children's reactions to a competitive situation. Specifically, the older children in their sample of participants (age range 24 to 60 months) showed greater affective reactions to winning (i.e., finishing a task first) than did the younger children. However, even for the oldest children, finishing the task appeared to be a more critical determinant of how they felt about themselves than did winning.

Another interesting perspective regarding young children's use of simple task accomplishment as a major source of competence information may be the emphasis they place on the "effect" of their task performance. This notion is based on Robert White's (1959) early contention that individuals in general are motivated to have an effect on their environment. That is, when individuals' actions (mastery attempts) do result in an effect (i.e., their actions produce a desirable change in their environment), then those individuals are generally motivated to continue such actions or mastery attempts. For young children (i.e., those in the early childhood years), evidence of such an environmental effect may have to be very concrete in nature. Thus, a very young child may be motivated to continue (often to her adult caregiver's dismay) banging the bottom of a metal pot with a spoon because her physical actions (slamming the spoon on the pot) produce a very loud noise and an observable "cringing" behavior on the part of any adult within hearing distance. Similarly, we probably have all observed a child sitting in a high chair who deliberately dumps his bowl of cereal to the floor and then stares intently and with quite obvious interest at the "effects" of his actions (i.e., the way in which the cereal and milk has splattered all over the floor and cupboards). In a more sport-oriented setting, a similar example might be that a group of kindergarten children may show more motivation, more joy, and more behavioral persistence when asked to practice throwing at a target on the wall which "squeaks" or "lights up" when it is hit by the ball than they would if they were just asked to practice throwing at a non-interactive target face on the wall. Although White contended that individuals of all age ranges are motivated in achievement situations to produce an effect on their environment, for young children, the "effects" may need to be more concrete (i.e., easily retrievable by one of the senses) because young children think and process information in very concrete ways.

A second source of competence information for young children is the feedback they receive from significant adults (Stipek et al., 1992; Stipek and Mac Iver, 1989). Thus, many children may base their perceptions of competence on what their parents, teachers, or coaches say. Example statements would be: "I know that I am a good runner because my mom says I am" or "My teacher says I can bat really good!" These children are basing their competence judgments on evaluative feedback they receive from significant adults concerning their performance. It is important to note here that young children take adult praise at "face value." Thus, even if a particular child obviously cannot bat as well as other children in her or his class, the positive feedback from the teacher appears to supersede or override other competence information.

Third, research in the developmental psychology area with young children suggest that they equate effort and ability (e.g., Nicholls and Miller, 1984). Thus, working hard at a task indicates or signifies high ability, as in the statement, "I know that I am good at jumping because I tried and tried to jump high, and then I did." Similarly, a child may say, "Well, I know that I am good at basketball because I practice a lot." These children are equating effort and ability (i.e., if I work hard at a task, then I must be good).

As noted earlier, several research studies have found that children in the preschool and early school years may exhibit generally high perceptions of competence. This finding may be understandable given that most (but certainly not all) caregivers are generally positive in their feedback to children in achievement contexts (Ames, 1992a; Stipek and Mac Iver, 1989; Stipek et al., 1992). Thus, teachers in preschool gymnastics programs and academically-oriented programs may tend to praise children for all of their task efforts. Furthermore, performance feedback to individual children may typically be given based on task accomplishment or mastery (e.g., finishing a task) or on effort (e.g., trying to kick the ball into the goal) rather than on task quality, performance outcome, or peer comparison. Generally, too, most parents (but certainly not all) may tend to respond positively to children's academic and physical task attempts. If children are criticized by adults at this age level, it is typically for behavioral or rules violations (e.g., failing to stay in line, not waiting for one's own turn, not following directions) rather than for lack of achievement on the task. Thus, at this stage of development, the sport or physical activity environment generally may tend to support high perceptions of competence in children. In support of this notion, Stipek and Daniels (1988) have provided evidence to show that kindergarten children who are exposed to a normatively-based classroom environment (i.e., classrooms where a high emphasis is placed on peer comparison and grades are given in a highly public manner) have lower perceptions of academic competence than do kindergarten children in classrooms described as less peer comparison-oriented (i.e., emphasis is placed on individual progress within the curriculum and more of the work is done in small group format). Based on these results, it could be hypothesized that young children enrolled in sport or motor skill programs that place heavy emphasis on "being the best" and on "winning" would also acquire or develop lower perceptions of their physical competence.

Assuming that we, as interested adults, want to facilitate high perceptions of competence in children who are in the early childhood years, recommendations to individuals working with children of this age would include two primary things. First, try to provide children with multiple opportunities to demonstrate mastery or task accomplishment experiences. In a preschool movement education program, for example, if the task is to complete an obstacle course, the teacher should make sure that all children (even the later maturing and less physically well developed) can accomplish the task (i.e., finish the course). Because children at this age (especially those at preschool age) do not really use peer comparison to evaluate their competence, it doesn't matter that some children (the less motorically proficient) may need some assistance from the teacher to complete the obstacle course and/or may take longer to finish the course. It only matters that each child accomplish the task (i.e., complete the course). These mastery experiences do not necessarily have to be provided within an instructional context, but certainly can be facilitated by parents or other care-givers in unstructured or play-oriented settings. Again, what is important here is that the child is given many opportunities to demonstrate mastery of some aspect of her or his physical environment—whether that is kicking a soccer ball from one point to another, walking on a low balance beam, or running from here to the wall. Additionally, if the child's task accomplishment or task mastery can be highlighted by providing him or her with a clearly retrievable task-completion sensory effect (i.e., child's task completion results in him or her hearing a noise, seeing a movement, smelling a scent, or feeling some stimuli), then the young child's joy, motivation, and perception of competence may certainly be enhanced.

Second, all children need to get positive feedback from significant adults (e.g., parents, teachers, coaches) for their performance accomplishments. As Stipek et al. (1992) suggest in their monograph, positive adult feedback given in response to a child's successful task accomplishment may enhance, or add to, the intrinsic pleasure the child already felt at the accomplishment itself. Thus, praise by significant adults can certainly facilitate the child's perception of her or his physical competence. However, it is important to point out that adult praise at this stage should be contingent on (or given in response to) task accomplishment or completion rather than on other factors, such as peer comparison or on adult-determined task criteria (e.g., doing skill "correctly"). That is, adults should not, at this stage of the game, subvert the emphasis that the children themselves place on simple task accomplishment or completion. Personally, we have seen four year old children enrolled in a tennis instructional program get as much enjoyment out of hitting the ball into the net as they did when they hit the ball into the right service court. The simple joy was in hitting the ball with their rackets (and causing a visible movement of the net or possibly a "smacking" sound as the ball hit the net tape) and not on the "correctness" of the response. Similarly, we have seen young soccer players (ages 4–6) not only take great pleasure in kicking their own soccer ball into the goal (again causing the net to move) but also celebrating the fact that their friend can do it even harder. Thus, even though children at this stage are able to compare their performance with that of their peers, it is not a very critical source of competence information (i.e., they do not appear to use this information to judge their performance competence). If, however, parents, teachers, or coaches place very high emphasis on the results of the peer comparison process, then the child's natural or intrinsic joy at hitting a ball (feeling the impact of the ball on the bat or racquet) or jumping on a trampoline (causing the tramp to bend and the child to rebound up) may be subverted. If, for example, a kindergartener comes home from school and says excitedly, "Guess what, Mom, I did 15 sit-ups in gym class today," and the mother responds with "How many did the other kids do," the child is learning that his performance is best judged by comparing it with that of peers. In contrast, if the mother responds with, "That's great. You must have worked hard to get that many," the child is learning that his performance is best judged by whether or not he tried to do as many as he could. It is true, then, that the type, frequency, and intensity of the feedback adults give to young children not only tells them how good they are at that task but also how valuable that competency is relative to other aspects of life (i.e., sport competency is more, less, or equally as important as competency in music, reading, etc.) and how their performance in each domain will be or should be evaluated. Thus, even if the children themselves tend to emphasize task accomplishment as a primary source of competence information, adult feedback can be critical in either enhancing or subverting this competence information source.

Childhood Years

Over the elementary and middle school years (ages 7 to 12), children exhibit a number of developmental changes in regard to their perceptions of sport or physical competence. First, the generally high perceptions of competence that are seen in preschoolers and early elementary age children (Kindergarten and first grade) appear to diminish somewhat over the next couple of years (second and third grade) (Ulrich, 1987; Ulrich and Ulrich, 1997) but then may remain fairly stable from age 8 to 12 years (Feltz and Brown, 1984; Horn and Hasbrook, 1986). It should be noted that a few researchers have found some continued declines in perceived physical competence across the elementary and middle school years (e.g., Harter, 1985; Uhich, 1987). It is possible that such inconsistencies across studies in the stability or instability of children's perceived competence scores across the middle and late childhood years are due to differences in study samples (i.e., sample drawn from athletes only or from a more general population) and assessment reference (i.e., assessment of perceived general physical competence or assessment of perceived sport-specific competence). Further research is certainly needed to address this developmental phenomenon.

In regard to the accuracy of children's self-assessments, the available research rather consistently suggests that children's ability to judge the quality of their performance increases linearly over this same age range (i.e., they become more accurate with increasing age) (Feltz and Brown, 1984; Harter, 1998; Horn and Weiss, 1991). From a motor development perspective, such age-related increases across the early, middle, and late childhood years in the accuracy with which children judge their sport or physical abilities is understandable given that the results of younger children's motor performance attempts are often quite variable. Thus, children at these early stages of motor proficiency may be getting inconsistent or varying performance feedback concerning their abilities (Parker, Larkin, and Ackland, 1993). As children mature and gain more motor or sport skill experience, their performance will show less variability from one skill attempt to the next. This decrease in variability could then result in increased accuracy in judging performance ability (Plumert, 1995).

As documented in the previous two paragraphs, it does appear as if children's perceptions of their physical competencies do change with increasing age. However, such age-related changes should be interpreted with some caution as they are based predominantly on cross-sectional research and on statistical techniques that compare one age group mean with that of other age groups. As Duncan and Duncan (1991) have argued, longitudinal research designs that allow for an examination of developmental changes in the same group of children over time and which use measures of biological age rather than chronological age may reveal considerably different developmental trends in regard to children's perceptions of physical competence. Further research of this type is certainly necessary if we are to get a clear picture of the changes that may occur within any age range.

Although some researchers have found gender differences (males higher than females) in children's perceptions of physical or sport competence during the childhood years (e.g., Brustad, 1993; Eccles and Harold, 1991), others have not (e.g., Horn and Hasbrook, 1987). This inconsistency in research findings may be due again to variability across studies in participant samples and/or in the context within which the self-assessments are taken. That is, it is possible that gender differences in perceived competence or perceived ability are more apt to be found when the study sample is drawn from a more general population (i.e., students in a required physical education class or in a very recreationally-based sport program) but less likely to be found when the study sample is drawn from a more homogeneous population (i.e., male and female athletes who are engaged in a competitive sport program or who are enrolled in a voluntary instructionally-based sport program such as a summer camp). This possibility is supported by research indicating that females tend to show more situational variability in self-assessments than do males (e.g., Lenney, 1977; Ulrich and Ulrich, 1997). Thus, it appears as though gender differences in regard to perceived physical or sport competence, while evident in certain groups and in certain sport contexts, may not be consistently found across all ages or in all sport situations.

In regard to the processes children in this age range use to form their perceptions of physical or sport competence, the available research shows considerable change from the preschool years but also reveals changes that occur across this particular age range itself. To begin with, towards the end of the preschool years or early in the childhood years (e.g., ages four through seven), children begin using the peer comparison process to evaluate their own performance. That is, they judge their own competence or ability in a physical task or sport based on how their performance at the task or sport compares with that of their peers. Thus, children may reason that "I know that I'm good at running because I can beat all of my friends." or "I'm not really good at basketball because I am always the last one picked for a team in gym class." Our research in this area (Horn and Hasbrook, 1986; Horn and Weiss, 1991) shows that the use of peer comparison to judge one's own competence increases steadily in importance until for many, if not most, children it becomes, by the age of 12, the most important source of ability information. A similar age-related increase across the late childhood and early adolescent years in the use of peer comparison has recently been documented by McKiddie and Maynard (1997) in regard to the sources of information used by physical education students.

Correspondingly, we have found that children's use of feedback from parents declines in importance from age 8 to 14, whereas children's use of evaluative feedback from peers and possibly from coaches increases in importance (Horn and Hasbrook, 1986; Horn and Weiss, 1991). Interestingly, it also appears as if children at the older end of this age range (11 and 12 years) may no longer take an adult's feedback at "face value," but, rather, evaluate that feedback relative to other sources of information (Barker and Graham, 1987; Meyer, Bachmann, Biermann, Hempelmann, Ploger and Spiller, 1979). Assume, for example, that a child, whose performance on a soccer drill is not as good as that of his teammates, receives very positive feedback from his coach in the form of a general statement such as "Good job, Jimmy" while his teammates, who are actually performing at a higher level of competence, get no praise. In this instance, Jimmy does not take his coach's comment at face value but rather evaluates it relative to peer comparison and comes up with the conclusion that "I must be really bad if my coach thinks this is a good performance for me." Thus, the coach's positive feedback is actually interpreted by Jimmy as negative ability information. Similarly, a child who receives criticism from an adult for a particular performance attempt may perceive higher personal ability than does a child who exhibits the same level of performance but gets no feedback. Thus, it appears that children at this age do use adult feedback as a source of competence information but that this feedback is interpreted relative to other performance indicators.

In addition to the preceding points, the available research (e.g., Horn and Hasbrook, 1986; Watkins and Montgomery, 1989) has also indicated that children (especially those at the younger ages) within this age range use performance outcomes (winning/losing) as important sources of ability information. Not only does this mean that they use personal performance outcomes (i.e., whether I win or lose a wrestling or tennis match) but also that they may use team performance outcomes to judge their own ability. Thus, it would not be unusual for a 9-year old child to say, "I guess I'm a really bad soccer player, and I know that because my team loses all the time." It may be, then, that children (especially those under ten years) are not very good at separating their own personal competence from that of their team.

The developmental changes in regard to the processes children use to form perceptions of competence that have been described in the previous paragraphs can be interpreted from a broader developmental perspective. Specifically, given that children in the early and middle childhood years tend to be very concrete thinkers, it is understandable that their primary sources of competence information (e.g., peer comparison, evaluative feedback from teachers, coaches, peers, and parents, win-loss outcomes) tend to be very concrete in nature. That is, these sources of information are readily available in most sport-oriented contexts and provide easily visible and interpretable evaluations of personal competence.

Second, the broader developmental literature supports the notion that peers gradually become a more important source of information for children as they reach the end of the childhood years and progress into early adolescence (Adams, 1980; Harter, 1987, 1990). In addition, research and theory in the developmental and child psychology literatures clearly establishes the notion that peer acceptance and friendship quality are important contributors to psychosocial growth and maturation in children and early adolescents (Berndt, 1996; Hartup, 1995, 1996; Parker and Asher, 1993; Sullivan, 1953). In the sport domain as well, the desire for affiliation and the development of new friendships has consistently been cited by children and adolescents as one of the most important motives for their participation in competitive sport programs (see reviews by Weiss and Ferrer-Caja, in press and Weiss and Petlichkoff, 1989). Given this emphasis on peer relationships, especially during the late childhood and early adolescent years, it is understandable that peer comparison and peer evaluation become significantly more important sources of competence information for children as they move from the middle childhood to the later childhood years.

From a more physiologically-oriented perspective, the increase in the use of peer comparison across the middle and late childhood years can best be understood by considering the physical growth and development process. Specifically, as children approach the later end of the childhood years and move into early adolescence (ages 10–14), they enter the preadolescent growth spurt. Due to the wide variability between children both in regard to the chronological age at which this growth spurt begins and in the rate at which individual children pass through this pubertal growth phase, there often is considerable variability between children in this age and grade range (fifth through eighth grades) in their body size, shape, and composition. This inter-individual variability is evident both within and between the genders. That is, boys generally appear to be somewhat later than girls to enter the pre-adolescent growth spurt. Such inter-individual variability in age of entry into the pubertal growth spurt results in considerable differences between and among boys and girls in the late middle and junior high school years in height, weight, and body composition (e.g., amount of muscle mass, body fat). Such obvious inter-individual variability may certainly enhance children's tendencies to use the peer comparison process as a pertinent source of ability information.

From the cognitive-developmental literature (e.g., Nicholls, 1989), we know that children's perceptions of, or understanding regarding, the concept of ability changes significantly from the early childhood to the late childhood years (ages 5–12). Specifically, Nicholls' theory suggests that children will reach a mature understanding of ability (typically around 12 years) as they acquire the cognitive capabilities that are necessary to distinguish between such concepts as luck, effort, and normative task difficulty, especially as these components variously contribute to performance in achievement contexts. The relevance of these cognitive-developmental stages to the physical domain has recently been demonstrated in a series of studies conducted by Fry (2000, in press; Fry and Duda, 1997) with children ranging in age from 5 to 13 years. As the combined results of these studies clearly show, there are strong developmental trends in children's ability to differentiate the concepts of luck, effort, and task difficulty as contributors to achievement performance. Given such developmental changes in children's ability to determine the relative causes of performance successes and failures, it is also understandable, then, that the sources of information they use to evaluate their own competence will change as their cognitive capabilities mature.

In addition to the maturational changes discussed in the preceding paragraphs, the developmental changes that we see in the processes that children in this age range use to form their perceptions of competence must also be interpreted relative to changes in the sport environment. One of the primary changes that occurs for children moving from very early youth sport programs to childhood and junior high programs is that the emphasis in such programs changes from an instructional orientation to that which is more competitive in nature. Specifically, many (but certainly not all) sport-oriented programs for children in the early childhood years (ages three to six) are conducted in a more instructional way. That is, more emphasis is placed on teaching children the fundamental sport skills and on encouraging the participation of all children. Beginning around the age of six or seven, however, the emphasis switches to a progressively more competitive orientation. Now, leagues are formed, team and/or individual standings are kept, end-of-season trophies are awarded, all-star teams are added, tryouts are introduced, and some children may be "cut" from programs or at least tracked into a "lower" ability level. Even a cursory analysis of these changes suggests that the primary basis for decision-making in regard to children's status within these programs is on peer comparison and performance outcomes. That is, children are "cut" from teams or "tracked" into a lower ability level on the basis of personal performance scores (e.g, batting averages, shooting percentages, agility run scores) that are compared with those of their peers (i.e., children with higher scores are kept on the team or placed in the higher ability programs). Furthermore, awards (team trophies, individual awards) are most often given based either on win-loss outcomes (e.g., which team has the best win-loss record) or again on the peer comparison process. Thus, it is clear that the sport environment increasingly conveys to children the idea that their sport competence is best evaluated or judged by using performance outcomes and peer comparison (Chaumeton and Duda, 1988). Therefore, the increasing tendency of children between the ages of 7 and 13 years to use peer comparison and win-loss outcomes may certainly be due to maturational changes in cognitive and psychological abilities but can also be a function of relevant changes in the sport environment.

A second important change that occurs in regard to the sport environment is that coaches become a more credible source of ability information for children as they progress from early childhood sport-oriented programs into youth sport and then junior high programs. Adults who coach at the early youth sport levels (e.g., preschool and early elementary levels) may be selected (or recruited) for their coaching roles more for their nurturing and emotionally supportive skills (i.e., they are parents) than for their technical knowledge of the sport. Also, the program philosophies for children at this age tend to emphasize the notions that all children should play in all games and in all field positions and that the primary goal is to have fun. Thus, the coaches are presented more as supporters or facilitators of children's sport experience. However, when children move up in youth sport programs (i.e., go from early instructional to the more competitive levels), the coach is presented as more of an authority figure. He (or, less often, she) may be marketed to parents and children as particularly "knowledgeable" about sport and/or as "experienced" (as an athlete or coach) in the sport process. In addition, now that players are "cut" or "tracked" on the basis of ability and that all kids may not have equal playing time (i.e., some will be regular starters and/or play a lot and some will not), the coach is necessarily perceived by the athletes (and their parents) as the controller of important resources (i.e., as the determiner of who will make the team, who will play, what positions each child will play). Given this important environmental change, it is not surprising that young athletes show an increasing tendency from ages 8 to 14 years to base their perceptions of sport competence on their coach's feedback and a corresponding decrease in use of feedback from parents. After all, even if mom and/or dad thinks a child is good, it is ultimately the coach's evaluation of the child's ability that will determine if he or she makes the team and gets playing time. Thus, the coach's feedback obviously becomes more critical to the child's status in the sporting context than does the parent's feedback.

Based on the information provided in the previous paragraphs concerning the way in which children think about sport and their position within it, what can we, as interested adults, do to facilitate positive self-perceptions in all children? First, because there is so much variation between children in their maturation rates, it is important that we provide each of them with optimally challenging skill activities. Children in this age range appear to be very sensitive to performance successes and failures (e.g., how many free throws they can make out of 10; how many tennis serves they can get in the service court) as ways to evaluate their sport competence. Therefore, if a child is engaged in a sport activity in which the task demands greatly exceed her or his actual motor ability, then that child will have difficulty seeing any objective performance success (i.e., if a child does not have enough upper body strength to shoot a basketball from the 10-foot line, that child cannot ever "see" the shot go into the basket). The slower-maturing child, then, is at risk for developing a low perception of competence. Thus, it is important that the physical facilities, the equipment, and the game rules be modified to provide children with optimal challenge so that they can achieve at least some performance success. Instructional strategies that coaches and parents can use to provide children with optimal challenge have been described in some detail by Weiss (1987) and by Weiss and Ebbeck (1996).

Second, it would be helpful to reduce or decrease the emphasis on peer comparison and performance outcomes as a means to evaluate personal competence. As noted earlier, the use of peer comparison appears to begin in the early elementary years (ages 4 to 7) and then increases in importance until by age 12 or 13 years, it becomes for many (if not most) children the primary source of competence information. As researchers and practitioners, we need to recognize that peer comparison and performance outcomes are not necessarily bad sources of information. (We, as adults, use them all the time to judge our competence!) The problem, however, arises when one and/or the other become the only source (sources) of information that children use to judge their sport ability. Because only a few children within any group (team, physical education class) can fare well in the peer comparison process (i.e., only a few can be picked first for athletic teams, selected to all-star teams, receive most-valuable-player awards), the majority of children within that group are not receiving positive information about their competence via the peer comparison process.

Thus, if any single child is almost solely dependent on peer comparison as a means to judge sport ability, then that child is really at risk for low perceptions of competence.

As noted earlier in this chapter, part of the reason why children at the upper end of this age range may rely so heavily on these two sources of ability information (peer comparison and performance outcomes) is because they constitute very concrete sources of information in the sport setting. That is, although an individual child's low test score in the academic classroom can, with some effort, be hidden from other children, a strike-out by a batter in a softball game or a missed free throw in a basketball game is very easily visible not only to the child her- or himself but also to everyone else. In addition, of course, as was noted earlier, youth sport programs (especially at the older ages) are very much structured to emphasize peer comparison and performance outcomes as primary ways to evaluate each child's sport ability.

Given this socioenvironmental situation, what can coaches or parents do to de-emphasize the use of these two sources of competence information? We can work with the individual child or groups of children to help them decrease their individual dependence on peer comparison and performance outcomes. We can do that by encouraging them to turn instead to the use of self-comparison. Self-comparison involves the use of skill improvement over time or the achievement of self-set goals. We might help the child to see that even though she may not be in the starting line-up for her club volleyball team, she has improved her skill performance from last season or she is acquiring some very nice skill patterns. What we are trying to do here is help the child see that there are other ways to evaluate or judge personal competence.

It is important to note again that most children may not spontaneously use self-comparison. The fact that they don't is likely due to the fact that the sport environment is structured to enhance the peer comparison and performance outcome process. In addition, because children at this stage are very concrete thinkers, it may be more difficult for them to use a comparison process that requires a time element (i.e, individual child must compare performance in today's game with her/his performance in a game that occurred last week). Given that individual children may even have difficulty remembering what they had for lunch today or where they left their shoes, it is understandable that self-comparison is more difficult for them. Coaches and parents can, however, make the self-comparison process more concrete. Examples include: (a) use of a personal performance improvement chart that maps individual children's progress at specific skills across the season; (b) incorporation of practice drills in which individual or group progress or improvement can be concretely measured across time; (c) use of individual accomplishment awards (e.g. skill mastery awards) for each game rather than best offensive or best defensive player awards; (d) use of goal-setting techniques; (e) provision of opportunities within each practice session to show children in concrete and easily visible ways that they have improved. These programmatic techniques can facilitate or promote what Ames (1992a, 1992b) has referred to as a mastery motivational climate. This type of climate characterizes a sport environment in which success is defined in terms of the individual child's progress on a skill continuum rather than as a function of normative comparison or performance outcomes (see also Duda's chapter in this text as well as Treasure and Roberts, 1995, and Weiss and Ebbeck, 1996).

Third, it is important that parents, teachers, and coaches, as well as the children themselves, be taught about the wide variability in maturation that occurs between children during this age range. Because some children on a youth sport team are early maturers and others are late maturers, there is bound to be considerable differences between these children not only in size, speed and strength but also in motor and sport skill proficiency. This situation, again, may encourage children to use peer comparison to evaluate personal competence and place the later maturing children at particular risk for low perceived competence. As detailed elsewhere (Horn, Lox, and Labrador, 2001), coaches who are unaware that there is wide variability between children in maturation rates may assume that late maturing children are just unathletic (i.e., that they have no innate athletic ability and never will have) and thus act toward these children in ways that impede their skill progress. If coaches (and parents) are made aware of the variation in maturation, then such expectancy-biased behavior on the part of the coaches and parents may be at least somewhat alleviated.

As a final recommendation for this age range, coaches and parents must provide children with appropriate and contingent performance feedback. That is, feedback should be given contingent to the level of performance that is exhibited. As previously noted, children at the upper end of this age range no longer take adults' praise and criticism at "face value" but rather evaluate it relative to other sources of competence information. Coaches who give inappropriate and/or non-contingent praise and criticism not only risk losing credibility as information-givers but can also be exerting a negative effect on their athletes' self-perceptions (see Horn, 1987 and Horn et al., 2001, for further discussion of this topic). Therefore, coaches, teachers, and parents must be careful in regard to the type of feedback they give young athletes (see also recommendations provided in Chapters 9 and 10 of this volume).

In addition, adults need to remember that their performance feedback to children (i.e., the praise and criticism they direct to individual children or groups of children in response to performances) not only provides children with information concerning the coach's judgment of their performance ability but also informs kids as to how their performance will be judged within that sport context. For example, coaches who give praise and criticism to players contingent only on performance outcomes (e.g., whether a shot is made, a runner is thrown out, a rally point is won or lost) are telling their players that their personal competence can only be judged on the basis of outcome (i.e., if you win, you are talented and if you lose, you are a failure). In contrast, coaches who give praise and criticism contingent on skill technique (e.g, whether player used the correct movement pattern regardless of whether the outcome was successful) are telling their players that their performance will be judged on the basis of skill learning, performance improvement, amount of effort exerted, and/or basic skill execution.

Given the vast differences between children in this age range in regard to physical maturation, motor skill proficiency, body control, and sport background, it makes sense that coaches' feedback would place greater emphasis on skill technique than on performance outcomes. That is, from a long-term goal perspective, it is more important for children at this age to learn the fundamental motor (throwing, catching, kicking) and sport skills (shooting lay-ups, hitting a baseball, serving a tennis ball) than it is to win. A corollary to this is that skill technique is something that almost all children (with few exceptions) can control. That is, an individual child on a Little League baseball team may not yet have enough strength or speed to beat out a bunt but she can learn and execute the correct skill pattern. Similarly, another child may not yet have the height, upper body strength, or jumping ability to be a powerful hitter in volleyball, but he can learn and execute the correct skill pattern. Thus, from multiple perspectives, it makes greater sense for coaches and parents to emphasize skill development rather than performance outcomes in youth sport settings.

Adolescence

During the adolescent years (ages 13–18), many additional changes occur in regard to children's perceptions of competence. Although researchers in the educational and developmental psychology literature have found that there is a rather significant decline in children's perceptions of competence and control from late childhood to early adolescence (see Stipek and Mac Iver, 1989), no comparable and consistent age-related declines have yet been reported in regard to perceptions of physical competence. In fact, a few researchers have found increases in perceived competence from early to later adolescence (Duncan and Duncan, 1991; Petlichkoff, 1993). In addition, gender differences in self-perceptions have been found in several adolescent study samples (e.g., Black and Weiss, 1992; Eccles and Harold, 1991).

Specifically, males have been found to exhibit higher scores on perceived competence or perceived ability than did their female peers. However, as Vealey (1988) pointed out, gender differences in self-perceptions may not be consistently found across all study samples. In her study, gender differences in trait sport-confidence, although evident in high school and college athletes, were not found in elite athletes. Thus, again, the degree of gender differences may vary as a function of the study participants and the situational sport context.

In regard to the processes adolescents use to judge their performance competence, Horn and colleagues (Horn, Glenn, and Wentzell, 1993) found a number of developmental changes that occur between the ages of 14 to 18 years. First, athletes in the younger end of this age range (athletes from freshmen and sophomore teams) showed a greater tendency than did older athletes (high school juniors and seniors) to use evaluative feedback from peers to judge their sport ability. Second, athletes in the older group showed greater use of self-comparison processes (skill improvement over time), internalized or self-determined performance standards (achievement of self-set goals) and internal information (e.g., pre-event self-confidence, ability to motivate self, enjoyment of sport activity) to evaluate how competent they are at a particular sport.

A similar age-related trend was found in research by Vealey and Campbell (1988), who examined the competitive orientations of 13–18 year old elite ice skaters. Examination of this data showed that a performance orientation (i.e., tendency to base performance satisfaction and feelings of competence on performing well) increased with age whereas an outcome orientation (a tendency to base performance satisfaction and feelings of competence on winning) declined. Also, Watkins and Montgomery (1989), in a study examining children's and adolescents' reasoning about athletic excellence, found that adolescents showed a greater tendency than did younger children to use covert, or more abstract factors (e.g., cognitive and attitudinal skills such as concentration, confidence, strategies) to explain differences between excellent athletes and others. Thus, there appears to be an increasing trend over the adolescent years to use more internally-based criteria as a means to evaluate sport competence.

In addition to these age differences, rather consistent gender differences have also been found (e.g., Gill, in press; Horn et al., 1993; McKiddie and Maynard, 1997; Petlichkoff, 1993) in this adolescent age group. Specifically, male athletes are more oriented toward the use of winning and peer comparison as means to evaluate their sport ability, whereas female athletes are more apt to use self-comparison (skill improvement) processes, internalized performance standards (e.g., achievement of self-set goals), and the feedback of others (coaches, peers) to judge their sport ability. The fact that there are gender differences in the criteria adolescents use to judge their sport competence is particularly interesting given that few, if any, differences are found in younger children. Thus, these gender differences appear to emerge, or perhaps intensify, sometime during the early adolescent years. This notion that gender differences in achievement-related cognitions may first appear in early adolescence is consistent with research in the developmental psychology literature (Eccles et al., 1998; Phillips and Zimmerman, 1990).

The age-related changes that occur during the adolescent years in perceptions of competence must be examined in light of other broader developmental changes that are occurring within the individual and within the context of the sport environment. In regard to maturational changes, it is important to understand that many physical changes are occurring from early to late adolescence in body size, shape, composition and functioning (see also Chapter 11 of this text). In addition, the variability between children in regard to rate of maturation, which was discussed in the previous section of this chapter, continues and may even intensify. Some adolescents are early maturers, and others are late maturers. What complicates things now, however, is that this variability becomes uniquely obvious. We can, for example, have an early maturing 14-year old boy on a freshmen basketball team whose physique is already similar to that of an adult male while his teammate still has the size and linear physique that is characteristic of a prepubescent child. Similar variability occurs in regard to early- and late-maturing girls. The intensity, visibility, and variability of the physical changes that occur in the early adolescent years may contribute to early adolescents' tendencies to use peer comparison and peer feedback as primary sources of competence information.

From a cognitive perspective, children between the ages of 11 and 18 years develop more abstract reasoning or processing skills. Such cognitive maturation could certainly cause, or at least be associated with, corresponding changes in the processes/information adolescents use to judge their sport ability. For example, although researchers have found that adolescents continue to use peer comparison as a means to evaluate their sport competence, it has been hypothesized (but not yet tested) (Horn et al., 1993; Stipek and Mac Iver, 1989) that whereas children in the earlier age range (ages 8 to 12) may use a familiar or "known" peer comparison group (i.e., all the players on my team or in my league or my fifth grade class), adolescents begin using a more extended peer comparison group, a group that includes known peers but is also expanded to include abstract peers (i.e., how do I compare with all high school juniors in the state?). This expanded comparison process may be more likely for adolescents because of their increased ability to reason in a more abstract form. This notion concerning an age-related increase over the adolescent years in individuals' use of the extended peer group to make judgments about their own competence is consistent with Harter's developmentally-based work (1987; 1990) on the sources contributing to adolescents' sense of self-worth. Obviously, this aspect needs to be further explored in the physical domain.

Another possible correlate of adolescents' cognitive maturation is their increasing ability to internalize achievement standards (Adams, 1980; Harter, 1981, 1990). That is, during the period from late childhood through adolescence, children acquire the ability to develop an internal set of performance criteria or standards that they can then use in subsequent performance situations to make independent judgments of their skill competence. The result of such internalization is that older adolescents probably become less dependent on such external sources of information as win/loss outcomes and evaluative feedback from others.

Third, a more abstract reasoning ability may also explain the fact that adolescents are able to integrate information concerning their sport ability from multiple sources. That is, unlike children in the earlier age group, who may depend on only one or two of the most visible information sources, adolescents may be able to integrate and synthesize information from a variety of sources. Along these same lines, adolescents may show less dependence on group performance outcomes (i.e., team win-loss record) to evaluate their own ability because they are now cognitively able to dissociate personal performance from that of the group.

Fourth, the use of effort as a source of competence information appears to undergo a change during the early adolescent years. As noted earlier, young children view effort as a primary indicator of ability (e.g., "If I try hard, I must be good"). Thus, the two constructs (effort and ability) are not well differentiated by young children (Nicholls, 1989; Nicholls and Miller, 1984). By the age of 11 or 12, however, children begin to see that ability and effort are independent entities. Furthermore, ability may now be perceived to be a stable, even innate, trait which is unaffected by effort (Dweck, 1996; Dweck and Leggett, 1988). Such perceptions can certainly affect how adolescents judge their performance abilities. For example, an adolescent who perceives that she had to exert a considerable amount of effort to achieve success at a fairly easy task may conclude that she must have low competence. Similarly, such reasoning may affect how the adolescent interprets evaluative feedback. If, for example, two adolescents achieve the same level of performance, but one receives effort-related criticism from his/her coach (e.g., "You didn't try hard enough."), while the other one does not, the individual who receives no feedback may conclude that she/he is low in ability (i.e., "My coach does not think I can get better even with more effort. Thus, I must have low ability.").

Fifth, research and theory from the developmental psychology literature indicates that peers become a very salient reference group beginning in the late childhood years and continuing into, or perhaps peaking in, adolescence. Harter (1987; 1990), for example, indicates that adolescents' perceptions of their social adequacy within their peer group and their evaluation of the quality of the social support they receive from their peers are strong predictors of their overall or global self-worth. Within the sport domain, recent studies by Weiss and Smith and their colleagues (Duncan, 1993; Smith, in press; Weiss and Smith, 1999; Weiss, Smith, and Theeboom, 1996) have demonstrated the importance of studying peer relations in sport contexts and have verified the link that exists between children's and adolescents' perceptions of friendship quality, peer support, and peer acceptance and their scores on such positive psychosocial outcomes as physical self-worth, self-esteem, intrinsic motivation and positive affect in physical activity contexts. Thus, researchers and practitioners interested in examining, facilitating, and enhancing adolescents' perceptions of themselves and their physical competencies should consider the role that peers play.

In addition to developmental changes that occur over the adolescent years in physical and cognitive abilities, there are also numerous changes in the sport environment. Specifically, the emphasis on competition (and winning) increases. In addition, membership on athletic teams gets increasingly more selective. That is, while many children may "make" their junior high basketball team, relatively few will "make" their high school varsity team. This increased selectivity may account for the higher perceptions of physical competence that have been found in varsity level athletes (high school juniors and seniors) as compared to their younger counterparts (Pethchkoff, 1993). Over the high school years, too, the emphasis on extended peer groups increases. For example, early in an athlete's high school career (e.g., freshman level), coaches, parents, and others may compare individual athletes to their peers within the program (i.e., "Are you the best shooter on your team?") or maybe even within the league (i.e, "Are you the best point guard in the league?"). But, at the varsity level, the comparison may be extended. That is, we now not only have all-league teams (best athletes within a league) but also all-city, and all-state teams. Obviously, this represents an extension of the peer comparison group. Furthermore, those athletes who are superstars on their own high school team and even within their own city and state are additionally compared to an even larger peer group (all nation) for purposes of college recruitment (i.e., Who are the top 25 high school players in the country?). Thus, again the sport environment facilitates the progressive expansion of the peer group in regard to the evaluation of each athlete's sport competence.

Along with this, we also see an increase in training demands, and participation becomes increasingly more regimented. That is, athletes cannot miss practices or games, and they must follow prescribed training rules in regard to diet, bedtime, social life, etc. Based on anecdotal evidence (informal conversations with youth sport and adolescent athletes), it also may be that coaches become more controlling as their athletes increase in age and skill. Specifically, coaches of adolescent athletes may be more apt than are coaches of younger athletes to act in practices and games in ways that are designed to show athletes that the coach is "in control." These behaviors not only include making the athletes do everything the coach says without providing an opportunity to discuss and/or respond but also giving the athletes non-contingent feedback. That is, if a very highly skilled athlete executes a good play, the controlling coach may give her or him critical feedback anyway just to show the player who is "in control" and/or to "reduce the super-star player down to size." Certainly, not all coaches of adolescent athletes are controlling in their behavior, but the percentage of such coaches may increase as athletes get older, more knowledgeable, and more skilled, and as the pressure on the coach to win increases. Thus, the socioenvironmental climate may change as the athletes progress from junior high to high school programs. These environmental changes may cause athletes to perceive that their behavior and their performance are no longer under their own control. Such perceptions may cause a decrease in the athletes' intrinsic motivation and also interfere with the athletes' ability to internalize a set of performance standards (Ames, 1992b; Horn and Hasbrook, 1987; Vallerand and Losier, 1999; Vallerand, Deci, and Ryan, 1987).

Finally, it is also likely that the sport and social environment may change in unique ways for girls during this adolescent period. Specifically, female athletes, especially those in the early adolescent years, may be given conflicting messages concerning the appropriateness of sport participation. As their bodies mature, girls may be overtly discouraged from continuing their sport participation or given subtle messages suggesting that they should not become too competent in sport. As Gill (in press) explains, gender stereotypes concerning both male and female athletes abound in both the broader social and the more specific sport context. Thus, girls who continue to participate in sport throughout the adolescent years may be subjected to different environmental conditions than are boys. Since sport is perceived to be more appropriate and more suited to boys, the expectations that coaches hold for adolescent girls may be significantly lower than that of which they are capable (see Horn et al., 2001). Thus, girls at this age level may be given messages that suggest they have less competence in the sport context. Such socienvironmental messages may leave adolescent girls at risk for lower perceptions of sport competence and thus may help to explain why there appears to be more gender differences in competence perceptions during the adolescent years than in the earlier childhood years.

The developmental and socioenvironmental patterns that have been described in the previous paragraphs can be used to identify the techniques and strategies that adults should use in working with adolescent athletes. Some of these techniques are described in the following paragraphs.

First, we, as adults, should hold high expectations for all adolescents (e.g., males and females, early and late maturers, low- and high-skilled performers). However, and this is very important, our expectations for each child should be realistic or achievable, and these expectations should be held only for controllable skills and behaviors. As a baseball coach, for example, it would be unrealistic for me to expect all of my junior high players to be able to bat above .300 or to hit 20 home runs. I can, however, expect all players to use the correct batting techniques. Similarly, due to variable maturation rates, not all of my ninth grade volleyball players may yet be tall enough or strong enough to execute a good block, but they can all be expected to learn the correct skill pattern and to get themselves into good position at the net. The key point here is that we, as adults, are careful not to convey low expectations for certain players (e.g., females, late maturers) by "letting them get away with sloppy techniques."

Second, we should try to encourage each adolescent to develop an internalized set of performance standards. It is important, however, that the internalized performance standards be challenging but still realistic. Adolescents who internalize a performance standard that is too low will be satisfied with a lower level of exhibited performance, and motivation will be low. Conversely, adolescents whose standard for performance is too high will likely experience anxiety because failure is almost virtually assured, and perceptions of competence will be consistently low. As a corollary to this, it should also be noted that some children do not develop an internalized structure but continue to be dependent on external sources of competence information (Horn and Hasbrook, 1987). It is possible that the inability of some children to develop an internalized set of performance standards may be due either to the absence of performance feedback during the childhood and early adolescent years or to the inconsistency of such feedback. Either situation may make it more difficult for an individual child to internalize a consistent set of standards for his or her performance.

One way to encourage all children to develop an internal structure may be to incorporate specific classroom or practice (and game) strategies that teach children to assume more responsibility for both their practice effort and for the evaluation of their performance. These strategies have been referred to by various labels including self-regulatory teaming (Schunk, 1989; Weiss, 1995) and mastery motivational orientation strategies (Ames, 1992a, 1992b). The primary emphasis of these techniques is to involve the children (adolescents) in the teaming process and to encourage them to engage in self-monitoring, self-evaluative, and self-rewarding behaviors. Research has supported the value of these strategies in regard to adolescents' performance and behavior in achievement contexts.

Third, as coaches, we should try to develop a more autonomous, rather than a controlling, coaching style. As suggested earlier, the primary goal of controlling coaches is to demonstrate and exert "control" over their athletes. In contrast, the primary goal of an autonomous coach is to get athletes to take responsibility for their own behavior (i.e., to "internalize" motivation so that athletes are working hard because they want to get better or to achieve a certain self-set goal). Thus, an autonomous coaching style is more consistent with the strategies identified in the previous paragraph. Initial research in the athletic setting (see reviews by Horn, 2001, and Vallerand and Losier, 1999) has revealed that an autonomous coaching style is associated with higher intrinsic motivation in athletes than is a controlling coaching style.

Fourth, because adolescents have the cognitive ability to integrate information from multiple sources, we need to help them do so. At this age, they should no longer focus exclusively on only one source of competence information but should be able to use multiple pieces of information to evaluate individual progress and competence in their sport.

Fifth, given the important role which peers play in the formation of adolescents' self-perceptions and affective reactions, it seems important that we, as coaches and parents, would try to facilitate positive peer relationships. Specifically, the research and theory indicates that adolescents need to feel accepted, liked, and respected by their peers and that they need to have both close friendships as well as to receive high quality social support from their peers (e.g., Harter, 1987; 1990; Hartup, 1995, 1996; Sullivan, 1953). Because athletic teams have the *potential* to provide feelings of unity, bondedness, and group cohesion (Widmeyer, Brawley, and Carron, in press), it would seem that coaches would have a unique opportunity to facilitate such group dynamics and thus to have a significant effect on the psychosocial growth of adolescents. However, it is also important to note that coaches can, and often do, undermine athletes' peer relationships and team cohesion through coaching techniques and practices that overemphasize competition between and among members of the same team and that create a team climate that encourages members to denigrate and devalue the contributions each player makes to the team as a whole. There are also coaches who adhere to negative stereotypes concerning race, class, gender, and sexual orientation. Typically, such coaches allow their stereotyped beliefs to influence their behavior in practices and games (see Horn, in press, for more detail) and thus to cause divisiveness among team members. Specifically, the stereotyped views of these coaches tend to encourage the formation of very exclusive and separate groups within a team and to facilitate the development of a very hierarchical social status within a team. These practices can certainly lead to social isolation for some athletes. Certainly, more research needs to be conducted on the types of coaching behaviors and/or practices that will most facilitate (or undermine) peer relationships within the athletic team context. At this point, however, the best available research seems to point toward an autonomous and democratically-oriented coaching style (see reviews by Horn, in press, and Vallerand and Losier, 1999) and toward the establishment of a mastery- (or task-) oriented team climate (see chapter by Duda in this text) as ways in which coaches can best enhance positive peer relationships and team/group cohesion. Other suggestions regarding the enhancement of team or group cohesion have been forwarded by Carron, Spink and Prapavessis (1997).

Finally, as coaches, teachers, and parents, we need to continue to provide effective performance feedback. Our research clearly shows that adult feedback is an important factor in facilitating positive self-perceptions in children at all developmental levels (Horn, in press). However, as noted earlier, children above the age of 10 no longer take adults' praise and criticism at "face value" but evaluate it relative to other sources of competence information. Thus, it is strongly recommended that coaches give feedback which is contingent to the athlete's performance (e.g., athletes get praise if they executed skill well and corrective feedback if they did not). Based on anecdotal evidence provided by the athletes themselves, it appears as if controlling coaches do not give contingent feedback but rather use their feedback to play "mind games" with their athletes (i.e., they "mess with the minds" of super-star athletes so that they begin to doubt personal competence). In contrast, autonomous coaches give feedback that is directly related to the performance itself (i.e., such coaches are more consistent in how they evaluate athletes' performance). Thus, the way in which adults give performance feedback may be critical in either facilitating or undermining athletes' perceptions of their sport competence.

Summary

As this chapter has illustrated, children's perceptions of their physical and sport competence change both quantitatively and qualitatively with age. Such developmental changes or patterns are important to identify and to understand because of the impact that perceptions of competence have on children's and adolescents' performance and behavior. Given the importance of perceived competence for children of all ages, further developmentally-based research on this topic is certainly warranted. We have probably only begun to understand how children's self-perceptions change as they grow and develop.

References

Adams, J. (1980). Understanding adolescents. In J. F. Adams (Ed.), *Understanding adolescence: Current developments in adolescent psychology* (pp. 2–29). Boston: Allyn and Bacon.

Ames, C. (1992a). Achievement goals, motivational climate, and motivational processes. In G. C. Roberts (Ed.), *Motivation in sport and exercise* (pp. 161–176). Champaign, IL: Human Kinetics.

Ames, C. (1992b). Classrooms: Goals, structures, and student motivation. *Journal of Educational Psychology, 84*, 261–271.

Barker, G. P., and Graham, S. (1987). Developmental study of praise and blame as attributional cues. *Journal of Educational Psychology, 79*, 62–66.

Berndt, T. J. (1996). Exploring the effects of friendship quality on social development. In W. M. Bukowski, A. F. Newcomb, and W. W. Hartup (Eds.), *The company they keep: Friendship in childhood and adolescence* (pp. 346–365). NY: Cambridge University Press.

Black, S. J., and Weiss, M. R. (1992). The relationship among perceived coaching behaviors, perceptions of ability, and motivation in competitive age-group swimmers. *Journal of Sport and Exercise Psychology, 14*, 309–325.

Brustad, R. (1993). Who will go out and play? Parental and psychological influences on children's attraction to physical activity. *Pediatric Exercise Science, 5*, 210–223.

Boyd, M., and Yin, Z. (1996). Cognitive-affective sources of sport enjoyment in adolescent sport participants. *Adolescence*, LI, 283–295.

Carron, A. V., Spink, K. S., and Prapavessis, H. (1997). Team building and cohesiveness in the sport and exercise setting: Use of indirect interventions. *Journal of Applied Sport Psychology, 9*, 61–72.

Chaumeton, N., and Duda, J. (1988). Is it how you play the game or whether you win or lose?: The effect of competitive level and situation on coaching behaviors. *Journal of Sport Behavior, 11,* 157–174.

Duncan, S. C. (1993). The role of cognitive appraisal and friendship provisions in adolescents' affect and motivation toward activity in physical education. *Research Quarterly for Exercise and Sport, 64*, 314–323.

Duncan, T., and Duncan, S. (1991). A latent growth curve approach to investigating developmental dynamics and correlates of change in children's perceptions of physical competence. *Research Quarterly for Exercise and Sport, 62*, 390–398.

Dweck, C. (1996). Implicit theories as organizers of goals and behaviors. In P. Gollwitzer and J. Bargh (Eds.), *The psychology of action* (pp. 69–90). NY: Guilford Press.

Dweck, C., and Leggett, E. (1988). A social-cognitive approach to motivation and personality. *Psychological Review, 95*, 256–273.

Ebbeck, V., and Weiss, M. R. (1998). Determinants of children's self-esteem: An examination of perceived competence and affect in sport. *Pediatric Exercise Science, 10*, 285–298.

Eccles, J., and Harold, R. (1991). Gender differences in sport involvement: Applying the Eccles' expectancy-value model. *Journal of Applied Sport Psychology, 3*, 7–35.

Eccles, J. S., Wigfield, A. W., and Schiefele, U. (1998). Motivation to succeed. In W. Damon (Series Ed.) and N. Eisenberg (Vol. Ed.), *Handbook of child psychology (5th ed., Vol, 3): Social, emotional, and personality development* (pp. 1017–1095). NY: Wiley.

Feltz, D., and Brown, E. (1984). Perceived competence in soccer skills among young soccer players. *Journal of Sport Psychology, 6*, 385–394.

Fry, M. D. (2000). A developmental analysis of children's and adolescents' understanding of luck and ability in the physical domain. *Journal of Sport and Exercise Psychology, 22*, 145–166.

Fry, M. D. (in press). A developmental examination of children's understanding of task difficulty in the physical domain. *Journal of Applied Sport Psychology*.

Fry, M. D. and Duda, J. L. (1997). A developmental examination of children's understanding of effort and ability in the physical and academic domain. *Research Quarterly for Exercise and Sport, 68*, 331–344.

Gill, D. (in press). Gender and sport behavior. In T. S. Horn (Ed.), *Advances in Sport Psychology* (2nd Ed.). Champaign, IL: Human Kinetics.

Harter, S. (1981). A model of intrinsic mastery motivation in children: Individual differences and developmental change. In W. A. Collins (Ed.), *Minnesota Symposium on Child Psychology* (Vol. 14, pp. 215–255). Hillsdale, NJ: Erlbaum.

Harter, S. (1985). *Manual for the Self-Perception Profile for Children*, Denver, CO: University of Denver.

Harter, S. (1987). The determinants and mediational role of global self-worth in children. In N. Eisenberg (Ed.), *Contemporary topics in developmental psychology* (pp. 219–242). NY: Wiley.

Harter, S. (1990). Causes, correlates, and the functional role of global self-worth: A lifespan perspective. In R. J. Sternberg and J. Kolligian (Eds.), *Competence considered* (pp. 67–97). New Haven, CT: Yale University Press.

Harter, S. (1998). The development of self-representations. In W. Damon (Series Ed.) and N. Eisenberg (Vol. Ed.), *Handbook of child psychology (5th Ed., Vol, 3): Social, emotional, and personality development* (pp. 553–618). NY: Wiley.

Harter, S., Pike, R., Efron, C., Chao, C., and Bierer, B. (1983). *Pictorial Scale of Perceived Competence and Social Acceptance for Young Children*. Denver: University of Denver.

Hartup, W. W. (1995). The three faces of friendship. *Journal of Social and Personal Relationships, 12*, 569–574.

Hartup, W. W. (1996). The company they keep: Friendships and their developmental significance. *Child Development, 67*, 1–13.

Horn, T. S. (1987). The influence of teacher-coach behavior on the psychological development of children. In D. Gould and M. Weiss (Eds.), *Advances in pediatric sport sciences* (Vol. 2, pp. 121–142). Champaign, IL: Human Kinetics.

Horn, T. S. (in press). Coaching effectiveness in the sport domain. In T. S. Horn (Ed.), *Advances in sport psychology* (2nd Ed.), Champaign, IL: Human Kinetics.

Horn, T. S., and Hasbrook, C. (1986). Informational components influencing children's perceptions of their physical competence. In M. Weiss and D. Gould (Eds.), *Sport for children and youths: Proceedings of the 1984 Olympic Scientific Congress* (pp. 81–88). Champaign, IL: Human Kinetics.

Horn, T. S., and Hasbrook, C. (1987). Psychological characteristics and the criteria children use for self-evaluation. *Journal of Sport Psychology, 9*, 208–221.

Horn, T. S., Lox, C., and Labrador, F. (2001). The self-fulfilling prophecy theory: When coaches' expectations become reality. In J. M. Williams (Ed.), *Applied sport psychology: Personal growth to peak performance* (4th Ed., pp. 63–81). Mountain View, CA: Mayfield.

Horn, T. S., and Weiss, M. R. (1991). A developmental analysis of children's self-ability judgments in the physical domain. *Pediatric Exercise Science*, 3, 310–326.

Horn, T. S., Glenn, S. D., and Wentzell, A.B. (1993). Sources of information underlying personal ability judgments in high school athletes. *Pediatric Exercise Science, 5*, 263–274.

Kimiecik, J. C., Horn, T. S., and Shurin, C. S. (1996). Relationships among children's beliefs, perceptions of their parents' beliefs, and their moderate-to-vigorous physical activity. *Research Quarterly for Exercise and Sport, 67*, 324–336.

Lenney, E. (1977). Women's self-confidence in achievement settings. *Psychological Bulletin*, 84, 1–13.

McKiddie, B., and Maynard, I. W. (1997). Perceived competence of school children in physical education. *Journal of Teaching in Physical Education, 6*, 324–339.

Meyer, W., Bachmann, M., Biermann, V., Hempelmann, P., Ploger, F., and Spiller, H. (1979). The informational value of evaluative behavior: Influence of praise and blame on perceptions of ability. *Journal of Educational Psychology, 71,* 259–268.

Nicholls, J. G. (1989). *The competitive ethos and democratic education.* Cambridge, MA: Harvard University Press.

Nicholls, J., and Miller, A. (1984). Development and its discontents: The differentiation of the concepts of ability. In J. Nicholls (Ed.), *Advances in motivation and achievement: The development of achievement motivation* (pp. 185–218). Greenwich, CT: JAI.

Ommundsen, Y., and Vaglum, P. (1991). Soccer competition anxiety and enjoyment in young boy players: The influence of perceived competence and significant others' emotional involvement. *International Journal of Sport Psychology, 22,* 35–49.

Parker, J. G., and Asher, S. R. (1993). Friendship and friendship quality in middle childhood: Links with peer group acceptance and feelings of loneliness and social dissatisfaction. *Developmental Psychology, 29,* 611–621.

Parker, H. E., Larkin, D., and Ackland, T. R. (1993). Stability and change in children's skill. *Psychological Research, 55,* 182–189.

Petlichkoff, L. (1993). Relationship of player status and time of season to achievement goals and perceived ability in interscholastic athletes. *Pediatric Exercise Science, 5,* 242–252.

Phillips, D. A., and Zimmerman, M. (1990). The developmental course of competence and incompetence among competent children. In R. J. Sternberg and J. Kolligan, Jr. (Eds.), *Competence considered* (pp. 41–66). New Haven, CT: Yale University Press.

Plumert, J. M. (1995). Relations between children's overestimation of their physical abilities and accident proneness. *Developmental Psychology, 31,* 866–876.

Rudisill, M. (1989). Influence of perceived competence and causal dimension orientation on expectations, persistence, and performance during perceived failure. *Research Quarterly for Exercise and Sport, 60,* 166–175.

Scanlan, T., and Lewthwaite, R. (1986). Social psychological aspects of competition for male youth sport participants: IV. Predictors of enjoyment. *Journal of Sport Psychology, 8,* 25–35.

Schunk, D. (1989). Social-cognitive theory and self-regulated learning. In B. J. Zimmerman and D. H. Schunk (Eds.), *Self-regulated learning and academic performance* (pp. 83–110). New York: Springer-Verlag.

Smith, A. L. (in press). Peer relationships and physical activity participation in early adolescence. *Journal of Sport and Exercise Psychology.*

Stipek, D., and Daniels, (1988). Declining perceptions of competence: A consequence of changes in the child or in the educational environment? *Journal of Educational Psychology, 80,* 352–356.

Stipek, D., and Mac Iver, D. (1989). Developmental change in children's assessment of intellectual competence. *Child Development, 60,* 521–538.

Stipek, D., Recchia, S., and McClintic, S. (1992). *Self-evaluation in young children, With commentary by Michael Lewis*. Monographs of the Society for Research in Child Development, *57* (1, Serial No. 226).

Sullivan, H. S. (1953). *The interpersonal theory of psychiatry*. NY: W. W. Norton and Company.

Treasure, D. C., and Roberts, G. C. (1995). Applications of achievement goal theory to physical education: Implications for enhancing motivation. *Quest, 47,* 475–489.

Ulrich, B. (1987). Perceptions of physical competence, motor competence, and participation in organized sport: Their interrelationships in young children. *Research Quarterly for Exercise and Sport, 58,* 57–67.

Ulrich, B. D., and Ulrich, D. A. (1997). Young children's perceptions of their ability to perform simple play and more difficult motor skills. In M. E. Clark and J. H. Humphrey (Eds.), *Motor development: Research and reviews, Volume I* (pp. 24–45). Reston, VA: National Association of Sport and Physical Education.

Vealey, R. (1988). Sport-confidence and competitive orientation: An addendum on scoring procedures and gender differences. *Journal of Sport and Exercise Psychology, 10,* 471–478.

Vealey, R., and Campbell, J. (1988). Achievement goals in adolescent figure skaters: Impact on self-confidence, anxiety, and performance. *Journal of Adolescent Research, 3,* 227–243.

Vallerand, R. J., and Losier, G. F. (1999). An integrative analysis of intrinsic and extrinsic motivation in sport. *Journal of Applied Sport Psychology, 11,* 142–169.

Vallerand, R. J., Deci, E. L., and Ryan, R. M. (1987). Intrinsic motivation in sport. In K. B. Pandolf (Ed.), *Exercise and sport sciences reviews* (Vol. 15, pp 389–425). New York: Macmillan.

Watkins, B., and Montgomery, A. (1989). Conceptions of athletic excellence among children and adolescents. *Child Development, 60,* 1362–1372.

Weiss, M. R. (1987). Self-esteem and achievement in children's sport and physical activity. In D. Gould and M. R. Weiss (Eds.), *Advances in pediatric sport sciences, Volume 2: Behavioral issues* (pp. 87–120). Champaign, IL: Human Kinetics.

Weiss, M. R. (1995). Children in sport: An educational model. In S. Murphy (Ed.), *Sport psychology interventions* (pp. 39–69). Champaign, IL: Human Kinetics.

Weiss, M. R., and Ebbeck, V. (1996). Self-esteem and perceptions of competence in youth sport: Theory, research, and enhancement strategies. In O. Bar-Or (Ed.), *The encyclopaedia of sports medicine, Volume VI:. The child and adolescent athlete* (pp. 364–382). Oxford: Blackwell Science Ltd.

Weiss, M. R., and Ferrer-Caja, E. (in press). Motivational orientations and sport behavior. In T. S. Horn (Ed.), *Advances in sport psychology* (2nd ed.). Champaign, IL: Human Kinetics.

Weiss, M. R., and Petlichkoff, L. M. (1989). Children's motivation for participation in and withdrawal from sport: Identifying the missing links. *Pediatric Exercise Science, 1,* 195–211.

Weiss, M. R., and Smith, A. L. (1999). Quality of youth sport friendships: Measurement and validation. *Journal of Sport and Exercise Psychology, 21,* 145–166.

Weiss, M., Bredemeier, B., and Shewchuk, R. (1986). The dynamics of perceived competence, perceived control, and motivational orientation in youth sports: In M. R. Weiss and D. Gould (Eds.), *Sport for children and youths Proceedings of the 1984 Olympic Scientific Congress* (pp. 89–101). Champaign, IL: Human Kinetics.

Weiss, M. R., Smith, A. L., and Theeboom, M. (1996). "That's what friends are for": Children's and teenagers' perceptions of peer relationships in the sport domain. *Journal of Sport and Exercise Psychology, 18,* 347–379.

Weiss, M. R., McAuley, E., Ebbeck, V., and Wiese, D. M. (1990). Self-esteem and causal attributions for children's physical and social competence in sport. *Journal of Sport and Exercise Psychology, 12,* 21–36.

White, R. W. (1959). Motivation reconsidered: The concept of competence. *Psychological Review, 66,* 297–330.

Widmeyer, W. N., Brawley, L. R., and Carron, A. V. (in press). Group dynamics in sport. In T. S. Horn (Ed.), *Advances in sport psychology* (2nd Ed.). Champaign, IL: Human Kinetics.

CHAPTER 19

Enhancing Children's Sport and Life Experiences

Terry Orlick, University of Ottawa

Early sport experiences have a profound effect on the life of every child. These experiences, whether positive or negative, set the foundations for love or avoidance of sport and physical activity. Positive beginnings nourish future involvement in sport and physical activity—for pure joy, for the pursuit of excellence, or as a career. Early sport experiences have an enormous impact on how a child feels about himself or herself, not only in relation to sport and physical activity, but also with respect to global self-esteem. Children want and need an abundance of positive experiences in sport and in life. They want to play, not merely watch others play; they want to pursue their own goals, not only adult goals; they want less emphasis on winning and more freedom to have fun and learn at their own pace (Orlick, 1986, 1998a). Unfortunately, what children want and need most from sport is sometimes overshadowed by narrow visions of children's sport. The joy of play and the joy of a natural progression of skill development is overshadowed by emphasis on winning. This is reflected by the recruitment of bigger, more intimidating young players, high dropout rates, early specialization, and discrimination in team selection against children who are smaller, less physically mature, and less assertive. Some children face enormous pressure from coaches and parents to perform on demand and, if they do not, are subjected to what borders on child abuse—being humiliated in front of others, screamed at, ignored, left out, made to feel worthless or like a failure. Clearly this is not what children want or need from their early sport experiences. To help children fully benefit from their early sport experiences, positive change can come from a number of directions. This chapter targets two areas: (1) providing an alternative to the competitive model, and (2) enhancing children's capacity to cope with and benefit from their sport experience through mental skills training.

Alternatives to the Competitive Model

One way to help children experience more positive beginnings in sport is to change the environment in which they play and compete. A more positive and supportive environment will help to ensure that more children enjoy and gain from their early sport experiences. One of the dangers in an overemphasis on competition in children's sport is that it can lead to children's "free time" being monopolized by outcome oriented play, or competitive activities, with no play time to balance their lives or values. By turning everything into a competition, or even a quest for mastery, we rob children of an important life perspective—one of balance and joy. Children and adults desperately need time away from the demands of school or work or competition—to relax, re-energize and embrace life's simple joys (Orlick, 1998b). If we can't have joy and balance in our lives as children, when can we ever have them?

Cooperative games provide one joyful alternative where children learn to cooperate and play with more joy, without judgment and without worrying about living up to the performance expectations of others. Sport can also be played in a more respectful, joyful, and healthy manner. One of the best ways to help keep sport in perspective is for parents, coaches, and children to remember why they play in the first place—for fun, for joy, for developing friends and learning new skills. We can do a better job at respecting children's reasons for being there and teach them positive ways of coping with the potential stresses that may come their way (Orlick, 1998a).

The Challenge of Cooperative Sport and Games

A message that children often receive through television, professional sport, the media, school or community is that all that matters is the final product—winning. Many children are funneled through systems that appear to value only results or winning, as opposed to embracing ongoing learning and enjoyment. They often learn to evaluate their overall worth by results or numbers, to live only for the future, and to accept that there is no place free from evaluation. Many children and youth feel that they are always being judged or evaluated and must always do their best or suffer the consequences of being a failure. One way to eliminate or dramatically reduce the stress and related problems experienced in highly competitive children's sport is to simply alter the basic game structure. For example, change the rules, remove the need to compete, reduce the rewards for winning or for demonstrating mastery over others.

The distinctive feature of cooperative games, which separates them from all other games, is their structural makeup. For example, in the traditional game of Musical Chairs, children not quick enough to sit on one of the remaining chairs when the music stops are eliminated. In the end, one winner is left and all the rest are losers. This game has a competitive structure, the rules dictate that players act against one another to win, and in the end only one child attains the stated object of the game. All the rest are losers.

In the cooperative version, as the number of chairs decreases, the children sitting on those chairs increase until all the children are either sitting on the last chair or sitting on or touching someone who is sitting on the last chair. This version frees the players from the pressure to compete, eliminates the need for destructive behavior, includes everyone for the duration of the game, and by design encourages cooperation and fun-filled interaction (Orlick, 1978, 1982). The concept is simple: People play *with* one another rather than *against* one another; they play to overcome challenges, not to overcome other people; and they are freed by the very structure of the activity to enjoy the game itself. No child needs to find himself or herself a benchwarmer nursing a bruised self-image. When games are designed so that cooperation among players is necessary to achieve the game objective(s), children play together for common ends rather than against one another for mutually exclusive ends. In the process, they learn in a fun way how to become more considerate of one another, more aware of how other people are feeling, and more willing to operate in one another's best interests.

Over the past 25 years I have developed and collected hundreds of cooperative games for various ages and abilities, from infants to the aged. Anyone can enjoy these games and most can be played virtually anywhere with almost no equipment. When these games are appropriately selected or adapted for a specific age group, they almost always result in total involvement, feelings of acceptance, cooperative contribution by all players, and lots of smiling faces (Orlick, 1975, 1978, 1982; Orlick and Pitman-Davidson, 1989; Orlick, 1995). Other books that have presented positive alternatives for children's competition and cooperation include those by Botterill and Patrick (2000), Fine and Sachs (1997), Michaelis and Michaelis (1977), Morris (1980, 1978b), and Weinstein and Goodman (1980).

Cooperative Values in Day-to-Day Living

Studies conducted on the effects that cooperative games can have on young children have shown significant positive effects with respect to increased empathy and cooperative behavior. They also show that learning through play has great transferability to human development outside of play or sport (Jensen, 1979; Orlick, 1981a, 1981b; Orlick and Foley, 1976; Orlick, McNally, and O'Hara, 1978; Pines, 1979; Provost, 1981; Witt, 1980). Positive beginnings with respect to learning about the value of cooperation and empathy are extremely important to children and society as a whole (Orlick, 1995). However, some pervasive problems exist that may negate the potential long-term positive impact of early exposure to cooperative play and games. First, the number of children currently engaged in high quality, active, cooperative learning opportunities is relatively low. Children's time involvement in these cooperative activities is often minimal, and programs may not be continued from one age to the next (or from year to year).

Second, children who are fortunate enough to experience early, positive, cooperative learning opportunities at home, in their schools or community, live in a society that often supports contrary models of behavior (for example, through violent or non-empathetic models or heroes in television programming, professional sport, video-games, and videos/movies). They also experience highly competitive structures in school, sport, or community programs. The mediums of television, video-games, school, and sport provide a powerful, yet often insensitive model to overcome with respect to the promotion of cooperative play and empathetic living (Orlick, 1983, 1995, 1998).

Many positive human interaction skills can be learned within cooperative settings and cooperative play, and if these ways of interacting are fostered, they will become a part of everyday life. The way we interact with children from the very beginning has a profound effect on the extent to which they develop humanistic qualities. These qualities—shared empathy, flexibility of thought, creativity, respect, joy and humor—can be nurtured through a variety of mediums, a primary one being the medium of cooperative play. These qualities often surface naturally in young children. The only reason they fade as children grow is that they are not nurtured. What kind of an example or model do you see for children at home, at school, at play, and in the sport environment? Are you, and others who interact with children, modeling the perspectives, actions, and interactions that are likely to be of most value to children?

The paths for helping children grow in warm and loving ways are numerous. Here are some suggestions for parents, teachers, and coaches (Orlick, 1983, 1995):

- Acknowledge and encourage any positive gestures exhibited by children toward others.
- Discuss with children how others might feel when someone is not nice on their feelings. For example, if you witness an inconsiderate act during play or in a game, point it out and discuss it. Seize teachable moments to provide and reinforce more respectful ways of responding, wherever they occur.
- Voice your dissatisfaction with inconsiderate or disrespectful behavior on the part of any child. For example, if one child hits or hurts another child, physically or emotionally, tell him or her that it is unacceptable and respectfully explain why. Wherever possible, suggest and have children practice more positive responses that are more respectful of other people's feelings; for example, they can practice saying something positive or sharing, as an alternative to hitting or excluding. Challenge the child to be more positive and respectful "next time."
- Recognize and express appreciation for the contributions, positive perspectives, and positive actions of others, and encourage children to do likewise.
- Freely discuss your respect, concern and love for children and their positive attributes.

Cooperation during Competition

In many present day games and sports, a basic organizational structure exists where two or more people or teams want what only one can have—the goal, the ball, the space, or the victory. In such situations, issues of human values arise which include: How far will each person or organization go to achieve the goal? How will people react if they do not achieve the outcome goal? What will be the reactions of the "winners" and the "losers" towards the "winners" and the "losers"? One way to alleviate potential problems within competitive structures is to work on helping people bring more respectful perspectives into that structure.

At its best, competition can be a forum for the positive pursuit of personal excellence—a medium where participants can explore their personal potential and push beyond previous limits. At its worst, competition can pit person against person in destructive rivalry, resulting in high levels of anxiety, self-depreciation, insensitivity toward others, cheating, and destructive aggression.

Competitive games can be played in a more cooperative and humanistic fashion by helping children learn how to gain control over themselves and over the game. Within competitive structures there are countless opportunities for teaching important human values. What better place than in the midst of a game to discuss the true meaning of winning, losing, success, failure, anxiety, rejection, fair play, acceptance, friendship, cooperation, and healthy competition? What better place to help children become aware of their own feelings and more sensitive to the feelings of others? What better place to encourage children to help one another and to learn how to cope constructively with some of the concerns they face? A time-out can be called to take advantage of any meaningful learning opportunity. A value (or devaluation) can be discussed quickly, the behavior can be reinforced or a change in behavior recommended, and play can resume. With little direction, children can decide for themselves what they want to get out of a game and how they want to treat one another. They can discuss what other children do that makes them feel good or bad, how they think children should treat one another, how to help one another, and how to encourage one another to follow the values or action guidelines they feel are important. Orlick (1979a, 1979b, 1979c, 1980, 1981b, 1990, 1992, 1993, 1995, 1998, 2000), Orlick and Botterill (1975), Botterill (1978), and Halas (1987) have some good practical suggestions on how to carry out activities that promote cooperation, respect, and healthy competition.

Cooperative games are one way of meeting children's needs for early positive play and sport experiences. They have the added benefit of teaching prosocial values that can be applied to life outside of the sport context. Competitive games can also be a positive experience if the pursuit is kept in perspective, guided by respect, and centered on goals of personal growth or personal mastery. Unfortunately, healthy sport environments that are respectful and centered on children's needs are not always what children face. At times, children in these environments need and gain from developing a repertoire of positive coping skills.

Mental Training with Children

Although positive modifications to the competitive model for children are occurring in a number of areas, it will take greater personal commitment on the part of sport organizations, coaches, teachers, and parents to positively influence the real experiences of children in sport. Positive change takes effort and time, and many issues children are facing are beyond the direct control of those children. While we continue to pursue positive change, teaching children how to deal with the sport environment they find themselves facing is another important consideration.

In the sport world, the importance of mental training has been well established at the elite level. Personal excellence and satisfaction with performance achievements are largely due to mental readiness and positive coping skills (Orlick and Partington, 1988; Orlick, 2000). Mental skill training not only helps athletes maximize their potential, it also helps them deal with the potential stresses of competition, victory, loss, errors, and unmet goals. Children and young athletes can also benefit from mental skills training. The skills of mental readiness, relaxation, mental imagery, focusing, distraction control, and constructive evaluation for ongoing learning are useful in sport but are equally important in all other areas of life. They provide positive perspectives and skills for performance enhancement, handling stressful situations, and for enhancing the quality of daily life.

Teaching Mental Skills to Young Athletes

In the past 25 years, my colleagues and I have implemented many mental training programs with children and young athletes. The emphasis of these programs is on teaching children the skills of mental planning, relaxation, imagery, focusing, refocusing, and constructive evaluation to assist them with mental and physical skill learning and in maximizing their potential. Helping children to gain and maintain a healthy perspective toward sport, school, and life is also an important goal in these programs (Orlick, 1998).

Our work in providing mental training services for young athletes has shown that children are highly capable of learning and applying a variety of mind/body skills (Zhang, Ma, Orlick, and Zitzelsberger, 1992). We have found that many of the skills and techniques we teach high performance athletes are relevant for children, as long as the strategies and perspectives are explained, adapted, simplified, and presented in terms the children understand. Most children enjoy doing these activities and learning these skills, including mental imagery and simple relaxation procedures. They gain from developing simple individualized plans or routines for pre-practice and pre-competition situations and have some very creative ideas for dealing with hassles, stress, or distractions. We have also found that their mental skills improve dramatically with practice. For this reason we try to integrate mental skill improvement and refinement into their daily or weekly practice sessions.

The ideal situation is to incorporate mental skills (such as imagery or focusing) into the execution of technical/physical skills during practice sessions. For example, a young diver can be encouraged to get into a routine of correctly "feeling" the take-off, the dive, and the entry, in his or her mind and body, before doing the dive, and then fully focus on executing that image. Consistent positive input and positive reminders are often necessary to ensure that children and youth integrate their mental skills with their physical skills on a consistent basis.

Teaching Mental Skills in the School System

Our focus with children in the past 10 years has been on developing and refining a highly effective mental skills program for elementary school children from kindergarten through Grade 6. The program consists of a series of fun games and activities that guide children through the development of their mental strengths and stress control skills. Activities include positive thinking, positive perspective training, relaxation, imagery, focusing, and refocusing. We also help children to develop more confidence in themselves and more positive perspectives towards life through exercises that teach them to think in positive ways, to look for highlights in each day (the good things in the day, small or large), to put away small stresses and to switch from negative thoughts to a more positive frame of mind (Orlick, 1998).

In the early 1990s, we began to test this program in a number of elementary schools. We received very positive feedback from teachers, students, parents, and administrators. The children not only found the games, exercises and activities fun, but they also were able to take the concepts and strategies and use them effectively in school, at home, and in sport. The best of these games and activities have been turned into a comprehensive program for teachers, parents and coaches. Not only do children benefit from learning these skills, but teachers, parents, and coaches also benefit from a class of students or group of youngsters who are positive, cooperative, and more capable of managing ongoing stressful situations in a more healthy way (Orlick, 1998).

Approaches That Work with Children

When we are effective with children, whether they are young athletes or children in another setting (e.g., school, hospital, summer camps), we have a meaningful impact with respect to enhancing life skills, coping skills, performance skills, self-confidence, and/or quality of living. To have a positive effect on children's lives, the following guidelines appear to work best.

Simple strategies. Use simple approaches that allow children to form a clear image or feeling of what they are attempting to accomplish. For example, a child can pretend he is a piece of cooked spaghetti to relax, imagine she is changing channels of a TV to change the focus in her mind from negative to positive, use a little marble bag ("stress bag") to place worries in, create internal performance images and positive feelings while watching a video of someone performing a skill, practice focusing on cornflakes by focusing on one flake and then finding it among a number of others (for additional examples see Orlick, 1998).

Keep it fun. When working with children, it is important to keep an element of fun in your approach or integrate some fun into the strategy itself. A young child does not have fun going through a dry, matter-of-fact progressive muscle relaxation procedure. However, children do have fun pretending they are a piece of warm, cooked spaghetti curling up on a plate. Turning an exercise into playing a game is the best way to get concepts across to children and ensure they will continue to practice them.

Concrete, physical component. Strategies that allow a child to physically act out the removal of stress or physically act out an image seem to work best. For example, with respect to refocusing or shifting the focus away from worry, children relate well to putting "it" into a tree, a match box, or a stress bag. In a sport like gymnastics, putting the handgrips used for one event into a gym bag is an effective way to put away the last event and focus on the next.

Individualized approach. Getting to know a child as a unique individual is very important. The better you get to know a child, the better you can understand her specific needs, draw upon her input, and adapt your approach to fit the reality of her situation.

Multiple approaches. If one approach does not work for a particular child, try another. As you get to know children better and they begin to understand their options more clearly, approaches that fit the situation become more prevalent.

Be positive and hopeful. Whether you are working with children in sport or in another setting (e.g., school, hospital), it is important that you project a positive belief in that child, in his or her strengths, and in his or her capacity to overcome obstacles and pursue personal goals.

Use role models. Most children respond well to the use of role models. If well chosen, a role model can set a positive example to emulate with respect to mental skills, physical skills, a healthy perspective, persistence, or anything else one might want to pursue. We often use videos of respected high-performance athletes to help younger athletes form a clearer image of moves they might like to do.

Involve parents. Draw upon all the support systems possible when working with children. Parents are central. Wherever possible, solicit their support for reinforcing the concepts, positive approaches, and healthy perspectives you are attempting to teach. Talk with parents about what you are attempting to do, explain why it is important, and request their ongoing assistance in encouraging these important objectives.

Until our current societal values change in a substantial way, children will be forced to deal with stress in sport, school, and life. As concerned coaches, teachers, parents, or mental trainers, we need to continue to push for ways to improve the sport and life experiences of children—to place them more in keeping with what children themselves want. Providing children with opportunities to play free from expectation and evaluation is very important, as is helping them develop positive mental skills for stress control and self-growth.

Our ultimate goal with children is to teach them relevant cooperative values, mental skills, and positive perspectives that will enhance their quality of living. There is a great advantage in beginning this process at an early age to establish a concrete foundation of belief in themselves and in their capacity to directly influence the course of their lives. Children who learn positive mental skills and healthy perspectives early have more time to apply them to living their lives and pursuing their goals.

References

Botterill, C., and Patrick, T. (2000). *A guide for sport parents*. Sport Manitoba (www.sport.mb.ca).

Botterill, C. (1978, July). Psychology of coaching. *Coaching Review,* pp. 45–57.

Fine, A. H., and Sachs, M. L. (1997). *The total sport experience for kids*. South Bend, IN: Diamond Communications.

Halas, J. (1987). *The effect of a social learning intervention program on a grade seven physical education program*. Unpublished master's thesis, University of Ottawa, Ontario.

Jensen, P. (1979). *The effect of a cooperate games program on subsequent free play of kindergarten children*. Unpublished doctoral dissertation, University of Alberta, Edmonton.

MacGregor, R. (1993, November 20). The great Canadian dream fades. *The Ottawa Citizen*, pp. B1–B2.

Michaelis, B., and Michaelis, D. (1977). *Learning through noncompetitive activities and play*. Palo Alto, CA: Learning Handbooks.

Morris, G. (1980). *How to change the games children play* (2nd ed.). Minneapolis: Burgess.

Orlick, T. (1978a). *The cooperative sports and game book*. New York: Pantheon.

Orlick, T. (1978b). *Winning through cooperation: Competitive insanity, cooperative alternatives*. Washington, DC: Acropolis Press.

Orlick, T. (1979a). Children's games: Following the path that has heart. *Elementary School Guidance and Counseling, 114*, 156–161.

Orlick, T. (1979b). Cooperative games: Cooperative lives. *Recreation Research Review, 6,* 9–12.

Orlick, T. (1979c, January). What do parents want for their kids, coach? *Coaching Review*, pp. 19–21.

Orlick, T. (1980). Cooperative play and games. In J. Knight (Ed.), *All about play: A handbook of resources on children's play* (pp. 46–59). Ottawa, Ontario: Canadian Council on Children and Youth.

Orlick, T. (1981a). Cooperative play socialization among preschool children. *Journal of Individual Psychology, 37*, 54–64.

Orlick, T. (1981b). Positive socialization via cooperative games. *Developmental Psychology, 17*, 426–429.

Orlick, T. (1982). *The second cooperative sports and games book*. New York: Pantheon.

Orlick, T. (1983, June). Enhancing love and life mostly through play and games. *Humanistic Education*, pp. 153–164.

Orlick, T. (1986). Evolution in children's sport. In M. R. Weiss and D. Gould (Eds.), *Sport for children and youths* (pp. 169–178). Champaign, IL: Human Kinetics.

Orlick, T. (2000). *In pursuit of excellence: How to win in sport and life through mental training*. Champaign, IL: Leisure Press.

Orlick, T. (1995). *Nice on my feelings: Nurturing the best in children and parents*. Carp, Ontario: Creative Bound,

Orlick, T. (1998). *Feeling great: Teaching children to excel at living*. Carp, Ontario: Creative Bound.

Orlick, T., and Botterill, C. (1975). *Every kid can win*. Chicago: Nelson-Hall.

Orlick, T., and Foley, C. (1976). Pre-school cooperative games: A preliminary perspective. In A. Yiannakis, T. McIntyre, M. Melnick, and D. Hart (Eds.), *Sport sociology: Contemporary themes* (2nd ed., pp. 266–273). Dubuque, IA: Kendall/Hunt.

Orlick, T., and Pitman-Davidson, A. (1989). Enhancing cooperative skills in games and life. In F. L. Smoll, R. A. Magill, and M. J. Ash (Eds.), *Children in sport* (3rd ed., pp. 149–160). Champaign, IL: Human Kinetics.

Orlick, T., McNally, J., and O'Hara, T . (1978). Cooperative games: Systematic analysis and cooperative impact. In F. L. Smoll and R. E. Smith (Eds.), *Psychological perspectives in youth sports* (pp. 203–225). Washington, DC: Hemisphere.

Orlick, T., and Partington, J. (1988). Mental links to excellence. *The Sport Psychologist, 2*, 105–130.

Pines, M. (1979, January). Good samaritans at age two. *Psychology Today*, pp. 66–77.

Provost, P. (1981). *Immediate effects of film-mediated cooperative games on children's prosocial behaviour*. Unpublished master's thesis, University of Ottawa, Ontario.

Weinstein, M., and Goodman, J. (1980). *Play fair: Everybody's guide to non-competitive play*. San Luis Obispo, CA: Impact.

Witt, W. (1980). *Comparison of a traditional program of physical education and a cooperative games program on the cooperative classroom behaviour of kindergarten children*. Unpublished master's thesis, Temple University, Philadelphia.

Zhang, L., Ma, Q., Orlick, T., and Zitzelsberger, L. (1992). The effect of mental-imagery training on performance enhancement with 7–10 year old children. *The Sport Psychologist, 6*, 230–142.

CHAPTER 20

Expertise in Youth Sport: Relations Between Knowledge and Skill

Jere D. Gallagher, University of Pittsburgh
Karen E. French, University of South Carolina
Katherine T. Thomas, Iowa State University
Jerry R. Thomas, Iowa State University

In recent years, motor development researchers have analyzed how children learn and perform sport skills in complex and varying environments. Emphasis has been placed on the evaluation of motor and cognitive skills and their role in children's development of sport expertise (for comprehensive reviews see French and McPherson, 1999; Starkes, Helsen, and Jack, 2001). In this paradigm, the development of cognitive (perception, attention, decision making, paramaterization, knowledge base, etc.) and motor skill (response execution) components of sport performance are considered to be closely linked, both being necessary if the goal is for children to achieve higher levels of sport performance. Sport practice that requires intense physical effort and mental concentration is also considered to be the most enjoyable (Starks et al., 2001). With the connection between cognition and physical demands and the knowledge that it takes approximately 10 years to become an expert (Ericsson, Krampe, and Tesch-Romer, 1993), research needs to determine "best practice" for acquiring sport expertise.

The major goal of this chapter is to tease apart differences between experts and novices to assist in the development of expertise. Research has documented numerous differences in perceptual and cognitive abilities of adult expert and novice sport performers. Adult experts exhibit superior perceptual skills in anticipating the flight of objects (Abernethy, 1988: Abernethy and Russell, 1987a, badminton; Bard and Fleury, 1981, ice hockey; Jones and Miles, 1978, tennis), use different visual cues or visual search strategies (Abernethy, 1988; Abernethy and Russell, 1987b, badminton; Bard and Fleury, 1976, basketball; Helsen and Bard, 1989, soccer), detect the presence or absence of game-related stimuli (Allard and Starkes, 1980, volleyball), and recognize sequences of movements more accurately (Vickers, 1986, gymnastics).

A number of cognitive differences between expert and novice adult performers have also been determined. For example, experts recall game structured information more accurately than novices (Allard and Burnett, 1985; Allard, Graham, and Paarsula, 1980; Starkes, 1987), make faster and more accurate sport decisions (Bard and Fleury, 1976, basketball; Helsen and Bard, 1989, soccer; Starkes, 1987, field hockey), and employ different problem representations and cognitive processes to monitor current game situations, predict possible game scenarios, and plan actions in advance (McPherson, 1993a).

Since a major goal of youth sport is to improve the cognitive and motor skills of children to participate with skill and confidence, this chapter focuses on the perceptual, cognitive and decision making factors that impact the development of expertise in athletes of varying ages and concludes with our best practice guidelines. In the first section we present a sport acquisition research model that establishes a link between the development of motor and cognitive skills. We then review the development of memory and the influence of memory strategy use on knowledge base. Next we focus on the content of knowledge base and how a well-developed knowledge base facilitates memory strategy use and decision making even in young children. We conclude with application for youth sport coaches to interweave the development of skill and cognition during practice.

Sport Acquisition Research Model

An important question is whether the research on expertise has any impact on practice (Thomas and Thomas, 1999). Each sport has a complex set of rules, strategies, and skills that provide opportunities to gain understanding about how competence is developed. In fact, Ornstein and Naus (1985) make this very point when they indicate the need to determine what children of various ages know about specific content domains. Further, the sport-specific rules, strategies, and skills (a specific content domain for each sport) are of great interest to children over many years—in some instances over the life span. Thus motivation, interest, and persistence are inherent in the sport.

Coaches, instructors, and performers benefit in applied ways from a sport-specific research model. Much information is acquired about ways to structure practice; what types of skill to teach first, how knowledge can be organized for effective instruction; techniques for teaching sport-specific strategies; and rates at which skill, knowledge, and strategies are learned and how they interact. This chapter integrates research using a sport-specific model to contribute to both theory and application.

Whether an open or closed environment, sport provides the athlete with a dynamic situation. For open sports, the environment is rapidly changing and the athlete needs to attend to the important cues in the environment while ignoring the irrelevant information yet remaining vigilant to any unexpected important changes. Quick decision making is imperative. The situation changes rapidly when playing soccer. Closed sports require the individual to make complex decisions but the individual can plan ahead. Whether the sport is open or closed, to compete the athlete needs to attend to the appropriate environmental information, make the best decision, and execute the movements. The next section of this chapter reviews the memory components that impact the selection of environmental information and decision making.

Memory Development

Past research in the cognitive literature has investigated the role of children's memory processes on acquisition and retention of information (Bjorklund, 1985; Bjorklund and Thompson, 1983; Brown and Deloach, 1978; Chi, 1976, 1977, 1978, 1982; Ornstein and Naus, 1985; Piaget, 1969). These researchers have indicated three factors affecting memory development: capacity, strategies, and knowledge. In the next sections, we briefly address the controversy concerning memory capacity and then cover perception prior to returning to how memory strategies influence both capacity and perception.

The capacity hypothesis states that the improvement in memory performance with increasing age can be partially explained by an increase in memory capacity. The predominant explanation is that as children mature, memory capacity increases, allowing them to retain more (Piaget, 1969). The underlying metaphor was to view the mind as a container. As posited by Brown and Deloach (1978): "Little people have little boxes or jars in their heads, and bigger people have bigger ones" (p. 45). According to this view, any developmental difference in memory performance could be attributed to the capacity limitations of the younger groups.

The capacity hypothesis was challenged in the early 1970s by human information-processing theory. In this paradigm, cognitive researchers (Craik and Lockhart, 1972; Flavell, 1970) argued for a more active role of the memory system. Memory was viewed as a sequence of elaborate mental processes beginning with an initial stimulus and concluding with a response. The information received from the environment (perception) is held in various successive and temporary stores (working memory) until, through recoding and other transformations, it reaches a permanent store (long-term memory). Through perception the initial contact with memory established. The next sections review the research on perception, developmental strategy use changes in working memory, and long-term memory.

Perception

Prior to perception, information is maintained in a sensory store. Sensory store has unlimited capacity but is fleeting. If information is not attended to in sensory store, the information is lost from further use. The use and interpretation of information in sensory store is perception. With age, intrasensory discrimination (Thomas and Thomas, 1987) and intersensory integration improve (Williams, 1983). Improvement in intrasensory discrimination has been well documented for visual, auditory and kinesthetic systems.

The intrasensory development of the visual systems specifically related to sport performance includes visual acuity, spatial orientation, peripheral vision, perception of movement, and visual-motor coordination. Dynamic visual acuity, or the ability to perceive detail in a moving object, improves up to about 12 years of age, after which it remains stable (Gabbard, 2001). Gabbard (2001) indicates that children acquire adult-like perception at the following ages: visual acuity at 12 months, field of vision at 5 years, spatial orientation at 8 years, perceptual constancy by 11 years, depth perception and perception of movement by 12 years and figure-ground perception by 13 years. By about 11 years of age children are able to accurately judge the flight of a moving object. However, age is not the best predictor of coincident timing antici-pation. Kuhlman and Beitel (1997) found that a combination of the time spent playing video games and the time spent playing sport was a better predictor of ability than age.

In addition to improved intrasensory perception of vision, auditory perception also improves with age and experience. Basic auditory skills are evident by the age of 3 years but refinement continues until approximately 13 years of age when near adult levels are reached.

As children age they are more accurate with kinesthetic perception as evidenced by their increasing ability to position a limb (Thomas and Thomas, 1987; Williams, Temple, and Bateman, 1979), and discriminate touch (VanDyne, 1973). Included in kinesthetic perception is body awareness, spatial and directional awareness, vestibu-lar awareness and rhythmic awareness. By age 7 years the majority of children can identify both large and small body parts (Gabbard 2001). In the development of spatial awareness the individual is able to locate their body in space in relation to the environment. Thomas, Thomas, Lee, Testerman and Ashy (1983) found that providing cues to children as young as 5 years helped them to remember spatial locations and distances.

Directional concepts develop in a given sequence beginning around 3 years: up-down, front-back, side (Kuczaj and Maratson, 1975). Between 9 to 12 years children refine their ability to locate objects without reference to themselves (e.g. The ball was thrown over the head of the batter). Vestibular awareness (awareness of where one is in space) and balance improves into adolescence (Ulrich and Ulrich, 1985). Rhythmic awareness significantly improves around age 6 and continues until adolescence or early adulthood (Keogh and Sugden, 1985).

Improved discrimination within a sensory system gives the individual higher quality information with which to make decisions for response selection, adaptation of the response to meet environmental demands, and detection and correction of errors. An example of improved intrasensory discrimination is the child's ability to discriminate differences in speed or detect differences in weight. The coach is also able to present information to an older child in a more refined manner. The older child could detect smaller differences in error. Generally it appears that into adolescence we see improvement in discrimination that the coach needs to take into account when planning practice.

Intersensory development parallels improvements in intrasensory development. The use of better processing strategies (Millar, 1974) and improved intrasensory functioning (Bryant, 1968) are the basis for improved intersensory functioning. It appears that visual-tactile integration abilities, the most advanced in 5-year-olds, precedes development of visual-kinesthetic integration. Anticipation timing, requiring visual-kinesthetic integration, improves with age (Dunham and Reid, 1987; Thomas, Gallagher, and Purvis, 1981). Visual-auditory integration starts around 4 months of age but continues to develop until about 12 years of age.

The key message in this section is that the coach needs to consider maturational differences in the child. Coaches need to be aware of these perceptual changes and understand that although many abilities can be influenced by practice some require biological maturation. For perception to occur, the environmental information must be attended. After attention to and perception of the information, the individual must then manipulate the information. This occurs as an interaction of both working memory and long-term memory. Working memory processes are covered next, followed by changes in long-term memory.

Working Memory

The concept of short-memory (STM) is controversial, and the need for a separate STM system has been questioned (Dempster, 1988). Short-term memory has historically been defined as a passive rehearsal buffer for information (Atkinson and Shiffrin, 1968), but current research approaches STM as the active portion of long-term memory (Dempster, 1988). A dynamic, integrated memory system emphasizes active processing as opposed to merely a separate store. Thus the term short-term memory has been replaced by the term working memory to convey the idea of more than just a warehouse of information. The processing of information in working memory is accomplished through memory strategy use.

Of concern to contemporary researchers are developmental questions relating to the effectiveness of a particular strategy and conditions under which a strategy will be used and generalized. Much of the initial research focused on laboratory oriented tasks (Gallagher and Thomas, 1984) but has recently shifted to ecologically valid tasks including basketball (French and Thomas, 1987), baseball (French, Nevett, Spurgeon, Graham, Rink, McPherson, 1996; Nevett and French, 1997), and soccer, (McMorris and Graydon, 1996). Ornstein, Baker-Ward, and Naus (1988) view development of children's memory strategies as a process analogous to the development of skill. With increases in age and experience, the various cognitive operations that are involved in strategy production and execution become increasingly routinized and thus less demanding of attentional capacity and effort. The memory strategies reviewed here include attention, labeling, rehearsal, and organization.

Attention. A global term, attention, has been used to address a variety of proc-esses, ranging from concentration and vigilance to mental set and arousal (Abernethy, 1993). When performing a motor skill, the individual must deal with a wealth of exteroceptive and proprioceptive information. While moving, performers at times need to focus their attention on selected information and at other times divide their attention between several items of information, often shifting attention from one stimulus to another, all while ignoring irrelevant information (Kay and Ruskin, 1990). Throughout the performance the individual must scan the environment since the important cues appear at various locations. In this section we review the information-processing viewpoint of attention to include attention capacity (size of working memory), attention span (how long one attends to information), and selective atten-tion (the focus of attention).

Attentional capacity has been used interchangeably with memory capacity. As mentioned previously, the increase in the physical aspects of the memory system (the size of memory) appear to be minimal, with memory strategies and the amount of information in long-term memory playing a greater role (Gallagher and Thomas, 1984, 1986; Thomas, 2000). Kail (1988) argues that a general developmental change in memory is due to the efficient allocation of processing resources and mental effort. However, Abernethy, Thomas, and Thomas (1993) suggest that expertise is a product of encoding strategies rather than overall memory capacity. An example of an encod-ing strategy is naming or labeling and is covered later. The reasons for the capacity demands of strategy use decreasing with age are: practice, and increase and/or reorganization of the general knowledge base or more efficient and effective resource allocation of strategies (Guttentag and Ornstein, 1990). Younger children are re-garded as less capable of controlling their attentional resources than are older children and adults (Barrett and Shepp, 1988).

Reviewing the developmental literature, Guttentag and Ornstein (1990) concluded that the capacity demands of strategy execution generally decline with age, thereby affecting the complexity of the strategies that children are able to deploy. Guttentag (1989) found that young children must exert greater mental effort than older children to execute the same procedures or use a less effective procedure than older children while exerting the same level of mental effort. Spontaneous strategy deployment for children in grades 3 through 5 was predicted by the attentional demands of the strategy (Guttentag, 1989). These findings suggest that the high capacity demands of strategy execution do not prevent the younger children from being able to execute the strategy effectively; however, spontaneous strategy use was affected.

Paris (1988) suggests that age-related changes in spontaneous strategy selection are also influenced by interactions among the children's changing judgments of the effort required to use the strategy, their perceptions of the relative effectiveness of the strategy, and in their perceived level of required performance. Since young children have higher perceived costs of strategy use than older children, they may be unwilling to use the strategy due to the mental effort required.

A concept related to mental effort is metamemory. Research on metamemory determines the child's understanding of the working of the memory system and also determines whether the understanding of memory facilitates memory strategy use. Young children have some degree of awareness of the usefulness of memory strategies (Schneider and Sodian, 1988). Results from a study by Fabricius and Cavalier (1989) on labeling task-appropriate cues demonstrated that children's conceptions of how labeling worked predicted their self-initiated use of a labeling strategy. The results suggest that the effects of increasing accessibility and increasing strategy effectiveness on strategy acquisition are mediated through children's casual theories of memory. However, when faced with novel situations, children tend to abandon a strategy if they do not understand the benefits of the strategy (Rao and Moley, 1989). Bjorklund and Buchanan (1989) and Rabinowitz (1988) indicate a higher probability of training effectiveness for familiar material.

Attention span is also related to attentional effort. Attention span refers to the amount of time that an individual focuses on a task. Typically, older children and adults have longer attention spans than younger children. However, given motivation and interest, younger children can attend for long periods of time.

Once the child attends to the task, the next question is: Does the child know what to attend to? *Selective attention* serves in the perceptual encoding of task-appropriate cues and as a control process to continually maintain relevant information in working memory. What the individual attends to in the environment is extremely important. Chi (1997) and McPherson (1993a, 1993b) indicate how the individual initially represents the task at hand guides the retrieval and use of relevant information.

Research on selective attention has moved from a description of the development of selective attention (Ross, 1976; Stratton, 1978) to determining the mechanisms of selective attention and the relationship between perception and attention. Next, we cover the development of selective attention followed by the mechanisms of selective attention and the relationship between perception and attention.

Ross (1976) has proposed three levels in the development of selective attention: overexclusive, overinclusive, and selective attention. Up to 5 or 6 years of age, the child focuses on a limited number of cues that are not necessarily related to task appropriateness (underinclusive phase). The overinclusive child attempts to attend to a larger amount of environmental cues (between 6 and 7, and 11 and 12 years of age), and environmental distractors significantly impact task performance. At approximately 11 years of age the child develops the ability to selectively attend to task-appropriate cues and ignore irrelevant information. Impacting selective attention, children and adults or experts and novices might differ in whether they perceive the information in parts or as an integral whole and the type of visual search strategies used.

An important factor in determining the development of selective attention is understanding the relationship between perception and attention. During the past 20 years the joint development of perceptual organization and attention has been researched (Barrett and Shepp, 1988). One finding that has dominated the research is that young children perceive objects as integral wholes, whereas older children and adults perceive the same objects as aggregates of features. An implication from the interaction of perception and attention is that questions about the development of attention must also address the issue of perceived structure. If aspects of the stimuli are perceptually independent, the development of attention can be directly assessed. If, however, a child perceives an object as a whole the failure to attend to a feature of the object cannot be attributed to an inability to attend but must be attributed to the nature of the perceived structure. Research supports this linkage of perceptual and attentional development (Shepp, Barrett, and Kolbert, 1987). Most stimuli are integral for young children but become increasingly separate with increasing age. A series of studies by Shepp et al. (1987) concluded that the development of perceived structure is enhanced by the flexibility of attention that accompanies perceptual development. Accordingly, the young child attends primarily to holistic properties; but with increasing age and experience the child becomes increasingly proficient in extracting either featural or holistic properties.

Investigating visual search strategies when selecting environmental information, there has been a controversy as to whether experts search the environment with more fixations of shorter durations (Williams and Davids, 1998) or if due to superior selective attention strategies they have fewer fixations of longer duration (Helsen and Starkes, 1999; Ripoll, 1991). According to Paull and Glencross (1997) and Starks et al. (1999) the issue is not how the individual searches the environment but how the athlete makes use of that information.

Reviewing the question of on what should the athlete focus, French and McPherson (1999) concluded that the number of irrelevant concepts identified in a game situation decreased with age and expertise. Thus the athlete's ability to selectively attend to task appropriate cues improved. French, Werner, Rink, Taylor and Hussey (1996) suggest that experts focused their attention and cognitive resources on the task at hand, whereas novices divided their attention even further and uttered irrelevant emotional statements. Nevett and French (1997) found that high school shortstops focused their attention almost exclusively on information relevant to the game situation.

French and McPherson (1999) concluded that youth and adult novices attended to irrelevant conditions in the environment. The novices attended to characteristics of their own play and seldomly attended to their opponent, the environmental conditions, or other player positions. Since the players did not attend to their opponents, they did not diagnose their opponent's strengths, weaknesses, or tendencies to assist them in decision making. Nougier, Stein and Bonnel (1991) suggest that experts have developed a sport specific attentional organization that allows them to identify and use the behavioral cues produced by the opponent.

A different line of research is attempting to determine the KEY task appropriate cues during a game. Williams and Davids (1998) required expert and novice soccer players to predict directions of movement with various parts of the kicker/dribbler occluded and found the most appropriate place to focus was the hips and legs.

Since elementary school children have not developed a selective attention strategy, the question is: How do we teach children to attend to task-appropriate cues? There is a wealth of information in visual space; at times the individual has to focus attention on a specific aspect of performance while continuing to be vigilant of unexpected events (Ripoll and Benguigui, 1999). Since the environment surrounding any movement task is complex, with high levels of irrelevant information present and often times having to select a response within a short time frame, do children need to be taught the skill under low or high levels of interference? Thomas and Stratton (1977) and Ladewig and Gallagher (1992) and Ladewig, Cuthma, Martins, and Gallagher (2000) have conducted research manipulating levels of interference during practice. The results from these studies demonstrated that low interference early in practice had a positive result during acquisition, but subjects exposed to high levels of interference early in practice had poor performance. During a retention test with high levels of interference, results indicated a reversal. Subjects exposed to high levels of interference early in practice performed the retention task better. Thus the subjects performed better when there was low interference but did not develop the strategies to use when performing under high interference conditions. These results demonstrate the benefit of providing high interference early in practice as long as the subjects are given cues to focus attention. For this research, the task-appropriate information remained in the same location throughout the study. Future research needs to answer the question: When task complexity is increased such that the relevant information can be found in various locations in the environment, can the children still deal with the high amount of interference during early learning?

In contrast to Thomas and Stratton (1977) and Ladewig and Gallagher (1992) and Ladewig et al. (2000), McMorris (1999) feels that to develop decision making skills during early learning, the amount of relevant and irrelevant cues should be restricted. For example, he feels that athletes should play singles prior to doubles, play one-on-one team sports prior to adding teammates. These situations are far more complex than those tested by Thomas and Stratton (1977) and Ladewig and Gallagher (1992, 2000).

Attention to task appropriate cues is critical for learning and performance. Selective attention allows the encoding of information into memory while memory strategies allow the individual to maintain the information in memory and move it to long term memory. Memory strategy use changes with age and experience assisting the athlete in developing their long-term memory. Next we cover the development of the memory strategies of labeling, rehearsal and organization.

Labeling. A strategy related to the development of selective attention is labeling. Labeling is one aspect of perception, and increasing the meaningfulness of the label improves performance. The use of labels has improved children's recall performance for memory of location (Winther and Thomas, 1981), movement series (Miller, 1990;

Weiss, 1983; Weiss and Klint, 1987), and closed movement skills (head stands and forward rolls, Masser, 1993). Additionally, labels have facilitated the performance of children with a learning disability (Miller, 1990).

Using dancers as subjects, Poon and Rodgers (2000) found that a strategy used widely by all dancers to facilitate remembering dance routines was counting while the advanced dancers expanded this to include musical cues as labels. For example, high and low notes, specific instrumental highlights, and rhythmic information were associated with specific movements. The strategies adopted by the advanced dancers was a combination of verbal labels with counting, the music, and frequently they even created their own song to represent the dance. On the other hand, novice dancers used isolated verbal labels to represent certain movements or movement patterns.

Studying children in a sport environment, McPherson (1999a, 1999b) found that adult experts used verbal labels for error correction. The youth experts did not respond at the same level as the adult experts. Ille and Cadopi (1999) found that by age 10 or 11 labeling was the principal strategy used to remember gymnastic routines, although those who used labeling did not demonstrate improved performance.

Rehearsal. Another strategy in working memory that facilitates performance is rehearsal. Rehearsal is important to maintain information in memory with transfer to knowledge base. The importance of active rehearsal has been demonstrated in a study by Gallagher and Thomas (1984). Given a series of eight movements, 5- and 7-year-old children chose to rehearse on an instance-by-instance basis, whereas 11- and 19-year-old subjects grouped the movements for recall. When forced to rehearse in an adult fashion the 5- and 7-year-old children's performance improved. Similar findings have been reported for children with mental retardation (Reid, 1980; Schroeder, 1981).

Nevett and French (1997) found that high school shortstops rehearsed their action sequences more in certain situations (double play) when compared to younger players. In other situations their level of rehearsal did not differ (look runner back, critical run). The high school shortstops rehearsed combinations of high level conditions with their action sequences.

Investigating the rehearsal practices of dancers, Poon and Rogers (2000) found that novice dancers rehearsed dance movements in a child-like fashion. They started at the beginning of the dance and continued to add segments. For each new learning trial novice dancers would rehearse the routine from the beginning and add on the next segment. Expert dancers, on the other hand, rehearsed segments of the dance individually, creating chunks of movements.

Organization. Organization is a strategy used to combine meaningful information to reduce cognitive demands. Instead of thinking of separate pieces of information, the individual groups and recodes the information into one unit. A simple example of organization is how we remember telephone numbers; we tend to chunk or group the first three numbers followed by the last four. Studying organization of a series of eight movements Gallagher and Thomas (1986) manipulated the degree of organization in the material. Results indicated that 5-year-old children were unable to increase performance regardless of organization strategy or input of information. The 7-year-old children were able to use organized input to facilitate recall but the strategy failed to transfer to a new task. Eleven-year-old children's performances, with the exception of the unorganized input group, conformed to the predictions. It was anticipated that the 11-year-old children used organized input and showed some transfer of strategy. However, they could not restructure the information or produce a self-generated organizational strategy. Nineteen-year-old subjects organized the information regardless of input.

Integrating the studies on rehearsal and organization of input, Gallagher and Thomas (1986) indicated that forcing the use of the strategies was of greater importance to younger children; it had less effect on older children and adults. The older children and adults were using the strategies when not forced to do so, whereas the younger children were not. Even though the 5-year-old children were given organizational cues, they failed to recall the movements in order (from short to long). Forcing rehearsal, on the other hand, aided recall of the 5-year-old children. The 7-year-old children used the organizational strategy to recall eight movements. The older children and adults in the self-determined strategy were similar in recall to the organization strategy. They rehearsed spatially similar groups of movement.

Poon and Rodgers (2000) found that the major difference between the advanced and novice dancers was that when labeling, the advanced dancers chunked information and the novices tried to remember each step separately. The experts and novice dancers also differed in the way they organized the movements in the dance routine. The advanced dancers had fewer but larger segments of movements, while novices had more but smaller segments. The experienced dancers segmented the routines in a dance-specific manner using musical phrases, thus relying on domain-specific knowledge. The novice dancers had more randomly separated sections that were not directly organized in either a step-by-step or movement-by-movement fashion. The advanced dancers learned these chunks separately and not necessarily in the order of the routine. In addition to increasing the spontaneous use of strategies with experience, the individual begins to combine strategies.

Ille and Cadopi (1999) found evidence that 10- to 13-year old experts used an organization strategy when recalling gymnastics movements. They recalled second and third movements as often as first movements, thus suggesting chunking of the first three movements. The skilled gymnasts also indicated that they combined movements into "subsets."

In summary, younger children do not spontaneously use memory strategies. However, as Chi (1982) has suggested, this could be due to an inefficient knowledge base. Children's earliest successful memory strategies begin with highly familiar information, as do successful training efforts. A noticeable difference between novices and experts is the experts' ability to combine several strategies together and use them simultaneously, thereby making their encoding and retentions processes more effective. The automatization of these strategies occurs as a result of practice and experience, reducing the mental effort required to perform the strategy and lead to a functional enlargement of the space available in working memory for the handling of information-processing operations.

Long-Term Memory

Age-related changes in both the contents and familiarity of the knowledge base (long-term memory) have significant implications for the deployment of strategies. Knowledge base theorists postulate that knowledge is represented more elaboratively with increased practice; thus, information is accessed with less mental effort, leaving more mental resources available for the execution of strategies.

To this point, the various aspects of memory have been discussed with adult/child differences highlighted. Bjorklund (1985) and Ornstein and Naus (1985) have suggested there are long-term effects of changes in knowledge base on the developmental use of strategies, whereas Chi (1985) suggests that the relationship between strategy and knowledge is interdependent. Abernethy, Thomas, and Thomas (1993) state that it is limited long term memory store that causes the most problems for the child in processing information, and hence making decisions

Adult experts exhibited two types of memory profiles: action plan profiles and current event profiles (McPherson, 1999a, b, 2000). Action plan profiles are rule governed prototypes stored in long term memory that match conditions with appropriate actions or position moves. McPherson concluded that young baseball players and novice tennis players (youth and adult) exhibited weak or less advanced action plan profiles. Both adult tennis experts and older baseball experts were more consistent in terms of solutions regarding the best possible tactics.

Current event profiles are tactical scripts the athlete uses to develop and continually modify task relevant information during competition. A current script of game events potentially allows experts quick access and retrieval of information needed to make decisions during competition (Ericsson and Kintsch, 1995). Novices (both adult and youth) did not show evidence of current event profiles. Only the older experts in tennis and baseball displayed current event profiles during competition and used these profiles to modify and adjust responses to changing conditions.

A major reason to review strategy use, working memory and long term memory is to determine how adults and novices make decisions during competition. We next review the research on how knowledge is represented and then present information on decision making.

How Knowledge May Be Represented

This section deals with the type of information stored in the knowledge base, or long-term memory (LTM), and the quality of that information. Sport information is placed in LTM purposefully as a result of practice and experience. Increased knowledge is believed to be related to increases in skill level and experience (Abernethy et al., 1993). Two dimensions of sport performance are execution (motor skill) and decision making (cognitive). Information about each of these must be represented in memory. Execution knowledge is information about the mechanics of movement and movement parameters. Decision-making includes selecting a response and evaluating the outcome. As skill level improves from novice to expert, the quantity and quality of information in the knowledge base increases (McPherson, 1993b; McPherson, Dovenmuehler, and Murray, 1992; McPherson and Thomas, 1989).

Research on expertise has been conducted in many domains, for example, dinosaurs (Chi and Koeske, 1983), chess (Chase and Simon, 1973), and teaching (Berliner, 1986), resulting in a consensus that knowledge falls into three categories. These are declarative, procedural, and strategic knowledge (Chi, 1982). Research on sport has used the same categories to define knowledge (Chiesi, Spilich and Voss, 1979; French and Thomas, 1987; McPherson and Thomas, 1989).

Declarative knowledge includes factual information. Rules, definitions, and other facts about the sport are categorized as declarative knowledge. Experts typically have more declarative knowledge than novices, including more concepts and more information describing each concept (Chase and Simon, 1973; Chi, 1978; Chi and Koeske, 1983; French and Thomas, 1987). Declarative knowledge is consistent and typically organized in similar patterns among experts within a domain (Chiesi et al., 1979; Murphy and Wright, 1984). Declarative knowledge is possessed by all experts but can be observed in novices. In other words, to become an expert, an athlete must know the rules, facts, and other basic information about the sport and the movements' in the sport. However, this information does not guarantee that the athlete will become an expert.

Experts also have greater procedural knowledge than novices (Adelson, 1984; Chi, Feltovich, and Glaser, 1981; French and Thomas, 1987). Procedural knowledge, based on declarative knowledge, is knowing how to do something which is related to problem solving and decision making. Experts have more potential solutions and organize these in a way that leads to a logical solution. McPherson and Thomas (1989) called the connections between situations and outcomes *linkages*. Linkages were found to be a potent force in expert tennis players' ability to make good decisions. The tennis players had if-then statements that allowed them to select potential responses that were appropriate. The accuracy, number, and size of their selections increased with expertise. In some sports the number of concepts is more similar between experts and novices, but the experts have more connections among concepts and complexity within concepts (McPherson, 1993b). Athletes who have more potential solutions to problems in their sport with greater depth of understanding to those solutions tend to be more expert. The organization of these representations is critical to ensuring expertise. Once again, procedural knowledge is required for expertise but does not guarantee expertise.

Strategic knowledge is the use of general rules or control processes to facilitate cognitive processing. Chi and Koeske (1983) found that a child who was an expert on dinosaurs would use rehearsal and encoding strategies, within the domain of dinosaurs, that were beyond what a child of that age should use. However. those same control processes were not used by that child in other domains. This suggests a relationship among the three types of knowledge, indicating that strategic knowledge may be linked more to experience rather than being age dependent. The three types of knowledge are viewed as hierarchical in nature. Each succeeding level is somewhat dependent upon the previous level and more complex than the preceding level(s).

Movement information is stored or represented first as declarative—facts and rules. The movements become increasingly automatic, so the performer may be relatively unaware of response programming (e.g., selecting movement parameters). One thing is clear: Experts have considerable information about how to execute their sport skills and they are able to translate this into action, even when some experts have difficulty verbalizing the motor skill knowledge (Davis, Thomas, and Thomas, 1991; Thomas and Lee, 1992). In studies of golfers and swimmers, experts had more declarative and procedural knowledge about execution than novices. Thus skill execution and knowing about skill appear to be limiting factors in sport performance. This means that athletes must have cognitive representations of the efficient motor patterns associated with their sport and be able to execute those patterns to become experts.

Coaches and teachers may have limited influence over skill execution due to a wide variety of biological factors such as size, muscle type, and physique, but the potential of athletes should not be limited by skill knowledge (Davis et al., 1991). Compelling evidence from swimmers and golfers suggests the importance of skill knowledge. All experts in both sports were able to recognize or recall many concepts about execution; this information was represented differently, however, depending on the age of the individual. Child experts could pantomime or demonstrate the important points of form and efficiency. Adults could distinguish between written statements of correct and incorrect form. Novices in both sports did not know as much about the form of the skill and were less often able to actually execute the correct form. The novice golfers were often confident that they knew the correct form, even when they did not. These golfers were often doing exactly what they believed to be correct, when in fact the movement was not effective or efficient. Age-group swimmers often commented that coaches did not care how they swam, as long as it was fast. For athletes to maximize their talent, coaches and teachers must help them build correct cognitive representations of the important skills (Davis et al. 1991; Thomas and Lee, 1992).

In sum, information represented in long-term memory can be about the motor skill (execution) or decision making process (cognitive). Knowledge can be categorized as either declarative, procedural, or strategic. Higher levels of knowledge are associated with expertise, and lower levels limit sport performance. The next section reviews differences between experts and novices in decision making.

Decision Making

If given the opportunity to practice decision-making skills, children demonstrate levels of performance that are better than might be expected for their chronological age (French and Thomas, 1987; McPherson and Thomas, 1989). However, if a child is given a new problem without help, the child may not be able to determine relevant from irrelevant information and will have difficulty making a decision. Children need to be introduced to more complex displays and decisions that require them to develop restructuring skills.

French and McPherson (1999) indicate that decision making skills are intricately tied to an athlete's specific motor skills. During competition, the athlete will more likely choose the well-learned sport skills that are reliable (French, Nevett, Spurgeon, Graham, Rink and McPherson, 1996). Their decision is based upon confidence in their performance for a given skill (McPherson, 1999b). Finally, decisions are influenced by the game complexity, game context, or level of competition (i.e., changes in rules of the game at different ages, skill of teammates or opponent; French, Nevett, Spurgeon, Graham, Rink and McPherson, 1996).

Children should think ahead and pre-plan decisions. Younger baseball experts do not generate a plan in most baseball situations. Anticipating what the opponent will do next is important and helps the athlete in planning ahead. With increasing age, years of competition, and expertise, players more consistently generated multiple action plans and either rehearsed the alternative plans or modified and updated plans based on changing environmental conditions. The accuracy and sophistication of predictions improved with increasing age and expertise.

French, Spurgeon, and Nevett (1995) found that cognitive decision making does not discriminate skill levels in baseball game performance. For baseball, the frequency of occurrence of complex decisions is low, therefore the athletes are unable to practice. Secondly, coaches cue players concerning what to do between pitches. Also, frequently parents and spectators would loudly verbalize where to throw during a given play. This type of cueing and constant reinforcement of what to do before the ball is hit is very effective in producing higher percentages of correct game decisions. The bigger issue is, however, whether this is the most effective way to produce knowledgeable players who can make good decisions without prompting.

It appears likely that overreliance on coaches' and spectators' prompting encourages players to wait for coaches' prompts and not internalize or process game information at levels that lead to more effective knowledge representations. Like instances where more frequent feedback or knowledge of results (KR) can lead to poorer motor skill learning, high frequencies of prompting may lead to the same type of shallow processing that deters long-term benefits to knowledge and decision development. Coaches should provide practice opportunities for players to generate decisions in situations that occur frequently and infrequently. The emphasis should be on players choosing the correct response themselves (choice or responses) without prompts, rather than just drilling the appropriate response to one situation over and over.

Which Develops First: Cognitive or Motor Skill?

Development of both cognitive and motor skill components takes hours of practice and years to develop to high levels of performance. Few studies have been conducted longitudinally, following changes in cognitive and motor skills, over some period of time (season) or instruction. Some findings suggest that cognitive decision-making skills at low sophistication levels develop faster than motor skills (French and Thomas, 1987, basketball; McPherson and French, 1991, tennis).

French and McPherson (1999) suggest that knowledge and decision making processes may develop faster than motor skills. Van Geert (1993) claims that a limited working memory capacity means that the child can concentrate on developing one domain at a time. This brings into question attempts to teach decision-making and technique at the same time. French and associates (French, Werner, Rink, Taylor and Hussey, 1996; French, Werner, Taylor, Hussey and Jones, 1996) showed that adolescent children could learn both techniques and decision-making skills in tennis. However, if they tried to teach both simultaneously then learning was slower than when teaching one aspect only.

Other research suggests that what develops is at least in part determined by the focus of instruction or practice. Cognitive skills progressed faster in the French and Thomas (1987) study because players focused on cognitive skills more frequently in practice. Adult novices followed over a period of skill instruction and tactical instruction improved tennis skill only when direct instruction of the skills became a focus of practice (McPherson and French, 1991). Some improvement in low-level cognitive skills was made when instruction was primarily skill oriented. However, the development of procedural knowledge structures in tennis were much more advanced when instruction focused on building cognitive decision-making skills (McPherson, 1991).

Some developmental limitations appear to influence both cognitive and sport skill development. Anticipation timing and reaction time show developmental trends that are not always overcome by expertise at young ages as evidenced by French, Spurgeon, and Nevett (1995, batting, catching performance), Abernethy (1988, temporal occlusion), and Johnson, (1991, reaction time). Also, maturation constrains skill improvement in sport skills that require force production (throwing, kicking, etc.). Selection of the skill to use (Johnson, 1991) may be biased since the individual does not have confidence in performance of the skill.

Thus, constraints on cognitive and skill development exist during childhood and early adolescence. For some sports, readiness for certain sport skills and sport tactics is an issue. Most youth sport leagues modify the rules, equipment, and game to accommodate the skill levels of age-grouped participants (i.e., T-ball, coaches pitch, player pitch). Some sports, such as soccer, have specified age-appropriate skills and tactics in a youth coach's manual (Rees, 1987). In some cases, coaches modify the game strategies in a positive way to meet the skill levels of their individual players; for example, positioning a teammate to help relay the ball to the cutoff when outfielders can not throw all the way to second base.

The problem with modifying strategies to accommodate skill levels at young ages is that many coaches end up with strategies that eliminate lesser-skilled players from full participation in the game. Therefore, coaches need to carefully think about the reasons for modifying strategies and the potential impact of these modifications on every child's opportunity to learn the skills and tactics of the game.

Since youth sport coaches are relatively limited in identifying characteristics of expertise (Starkes, 1987) and expert level coaches are not in the developmental process until after expertise is well-established, coaches need to provide quality experiences for the young athletes. In the final section we apply the research and provide guidelines for youth sport coaches.

Application for Youth Sport Coaches

Throughout this chapter, we have stressed the interaction of cognitive and motor skill performance. When planning practice, the youth sport coach needs to emphasize both, in addition to providing situations in which the athletes are given practice at decision making. Skill execution and knowing how and when to execute the specific skills appear to be limiting factors in sport performance. The coach needs to be aware that athletes make decisions that are biased by skill constraints.

The type of experience that did seem to discriminate skilled players from lesser-skilled players was the amount of practice time outside of organized practices and games. Parents estimated the amount of time their child spent practicing skills with a number of significant others (e.g., father, mother, brother, friend). Across all ages, skilled players spent almost twice the amount of time practicing with a friend than the lesser-skilled players. This suggests that the skilled players were initiating practice of skills themselves rather than being externally motivated by a parent or father to practice. Thomas and Thomas (1999) found similar results when interviewing expert physical education teachers. Each teacher taught a nationally recognized athlete when the athlete was in elementary school. The teacher was asked what differentiated the national athletes when they were in elementary school from the other children. The teachers continually indicated practice, hard work, thinking, attitude and coordination.

The perceptual and memory adaptations uncovered thus far raise important issues and questions regarding what types of instruction and practice experiences may facilitate building more sophisticated knowledge structures, particularly the current event profile; focus of practice activities certainly influences what outcomes are learned. The challenging task is to uncover what types of practice produce what types of response selection and execution performance. The coach must remember that children are not miniature adults, expectations have to be related to their developing perceptual abilities and to their developmental level.

During practice the athlete needs to learn how to execute the skill while developing the decision-making skills to translate knowledge into action. The correct cognitive representation of the important skills needs to be provided to develop an error detection and correction mechanism. Links between gamelike situations and outcomes are important for the athlete to appropriately select the correct parameters of the skill (e.g. How hard do I need to throw the ball for it to go to the player on first base).

Improvement in a cognitive or skill component is not guaranteed by participation alone. Coaches need to provide practice opportunities that allow athletes to generate decisions to situations that occur both frequently and infrequently. Cueing and constant reinforcement by the coach during practice and game situations might be good for immediate performance but not for learning. The coach needs to remember that telling the children what to do during the game can help immediate performance (winning the individual game) but has a detrimental long term effect. The child does not develop the appropriate decision making capabilities.

Since there are age differences in the production and quality of sport-specific strategies associated with planning, the coach needs to assist the novices in adopting these strategies, developing plans in advance and continually updating their plans as the game situation changes. The coach can help the player attend to the appropriate cues and not waste valuable memory capacity by engaging in chatter. To help expand the alternative decisions, the coach can also help the child develop new techniques and develop confidence in those techniques. Players need to be taught to critically monitor the environment and relate the new information to information in long term memory (Rink, 1993). Coaches can have the children verbalize their plans in order to check thought processes. Based upon what the child is thinking, the coach can provide appropriate feedback (Rink, 1993).

Thomas and Thomas (1999) indicate that coaches should teach children what to do (procedural knowledge). Practice needs to be designed for quality. Effort and hard work need to be related to success. Clear goals need to be provided and improvement noticed.

Motivation is important. Skilled players initiate practice of the skills with other players, rather than being externally motivated by a parent or coach. Thus, coaches need to assist athletes in developing intrinsic motivation. Finally, children need to perceive the sporting experience as challenging yet fun!

References

Abernethy, B. (1988). The effects of age and expertise upon perceptual skill development in a racket sport. *Research Quarterly for Exercise and Sport, 59,* 210–220.

Abernethy, B. (1993). Attention. In R. Singer and G. Murphy and K. Tennant (Eds.), *Handbook on research on sport psychology* (pp. 127–170). New York: Macmillan.

Abernethy, B., and Russell, D. (1987a). Expert-novice differences in an applied selective attention task. *Journal of Sport Psychology, 9,* 326–345.

Abernethy, B., and Russell, D. (1987b). The relationship between expertise and visual search strategy in a racquet sport. *Human Movement* Science, *6,* 283–319.

Abernethy, B., Thomas, J., and Thomas, K. (1993). *Strategies for improving understanding of motor expertise.* Amsterdam: Elsevier.

Adelson, B. (1984). When novices surpass experts: The difficulty of the task may increase with expertise. *Journal of Experimental Psychology: Learning, Memory and Cognition, 10,* 483–356.

Allard, F., and Burnett, N. (1985). Skill in sport. *Canadian Journal of Psychology, 39,* 294–312.

Allard, F., Graham, K., and Paarsula, M. (1980). Perception in sport: Basketball. *Journal of Sport Psychology, 2,* 14–21.

Allard, F., and Starkes, J. (1980). Perception in sport: Volleyball. *Journal of Sport Psychology, 2, 22–23.*

Atkinson, R., and Shiffrin, R. (1968). Human memory: A proposed system and its control processes. In K. Spence and J. Spence (Eds.), *The psychology of learning and motivation* (Vol. 2). New York: Academic Press.

Bard, C., and Fleury, M. (1976). Analysis of visual search activity during sport problem situations. *Journal of Human Movement Studies, 3, 214–222.*

Bard, C., and Fleury, M. (1981). Considering eye movement as a predictor of attainment. In I. M. Cockerill and W. W. MacGillivary (Eds.), *Vision and sport* (pp. 28–41). Cheltonham, England: Stanley Thomas.

Barrett, S., and Shepp, B. (1988). Developmental changes in attentional skills: The effect of irrelevant variations on encoding and response selection. *Journal of Experimental Child Psychology, 45, 382–399.*

Berliner, D. (1986). In pursuit of the expert pedagogue. *Educational Researcher, 15*(7), 5–13.

Bjorkland, D. (1985). The role of conceptual knowledge in the development of organization in children's memory. In C. Brainerd and M. Pressley (Eds.), *Basic processes in memory development: Progress in cognitive development research* (pp. 103–142). New York: Springer-Verlag.

Bjorkland, D., and Thompson, B. (1983). Category typicality effects in children's memory performance: Qualitative and quantitative differences in the processing of category information. *Journal of Experimental Child Psychology, 35,* 329–344.

Bjorklund, D., and Buchanan, J. (1989). Developmental and knowledge base differences in the acquisition and extension of a memory strategy. *Journal of Experimental Child Psychology, 48,* 451–471.

Brown, A., and Deloach, J. (1978). Skills, plans, and self-regulation. In R. Siegler (Ed.), *Children's thinking: What develops* (pp. 3–35). Hillsdale: Erlbaum.

Bryant, P. (1968). Comments on the design of developmental studies of cross-modal matching and cross-modal transfer. *Cortex, 4,* 127–137.

Chase, W., and Simon, H. (1973). Perception in chess. *Cognitive Psychology*, 4, 55–81.

Chi, M. T. H. (1976). Short-term memory limitations in children: Capacity of processing deficits? *Memory and Cognition, 4.*

Chi, M. T. H. (1977). Age differences in memory span. *Journal of Experimental Child Psychology, 23,* 266–281.

Chi, M. T. H. (1978). Knowledge structures and memory development. In R. Siegler (Ed.), *Children's thinking: What develops* (pp. 73–105). Hillsdale, NJ: Erlbaum.

Chi, M. T. H. (1982). Knowledge development and memory performance. In M. Friedman and J. Das and N. O'Connor (Eds.), *Intelligence and learning* (pp. 221–230). NY: Plenum Press.

Chi, M. T. H. (1985). Interactive roles of knowledge and strategies in the development of organized sorting and recall. In S. Chipman and R. Segal and R. Glaser (Eds.), *Thinking and learning skills: Vol 2 Research and open questions* (pp. 457–483). Hillsdale, NJ: Erlbaum.

Chi, M. T. H. (1997). Quantifying qualitative analyses of verbal data: A practical guide. *The Journal of the Learning Sciences, 6,* 271–315.

Chi, M. T. H., Feltovich, P., and Glaser, R. (1981). Categorizations and representation of physics problems by experts and novices. *Cognitive Science, 5,* 121–152.

Chi, M. T. H., and Koeske, R. (1983). Network representation of a child's dinosaur knowledge. *Developmental Psychology, 19,* 29–39.

Chiesi, H., Spilich, G., and Voss, J. (1979). Acquisition of domain related information in relation to high and low domain knowledge. *Journal of Verbal Learning and Verbal Behavior, 18,* 257–273.

Craik, F., and Lockhart, R. (1972). Levels of processing: A framework for memory research. *Journal of Verbal Learning and Verbal* Behavior, *11,* 671–684.

Davis, C., Thomas, K., and Thomas, J. (June 1991). Relations between knowledge and expertise in breaststroke swimming. Paper presented at the North American Society for the Psychology of Sport and Physical Activity, Asilomar, CA.

Dempster, F. (1988). Short-term memory development in childhood and adolescence. In C. Brainerd and M. Pressley (Eds.), *Basic processes in memory develop-*

ment: *Progress in cognitive development* research (pp. 209–248) New York: Springer-Verlag.

Dunham, P., and Reid, D. (1987). Information processing: Effect of stimulus speed variation on coincidence-anticipation of children. Journal *of Human Movement Studies, 13*, 151–156.

Ericsson, K., and Kintsch, W. (1995). Long term working memory. *Psychological* Review, *102*, 211–245.

Ericsson, K., Krampe, R., and Tesch-Romer, C. (1993). The role of deliberate practice in the acquisition of expert performance. *Psychological* Review, *100*, 363–406.

Fabricius, W., and Cavalier, L. (1989). The role of causal theories about memory in young children's memory strategy choice. *Child Development, 60,* 298–308.

Flavell, J. (1970). *Cognitive development.* Englewood Cliffs: Prentice-Hall.

French, K., and McPherson, S. (1999). Adaptations in response selection processes used during sport competition with increasing age and expertise. *International Journal of Sport Psychology, 30*, 173–193.

French, K., Nevett, M., Spurgeon, J., Graham, K., Rink, J., and McPherson, S. (1996). Knowledge representation and problem solution in expert and novice youth baseball players. *Research Quarterly for Exercise and Sport, 67,* 386–395.

French, K., Spurgeon, J., and Nevett, M. (1995). Expert-novice differences in cognitive and skill execution components of Youth Baseball performance. *Research Quarterly for Exercise and Sport, 66*, 194–201.

French, K., and Thomas, J. (1987). The relation of knowledge development to children's basketball performance. *Journal of Sport Psychology, 2,* 15–32.

French, K., Werner, P., Rink, J., Taylor, K., and Hussey, K. (1996). The effects of a 3-week unit of tactical, skill or combined tactical and skill instruction on badminton performance of ninth grade students. *Journal of Teaching in Physical Education, 15*, 418–438.

French, K., Werner, P., Taylor, K., Hussey, K., and Jones, J. (1996). The effects of a 6-week unit of tactical, skill or combined tactical and skill instruction on badminton performances of ninth grade students. *Journal of Teaching in Physical Education, 15*, 439–463.

Gabbard, C. (2001). *Lifelong motor development* (3rd ed.). Boston: Allyn and Bacon.

Gallagher, J., and Thomas, J. (1984). Rehearsal strategy effects on developmental differences for recall of a movement series. *Research Quarterly for Exercise and Sport, 55*, 123–128.

Gallagher, J., and Thomas, J. (1986). Developmental effects of grouping and recoding on learning a movement series. *Research Quarterly for Exercise and Sport, 57*, 117–127.

Guttentag, R. (1989). Age differences in dual-task performance procedures assumptions and results. *Developmental* Review, *9*, 146–170.

Guttentag, R., and Ornstein, P. (1990). Attentional capacity and children's memory strategy use. In J. Ennis (Ed.) *The development of attention: Research and theory* (pp. 305–319) North Holland: Elsevier Science Publishers.

Helsen, W., and Bard, C. (1989). The relation between expertise and visual information processing in sport. Paper presented at the International Conference on Youth, Leisure, Physical Activity, and Kinathropometry IV, Brussels Belgium.

Helsen, W., and Starkes, J. (1999). A multidimensional approach to skilled perception and performance in sport. *Applied Cognitive Psychology, 13*, 1–27.

Ille, A. A., and Cadopi, M. (1999). Memory for movement sequences in gymnastics: effects of age and skill level. *Journal of Motor Behavior, 31*, 290–300.

Johnson, D. (1991). Off the ball decision making in soccer., University of South Carolina, Columbia, SC.

Jones, C., and Miles, T. (1978). Use of advance cues in predicting the flight of a lawn tennis ball. *Journal of Human Movement* Studies, *4*, 231–235.

Kail, R. (1988). Developmental functions for speeds of cognitive processes. *Journal of Experimental Child Psychology, 45*, 339–364.

Kay, D., and Ruskin, E. (1990). The development of attentional control mechanisms. In J. Ennis (Ed.) *The development of attention: Research and theory* (pp. 227–244) North Holland: Elsevier Science Publishers. North-Holland: Elsevier Science Publishers.

Keogh, J., and Sugden, D. A. (1985). *Movement skill development*. New York: Macmillan.

Kuhlman, J., and Beitel, P. (1997). Development/learning of coincidence anticipation. *Journal of Sport and Exercise Psychology, 19*, s76.

Ladewig, I., Cuthma, C., Martins, D., and Gallagher, J. (2000). Attention instructors: Use cues to improve your student's selective attention. *Journal of Sport and Exercise Psychology, 21,* s63.

Ladewig, I., and Gallagher, J. (1992). Development of selective attention strategies in children. Paper presented at the North American Society for the Psychology of Sport and Physical Activity, Pittsburgh, PA.

Masser, L. (1993). Critical cues help first grade student's achievement in handstands and forward rolls. *Journal of Teaching in Physical Education, 12*, 301–312.

McMorris, T. (1999). Cognitive development and the acquisition of decision-making skills. *International Journal of Sport Psychology, 30*, 151–172.

McMorris, T., and Graydon, J. (1996). The contribution of the research literature to the understanding of decision making in team games. *Journal of Human Movement Studies, 33*, 69–90.

McPherson, S. (1993a). Knowledge representation and decision making in sport. In J. Starkes and F. Allard (Eds.), *Cognitive issues in motor expertise* (pp. 159–188). Amsterdam: Elsevier Science.

McPherson, S. (1993b). The influence of player experience on problem solving during batting preparation in baseball. *Journal of Sport and Exercise Psychology, 15*, 304–325.

McPherson, S. (1994). The development of sport expertise: Mapping the tactical domain. *Quest, 46,* 223–240.

McPherson, S. (1999a). Expert-novice differences in performance skills and problem representations of youth and adults during tennis competition. *Research Quarterly for Exercise and Sport, 70,* 233–251.

McPherson, S. (1999b). Tactical differences in problem representations and solutions in collegiate varsity and beginner women tennis players. *Research Quarterly for Exercise and Sport, 70,* 369–384.

McPherson, S. (2000). Expert-novice differences in planning strategies during collegiate singles tennis competition. *Journal of Sport and Exercise Psychology, 22,* 39–62.

McPherson, S., Dovenmuehler, A., and Murray, M. (1992). Player differences in representation of strategic knowledge and use during a modified volleyball game situation. Paper presented at the North American Society for the Psychology of Sport and Physical Activity, Pittsburgh, PA.

McPherson, S., and French, K. (1991). Changes in cognitive strategies and motor skill in tennis. *Journal of Sport and Exercise Psychology, 13*, 26–41.

McPherson, S., and Thomas, J. (1989). Relation of knowledge and performance in boys' tennis: age and expertise. *Journal of Experimental Child Psychology, 48*, 190–211.

Millar, S. (1974). Tactile short-term memory by blind and sighted children. *British Journal of Psychology, 65*, 253–263.

Miller, M. (1990). The use of labeling to improve movement recall involving learning-disabled children., University of Pittsburgh, Pittsburgh, PA.

Murphy, G., and Wright, J. (1984). Changes in conceptual structure with expertise: Differences between real-world experts and novices. *Journal of Experimental Psychology: Learning, Memory and Cognition, 190*, 144–155.

Nevett, M., and French, K. (1997). The development of sport-specific planning, rehearsal, and updating of plans during defensive youth baseball game performance. *Research Quarterly for Exercise and Sport, 68*, 203–214.

Nougier, V., Stein, J., and Bonnel, A. (1991). Information processing in sport and orienting of attention. *International Journal of Sport Psychology, 22*, 307–327.

Ornstein, P., Baker-Ward, L., and Naus, M. (1988). The development of mnemonic skill. In F. Weinert and M. Perlmutter (Eds.), *Memory development: Universal changes and individual* differences (pp. 31–50). Hillsdale, NJ: Erlbaum.

Ornstein, P., and Naus, M. (1985). Effects of knowledge base on children's memory strategies. In H. Reese (Ed.), *Advances in child development and behavior* (pp. 113–148). New York: Academic Press.

Paris, S. (1988). Motivated forgetting. In F. Weinert and M. Perlmutter (Eds.), *Memory development: Universal changes and individual differences*. Hillsdale, NJ: Erlbaum.

Paull, G., and Glencross, D. (1997). Expert participation and decision making in baseball. *International Journal of Sport Psychology, 28*, 35–56.

Piaget, J. (1969). *On the development of memory and identity*. Worchester, MA: Clark University Press and Barre,

Poon, P., and Rodgers, W. (2000). Learning and remembering strategies of novice and advanced jazz dancers for skill level appropriate dance routines. *Research Quarterly for Exercise and Sport, 71,* 135–144.

Rabinowitz, M. (1988). On teaching cognitive strategies: The influence of accessibility of conceptual knowledge. *Contemporary Educational Psychology, 13*, 229–235.

Rao, N., and Moley, B. (1989). Producing memory strategy maintenance and generalization by explicit or implicit training of memory knowledge. *Journal of Experimental Child Psychology, 48*, 335–252.

Rees, H. (1987). *The manual of soccer coaching*. Spring, TS: Annbon, Inc.

Reid, G. (1980). The effects of motor strategy instruction in the short-term memory of the mentally retarded. *Journal of Motor* Behavior, *12*, 221–227.

Rink, J. (1993). Teaching physical education for learning (2nd ed.). St. Louis: Mosby.

Ripoll, H. (1991). The understanding-acting process in sport: the relationship between the semantic and the sensorimotor visual function. *International Journal of Sport Psychology, 22*, 221–250.

Ripoll, H., and Benguigui, N. (1999). Emergence of expertise in ball sports during Child Development. *International Journal of Sport Psychology, 30*, 235–245.

Ross, A. (1976). *Psychological aspects of learning disabilities and reading disorders*. New York: McGraw-Hill.

Schneider, W., and Sodian, B. (1988). Metamemory—memory behavior relationships in young children: Evidence from a memory-for-location task. *Journal of Experimental Child Psychology, 45,* 209–233.

Schroeder, R. (1981). The effects of rehearsal on information processing efficiency of severely/profoundly retarded normal individuals. Louisiana State University, Baton Rouge, LA.

Shepp, B., Barrett, S., and Kohlbert, L. (1987). The development of selective attention: Holistic perception versus resource allocation. *Journal of Experimental Child Psychology, 43*, 159–180.

Smyth, M., and Pendleton, L. (1994). Memory for movement in professional ballet dancers. *International Journal of Sport Psychology, 25*, 282–294.

Starkes, J. (1987). Skill in field hockey: The nature of the cognitive advantage. *Journal of Sport Psychology, 9*, 146–160 7/7

Starkes, J., Helsen, W., and Jack, R. (2001). Expert performance in sport and dance. In R. Singer and H. Hausenblas and C. Janelle (Eds.), *Handbook of sport psychology* (pp. 174–201). NY: John Wiley and Sons.

Stratton, R. (1978). Information processing deficits in children's motor performance: Implications for instruction. *Motor Skills: Theory into practice, 3*, 49–55.

Thomas, J. (2000). C. H. McCloy lecture: Children's control, learning and performance of motor skills. *Research Quarterly for Exercise and Sport, 71*, 1–9.

Thomas, J., Gallagher, J., and Purvis, G. (1981). Reaction time and anticipation time: Effects of development. *Research Quarterly for Exercise and Sport, 52*, 359–367.

Thomas, J., and Lee, C. (June 1992). A description of skill, knowledge, selected fitness measures and golf play in women over 50 years of age. Paper presented at the North American Society for Psychology of Sport and Physical Activity, Pittsburgh, PA.

Thomas, J., and Stratton, R. (1977). Effect of divided attention on children's rhythmic response. *Research Quarterly, 48*, 428–435.

Thomas, J., and Thomas, K. (1999). What squirrels in the trees predicts about expert athletes. *International Journal of Sport Psychology, 30*, 221–234.

Thomas, J., Thomas, K., Lee, A., Testerman, E., and Ashy, M. (1983). Age differences in use of strategy for recall of movement in a large scale environment. *Research Quarterly for Exercise and Sport, 54*, 264–272.

Thomas, K., and Thomas, J. (Eds.). (1987). Perceptual development and its differential influence on limb positioning under two movement conditions in children. In J. Clark and J. Humphrey (Eds.), *Motor development: Current selected research (Vol. 1).* (pp. 83–96). Baltimore, MD: AMS press.

Ulrich, B., and Ulrich, D. (1985). The role of balancing in performance of fundamental motor skills in 3-, 4-, and 5-year-old children. In J. Clark and J. Humphrey (Eds.), *Motor development: Current selected research (Vol. 1).* Princeton, NJ: Princeton Book Co.

van Geert, P. (1993). *A dynamic systems model of cognitive growth: Competition and support under limited resource conditions.* Cambridge: MIT Press.

VanDyne, H. (1973). Foundations of tactical perception in three to seven year olds. *Journal of the Association of Perception, 8*, 1–9.

Vickers, J. (1986). The resequencing task: Determining expert-novice differences in the organization of a movement sequence. *Research Quarterly for Exercise and Sport, 57*, 260–264.

Weiss, M. (1983). Modeling and motor performance: A developmental perspective. *Research Quarterly for Exercise and Sport, 54*, 190–197.

Weiss, M., and Klint, K. (1987). "Show and tell" in the gymnasium: An investigation of developmental differences in modeling and verbal rehearsal of motor skills. *Research Quarterly for Exercise and Sport, 58*, 234–241.

Williams, A., and Davids, K. (1995). Declarative knowledge in sport: A byproduct of experience or a characteristic of expertise? *Journal of Sport and Exercise Psychology, 17,* 259–278.

Williams, A., and Davids, K. (1998). Visual search strategy, selective attention, and expertise in soccer. *Research Quarterly for Exercise and Sport,* 6–9, 111–128.

Williams, H. (1983). *Perceptual and motor development.* Englewood Cliffs, NJ: Prentice-Hall.

Williams, H., Temple, J., and Bateman, J. (1979). A test battery to assess intrasensory and intersensory development of young children. *Perceptual and Motor Skills, 48,* 643–659.

Winther, K., and Thomas, J. (1981). Developmental differences in children's labeling of movement. *Journal of Motor Behavior, 13,* 77–90.

CHAPTER 21

Sport Performance Anxiety in Young Athletes

Ronald E. Smith, University of Washington
Frank L. Smoll, University of Washington
Michael W. Passer, University of Washington

Sport scientists have emphasized that youth sports provide socialization opportunities and place adaptive demands on participants that parallel those of other important life experiences (Brustad, 1993; Coakley, 1993; Ewing, Seefeldt, and Brown, 1997; Martens, 1993; Scanlan, this volume; Smoll, 1989). For this reason, organized athletic experiences are regarded as potentially important in child and adolescent development, and participation is believed to have direct relevance to the development of prosocial attitudes and behaviors such as respect for authority, cooperation, self-discipline, risk-taking, and the abilities to tolerate frustration and delay gratification. Unfortunately, however, some programs have become more highly structured, and adults have often shaped them to reflect a win-oriented professional sport model. Consequently, critics have charged that extreme pressures are being placed on youngsters before they are developmentally prepared to cope with them (e.g., Brower, 1979; Kamm, 1997; Nash, 1987; Ogilvie, 1979; Sayre, 1975; Smilkstein, 1980). This type of concern was reflected in the results of a questionnaire administered to sport psychologists and to nonschool youth sport coaches and administrators; "competitive stress placed on young athletes" and "helping young athletes cope with competitive stress" were among the five topics rated most important for study (Gould, 1982). In view of this, it is not surprising that competitive stress in youth sports has been the focus of considerable empirical attention.

Given the range of practical and theoretical issues that can be addressed, the study of sport performance anxiety has attracted the attention of scientists for many years. In the past decade, however, a notable upsurge of scientific activity has occurred, due largely to theoretical advances (Jones, 1995), the development of sport-specific measures of anxiety (see Burton, 1998; Smith, Smoll, and Wiechman, 1998) and increased interest among sport psychologists in developing anxiety reduction intervention programs for athletes (Apitzsch, 1983; Crocker, Alderman, and Smith, 1988;

Hackfort and Spielberger, 1989; Smith, 1989; Suinn, 1989; Zaichkowsky and Tak-enaka, 1993).

This chapter begins with a review of anxiety-related terminology and concepts, after which we present a conceptual model of athletic performance anxiety. We then review research on situational and personal determinants of anxiety experienced by young athletes. Next, we consider the negative consequences of competitive anxiety, and the question of whether youth sports are too stressful. The chapter concludes with coverage of several intervention strategies that are designed to reduce young athletes' performance anxiety.

Arousal, Stress, and Anxiety

Before discussing the nature of sport performance anxiety, distinctions should be drawn between the related concepts of arousal, stress, and anxiety. These terms are often used interchangeably, resulting in no small measure of confusion within the literature.

Arousal is the most general of the three terms. Cannon (1929) used the term to refer to physiological and energy mobilization in response to situations that threatened the physical integrity of the organism. The concept of arousal has also occupied a prominent position in the theoretical formulations of Berlyne (1960), Duffy (1962), Hebb (1949), Malmo (1959), and others. If behavior is viewed as varying along two basic dimensions of direction and intensity, then arousal is the intensity dimension. Arousal, often used interchangeably with other intensity-related terms such as tension, drive, and activation, can vary on a continuum ranging from deep sleep to peak excitement.

The term *stress* is used in two different but related ways. First it is used in relation to situations (termed *stressors*) which place significant demands on the organism. This situational definition of stress is frequently couched in terms of the balance between situational demands and the resources of the individual (e.g., Lazarus and Folkman, 1984). The second use of the term stress refers to the responses of individuals to stressors. Used in this sense, stress refers to a cognitive-affective response involving appraisal of threat and increased physiological arousal (Lazarus and Folkman, 1984; Spielberger, 1989). Though less general than arousal, the term stress is typically used to refer to a range of aversive emotional states, such as anxiety, depression, and anger.

Anxiety is one variety of stress response, and it is a multifaceted construct. On the one hand, it is a subjectively aversive emotional response and an avoidance motive characterized by worry and apprehension concerning the possibility of physical or psychological harm, together with increased physiological arousal resulting from the appraisal of threat. As a motivational state, anxiety is an avoidance motive that helps strengthen successful coping and/or avoidance responses through negative reinforcement (i.e., response-contingent anxiety reduction).

The concept of anxiety has undergone considerable theoretical refinement over the years, and these refinements have been reflected in the measuring instruments used to operationally define the construct. Four sets of distinctions have been particularly important. The first is the state-trait distinction. The second differentiates between general or global anxiety and situation-specific forms of anxiety. The third involves the multidimensional nature of anxiety, particularly its cognitive and somatic components. The fourth is a more recent distinction in the sport literature between debilitative and facilitative anxiety states.

The State-Trait Anxiety Distinction

The emotional reaction of anxiety varies in intensity and fluctuates over time. Physiological and psychological calmness and serenity indicate the absence of an anxiety response. Moderate levels of anxiety involve apprehension, nervousness, worry, and tension. Very high levels of anxiety may involve intense feelings of fear, catastrophic thoughts, and high levels of physiological arousal. The momentary level of anxiety experienced by an individual is termed *state anxiety*.

Spielberger (1966) highlighted the important distinction between state anxiety and trait anxiety. *Trait anxiety* refers to relatively stable individual differences in anxiety proneness that are regarded as a personality disposition or trait. That is, people who are high in trait anxiety are more anxiety prone in that they perceive or appraise a wider range of situations as threatening than do individuals who are low in trait anxiety. High trait-anxious people are thus more likely to experience state anxiety, and their anxiety responses tend to be of greater intensity and duration.

It is now generally accepted that a comprehensive theory of anxiety must distinguish between anxiety as a transitory emotional state (A-state) and individual differences in the relatively stable personality trait of anxiety (A-trait). An adequate model of anxiety should also specify the nature of the cognitive processes that mediate the appraisal of threat as well as the consequences of such appraisals.

The General-Specific Anxiety Distinction

Because A-state is defined as a transitory emotional response, it is always measured within specific situations. Trait measures of anxiety, on the other hand, fall into two general categories. Some instruments measure anxiety as a global transituational trait, while others are designed to assess the tendency of individuals to experience anxiety within particular types of situations such as tests, social situations, or athletics. The study of situation-specific anxiety has been stimulated in part by interactional approaches to personality (e.g., Magnusson and Endler, 1977), in which behavior is assumed to be determined by the reciprocal interaction of personal traits and the characteristics of situations. If anxiety is a learned response to particular classes of situations, then we should expect that situation-specific anxiety measures would relate more strongly to behavior in the critical situations than would general transituational anxiety. An impressive array of research results supports this prediction. For example, test anxiety measures are more strongly related to test performance than are measures of general anxiety (Sarason and Sarason, 1990). Moreover, situation-specific A-trait measures are better predictors of elevation in state anxiety for a particular class of stress situations than are generalized A-trait measures (Martens, 1977; Sarason and Sarason, 1990; Spielberger, 1972).

The Multidimensional Nature of Anxiety

Conceptualizations of anxiety as a multidimensional construct are based on the distinction between its cognitive and physiological components (e.g., Borkovec, 1976; Davidson and Schwartz, 1976; Liebert and Morris, 1967; Martens, Vealey, and Burton, 1990; Sarason, 1984; Smith, 1989; Smith and Smoll, 1990; Smith, Smoll, and Schutz, 1990). Cognitive anxiety is characterized by negative appraisals of situation and self, worry, and aversive mental imagery, whereas somatic anxiety is reflected in increased physiological arousal as typified by rapid heart rate, shortness of breath, and increased muscle tension. Multidimensional conceptions of anxiety were stimulated in part by behavior therapy research in the 1960s and 1970s that revealed three separate and largely independent cognitive, physiological, and behavioral response dimensions (Borkovec, 1976; Lang, 1971). Measurement of anxiety responses by means of self-report, physiological, and behavioral measures of anxiety in laboratory stress studies and in behavior therapy research often indicated that these three response systems were only loosely correlated with one another.

Factor analytic studies of trait anxiety scales have likewise revealed the existence of separate cognitive (e.g., worry) and somatic (e.g., physiological response) dimensions of anxiety (Morris, Davis, and Hutchings, 1981; Sarason, 1984; Smith et al., 1990). The discovery that the cognitive and physiological dimensions of anxiety can have various degrees of statistical independence and that the components can relate differentially to other behaviors spurred the development of multidimensional sport anxiety scales. The Sport Anxiety Scale (Smith et al., 1990) provides separate trait subscales for somatic anxiety and two variants of cognitive anxiety, namely, worry and concentration disruption. Multidimensional state anxiety can be assessed using the Competitive State Anxiety Inventory-2 (Martens, Burton, Vealey, Bump, and Smith, 1990), which contains separate subscales for somatic and cognitive anxiety, plus a self-confidence subscale. Like the Sport Anxiety Scale, this measure was developed using adolescent and young adult samples, and far less work has been done with children.

Debilitative and Facilitative Anxiety

Traditionally, anxiety has been viewed as an emotional state that, particularly at high levels, interferes with performance. This conception is, however, at odds with reports by some people that "anxiety" helps enhance their performance. For example, some students believe that test anxiety facilitates their performance, whereas most report that it degrades test performance. On the Achievement Anxiety Test developed by Alpert and Haber (1960) to measure these constructs, facilitative anxiety is measured by items such as "Nervousness while taking a test helps me do better," whereas debilitative anxiety is indexed by items such as "Nervousness while taking an exam hinders me from doing well." Such reports are differentially related to academic test scores, facilitative anxiety in a positive direction and debilitative anxiety exhibiting a negative correlation (Alpert and Haber, 1960; Raffety, Smith, and Ptacek, 1997).

The facilitative-debilitative distinction has been carried into the sport arena by Graham Jones and coworkers (Jones, 1995; Jones and Swain, 1995). They modified the CSAI-2 to provide measures of both the intensity and the direction (facilitative/debilitative) of cognitive and somatic state anxiety. Using this scale with college basketball players, Swain and Jones (1996) found that the direction of pregame cognitive and somatic state anxiety accounted for more performance variance than did the normal CSAI-2 anxiety intensity scores.

As Jones (1995) points out, the facilitative-debilitative distinction is not universally accepted by anxiety researchers. Some question whether the facilitative construct is truly anxiety. As Jones notes, "It is likely, of course, that a state in which cognitive and physiological symptoms, however intense, are perceived as being facilitative to performance does not represent 'anxiety' at all. Instead, it will probably be labeled by the performer as 'anticipatory excitement' or being 'psyched up' (1995, p. 464). Jones's statement points to the importance of cognitive appraisal and labeling processes in the experiencing and effects of affective states. We therefore turn to a model of performance anxiety that considers the interacting roles of personality, situational, cognitive, physiological, and behavioral factors.

The Dynamics of Sport Performance Anxiety

As a trait construct, sport performance anxiety may be defined as "a predisposition to respond with cognitive and/or somatic state anxiety to competitive sport situations in which the adequacy of the athlete's performance can be evaluated" (Smith et al., 1998, p. 107). Although a number of specific sources of threat (including the possibility of physical harm) may reside in the sport situation, probably the most salient sources of threat are the possibilities of failure and of disapproval by significant others who are evaluating the athlete's performance in relation to some standard of excellence (e.g., Dunn, 1999). Athletic performance anxiety is thus part of a family of performance-related fear-of-failure constructs that include test anxiety, speech anxiety, and the "stage fright" that actors, musicians, and dancers can experience within their evaluative performance situations (Kendrick, Craig, Lawson, and Davidson, 1982; Steptoe and Fidler, 1987). Like other forms of anxiety, sport performance anxiety has separate but related cognitive, affective, and behavioral components.

A conceptual model of athletic performance anxiety is presented in Figure 21.1 (Smith et al., 1998). This model, derived from conceptions of emotionality and anxiety advanced by Arnold (1960), Ellis (1962), Lazarus (2000), Mandler and Sarason (1952), Smith (1989), and Spielberger (1966), includes both the trait-state distinction and the differentiation between situational, cognitive, physiological, and behavioral components of the process of anxiety. The model also accounts for the distinction between debilitative and facilitative anxiety states.

The cognitive and somatic components of competitive A-state are shown within the appraisal and physiological response panels of the figure. The intensity and duration of the A-state response are assumed to be influenced by three major factors. The first of these factors is the nature of the competitive situation in which the athlete is involved. Obviously, such situations differ in the demands they place upon the athlete, as well as the degree of threat that they pose to successful performance. Such factors as strength of opponent, importance of the contest, presence of significant others, and degree of social support received from coaches and teammates can affect the amount of threat that the situation is likely to pose for the individual. It should also be noted that A-trait influences the situations to which people will expose themselves. Thus, people with excessively high performance anxiety may choose to avoid the sport situation altogether. As an individual difference variable, A-trait thus represents a relatively stable set of cognitive and affective tendencies that interact with the situation to determine the level of A-state that is experienced.

The objective situation and the performer's level of A-trait are assumed to influence the performer's appraisal processes. Four classes of appraisal are particularly important: (a) appraisal of the situational demands; (b) appraisal of the resources available to deal with them; (c) appraisal of the nature and likelihood of potential consequences if the demands are not met (that is, the expectancies and valances relating to potential consequences); and (d) the personal meaning that the consequences have for the individual. The meanings attached to the consequences derive from the person's belief system, and they often involve the individual's criteria for self-worth (Ellis, 1962; Rogers, 1959). Thus, a child athlete who defines the present situational demands as overwhelming, who appraises his or her resources and skills as insufficient to deal with the demands, who anticipates failure and/or disapproval as a result of the demands/resources imbalance, and who defines his or her self-worth in terms of success and/or the approval of others will clearly perceive this competitive situation as threatening or dangerous. It is assumed that differences in the worry component of cognitive anxiety are especially important determinants of the kinds of appraisals that are made. Worriers perceive an unfavorable balance between demands and resources and expect the worst to occur.

Negative appraisals are likely to generate high levels of physiological arousal, and this arousal, in turn, feeds back into the ongoing process of appraisal and reappraisal (Lazarus, 2000). High levels of arousal may convince the athlete that he or she is "falling apart" and help generate even more negative appraisals. Athletes

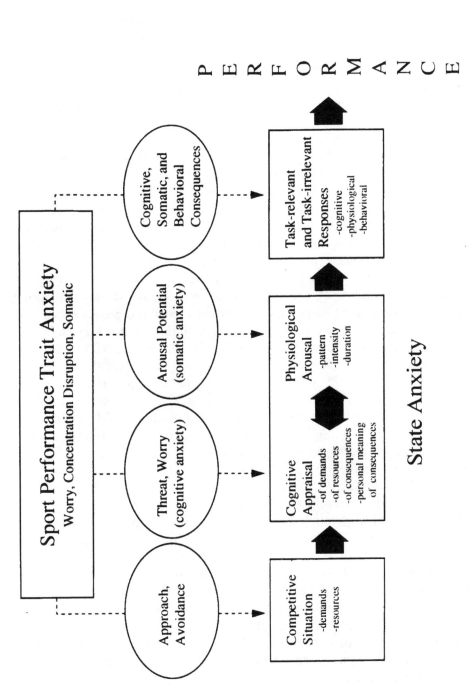

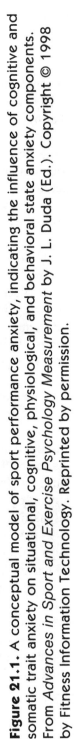

Figure 21.1. A conceptual model of sport performance anxiety, indicating the influence of cognitive and somatic trait anxiety on situational, cognitive, physiological, and behavioral state anxiety components. From *Advances in Sport and Exercise Psychology Measurement* by J. L. Duda (Ed.). Copyright © 1998 by Fitness Information Technology. Reprinted by permission.

clearly differ in the amount of physiological arousal they report, and individual differences in the trait of somatic anxiety are likely to predispose athletes to differ in this regard. As behavior genetics research is demonstrating, some portion of the variance in somatic anxiety potential may be attributable to genetically-based constitutional factors (Buss, 1995). This is a topic that deserves empirical attention, and such research may be facilitated by the existence of a multidimensional anxiety scale that permits the calculation of separate heritability indices for somatic and cognitive anxiety dimensions.

Since the relation between anxiety and performance has always been a central focus of sport anxiety research, we have included mechanisms assumed to influence performance. As Mandler and Sarason (1952) have noted, motivational and emotional states may generate two broad classes of task-related responses. Some of these responses (task-relevant responses) facilitate task performance, whereas others (task-irrelevant responses) are detrimental to performance. We suggest that the task-relevant and task-irrelevant responses may be cognitive, physiological, or behavioral in nature. Thus, cognitive responses such as perceived control over the situation, positive expectations of goal attainment, concentration on the task, and strategic planning may be considered task-relevant responses that would contribute positively to performance. These cognitive responses (including the appraisal that the affective response being experienced is a "psyching up" that will facilitate performance) are assumed to underlie some performers' reports that anxiety facilitates their performance (e.g., Jones and Swain, 1995). Conversely, task-irrelevant cognitive responses such as expectations of an inability to cope, failure in goal attainment, worry about the reactions of others, and catastrophic thinking could readily interfere with task performance by disrupting attentional and problem-solving processes. Both the worry and concentration-disruption components of A-trait are assumed to be negative predisposing factors of debilitative anxiety (Smith, 1996). Likewise, depending on the nature (especially the complexity) of the task, certain classes and intensities of physiological responding might facilitate task performance, whereas other types and intensities of physiological responding might interfere with task performance (Jones, 1995). Thus, high physiological may enhance a sprinter's performance while degrading a golfer's. Finally, behavioral responses such as persistence and smooth execution of motor responses would facilitate performance, while impulsive or inappropriate behaviors would interfere with it. These task-irrelevant responses contribute to debilitative anxiety effects. The balance between task-relevant and task-irrelevant responses and the manner in which they are affected by the performer's anxiety level will thus affect the adequacy of performance. It should also be noted that ongoing appraisal of performance adequacy can influence the four basic cognitive appraisal elements shown in the figure.

Determinants of Competitive Anxiety

A substantial amount of research has been devoted to examining situational and individual difference (e.g., personality, attitudinal, motivational) factors associated with anxiety experienced by young athletes prior to, during, and following competitive events. Most of the field studies investigating pre- and postcompetition anxiety have employed variations of the following methodological paradigm: Individual difference factors (e.g., trait anxiety, self-esteem) thought to be predictive of anxiety were assessed several weeks before a competitive event. On the day of competition, characteristic pregame thoughts and worries as well as youngsters' perceptions of adults were assessed a few hours before the contest. Ten to 20 minutes prior to the event, young athletes completed measures of personal and team performance expectancies and either the State Anxiety Inventory for Children (Spielberger, 1973) or the children's version of the Competitive State Anxiety Inventory-1 (Martens, Burton, Rivkin, and Simon, 1980). Postevent measures of A-state and assessments of the amount of fun experienced during the competition were made immediately after the contest. A smaller number of studies have employed psychophysiological measures to assess arousal during actual youth sport competition. The findings are highlighted below and are discussed in greater detail elsewhere (see Passer, 1988; Smith and Smoll, 1990).

Precompetition Anxiety: Situational Factors

Some research has been conducted to determine whether certain types of sports are more anxiety-inducing than others. The results of Griffin (1972) and those of Simon and Martens (1979) are consistent in revealing that individual sports, which maximize the social evaluation potential of competition, generally elicit higher levels of precompetition anxiety than team sports. In addition to the type of sport, caliber of the opposition and criticality of the contest are situational factors that influence precompetition anxiety. Thout, Kavouras, and Keneflick (1998) measured adolescents' A-state prior to basketball games, at home and away, against opponents who differed in ability level. Significantly higher somatic and cognitive anxiety and lower self-confidence were reported as the ability of the opposition increased. Away games evoked more somatic anxiety and lower self-confidence than did home games. Studies have generally shown that more important events (e.g., championship games or matches) are more stressful than less important events (Feltz and Albrecht, 1986; Gould, Horn, and Spreeman, 1983b; Lowe and McGrath, 1971). The temporal countdown to competition is a third factor that affects precompetition anxiety. As one might expect, anxiety increases as the time of competition nears (Gould, Horn, and Spreeman, 1983a; Gould, Petlichkoff, and Weinberg, 1984).

Precompetition Anxiety: Individual Difference Factors

The amount of anxiety experienced in a particular sport setting varies considerably from one athlete to another. Some youngsters may feel very anxious before the start of a contest, while others feel relatively calm and relaxed. This has prompted researchers to identify individual difference factors that might account for such differences. One such factor is performance trait anxiety. In several laboratory experiments and field studies, findings consistently indicated that prior to competition, high trait anxious boys and girls experience higher state anxiety than low trait anxious children (Gill and Martens, 1977; Martens and Gill, 1976; Scanlan and Lewthwaite, 1984; Scanlan and Passer, 1978, 1979). Similarly, low self-esteem children experience more competitive anxiety than do high self-esteem children (Scanlan and Passer, 1978, 1979).

Precompetition anxiety is also related to several individual difference factors that do not represent personality dispositions. Specifically, research with team (soccer) and individual (wrestling) sports has revealed that young athletes who experience high levels of A-state are characterized by low team and individual performance expectancies (Scanlan and Lewthwaite, 1984; Scanlan and Passer, 1978, 1979); they tend to worry more about failure, adult expectations and social evaluation; and they perceive more parental pressure to participate (Scanlan and Lewthwaite, 1984).

Finally, precompetition A-state appears to be *unrelated* to certain individual difference factors. Research has shown that neither gender (Gill and Martens, 1977; Martens and Gill, 1976; Scanlan and Passer, 1978, 1979), age (Gould et al., 1983a), nor amount of sport experience (Gould et al., 1984) consistently relate to young athletes' competitive stress.

Anxiety During Competition

As we have seen, several situational factors are related to how much anxiety youngsters experience prior to competing. Other investigations have examined how young athletes' anxiety during competition is affected by specific situational factors that accompany or occur within a particular contest. Lowe and McGrath (1971) examined the effects of game and situation criticality on the pulse and respiration rates of 60 boys throughout an entire season of Little League Baseball. As predicted, players showed greater arousal as the criticality of the contest increased (e.g., when opposing teams were closer in ranking, as fewer games remained in the season) and as the criticality of the situation within the contest increased (e.g., when players were on base, when the score was close). Overall, game criticality seemed to have a greater effect on players' arousal than did situation criticality, which led Lowe and McGrath to suggest that the importance of the total situation (i.e., the game) may be a greater determinant of arousal than specific events within the situation.

In a study by Hanson (1967), the heart rates of 10 Little League Baseball players were monitored by telemetry during the course of a single game. Recordings were taken when the player was at bat, standing on base after a hit, sitting in the dugout after making an out, standing in the field, and sitting at rest before and after the game. When at bat, players' heart rates escalated dramatically to an average of 166 beats per minute (bpm), which was 56 bpm above their mean pregame resting rate. No other game situation caused arousal increases that even closely approximated the levels experienced when batting.

The studies by Hanson (1967) and Lowe and McGrath (1971) provided information about young athletes' physiological reactions to various game conditions. Several laboratory experiments have used self-report rather than physiological measures to assess children's anxiety during competition. For example, Martens and Gill (1976) and Gill and Martens (1977) had children compete at a motor skills task over a series of trials, with the won-lost outcome of each trial controlled by the experimenters. A-state was measured during midcompetition by Spielberger's (1973) State Anxiety Inventory for Children. The findings indicated that children who lost the early trials became more anxious than children who found themselves ahead. Research with adults suggests that the cognitive component of state anxiety covaries more strongly with performance expectancy changes during subsequent performance than does somatic anxiety (Morris and Engle, 1981; C. A. Smith and Morris, 1976), but more work on this topic is needed with children.

The Russian sport psychologist Yuri Hanin has advanced a Zone of Optimal Functioning (ZOF) model to capture individual differences in the anxiety-performance relation during competition (Hanin, 2000; Raglin and Hanin, 2000). This zone is identified in reference to the athlete's precompetition level of state anxiety. Slight departures above or below this level define the state anxiety zone within which the athlete is most likely to perform well during competition. Although some empirical support has been found with older athletes, research with children and adolescents is needed.

A final factor affecting anxiety during competition merits attention, namely, performance trait anxiety. The studies cited earlier indicated that prior to competition, high trait anxious children experience greater state anxiety than low competitive trait anxious children. During competition, a similar but slightly weaker relation has been obtained as ongoing success-failure outcomes begin to influence youngsters' anxiety (Gill and Martens, 1977; Martens and Gill, 1976).

Postcompetition Anxiety

Two major predictors of postcompetition anxiety have been identified. These include (a) the situational factor of victory versus defeat, and its various gradations, and (b) the individual difference variable involving the amount of fun athletes report having had during the event. The effects of won-lost outcomes were examined in research with male and female youth soccer players (Scanlan and Passer, 1978, 1979) and with male junior wrestlers (Scanlan and Lewthwaite, 1984). The studies found that boys and girls who lose a contest experience greater postcompetition stress than children who win. Relatedly, children who lose experience a significant increase in pre- to postcompetition stress, while children who win manifest a significant decrease.

In their study of male players, Scanlan and Passer (1978) also examined the relation between game closeness and postcompetition anxiety. The closeness of the game did not influence the postgame anxiety of winners, suggesting that a victory by any margin was sufficient to minimize anxiety. Game closeness, however, did affect losers' anxiety. Boys who lost a game by a very close margin had higher postgame anxiety than boys who lost by greater margins.

Because several games in Scanlan and Passer's studies happened to end in a tie, this allowed them to examine the effects of a tied outcome on players' anxiety. Players experienced a significant increase in pre- to postgame state anxiety after tie matches; they had greater postcompetition anxiety than winners, but less than losers (Passer and Scanlan, 1980; Scanlan and Passer, 1978). The findings thus suggested that a tie is perceived as an aversive outcome, not a neutral one.

In addition to won-lost outcome, the amount of fun experienced while competing has been found to be a strong and consistent predictor of postcompetition anxiety for both genders across diverse sport contexts. Boys and girls who report having less fun during a game or match experience greater postcompetition anxiety than children who report having more fun (Scanlan and Lewthwaite, 1984; Scanlan and Passer, 1978, 1979). Moreover, and perhaps most importantly, the inverse relation between fun and anxiety is independent of victory or defeat. In other words, it is not simply the case that winners have more fun than losers. This suggests that even among losing athletes, anxiety might be reduced by making the process of competition as enjoyable as possible.

The Impact of Competitive Anxiety on Young Athletes

The youth sport environment is an important achievement arena where ability is publicly tested, scrutinized, and evaluated by highly significant people, including coaches, parents, and peers (Brustad, this volume; Passer, 1988; Scanlan, this volume). Because of this, youngsters must learn to cope with the demands and pressures of competition if they are to enjoy and succeed in sports. Fortunately, some athletes develop effective ways of coping with potential sources of anxiety. Others are prone to suffer adverse psychological, behavioral, and health-related effects. Consideration is now given to the negative consequences of excessive competitive anxiety (Figure 21.2).

Fear and anxiety are unpleasant emotions that most people try to avoid. There is evidence that this is precisely what many anxiety-ridden athletes do. *Avoidance* of sports is one of the ways some youngsters cope with an activity they find threatening rather than pleasant (Orlick and Botterill, 1975; Pierce, 1980). Evidence also suggests

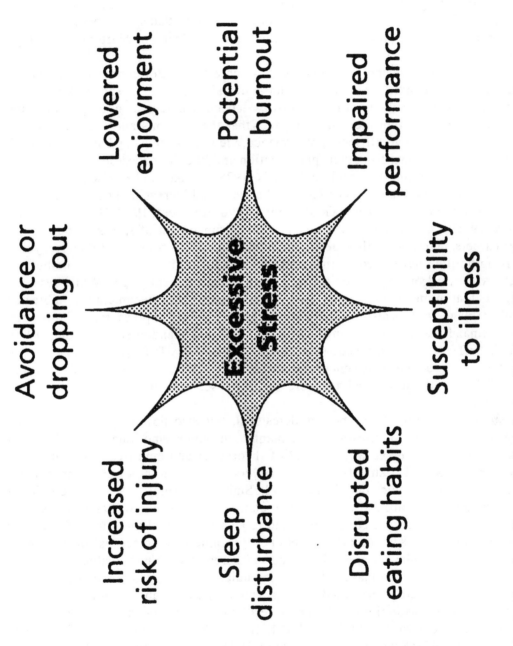

Figure 21.2. Negative effects of excessive anxiety in youth sports.

that competitive anxiety contributes significantly to *attrition* in youth sports (Burton and Martens, 1986; Gould, Feltz, Horn, and Weiss, 1982). For example, a study of over 1,000 age-group swimmers indicated that too much pressure, conflict with coaches, and insufficient success were among the reasons that swimmers reported for why their teammates dropped out of competition (McPherson, Marteniuk, Tihanyi, and Clark, 1980).

In addition to influencing decisions about entering and/or continuing to partici-pate, competitive anxiety can detract from athletes' *enjoyment* of sports. Youngsters who play for relatively punitive or critical coaches perceive more pressure and negative responses from their mothers, feel that their parents and coaches are less satisfied with their overall sport performance, view themselves as having less skill, express less enjoyment from their participation and like their sport less (Scanlan and Lewthwaite, 1986; Smith, Smoll, and Curtis, 1978; Wankel and Kreisel, 1985).

In recent years, the notion of *burnout* has received increasing attention in sports (Brustad, 1993; Coakley, 1992; Gould, 1993, 1996; Hellstedt, 1988; Henschen, 2001; Smith, 1986b). Elite athletes and coaches have dropped out of sports at the peak of their careers, maintaining that they are too "burned out" to continue. Likewise, youth sport authorities have become increasingly concerned about the large numbers of youth who are dropping out of sports during the adolescent years. While research suggests that in many cases, children drop out because they become more interested in other things, there is also evidence that intense competitive pressures and too many sport demands cause some youngsters to burn out and abandon sports (Cohn, 1990; Gould, Tuffey, Udry, and Loehr, 1996, 1997; Gould, Udry, Tuffey, and Loehr, 1996). Sport burnout is a legitimate concern, since burned out athletes often show depression, loss of drive and energy, and a lowered sense of self-esteem that carries over into other areas of their lives.

Anxiety not only affects how athletes feel, but also how they *perform*. Thus, because of practical implications, the manner in which emotional arousal affects performance has received a great deal of theoretical and empirical attention. It is widely recognized that anxiety can have adverse effects on motor skill and athletic performance (see Gould and Krane, 1992; Smith and Smoll, 1990). In empirical investigations of the arousal-performance relation, sport psychologists have assessed anxiety prior to or during competition and related it to actual measures of perform-ance. For example, Klavora (1978) obtained pregame A-state scores for male high school basketball players and related the measures to coaches' evaluations of the individual player's performance. The results indicated that approximately 10% of the time the players were overexcited, during which time their ability to function up to normal capacity was inhibited. Although results of other studies are less consistent than one might expect (Gould, Eklund, Petlichkoff, Peterson, and Bump, 1991; Lowe and McGrath, 1971; Scanlan and Lewthwaite, 1984), it is generally held that excessive anxiety causes impaired performance in young athletes.

The development of multidimensional anxiety measures has permitted the study of cognitive and somatic anxiety effects on performance. Cognitive and somatic anxiety may have differential effects on performance, depending upon the nature of the task. Although worry and emotionality are correlated with one another, only worry appears to be consistently related to performance decrements on cognitive tasks under evaluative stress conditions (Deffenbacher, 1980; Sarason, 1984; Tryon, 1980). On the other hand, somatic anxiety can negatively affect performance on motor tasks, particularly those requiring fine neuromuscular behaviors that might be disrupted by high arousal. To this point, most research on this question has been based on adult samples. Using the Competitive State Anxiety Inventory-2, Gould, Petlichkoff, Simons, and Vevera (1987) found a curvilinear (inverted U) relation between somatic A-state scores and adults' pistol shooting performance, whereas cognitive anxiety was unrelated to performance. In a study of competitive swimmers, Burton (1988) reported a similar curvilinear relation between somatic A-state and performance, but a negative linear relation between cognitive A-state and performance. It thus appears that, depending upon the nature of the task, cognitive and somatic anxiety may be differentially related to performance, either in the magnitude or in the form of the relation. However, although different anxiety theories differ on the details, there seems little question that high levels of both cognitive and somatic state anxiety impair performance (Jones, 1995).

Another approach to assessing the arousal-performance relation involves having youngsters report how they feel their performance typically is affected by anxiety. Pierce (1980) found that 31% of a sample of youth sport participants and 50% of sport dropouts reported that various worries prevented them playing up to their capabilities. On the other hand, 39% of a sample of elite wrestlers (Gould et al., 1983a) and 50% of junior elite runners (Feltz and Albrecht, 1986) reported that anxiety and nervousness helped their performance, providing evidence for the distinction between debilitative and facilitative anxiety. Thus, although results are equivocal, it appears that some young athletes feel anxiety usually hurts their performance, whereas others report positive effects of pre-event "nervousness." Apparently, in this latter group, this state helps evoke task-relevant responses that facilitate subsequent performance.

Several other effects of competitive anxiety should be noted. The physical nature of the anxiety response taxes the resources of the body and appears to increase susceptibility to *illness* and disease. For example, the unfortunate effects of severe competitive pressures are all too frequently seen in young athletes who develop anxiety-related headaches, stomachaches, and dermatological problems (Nash, 1987; Olerud, 1989). In addition, disruption of youngsters' *eating and sleeping patterns* is directly related to competitive anxiety (Gould et al., 1983a; Skubic, 1956; Universities Study Committee, 1978). This is surely a high and unnecessary price to pay for the pursuit of athletic excellence!

Anxiety affects physical well-being in yet another way. The widely recognized contribution of life change to the development of physical illness and psychological distress has stimulated research on the possible role of anxiety in *athletic injuries* (see Williams and Roepke, 1993). Several studies have examined whether athletes who experience a high degree of "life stress" are at greater risk for athletic injury. Studies of college football players have shown injury rates of 68% to 73% in athletes who had recently experienced major life changes, compared with rates of 30% to 39% in athletes who had not experienced such events (Bramwell, Masuda, Wagner, and Holmes, 1975; Cryan and Alles, 1983). In another study of college football players, Passer and Seese (1983) obtained partial support for an association between injury and object loss (a subgroup of negative life events involving the actual or threatened loss of a close personal relationship). In a study of younger athletes, Coddington and Troxell (1980) found no association between overall life stress and injury rates among high school football players. However, athletes who suffered the actual loss of a parent were five times more likely to be injured than teammates who had experienced no such loss.

The most compelling suggestions of an association between life stress and injuries have occurred in studies of football players. However, May, Veach, Southard, and Herring (1985) reported life change units to be related to injuries in a diverse group of male and female athletes, including gymnasts, figure skaters, basketball players, and biathletes. Unfortunately, the injury data were derived from athlete self-reports rather than from medical records, introducing the possibility of reporting bias.

Although there appears to be a reasonable basis for considering life stress as a potential risk factor in athletic injuries, stressors do not affect people in a uniform fashion. Some individuals are highly susceptible, whereas others are quite resilient. Results from a study involving 451 high school male and female athletes suggest that the stress-injury relation may be enhanced dramatically by a combination of poor psychological coping skills and low social support (Smith, Smoll, and Ptacek, 1990). Major negative life changes in themselves were essentially unrelated ($r = .09$) to a measure of subsequent injury (time loss from participation). However, among athletes whose scores fell in the lower quartiles in *both* social support and coping skills, a correlation of .55 was found between the number of major negative life events experienced in the 6 months prior to the start of the season and subsequent injury. No other low-high combination of social support and coping skills yielded a statistically significant stress-injury correlation. Thus, coping skills and social support operated as moderator variables in an interactive manner; low levels of both variables were required for injury vulnerability in the face of high life stress. In subsequent research, Smith, Ptacek, and Smoll (1992) reported evidence suggesting that the relation between major negative sport-specific life events and ensuing injury-related time loss may be most profound for athletes who have a lower tolerance for arousal than their high sensation seeking counterparts. More recently, research on ballet dancers have shown that social support and trait anxiety both serve to influence the relation between life stress and injury time loss. Consistent with the previously discussed evidence that social support serves to buffer the effects of situational stressors, Patterson, Smith, and Everett (1998) found a strikingly high positive correlation (r = .71) between recent life stress and subsequent injury time loss in dancers who reported low levels of social support in their lives. In those reporting high social support, no relation was found between negative life events and subsequent injuries (r = -.02).

Consistent with the hypothesis that trait anxiety predisposes the tendency to experience higher levels of somatic and cognitive state anxiety, a more recent analysis of these ballet data revealed that high somatic, worry, and concentration disruption scores on the Sport Anxiety Scale (modified slightly to refer to the ballet performance environment) all served to increase the relation between life stress and injury (Smith, Ptacek, and Patterson, 2000). These findings suggest the possibility that both somatic arousal (including muscle tension and reduced joint flexibility) and worry place athletes at greater risk for injury, as does concentration disruption.

In addition to being at greater risk for injury, sports medicine specialists have observed that athletes who find participation to be stressful and unpleasant often appear to take longer to recover from injuries (May and Sieb, 1987; Williams, Rotella, and Scherzer, 2001). Depression, anxiety, and anger are frequently experienced by injured athletes, but the impact of such reactions on recovery are unclear. Speculation exists that athletes who are high in fear of failure might find an injury a socially acceptable means of avoiding exposure to the sources of stress, resulting in a longer required recovery period. In other words, some athletes may find an injury to be a temporary and legitimate haven from the stresses of competition.

In view of the above, it seems appropriate to ask an obvious question: Are youth sports *too* stressful? Although there is no simple answer, research results indicate that for most youngsters, sport participation is not exceedingly stressful, especially in comparison with other activities involving performance evaluation (see Gould and Eklund, 1996; Smoll and Smith, 1996). Indeed, the amount of stress in youth sports does not appear to be as widespread or as intense as critics have claimed. But it is equally clear that the sport setting is capable of producing high levels of anxiety for a *minority* of youngsters. And, for the United States alone, if only 5% to 10% of the estimated 47 million youth sport participants (Ewing and Seefeldt, this volume) experience excessive stress, this would involve about 2.3 to 4.7 million youngsters. Instead of finding athletic competition enjoyable and challenging, these young athletes undoubtedly endure anxiety and discomfort, which can have harmful psychological, behavioral, and health-related effects. Because of this, priority should be given to minimizing sources of undue stress in youth sports and to identifying individuals who are at high risk for suffering adverse effects of competitive anxiety.

Stress Reduction Strategies

The conceptual model of stress not only provides a frame of reference for analyzing the dynamics of sport performance anxiety, but it also suggests a number of points at which intervention strategies might be applied. In a general sense, any of the model's components may be a target for intervention. It is important to reiterate, however, that the model is a reciprocally interactive and recursive one, so that measures taken to modify any one of the components will almost certainly affect others as well. We now consider how intervention might be directed at each of the four core components of the model.

The Situational Component

The most practical approach to solving stress-related problems involves taking measures at the situational level to alter its capacity to generate stress. Reduction of situational sources of stress is addressed relative to (a) changes in certain features of the sport itself, (b) the role of coaches in creating a psychologically healthy environment, and (c) the role of parents in combating competitive anxiety.

Modification of the sport. The organization and administration of a sport program can be the focus of environmental change aimed at eliminating potential sources of stress. In this regard, it is well known that children vary greatly in physical and psychological maturation. Diverse programs should therefore be offered to provide for varied levels of athletic skill as well as degrees of competitive intensity. With adult counseling and guidance, youngsters can then select the level at which they prefer to play.

Other methods of matching children to the appropriate level of competition can serve to combat stress associated with inequity of competition and risk of injury. Some youth leagues utilize homogeneous grouping procedures so that athletes compete against others of their own ability and size. Examples of homogeneous grouping procedures include (a) keeping the age range as narrow as possible (i.e., leagues for 9- and 10-year-olds and 11- and 12-year-olds, rather than 9- to 12-year-olds), (b) using measures of height and weight in conjunction with chronological age for grouping purposes, and (c) using sport-skills tests to group participants (Martens and Seefeldt, 1979).

Organizational modification might also involve attempts to minimize situational demands that many youngsters find stressful. For example, to eliminate the stress-related emphasis on winning, some programs do not keep game scores, league standings, or individual performance statistics.

A more direct approach to change at the situational level involves modification of the sport itself. The purpose here is to decrease performance demands on growing children, thereby maximizing their chances of success and enjoyment. For example, Potter (1986) identified four categories in which sports are modified in the Eugene (Oregon) Sports Program: equipment, dimensions of the playing area, length of the contest, and rules changes. Examples of equipment changes include reduced ball size and lowered hoops in basketball, and lowered nets in volleyball. In addition to reducing the overall dimensions of the playing area, appropriate scaling modifications are applied to restraining lines for particular skills, such as serving in volleyball and shooting free throws in basketball. The length of the contest for all sports is shortened until at least the middle-school grades. Finally, specific rules changes are implemented to reduce demands on players. Examples include no press defense in basketball, no fumble recovery in football (i.e., ball is dead), and no stealing in baseball and softball.

The kinds of sport modifications described herein are highly desirable improvements. However, they may not be entirely appropriate for adolescent-level athletics. Additionally, because administrators are often reluctant to implement change, proposals to modify a particular policy or practice should include a rationale based on (a) growth and developmental status of young athletes, (b) biomechanics of young athletes' skill performance, and/or (c) systematically obtained empirical evidence substantiating the benefits of the modification (Haywood, 1986). For example, research has shown that the use of a smaller basketball results in better ball-handling skills and slightly better shooting for 9- to 13-year-old children (Haywood, 1978).

Coaching roles and relationships. Within the youth sport environment, coaches exert a major impact on the nature and quality of the total experience, and they can play an especially influential role in the processes that affect the development and maintenance of performance anxiety. Some coaches cause performance anxiety by constantly reminding athletes about the uncertainty of winning, which makes them feel uncertain about their capability of meeting the demands of the competitive situation (Martens, 1988). Moreover, coaches provide athletes with extensive evaluative feedback about their ability and performance, and they administer response-contingent approval and disapproval. Critical or punitive feedback from coaches can evoke high levels of negative affect in youngsters who fear failure and disapproval, thereby contributing to a threatening athletic situation (Baker, Cote, and Hawes, 2000; Passer, 1988; Roberts, 1986; Scanlan, Stein, and Ravizza, 1991). In contrast with children who have negative interactions with their coaches, children who perceive their coaches as supportive of their efforts experience higher levels of sport enjoyment (Scanlan and Lewthwaite, 1986; Smoll, Smith, Barnett, and Everett, 1993). Ryska and Yin (1999) found that athlete-perceived coach support was significantly related to prematch state anxiety in adolescent tennis players who were high in performance trait anxiety. No relationship between coach support and state anxiety were found in low trait anxiety athletes. It thus appears that supportive coaching behaviors serve to buffer the impact of competitive anxiety, particularly in athletes who have high trait anxiety. Given the significant role that coaching behaviors can have on the emotional reactions of young athletes and their continuation in sports, the potential value of educational interventions designed to train coaches to provide a positive and supportive athletic environment seems self-evident.

As indicated in Chapter 9 (Smoll and Smith, this volume), Coach Effectiveness Training (CET) is an empirically supported and economical intervention that provides instruction for coaches in creating a more positive interpersonal environment for athletes. The core of CET consists of a series of coaching guidelines based primarily on social influence techniques that involve (a) principles of positive control rather than aversive control, and (b) the conception of success or "winning" as giving maximum effort. Field research has confirmed that this educational program favorably impacts the behaviors of coaches and the experiences of young athletes. Experimental group coaches who attended a preseason CET workshop were later judged by trained observers and by their players as behaving in a manner consistent with the coaching guidelines. In comparison with control group (untrained) coaches, CET coaches were better liked and rated as better teachers, and players on their teams liked one another more. Children who played for these coaches enjoyed their sport experience more, exhibited an increase in self-esteem, and had a lower attrition rate than players of control group coaches (Barnett, Smoll, and Smith, 1992; Smith, Smoll, and Curtis, 1979; Smoll et al., 1993). Moreover, youngsters who played for CET coaches showed a significant reduction in competitive A-trait over the course of the season, while a nonsignificant decline was found in players of untrained coaches (Smith, Smoll, and Barnett, 1995).

An understanding of how CET affects athletes' competitive anxiety is important for both theoretical and practical reasons. In this regard, several features of the program might serve to reduce the anxiety-arousing potential of the sport environment. First, CET might be viewed, at least in part, as a social support enhancement program (Smith and Smoll, 1991), and there is considerable evidence that social support has stress-reducing properties (Cutrona and Russell, 1990; Heller and Swindle, 1983; Linder, Sarason, and Sarason, 1988; Windle, 1992). Second, the program's emphasis on encouraging and positively reinforcing effort as opposed to outcome might also reduce stress, for it is generally recognized that increasing perceptions of personal control is one method of reducing stress (Folkman, 1984; Holahan and Moos, 1990). By encouraging coaches to focus on personal effort and improvement rather than on winning, the CET guidelines emphasize an area over which children have relatively greater personal control. Third, the more supportive environment, coupled with effective instructional strategies learned by the coaches, may increase the skill level of the athletes and create a more favorable balance between the demands of the situation and the personal coping resources of the athletes, thus reducing stress (Lazarus and Folkman, 1984). Finally, a strong emphasis is placed on the outcome of "having fun," a factor that has been found to be inversely related to competitive stress (Scanlan and Lewthwaite, 1984; Scanlan and Passer, 1978, 1979). Thus, to the extent that the behavioral guidelines of the CET program are implemented by coaches, the two major sources of performance anxiety—fear of failure and fear of negative social evaluation—should be reduced. At this time, it is not known which of the four factors has the greatest stress-reducing effect, nor is it known whether the factors operate independently or in some combination. These issues await further empirical attention.

Parent-induced stress. Although coaches have the most direct contact with children within the sport environment, parents also play an important role. The literature on sport socialization confirms that parents are instrumental in determining children's sport involvement (Greendorfer, Lewko, and Rosengren, this volume; McPherson and Brown, 1988). Moreover, the negative impact that parents can have on young athletes is all too obvious. Some parents assume an extremely active role in their children's sport involvement, and in some instances, their influence becomes an important source of stress (Brustad, 1993, this volume; Passer, 1984; Scanlan, 1986; Smith, 1986a).

What might constitute the underlying basis of parent-induced stress? One factor is what we have termed the *reversed-dependency phenomenon* (Smith, Smoll, and Smith, 1989). All parents identify with their children to some extent and thus want them to do well. Unfortunately, in some cases, the degree of identification becomes excessive, and the child becomes an extension of the parents. When this happens, parents begin to define their own self-worth in terms of how successful their son or daughter is. The father who is a "frustrated jock" may seek to experience through his child the success he never knew as an athlete. Or the parent who was a star may be resentful and rejecting if the child does not attain similar achievements. Some parents thus become "winners" or "losers" through their children, and the pressure placed on the children to excel can be extreme. A child *must* succeed or the parent's self-image is threatened. Much more is at stake than a mere game, and the child of such a parent carries a heavy burden. When parental love and approval depend on how well the child performs, sports are bound to be stressful (Smoll and Smith, 1999).

The definition of "success" communicated by parents may affect the child's trait anxiety. White (1998) studied the relation between athletes' trait anxiety and their perceptions of their parents' achievement goal orientation. Athletes rated their parents' ego (emphasis on winning, comparison with others) and task (emphasis on learning and enjoyment, meeting one's own standards) orientations toward their child's sport experience. Adolescents whose parents were rated as high in ego orientation and low in task orientation reported their fathers as causing them worry about making mistakes. This group obtained the highest trait anxiety scores. A more recent study by Voight, Callaghan, and Ryska (2000) reported a similar relation between an ego achievement goal orientation and trait anxiety among female athletes who reported low self-confidence. Finally, higher anxiety levels associated with an ego orientation have been found in a within-subject design in which junior high school children were exposed to both task-involving and ego-involving task conditions (Papaioannou and Kouli, 1999). It thus appears that parents would be well advised to encourage the development of an achievement orientation that emphasizes a focus on enjoyment of the activity for its own sake, on giving maximum effort in learning and striving for personal improvement, and a reduced emphasis on winning and besting others. A "win at all costs" philosophy has negative implications not only for the youth sport environment, but also for the developing athlete.

Because of the harmful consequences caused by overzealous and unknowing adults, some youth leagues have banned parents from attending games in order to reduce the stress placed on young athletes and officials. We view this as an unfortunate example of situational change, as parents can strongly and positively affect the quality of their children's sport experience. More desirable and constructive efforts are reflected in an increasing number of books devoted to educating sport parents about their roles and responsibilities (e.g., Fine and Sachs, 1997; Murphy, 1999; Smith et al., 1989; Smoll and Smith, 1999; Wolff, 1997). Workshops for parents similar to those developed for coaches can be another vehicle for reaching parents and influencing the ways in which they interact with their child athlete. Elsewhere, we have advanced a set of guidelines for parents that parallel those emphasized in Coach Effectiveness Training (Smoll and Smith, 1999), and we have also provided coaches with guidelines for conducting a workshop with the parents of the athletes they are coaching (Smith and Smoll, 2002; Smoll, 2001). However, it should be noted that, in contrast to the empirical base for CET, no outcome data are currently available for assessing the efficacy of the parent program we have developed.

The Cognitive and Physiologic Components

Given that the amount of stress experienced by the young athlete is a joint function of the intensity of environmental stressors and the way the individual appraises and copes with them, it follows that actively assisting youngsters in developing coping skills can increase their ability to deal effectively with athletic stress. Reduction of stress at the cognitive and physiological levels is the focus of stress management programs that seek to teach specific cognitive and physiological coping skills. Stress Management Training (SMT), developed by Smith (1980), consists of a number of clinical treatment techniques combined into an educational program for self-control of emotion. SMT was originally developed for individual and group psychotherapy clinical populations. The program components have been adapted to form a training package that has been used successfully with a variety of populations, including preadolescent, college, and professional athletes (Crocker, 1989; Crocker, Alderman, and Smith, 1988; Smith, 1984; Ziegler, Klinzing, and Williamson, 1982), test-anxious college students (Smith and Nye, 1989), problem drinkers (Rohsenow, Smith, and Johnson, 1985), and medical students (Holtzworth-Munroe, Munroe, and Smith, 1985).

When presented to athletes, the SMT program is labeled "mental toughness training," the latter being defined as the ability to control emotional responses that might interfere with performance and to focus attention on the task at hand. Ordinarily, the training involves six 1-hour group training sessions held twice a week, a series of specific homework assignments geared to self-monitoring, and the development and rehearsal of coping skills.

Part of SMT is directed at helping athletes to acquire specific coping skills at the physiologic level. Specifically, athletes are taught muscle relaxation skills that can be used to prevent or lower excessive arousal. The rationale underlying relaxation training is that the relaxation response is incompatible with physiologic arousal, and, to the extent that athletes can voluntarily control their level of relaxation, they can also control stress responses. It is important to note that the purpose is *not* to eliminate arousal completely, as some degree of arousal enhances athletic performance. Rather, the goal of the training is to give young athletes greater control over emotional responses, enabling them to reduce or prevent high and aversive levels of arousal that interfere with performance and enjoyment.

Because of their generally superior ability to control motor responses, athletes tend to learn relaxation skills rather quickly. Acquiring such skills also helps athletes to become more sensitive to their bodily arousal, so that they can apply their coping skills before their level of arousal becomes excessive and difficult to manage.

In SMT, a variant of progressive muscle relaxation (Jacobson, 1938) and deep breathing are taught as methods of lowering physiologic arousal. Individual muscle groups are tensed, slowly relaxed half way, and then slowly relaxed completely. This procedure is designed to enhance discrimination of slight changes in muscle tension. The written training exercises are presented elsewhere (Smith et al., 1989, pp. 130–134). As training proceeds, athletes are taught to breathe slowly and deeply and to emit the mental command, "Relax," while they exhale and voluntarily relax their muscles. The mental command is repeatedly paired with the relaxation that occurs with exhalation; with time, the command becomes a cue for inducing relaxation.

In SMT, training in cognitive coping skills is carried out concurrently with relaxation training. This part of the program is targeted at dysfunctional thoughts that play a major role in the stress process. As noted earlier, stress responses are not directly triggered by the situation but rather by what people tell themselves about the situation and about their ability to cope with it. SMT thus includes two related procedures to modify cognitive processes. *Cognitive restructuring* (Goldfried and Davison, 1976; A. Lazarus, 1972) is directed at identifying and altering irrational beliefs that cause athletes to appraise the competitive situation as threatening. Dysfunctional stress-producing ideas (e.g., "It would be awful if I failed or if someone disapproved of me.") are rationally analyzed, challenged, and replaced with self-statements that are both rationally sound and likely to reduce or prevent a stress response (e.g., "All I can do is give 100%. No one can do more.") In *self-instructional training* (Meichenbaum, 1977), athletes are taught to emit specific covert instructions designed to enhance attentional and problem-solving processes. In so doing, they are assisted in developing and using specific self-commands that can be employed in relevant situations (e.g., "Don't get shook up. Just focus on what you have to do.").

Eventually, the relaxation and cognitive coping responses are combined into an *integrated coping response* that ties both into the breathing cycle. As the athlete inhales, an antistress self-statement is emitted (e.g., "I'm in control."). At the peak of inhalation, the word, "So" is mentally said. Then, during exhalation, the athlete gives the mental self-command, "Relax," which was built into the relaxation training. This cognitive-behavioral coping response can be utilized instantaneously and as often as necessary in stressful situations.

Stress-coping skills are no different than any other kind of skill. In order to be most effective, they must be practiced under conditions that approximate real-life situations. For this reason, the skill-rehearsal phase of SMT includes a variant of a psychotherapeutic procedure known as *induced affect* (Smith and Ascough, 1985). With this technique, athletes are asked to imagine as vividly as possible stressful sport situations. They are then asked to focus on the feeling that the imagined situation elicits. The trainer suggests that when focused upon, the feeling becomes increasingly stronger. When a heightened state of arousal is produced, the athlete is asked to "turn it off" with the relaxation-coping skill. In a later rehearsal, antistress self-statements alone are used. Finally, the integrated coping response is used.

The SMT program ends with training in Benson's (1976) meditation procedure. The meditation technique cannot ordinarily be used in stressful athletic situations, but it is a general relaxation and tension-reducing technique that can be used in situations that do not require the athlete to perform. Many athletes find it useful in reducing pre-event stress.

The Behavioral Component

At the behavioral level, it is intuitively obvious, as well as theoretically consistent, that increasing the young athlete's physical prowess can make athletic demands easier to cope with (Roberts, 1986). It follows that training to improve sport skills should be one way to reduce competitive stress, as youngsters' anxiety reactions are derived in part from perceived deficits in ability. Specifically, feelings of insecurity and heightened anxiety might arise because of perceived lack of skill to cope with a situation. Support for this assumption is provided by research indicating that all-star athletes had significantly lower competitive trait anxiety scores than playing substitutes (T. Smith, 1983). However, other research is equivocal as to whether high competitive trait-anxious athletes experience competitive stress due to a lack of athletic ability (Gould et al., 1983a; Magill and Ash, 1979; Passer, 1983; Passer and Scanlan, 1980). For some youngsters, increasing their level of skill may serve to reduce the perceived imbalance between athletic demands and resources, but for others skill improvement may not be sufficient to reduce anxiety. For the latter, assistance in changing excessively high performance standards or distorted fears of the consequences of possible failure may be required.

Concluding Comments

Some degree of stress is inherent in all competitive situations. Like striving for victory, it is an integral part of sports. But some young athletes experience excessive and chronic stress that can contribute to a variety of psychological as well as physical maladies. This chapter has emphasized that an understanding of the antecedents, dynamics, and consequences of athletic stress can pave the way for preventive and remedial measures. Sport psychologists can play an important role in helping coaches, parents, and athletes to keep competition within a healthy perspective. Through our professional efforts, we can help to alleviate needless stress within sports and thus provide child and adolescent athletes with enjoyment and personal growth.

References

Alpert, R., and Haber, R. N. (1960). Anxiety in academic achievement situations. *Journal of Abnormal and Social Psychology, 61,* 207–215.

Apitzsch, E. (Ed.). (1983). *Anxiety in sport.* Magglingen, Switzerland: Guido Schilling, ETS.

Arnold, M. B. (1960). *Emotion and personality.* New York: Columbia University Press.

Baker, J., Cote, J., and Hawes, R. (2000). The relationship between coaching behaviours and sport anxiety in athletes. *Journal of Science and Medicine in Sport, 3,* 110–119.

Barnett, N. P., Smoll, F. L., and Smith, R. E. (1992). Effects of enhancing coach-athlete relationships on youth sport attrition. *The Sport Psychologist, 6,* 111–127.

Benson, H. (1976). *The relaxation response.* New York: Avon.

Berlyne, D. E. (1960). *Conflict, arousal, and curiosity.* New York: McGraw-Hill.

Borkovec, T. D. (1976). Physiological and cognitive processes in the regulation of anxiety. In G. Schwartz and D. Shapiro (Eds.), *Consciousness and self-regulation: Advances in research* (Vol. 1, pp. 261–312). New York: Plenum.

Bramwell, S. T., Masuda, M., Wagner, N. N., and Holmes, T. H. (1975). Psychosocial factors in athletic injuries: Development and application of the Social and Athletic Readjustment Rating Scale (SARRS). *Journal of Human Stress, 1,* 6–20.

Brower, J. J. (1979). The professionalization of organized youth sport: Social psychological impacts and outcomes. *Annals of the American Academy of Political and Social Science, 445,* 39–46.

Brustad, R. J. (1993). Youth in sport: Psychological considerations. In R. N. Singer, M. Murphey, L. K. Tennant (Eds.), *Handbook of research on sport psychology* (pp. 695–717). New York: Macmillan.

Brustad, R. J., and Partridge, J. A. (2002). Parental and peer influence on children's psychosocial development through sport. In F. L. Smoll and R. E. Smith (Eds.), *Children and youth in sport: A biopsychosocial perspective* (2nd ed., pp. 187–210). Dubuque, IA: Kendall/Hunt.

Burton, D. (1988). Do anxious swimmers swim slower? Reexamining the elusive anxiety-performance relationship. *Journal of Sport and Exercise Psychology, 10,* 45–61.

Burton, D. (1998). Measuring competitive state anxiety. In J. L. Duda (Ed.), *Advancements in sport and exercise psychology measurement* (pp. 129–148). Morgantown, WV: Fitness Information Technology.

Burton, D., and Martens, R. (1986). Pinned by their own goals: An exploratory investigation into why kids drop out of wrestling. *Journal of Sport Psychology, 8,* 183–195.

Buss, A. H. (1995). *Personality: Temperament, social behavior, and the self.* Boston: Allyn and Bacon.

Cannon, W. B. (1929). The mechanism of emotional disturbance of bodily functions. *New England Journal of Medicine, 198,* 877–884.

Coakley, J. (1992). Burnout among adolescent athletes: A personal failure or social problem? *Sociology of Sport Journal, 9,* 271–285.

Coakley, J. (1993). Social dimensions of intensive training and participation in youth sports. In B. R. Cahill and A. J. Pearl (Eds.), *Intensive participation in children's sports* (pp. 77–94). Champaign, IL: Human Kinetics.

Coddington, R. D., and Troxell, J. R. (1980). The effect of emotional factors on football injury rates: A pilot study. *Journal of Human Stress, 6,* 3–5.

Cohn, P. J. (1990). An exploratory study on sources of stress and athlete burnout in youth golf. *The Sport Psychologist, 4,* 95–106.

Crocker, P. R. E. (1989). A follow-up of cognitive-affectetive stress management training. *Journal of Sport and Exercise Psychology, 11,* 236–342.

Crocker, P. R. E., Alderman, R. B., and Smith, F. M. R. (1988). Cognitive-affective stress management training with high performance youth volleyball players: Effects on affect, cognition, and performance. *Journal of Sport and Exercise Psychology, 10,* 448–460.

Cryan, P. D., and Alles, W. F. (1983). The relationship between stress and college football injuries. *Journal of Sports Medicine, 23,* 52–58.

Davidson, R. J., Schwartz, G. E. (1976). The psychobiology of relaxation and related states: A multi-process theory. In D. Mostofsky (Ed.), *Behavioral control and modification of physiological activity* (pp. 399–442). Englewood Cliffs, NJ: Prentice-Hall.

Deffenbacher, J. L. (1980). Worry and emotionality in test anxiety. In I. G. Sarason (Ed.), *Test anxiety: Theory, research, and applications* (pp. 111–128). Hillsdale, NJ: Erlbaum.

Dunn, J. G. H. (1999). A theoretical framework for structuring the content of competitive worry in ice hockey. *Journal of Sport and Exercise Psychology, 21,* 259–279.

Duffy, E. (1962). *Activation and behavior.* New York: Wiley.

Ellis, A. (1962). *Reason and emotion in personality.* New York: Lyle Stuart.

Ewing, M. E., and Seefeldt, V. (2002). Patterns of participation in American agency-sponsored youth sports. In F. L. Smoll and R. E. Smith (eds.), *Children and youth in sport: A biopsychosocial perspective* (2nd ed., pp. 39–56). Dubuque, IA: Kendall/Hunt.

Ewing, M. E., Seefeldt, V. D., and Brown, T. P. (1996). Role of organized sport in the education and health of American children and youth. In A. Poinsett (Ed.), *The role of sports in youth development* (pp. i-157). New York: Carnegie Corporation.

Feltz, D. L., and Albrecht, R. R. (1986). Psychological implications of competitive running. In M. R. Weiss and D. Gould (Eds.), *Sport for children and youths* (pp. 225–230). Champaign, IL: Human Kinetics.

Fine, A. H., and Sachs, M. L. (1997). *The total sports experience for kids: A parents' guide to success in youth sports*. South Bend, IN: Diamond Communications.

Folkman, S. (1984). Personal control and stress and coping processes: A theoretical analysis. *Journal of Personality and Social Psychology, 46*, 839–852.

Gill, D. L., and Martens, R. (1977). The role of task type and success-failure in group competition. *International Journal of Sport Psychology, 8*, 160–177.

Goldfried, M. R., and Davison, G. (1976). *Clinical behavior therapy*. New York: Holt, Rinehart, and Winston.

Gould, D. (1982). Sport psychology in the 1980s: Status, direction, and challenge in youth sports research. *Journal of Sport Psychology, 4*, 203–218.

Gould, D. (1993). Intensive sport participation and the prepubescent athlete: Competitive stress and burnout. In B. R. Cahill and A. J. Pearl (Eds.), *Intensive participation in children's sports* (pp. 19–38). Champaign, IL: Human Kinetics.

Gould, D. (1996). Personal motivation gone awry: Burnout in competitive athletes. *Quest, 48*, 275–289.

Gould, D., and Eklund, R. C. (1996). Emotional stress and anxiety in the child and adolescent athlete. In O. Bar-Or (Ed.), *The child and adolescent athlete* (pp. 383–398). Osney Mead, Oxford: Blackwell Science.

Gould, D., and Krane, V. I. (1992). The arousal-athletic performance relationship: Current status and future directions. In T. Horn (Ed.), *Advances in sport psychology* (pp. 119–142). Champaign, IL: Human Kinetics.

Gould, D., Eklund, R. C., Petlichkoff, L., Peterson, K., and Bump, L. (1991). Psychological predictors of state anxiety, and performance in age-group wrestlers. *Pediatric Exercise Science, 3*, 198–208.

Gould, D., Feltz, D., Horn, T., and Weiss, M. (1982). Reasons for discontinuing involvement in competitive youth swimming. *Journal of Sport Behavior, 5*, 155–165.

Gould, D., Horn, T., and Spreeman, J. (1983a). Competitive anxiety in junior elite wrestlers. *Journal of Sport Psychology , 5*, 58–71.

Gould, D., Horn, T., and Spreeman, J. (1983b). Sources of stress in junior elite wrestlers. *Journal of Sport Psychology, 5*, 159–171.

Gould, D., Petlichkoff, L., and Weinberg, R. S. (1984). Antecedents of, temporal changes in, and relationships between CSAI-2 subcomponents. *Journal of Sport Psychology, 6*, 289–304.

Gould, D., Petlichkoff, L., Simons, J., and Vevera, M. (1987). The relationship between Competitive State Anxiety Inventory-2 subscale scores and pistol shooting performance. *Journal of Sport Psychology, 9*, 33–42.

Gould, D., Tuffey, S., Udry, E., and Loehr, J. (1996). Burnout in competitive junior tennis players: II. A qualitative analysis. *The Sport Psychologist, 10*, 341–366.

Gould, D., Tuffey, S., Udry, E., and Loehr, J. (1997). Burnout in competitive junior tennis players: III. Individual differences in the burnout experience. *The Sport Psychologist, 11*, 257–276.

Gould, D., Udry, E., Tuffey, S., and Loehr, J. (1996). Burnout in competitive junior tennis players: I. A quantitative psychological assessment. *The Sport Psychologist, 10*, 322–340.

Greendorfer, S. L., Lewko, J. H., and Rosengren, K. S. (2002). Family and gender-based influences in sport socialization of children and adolescents. In F. L. Smoll and R. E. Smith (Eds.), *Children and youth in sport: A biopsychosocial perspective* (2nd ed., pp. 153–186). Dubuque, IA: Kendall/Hunt.

Griffin, M. R. (1972, Spring). An analysis of state and trait anxiety experienced in sports competition at different age levels. *Foil*, 58–64.

Hackfort, D., and Spielberger, C. D. (Eds.). (1989). *Anxiety in sports: An international perspective*. New York: Hemisphere.

Hanin, Y. L. (Ed.) (2000). *Emotions in sport*. Champaign, IL: Human Kinetics Publishers.

Hanson, D. L. (1967). Cardiac response to participation in Little League baseball competition as determined by telemetry. *Research Quarterly, 38*, 384–388.

Haywood, K. M. (1978). *Children's basketball performance with regulation and junior-sized basketballs*. St. Louis: University of Missouri-St. Louis. (ERIC Document Reproduction Service No. ED 164 452).

Haywood, K. M. (1986). Modification in youth sport: A rationale and some examples in youth basketball. In M. R. Weiss and D. Gould (Eds.), *Sport for children and youths* (pp. 179–185). Champaign, IL, Human Kinetics.

Hebb, D. O. (1949). *The organization of behavior*. New York: Wiley.

Hellstedt, J. C. (1988). Kids, parents and sports: Some questions and answers. *The Physician and Sportsmedicine, 16*, 59–62, 69–71.

Henschen, K. P. (2001). Athletic staleness and burnout: Diagnosis, prevention, and treatment. In J. M. Williams (Ed.), *Applied sport psychology: Personal growth to peak performance* (4th ed., pp. 445–455). Mountain View, CA: Mayfield.

Holahan, C. J., and Moos, R. H. (1990). Life stressors, resistance factors, and improved psychological functioning: An extension of the stress resistance paradigm. *Journal of Personality and Social Psychology, 58*, 909–917.

Holzworth-Munroe, A., Munroe, M., and Smith, R. E. (1985). Effects of a stress-management training program on first- and second-year medical students. *Journal of Medical Education, 60*, 417–419.

Jacobson, E. (1938). *Progressive relaxation*. Chicago: University of Chicago Press.

Jones, G. (1995). More than just a game: Research developments and issues in competitive anxiety in sport. *British Journal of Psychology, 86*, 449–478.

Jones, G., and Swain, A. (1995). Predisposition to experience debilitative and facilitative anxiety in elite and nonelite performers. *The Sport Psychologist, 9,* 201–211.

Kamm, R. L. (1997, June 29). Out of Williamsport, into the parent trap. *The New York Times*, p. Y19.

Kendrick, M. J., Craig, K. D., Lawson, D. M., and Davidson, P. O. (1982). Cognitive and behavioral therapy for musical-performance anxiety. *Journal of Consulting and Clinical Psychology, 50,* 353–362.

Klavora, P. (1978). An attempt to derive inverted-U curves based on the relationship between anxiety and athletic performance. In D. M. Landers and R. W. Christina (Eds.), *Psychology of motor behavior and sport—1977* (pp. 369–377). Champaign, IL: Human Kinetics.

Lang, P. J. (1971). The application of psychophysiological methods to the study of psychotherapy and behavior modification. In A. E. Bergin and S. L. Garfield (Eds.), *Handbook of psychotherapy and behavior change* (pp. 75–125). New York: Wiley.

Lazarus, A. (1972). *Behavior therapy and beyond*. New York: McGraw-Hill.

Lazarus, R. S. (2000). How emotions influence performance in competitive sports. *The Sport Psychologist, 14,* 229–252.

Lazarus, R. S., and Folkman, S. (1984). *Stress, appraisal, and coping*. New York: Springer.

Liebert, R. M., and Morris, L. W. (1967). Cognitive and emotional components of test anxiety: A distinction and some initial data. *Psychological Reports, 20,* 975–978.

Linder, K. C., Sarason, I. G., and Sarason, B. R. (1988). Assessed life stress and experimentally provided social support. In C. D. Spielberger and I. G. Sarason (Eds.), *Stress and anxiety* (Vol. 11, pp. 231–240). Washington, DC: Hemisphere.

Lowe R., and McGrath, J. E. (1971). *Stress, arousal and performance: Some findings calling for a new theory* (Report No. AF 1161-67). Washington, DC: Air Force Office of Strategic Research.

Magill, R. A., and Ash, M. J. (1979). Academic, psycho-social, and motor characteristics of participants and nonparticipants in children's sport. *Research Quarterly, 50,* 230–240.

Magnusson, D., and Endler, N. S. (Eds.). (1977). *Personality at the crossroads: Current issues in interactional psychology*. Hillsdale, NJ: Erlbaum.

Malmo, R. B. (1959). Activation: A neurophysiological dimension. *Psychological Review, 66,* 367–386.

Mandler, G., and Sarason, S. B. (1952). A study of anxiety and learning. *Journal of Abnormal and Social Psychology, 47,* 166–173.

Martens, R. (1977). *Sport Competition Anxiety Test*. Champaign, IL: Human Kinetics.

Martens, R. (1988). Competitive anxiety in children's sports. In R. M. Malina (Ed.), *Young athletes: Biological, psychological, and educational perspectives*. (pp. 235–244). Champaign, IL: Human Kinetics.

Martens, R. (1993). Psychological perspectives. In B. R. Cahill and A. J. Pearl (Eds.), *Intensive participation in children's sports* (pp. 9–17). Champaign, IL: Human Kinetics.

Martens, R., and Gill, D. L. (1976). State anxiety among successful and unsuccessful competitors who differ in competitive trait anxiety. *Research Quarterly, 47,* 698–708.

Martens, R., and Seefeldt, V. (1979). *Guidelines for children's sports*. Washington, DC: American Alliance for Health, Physical Education, Recreation, and Dance.

Martens, R., Burton, D., Vealey, R. S., Bump, L. A., and Smith, D. E. (1990). Development and validation of the Competitive State Anxiety Inventory-2 (CSAI-2). In R. Martens, R. S. Vealey, and D. Burton (Eds.). (1990). *Competitive anxiety in sport*. Champaign, IL: Human Kinetics.

Martens, R., Burton, D., Rivkin, F., and Simon, J. (1980). Reliability and validity of the Competitive State Anxiety Inventory (CSAI). In C. H. Nadeau, W. R. Halliwell, K. M. Newell, and G. C. Roberts (Eds.), *Psychology of motor behavior and sport— 1979* (pp. 91–99). Champaign, IL: Human Kinetics.

Martens, R., Vealey, R. S., and Burton, D. (Eds.). (1990). *Competitive anxiety in sport*. Champaign, IL: Human Kinetics.

May, J. R., and Sieb, G. E. (1987). Athletic injuries: Psychosocial factors in the onset, sequelae, rehabilitation, and prevention. In J. R. May and M. J. Asken (Eds.), *Sport psychology: The psychological health of the athlete* (pp. 157–185). New York: PMA Publishing.

May, J. R., Veach, T. L., Southard, S. W., and Herring, M. (1985). The effects of life change on injuries, illness, and performance in elite athletes. In N. K. Butts, T. T. Gushikin, and B. Zarins (Eds.), *The elite athlete* (pp. 171–179). Jamaica, NY: Spectrum.

McPherson, B. D., Brown, B. A. (1988) The structure, processes, and consequences of sport for children. In F. L. Smoll, R. A. Magill, and M. J. Ash (Eds.), *Children in sport* (3rd ed., pp. 265–286). Champaign, IL.

McPherson, B., Marteniuk, R., Tihanyi, J., and Clark, W. (1980). The social system of age group swimmers: The perception of swimmers, parents and coaches. *Canadian Journal of Applied Sport Sciences, 4,* 142–145.

Meichenbaum, D. (1977). *Cognitive-behavior modification*. New York: Plenum.

Michener, J. A. (1976). *Sports in America*. New York: Random House.

Morris, L. W., and Engle, W. B. (1981). Assessing various coping strategies and their effects on test performance and anxiety. *Journal of Clinical Psychology, 37,* 165–171.

Morris, L. W., Davis, D., and Hutchings, C. (1981). Cognitive and emotional components of anxiety: Literature review and revised worry-emotionality scale. *Journal of Educational Psychology, 73*, 541–555.

Murphy, S. (1999). *The cheers and the tears: A healthy alternative to the dark side of youth sports today.* San Francisco: Jossey-Bass.

Nash, H. L. (1987). Elite child-athletes: How much does victory cost? *The Physician and Sportsmedicine, 15*, 128–133.

Ogilvie, B. (1979). The child athlete: Psychological implications of participation in sport. *Annals of the American Academy of Political and Social Sciences, 445*, 47–58.

Olerud, J. E. (1989). Acne in a young athlete. In N. J. Smith (Ed.), *Common problems in pediatric sports medicine* (pp. 219–221). Chicago: Year Book Medical Publishers.

Orlick, T. D., and Botterill, C. (1975). *Every kid can win.* Chicago: Nelson-Hall.

Papaioannou, A., and Kouli, O. (1999). The effect of task structure, perceived motivational climate and goal orientations on students' task involvement and anxiety. *Journal of Applied Sport Psychology, 11*, 51–71.

Passer, M. W. (1983). Fear of failure, fear of evaluation, perceived competence, and self-esteem in competitive-trait-anxious children. *Journal of Sport Psychology, 5*, 172–188.

Passer, M. W. (1988). Determinants and consequences of children's competitive stress. In F. L. Smoll, R. A. Magill, and M. J. Ash (Eds.), *Children in sport* (3rd ed., pp. 203–227). Champaign, IL, Human Kinetics.

Passer, M. W., and Scanlan, T. K. (1980). The impact of game outcome on the postcompetition affect and performance evaluations of young athletes. In C. H. Nadeau, W. R. Halliwell, K. M. Newell, and G. C. Roberts (Eds.), *Psychology of motor behavior and sport—1979* (pp. 100–111). Champaign, IL: Human Kinetics.

Passer, M. W., and Seese, M. D. (1983). Life stress and athletic injury: Examination of positive versus negative events and three moderator variables. *Journal of Human Stress, 9*, 11–16.

Patterson, E. L., Smith, R. E., and Everett, J. J. (1998). Psychosocial factors as predictors of ballet injuries: Interactive effects of life stress and social support. *Journal of Sport Behavior, 21*, 101–112.

Pierce, W. J. (1980). *Psychological perspectives of youth sport participants and nonparticipants.* Unpublished doctoral dissertation, Virginia Polytechnic Institute and State University, Blacksburg.

Potter, M. (1986). Game modifications for youth sport: A practitioner's view. In M. R. Weiss and D. Gould (Eds.), *Sport for children and youths* (pp. 205–208). Champaign, IL: Human Kinetics.

Raffety, B. D., Smith, R. E., and Ptacek, J. T. (1997). Facilitating and debilitating trait anxiety, situational anxiety, and coping with an anticipated stressor: A process analysis. *Journal of Personality and Social Psychology, 72*, 892–906.

Raglin, J. S., and Hanin, Y. L. (2000). Competitive anxiety. In Y. L. Hanin (Ed.). *Emotions in sport*. Champaign, IL: Human Kinetics Publishers.

Roberts, G. C. (1986). The perception of stress: A potential source and its development. In M. R. Weiss and D. Gould (Eds.), *Sport for children and youths* (pp. 119–126). Champaign, IL: Human Kinetics.

Rogers, C. R. (1959). A theory of therapy, personality and interpersonal relationships as developed in the client-centered framework. In S. Koch (Ed.), *Psychology: A study of a science* (Vol. 3, pp. 67–102). New York: McGraw-Hill.

Rohensenow, D. J., Smith, R. E., and Johnson, S. (1985). Stress management training as a prevention for heavy social drinkers: Cognitions, affect drinking, and individual differences. *Addictive Behaviors, 10*, 45–54.

Ryska, T. A., and Yin, Z. (1999). Testing the buffering hypothesis: Perceptions of coach support and pre-competitive anxiety among male and female high school athletes. *Current Psychology, 18*, 381–393.

Sarason, I. G. (1984). Stress, anxiety, and cognitive interference: Reactions to tests. *Journal of Personality and Social Psychology, 46*, 929–938.

Sarason, I. G., and Sarason, B. R. (1990). Test anxiety. In H. Leitenberg (Ed.), *Handbook of social and evaluation anxiety* (pp. 475–495). New York: Plenum.

Sayre, B. M. (1975). The need to ban competitive sports involving preadolescent children. *Pediatrics, 55*, 564.

Scanlan, T. K. (1986). Competitive stress in children. In M. R. Weiss and D. Gould (Eds.), *Sport for children and youths* (pp. 113–118). Champaign, IL: Human Kinetics.

Scanlan, T. K. (2002). Social evaluation and the competition process: A developmental perspective. In F. L. Smoll and R. E. Smith (Eds.), *Children and youth in sport: A biopsychosocial perspective* (2nd ed., pp. 393–407). Dubuque, IA: Kendall/Hunt.

Scanlan, T. K., and Lewthwaite, R. (1984) Social psychological aspects of competition for male youth sport participants: I. Predictors of competitive stress. *Journal of Sport Psychology, 6*, 208–226.

Scanlan, T. K., and Lewthwaite, R. (1986). Social psychological aspects of competition for male youth sport participants: IV. Predictors of enjoyment. *Journal of Sport Psychology, 8*, 25–35.

Scanlan, T. K., and Passer, M. W. (1978). Factors related to competitive stress among male youth sports participants. *Medicine and Science in Sports, 10*, 103–108.

Scanlan, T. K., and Passer, M. W. (1979). Sources of competitive stress in young female athletes. *Journal of Sport Psychology, 1*, 151–159.

Scanlan, T. K., Stein, G. L., and Ravizza, K. (1991). An in-depth study of former elite figure skaters: III. Sources of stress. *Journal of Sport and Exercise Psychology, 13*, 103–120.

Simon, J. A., and Martens, R. (1979). Children's anxiety in sport and nonsport evaluative activities. *Journal of Sport Psychology, 1*, 160–169.

Smilkstein, G. (1980). Psychological trauma in children and youth in competitive sport. *Journal of Family Practice, 10*, 737–739.

Smith, C. A., and Morris, L. W. (1976). Effects of stimulative and sedative music on two components of test anxiety. *Psychological Reports, 38*, 1187–1193.

Smith, R. E. (1980). A cognitive-affective approach to stress management training for athletes. In C. H. Nadeau, W. R. Halliwell, K. M. Newell, and G. C. Roberts (Eds.), *Psychology of motor behavior and sport—1979* (pp. 54–72). Champaign, IL: Human Kinetics.

Smith, R. E. (1984). Theoretical and treatment approaches to anxiety reduction. In J. M. Silva and R. S. Weinberg (Eds.), *Psychological foundations of sport* (pp. 157–170). Champaign, IL: Human Kinetics.

Smith, R. E. (1986a). A component analysis of athletic stress. In M. R. Weiss and D. Gould (Eds.), *Sport for children and youths* (pp. 107–111). Champaign, IL: Human Kinetics.

Smith, R. E. (1986b). Toward a cognitive-affective model of athletic burnout. *Journal of Sport Psychology, 8*, 36–50.

Smith, R. E. (1989). Athletic stress and burnout: Conceptual models and intervention strategies. In D. Hackfort and C. D. Spielberger (Eds.), *Anxiety in sports: An international perspective* (pp. 183–201). New York: Hemisphere.

Smith, R. E. (1996). Performance anxiety, cognitive interference, and concentration enhancement strategies in sports. In I. G. Sarason, G. R. Pierce, and B. R. Sarason (Eds.), *Cognitive interference: Theories, methods, and findings* (pp. 261–284). Mahwah, NJ: Lawrence Erlbaum Associates.

Smith, R. E., and Ascough, J. C. (1985). Induced affect in stress management training. In S. R. Burchfield (Ed.), *Stress: Psychological and physiological interactions* (pp. 359–378). New York: Hemisphere.

Smith, R. E., and Nye, S. L. (1989). A comparison of induced affect and covert rehearsal in the acquisition of stress-management coping skills. *Journal of Counseling Psychology, 36*, 17–23.

Smith, R. E., Ptacek, J. T., and Patterson, E. (2000). Moderator effects of cognitive and somatic trait anxiety on the relation between life stress and physical injuries. *Anxiety, Stress, and Coping, 13*, 269–288.

Smith, R. E., and Smoll, F. L. (1990). Sport performance anxiety. In H. Leitenberg (Ed.), *Handbook of social and evaluation anxiety* (pp. 417–454). New York: Plenum.

Smith, R. E., and Smoll, F. L. (1991). Behavioral research and intervention in youth sports. *Behavior Therapy, 22*, 329–344.

Smith, R. E., and Smoll, F. L. (2002). *Way to go, coach! A scientifically-proven approach to coaching effectiveness* (2nd ed.). Portola Valley, CA: Warde.

Smith, R. E., Ptacek, J. T., and Smoll, F. L. (1992). Sensation seeking, stress, and adolescent injuries: A test of stress-buffering, risk-taking, and coping skills hypotheses. *Journal of Personality and Social Psychology, 62*, 1016–1024.

Smith, R. E., Smoll, F. L., and Barnett, N. P. (1995). Reduction of children's sport performance anxiety through social support training and stress-reduction training for coaches. *Journal of Applied Developmental Psychology, 16*, 125–142.

Smith, R. E., Smoll, F. L., and Curtis, B. (1978). Coaching behaviors in Little League Baseball. In F. L. Smoll and R. E. Smith (Eds.), *Psychological perspectives in youth sports* (pp. 173–201). Washington, DC: Hemisphere.

Smith, R. E., Smoll, F. L., and Curtis, B. (1979). Coach effectiveness training: A cognitive-behavioral approach to enhancing relationship skills in youth sport coaches. *Journal of Sport Psychology, 1*, 59–75.

Smith, R. E., Smoll, F. L., and Ptacek, J. T. (1990). Conjunctive moderator variables in vulnerability and resiliency research: Life stress, social support and coping skills, and adolescent sport injuries. *Journal of Personality and Social Psychology, 58*, 360–370.

Smith, R. E., Smoll, F. L., and Schutz, R. W. (1990). Measurement and correlates of sport-specific cognitive and somatic trait anxiety: The Sport Anxiety Scale. *Anxiety Research, 2*, 263–280.

Smith, R. E., Smoll, F. L., and Smith, N. J. (1989). *Parents' complete guide to youth sports*. Reston, VA: American Alliance for Health, Physical Education, Recreation, and Dance.

Smith, R. E., Smoll, F. L., and Wiechman, S. A. (1998). Measurement of trait anxiety in sport. In J. L. Duda (Ed.), *Advancements in sport and exercise psychology measurement* (pp. 105–127). Morgantown, WV: Fitness Information Technology.

Smith, T. (1983). Competitive trait anxiety in youth sport: Differences according to age, sex, race, and playing status. *Perceptual and Motor Skills, 57*, 1235–1238.

Smoll, F. L. (1989). Sports and the preadolescent: "Little league" sports. In N. J. Smith (Ed.), *Common problems in pediatric sports medicine* (pp. 3–15). Chicago: Year Book Medical Publishers.

Smoll, F. L. (2001). Coach-parent relationships in youth sports: Increasing harmony and minimizing hassle. In J. M. Williams (Ed.), *Applied sport psychology: Personal growth to peak performance* (4th ed., pp. 150–161). Mountain View, CA: Mayfield.

Smoll, F. L., and Smith, R. E. (1996). Competitive anxiety: Sources, Consequences, and intervention strategies. In F. L. Smoll and R. E. Smith (Eds.), *Children and youth in sport: A biopsychosocial perspective* (pp. 359–380). Dubuque, IA: WCB/McGraw-Hill.

Smoll, F. L., and Smith, R. E. (1999). *Sports and your child: A 50-minute guide for parents*. Portola Valley, CA: Warde.

Smoll, F. L., and Smith, R. E. (2001). Conducting sport psychology training programs for coaches: Cognitive-behavioral principles and techniques. In J. M. Williams (Ed.), *Applied sport psychology: Personal growth to peak performance* (4th ed., pp. 378–400). Mountain View, CA: Mayfield.

Smoll, F. L., and Smith, R. E. (2002). Coaching behavior research and intervention in youth sports. In F. L. Smoll and R. E. Smith (Eds.), *Children and youth in sport: A biopsychosocial perspective* (2nd ed., pp. 211–233). Dubuque, IA: Kendall/Hunt.

Smoll, F. L., Smith, R. E., Barnett, N. P., and Everett, J. J. (1993). Enhancement of children's self-esteem through social support training for youth sport coaches. *Journal of Applied Psychology, 78*, 602–610.

Spielberger, C. D. (1966). Theory and research on anxiety. In C. D. Spielberger (Ed.), *Anxiety and behavior* (pp. 3–20). New York: Academic Press.

Spielberger, C. D. (1972). Anxiety as an emotional state. In C. D. Spielberger (Ed.), *Anxiety: Current trends in theory and research* (pp. 23–49). New York: Academic Press.

Spielberger, C. D. (1973). *Preliminary test manual for the State-Trait Anxiety Inventory for Children*. Palo Alto, CA: Consulting Psychologists,

Spielberger, C. D. (1989) Stress and anxiety in sports. In D. Hackfort and C. D. Spielberger (Eds.), *Anxiety in sports: An international perspective* (pp. 3–17). New York: Hemisphere.

Steptoe, A., and Fidler, H. (1987). Stage fright in orchestral musicians: A study of cognitive and behavioural strategies in performance anxiety. *British Journal of Psychology, 78*, 241–249.

Suinn, R. M. (1989). Behavioral intervention for stress management in sport. In D. Hackfort and C. D. Spielberger (Eds.), *Anxiety in sports: An international perspective* (pp. 203–214). New York: Hemisphere.

Swain, A., and Jones, G. (1996). Explaining performance variance: The relative contribution of intensity and direction dimensions of competitive state anxiety. *Anxiety, Stress, and Coping: An International Journal, 9*, 1–18.

Thout, S. M., Kavouras, S. A., and Keneflick, R. W. (1998). Effect of perceived ability, game location, and state anxiety on basketball performance. *Journal of Sport Behavior, 21*, 311–321.

Tryon, G. S. (1980). The measurement and treatment of test anxiety. *Review of Educational Research, 50*, 343–372.

Universities Study Committee. (1978). *Joint legislative study on youth sports programs: Phase II. Agency sponsored sports*. East Lansing, MI: Michigan Institute for the Study of Youth Sports.

Voight, M. R., Callaghan, J. L., and Ryska, T. A. (2000). Relationship between goal orientations, self-confidence and multidimensional trait anxiety among Mexican-American female youth athletes. *Journal of Sport Behavior, 23*, 271–288.

Wankel, L. M., and Kreisel, P. S. J. (1985). Factors underlying enjoyment of youth sports: Sport and age group comparisons. *Journal of Sport Psychology, 7*, 51–64.

White, S. A. (1998). Adolescent goal profiles, perceptions of the parent-initiated motivational climate and competitive trait anxiety. *Sport Psychologist, 12*, 16–28.

Williams, J. M., and Roepke, N. (1993). Psychology of injury and injury rehabilitation. In R. N. Singer, M. Murphey, and L. K. Tennant (Eds.), *Handbook of research on sport psychology* (pp. 815–839). New York: Macmillan.

Williams, J. M., Rotella, R. J., and Scherzer, C. B. (2001). Injury risk and rehabilitation: Psychological considerations. In J. M. Williams (Ed.), *Applied sport *psychology: Personal growth to peak performance* (4th ed., pp. 456–479). Mountain View, CA: Mayfield.

Windle, J. D. (1992). A longitudinal study of stress buffering for adolescent problem behaviors. *Developmental Psychology, 28*, 522–530.

Wolff, R. (1997). *Good sports: The concerned parent's guide to competitive youth sports*. Champaign, IL: Sagamore.

Zaichkowsky, L., and Takenaka, K. (1993). Optimizing arousal levels. In R. N. Singer, M. Murphey, L. K. Tennant (Eds.), *Handbook of research on sport psychology* (pp. 511–527). New York: Macmillan.

Ziegler, S. G., Klinzing, J., and Williamson, K. (1982). The effects of two stress management training programs on cardiorespiratory efficiency. *Journal of Sport Psychology, 4*, 280–289.

CHAPTER 22

Character Development and Children's Sport

David Light Shields, University of Notre Dame
Brenda Light Bredemeier, University of Notre Dame
F. Clark Power, University of Notre Dame

We've all heard the phrase "sport builds character." Whether there is any truth to this old adage or not is hotly debated. Unfortunately, this debate is often rooted more in ideological stance than in any real valid and reliable evidence. Perhaps this is not surprising, since the central terminology is ill-defined and the science is at an embryonic stage. In this chapter, we will seek to offer an approach to character that is rooted in current theory and research and review the state of knowledge relevant to answering this important question.

What Is "Character"?

The concept of "character" is an elusive one in our everyday conversation as well as in the fields of psychology and education. The term "character" originally meant a distinctive mark, and later became a rough equivalent to personality in the psychological lexicon. But the term has also consistently had a moral connotation. People of "good character" are thought to be people who exhibit moral virtues, such as honesty and justice, or socially valued achievement related virtues, such as diligence and perseverance. Although we sometimes attribute good character to individuals when they exhibit a single virtue (for example, sportscasters extol players who keep hustling even when the game is out of reach), we more often think of character as a complex of virtues that help to define the person as a whole. Taking this holistic perspective on human development, John Dewey (1922/1988) described character as the "interpenetration of habits" (p. 29).

The extent to which habits relate to each other to form a unified whole has been a matter of dispute in philosophy and psychology going back to the time of Plato and Aristotle. Plato believed that virtue was one. Aristotle (323 B.C./1985), on the other hand, adopted a pluralistic approach to the virtues. Aristotle, nevertheless, claimed that although the virtues were not identical, they were inseparable from each other because they all involve the intellectual virtue of *phronesis*, commonly translated as practical wisdom (NE 1145a1). Dewey (1922/1928) attempted to account for the "interpenetration of habits" through his understanding of the continuity of human experience. However we account for the relatedness of the virtues, it is difficult to use the term character without assuming such a relatedness.

Aristotle and Dewey's understanding of character builds on the popular notion that character is manifested in action. In fact, we cannot really know about a person's character apart from that person's actions. A person's beliefs, values, and feelings may reveal a great deal about a person, but character or a lack of character depends upon how one acts. In the realm of sports, we can think of countless examples of athletes who fail to live up to their potential, which is often attributed to a lack of character. In the moral domain, we are acutely aware of the gap between the values that one espouses and the values that one puts into practice.

Not only is character revealed in action, but many also assume that character is developed through action. Aristotle and Dewey describe character development as taking place through a process of habituation. Habituation is a term that can be easily misunderstood, particularly in the context of sport, with its emphasis on the acquisition of quasi-automatic motor skills through repetition. A better analogy for habituation with respect to character is to think of how we develop children into basketball players. Part of the task is to teach them the rules of the game; another part is to have them acquire the skills of dribbling, shooting, and passing; a third part is to help them to understand and apply various competitive strategies on offense and defense; and yet another part is to have them acquire a love and appreciation for the game itself in its many facets. We can best accomplish all of these tasks by having children actually play the game of basketball regularly and by doing all that we can to make the game fun for them, even if this initially requires the use of external rewards, like snacks at the end of practice. If the process of habituation goes well, children will become accomplished in the skills of the game and experience the joys that are intrinsic to the game.

Although there are similarities between being a person of character and being a good ballplayer, there is an important difference. Ballplayers tend to be judged on actions alone. If they are productive (e.g., shoot and defend well), we will regard them highly. Judgments of character depend upon having the right intentions or motives in addition to performing the right actions. For example, if a person acts kindly to an aging relative for the purpose of being included in her will, we would not judge him to be a person of good character. One of the most vexing questions for habituation approaches to character education is how children develop autonomous moral judgment such that they are able to decide for themselves upon the right course of action for the right reasons.

The Legacy of Hartshorne and May

The construct of character has had a significant history in the field of psychology over the past century. A brief review of that history, and how it relates to research in sport, will help us frame our discussion of the nature of character and how children's sport experience may influence their character development.

The understanding of character as a set of behavioral habits and mental rules was prevalent in the early part of the twentieth century and it served as the backdrop for the monumental—and devastating—studies of Hartshorne, Maller, May and Shuttleworth carried out in the 1920s and published in three volumes: *Studies in Deceit* (1928), *Studies in Service and Self-Control* (1929), and *Studies in the Organization of Character* (1930). These researchers sought to determine how stable character "traits" were, and how congruent were a person's beliefs, attitudes, and actual behavior. They gave 11,000 elementary and high schools students some 33 different behavioral tests of altruism, self-control, and honesty. Some of the tests were in the home, others in the classroom or church, still others in play settings or sport contexts. They were alarmed to discover that children do not have stable character traits, but rather would cheat in one situation but not another; would lie in one instance but later tell the truth; would help someone at time one but fail to help at time two, and so on. Moreover, it made little difference to actual behavior what a child claimed to believe about right and wrong. Hartshorne and May developed the "doctrine of specificity," which held that it is situations that determine moral or ethical behavior, not internal character traits. While their results have sometimes been overstated (see Rushton, 1982), their findings certainly raised critical questions about the nature and stability of character.

The Hartshorne and May results, combined with the ascendence of behaviorist approaches to psychology, led to the nearly total removal of the term "character" from the psychological lexicon for almost 30 years. Lawrence Kohlberg's research into "moral development" helped to revive psychological investigations into constructs related to character. Following the lead of Jean Piaget (1932), Kohlberg studied the structural pattern of reasoning that children and adolescents used to resolve moral conflicts (Kohlberg, 1981, 1984). By identifying a sequence of age-related developmental stages through which children progress in their march toward moral reasoning maturity, Kohlberg recovered the possibility that something internal to the child could account for much of their moral behavior. By focusing on underlying cognitive structures, rather than observable behavior or attitudes, his theory helped to explain why children at the earlier stages of moral development would be vulnerable to certain situational pressures to transgress moral norms. Moreover, because the same underlying cognitive moral stage structure could lead a person to believe that cheating was wrong in one situation but appropriate in another, the contextual variability that Hartshorne and May observed no longer needed to be interpreted as disconfirming the possibility of individual character. When researchers turned from external behavior and simple cognitive beliefs to an investigation of the pattern of moral judgment, individuals were found to be remarkably consistent in their approach to moral problems.

Kohlberg also asserted that beyond the domain of moral development, there was a wider consistency that encompassed how individuals made sense of their physical and social worlds, including their experience of themselves. That broader unity Kohlberg referred to as ego development, and he cited Loevinger's (1976) stage model as exemplifying and supporting his view. Loevinger (1976) uses the terms "ego" and "character" interchangeably. Although Loevinger contends, "Kohlberg's concern is the development of moral character" (1976; p. 119), Kohlberg never used the term character to refer to his or Loevinger's theory. In fact, Kohlberg (1971) sharply criticized character psychology and education for assuming that character consists of a relativistic, culturally transmitted "bag of virtues." In his later work, however, as he reflected on his just community alternative school experiments in moral education, Kohlberg acknowledged that the Aristotlean approach to character and virtue was more compatible with his own theory than he had originally thought (e.g., Kohlberg, 1981). He noted that the experience of participating in a small, democratically governed alternative school not only fostered students' moral reasoning but their sense of responsibility as members of a moral community (Power, Higgins, and Kohlberg, 1989). As he reflected more broadly on the relationship between moral judgment and moral action, he returned once again to Hartshorne and May, noting that "empirical studies relating the two [moral judgment and conduct] begin to build a theory of character, rather than such a theory being a starting point for research" (p. 509). Unfortunately, Kohlberg did not live long enough to elaborate that insight into a developmental theory of character.

We agree with Kohlberg that a theory of character must be built by carefully delineating the psychological processes involved in arriving at judgments and executing judgments as actions. We will use Rest's (1983, 1984) original "Four Component Model" to help identify those processes.

The Four Components of Morality

One critique of Kohlberg's model was that it focused on moral judgment and not on the totality of moral experience, a fact that Kohlberg readily acknowledged (e.g., Kohlberg, 1986). To help redress this problem, Rest developed the four component model of morality (Narvaez and Rest, 1995; Rest, 1983, 1984; Rest Narvaez, Bebeau and Thoma, 1999). Rest began to develop the model by asking a straight-forward question: What do we need to presume went on in the head of someone who has acted morally? In response, he identified four psychological processes that invariably need to occur for a person to act morally. The first (Process I) is labeled *interpretation;* it is a process that encompasses perception of key elements within the situation, perceiving the moral issues involved, anticipating various outcomes, and so on. Process II is *moral judgment* which entails determining what is the best or optimal moral action to pursue in the particular situation. Process III is *choice* and involves weighing the moral values against other nonmoral values that might also be pursued (such as personal interest) and deciding which value to pursue. Finally, Process IV is *imple-*

mentation and involves mustering the internal resources to actually implement the moral action, even when the situation may present obstacles or temptations.[1] Table 22.1 presents these four processes in more detail.

In Rest's own work (e.g. Rest et al., 1999), character is equated with Process IV and is roughly equivalent to "ego strength" or "having the strength of one's convictions." It is the ability to persist in the face of temptation, to overcome obstacles, and so on. We believe this is an important dimension of character, but, in itself, represents a truncated view.

Character: A Synthesis of Components

We will now seek to offer our own approach to character, congruent with what has been said above. We have found Rest's four component model of morality to be very useful, and elsewhere we have elaborated it by identifying specific types of influence that shape how each of the four processes operate in specific situations, focusing particularly on sport (Shields and Bredemeier, 1995). In our view, the four processes can be broken down into two groups: the first, consisting of Processes I and II, help define the moral domain. Morality consists of moral sensitivity (a part of interpretation) and moral judgment, each of which can be elaborated in a number of important ways. The second set of processes (Processes III and IV) consist of the psychological requisites to fulfill one's moral vision. One has to be motivated to do so (Process III) and have the capacity to sustain one's moral motivation over time and circumstance (Process IV). What is lacking from the model, however, is an integrative core. We propose "character" as the integrative core that brings coherence to the various components of the moral action model.

All "constructivists" hold that persons actively interpret the environment, rather than just react to stimuli in accordance with principles of modeling and reinforcement. Humans are meaning-creators and generators of purpose and intention. But, according to Blasi (1983a, 1983b, 1984, 1985, 1988, 1989), most psychological theories are deficient in that they do not have an adequate construct of the self-as-subject. How do we describe the inner agency that constructs meaning? Borrowing from Erikson (1968), Blasi refers to identity when referring to the person's interior, integrating, agentic self. Identity is the organizing center of personality. It is the person's inner sense of self-agency wherein a person owns her actions, feelings, and thoughts as self-expressions. We propose that moral identity is the core of what we mean by character. Character refers to the inner dimension of self-agency in which the various processes of moral action become synthesized, coordinated, and "owned" as self-expressions.

---

1. In recent work (e.g., Rest et al., 1999), Rest has reconceptualized the four components and now labels them "moral sensitivity," "moral judgment," "moral motivation," and "character." We find the earlier component labels more descriptive and continue to use them in our work.

Table 22.1   Rest's Four Component Model of Moral Action Processes

Process One: Interpretation

Major function: To interpret the situation in terms of how one's actions affect the welfare of others.

Cognitive-affective interactions: Drawing inferences about how the other will be affected, and feeling empathy, disgust, and so on, for the other.

Situational factors influencing component: Ambiguity of people's needs, intentions, and actions; familiarity with the situation; amount of time available; degree of personal danger and susceptibility to pressure; sheer number of elements involved and the saliency of crucial cues; complexity of cause-effect links; preconceptions and prior expectations.

Process Two: Judgment

Major function: To formulate what a moral course of action would be.

Cognitive-affective interactions: Both abstract-logical and attitudinal-valuing aspects are involved in the construction of moral meaning; moral ideals are composed of both cognitive and affective elements.

Situational factors influencing the process: Factors affecting the application of particular social norms or moral ideals; delegation of responsibility to someone else; prior conditions or agreements; the particular combination of moral issues involved; preempting of one's sense of fairness by prior commitments to some ideology or code.

Process Three: Choice

Major function: To select from among competing value outcomes or ideals the one to act on.

Cognitive-affective interactions: Calculation of relative utilities of various goals; mood influencing outlook; defensive distortion of perception.

Situational factors affecting the process: Factors that activate different motives other than moral motives; factors that influence estimates of costs and benefits; factors that influence subjective estimates of the probability of certain occurrences; factors that affect one's self-esteem and willingness to risk oneself, defensively reinterpreting the situation by blaming the victim, denying need or deservingness.

Process Four: Implementation

Major function: To execute and implement what one intends to do.

Cognitive-affective interactions: Task persistence as affected by cognitive transformation of the goal.

Situational factors influencing the process: Factors that physically prevent one from carrying out a moral plan of action; factors that distract, fatigue, or disgust a person; cognitive transformations of the goal; timing difficulties in managing more than one plan at a time.

Identity in this sense plays a unifying role in development that supplements the organization supplied by cognition. In calling attention to the role of identity, we should not lose sight of Kohlberg's critique of character as the embodiment of a culturally defined and socialized "bag of virtues." Character cannot be equated with a culturally preferred set of values or virtues that become "internalized" in the child. Yet character is influenced by culture. Character develops through the interaction between the individual, who actively interprets experience and makes judgments about right and wrong, and the world as organized by culture. Virtues, like honesty and altruism, do not exist apart from the principles used to define good and bad, right and wrong. As we noted earlier, we cannot determine character from external appearance alone, but must look within to determine as far as possible the intentionality that gives rise to action.

We said that the concept of character (or the moral identity) helps to provide an integrative core to the four moral action processes identified by Rest. Let us now briefly elaborate on that theme. Interpretation is the first component of Rest's model. But just what moral issues one is sensitive to, to what degree, and how those sensitivities inform attributions of responsibility and culpability, for example, relate to how morality is integrated within personality, to the person's sense of moral self-agency, to character. It is also the case that mature moral judgment reflects an ability to make autonomous moral decisions, requiring a heightened sense of moral self-agency. The degree to which a person is able to make reflective moral judgments and enter into moral dialogue with others as an autonomous, but interdependent, agent is a reflection of character. Choice is the third component of Rest's model, and it is easy to see how it is an expression of character, as we have defined it. As morality becomes more central to a person's identity, there is an enhanced motivation to act in moral ways to maintain self-consistency. Finally, character is related to Process IV in that mustering the inner resources to actually carry out intended moral actions is central to maintaining an inner sense of moral self-efficacy.

Figure 22.1 presents our view of character and its relation to the four components of moral action. We view moral character as equally engaged with each of the four processes and as providing an integrative core. Note that all lines are dotted, suggesting that there are no hard and fast distinctions among the processes, and that they all interact with each other. The model is also circular, rather than linear, in recognition of the fact that the four processes, as they operate psychologically, do not necessarily occur in the linear progression that might be suggested by the logical relations among them.

If character is that which enables the consistent display of mature moral behavior, then Rest's model of moral action components can provide a useful framework for understanding constituent elements in the development of character. The first step is to identify the psychological competencies, dispositions, or skills that enable the optimal functioning of each of the four components of the model. The second step is to identify the developmental processes related to each of these competencies, dispo-

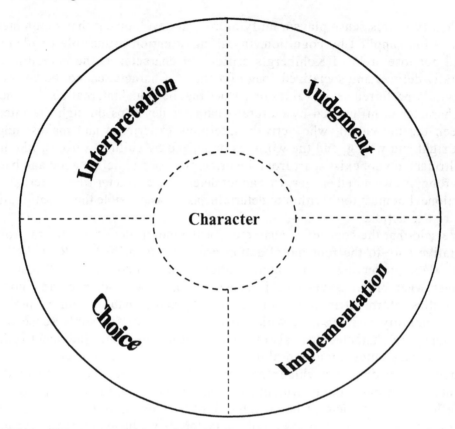

Figure 22.1. Character and moral action processes.

sitions, or skills. And, finally, it is important to examine the path of development of character itself as the integrative core that works to synthesize and coordinate the activities related to each of the four component processes. Completing such a series of steps would be a monumental undertaking and is far beyond the scope of the present chapter. However, we would like to sketch an outline of a response since it will provide the scaffolding for a discussion of how children's sport experience may influence their character development.

Character and Competence

The four processes identified in Rest's model (interpretation, judgment, choice, and implementation) do not designate distinct psychological constructs. Rather, they are names that identify the outcomes that come from the operation of a number of underlying psychological processes. Thus, when the various psychological operations associated with Process I are completed, the situation is interpreted. When the various psychological operations associated with Process II are completed, a moral judgment is formed. To identify all of the specific psychological competencies and processes that underlie each of the four components of Rest's model would be a formidable task. For our purposes, we identify a single psychological competency or characteristic for each of the four components of the model. We hope that this will enable the researcher to investigate the operation of each component, and the practitioner to get a handle on how a particular process can be enhanced. Clearly, our list of underlying psychological constructs is incomplete. We offer only exemplars of psychological underpinnings. Nonetheless, we believe that the list of psychological competencies and characteristics is sufficiently robust that a very significant portion of the variance in observable moral behavior may be attributable to the set of identified constructs.

We identify *empathy* as a critical psychological competence undergirding Process I, interpretation. As empathy develops, people have an increased capacity to apprehend the thought, feelings, motives, and intentions of others. These are critical skills necessary for recognizing moral situations and anticipating the outcomes of various action alternatives.

We identify *moral reasoning* as a critical competence supporting Process II, moral judgment. Clearly, as moral reasoning competence improves, moral judgments are likely to reflect more comprehensive and differentiated moral information, and are likely to be more adequate from an ethical standpoint.

We identify *motivational orientation* as a central psychological characteristic tethered to moral motivation. Particularly in achievement contexts like sport, motivational orientation is an important influence on moral motivation. As individuals become more "task oriented" (i.e., motivated by self-referenced goals) rather than "ego oriented" (i.e., motivated by the desire to demonstrate superior performance over others), they are more likely to choose moral values over nonmoral values when the two come into conflict.

Finally, we identify *ego strength* as a psychological characteristic that helps to undergird the fourth process, that of implementation. Ego strength refers to what philosophers traditionally call the will, and psychologists going back to William James (1920) study as attention. In order to carry out a moral decision, the individual must have the perseverance and determination to remain focused on achieving their moral goal and to resist distractions and temptations.

Empathy, moral reasoning competence, motivational orientation, and ego strength are important dimensions of character. Still, character is not reducible to this or any other set of psychological characteristics. Rather, these are "indicators" of character. Character itself, as we have said, refers to the person's inner sense of moral self-agency that draws from these capacities, integrates them, "owns" them, and gives expression to them.

We also can identify two dimensions of character that reflect its integrative, synthesizing dimension. These are dimensions of what Blasi (1983a, 1983b, 1984, 1985, 1988, 1989) called the "moral self." In earlier writings (Bredemeier and Shields,

1994; 1996; Shields and Bredemeier, 1995), we connected these dimensions of self-structure specifically with Process III of Rest's model, though we now prefer to think of them as cutting across the processes. The two dimensions pertain to moral salience and moral content.

For some people, morality is central to how they see themselves. For others, morality is less salient in self-definition. How important morality is to self-definition is a function of both development (cf. Damon, 1984) and individual differences. For children, moral concepts are unlikely to be important to self-definition, but by the time the person enters middle adolescence, sufficient cognitive and social development has taken place to open the possibility of integrating moral concepts within identity. But not all people will do so, or do so in the same way. It might be hypothesized that the more salient morality is to self-definition, the more adequate will be the integration or coordination of the four processes.

The other dimension of character as self-structure refers to the specific content of the morality that one incorporates into self-definition. In our view, morality is multidimensional and highly nuanced. Just what moral issues or themes are considered important varies from one person to another. As an example, one person may see compassion as essential to his identity, while another sees fairness and justice as central to hers. Again, there are likely to be developmental and individual differences that influence the moral content that becomes central to a person's self-definition.

To answer the question of how character develops would require a detailed discussion of each of the competencies and characteristics identified above. Since our focus here, however, is on how children's sport experience may relate to the development of character, we will now turn to a discussion of the current state of knowledge relevant to this question.

Does Sport Build Character?

Scientific answers to the question of whether sport builds character are unlikely to ever be conclusive. Character itself is too elusive of a construct, sport experiences are too widely varied, and in any given sport experience, there are usually both positive and negative dimensions. Having said that, there is still good reason to develop heuristic methods to unravel some of the complexity and examine the issue empirically. By identifying some of the constituent elements that go into (but don't define) character, we have provided one avenue for such research. We can begin to address the question of whether sport builds character by asking: What is the impact of sport on the development of empathy, moral reasoning, motivational orientation, and ego strength? We can also ask about how the formation of moral identity is influenced by sport experience, noting, for example, the value priorities that tend to be nurtured through involvement in sport.

Sport and Empathy

Empathy has long been recognized as a critical component of moral functioning (Hume, 1777; Mead, 1934) and has held an important place in various approaches to psychology, such as the psychoanalytic (e.g., Sullivan, 1953), social learning (e.g., Bandura, 1986), and structural-developmental (e.g., Hoffman, 1991). Though there is no agreed upon definition of empathy, nor a reliable way of measuring it, there is enough overlap in approach to keep the construct viable. Empathy involves the ability to apprehend the inner state of another and vicariously experience similar emotion. Empathy makes it more likely that a person will notice moral dimensions of situations and the needs and concerns of others. It makes possible compassion and benevolence.

There is no direct evidence regarding the impact of sport experience on the development of empathic responsiveness. Lacking such evidence, we can only surmise the likely impact of sport, based on what is known about the development of empathy in other contexts. Even here, the research base is thin. Duquin and Schroeder-Braun (1996) suggest that cross-cultural studies indicate that empathy is nurtured in societies where trust and respect are valued, where little physical discipline or punishment occur, and where there are supportive networks of mutual obligations and responsibilities. In contrast, empathy is less likely to be nurtured in societies where power and superiority are valued, where physical punishment is common, and where compassion is seen as a weakness rather than a strength.

It is likely that there are at least two major ways in which sport may contribute to or deter the development of empathy. In our view, empathy is neither purely cognitive nor affective but reflects a synthesis of the two. As a cognitive activity, empathy is dependent on social perspective-taking ability. Social perspective-taking refers to the ability to see social situations from multiple vantage points and coordinate those perspectives (cf. Selman, 1980). Sports, particularly team sports, are likely to provide a rich context for promoting social perspective taking, since the ability to "see" the game from multiple vantage points enables the player to anticipate the moves of the opponent and coordinate action with teammates.

Empathy also involves "feeling with" another. Here many sport experiences may be less supportive of empathic responsiveness. The milieu of many sports includes an acceptance of violence and a division of self from others (Curry, 1991). Athletes are sometimes encouraged to disassociate mind from body (e.g., "play with pain") and to suppress feelings for others (Duquin, 1994). Even in relatively positive sport environments, the emphasis that often occurs on hierarchy, function, and efficiency may lead to a suppression of empathy and moral sensitivity (Kitwood, 1990; Lord and Kozar, 1989). Clearly, the relationship between sport participation and empathy is ripe for research.

Sport and Moral Reasoning

Moral reasoning refers to the process of arriving at a moral judgment about what is good or right behavior, from an ethical viewpoint, in a particular situation. Though specific conceptions of the process vary, most theorists concur that moral reasoning undergoes changes in the course of the child's development and, consequently, it can be more or less adequate, more or less mature (Haan, 1991; Kohlberg, 1984; Rest, 1979). Within sport, moral reasoning has been shown to relate to aggression and its perceived legitimacy (Bredemeier, 1985, 1994; Bredemeier, Weiss, Shields and Cooper, 1986, 1987; Bredemeier and Shields, 1984b, 1986a; Stephens, 2000; Stephens and Bredemeier, 1996) and beliefs about fair play (Stephens, Bredemeier and Shields, 1997). It did not, however, relate to perceptions of the legitimacy of gender stratification in sport (Solomon and Bredemeier, 1999), though attributes of the moral reasoning scale used may have been a factor in the nonsignificant findings. The literature also suggests that moral reasoning about issues occurring in sport may differ significantly from moral reasoning about issues in other contexts (Bredemeier, 1995; Bredemeier and Shields, 1984a, 1985, 1986b).

The literature on the relationship between sport participation and moral reasoning has not been encouraging. In one study of high school and collegiate basketball players, the collegiate athletes were found to have less mature moral reasoning than their nonathlete peers, though no differences were found at the high school level (Bredemeier and Shields, 1986c). However, in another study, high school team sport athletes were found to score lower on a measure of moral reasoning than high school nonathletes (Beller and Stoll, 1995). In a study of children in the 4th through 7th grade, it was found that boys who participated in high contact sports and girls who participated in medium contact sports (the highest level of contact sport experience they reported) were significantly less mature in their moral reasoning than children who had participated in other sports or had not participated in any organized sport program (Bredemeier et al., 1986).

Though the literature reviewed above suggests that sport may not be a good context for promoting moral reasoning, several studies have also demonstrated that sport experiences can be designed effectively to promote moral growth (Bredemeier, Weiss, Shields and Shewchuk, 1986; Romance, Weiss and Bockoven, 1986; Wandzilak, Carroll and Ansorge, 1988). Thus, when moral development is adopted as an explicit goal and appropriate strategies implemented, sport experience can stimulate the development of moral reasoning.

Sport and Motivational Orientation

In any achievement context like sport, people give meaning to their investment through the goals they endorse and pursue. Drawing from the work of Nicholls (1983, 1989) and Duda (1987, 1989), we use the term motivational orientation to refer to whether one is oriented primarily to demonstrating competence relative to others (i.e., defeating others) or relative to self-referenced goals. Nicholls defines the orientation that measures success relative to others as an "ego" orientation, and the orientation that measures success relative to one's own past performance and self-referenced goals as a "task" orientation. Nicholls explicitly linked these orientations to moral motivations, suggesting that high "task" orientation leads to greater weight being given to moral concerns. Evidence within the sport domains supports this contention of a link between motivational orientation and moral priorities (Duda, Olson and Templin, 1991; Dunn and Dunn, 1999; Guivernau and Duda, 1998; Kavussanu and Ntoumanis, 2001; Kavussanu and Roberts, in press; Stephens and Bredemeier, 1996). Since it is likely to orient the person to choose moral values over nonmoral values when the two conflict, we identify high "task" motivation as a constituent of good character. However, the two orientations are not mutually exclusive, and high task orientation does not necessarily imply low ego orientation.

Motivational orientations are malleable and are influenced by the structure and characteristics of the social environment (Ames, 1992; Dweck, 1999; Nicholls, 1989). Such issues as how standards are set, the methods of evaluation employed, the patterns of recognition given, the sources and characteristics of authority, the way discipline is administered, and how tasks are structure and by whom, all congeal to form a "motivational climate" that tends to augment one motivational orientation more than the other. "Mastery climates," which tend to augment task motivation, emphasize such things as continual learning, personal goal-setting, and effort. In contrast, "perform-ance climates," which tend to augment ego orientation, place a premium on compara-tive standards of evaluation, competitive outcome, and extrinsic rewards.

There is limited direct evidence that participation in sport tends to augment ego orientation (White and Duda, 1994). Indirect evidence comes from the professionali-zation literature (for reviews, see Shields and Bredemeier, 1995; Knoppers 1985) which suggests that the longer a person stays involved with sport, and the higher the level at which they participate, the more they come to value winning over other values. An important question for future research is whether an emphasis on task orientation is possible (and desirable) within highly competitive sport programs that seek to foster peak athletic performance. Is there a necessary trade-off between focusing on char-acter goals and competitive performance? We do not believe so, but there is no empirical evidence that definitively addresses this question.

Sport and Ego Strength

There is very little research on the role that ego strength plays in the actual execution of one's moral judgments. Grim, Kohlberg, and White (1968) found that ego strength inhibited the temptation to cheat among sixth graders but not first graders. They accounted for this difference by hypothesizing an interaction between moral reasoning development and ego strength. Krebs and Kohlberg (1984) substan-tiated that hypothesis by finding that ego strength predicted reduced cheating by the conventional participants but not by the pre-conventional participants.

In the sport literature, considerable research has been conducted on the role that attention plays in effective performance (Abernethy, 2001) and techniques have been designed to enhance attention control (Nideffer, 1993). Although no studies have been done on the relationship between moral judgment and ego control in sports contexts, White and Duda (1991) and Newton and Duda (1993) found a significant relationship between motivational orientation and concentration, as measured by the Thoughts Occurrence Questionnaire (TOQ; Sarason, Sarason, Keefe, Hayes, and Shearin, 1986). Concentration appears to be essential to the maintenance of a high level of performance, especially under conditions of fatigue and stress, as content analyses of reports of athlete's peak experiences suggest (e.g., Csikzentmihaly, 1971). As we have noted, we often praise athletes for demonstrating character when they manage to sustain their performances in the face of adversity. We are very much in need of studies that explore the role that ego strength plays in specifically moral situations.

Can Sport Build Character?

In the above section, we inquired as to whether sport, as typically practiced, builds character. Not surprisingly, the answer was ambiguous. Perhaps the more critical question is whether interventions within a sport context can lead to improved social outcomes. Unfortunately, relatively few studies have been conducted that address this question. There is some research that suggests that physical education can be structured so as to promote social and moral development, but research conducted within a physical education context cannot be generalized to sport. Nonetheless, this research will be reviewed because it may provide insights and direction for those working within a sport context.

Romance, Weiss, and Bockovan (1986) used a physical education context to investigate the effectiveness of interventions rooted in structural developmental theory. They found that an 8-week intervention program with 5th grade children significantly improved their moral reasoning. Miller and his colleagues (Miller, Bredemeier and Shields, 1997) used the Shields and Bredemeier (1995) model of moral action processes to design a physical education curriculum for upper-elementary at-risk youth. The curriculum incorporated cooperative learning, building moral community, creating a mastery-oriented motivational climate, and promoting self-responsibility as primary learning processes. Though a detailed presentation of outcomes is lacking from the published report, the authors provide anecdotal evidence of program effectiveness.

Hellison (De Busk and Hellison, 1989; Hellison, 1978, 1983, 1985, 1995; Hellison, Lifka, and Georgiadis, 1990) has developed a physical education model for teaching self-responsibility. Hellison and his colleagues report the successful use of physical education instruction with at-risk youth in promoting self-control, respect for the rights of others, and prosocial behavior. Hellison's field work has yielded important insights, but more empirical research is needed to test instructional strategies and establish causal relationships. Similar points could be made about the work of Solomon (1997a,b) who is, likewise, developing promising approaches to the teaching of physical education.

In a preliminary investigation to determine whether theoretically-based instructional strategies can be efficacious in promoting moral growth in a sport context, Bredemeier, Weiss, Shields, and Shewchuk (1986) conducted a field experiment designed to explore the effectiveness of a moral development program in a summer sport camp. After the 6-week intervention program, the experimental groups showed improvement in moral reasoning.

Comprehensive approaches to promoting character through sport have not yet been developed and tested. Thompson (1993), Beedy (1997) and Yeager, Buxton, Baltzell and Bzdell (2001) have published books on promising sport models that incorporate character development goals, but the models have yet to be tested empirically. These authors identify coaches as critical influences on the quality of the sport experience and offer approaches to coaching that they believe will lead to positive character development among participants. In the concluding section of this chapter, we would like to offer a preliminary description of an approach to promoting character through sport that we are developing at the University of Notre Dame's Mendelson Center for Sport, Character and Culture.

Sport Teams as Moral Communities

We have drawn upon the literature on the "just community" approach to moral and character education in the schools (e.g., Power, Higgins and Kohlberg, 1989) to develop a "moral community" approach to character education in sport. This approach recognizes that people develop in the context of social relations and that the shared norms and values of the group are important influences on what individuals come to value and how they act. Those sport teams, for example, in which collective norms are lenient when it comes to the use of aggression are more likely to have players who accept aggression as legitimate (Guivernau and Duda, 1998; Shields, Bredemeier, Gardner and Bostrom, 1995; Stephens and Bredemeier, 1996).

The moral community approach to sport has two critical dimensions. First, it attempts to build a sense of community within the team that features shared norms for ethical behavior. At the heart of the approach is the team meeting in which team rules and goals are established, strategies are taught, and performances are assessed, all with the aim of accentuating the moral dimension of the sport experience. The moral community approach requires that players participate to the fullest extent possible in such meetings by discussing and deciding upon disciplinary rules and punishments and offering suggestions and feedback about strategies and performances. Participation in such team meetings should help players to develop shared norms that express and realize ideals of cooperation, fair play, and respect for officials and opponents. In team meetings, players learn the democratic skills of self-expression, listening, and deliberating about the common good. Team meetings also clarify the special role of the coach as the team leader. The moral community approach encourages coaches and players to respond to play-related mistakes and misbehavior in ways that are instructive and supportive of the sense of community.

The second critical element of the moral community approach is the promotion of a mastery-oriented achievement climate. The most efficacious way to influence motivational orientation, a critical psychological characteristic associated with Process III, may be through a careful structuring of the environment (Duda, 1987; Nicholls, 1989; Nicholls and Miller, 1984). Promoting a *mastery climate* encourages or augments task motivation, while a *performance climate* encourages or augments ego motivation. Mastery climates are associated with students' use of effective learning strategies, preference for challenging tasks, positive attitudes, and the beliefs that effort leads to success (Ames, 1992; Ames and Archer, 1988; Burton, 1989; Hall; 1988; Newton, 1994; Newton and Duda, 1998; Seifriz, Duda, and Chi, 1992; Treasure, 1993; Treasure and Roberts, 1998; Walling, Duda and Chi, 1993). Performance climates, on the other hand, correlate with lower levels of satisfaction/enjoyment, poorer performance, higher anxiety and performance worries, and an overemphasis on innate ability to explain success and failure (e.g., Ames and Archer, 1988; Duda and Chi, 1989; Seifriz, Duda and Chi, 1992; Treasure and Roberts, 1994; Walling, Duda and Chi, 1993). Fortunately, promoting a mastery climate is very congruent with forming a sense of moral community. Future research will determine whether this and/or other models of character education through sport can be efficacious in benefitting our youth.

It is our hope that the moral community approach to sport can nurture the development of empathy, moral reasoning, a task motivational orientation, and enhanced ego strength. It may also increase the salience of morality within the self-structure. There is much research to be done. It is also the case that those who work with children in sport need not wait for definitive studies. Love of the game and love of children will go a long way.

References

Abernathy, B. (2001). Attention. In R. Singer , H. Hausenblas, and C. Janelle (Eds.), *Handbook of research on sports psychology* (2nd ed., pp. 53–85). New York: John Wiley and Sons.

Ames, C. (1992). Achievement goals, motivational climate, and motivational processes. In G. Roberts (Ed.), *Motivation in sport and exercise* (pp. 161–176). Champaign, IL: Human Kinetics.

Ames, C., and Archer, J. (1988). Achievement goals in the classroom: Students' learning strategies and motivation processes. *Journal of Educational Psychology, 80*, 260–267.

Aristotle (323 B.C./1985). *Nicomachean ethics.* (T. Irwin, Trans.) Indianapolis: Hacket.

Bandura, A. (1986). *Social foundations of thought and action: A social cognitive theory.* Engelwood Cliffs, NJ: Prentice-Hall.

Beedy, J. (1997). *Sports PLUS: Developing youth sports programs that teach positive values.* Hamilton, MA: Project Adventure.

Beller, J., and Stoll, S. (1995). Moral reasoning of high school student athletes and general students: An empirical study versus personal testimony. *Pediatric Exercise Science, 7,* 352–363.

Blasi, A. (1983a). Moral cognition and moral action: A theoretical perspective. *Developmental Review, 3,* 178–210.

Blasi, A. (1983b). The self and cognition: The roles of the self in the acquisition of knowledge, and the role of cognition in the development of the self. In B. Lee and G. Noam (Eds.), *Psychological theories of the self* (Vol. 2, pp. 1–25). New York: Plenum.

Blasi, A. (1984). Moral identity: Its role in moral functioning. In W. Kurtines and J. Gewirtz (Eds.), *Morality, moral behavior, and moral development* (pp. 128–39). New York: Wiley.

Blasi, A. (1985). The moral personality: Reflections for social science and education. In M. Berkowitz and F. Oser (Eds.), *Moral education: Theory and application* (pp. 433–444). Hillsdale, N.J.: Lawrence Erlbaum.

Blasi, A. (1988). Identity and the development of the self. In D. K. Lapsley and F. C. Power (Eds.), *Self, ego, and identity: Integrative approaches* (pp. 226–242). New York: Springer-Verlag.

Blasi, A. (1989). The integration of morality in personality. In I. E. Bilbao (Ed.), *Perspectivas acerca de cambio moral: Posibles intervenciones educativas.* San Sebastian: Servicio Editorial Universidad del Pais Vasco.

Bredemeier, B. J. (1985). Moral reasoning and the perceived legitimacy of intentionally injurious sport acts. *Journal of Sport Psychology, 7,* 110–124.

Bredemeier, B. J. (1994). Children's moral reasoning and their assertive, aggressive, and submissive tendencies in sport and daily life. *Journal of Sport and Exercise Psychology, 16,* 1–14.

Bredemeier, B. J. (1995). Divergence in children's moral reasoning about issues in daily life and sport specific contexts. *International Journal of Sport Psychology, 26,* 453–463.

Bredemeier, B. J. and Shields, D. L. (1984a). Divergence in moral reasoning about sport and life. *Sociology of Sport Journal, 1,* 348–357.

Bredemeier, B. J., and Shields, D. L. (1984b). The utility of moral stage analysis in the investigation of athletic aggression. *Sociology of Sport Journal, 1,* 138–149.

Bredemeier, B. J., and Shields, D. L. (1985). Values and violence in sport. *Psychology Today, 19,* 22–32.

Bredemeier, B. J., and Shields, D. L. (1986a). Athletic aggression: An issue of contextual morality. *Sociology of Sport Journal, 3,* 15–28.

Bredemeier, B. J., and Shields, D. L. (1986b). Game reasoning and interactional morality. *Journal of Genetic Psychology, 147*, 257–275.

Bredemeier, B. J., and Shields, D. L. (1986c). Moral growth among athletes and nonathletes: A comparative analysis. *Journal of Genetic Psychology, 147*, 7–18.

Bredemeier, B. L., and Shields D. L. (1994). Applied ethics and moral reasoning in sport. In J. Rest and D. Narvaez (Eds), *Moral development in the professions* (pp. 173–187). Hillsdale, NJ: Lawrence Erlbaum.

Bredemeier, B., and Shields, D. (1996). Moral development and children's sport. In F. L. Smoll and R. E. Smith (Eds), *Children and youth in sport: A biopsychosocial perspective* (pp. 381–401). Madison, WI: Brown and Benchmark.

Bredemeier, B., Weiss, M., Shields, D., and Cooper, B. (1986). The relationship of sport involvement with children's moral reasoning and aggression tendencies, *Journal of Sport Psychology, 8*, 304–318.

Bredemeier, B., Weiss, M., Shields, D., and Cooper, B. (1987). The relationship between children's legitimacy judgments and their moral reasoning, aggression tendencies and sport involvement. *Sociology of Sport Journal, 4*, 48–60.

Bredemeier, B., Weiss, M., Shields, D., and Shewchuk, R. (1986). Promoting moral growth in a summer sport camp: The implementation of theoretically grounded instructional strategies. *Journal of Moral Education, 15*, 212–220.

Burton, D. (1989). Winning isn't everything: Examining the impact of performance goals on collegiate swimmers' cognitions and performance. *The Sport Psychologist, 2*, 105–132.

Csikszentmihaly, M. (1977). *Beyond boredom and anxiety: The experience of play in work and games.* San Francisco: Jossey-Bass.

Curry, T. J. (1991). Fraternal bonding in the locker room: A profeminist analysis of talk about competition and women. *Sociology of Sport Journal, 8*, 119–135.

Damon, W. (1984). Self-understanding and moral development from childhood to adolescence. In W. M. Kurtines and Gewirtz (Eds.), *Morality, moral behavior, and moral development* (pp. 109–127). New York: Wiley.

DeBusk, M., and Hellison, D. (1989). Implementing a physical education self-responsibility model for delinquency-prone youth. *Journal of Teaching Physical Education, 8*, 104–112.

Dewey, J. (1922/1988). *Human nature and conduct.* Southern Illinois Press.

Duda, J. L. (1987). Toward a developmental theory of achievement motivation in sport. *Journal of Sport Psychology, 9*, 130–145.

Duda, J. L. (1989). Goal perspectives and behavior in sport and exercise settings. In C. Ames and M. Maehr (Eds.), *Advances in motivation and achievement* (Vol. 6, pp. 81–115). Greenwich, CT: JAI Press.

Duda, J. L., and Chi, L. (1989, September). *The effect of task and ego-involving conditions on perceived ability and causal attributions in basketball.* Paper presented at the annual meeting of the Association for the Advancement of Applied Sport Psychology, Seattle, WA.

Duda, J. L., Olson, L. K., and Templin, T. J. (1991). The relationship of task and ego orientation to sportsmanship attitudes and the perceived legitimacy of injurious acts. *Research Quarterly for Exercise and Sport, 62*, 79–87.

Duquin, M. (1994, Winter). The Body Snatchers and Dr. Frankenstein revisited: The social construction and deconstruction of bodies and sport. *Journal of Sport and Social Issues*, 268–281.

Duquin, M., and Schroeder-Braun, K. (1995). Power, empathy, and moral conflict in sport. *Peace and Conflict: Journal of Peace Psychology, 2*, 351–367.

Dunn, J. G. H., and Dunn, J. C. (1999). Goal orientations, perceptions of aggression, and sportspersonship in elite male youth ice hockey players. *The Sport Psychologist, 13*, 183–200.

Dweck, C. S. (1999). *Self-theories and goals: Their role in motivation, personality, and development*. Philadelphia: Taylor and Francis.

Erikson, E. H. (1968). *Identity: Youth and crisis*. New York: Norton.

Grim, P., Kohlberg, L., and White, S. (1968). Some relationships between conscience and attentional processes. *Journal of Personality and Social Psychology, 8*, 239–253.

Guivernau, M., and Duda, J. (1998). Integrating concepts of motivation and morality: The contribution of norms regarding aggressive and rule-violating behavior, goal orientations, and the perceived motivational climate to the prediction of athletic aggression. *Journal of Sport and Exercise Psychology, Supplement, S13*.

Haan, N. (1991). Moral development and action from a social constructivist perspective. In W. Kurtines and J. Gewirtz (Eds.), *Handbook of moral behavior and development, Vol. 1: Theory* (pp. 251–273). Hillsdale, NJ: Lawrence Erlbaum Associates, Inc.

Hall, K. H. (1988). *A social-cognitive approach to goal setting: The mediating effects of achievement goals and perceived ability*. Unpublished doctoral dissertation, University of Illinois at Urbana-Champaign.

Hartshorne, H., and May, M. A. (1928). *Studies in the nature of character (Vol. 1): Studies in deceit*. New York: Macmillan.

Hartshorne, H., May, M. A., and Maller, J. B. (1929). *Studies in the nature of character (Vol. II): Studies in service and self-control*. New York: Macmillan.

Hartshorne, H., May, M. A., and Shuttleworth, F. K. (1930). *Studies in the nature of character (Vol. III): Studies in the organization of character*. New York: Macmillan.

Hellison, D. (1978). *Beyond balls and bats: Alienated (and other) youth in the gym*. Washington, D.C.: AAHPERD.

Hellison, D. (1983). Teaching self-responsibility (and more). *Journal of Physical Education, Recreation, and Dance, 54*, 23ff.

Hellison, D. (1985). *Goals and strategies for teaching physical education*. Champaign, IL: Human Kinetics.

Hellison, D. (1995). *Teaching responsibility through physical activity.* Champaign, IL: Human Kinetics.

Hellison, D., Lifka, B., and Georgiadis, N. (1990). Physical education for disadvantaged youth: A Chicago story. *Journal of Physical Education, Recreation and Dance, 61,* 36–46.

Hoffman, M. L. (1991). Empathy, social cognition, and moral action. In W. Kurtines and J. Gewirtz (Eds.), *Handbook of moral behavior and development, Vol. 1: Theory,* (pp. 275–301). Hillsdale, NJ: Lawrence Erlbaum.

Hume, D. (1777). *Enquiries concerning the human understanding and concerning the principles of morals* (2nd ed.). Oxford, England: Clarendon.

James, W. (1920/1985). *Psychology: A Briefer course.* Notre Dame, IN: University of Notre Dame Press.

Kavussanu, M., and Ntoumanis, N. (2001, May). Participation in sport and moral functioning: The mediating role of ego orientation. Paper presented at the 10th World Congress of Sport Psychology, Skiathos Island, Greece.

Kavussanu, M., and Roberts, G. (in press). Moral functioning in sport: An achievement goal perspective. *Journal of Sport and Exercise Psychology.*

Kirkwood, T. (1990). *Concern for others: A new psychology of conscience and morality.* New York: Routledge.

Knoppers, A. (1985). Professionalization of attitudes: A review and critique. *Quest, 37,* 92–102.

Kohlberg, L. (1971). Stages of moral development as a basis for moral education. In C. M. Beck, B. S. Crittenden, and E. V. Sullivan (Eds.), *Moral education: Interdisciplinary approaches* (pp. 23–92). Toronto: University of Toronto Press.

Kohlberg, L. (1986). A current statement on some theoretical issues. In S. Modgil and C. Modgil (Eds.), *Lawrence Kohlberg: Consensus and controversy* (pp. 485–546). Philadelphia: Falmer.

Kohlberg, L. (1981). *Essays on moral development: Vol. 1: The philosophy of moral development.* San Francisco: Harper and Row.

Kohlberg, L. (1984). *Essays on moral development: Vol. 2: The psychology of moral development.* San Francisco: Harper and Row.

Krebs, D., and Kohlberg, L. (1984). Moral judgement and ego controls as determinants of resistance to cheating. Unpublished manuscript cited in Kohlberg, L. (1984). *Essays on moral development, Volume II: The psychology of moral development.* San Francisco: Harper and Row.

Lord, R. H., and Kozar, B. (1989). Pain tolerance in the presence of others: Implications for youth sports. *Physician and Sports Medicine, 17,* 71–77.

Loevinger, J. (1976). *Ego development: Conceptions and theories.* San Francisco: Jossey-Bass.

Mead, G. H. (1934). *Mind, self, and society.* Chicago: University of Chicago Press.

Miller, S., Bredemeier, B., and Shields, D. (1997). Sociomoral education through physical education with at-risk children. *Quest, 49*, 114–129.

Narvaez, D., and Rest, J. (1995). The four components of acting morally. In W. Kurtines and J. Gewirtz (Eds.), *Moral behavior and moral development: An introduction* (pp. 385–400). New York: McGraw-Hill.

Newton, M. (1994). *The effect of differences in perceived motivational climate and goal orientations on motivational responses of female volleyball players*. Unpublished Doctoral dissertation. Purdue University.

Newton, M., and Duda, J. L. (1998). The interaction of motivational climate, dispositional goal orientations, and perceived ability in predicting indices of motivation. *International Journal of Sport Psychology, 29*, 1–20.

Nicholls, J. G. (1983). Conceptions of ability and achievement motivation: A theory and its implications for education. In S. G. Paris, G. M. Olson, and H. W. Stevenson (Eds.), *Learning and motivation in the classroom*. Hillsdale, N.J.: Erlbaum.

Nicholls, J. G. (1989). *The competitive ethos and democratic education*. Cambridge, MA: Harvard University Press.

Nicholls, J., and Miller, A. (1984). Development and its discontents: The differentiation of the concept of ability. In J. Nicholls (Ed.), *Advances in Motivation and Achievement: The Development of Achievement Motivation* (pp. 185–218). Greenwich, CT: JAI Press.

Nideffer, R. N. (1993). Attention control training. In R. Singer, M. Murphy, and L. K. Tennant (Eds.), *Handbook of research on sports psychology* (pp. 542–556). New York: Macmillan.

Piaget, J. (1932/1965). *Moral judgment of the child*. New York: Free Press.

Power, F. C., Higgins, A., and Kohlberg, L. (1989). *Lawrence Kohlberg's approach to moral education*. New York: Columbia University Press.

Rest, J. R. (1979). *Development in judging moral issues*. Minneapolis: University of Minnesota Press.

Rest, J. R. (1983). Morality. In P. Mussen (Gen. Ed.), *Manual of child psychology: Cognitive development* (pp. 556–629), J. Flavell and E. Markman (eds), 4th ed. New York: John Wiley and Sons.

Rest, J. R. (1984). The major components of morality. In W. Kurtines and J. Gewirtz (eds.), *Morality, moral behavior, and moral development* (pp. 356–629). New York: John Wiley and Sons.

Rest, J., Narvaez, D., Bebeau, M., and Thoma, S. (1999). *Postconventional moral thinking: A neo-Kohlbergain approach*. Mahwah, NJ: Erlbaum.

Romance, T. J., Weiss, M. R., and Bockoven, J. (1986). A program to promote moral development through elementary school physical education. *Journal of Teaching in Physical Education, 5*, 126–136.

Rushton, P. (1982). Social learning theory and the development of prosocial behavior. In N. Eisenberg (Ed.), *The development of prosocial behavior* (pp. 77–105). New York: Academic Press.

Sarason, I. G., Sarason, B., Keefe, D., Hayes, B., and Shearin, E. (1986). Cognitive interference: Situational determinants and traitlike characteristics. *Journal of Personality and Social Psychology, 51*, 215–226.

Seifriz, J. J., Duda, J. L., and Chi, L. (1992). The relationship of perceived motivational climate to intrinsic motivation and beliefs about success in basketball. *Journal of Sport and Exercise Psychology, 14*, 375–391.

Selman, R. L. (1980). *The growth of interpersonal understanding*. New York: Academic.

Shields, D., and Bredemeier, B. (1995). *Character development and physical activity*. Champaign, IL: Human Kinetics.

Shields, D., Bredemeier, B., Gardner, D., and Bostrom, A. (1995). Leadership, cohesion and team norms regarding cheating and aggression. *Sociology of Sport Journal, 12*, 324–336.

Solomon, G. (1997a). Character development: Does physical education affect character development in students? *The Journal of Physical Education, Recreation and Dance, 68*, 38–41.

Solomon, G. (1997b). Fair play in the gymnasium: Improving social skills among elementary school students. *The Journal of Physical Education, Recreation and Dance, 68*, 22–25.

Solomon, G., and Bredemeier, B. (1999). Children's moral conceptions of gender stratification in sport. *International Journal of Sport Psychology, 30*, 350–368.

Stephens, D. (2000). Predictors of likelihood to aggress in youth soccer: An examination of coed and all-girls teams. *Journal of Sport Behavior, 23*, 311–325.

Stephens, D., and Bredemeier, B. (1996). Moral atmosphere and judgments about aggression in girls' soccer: Relationships among moral and motivational variables. *Journal of Sport and Exercise Psychology, 18*, 158–173.

Stephens, D., Bredemeier, B., and Shields, D. (1997). Construction of a measure designed to assess players' descriptions and prescriptions for moral behavior in youth sport soccer. *International Journal of Sport Psychology, 28*, 370–390.

Sullivan, H. S. (1953). *The interpersonal theory of psychiatry*. New York: Norton.

Thompson, J. (1993). *Positive coaching: Building character and self-esteem through sports*. Dubuque, IA: Brown and Benchmark.

Treasure, D. C. (1993). *A social-cognitive approach to understanding children's achievement behavior, cognitions and affect in competitive sport*. Unpublished Doctoral dissertation. University of Illinois. Urbana-Champaign.

Treasure, D. C., and Roberts, G. C. (1994). Cognitive and affective concomitants of task and ego goal orientations during the middle school years. *Journal of Sport and Exercise Psychology, 16*, 15–28.

Treasure, D. C., and Roberts, G. C. (1998). Relationship between female adolescents' achievement goal orientations, perceptions of the motivational climate, belief about success and sources of satisfaction in basketball. *International Journal of Sport Psychology, 29*, 211–230.

Walling, M. D., Duda, J. L., and Chi, L. (1993). The Perceived Motivational Climate in Sport Questionnaire: Construct and predictive validity. *Journal of Sport and Exercise Psychology, 15*, 172–183.

Wandzilak, T., Carroll, T., and Ansorge, C.J. (1988). Values development through physical activity: Promoting sportsmanlike behaviors, perceptions, and moral reasoning. *Journal of Teaching in Physical Education, 8*, 13–22.

White, S. A. and Duda, J. L. (1991). The interdependence between goal perspectives, psychological skills and cognitive interference among elite skiers. Paper presented at the annual meeting of the Association of Applied Sports Psychology, Savannah, Georgia.

White, S. A., and Duda, J. L. (1994). The relationship of gender, level of sport involvement, and participation motivation to task and ego orientation. *International Journal of Sport Psychology, 25*, 4–18.

Yeager, J., Buxton, J., Baltzell, A., and Bzdell, W. (2001). *Character and coaching: Building virtue in athletic programs*. New York: Dude Publishing.

Part Six

Future
Directions

The first part of the book presented a historical account of the development of youth sports in America and a view of their current status. In the parts that followed, youth sports were considered from a variety of perspectives. The main thrust was to synthesize information about children's readiness for participation, the social processes involved, anatomical and physiological concerns, and psychological issues. Consideration was given to the effects of participation on young athletes as well as how to deal with some of the problems associated with youth sports. Although significant progress has been made, one of the common conclusions was that we do not know enough about youth sport phenomena, either in terms of knowledge about the participants or about the appropriate role of youth sports in society. These concerns are the focus of the concluding part, the ultimate goal of which is to promote changes that will enable youth sports to fulfill their potential as a valuable developmental experience for children and youth.

In Chapter 23, Daniel Gould looks at the future from the perspective of sport psychology research. If we are to understand the psychological effects of youth sport participation, and if we are to effectively deal with problematic psychological issues, more research-based information is clearly needed. Gould emphasizes this need and suggests that researchers conduct youth sports investigations with three major objectives in mind: (a) to discover psychological information that will help those involved in youth sports provide its participants with positive and productive experiences, (b) to test existing theory in a sport setting, and (c) to develop new theory. Given these objectives, key lines of previous research are identified, and two of these areas are reviewed (coaching effectiveness research; competitive stress and burnout in young athletes). These investigations were characterized by several features that enabled them to yield the most useful and meaningful information. From this base, the author concludes that if sport psychologists are to conduct socially-relevant research that will have a maximum pay-off for youth sports, three issues must be addressed. First, critical questions of both theoretical and practical importance must be identified. Second, he argues that descriptive, evaluation, and systems research are all needed, and examples of each type of research are presented. The third issue is the need for sport psychologists to realize that no single method is always best, and that varied as well as innovative methodological procedures must be employed. In this regard, a shift is suggested from traditional methodologies (i.e., linear causation and ANOVA categories models) to multivariate longitudinal designs and to employment of qualitative research methods to a greater degree. Finally, Gould concludes that to conduct youth sport research with major impact, sport psychologists must consider all the discussed practical, theoretical, and methodological issues.

A different view of the future is provided by Vern Seefeldt and Michael A. Clark in the final chapter. Rather than being solely concerned with future research, they prophesy about what is needed if youth sport proponents are to be proactive in seeking solutions to problems. As a prelude, a detailed account is presented of changing demographics that will profoundly influence the future of youth sports. In this regard, dramatic changes in the characteristics of participants—ethnicity, geographic location, and gender—are expected to play a major role in determining the type, frequency, and intensity of involvement. For example, projections based on the year 2000 census indicate that the numbers of white and African-American youth will decline slightly, but Hispanic and Asian/Pacific Islander youth will increase significantly; population shifts will continue to move from the Northeast and Midwest to the South and Southwest; and girls will participate more fully in agency-sponsored and interscholastic programs as they strive for equality in opportunities to be active in sports. In addressing the on-going reformation in youth sports, five categories of adult leaders are identified as primary agents of change—administrators and professors from institutions of higher learning, directors of recreation programs, state high school associations, administrators of single-sport agencies, and public school physical education teachers and coaches. Consideration is given to what each "agent of reform" must do to bring about progress. Seefeldt and Clark then predict what the future holds with respect to several salient issues, including the following: the increasing role of scientific inquiry in deriving answers to critical questions, the incidence and severity of sport-related injuries in children and adolescents, the changing roles of litigation and legislation in youth sports, the proliferation of educational programs for volunteer coaches, greater reliance on programs conducted under the auspices of municipal recreation departments, greater dependence on volunteer workers to conduct the programs, implementation of policies and procedures designed to guard against the abuse of power in athletic settings, and the integration of mentally and physically handicapped individuals into traditional programs. The result is a chapter that provides a stimulating basis for discussion about the direction of youth sport programs in the next decade and why modifications are imminent.

CHAPTER 23

Sport Psychology: Future Directions in Youth Sport Research

Daniel Gould, University of North Carolina, Greensboro

Historical research by Berryman (this volume) and by Wiggins (this volume) has shown that athletic programs for children have existed in North America since the early 1920s.[1] Although these programs have a long heritage, their period of greatest growth has occurred within the last three decades. Not only is participation enormously popular, but also the participants are intensely involved. It has been found, for example, that, on the average, young athletes participate in these programs 12 hours a week during an 18-week season (Gould and Martens, 1979). The youth sport setting thus involves a large proportion of the population and constitutes an important part of children's lives.

Sport psychology researchers paid only scant attention to the study of youth sports until the late 1970s. Since that time, the topic has drawn considerable psychological interest. Yet, increased empirical efforts in the area have not always brought beneficial results of either a theoretical or an applied nature, nor will they in the future. Three decades of youth sports research has clearly shown that if our knowledge of the psychological aspects of youth sport participation is to be increased, long-range, systematic, and well-conducted research programs are needed. We can help ensure that this occurs by examining the existing literature in the area and determining current lines of research that have provided the greatest empirical and applied benefits. Thus, this chapter examines key lines of past youth sport research, identifies critical research questions, outlines appropriate theoretical and methodological approaches, and suggests future research directions.

---

1. This is an abridged and updated version of an article by Gould (1982).

Meaningful Lines of Youth Sport Research

In the late 1970s and early 1980s the number of youth sport psychological studies greatly increased, as evidenced by the large number of review articles summarizing existing research and outlining practical implications for coaches, parents, and administrators (e.g., Gerson, 1977; Roberts, 1980; Thomas, 1978). The majority of implications made in these reviews were based on research from the parent discipline of psychology and not from sport psychology research. Consequently, one found oneself asking why many of the sport psychological studies were telling us so little about youth sports! Although the youth sport research provided little practical information for a number of reasons (e.g., scant amount of research, infancy of the field), one of the primary reasons stemmed from the questions being asked. Many times we did not ask the most appropriate questions. To identify the most important research questions we needed to more closely examine the objectives of our research.

Three of the various objectives that sport psychologists may have for studying youth sport seemed most prevalent. These included the following:

1. *To provide psychological information that will help those involved in youth sports provide its young participants with positive and productive experiences.* Specifically, the methods of the behavioral sciences could be used to identify and evaluate behavioral guidelines and strategies that adult leaders could use to more effectively communicate with, reinforce, and instruct young athletes. Providing this type of information is important because most youth sport coaches have little formal coaching education and develop coaching guidelines based on experiences of trial and error or through the modeling of college and professional coaches, who work with vastly different populations.

2. *To test existing psychological theory in a sport setting.* Theory is the ultimate goal of science, and psychologists (Bronfenbrenner, 1977) and sport psychologists (Brustad, Babkes, and Smith, 2001; Gill, 2000; Martens, 1987; Smith and Smoll, 1978) alike have emphasized the need for the behavioral scientist to test existing psychological theory in complex and diverse social settings. The youth sport domain provides a readily accessible, naturalistic field setting where this can be accomplished.

3. *To develop new theory.* Although it is extremely important to test existing theory, a number of investigators (Martens, 1979, 1987; Siedentop, 1980) have suggested that existing psychological theory will not have all the answers for the sport psychologist. New theories that account for multivariate, highly complex athletic settings must be identified and tested. The youth sport setting is ideal for this purpose.

Given these objectives for conducting youth sport research, the body of knowledge in the area was examined for an earlier version of this chapter.[2] In addition, Brustad et al.'s recent (2001) comprehensive review of this body of knowledge was considered. Key studies were identified based on two criteria: (a) their practical significance, and (b) their contribution to the development or extension of psychological theory. Characteristics of these studies were also identified. The key lines of research identified were (a) the coaching effectiveness research of Smith, Smoll, and their associates, (b) predictors of state and trait anxiety and stress-induced burnout in young athletes initiated by Scanlan and her associates and later continued by a number of investigators, (c) young athlete self-esteem and motivation research best reflected in the work of developmental sport psychologist Maureen Weiss, (d) youth sport participation motive and attrition research as exemplified by the work of Petlichkoff (1996), (e) friendship and peer influence research such as that conducted by Weiss, Smith, and Theeboom (1996) and A. L. Smith (1999), and (f) investigations examining moral development and sportspersonship in young athletes spearheaded by Bredemeier, Shields, and Weiss. Space limitations prevent an examination of all six of these lines of research, so only the first two areas will be described here. For information about the other areas, the reader is referred to in-depth reviews by Brustad et al. (2001), Gould and Dieffenbach (in press), Shields, Bredemeier, and Power (this volume), Weiss (1993), and Weiss and Ebbeck (1996).

Coaching Effectiveness Research

The original coaching effectiveness research of Smith, Smoll, and their associates (Curtis, Smith, and Smoll, 1979; Smith, Smoll, and Curtis, 1978, 1979; Smith, Smoll, and Hunt, 1977; Smith, Smoll, Hunt, Curtis, and Coppel, 1979; Smoll, Smith, Curtis, and Hunt, 1978) can be categorized into three distinct phases. First, a Coaching Behavior Assessment System (CBAS) was developed over several years. This observational system consisted of behavioral categories derived from social learning theory and assessed individual differences in behavioral profiles of coaches. Both reactive and spontaneous coaching behaviors were assessed and included behaviors such as positive reinforcement, nonreinforcement, mistake-contingent encouragement, mistake-contingent technical instruction, punishment, punitive technical instruction, ignoring mistakes, keeping control behaviors, general technical instruction, general encouragement, organization, and general communication. The CBAS inventory was found to be a highly reliable and valid assessment instrument.

---

2. Due to space limitations it is not possible to include a comprehensive review of the psychological investigations conducted in the youth sport area. Therefore, the interested reader is referred to related reviews (Brustad et al., 2001; Gould, 1993; Gould and Seefeldt, 1981; Gould and Weiss, 1987; Seefeldt and Gould, 1980; Weiss, 1993; Weiss and Bredemeier, 1983) and, upon request from the author, may receive a detailed listing of the references reviewed.

In a second phase of the project, the relation between coaching behaviors of Little League Baseball coaches as assessed by the CBAS instrument ($N = 51$); and player perceptions ($N = 542$) of coaching behaviors, attitudes, and self-esteem were examined. It was found that coaches who were rated more positively by the children gave more technical instruction than general encouragement, gave more reinforcement and mistake contingent feedback, and engaged in more behaviors associated with keeping control. Negatively evaluated coaches generally were more punitive and gave more punitive technical instruction. Finally, children who played for the positively evaluated coaches had higher general and athletic self-concepts.

Because the results of this second phase were descriptive and no causal inferences could be made, a third phase was conducted. In this phase, 31 Little League Baseball coaches were randomly assigned to either an experimental group that received training in a positive approach to coaching (e.g., were given behavioral guidelines derived in the previous phase that emphasized the desirability of reinforcement, encouragement, and technical instruction) or to a control condition in which they coached as they normally would. The intervention program received by the experimental group of coaches consisted of a 2.5-hour coaching clinic, self-assessment of coaching behaviors, and observer feedback concerning emitted coaching behaviors. Dependent variables observed included coaching behaviors, self-perceived coaching behaviors, player perceptions of coaching behaviors, as well as attitudinal and self-esteem measures of 325 of their players. Findings revealed that the behavioral profiles of the experimental coaches differed from the control coaches in the expected direction. Moreover, the children who played for the experimental coaches, as compared with children who played for the control coaches, demonstrated greater enjoyment, a greater desire to play, rated their coaches as more knowledgeable, and rated their teammates higher in attraction.

The fourth phase of this line of research has been conducted and focused specific attention on how coaching behaviors affect self-esteem development and attribution rates in young athletes (Barnett, Smoll, and Smith, 1992; Smith and Smoll, 1990; Smoll, Smith, Barnett, and Everett, 1993). The relation between self-esteem enhancement and coaching behaviors was examined in 51 male Little League Baseball coaches and 542 of their players (Smith and Smoll, 1990). Children with low self-esteem responded most positively to coaches who exhibited reinforcing and encouraging behaviors as measured by the CBAS and most negatively to coaches who were low on supportiveness. Similarly, high levels of technical instruction were positively associated with enhanced self-esteem, whereas low levels of supportiveness were associated with lower self-esteem. Hence, a strong association was exhibited between high levels of technical instruction, encouragement, supportive behaviors, and self-esteem enhancement.

Next, Smoll et al. (1993) compared 8 youth baseball coaches, who attended a preseason workshop designed to increase supportiveness and instructional effectiveness, to 10 control group coaches, who did not participate in such a workshop. One hundred fifty-two boys who played for these coaches were interviewed pre- and postseason. The findings revealed that boys with low self-esteem experienced significant increases in general self-esteem across the season, whereas low self-esteem children who played for control group coaches did not. As was the case with other studies in the series, players who played for the trained coaches also evaluated their coaches more positively, had more fun, and exhibited higher intrateam attraction. No differences in won-loss records were evident between the trained and control group coaches.

As a follow-up to the previous study, Barnett et al. (1992) examined dropout rates in the children who played for the trained and control coaches. Results revealed that control group children exhibited a 26% dropout rate, whereas the attrition rate for experimental group players was only 5%. Interestingly, no differences were evident in won-loss records of the teams, and it was concluded that dropout rates were associated with negative sport experiences brought about by coaching behaviors exhibited during the previous season.

Taken together, then, the investigations in this four-phase project continued to add significantly to our understanding of the influence that coaching behaviors have on the affective reactions of young athletes. First, coaching behaviors were consistently associated with a variety of psychological reactions of players, including such attributes as the amount of fun experienced, liking of the coach, and liking of the game. Positive, instructional, and supportive coaching behaviors were also associated with enhanced self-esteem, especially for low self-esteem players. Second, these same patterns of coaching behaviors were also associated with motivation levels as players who played for coaches taught to be more positive, supportive, instructive, and encouraging evidenced lower dropout rates. Finally, it was shown that coaches could be trained to exhibit desirable coaching behaviors and, in turn, have positive effects on their young athletes motivation and psychological states.

Competitive Anxiety and Burnout Research

The second important line of research was initiated by Scanlan and her colleagues (Passer and Scanlan, 1980; Scanlan and Lewthwaite, 1984; Scanlan and Passer, 1978a, 1978b, 1979). These investigators examined the relations between competitive trait anxiety, self-esteem, team performance expectancies, personal performance expectancies, worries about failure, worries about adult expectations and social evaluation, parental pressure to participate, game or match outcome, perceived fun, and pre- and postcontest state anxiety in youth sport participants. In all, a series of three interrelated field studies was conducted using a similar methodological format. Competitive stress or state anxiety was assessed just prior to and immediately following competition and was correlated to various individual difference factors (e.g., trait anxiety, self-esteem, worries about adult expectations) taken well before the contests. In the first investigation, male youth soccer players, ages 10 to 12 years, were used as participants (Scanlan and Passer, 1978b). The second investigation replicated and extended the first by employing female youth soccer players of the same age (Scanlan and Passer, 1979). Finally, the final study in the series (Scanlan and Lewthwaite, 1984) extended the results of the soccer studies to the sport of wrestling, examining male youth wrestlers, ages 10 to 14.

Overall, the findings of these studies have shown that sport competition is perceived as anxiety producing by *some* children in some situations. In particular, the findings demonstrate that competitive trait anxiety, performance expectancies pertinent to the particular sport context, victory versus defeat and its varying degrees, and the amount of fun experienced while competing are strong and consistent predictors of competitive stress for both genders across diverse sport contexts. Self-esteem also was found to be a significant, although relatively weak, predictor of stress for boys and girls in the soccer studies and was significantly correlated with but not predictive of stress in wrestling. The final study in this series (Scanlan and Lewthwaite, 1984) identified additional factors associated with stress that focus on children's characteristic prematch thoughts and worries, as well as their perceptions of the significant adults in their lives (Scanlan, 1986, p. 117). Finally, many of these findings were replicated in an independent youth wrestling investigation conducted by Gould, Eklund, Petlichkoff, Peterson, and Bump (1991).

Although the previous studies focused on predictors of state anxiety in young athletes, several investigators have also begun to focus attention on factors associated with heightened competitive trait anxiety in young athletes, that is, factors that influence their personality disposition to perceive socially evaluative environments like competition as more or less threatening and respond with varying levels of state anxiety. And this is important because youngsters who experience the most state anxiety in sport environments have been consistently shown to be high trait anxious.

Passer (1983) was the first investigator to examine this issue when he compared 163 high and low trait anxious 10- to 15-year-old soccer players on performance expectancies, criticism for failure, self-esteem, perceived competence, and evaluative- and performance-related worries. His findings demonstrated that high as compared with low trait anxious players worried more frequently about losing; coach, parent, and teammate evaluations; and not playing well.

In a follow-up study, Brustad and Weiss (1987) compared 55 male and 55 female youth softball participants and found that high versus low trait anxious boys reported more performance worries and lower self-esteem. High versus low trait anxious girls, however, were not found to differ on any of these variables. Similar results for male and female participants did emerge in a second investigation of 207 youth basketball players conducted by Brustad (1988). Hence, both male and female high competitive trait anxious young athletes differed from their low trait anxious counterparts in that they exhibited higher levels of evaluative- and performance-based worries and lower self-esteem.

An important investigation by Newton and Duda (1992) also looked at predictors of competitive trait anxiety in young athletes. Male and female youth tennis players

(*M* age = 12 years) were studied, and it was found that an ego goal orientation (a tendency to base one's goals on winning or beating others versus self-improvement) was related to higher levels of multidimensional trait anxiety. Hence, youth tennis players whose goals focus on contest outcome (versus self-improvement) to judge athletic success are more threatened by social evaluation and competition.

Last, in an investigation linking the previously discussed coaching behavior research with the research on factors influencing trait anxiety in young athletes, Smith, Smoll, and Barnett (1995) found that the youth league coaches who took part in their Coach Effectiveness Training intervention were not only effective in positively influencing their athletes motivation and self-esteem but in lowering their trait anxiety as well. This is certainly an important finding as it suggests that high trait anxious children can gain much from the youth sport experience.

In summary, then, the research examining factors associated with increased trait anxiety in young athletes shows that high trait anxious children perceive failure and negative evaluation from significant others as more emotionally aversive and worry more about such concerns than their low trait anxious counterparts. These children also tend to adopt outcome, as opposed to mastery or self-referenced, goal orientations. An encouraging finding that needs replication is that coaches trained to be more encouraging, supportive, and instructive have positive effects in lowering trait anxiety in young athletes. Factors associated with heightened state anxiety include low self-esteem, low personal and team performance expectancies, and heightened trait anxiety. Children who experience high state anxiety during competition also report having less fun and satisfaction and frequently worry about adult evaluation and expectations.

In recent years, examining stress-related burnout in young athletes has extended the sport competition anxiety research. This research was spurred by Smith's (1986) cognitive-affective stress model of burnout. According to this conceptualization, burnout is defined as a psychological, physical, and emotional withdrawal from a formerly enjoyable and motivating activity resulting from prolonged or chronic stress. Specifically, the model posits that a demand of some type is placed on the young athlete (e.g., pressure to win by coaches and parents, excessive physical practice and training). Second, some young athletes will appraise that physical or psychological demand as more threatening or overwhelming than others. Third, when a demand is perceived as threatening, a physiological response occurs (e.g., anxiety, fatigue). Finally, the physiological response leads to some type of behavioral outcome or coping effort such as decreased performance, interpersonal difficulties, or withdrawal (burnout) from the activity.

Based on his model, Smith contends that although some individuals discontinue sport participation because of burnout, burnout is not the primary cause of sport withdrawal for most individuals (Smith, 1986). Rather, based on Thibaut and Kelly's (1959) social exchange theory, Smith indicates that individuals withdraw from sport when costs are viewed as outweighing benefits relative to alternative activities. For most young athletes, this means that they discontinue sport participation because of changing interests, conflicting time demands between activities, low perceived competence, and/or a lack of fun (Gould and Petlichkoff, 1988; Weiss and Chaumenton, 1992). Thus, for Smith, youth sport burnout only occurs when costs outweigh rewards for the young athlete and when the costs are stress-induced.

Using this model as a general guide, Gould, Tuffey, Udry, and Loehr (1996a, 1996b, 1997) conducted a three-phase study examining burnout in junior tennis players. The first phase of the study (Gould et al., 1996a) involved a retrospective survey of a national sample of 30 junior tennis players. All of these players were identified by U.S. Tennis Association regional staff members as having burned out of tennis in their junior years of play. A sample of comparison players of similar age, competitive experience, and age were also identified for comparison purposes. When the two groups of players were compared, the burned out players had significantly higher burnout scores, were more likely to play up in an older age division, had less input into their tennis training and tennis-related decisions, practiced fewer days (lessened their involvement), were higher in amotivation, were lower in external motivation, reported being more withdrawn, differed in perfectionism (especially relative to concern over mistakes, personal standards, parental criticism, parental expectations, and higher need for organization), were less likely to use planning coping strategies, and were lower on positive interpretation and growth coping. No differences between the groups were evident in the number of hours they trained, suggesting that for this sample of young athletes burnout was more psychologically than physically driven. It was also concluded that in addition to a variety of personal and situational factors, the personality disposition of perfectionism played a particularly important role in predicting burnout in junior tennis.

In the second phase of this study (Gould et al., 1996b), in-depth interviews were conducted with the 10 most burned out players identified in Phase 1. Signs and symptoms of burnout, how players dealt with their burned out feelings, factors viewed to lead to burnout, suggestions for preventing burnout, involvement of significant others in tennis, and advice to others were all issues examined. Results revealed that reasons for burning out included logistical concerns like time demands and too much travel, physical concerns such as being sick and not being satisfied with performance, and social interpersonal concerns such as dissatisfaction with social life and negative parental influence. Unexpectedly, the largest category of concerns focused on psychological issues and included such things as unfulfilled and unrealistic expectations and pressure. Recommendations for preventing and dealing with burnout for other players included playing for one's own reasons, balancing tennis with other activities such as school clubs or socializing with friends, stopping participation if playing tennis is no fun, focusing on making tennis fun, doing things to relax, and taking time off. The players recommended that to prevent burnout, parents reduce the importance they place on event and game outcome, have parent-coach role clarification, and solicit input from their junior player. The participants also indicated that some parent push is needed, but it must be an optimal amount as too much contributes to burnout.

In the third and final phase of the investigation (Gould et al., 1997), individual profiles of three players who represented different forms of burnout were presented. The cases included (a) a player characterized by high levels of perfectionism and over training who burned out primarily because of her personality orientation, (b) a player who experienced pressure from others and felt a strong need for a social life outside of tennis and burned out primarily due to social psychological factors, and (c) a player who was physically over trained, failed to get enough sleep, and burned out due to physical factors. It was concluded that burnout might best be viewed within a stress-related strain model, with a "physically-driven" strain resulting from physical over training and a "psychologically-driven" strain comprised of two additional substrains. One of the psychological substrains results from a young athlete having an "at risk" perfectionistic personality—a personality that predisposes them to burnout, even in nonpressure situations. The second psychological substrain focuses on burnout resulting from situational stress, such as coach or parent pressure to participate and perform. These three substrains are not totally independent.

Lastly, in a recent study of burnout, Raedeke (1997) tested sport commitment model predictions in 236 youth swimmers, ages 13 to 18. Based on sport commitment model theorizing, Raedeke contended that athletes experience stress and burn out of sport because their motives for being involved differ from athletes who do not burn out. Specifically, young athletes who burn out do so because they are committed to sport for solely entrapment-related reasons (e.g., athletes burn out when they feel that they "have to" maintain their involvement versus "want to" maintain their involvement).

Raedeke's initial test of his model was designed to examine whether youth swimmers with motivation profiles representing sport entrapment, sport attraction, and low commitment experience varying levels of burnout. The youth swimmers studied, all who trained 40,000 meters a week, completed a 21-item athletic burnout scale, as well as assessments of the benefits and costs of swimming, swimming enjoyment, personal investment in swimming, alternative activity attraction, social constraints, swim identity, and perceived control. The swimmers were statistically divided into profile groups (e.g., enthusiastic, indifferent) based on their psychological characteristics. Findings revealed that youth swimmers who were characterized by an entrapment profile (e.g., swam because they had to) had significantly higher burnout scores than swimmers who were characterized by an attraction profile (e.g., swam because they wanted to). Moreover, these swimmers were found to be entrapped because of their low perceived control (e.g., not having a say in what they do in swimming) and high social constraints (e.g., social norms and expectations that cause feelings of obligation to swim such as parental pressure). The results were consistent with many of the sport commitment model predictions.

While not presented in his original article, Gould and Dieffenbach (in press) used Raedeke's data to estimate the extent of burnout experienced by young athletes. Specifically, when those swimmers who scored 2 standard deviations above the mean on these various burnout subcategory scores and exhibited an overall burnout score of 4 (highest score possible) are grouped, approximately 3% to 5% of the athletes experienced some emotional and physical exhaustion, 3% to 5% of the athletes devaluation, and 1% to 2% of the athletes reduced accomplishment. Thus, between 1% and 5% of these 236 swimmers experienced some form of burnout.

Looking across all the burnout models and investigations, then, it is clear that burnout in young athletes occurs and results from a complex interplay of situational factors and personal characteristics. Numerous social and psychological factors beyond physical overtraining are involved. Dispositional factors such as perfectionism and motives such as entrapment are also involved in burnout. Hence, all these factors and their unique interactions must be considered when understanding burnout. It is also evident that even though the absolute number of athletes who experience excessive burnout is small, a significant portion of athletes do burn out.

What Have These Lines of Research Taught Us?

Examining both the coaching effectiveness and competitive anxiety/burnout lines of research (as well as the other meaningful lines of youth sport research not discussed here because of space), several lessons for future research are apparent. First and foremost, these lines of research focused on asking important questions of practical concern for youth sport personnel. What effect do coaching behaviors have on the psychological development of young athletes? What causes stress and anxiety in youth sport participants? Are young athletes burning out of sport? If so, under what conditions?

Second, these studies integrated previous research and directly tested theory or attempted to generate new theory to explain the relations between variables. For example, Smoll and Smith (1989) have developed a theoretical model of leadership in youth sports. This cognitive-behavioral model specifies how situational factors, individual difference factors, and cognitive processes mediate overt coaching behaviors and young athletes' reactions to them. Similarly, much of the youth sport anxiety and burnout research has been guided by anxiety theories developed in general psychology.

Third, these lines of research were methodologically sound. They examined more than a few isolated teams (entire leagues), were multivariate in nature, and involved more than one assessment. The junior tennis burnout research of Gould and his colleagues (1996a, 1996b; 1997) also shows how using quantitative and qualitative methods in the same line of studies can provide maximum information gain.

Finally, these projects were part of a systematic series of studies, not isolated, single studies. The research of Smith, Smoll, and associates, for instance, was conducted in four distinct phases (Phase 1—development of assessment instruments;

Phase 2—descriptive hypothesis-generating research; Phase 3—hypothesis-testing experimental research; Phase 4—special focus on understanding the coaching behavior self-esteem relationship) and provides a good model for future researchers to follow. Similarly, the factors related to competitive-stress/burnout investigations represent how a line of research can be conducted by groups of independent authors examining similar issues. It is also interesting to note that the initial state anxiety research that Scanlan and her associates conducted was part of a series of field studies, where the researchers tested theoretical principles derived from a line of laboratory research on competitive anxiety in a field setting. Conducting these three studies also allowed the investigators to replicate and extend their findings to young female athletes and across sports.

In contrast, a review of the literature revealed that youth sport studies that did not have the same impact as these lines of investigation did not reflect many of these characteristics. Investigations with less impact, for example, did not ask questions of practical importance, were often methodologically weak, and were not multivariate in their approach. Moreover, these investigations typically were not part of a systematic series of studies, nor did they integrate previous research into the design.

Conducting Youth Sport Research That Counts

Boring (1963), eminent historian of psychology, wrote, "one finds that he [or she] needs to know about the past, not in order to predict the future, but rather in order to understand the present" (p. 89). Thus, historically examining the youth sport literature will not let us predict what the future will bring. However, understanding the past research may help make our research efforts more fruitful and economical. If we agree with some of the leaders in the field (Martens, 1979, 1987; Siedentop, 1980; Smith and Smoll, 1978) and assume that one of the sport psychologist's major objectives is to conduct socially significant research that will make meaningful contributions to those involved in sport, then we must address three issues:

1. What questions should we ask if we are to have the greatest impact in providing information that ensures productive and healthful programs for children?
2. What types of research setting are needed if answers to these questions are to be derived?
3. What methodological approaches should be employed if valid and reliable answers are to be provided to these questions?

What Questions Should We Ask?

Do we ask important questions? Does our research really make a difference? All too often the answer to these questions has been no. More than 30 years ago, Locke (1969), stated the following:

> If you wiped out the last 50 years of research in physics or chemistry or medicine, life in our world would instantly change. If you wiped out the last 50 years of research in physical education, would physical education and physical educators continue to function as usual? The answer is usually an emphatic "yes." (p. 6)

Unfortunately, his conclusion is applicable to youth sport research today.

Psychologists like Bronfenbrenner (1977) and sport scientists like Martens (1979, 1987) and Siedentop (1980) have suggested that the time has come for sport psychologists to spend less time in their laboratories and more time on the playing fields, in the gymnasiums, and natatoriums. In essence, we must establish ecological validity for our theories (Bronfenbrenner, 1977). Siedentop (1980) warns that all too often applied research has been thought of as only extending laboratory research to practical settings. Behaviorists like Baer, Wolf, and Risely (1968), however, suggest that "the label applied in not determined by the research procedures used but by the interest which society shows in the problems being studied" (p. 12). Thus, if the sport psychologist conducting youth sport research is to have practical impact, then questions of practical importance must be identified.

To identify these issues, the author conducted a content analysis of the practical and empirical youth sport literature, and topics of psychological significance in youth sport were identified. A brief questionnaire was then formulated and administered to 23 sport psychologists working in youth sports throughout North America, as well as to 33 nonschool youth sport coaches and administrators. The results of this survey revealed that the following 10 topics were rated as most important by the combined sample:

- Reasons why young athletes stop participating
- Competitive stress placed on young athletes
- Helping young athletes cope with competitive stress
- Effects of competition on the psychological health and development of children
- Skills for enhancing communication with young athletes
- Strategies for developing self-confidence
- Why young athletes participate in sport
- Effects of winning and losing on young athletes
- What young athletes like and dislike about sport
- Effects of parent-child relationships on sport involvement and success.

Moreover, no differences were found between the groups on their ratings of the 10 topics ranked as most important for study.

Although not presented as a response in the previously discussed survey, several new topics have emerged as critically important to those interested in youth sports.

These include (a) parental conduct and involvement in the youth sport process, and (b) the role youth sports can play in life skills development.

Parental conduct has become an issue of concern as a result of increasing reports of parents interfering with youth league games, arguing with coaches, and verbally and physically fighting with each other as well as coaches and officials. In fact, there have even been reports of deaths as a result of parental misconduct. More needs to be known about the frequency of these problems, why they appear to be occurring more frequently, and what can be done to prevent such instances from happening.

Another critical topic that needs to be studied by youth sport researchers is the role of life skills development in youth sports. Life skills are those social, emotional and behavioral skills (e.g., the ability to set and achieve goals, anxiety management, leadership, emotional control strategies) a young athlete might develop or refine through sport participation that can be transferred to other areas of life (e.g., transfer setting goals from the athletic field to the classroom). Increasingly, many youth development agencies see sport as a vehicle for developing such life skills and hope that by doing so they can promote positive youth development off the field and reduce such problems as substance abuse and youth violence. Unfortunately, while programs focusing on teaching children involved in sport life skills such as goal setting and self-responsibility have been developed (e.g., Danish and Nellen, 1997; Martinek and Hellison, 1997), in-depth scientific evaluation of their effects are needed. Especially important is the need to verify that life skills were actually developed through sport participation and then successfully transferred to other life endeavors.

A number of sport psychology topics of practical significance for the youth sport researcher are evident then. However, asking questions of a practical significance does not mean the abandonment of theory, be it the testing of existing theory in youth sport field settings or the development of a new theory. Theory is the major goal of science, whether it is of basic or applied nature (Gill 2000; Kerlinger, 1973). Moreover, it has often been said that if one is interested in practical implications, nothing is more practical than good theory. The previously mentioned work of Scanlan and her associates, as well as the motivation and perceived competence research of Weiss (1991), are excellent examples of research that tests existing theory in youth sport settings while addressing practical problems.

It is also important to recognize that applying existing theory to sport can advance knowledge in sport psychology only so far. The sport psychologist must not only test existing theory but must also develop new sport-specific theories that better explain the complex interaction of personal and environmental variables in the naturalistic youth sport field setting (Martens, 1979, 1987; Siedentop, 1980; Smith and Smoll, 1978; Thomas, 1980). The need to test existing theory and to develop new theory is of paramount importance because we are sometimes blinded by the *zeitgeist* in which we work. For example, the early research on attributions in the youth sport setting primarily consisted on an extension of laboratory research findings to naturalistic environments. Although these findings were important in that they further verified previous research, the scientists were often blinded by the theory's assumptions and limitations.

One should have asked, are the four basic attributions found in the laboratory appropriate for sport settings? Some research (Roberts and Pascuzzi, 1979) indicated that alone they may not have been and, interestingly, attribution theory was later revised to be more inclusive (Weiner, 1985). In a related manner, why has the critical link between attributions and performance or participation in youth sport not been assessed to a greeter degree? Is it that we assume that attributions will automatically influence behavior because this is what is predicted from the general theoretical notions? Similarly, the feasibility of identifying learned-helpless young athletes and modifying their helpless states through attributional retraining has not been examined. In essence, whether we are testing existent theory and/or developing new theory, from time to time we must be able to step back and examine whether the *zeitgeist* or paradigm in which we are working is blinding us—preventing us from testing basic assumptions or asking theoretically important but forgotten questions.

When testing existing theory and developing new theory, the youth sport researcher must also remember that the young athlete is not a miniature adult. Too often we erroneously assume that psychological processes and theories that have been based on research with adults automatically transfer to younger age groups. Weiss and Bredemeier (1983) and Weiss (1991), however, have presented convincing evidence that shows that psychological processes systematically vary with age or the developmental level of the child. Thus, when testing existing theory and developing new sport-specific theories in youth sport, developmental factors must be considered.

The present review of the existing youth sport research clearly showed that the areas that have provided the most impact are ones where the investigators pursued a series of interrelated questions. Thus, in planning youth sport research, it is more fruitful for investigators to think in terms of lines of research, focusing on a number of interrelated questions and subquestions rather than on single, isolated questions. It may be fruitful to adopt elements of the method of strong inference developed by Platt (1964). That is, we should conduct lines of research in a logical fashion by attempting to devise and test alternative hypotheses, critically examining the results of previous studies and formulation questions in future investigations that will eliminate rival hypotheses.

A good example of this approach in the youth sport research is the work of Smith and Smoll and their associates. As already mentioned, this series of investigations was carried out in four phases. Phase 1 focused on the question of whether coaching behaviors could be reliably and validly assessed. After this was established, the question of what relation exists between coaching behaviors and player attitudes was explored. The researchers did not stop here, however. When stable relations were found between coaching behaviors and player attitudes and motivation, the next interrelated question was posed. Can coaching behaviors be changed, and will these changes result in changes in attitudes and motivation on the part of players? This question was answered in Phase 3. Phase 4 focused on examining the effects of coach behaviors and behavioral training on development of self-esteem and other psychological variables. Although not currently under way, strong inference would suggest that a next logical series of questions would focus on what specifically caused the changes in coaching behaviors and player affect. For instance, were the results of Phase 3 due to a placebo effect associated with the training program? Were they caused by the 2.5-hour coaching clinic, the self-assessment procedures employed, or the feedback given to the coaches about their actual behavior?

Although the strong inference process has much to offer the youth sport researcher, its limitations also must be recognized. Hafner and Presswood (1965), for example, suggest that the notion of strong inference is idealistic because alternative hypotheses do not always appear. Moreover, if we encounter an occasional mistake in observation, the idea that a systematic series of interrelated questions results in valid answers to a problem may be false. We may be systematically pursuing subquestions in the wrong direction! Similarly, Feltz (1989) convincingly argues that the strong inference notion that science can only advance by disproofs is faulty. In contrast, she contends that the sport psychology researcher must employ a planned critical multiplism approach, where a series of investigations are planned using multiple ways to formulate research questions, measure variables, design investigations, analyze results, and interpret findings. Consequently, sport psychologists conducting youth sport research must simultaneously consider sets of contending theoretical ideas, design and evaluate experiments with the greatest care, use multiple methods, replicate results, and view results from a single investigation with great care.

What Types of Research Settings Are Needed?

In preparing this chapter, a number of papers on the philosophy of science (Boring, 1955, 1963; Bronowski, 1973; Hafner and Presswood, 1965; Kuhn, 1970; Patton, 1990; Platt, 1964), the future direction of social psychology (Gergen, 1973; Helmreich, 1975; McGuire, 1973; Schlenkar, 1974), and direction of the research in sport psychology (Gill, 2000; Martens, 1979, 1987; Siedentop, 1980; Smith and Smoll, 1978; Thomas, 1980) were reviewed. One common theme in all of these papers was that we should beware of those who employ one method or instrument, either experimental or theoretical. If the state of knowledge in a field is to be advanced, diverse methods must be employed. Descriptive studies, evaluation research, and systems approach research are all types of research that are applicable in the psychological study of youth sport.

Descriptive research. In the early 1970s, if a particular sport psychology investigation was not theoretical, highly controlled, and conducted in the laboratory, it was more than likely not highly evaluated. Times have changed and we have come a long way since then. More and more field research is being conducted, and we now encourage new and different approaches to the field. We are still not completely open-minded, however. For example, the utility of descriptive research needs to be recognized and more highly supported, especially in the area of youth sports. Although theory is our ultimate goal, we must recognize that youth sports are conducted in a highly complex physical and social environment. We know relatively little about this environment; some feel it cannot be explained with existing laboratory-generated theories (Martens, 1979, 1987; Siedentop, 1980; Smith and Smoll, 1978). Thus, descriptive research could play an important role in helping us understand this complex setting and, in so doing, provide us with the groundwork needed for the development of new theory.

Descriptive research could also be extremely useful in answering practical problems. At the State of Michigan Institute for the Study of Youth Sports, for example, a descriptive study of the children's sport participation has been conducted (Ewing and Seefeldt, 1989; 1996). A descriptive study was selected because little was known about national patterns in children's sport participation. The number of participants involved; participation patterns; and children's motives for participation had never been extensively examined in a national sample. This survey of 8,000 youth, ages 10 to 18, has provided a wealth of data and results. For example, it was found that children's sport participation steadily increased up to the ages of 10, after which it markedly declined. They also found a number of interesting participation pattern differences by children of different races. Most notable was under-representation of Hispanic-American children in all sports. Information also was obtained on the reasons for children's involvement and discontinuation of participation. These findings have provided the staff of the Youth Sports Institute with valuable athletic motivation information to convey to youth sport coaches. Interestingly, however, little additional research like this has been conducted.

Descriptive research can also be extremely useful in solving controversial youth sport issues. Critics of youth sport, for example, suggest that coaches' overemphasis on winning places children under too much stress, that adult leaders demonstrate unsporting behavior, and that parents often stifle fun in children's sport programs. Sport psychologists could develop behavioral observation systems for assessing behaviors like these and examine the relations among these factors.

Finally, descriptive research does not have to be atheoretical. Descriptive methods could be used to provide support for theoretical formulations. For example, Bandura (1977) suggests that performance accomplishments are one primary means of influencing an individual's self-efficacy to be associated with various performance accomplishments over the course of a season. Similarly, changes in Harter's (1981) perceived competence scale scores could be examined over the course of several seasons, and relations between competence and various environmental factors (coaching behavior assessments, success) could be made.

Evaluation research. Edward Suchman (1976) indicates "evaluation research is a specific form of applied research whose primary goal is not the discovery of knowledge but rather a testing of the application of knowledge" (p. 75). Evaluation research includes the process of determining the value or amount of success in achieving some predetermined program objective or objectives (Patton, 1990; C. H. Weiss, 1972). In essence, evaluation research involves the careful planning of specific program objectives, the identification of criteria to measure the success of these objectives, determination and exploration of the degree of success, and recommendations for further program activity.

Although little evaluation research has been conducted by sport psychologists, this approach holds great promise for those interested in youth sports. A number of sport psychologists, for example, have been involved in making presentations in clinics and workshops held for youth coaches. Although it is easy for us to assume that we are contributing to the betterment of children's sport by conducting these programs, little empirical evidence exists outside of that of Smith, Smoll, and their associates to support this assumption. Do youth coaches conduct themselves in a more socially acceptable manner after receiving information on the psychology of sportspersonship? If so, do these behaviors affect the young athlete's moral attitudes and behaviors? Evaluation research could be used to answer these and related questions.

Evaluation research could also be used to provide information that could assist program administrators in ending controversies in children's sport. Martens, Rivkin, and Bump (1984) and Spieth (1977), for instance, compared the amount of activity youngsters experience in traditional versus nontraditional baseball leagues. Specifically, in both studies it was found that young athletes who played in a nontraditional league where their own coach pitched to them had more swings at pitches, made more contact with the ball, and had more balls hit to them in the field than children who played in traditional leagues. Similarly, Corbin and Laurie (1980) used evaluation research to assess the effects of rule changes in children's baseball on parental attitudes toward those rule changes. Specifically, it was found that parents generally supported program changes designed to reduce competition and focus attention on fun and skill development. These initial efforts demonstrate the practical implications that youth sport evaluation research can have.

Systems approach research. A third type of research that could be useful to the sport psychologist conducting youth sport research is systems approach research. Smith and Smoll (1978) indicate that because the youth sport setting involves the extensive interplay of a variety of social systems and subsystems, to fully understand the setting one must examine the various systems. Specifically, in the systems approach, the investigator (a) identifies all social systems and subsystems, (b) focuses on system change and factors related to change, (c) develops a model that describes causal patterns between systems and factors affecting systems, and (d) manipulates model elements to test their predicted effect on the system. This model would be especially appropriate in studying socialization into and through sport. Systems such as the child, teammates, and parents could be identified and observed simultaneously and longitudinally. Relations between systems could be examined, models developed, and predictions of the model tested.

What Methodological Approach Should Be Employed?

The sport psychologist can pose the appropriate and socially relevant questions and conduct research in the most appropriate setting to answer these questions, but unless good methodological procedures are utilized, all of his or her efforts are in vain. What is the best methodological format to follow when conducting naturalistic research in field settings? There is no one *best* method. The problem at hand determines which methods are most appropriate. For example, when conducting research in an underdeveloped area (e.g., parental relationship issues in youth athletes), noncausal survey techniques may be the most appropriate methods to employ. In essence, the primary purpose of this type of investigation would be the description of the phenomenon of concern and the identification of variables that covary with it. After a number of noncausal relations are established, however, the manipulation of various independent variables thought to influence the behavior of concern may be in order (e.g., parental educational strategies designed to develop positive parent-child athlete relationships), or statistical techniques such as structural equation modeling or path analyses may be employed, which will allow one to test theoretically derived paths or relations between variables.

It is becoming more apparent, however, that the same procedures that have guided both social psychologists in general and sport psychologists in particular are not always appropriate for field settings (Martens, 1979, 1987; Patton, 1990). Because we are investigating a complex phenomenon where a large number of internal and external factors are affecting the populations we sample, the traditional methodology of linear causation and convenient ANOVA categories are often inappropriate. For instance, in studying the effects of coaching behaviors on the attitudinal development of young athletes, isolating and assessing the effects of one particular coaching behavior (e.g., positive reinforcement) on attitudinal development will not be enough. Numbers of behaviors (e.g., positive reinforcement, punishment, technical instructions) of coaches and other role models (e.g., parents, peers) will need to be assessed in a variety of settings (games and practices) across time. Consequently, the sport psychologist interested in providing valid answers to many of the questions posed in this manuscript must consider multivariate longitudinal designs, use regression analyses that look at all subjects—not just dichotomized or trichotomized groups—and employ a wide range of quantitative and qualitative assessment procedures. In addition, answers to many of the complex questions involving children in sport do not reside in the psychological domain alone. Instead, they are influenced by the complex interplay of psychological, physiological, and kinesiological factors (Weiss, 1991). Thus, team research of a multidisciplinary nature is also needed.

Pediatric sport psychology researchers should also employ qualitative research methods to a much greater degree. Patton (1990), for instance, has convincingly shown that qualitative research methods such as in-depth interviews, case studies, and field observations provide a wealth of detailed information and depth of understanding not resulting from traditional quantitative methods. Using participant observation and interview techniques, for instance, Harris (1983) studied two youth baseball teams differing in their ethnic make-ups. Her results revealed that few ethnic group differences emerged between the teams. Moreover, players from both teams reflected their coaches' characterizations (most important concepts regarding the goals of the youth baseball experience) of youth baseball, partially redefining and adding to them. Similarly, Donnelly (1993) conducted in-depth interviews with former elite young athletes who had taken part in high-performance sports. In doing so, a number of important and previously undocumented negative side effects of participation, such as troubled family relationships, social relationship problems, identity concerns, and excessive behaviors like recreational drug use, were identified. Clearly, then, these initial studies show how conducting qualitative youth sport research can supplement and extend the excellent quantitative research knowledge base that has begun to develop in the area.

A final methodological issue that cannot be ignored focuses on sampling concerns. Too often, youth sport researchers select the most convenient sample of young athletes for their investigations, rather than choosing the most appropriate sample available for answering the questions posed. For example, Feltz and Ewing (1987) have indicated that many of the controversies surrounding sport competition for children are most prominent at the elite levels of involvement. They indicate, however, that few investigators have examined critical issues, such as burnout and excessive competitive stress, with samples of elite young athletes. Similarly, in a follow-up investigation to the previously discussed work of Smith, Smoll, and their colleagues, Horn (1985) has found that behaviors emitted by youth sport coaches differ depending on the sampling context, that is, whether coaching behaviors were observed in practices or competitions. These sampling context findings are of critical importance, as it was previously assumed that the pattern of observed coaching behaviors was similar across both practices and competitions. Finally, Brustad at al. (2001) emphasize the need to more often sample young athletes from around the world because the majority of research that has been conducted to date has been carried out on American and Canadian children. And in North America a need exists to be more inclusive in youth sport research sampling, including samples comprised of minority groups such African-American and Hispanic-American children. Hence, sport psychologists conducting youth sport research must pay particular attention to sampling issues and the effects of these issues on both their findings and their interpretation of findings.

A Final Comment

Social philosopher Herbert Marcuse (1964) has indicated that many times societal issues and problems remain unanswered, but not because those in the society are incapable of answering them. On the contrary, answers to these problems could be successfully achieved if the societal members only took the time to ask the appropriate questions. In many ways, the sport psychologist interested in studying youth sports is in a similar situation. We are in an emerging area and have the opportunity before us to conduct research that can have a tremendous impact on millions of youngsters. However, to conduct research that will have this practical significance, we need to stop, step back, and examine the major practical and theoretical issues in the field.

References

Baer, B., Wolf, M., and Risely, T. (1968). Current dimensions of applied behavior analysis. *Journal of Applied Behavior Analysis, 1*, 91–97.

Bandura, A. (1977). Self-efficacy: Toward a unifying theory of behavioral change. *Psychological Review, 84*, 191–215.

Barnett, N. P., Smoll, F. L., and Smith, R. E. (1992). Effects of enhancing coach-athlete relationships on youth sport attrition. *The Sport Psychologist, 6*, 111–127.

Berryman, J. W. (2002). The rise of boys' sports in the United States, 1900 to 1970. In F. L. Smoll and R. E. Smith (Eds.), *Children and youth in sport: A biopsychosocial perspective* (2nd. ed., pp. 5–17). Dubuque, IA: Kendall/Hunt.

Boring, E. G. (1955). Dual role of the zeitgeist in scientific creativity. *Scientific Monthly, 80*, 101–106.

Boring, E. G. (1963). Science and the meaning of its history. In R. I. Watson and D. T. Campbell (Eds.), *History, psychology and science: Selected papers* (pp. 87–91). New York: Wiley.

Bronfenbrenner, U. (1977). Toward an experimental ecology of human development. *American Psychologist, 32*, 513–531.

Bronowski, J. (1973). *The ascent of man.* Boston: Little, Brown.

Brustad, R. J. (1988). Affective outcomes in competitive youth sport: The influence of intrapersonal and socialization factors. *Journal of Sport and Exercise Psychology, 10*, 307–321.

Brustad, R. J., Babkes, M. L., and Smith, A. L. (2001). Youth in sport: Psychological considerations. In R. N. Singer, H. A. Hausenblas, and C. M. Janelle (Eds.), *Handbook of sport psychology* (2nd ed., pp. 604–635). New York: Wiley.

Brustad, R. J., and Weiss, M. R. (1987). Competence perceptions and sources of worry in high, medium, and low competitive trait-anxious young athletes. *Journal of Sport Psychology, 9*, 97–105.

Corbin, C. B., and Laurie, D. R. (1980, May). *Parental attitudes concerning modifications in baseball for young children.* Paper presented at the North American Society for Psychology of Sport and Physical Activity Conference, Boulder, CO.

Curtis, B., Smith, R. E., and Smoll, F. L. (1979). Scrutinizing the skipper: A study of leadership behaviors in the dugout. *Journal of Applied Psychology, 64*, 391–400.

Danish, S. J., and Nellen, V. C. (1997). New roles for sport psychologists: Teaching life skills through sport at-risk youth. *Quest, 49*, 100–113.

Donelley, P. (1993). Problems associated with youth involvement in high performance sport. In B. R. Cahill, and A. J. Pearl (Eds.), *Intensive participation in children's sports* (pp. 95–126). Champaign, IL: Human Kinetics.

Ewing, M. E., and Seefeldt, V. (1989). *Participation and attrition patterns in America's agency-sponsored and interscholastic sports: An executive summary.* North Palm Beach, FL: Sporting Goods Manufacturers Association.

Ewing, M. E., and Seefeldt, V. (1996). Patterns of participation and attrition in American agency-sponsored youth sports. In F. L. Smoll and R. E. Smith (Eds.), *Children and youth in sport: A biopsychological perspective* (pp. 31–45). Dubuque, IA: Brown and Benchmark.

Feltz, D. (1989). Future directions in theoretical research in sport psychology: From applied psychology toward sport science. In J. S. Skinner, C. B. Corbin, D. M. Landers, P. E. Marlin, and C. L. Wells (Eds.), *Future directions in exercise and sport research* (pp. 435–452). Champaign, IL: Human Kinetics.

Feltz, D., and Ewing, M. E. (1987). Psychological characteristics of elite young athletes. *Medicine and Science in Sport and Exercise, 19,* S98–S105.

Gergen, K. J. (1973). Social psychology as history. *Journal of Personality and Social Psychology, 26,* 309–320.

Gerson, R. (1977). Redesigning athletic competition for children. *Motor Skills: Theory into Practice, 2,* 3–14.

Gill, D. (2000). *Psychological dynamics of sport and exercise* (2nd ed.). Champaign, IL: Human Kinetics.

Gould, D. (1982). Sport psychology in the 1980's: Status, direction and challenge in youth sports research. *Journal of Sport Psychology, 4,* 203–218.

Gould, D. (1993). Intensive sport participation and the prepubescent athlete: Competitive stress and burnout. In B. R. Cahill and A. J. Pearl (Eds.), *Intensive participation in children's sports* (pp. 19–30). Champaign, IL: Human Kinetics.

Gould, D., and Dieffenbach, K. (in press). Psychological issues in youth sports: Competitive anxiety, over training and burnout. In R. M. Malina and M. A. Clark (Eds.), *Organized sports in the lives of children and adolescents.* Champaign, IL: Sagamore.

Gould, D., Eklund, R., Petlichkoff, L., Peterson, K., and Bump, L. (1991). Psychological predictors of state anxiety and performance in age-group wrestlers. *Pediatric Exercise Science, 3,* 198–208.

Gould, D., and Martens, R. (1979). Attitudes of volunteer coaches toward significant youth sport issues. *Research Quarterly, 50,* 369–380.

Gould, D., and Petlichkoff, L. (1988). Participation motivation and attrition in young athletes. In F. L. Smoll, R. A. Magill, and M. J. Ash (Eds.), *Children in sport* (3rd ed., pp. 161–178). Champaign, IL: Human Kinetics.

Gould, D., and Seefeldt, V. (1981). Youth sports research and practice: A selected bibliography. *Physical Educator*, (Suppl.).

Gould, D., Tuffey, S., Udry, E., and Loehr, J. (1996a). Burnout in competitive junior tennis players: I. A quantitative psychological assessment. *The Sport Psychologist, 10*, 322–340.

Gould, D., Tuffey, S., Udry, E., and Loehr, J. (1996b). Burnout in competitive junior tennis players: II. Qualitative analysis. *The Sport Psychologist, 10*, 341–366.

Gould, D., Tuffey, S., Udry, E., and Loehr, J. (1997). Burnout in competitive junior tennis players: III. Individual differences in the burnout experience. *The Sport Psychologist, 11*, 257–276.

Gould, D., and Weiss, M. R. (1987). (Eds.). *Advances in pediatric sport sciences Vol. 2: Behavioral issues*. Champaign, IL: Human Kinetics.

Haffner, E. M., and Presswood, S. (1965). Strong inference and weak interactions. *Science, 149*, 503–510.

Harris, J. C. (1983). Interpreting youth baseball player's understanding of attention, winning and playing the game. *Research Quarterly for Exercise and Sport, 54*, 330–339.

Harter, S. (1981). The development of competence motivation in the mastery of cognitive and physical skills: Is there a place for joy? In G. C. Roberts and D. M. Landers (Eds.), *Psychology of motor behavior and sport—1980* (pp. 3–29). Champaign, IL: Human Kinetics.

Helmreich, R. (1975). Applied social psychology: The unfulfilled promise. *Personality and Social Psychology Bulletin, 1*, 548–560.

Horn, T. S. (1985). Coaches' feedback and changes in children's perceptions of their physical competence. *Journal of Educational Psychology, 77*, 174–186.

Kerlinger, F. N. (1973). *Foundations of behavioral research*. New York: Holt, Rinehart and Winston.

Kuhn, T. S. (1970). *The structure of scientific revolutions*. Chicago: University of Chicago Press.

Locke, L. F. (1969). *Research in physical education*. New York: Teachers College Press.

Marcuse, H. (1964). *One-dimensional man*. Boston: Beacon.

Martens, R. (1979). About smocks and jocks. *Journal of Sport Psychology, 1*, 94–99.

Martens, R. (1987). Science, knowledge and sport psychology. *The Sport Psychologist, 1*, 29–55.

Martens, R., Rivkin, F., and Bump, L. A. (1984). A field study of traditional and nontraditional children's baseball. *Research Quarterly for Exercise and Sport, 55*, 351–355.

Martinek, T., and Hellison, D. R. (1997). Fostering resiliency in underserved youth through physical activity. *Quest, 49*, 34–46.

McGuire, W. J. (1973). The yin and yang of progress in social psychology: Seven koans. *Journal of Personality and Social Psychology, 26*, 446–456.

Newton, M. L., and Duda, J. L. (1992, June). *The relationship of goal perspectives to multidimensional trait anxiety in adolescent tennis players*. Paper presented at the North American Society for the Psychology of Sport and Physical Activity Conference, Pittsburgh, PA.

Passer, M. W. (1983). Fear of failure, fear of evaluation, perceived competence and self-esteem in competitive-trait anxious children. *Journal of Sport Psychology, 5*, 172–188.

Passer, M. W., and Scanlan, T. K. (1980). The impact of game outcome on the post competition affect and performance evaluations of young athletes. In C. H. Nadeau, W. R. Halliwell, K. M. Newell, and G. C. Roberts (Eds.), *Psychology of sport and motor behavior—1979* (pp. 100–111). Champaign, IL: Human Kinetics.

Patton, M. Q. (1990). *Qualitative evaluation and research methods* (2nd ed.). Newbury Park: Sage.

Petlichkoff, L. M. (1996). The dropout dilemma in sport. In O. Bar-Or (Ed.), *Encylopaedia of sports medicine: The child and adolescent athlete* (Vol. 6., pp. 418–430). Oxford, England: Blackwell Scientific.

Platt, J. R. (1964). Strong inference. *Science, 146*, 347–352.

Raedeke, T. D. (1997). Is athlete burnout more than just stress? A sport commitment perspective. *Journal of Sport and Exercise Psychology, 19*, 396–417.

Roberts, G. C. (1980). Children in competition: A theoretical perspective and recommendations for practice. *Motor Skills: Theory into Practice, 4*, 37–50.

Roberts, G. C., and Pascuzzi, D. (1979). Causal attributions in sport: Some theoretical implications. *Journal of Sport Psychology, 1*, 203–211.

Scanlan, T. K. (1986). Competitive stress in children. In M. R. Weiss and D. Gould (Eds.), *Sport for children and youths: 1984 Olympic Scientific Congress Proceedings* (Vol. 10, pp. 113–118). Champaign, IL: Human Kinetics.

Scanlan, T. K., and Lewthwaite, R. (1984). Social psychological aspects of competition for male youth sport participants: I. Predictors of competitive stress. *Journal of Sport Psychology, 6*, 208–226.

Scanlan, T. K., and Passer, M. W. (1978a). Anxiety inducing factors in competitive youth sports. In F. L. Smoll and R. E. Smith (Eds.), *Psychological perspectives in youth sports* (pp. 107–122). Washington, DC: Hemisphere.

Scanlan, T. K., and Passer, M. W. (1978b). Factors related to competitive stress among male youth sports participants. *Medicine and Science in Sports, 10*, 103–108.

Scanlan, T. K., and Passer, M. W. (1979). Sources of competitive stress in young female athletes. *Journal of Sport Psychology, 1*, 151–159.

Schlenkar, B. R. (1974). Social psychology and science. *Journal of Personality and Social Psychology, 29*, 1–15.

Seefeldt, V., and Gould, D. (1980). *The physical and psychological effects of youth sports competition*. Washington, DC: Eric Clearinghouse on Teacher Education.

Shields, D. L. L., and Bredemeier, B. J. L. (1995). *Character development and physical activity*. Champaign, Il: Human Kinetics.

Shields, D. L., Bredemeier, B. L., and Power, F. C. (2002). Character development and children's sport. In F. L. Smoll and R. E. Smith (Eds.), *Children and youth in sport: A biopsychosocial perspective* (2nd ed., pp. 537–559). Dubuque, IA: Kendall/Hunt.

Siedentop, D. (1980). Two cheers for Rainer. *Journal of Sport Psychology, 2*, 2–4.

Smith, A. L. (1999). Perceptions of peer relations and physical activity participation in early adolescence. *Journal of Sport and Exercise Psychology, 21*, 329–350.

Smith, R. E. (1986). Toward a cognitive-affective model of athletic burnout. *Journal of Sport Psychology, 8*, 36–50.

Smith, R. E., and Smoll, F. L. (1978). Sport and the child: Conceptual and research perspectives. In F. L. Smoll and R. E. Smith (Eds.), *Psychological perspectives in youth sports* (pp. 3–13). Washington, DC: Hemisphere.

Smith, R. E., and Smoll, F. L. (1990). Self-esteem and children's reactions to youth sport coaching behaviors: A field study of self-enhancement processes. *Developmental Psychology, 26*, 987–993.

Smith, R. E., Smoll, F. L., and Barnett, N. P. (1995). Reduction of children's sport performance anxiety through social support training and stress-reduction training for coaches. *Journal of Applied Developmental Psychology, 16*, 125–142.

Smith, R. E., Smoll, F. L., and Curtis, B. (1978). Coaching behaviors in Little League Baseball. In F. L. Smoll and R. E. Smith (Eds.), *Psychological perspectives in youth sports* (pp. 173–201). Washington, DC: Hemisphere.

Smith, R. E., Smoll, F. L., and Curtis, B. (1979). Coach effectiveness training: A cognitive-behavioral approach to enhancing relationship skills in youth sport coaches. *Journal of Sport Psychology, 1*, 59–75.

Smith, R. E., Smoll, F. L., and Hunt, E. (1977). A system for the behavioral assessment of athletic coaches. *Research Quarterly, 48*, 401–407.

Smith, R. E., Smoll, F. L., Hunt, E., Curtis, B., and Coppel, D. B. (1979). Psychology and the bad news bears. In G. C. Roberts and K. M. Newell (Eds.), *Psychology of motor behavior and sport—1978* (pp. 109–130). Champaign, IL: Human Kinetics.

Smoll, F. L., and Smith, R. E. (1989). Leadership behaviors in youth sports: A theoretical model and research paradigm. *Journal of Applied Sport Psychology, 19*, 1522–1551.

Smoll, F. L., Smith, R. E., Barnett, N. P., and Everett, J. J. (1993). Enhancement of children's self-esteem through social support training for youth sport coaches. *Journal of Applied Psychology, 78*, 602–610.

Smoll, F. L., Smith, R. E., Curtis, B., and Hunt, E. (1978). Toward a mediational model of coach-player relationships. *Research Quarterly, 49*, 528–541.

Spieth, W. R. (1977). Investigation of two pitching conditions as determinants for developing fundamental skills of baseball. *Research Quarterly, 48*, 408–412.

Suchman, E. A. (1967). *Evaluation research: Principles and practice in public service and social action programs*. New York: Russell Sage Foundation.

Thibaut, J. W., and Kelly, H. H. (1959). *The social psychology of groups*. New York: Wiley.

Thomas, J. R. (1978). Attribution theory and motivation through reward: Practical implications for children's sports. In R. A. Magill, M. J. Ash, and F. L. Smoll (Eds.), *Children in sport: A contemporary anthology* (pp. 149–157). Champaign, IL: Human Kinetics.

Thomas, J. R. (1980). Half a cheer for Rainer and Daryl. *Journal of Sport Psychology, 2,* 266–267.

Weiner, B. (1985). An attribution theory of achievement motivation and emotion. *Psychological Review, 92,* 548–573.

Weiss, C. H. (1972). *Evaluative research: Methods of assessing program effectiveness*. Englewood Cliffs, NJ: Prentice-Hall.

Weiss, M. R. (1991). Psychological skill development in children and adolescents. *The Sport Psychologist, 5,* 333–354.

Weiss, M. R. (1993). Psychological effects of intensive sport participation on children and youth: Self-esteem and motivation. In B. R. Cahill and A. J. Pearl (Eds.), *Intensive participation in children's sports* (pp. 39–69). Champaign, IL: Human Kinetics.

Weiss, M. R., and Bredemeier, B. J. (1983). Developmental sport psychology: A theoretical perspective for studying children in sport. *Journal of Sport Psychology, 5,* 216–230.

Weiss, M. R., and Bredemeier, B. J. (1990). Moral development in sport. *Exercise and Sport Sciences Reviews, 18,* 331–378.

Weiss, M. R., and Chaumeton, N. (1992). Motivational orientations in sport. In T. S. Horn (Ed.), *Advances in sport psychology* (pp. 61–69). Champaign, IL: Human Kinetics.

Weiss, M. R., and Ebbeck, V. (1996). Self-esteem and perceptions of competence in youth sports: Theory, research and enhancement strategies. In O. Bar-Or (Ed.), *The child and adolescent athlete* (pp. 364–382). Oxford: Blackwell Science.

Weiss, M. R., Smith, A. L., and Theeboom, M. (1996). "That's what friends are for": Children's and teenager's perceptions of peer relationships in the sport domain. *Journal of Sport and Exercise Psychology, 18,* 347–379.

Wiggins, D. K. (2002). A history of highly competitive sport for American Children. In F. L. Smoll and R. E. Smith (Eds.), *Children and youth in sport: A biopsychosocial perspective* (2nd ed., pp. 19–37). Dubuque, IA: Kendall/Hunt.

CHAPTER 24

The Continuing Evolution in Youth Sports: What Does the Future Hold?

Vern Seefeldt, Michigan State University
Michael A. Clark, Michigan State University

If you have trouble forecasting the future, do it frequently at very short intervals.

Ancient Proverb-Author Unknown
(In Prochnow and Prochnow, 1983, pg. 437)

Introduction

The words of the anonymous writer could be aptly applied to sports in the United States at the beginning of the millennium. Who, among yesterday's prognosticators, would have forecast that America's sport, baseball, would rank sixth among team sports in popularity, with a 20% loss in participation during the last decade (SGMA Report 2000), or that only 8% of children in urban Detroit would have access to summer sports programs (Seefeldt, 1995), at a time when the cost of new stadiums, arenas and players' salaries were reaching astronomical levels, or that the commissioner of the National Football League would feel compelled to publicly defend the reputation of the League's athletes at a time when violent crimes in the United States were at a 20-year low? These paradoxes suggest that the future of youth sports will be as turbulent and unpredictable as its recent past.

After 50 years of experience in the promotion, supervision and implementation of programs in youth sports, its advocates should have been aware of the issues that were apt to arise in conjunction with the exceptional growth of sports for children. However, tradition, rather than vision, was the watchword as problems descended on organizations that were not prepared to deal with them. Illustrations in point are: failure to provide equal opportunities in sports for girls; inability to provide appropriate educational mandates for an army of volunteer coaches; lack of cooperation between agencies and interscholastic associations; and the inability to curb elitism, in lieu of inclusion, burnout instead of developmentally-appropriate participation and the proliferation of overuse injuries at a time when our knowledge of the science and medicine of sport clearly discourages such incidents.

Apologists for youth sports agencies maintain that their rapid growth has placed insurmountable demands on organizations whose mission is often entrusted to volunteers. Such excuses are misleading for several reasons. (a) Numerous professional organizations whose members have a vested interest in the health and safety of children and youth have provided guidelines for the safe and rational conduct of youth sports. For example, the medical profession, chiefly through the American Academy of Pediatrics and the American College of Sports Medicine, has issued over 33 position stands, guidelines and opinion statements regarding competitive sports for youth (See Appendix). These guidelines are supported by an abundant literature in such areas as medicine, education, psychology, engineering and physiology, advocating changes that would contribute to the safety of young athletes. (b) There is a general assumption that program sponsors have a prerequisite responsibility for the psychological and physiological welfare of those who enroll in their programs. This premise has been supported so consistently in courts of law that standards of care are now available in textbook form (Herbert, 1994; Cotten and Cotten, 1997).

The continuing popularity of organized athletics for children implies that a significant number of adults believe that the inherent benefits of sport participation outweigh the potential detrimental effects. These increases in participation suggest that parents who enroll their children in competitive athletic programs either agree with the current philosophy and operation of the programs or they have sufficient confidence in the programs' sponsors to assume that the required changes will take place as soon as the conflict between tradition and new information can be resolved.

Whether the promoters of children's sport deserve the annual vote of confidence they receive from millions of parents who enroll their children in competitive athletics is an issue that has aroused considerable controversy. The media's persistent attention to the problems of youth sports has stimulated the scientific community to conduct investigations regarding the benefits and consequences of children's involvement in sport. Specialists in sports medicine, sport psychology, sport sociology, sport physiology, biomechanics, and motor behavior now consider children to be legitimate subjects in their investigations. The interdisciplinary focus on children and youth in the 1990s rivaled the attention that was formerly reserved for adults and elderly Americans.

The attention of scientists to the alleged problems of youth sports has resulted in two important outcomes that have been missing heretofore in its turbulent history: (a) An interdisciplinary account of what happens to children as a result of their athletic participation has gradually emerged, and (b) the conditions that have been proven to be detrimental to the welfare of children have prompted some changes in the rules and policies of the various sponsoring agencies. On the basis of the modifications made in youth sports during the last decade, proponents of youth sports have reason to believe that additional changes in the structure and conditions under which competition takes place will be forthcoming.

History of Youth Sports

Children's sport programs that are supervised by adults have been immersed in controversy almost from their modest beginning on the playgrounds of New York City at the turn of the century. Berryman (this volume) chronicled the growth of sport for children from the time sports emerged as an after-school recreational activity that was designed to prevent juvenile delinquency to the time nearly a century later when groups are again turning to youth sports and recreation as a means of structuring the nonschool hours of children and youth (Carnegie Corporation of New York, 1992). Berryman's review reveals several important historical facts that are commonly lost in the debate over the relative merits of school-based versus agency-sponsored sports: (a) that youth Sports were an outgrowth of the regular public school curriculum; (b) that sports were initiated as a diversionary activity to meet the perceived competitive needs of boys; and (c) that certain sports became highly competitive in a matter of years, even when they were under the auspices of public school personnel. Therefore the argument that youth sports are beset with problems because they are under the auspices of volunteers, primarily parents, does not seem to have historical validity.

The withdrawal of support for competitive athletics prior to high school age by public school educators in the 1930s has had a lasting influence on youth sport programs. The elimination of athletic competition from many elementary school programs ushered in an increase in the number of programs in physical education and intramural sports. The new school-based programs were to emphasize the acquisition of skills for all children, in lieu of the specialized attention that was reputed to be directed to a few highly skilled athletes in the interscholastic sports. However, withdrawal of public school sponsorship of competitive sports for children and youth prompted a number of family-oriented agencies such as the Young Men's Christian Association (YMCA), Young Women's Christian Association (YWCA), and the Police Athletic League (PAL) to begin offering competitive athletics in private facilities. These offerings became more numerous and diverse as additional agencies, created for the sole purpose of offering sport competition for children, were established.

The creation of nonschool agencies in the 1930s through 1950s for the specific purpose of teaching sports skills to children and youth created a paradox that persists to the present day. Schools that employ personnel who are educated to teach movement skills and to serve as coaches are offering limited opportunities for children and youth to learn the sports skills of their culture, whereas nonschool agencies are spending substantially greater amounts of time teaching sports skills to children—but under the direction of administrators and coaches who are generally not well qualified to conduct such programs. Transfer of responsibility for teaching sports skills to children and youth, from schools to agencies, is still in progress. The Centers for Disease Control and Prevention (2000) reported a dramatic decline in high school students who attended daily physical education classes (from 42% in 1991 to 29% in

1999) at the same time as the Sporting Goods Manufacturers' Association survey reported an increase in all organized team sports participation for children and adolescents (The SGMA Report 2000). Thus, the self-perception of children that they learn their sports skills in the youth sports arena, rather than in physical education classes, may be closer to reality today than when it was initially reported in 1978 (Joint Legislative Study of Youth Sports—Phase II).

This estrangement between the public schools and youth sports agencies is also reflected in memberships of professional organizations. For example, the professional organizations of physical educators have few members whose primary interest is interscholastic or recreational sports. Concomitantly, organizations that serve professional recreation seldom attract physical educators and coaches as members. The lack of professional fellowship has become a dilemma for interscholastic sports administrators who must frequently enter the ranks of agency sports to recruit coaches. Non-faculty coaches have been reluctant to acquire the minimum level of education that is deemed a prerequisite for entry-level coaches in scholastic sports (McCann, 1997).

The indifference of public school personnel to the agency-sponsored sport programs that sprang up as replacements for elementary school athletic programs frequently led to animosity and hostility between the two groups. This unfriendly attitude was fueled periodically by policy statements from the American Medical Association, the American Academy of Pediatrics, and the National Association for Health, Physical education and Recreation (Low, 1968), which opposed highly organized sports activities for children before the ninth grade. Despite these statements of position by educational and medical associations, the number of programs and participants in youth sports continued to grow, unmindful of the unsolicited advice that was directed at them.

By 1970 the opportunities for regional and national competition in children's athletics had expanded to include virtually every sport in which competition was available at the adult level. National sponsorship of programs also seemed to increase the intensity of competition to the point where even the agencies who proclaimed a philosophy of "everyone plays" contradicted their own mottoes by supporting national tournaments in which the elimination of all teams except the eventual victor was inherent in the structure of the competition. Children also became involved in sport at younger ages. Data from the *Joint Legislative Study on Youth Sports,* Phase II (1978) indicated a modal age of 8 years for boys and 10 years for girls (see Table 24.1) as the time when competition in a specific sport began, with many children already competing at 4 or 5 years of age. These data were supplemented by a study conducted nearly a decade later (Ewing and Seefeldt, 1989) that indicated the dropout or attrition in youth sports was well under way by 10 years of age in both boys and girls (see Table 24.2).

Table 24.1   Percentages Reflecting Ages When Children First Enrolled in an Organized Sport

Chronological Age	Boys	Cumulative Total	Girls	Cumulative Total
Before age 3	4	—	2	—
3	3	7	3	5
4	6	13	6	11
5	13	26	9	20
6	10	36	10	30
7	16	52	11	41
8	17	69	15	56
9	13	82	12	68
10	9	91	14	82
11	4	95	8	90
12	3	98	6	96
13	1	99	2	98
14	1	100	2	100

Source: *Joint Legislative Study on Youth Sports: Phase II* (1978), Copyright © 1978 by the Michigan State University Youth Sports Institute.

Evidence of a changing attitude about youth sports by physicians, educators, and administrators began to emerge in the 1970s. The culmination of this conciliatory position occurred at a meeting sponsored by the National Association for Sport and Physical Education in Washington, DC (R. Merrick, personal communication, November 5, 1976) in 1977. Two documents, *Youth Sports Guide for Coaches and Parents* (Thomas, 1977) and *Guidelines for Children's Sports* (Martens and Seefeldt, 1979), summarize the content of the historic meeting between two groups: those who formerly opposed children's sport and those who represented the nonschool sport agencies.

Table 24.2   Percentage of Participants, by Chronological Age, Who Indicated That They Will Not Play Next Year, a Sport They Played This Year

Sport	10	11	12	13	14	15	16	17	18
Baseball	8.5	12.5	14.9	14.0	13.9	13.8	9.7	6.6	2.7
Basketball	5.0	6.8	11.5	13.8	19.4	18.6	11.5	8.3	3.3
Football	3.3	8.1	9.6	12.1	14.8	17.7	13.4	13.3	5.6
Gymnastics	10.6	17.1	17.1	15.0	13.2	11.9	5.7	3.9	1.7
Softball	6.3	11.1	13.5	12.5	15.8	16.9	10.0	8.2	2.7
Swimming	9.7	14.7	12.8	12.1	14.1	11.3	10.9	8.3	2.5
Tennis	6.0	12.0	11.6	14.6	12.3	16.0	10.5	8.8	5.3
Volleyball	2.9	5.4	10.0	12.6	22.2	18.5	13.4	10.2	2.9
Wrestling	6.2	7.6	9.2	9.7	12.9	17.7	12.9	15.2	6.6
Ice hockey	2.9	6.7	11.5	19.2	15.4	10.6	15.4	12.2	4.8

From Ewing, M., and Seefeldt, V. (1989). *Participation and Attrition Patterns in American Agency Sponsored and Interscholastic Sports: An Executive Summary.* Sports Goods Manufacturer's Association, North Palm Beach, FL.

In essence, the two groups agreed to recognize that athletic competition for children had become an enduring part of our culture. The conditions under which healthful competition should occur were described in a "Bill of Rights for Young Athletes" (Martens and Seefeldt, 1979). A significant change in the attitudes that physicians and educators held about youth sports was now a matter of record. Instead of their previous disapproval of athletic competition for children, its former antagonists and protagonists now agreed to work together for more desirable conditions under which competition for children and youth should be organized and implemented. However, the latent resistance to organized sports for children lingered for some time, as reflected by the position statement issued in 1981 by the American Academy of Pediatrics, which gave reluctant approval, but enumerated the precautions that should be addressed prior to permitting children to participate in competitive sports.

Demographics and Youth Sports

Predictions regarding the future of sports are commonly based on the state of the economy and confidence of consumers, both of which are indirectly related to the sale of products used in recreation and leisure (State of the Industry: SGMA 2000, pg. 20). However, in youth sports it is inevitable that the factors of gender, ethnicity and geographical location play a major role in determining the type, frequency and intensity of participation. The following statistics indicate that it is no longer sufficient to describe the status of new data by simply adding to participation rates or to expect that the popularity of sports will retain the rank order of previous years. The first decade of the century promises to bring significant changes in the kinds of activities that are popular, determined by the ethnicity, gender and geographical location of the 5 to 18 year age group.

As indicated in Table 24.3, Table 24.4 and Figure 24.1, the 1990s were a period of rapid increase in the numbers of youth aged 5 to 17. This so-called "echo" of the Baby Boom resulted in a 14% increase in the population of this age group during the decade. Although sport-specific data were difficult to obtain, there is anecdotal evidence that the decade also saw an increase in organized youth sports. However, the projections for the 5 to 17 age group during the first decade of the new century should give all reason for concern. Table 24.3 indicates that there will be little growth in this segment of the population. Overall the number of youth will expand by a mere 1% during the years from 2000 to 2010. More importantly, growth will be focused in the older segment of the population—those 14 to 17 years of age. The 5 to 13 age group will actually decrease in total numbers.

No matter how striking the data appear at first glance, they describe only the broadest outline of the changes in store. To realize the extent of changes in ethnicity, it is necessary to look at other data to discover how the face of America will change in the coming decade. As Table 24.4 clearly shows, our society will become increasingly diverse, with all the growth in the youth population occurring among people of color. Whereas at the start of the decade, the population of white youth accounted for 64.8% of the total, by the end of the decade (2010) they will represent less than 60% of the population (59.5%). African-American youth, currently 14.8% of youth, will decline to 14.1 %. Less than 1% of the 5–17 age group will be Native Americans. Moreover, this will not be simply a decline in percentage; these segments of the population will literally decrease in number. On the other hand, the Hispanic/Latino and Asian/Pacific Islander segments will increase by a third. By 2010, 20% of youth will be Latinos, and 5.4%, Asian/Pacific Islanders. At the same time, there will be a small increase (approximately 0.1%) in the number of females.

In short, the 1990s were a decade of expansion, particularly among the younger age group. However, in the coming years this population will remain stable. The very youngest ages (5 to 13) will decrease in number, while the high school aged youth

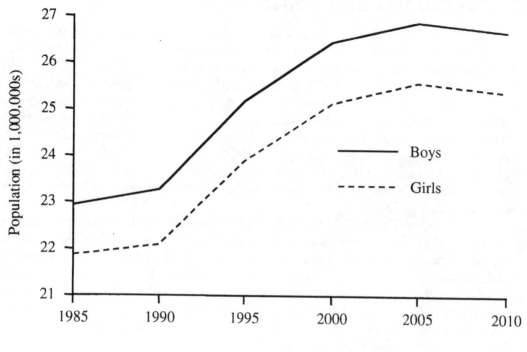

Figure 24.1. Population estimates and projections for the 5 to 17 age group, by gender, for several years. Source: U.S. Census Bureau figures available at http://www.census.gov/population/www/estimates/popest.html and http://www.census.gov/population/www/projections/popproj/html.

will continue to increase by about 6%. More dramatic will be the change in the ethnic make up of the youth population, as white and African-American youth become a smaller portion of the population. With an over all decrease in the 5 to 13 age group, program providers wanting to maintain their participation rates will have to attract older youth—who often are the very ones dropping out of sports (Seefeldt, 1995). Further, sponsors will be asked to provide services to an increasingly diverse population—one that involves more youth of color and slightly more females.

Table 24.3 Population Estimates and Projections (in 1000s) of Various Age Groups, by Gender and Total Population, for Selected Years, 1985 to 2010.

Population Groups	Age Groups	1985	1990	1995	2000	2005	2010	% Change 1985–2000	% Change 2000–2010
Males	5 to 13	15,300	16,386	17,506	18,309	18,144	18,056	19.7%	−1.4%
	14 to 17	7,627	6,849	7,632	8,096	8,709	8,583	6.1%	6.0%
	Sum 5 to 17	22,927	23,235	25,138	26,405	26,853	26,639	15.2%	0.9%
Females	5 to 13	14,592	15,617	16,689	17,465	17,331	17,265	19.7%	−1.1%
	14 to 17	7,263	6,473	7,196	7,637	8,222	8,098	5.1%	6.0%
	Sum 5 to 17	21,855	22,090	23,885	25,102	25,553	25,363	14.9%	1.0%
Totals	5 to 13	29,893	32,003	34,195	35,774	35,475	35,321	19.7%	−1.3%
	14 to 17	14,889	13,322	14,828	15,733	16,931	16,681	5.7%	6.0%
	Sum 5 to 17	44,782	45,325	49,023	51,507	52,406	52,002	15.0%	1.0%

Source: U.S. Census Bureau figures at http://www.census.gov/population/www/estimates/nat_80s_detail.html; estimates at http://www.census.gov/population/www/estimates/nation2.html; and population projections at http://www.census.gov/population/www/projections/natsum.html (January 30, 2001).

Table 24.4 Population Projections (in 1000s) Among Various Age Groups by Ethnicity for Selected Years, 2000 to 2010

Race/ Ethnicity	Age Groups	2000	2005	2010	% Change, 2000–2010
White	5 to 13	22,965	21,813	20,845	–9.2%
	14 to 17	10,407	10,707	10,087	–3.1%
	Total 5 to 17	33,372	32,520	30,932	–7.3%
Black	5 to 13	5,325	5,020	4,929	–7.4%
	14 to 17	2,297	2,588	2,413	5.1%
	Total 5 to 17	7,622	7,608	7,342	–3.7%
Hispanic	5 to 13	5,667	6,590	7,280	28.5%
	14 to 17	2,225	2,708	3,137	41.0%
	Total 5 to 17	7,892	9,298	10,417	32.0%
Asian/ Pacific Islander	5 to 13	1,471	1,726	1,933	31.4%
	14 to 17	640	753	887	38.6%
	Total 5 to 17	2,111	2,479	2,820	33.6%
Native American	5 to 13	346	325	334	–3.5%
	14 to 17	165	174	157	–4.8%
	Total 5 to 17	511	499	491	–3.9%

Source: U.S. Census Bureau population projections at http://www.census.gov/population/www/projections/natsum.html (January 30, 2001).

The demographics regarding the current status and projected changes in gender and ethnicity, by age group, are incomplete without information about the lifestyles and activity preferences of the various groups. Unfortunately, such data did not accompany the projections of population heterogeneity, forcing prognosticators to look elsewhere for clues to activity preferences.

The National Federation of State High School Associations (NFHS) provides reliable, comprehensive data on sports participation among older youth. The NFHS began reporting statistics in 1971 and now provides an annual report of students' sports participation in the nation's high schools. Figure 24.2 provides the total number of participants over the last 30 years. Note the dramatic increase in the number of girls playing sports in the first years after the adoption of Title IX; the relative stability of participation throughout the 1980s and early 1990s; the continued lag in participation of girls even 25 years after the passage of Title IX; the lack of growth in numbers of boys participating during the period from 1980 to 2000; the slight narrowing of the gap between participation by boys and girls in recent years.

If the trends suggested in Figure 24.2 continue, the total number of boys playing high school sports will change little over the next decade. In fact, the percentage of high school aged boys involved in sports increased less than 4% from 1985–86 (43.8%) to 1999–2000 (47.7%). The percentage of high school aged girls active in sports increased more sharply, from 24.9% in 1985–86 to 35.0% in 1999–2000. These data indicate that the gap in participation between the genders will continue to narrow as a result of a slightly higher participation rate among girls—and a continued recognition of their right to compete in organized sports programs.

The aggregate numbers for interscholastic sports participation by boys and girls are not nearly as revealing as the data for individual sports. Table 24.5 provides data reflecting the ten most popular high school sports. While there has been no change in the sports most attractive to boys, it is worth noting that seven of them actually have fewer participants than they did 25 years ago. Soccer has been the only sport to enjoy

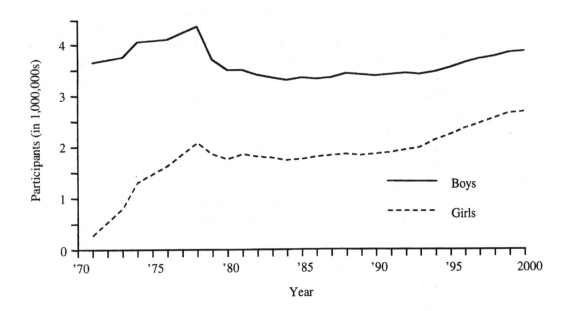

Figure 24.2. Total number of participants in high school sports, by gender, 1971–2000. Source: Plotted from data provided by the National Federation of State High School Associations, http://www.Nfhs.org/part_survey99-00.htm.

real growth among boys. For girls the numbers have grown dramatically: nearly two-thirds more girls were active in athletics in 2000 than were active in 1975. Although there has been some change among the most popular sports for girls, 7 of the 10 most popular in 1975–76 retained their popularity in the 1999–2000 school year.

Basketball and track and field have consistently been the most popular sports among girls, but their growth has been limited. Involvement in tennis, swimming and volleyball has expanded more rapidly. Two sports (cross-country and softball) saw huge increases, and soccer—once it became established—grew quickly. This may reflect social and historical factors. For example, in the early 1970s basketball and track and field were acceptable activities for girls, and even before Title IX schools occasionally included these sports in their programs. Thus, there was relatively less room for their expansion after 1972. Tennis and volleyball were often the next sports made available to girls. Softball and soccer tended to be later additions, and so their increases are larger. Finally, the 1999–2000 report (NFHS, 2000) included a new sport among the ten most popular: competitive cheer, which attracted significant numbers of girls shortly after its recognition as a varsity sport.

Projections from the data provided by NFHS indicate that nearly half of all high school boys will play sports, although they will less likely be involved in the traditional "big three" (i.e., football, basketball and track and field). Rather, boys more probably will play soccer, golf and baseball. Tennis seems destined to experience little change in participation, but numbers of participants in wrestling and swimming are declining. Among girls, all of the most attractive sports may well continue to increase in popularity. Potential increases depend upon the commitment of the schools and the allocation of resources to the programs. Expansion in girls basketball, volleyball and track and field is open to question, because these sports are so well established. On the other hand, there seems little doubt that soccer and competitive cheer have continued growth potential. Further, just as competitive cheer found a place among the most popular sports, there may be other sports whose popularity will grow. Some evidence suggests that ice hockey, water polo, bowling and lacrosse are developing a following among both boys and girls.

The changing demography of children and youth in the United States will influence the participation patterns in youth sports programs. Changes that will be most compelling are:

- Youth 5 to 13 will decrease in number.
- The 14 to 17 age group will grow by about 6%.
- Over 40% of young people will be youth of color.
- There will be a slight increase in the proportion of females.

These data indicate that the traditional participants in youth sports will decrease in number. No longer can program sponsors rely on young white males to fill their rosters

Table 24.5 Number of Participants in the Ten Most Popular High School Sports for Boys and Girls in Selected School Years[1]

	Boys					Girls				
	1975–76	1985–86	1995–96	1999–2000	% Change	1975–76	1985–86	1995–96	1999–2000	% Change
Football	1,077,599	953,516	957,573	1,002,734	-6.9%	—	—	—	—	—
Basketball	688,410	505,130	545,596	541,130	-21.4%	387,507	293,881	445,869	451,600	16.5%
Track/field	644,813	446,286	454,645	480,791	-25.4%	395,271	343,112	379,060	405,305	2.5%
Baseball/Softball	399,900	393,905	444,476	451,701	13.0%	133,458	220,459	305,217	343,001	157.0%
Wrestling	334,107	247,653	221,162	239,105	-28.4%	—	—	—	—	—
Cross-country	204,087	154,590	168,203	183,139	-10.3%	30,899	85,272	140,187	154,021	398.5%
Golf	154,457	112,602	140,011	165,857	7.4%	32,190	—	39,634	—	—
Tennis	143,970	128,820	136,534	139,507	-3.1%	112,166	119,944	146,573	159,740	42.4%
Swimming	125,234	81,516	81,000	86,640	-30.8%	85,013	83,204	111,360	138,475	62.9%
Soccer	112,743	196,028	283,728	330,044	192.7%	—	85,173	209,287	270,273	217.3%
Volleyball	—	—	—	—	—	245,032	279,601	357,576	382,755	56.2%
Field hockey	—	—	—	—	—	—	84,446	56,142	58,372	-30.9%
Gymnastics	—	—	—	—	—	79,461	34,474	—	21,620[2]	-72.8%
Skiing	—	—	—	—	—	5,367	—	—	4,225[2]	-21.3%
Competitive spirit	—	—	—	—	—	—	—	—	64,319	—
Total	4,109,021	3,344,275	3,634,052[3]	3,861,749[3]	-6.0%	1,645,039	1,807,121	2,367,936[3]	2,675,874[3]	62.7%

[1] Source: The National Federation of State High School Associations (2001).
[2] Drops out of the 10 most popular sports list.
[3] Does not include athletes in "combined sports." In some instances, these would be girls involved in wrestling or playing sports such as tennis, golf or hockey on teams otherwise identified as "boys" teams. In other cases, these are sports involving co-educational teams. The numbers range from 15,000 to 20,000 per year.

and replenish those who have outgrown the program's offerings. The difference will not only be in those who are playing but in the activities in which they participate.

Recent data on the activity preferences of the various ethnic groups are not available. However, Ewing and Seefeldt (1989) found important differences among the ethnic groups regarding their preferences for specific sports (see Figure 24.3) which indicate that the population identified as "White" fell near the middle of the range of interest in all sports. Concurrently, African-Americans indicated a strong preference for baseball, basketball and football. Respondents classified as "Oriental" were most interested in soccer, tennis, volleyball, softball and wrestling. The preferences by ethnic youth suggest that these sports may not be as seriously affected by population shifts. However, there is a major cause for concern to program sponsors in the responses of Hispanic subjects, because in nearly every instance, this group expressed the least interest in sports. In other words, the most rapidly growing segment of the population is least likely to look favorably on becoming involved in sports. Whatever the reason for this result, it bodes ill for participation levels, especially among the younger age group.

Consequences of the changes in demography suggest that:

- The overall youth population will not grow, so program sponsors will be drawing from a dwindling pool of participants. This will increase competition among sports for a smaller pool of potential clients.
- Because of the smaller pool of potential clients, sponsoring groups must develop new strategies for attracting participants.
- In the coming decade, participants are a bit more likely to be female and certainly more likely to be of color. Ethnic groups differ in their preference and sponsors must adapt program offerings accordingly.
- Girls have become involved in many of the traditional sports offered to them, but in recent years alternatives such as competitive cheer and lacrosse have become available and seem likely to attract increasing interest.
- As the Hispanic and Asian/Pacific Islander populations grow, certain sports may become more popular. Soccer is most likely to benefit, but so may tennis, track and field and volleyball.
- Because Hispanic youth report being less interested in sports, strategies to attract them will have to change. Alternative activities may have to be explored; new recruiting techniques may have to develop.
- Native Americans report being very interested in track and field, gymnastics, swimming, football and basketball. However, this population group is very small and appears to represent even smaller numbers in the future.

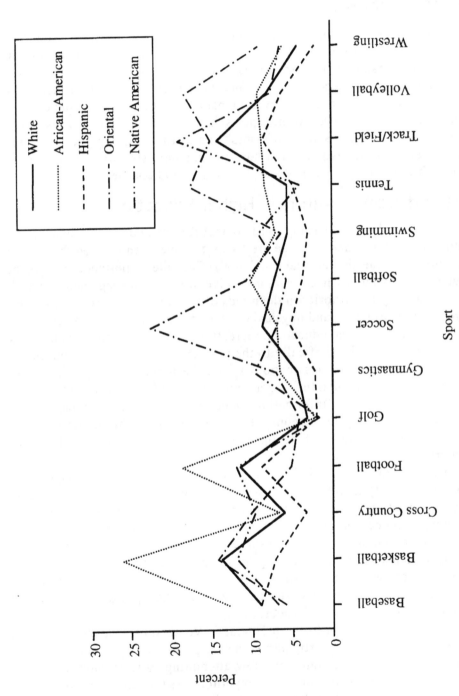

Figure 24.3. Percent of each ethnic group indicating an interest in participating in a particular scholastic sport offering. Source: M. Ewing and V. Seefeldt (1989). *Participation and Attrition Patterns in American Agency-Sponsored and Interscholastic Sports: An Executive Summary.* Sporting Goods Manufacturers' Association, North Palm Beach, Florida.

Agents of Reform

Changes in youth sports primarily depend on the degree to which the attitudes of its adult leaders can be modified. These modifications have generally received their impetus from the leadership at the institutions where teachers, recreation directors, sport managers, and coaches receive their formal education. This section identifies five categories of agents who are primarily responsible for the education and experiences of individuals who control youth sports in the United States. These five categories include administrators and professors from institutions of higher learning, directors of recreation, state high school associations, administrators of single-sport agencies, and public school physical education teachers and coaches.

Educators and Administrators in Higher Education

The attitudes and values concerning sport competition that coaches, teachers, and recreation directors support and advance are likely to have been derived from their former instructors. To the degree that curricula reflect the importance of subject matter, as determined by faculty in colleges and universities, the management of youth sports holds a relatively low priority in the minds of those who prepare professional workers in recreation, athletics, and physical education. Few courses in the curricula of students who choose physical education, recreation, or sport management as areas of concentration are devoted specifically to the problems and proposed solutions of age-group athletic competition. In situations where the topic is included in course offerings, it receives the treatment that is generally reserved for unimportant content. This direct or subtle omission of information about youth sports in the preparation of students who will eventually be responsible for guiding the athletic activities of children is an inexcusable form of negligence on the part of those in charge of academic programs.

In addition to providing current information about children's athletic competition, administrators and faculty members in higher education can influence the attention directed at youth sport by: (a) providing students with practical day-to-day experiences in planning, conducting, and evaluating sport programs, (b) encouraging students to become involved in basic and field-based research involving young athletes, and (c) placing students as interns into programs that are conducted according to an acceptable philosophy, with sound operating procedures. Placing students into situations where they can be closely supervised as they learn their profession is a model that has been used successfully for decades.

Although research pertaining to the problems in youth sports has not kept pace with the phenomenal increase of participation in such programs, many scientists who had previously concentrated on adults are now attempting to learn more about the effects of athletic participation on youthful competitors. As the intensity and duration of training programs for children have increased, we have learned that children encounter problems of a physiological and psychological nature similar to those observed for decades in adult competitors. Scientists, when working in the area of childhood, face the problems of defining additional intervening variables and determining their influence on an immature, growing system. Educators should apprise their students of the potential problems that exist in children's sport and, whenever possible, enlist their assistance in conducting research that seeks basic and practical solutions to these problems.

Directors of Recreational Programs

Directors of recreation are essential agents in any attempt to change youth sports because they usually have a direct involvement with the coaches and officials who actually conduct the practices and contests. Although sport-specific agencies with regional or national affiliations conduct many programs at the local level, the vast majority of youth sport programs exist under the auspices of the local recreation department. Even programs that are controlled through a national affiliation often depend on local facilities, administrators, and coaches for their implementation. Therefore, the philosophy and operational procedures promoted by the local recreation directors have the potential of exerting a profound influence on youth sports, even when the programs are not initiated or maintained by the Recreation Department.

Frequently, recreation directors have been accused of acting as "activity brokers" by relinquishing their responsibility for youth sports to any agency or service club that offers to conduct the programs. Another criticism is that recreation directors are more concerned about the number who participate than they are about the quality of their participation. Such criticism seems appropriate when recreation directors permit other agencies to conduct sports programs for youth in municipal facilities even when the philosophies of the two groups are incompatible.

An increasingly important role for directors of recreation is to serve as advocates for youth who participate in programs that accept a broad range of skills and abilities. Such support is needed to counteract the strong thrust from programs that serve only elite athletes. Adults are also demanding a greater share of the facilities that were once reserved for young athletes. Fiscal constraints have intensified the need for directors of recreation to sponsor pay-for-play activities, which favor adults and disenfranchise younger participants.

Desirable changes in youth sports depend on the acknowledgment by recreation directors that athletic competition involving children is here to stay, that it has potentially beneficial and detrimental effects, and that the potential for beneficial results can be influenced by strong leadership within the local recreation program. The abdication of responsibility for youth sport programs to other agencies by recreation directors will usually generate more problems than it solves.

State High School Associations

Associations that govern interscholastic athletics in the United States are the most stable and enduring of all youth sports governing bodies. Many of the interscholastic associations were established in the 1920s and '30s and have functioned as quasi-independent members of the National Federation of State High School Associations (NFHS) since its inception in 1920 (Forsythe, 1950). Not only have the state interscholastic associations provided constancy in the administration of school-based athletics, but they have been staunch guardians of amateurism and defenders of academic-based eligibility. Their stance in opposition to commercialism and undue influence also sets them apart from other sports-promoting organizations.

High school associations will continue their prevailing dominance of youth athletics for the 13–18 year age groups because their product—educational athletics—is unique and delivered with maximum efficiency. In addition to the orderly oversight and administration of athletic contests and tournaments, the interscholastic associations have launched exemplary school-wide programs that not only benefit athletes but the entire student body.

The following initiatives have been launched by the Michigan High School Athletic Association (MHSAA) (Roberts, 2001), cited here as examples of the leadership role that scholastic associations have had in the safe and sensible conduct of youth sports. (a) *The Women in Sports Leadership Conference,* now in its 13th year, encourages the participation of girls in sports, challenges girls and women to aspire to leadership roles in athletics, and honors past and present leaders. (b) *Program for Athletic Coaches' Education,* also in its 13th year, promoted and supported solely by the MHSAA, designed for entry-level and experienced coaches who seek accreditation commensurate with the National Standards for Athletic Coaches. (c) *Sportsmanship Summit,* a biennial conference to educate, encourage, reinforce and strategize about sportsmanship and its role in educational athletics. (d) *Legacy,* a program to encourage seniors in high school to become sports officials by working with mentors in every phase of officiating. (e) *Good Sports Are Winners,* a campaign that defines sportsmanship in practical terms and provides instruments for the self-assessment of the behavior of coaches, athletes and the student body. Enumerates the tangible and intangible awards available to those who advance exemplary sportsmanship. (f) *TWODAE,* a start-up program intended to attract women to sports officiating. Provides instruction, encouragement and support to female officials as they begin their careers in sports officiating.

The proactive accomplishments of the state high school associations in the areas of academic eligibility, amateurism, conduct of athletes, sportsmanship and resistance to commercialism distinguish them from agency-sponsored and intercollegiate sports programs. The unique role of interscholastic athletics and their potential demise were articulated succinctly by Robert Kanaby, Executive Director of the National Federation of State High School Associations (1993). He stated, "If anything is going to destroy high school sports in this country, it's going to be that people will believe that sports have lost their educational purpose. Once that happens, we're not going to have them anymore" (pg. 26). The millions of teen-aged Americans who annually benefit from interscholastic sports programs can be thankful for the prolonged leadership by the personnel who conduct school sports. Parents and promoters of youth sports everywhere are indebted to scholastic associations for their unremitting resistance to elements that would deter school sports from achieving their educational objectives.

Managers of Single-Sport Agencies

Single-sport agencies are defined here as organizations that promote and sponsor competition in a specific sport for children of designated age ranges (Seefeldt and Ewing, 1998). Examples of single-sport agencies are Little League Baseball, Pop Warner Football, USA Hockey, and the American Youth Soccer Organization. Single-sport agencies have been instrumental in elevating certain sports for children to their present levels of popularity and deserve much of the credit for the uniformity of rules and playing conditions throughout the nation. However, these agencies have also received much of the criticism for conducting programs in ways that some adults consider to be unacceptable to the welfare of children.

Single-sport agencies have generally been responsible for the standard rules and modifications that distinguish children's sport from the sport of their adult prototypes. They have also been instrumental in developing a system of adult volunteer leadership that permits these programs to operate at low overhead costs to local communities. Also ascribed to single-sport agencies by their detractors is a desire to maintain complete control over programs, to impose a set of inflexible playing conditions on local programs, to conduct "elitist" programs wherein only the skillful athletes are retained, and to extract membership fees in exchange for providing little more than playing rules and a tournament structure, while imposing on local residents the responsibility of implementing the program and instructing its participants. The amplified intensity associated with competition in interleague, regional, and national play is also attributed to sponsors of nationally affiliated programs.

If single-sport agencies are to maintain their roles as leaders in the organization and promotion of sport for children, they must adjust more readily to the suggestions for change that are supported by science and experimental evidence. In an era where litigation is the common recourse for negligent acts, the safety and welfare of youthful competitors has received greater attention in the 1990s and is likely to become even more prominent in the future. The current inflexibility of rules and lack of a willingness to adopt the safety features that accompany many of the scientifically-based modifications in equipment and playing rules for youthful competitors will become increasingly intolerable to adult leaders in local programs as they become more knowledgeable about the potential to promote greater safety through local control. A philosophy that places the single-sport agency in a role that facilitates, rather than controls, the leadership of local communities in sport-program management is likely to become the modus operandi at the local level in the future.

Public School Personnel

The concessions that educators made to the involvement of children in athletic competition (Martens and Seefeldt, 1979) were based on the assumption that great changes would occur in current operating procedure by organizers of sport programs. Implicit in these changes was the important role that physical education teachers, coaches, and public school administrators would have in bringing about the cooperation between personnel in the public schools and the youth agencies. Central to such negotiations were the resolution of such problems as overlapping seasons, eligibility of participants, frequency and intensity of competition, age when competition should begin, and the emphasis to be placed on the athlete's skill acquisition versus winning as the primary criterion for success. There are indications that some resolution to these problems has occurred, but changes have been slower than anticipated.

Evidence of changes that are designed to affect the safety of young athletes is most prominent in the design of equipment. For example, in baseball such changes as the visor on the batter's helmet, adjustable personalized helmets, low-compression baseballs, progressive-release bases, and the double base at first base have all been introduced in the last decade. The low rate of acceptance of some of these safety features is an indication of the traditional and conservative nature of adults who control children's sports.

Much of the control over athletic facilities and the expertise for teaching and managing sport programs currently lies with the coaches and administrators of public schools. Consequently, it appears that they are also in a position to make the greatest contribution to the youth sport movement. The "Bill of Rights for Young Athletes" argues distinctly that such a contribution is possible without compromising the principles upon which physical education, interscholastic athletics, and youth sport programs are based. Agency-sponsored youth sport programs can no longer be viewed as desirable substitutes for physical education programs or as farm systems for the interscholastic athletic program. If the emphasis in youth sport programs is to be on maximum participation and skill acquisition for all individuals, there is no need to fear that overexposure and exploitation will occur in agency-sponsored sports or that children's participation in them will be detrimental.

Projections for the Future of Youth Sports

The history of youth sports suggests that the future has room for both optimism and pessimism. The following projections for changes in youth sports are overwhelmingly optimistic. This does not imply, however, that youth sports are in a position where any change would be an improvement. In fact, any changes would be detrimental to the degree that they emulate the adult model of sport participation and ignore what has been learned about training, motivation, goal setting, and other parameters of competition as they relate to children and youth.

The optimism about the future of youth sports is generated by the abundance of information pertaining to youth sports from the scientific community and the widespread desire of administrators, officials, coaches and parents to provide the best possible experiences for children. These predictions are also influenced by variables such as population migration, energy costs, structure of the family and the changing attitudes toward persons with handicapping conditions. To the degree that these variables are incorporated into the plans of program providers, they will be instrumental in determining the direction of youth sport programs in the next decade.

Scientific Inquiry

The influence of science on youth sports during the 1990s has eclipsed the importance of any other variable because of the previously depressed status of knowledge concerning the development of children involved in intensive physical activity. Many training programs for children formerly were modeled after those of adults, but without the associated experimental evidence to support them. Knowledge about adults in stressful situations is relatively sophisticated because of the research that has been conducted during the past three decades. However, scientific inquiry into the influence of competitive stress on children has just begun (see Gould, this volume; Malina, this volume; Smith, Smoll, and Passer, this volume). Consequently, the changes that will be made in children's sport programs in the future are even more likely to be stimulated as the scientific information continues to evolve.

Two issues appear to have paramount importance in athletic competition for children: (a) the influence of physical stress on biological structure and function and (b) the psychological consequences and benefits of highly competitive situations. Many questions have been raised: How much physical and psychological stress is essential for optimum development and at what point does it become excessive? At what age should athletic competition begin? At what ages and in what sports can boys and girls compete on an equal basis on the same teams? What are the immediate and latent consequences of specific physically and emotionally stressful activities? Answers to such questions are becoming more numerous in the scientific literature. To hasten this process the leaders in youth sports must communicate their concerns to the scientific community, which must then conduct the applied kinds of research that will lead to solutions that can be incorporated into defensible practices.

Sports-Related Injuries

Extended sports seasons and greater intensity of training have contributed to the incidence and severity of sports-related injuries in children and adolescents. Epidemiologists at the Centers for Disease Control and Prevention (2001) reported that 775,000 children under the age of 15 are treated each year in hospital emergency rooms. Sports-related injuries are also the most frequent cause for visits to emergency rooms among children. Two startling facts accompany these statistics. (a) Visits to emergency rooms account for a small percent of the total injuries in children's sports. Most injuries are treated by family physicians and therefore are not recorded as emergencies. (b) Physicians and other health care providers estimate that from 50% to 90% of sports-related injuries to children and youth could be avoided by wearing proper protective equipment, appropriate training and conditioning, and mandatory minimum levels of competency/education for coaches (Baker et al., 1996; Flanders, 1995; Marchi et al., 1999; Schnirring, 2001; Vinger, 1997). As education of the general public approximates the gains made in medical science, consumers will be less tolerant of injuries, especially those that are avoidable through proper instruction and appropriate equipment.

Sports to Be Shaped by Litigation and Legislation

In a review of litigation in sports, Wong (1998) reported that the first course in sports law in the United States was offered in 1972; today there are over 100 law schools offering courses in sports law. In 1972 there were only a few reviews of sports law; today there are over 1000. In 1972 attorneys in sports law were generalists; today there are more than seven specialties within sports law. This proliferation of laws, courses and lawyers suggests that litigation, and perhaps legislation, will have prominent roles in the future of youth and scholastic sports (Tremper and Kostin, 1993). Issues that are candidates for discord are gender equity, waivers and releases of liability, questions regarding the assumption of risk by athletes, reckless and gross misconduct, physical and emotional abuse of athletes, inappropriate emergency care, unsafe venues, improper supervision, product liability, age limitations, and lack of compliance with the Americans with Disabilities Act.

Formal Education and Certification of Volunteer Coaches

The availability of new information about children in sport is currently interpreted and made available to volunteer coaches at a more rapid rate through various Internet sites such as:

- Coaching Association of Canada (http://www.coach.ca/cachome.htm)
- Positive Coaching Alliance (http://www.positivecoach.org/index.htm)
- National Youth Sports Safety Foundation (http://www.nyssf.org/wframeset.html)
- National Alliance for Youth Sports (http://www.nays.org/)
- Gatorade Sports Science Center (http://www.gssiweb.com/sciencecenter/)
- International Society of Biomechanics in Sports (http://www.sportscoach-sci.com/)
- Coaching Youth Sports (http://www.tandl.vt.edu/rstratto/CYS/)
- North American Youth Sports Institute (http://www.naysi.com/)

- Youth Sports Institute (http://ed-web3.educ.msu.edu/ysi/)
- Youth Sports.com (http://www.youth-sports.com/)
- American College of Sports Medicine (http://www.acsm.org/comments.htm)

Establishment of numerous organizations that have as their purpose the education of volunteer coaches has expedited the flow of materials in a form that hitherto has been inaccessible to most volunteer coaches. As managers of sport programs become aware of the information available to coaches, they must provide inducements for their coaches to become involved in programs that lead to certification. The number of organizations that provide educational programs for athletic coaches has grown steadily in the last decades (see Table 24.6). The national demand for certification will induce additional sport-specific organizations to develop their own programs. Minimum knowledge and competency in various subject matter areas has been identified (National Standards for Athletic Coaches, 1995). Credits or equivalent competencies acquired by volunteer coaches should be transferable across state and regional boundaries, similar to the reciprocity of certification in the education of teachers.

Table 24.6   Programs for Coaches' Education in North America

American Red Cross

American Sport Education Program

Canadian National Coaching Certification Program

Coach Effectiveness Training

Coalition of Americans to Protect Sports

National Federation Interscholastic Coaches Education Program

National Youth Sports Coaches Association

National Youth Sports Safety Foundation

North American Youth Sports Institute

Positive Coaching Alliance

Program for Athletic Coaches' Education

Special Olympics International

United States Olympic Committee

Youth Sports Research Council

United States Sports Academy

Source: *Youth Sports in the 21st Century: Organized Sport in the Lives of Children and Adolescents.* East Lansing, MI: Michigan State University (1999).

Local Ownership of Programs

As local managers become more knowledgeable about conducting sport programs for children, they will rely more on their own abilities to make sound decisions and depend less on regionally or nationally based agencies for guidance. To compete with locally controlled programs, nationally based agencies will have to restore to the local communities a greater share of the funds that they currently extract in the form of memberships and registrations. Increased services and education for coaches and administrators are two ways in which an infusion of resources would result in immediate changes. Providing educational programs for coaches, conducting research, and furnishing inducements such as insurance, certification, and newsletters are other examples of how a portion of the membership fees could be returned to communities. Greater representation in decisions that affect local programs and increased flexibility of rules to ensure greater participation in relation to local needs are additional concessions that nationally affiliated programs will have to make if they are to retain their status at the local level. The independence of local communities, emboldened by information, may be reflected in the attrition experienced by team sports that demand strict adherence to national regulations (the SGMA Report 2000).

Greater Reliance on Municipal Sport Programs

Municipal recreation programs will not only receive more frequent demands for competitive programs from displaced public school athletes, but their adult clients will demand more time and space as well. Parents are having fewer children and having them at a later age, thus freeing adults for their own recreation pursuits. The provisions of athletic programs for girls and women in high schools and colleges has resulted in greater numbers who seek single-gender athletic experiences beyond their formal education. The demands for coeducational sport programs for adults are also likely to increase as more women become involved in physical activities. Increased longevity has resulted in an additional generation of older, healthier adults competing for the facilities and personnel of local recreation departments. These demands for facilities and administrative expertise to conduct programs for adults poses potential problems for children and youth unless directors of recreation become more aggressive advocates for clients who are unable, financially and politically, to protect their own interests.

Increased Role for Volunteers

Financial constraints and the increased demand for services will cause municipal recreation departments to seek even more volunteer assistance for their professional staff members in the future. Dependence on volunteers creates a series of problems, foremost of which will be the need for programs to educate the volunteers. Sport programs that depend on volunteers, whether locally controlled or offered by national

Table 24.7 Estimated Participation Patterns in Nonschool Sports (1977–1984) for Children Aged 6–18 Years (in Millions)[1]

Sport	Boys		Girls		Combined		% Gain-Loss (Boys)	% Gain-Loss (Girls)
	1977	1984	1977	1984	1977	1984		
Baseball	4.20	3.91	0.79	0.62	4.99	4.53	−7	−12
Softball	1.97	2.10	2.41	2.62	4.38	4.72	+6	+9
Swimming	1.71	1.85	1.91	2.08	3.62	3.93	+8	+9
Bowling	2.07	2.07	1.51	1.50	3.58	3.57	0	−1
Basketball	2.13	2.13	1.22	1.22	3.35	3.35	0	0
Football (tackle)	1.56	1.16	0.29	0.10	1.85	1.26	−26	−66
Tennis	0.88	1.35	0.95	1.24	1.83	2.59	+53	+30
Gymnastics	0.59	0.75	1.17	1.50	1.76	2.25	+27	+28
Football (flag)	1.11	1.20	0.36	0.45	1.47	1.65	+8	+25
Track and field	0.76	1.00	0.54	0.75	1.30	1.75	+32	+39
Soccer	0.72	2.20	0.52	1.70	1.24	3.90	+305	+327
Wrestling	—	0.25	—	0.00	—	0.25	—	—
Other	1.24	1.00	0.79	0.80	2.03	1.80	−19	+1
Totals	18.94	20.97	12.46	14.58	30.41	35.55		
Percent by sex	62%	59%	38%	41%				

[1]Source: "Youth Sport in the USA" by R. Martens. In *Sport for Children and Youths* (p. 28) by M. R. Weiss and D. Gould (Eds.), 1986, Champaign, IL: Human Kinetics. Copyright 1986 by Human Kinetics.

sports governing bodies, must gradually demand certain levels of competence from their coaches and officials. The threat of lawsuits resulting from injuries, both physical and psychological, will force sponsoring agencies to require certain levels of competence that can most easily be assessed or certified through a formal instructional program. For this reason, required competence, as outlined in the National Standards for Athletic Coaches (1995), on the part of coaches will replace voluntary compliance.

Guarding Against Abuse of Power

The terms *abuse of power, sexual harassment* and *background checks* will become increasingly familiar in the next decade to administrators and coaches associated with youth sports programs (Women's Sports Foundation, 1995). Although sponsors of such programs have an obligation to protect the health and well-being of their young participants, there is a long history of psychological and physical abuse of young athletes by those whose duty it is to serve them.

The abuse of power in athletic settings is not confined to youth sports programs, but its incidence may be concentrated there because of two contributing factors (a) the potential victims are more vulnerable and (b) administrative control is often inadequate. The problem appears to be sufficiently common that a national publication devoted its cover story to the topic (Barrier, 1998), a national organization issued a position statement addressing the problem (Pope, 1998) and several national, non-profit organizations have established procedures to combat the problem (Patterson, 1997; Patterson, 1998).

The occurrence of aberrant behavior by coaches of young athletes has ushered in an administrative procedure commonly called *background checks,* designed to protect organizations from *negligent hiring.* Mandatory background checks may provide such information as an applicant's criminal record, credit history, professional credentials, education and personal references. However, improper use of information obtained in background checks could involve the initiating organization in violations of Federal law, claims of discrimination and invasion of privacy (Perry, 2000; Youth Today, 1994). The directive by courts of law that organizations are liable for risks created by their employee or representatives will cause more sponsors of youth sports to scrutinize certain histories of their coaches.

Coaching as a Male-Dominated Profession

A unique problem arises when youth sport programs are conducted by volunteers. Today many children are being raised in single-parent homes, most frequently by the mother (Carnegie Corporation of New York, 1992). However, with the exception of gymnastics, swimming, and figure skating, most of the youth sport coaches are males, including those in interscholastic programs (Bradley, 1994; Cataleno, 1996; Popke, 2000).

The lack of females as youth sport coaches may be to some degree associated with the lower participation rates and higher attrition rates of girls, but extenuating circumstances most likely account for the disparity. Convincing a single-parent female, who also works full time, that she should devote several evenings a week, plus weekends, to attend coaching workshops and to coach her child's athletic team may challenge the persuasive powers of any recreation director. The later age of child bearing also reduces the number of years a parent may be willing to assist as a volunteer coach, official, or administrator in a youth sport program.

Changes in Activity Patterns

The trend for adults to engage in activities that offer personal autonomy and less regimentation will also be evident in children's sport (Ewing and Seefeldt, 1989). Due to a prevailing philosophy that emphasizes personal needs, the shift to local ownership and control by recreation departments will bring a greater emphasis on personal growth and participation, with less emphasis on a philosophy that stresses "win at all costs." Goals of sport programs will be readjusted to incorporate the qualities of social development, fun, skill acquisition, and personal fitness that have historically been a part of children's motivation for participation but that have not always been evident in the conditions imposed on them by adults (Ewing and Seefeldt, 1989).

Sports that permit the attainment of personal goals and individual styles of play will become more popular, and those that require a high degree of regimentation will decrease in popularity. Racial and ethnic preferences will also determine the popularity of certain sports. An increasing proportion of children from African American and Latino origins and a decreasing proportion of Caucasian children in the population of the United States suggests that sports that are part of the culture of minority groups, namely, soccer, baseball, and basketball, will have an increase in the proportion of child participants, whereas gymnastics, wrestling, and swimming will decrease in popularity. Due to decreases in the age of eligibility for memberships, the absolute number of youth sport competitors will decrease through the remainder of this decade. As a point of reference, Martens's (1986) projection of youth sport participation from 1977 to 1984 is shown in Table 24.7 in contrast to newer projections into the twenty-first century.

Integration of Mentally and Physically Handicapped Children

Despite the mandates of PL 94-142, Education for All Handicapped Children Act, and PL 93–112, Section 504 of the Rehabilitation Act, little evidence is available to indicate that attempts to incorporate handicapped persons into youth sport programs have been successful (Shepard, 1990). Inquiries to representatives of six nationally affiliated sports governing bodies confirmed that all of these organizations welcome handicapped persons into their competitive programs (Seefeldt, Ewing, and Walk,

1992). However, only one of the programs had special provisions in its rules to accommodate such individuals, and only one provided incentives and encouragement for the enrollment of special populations.

The positive attitude of program leaders from national sports governing bodies indicates that the merger of sport programs for handicapped and able-bodied individuals is possible, but progress in this area will depend on how aggressively the advocates for persons with handicapping conditions pursue this opportunity (American Academy of Pediatrics, 1987; Shephard, 1990). Modification of rules involving equipment, playing conditions, eligibility, and skill requirements must occur prior to such a merger. Although the long-standing image that sport is reserved for the able-bodied will be difficult to overcome, the remainder of the twenty-first century will result in a gradual blending of available facilities and programs to accommodate more children and youths who have handicapping conditions (Dummer, 2001).

Summary

Youth sport programs are at a place in their natural history where change is imminent. Historically, programs for young athletes have been plagued by controversies brought on by rapid growth and lack of a firm knowledge base. Proponents of youth sports have frequently been defensive in their reactions to criticism rather than proactive in seeking solutions to problems. Five categories of adult leaders have been identified as the primary agents of change in youth sport. Among variables likely to influence the impending changes are:

- the greater availability of scientific information about the effects of stressful competition on children
- the proliferation of educational programs for volunteer coaches
- the continuing leadership of high school athletic associations
- a greater emphasis on athletic programs offered by recreation departments
- a greater dependence on volunteer workers to conduct the programs; and
- the integration of individuals with handicapping conditions into programs that have previously been reserved for able-bodied competitors.

The changing demographics of youth sports (including gender, ethnicity and place of residence) are the likely determinants of impending changes in sports programs for children and youth. The activity preferences of this emerging population will influence the sports offerings and determine the popularity of traditional American sports. The structure of program offerings will be determined by current and future litigation and legislation as information regarding the safety and welfare of young athletes becomes increasingly accessible through electronic sources.

References

American Academy of Pediatrics. (1981). Competitive sports for children of elementary school age. *Pediatrics, 67,* 927–928.

American Academy of Pediatrics. (1987). Exercise for children who are mentally retarded, policy statement, *The Physician and Sportsmedicine, 15,* 141–142.

Baker, M., Power, C., and Roberts, I. (1996). Injuries and the risk of disability in teenagers and young adults. *Archives of Diseases in Children, 75,* 156–158.

Barrier, M. (1998). Sexual harassment. *Nation's Business, 86(12),* 14–19.

Berryman, J. W. (2002). The rise of boys' sports in the United States, 1900 to 1970. In F. L. Smoll and R. E. Smith (Eds.), *Children and youth in sport: A biopsychosocial perspective* (2nd ed, pp. 5–17). Dubuque, LA. Kendall/Hunt.

Bradley, M. (1994). Cross-gender coaching. *Athletic Management, 6,* 18–26.

Carnegie Corporation of New York. (1992). *A matter of time: Risk and opportunity in the nonschool hours.* New York: Carnegie Council on Adolescent Development.

Catalano, J. (1996). Born to coach. *Athletic Management, 8,* 16–23.

Centers for Disease Control and Prevention. (2000). Youth risk behavior surveillance—United States, 1999. *Morbidity and Mortality Weekly Report 2000, 49(SS-5),* 1–94.

Centers for Disease Control and Prevention. (2001). *Sports injury prevention: Children and adolescents.* [On-line]. Available: http://www.cdc.gov/safeusa/sports/child.htm

Cotten, D., and Cotten M. (1997). *Legal aspects of waivers in sport, recreation and fitness activities.* Canton, OH: PRC Publishing.

Dummer, G. (2001). Including athletes with a disability. In V. Seefeldt and M. Clark (Eds.) *Program for Athletic Coaches' Education.* Traverse City, MI.: Cooper Publishing Group.

Ewing, M., and Seefeldt, V. (1989). *Participation and attrition patterns in America's agency-sponsored and interscholastic sports: An executive summary.* North Palm Beach, FL: Sporting Goods Manufacturer's Association.

Flanders, R. Z., and Mohandas, A. (1995). The incidence of oral facial injuries in sport: A pilot study in Illinois. *Journal of the American Dental Association, 126,* 491–496.

Forsythe, L. (I 950). *Athletics in Michigan high schools: The first 100 years.* New York: Prentice-Hall.

Gould, D. (2002). Sport psychology: Future directions in youth sport research. In F. L. Smoll and R. E. Smith (Eds.), *Children and youth in sport: A biopsychosocial perspective* (2nd ed., pp. 565–589). Dubuque, IA: Kendall/Hunt.

Herbert, D. (1994). *Legal Aspects of Preventative, Rehabilitative and Recreational Exercise Programs (3d ed.).* Canton, OH: PRC Publishing.

Joint legislative study on youth sports—Phase II report. (1978). Lansing: State of Michigan.

Kanaby, R. (1993). First and foremost, an educator. *Athletic Business, 17,* 25–32.

Low, M. (Chair). (1968). Competitive athletics for children of elementary school age. *Pediatrics, 42,* 703–704.

Malina, R. M. (2002). The young athlete: Biological growth and maturation in a biocultural context. In F. L. Smoll and R. E. Smith (Eds.), *Children and youth in sport: A biopsychosocial perspective* (2nd ed., pp. 261–292). Dubuque, IA: Kendall/Hunt.

Marchi, A., Bello, D., Messi, G., and Gazzola, G. (1999). Permanent sequela in sports injuries: A population-based study. *Archives of Diseases in Children, 81,* 324–328.

Martens, R. (1986). Youth sport in the USA. In M. R. Weiss and D. Gould (Eds.), *Sport for children and youths* (pp. 27–34). Champaign. IL: Human Kinetics.

Martens, R., and Seefeldt, V. (1979). *Guidelines for children's sports.* Reston, VA: American Alliance for Health, Physical Education, Recreation and Dance.

McCann, D. (1999). *Raising the standard. The 1999 national intercollegiate coaching requirements report.* Champaign, IL: Human Kinetics Publishers.

National Association for Sport and Physical Education. (I 994). *National standards for athletic coaches.* Reston, VA: Author.

National Federation of State High School Associations. (2001). *1999–2000 athletics participation summary.* [On-line]. Available: http://www.Nfhs.org/part-Survey99-00.htm

Patterson, J. (1997). *Screening volunteers to prevent child sexual abuse. A three-step action guide.* Washington, D.C.: National Assembly of National Voluntary Health and Social Welfare Organizations.

Patterson, J. (1998). *Staff screening tool kit.* Washington, D.C.: No-Profit Risk Management Center.

Perry, P. (2000). For the record. *Athletic Business, 24,* 40–43.

Pope, M. (1998). *Sexual harassment in athletic settings.* Reston, VA.: National Association for Sport and Physical Education.

Popke, M. (2000). Coaches wanted. *Athletic Business, 24,* 28–29.

Prochnow, H., and Prochnow, H. (1983). *A treasure chest of quotations for all occasions.* New York: Harper and Row.

Roberts, J. (2001). *Raising expectations: Commentaries for interscholastic athletics.* East Lansing, MI: Michigan High School Athletic Association.

Schnirring, L. (2001). Sports training and growth delay. *The Physician and Sportsmedicine, 29,* 23–27.

Seefeldt, V. (Ed.) (1995). *Recreating recreation and sports in Detroit, Hamtramck and Highland Park: Final report to the Skillman Foundation.* Detroit, MI: The Skillman Foundation.

Seefeldt, V., and Ewing, M. (1998). Youth sports in America. In C. Corbin and R. Pangrazi (Eds.) *Towards a better understanding of physical fitness and activity.* Scottsdale, AZ: Holcomb Hathaway Publishers.

Seefeldt, V., Ewing, M., and Walk, S. (1992). *An overview of youth sports programs in the United States.* Washington, DC: Carnegie Council on Adolescent Development.

Shephard, R. (1990), *Fitness in special populations.* Champaign, IL: Human Kinetics.

Smith, R. E., Smoll, F. L., and Passer, M. W. (2002). Sport performance anxiety in young athletes. In F. L Smoll and R. E. Smith (Eds.), *Children and youth* in *sport: A biopsychosocial perspective* (2nd ed., pp. 501–536). Dubuque, IA: Kendall/Hunt.

Sporting Goods Manufacturers' Association. (2000). *The SGMA report 2000. U.S. trends in team sports.* North Palm Beach, FL: Author.

Sporting Goods Manufacturers' Association. (2001). *State of the Industry: SGMA 2001.* North Palm Beach, FL: Author.

Thomas, J. R. (Ed.). (1977). *Youth sports guide for coaches and parents.* Washington, DC: American Alliance for Health, Physical Education, Recreation and Dance.

Tremper, C., and Kostin, G. (1993). *No surprises: Controlling risks in volunteer programs.* Washington, D.C.: Non-Profit Risk Management Center.

Vinger, P. F. (1997). Preventing eye injuries. *National Youth Sports Safety Foundation, 6,* 1–2.

Weiss, M. R., and Gould, D. (Eds.). (1986). *Sport for children and youths.* Champaign, IL.: Human Kinetics.

Women's Sports Foundation. (1995). *An educational resource kit for the athletic administrator: Prevention of sexual harassment in athletic settings.* East Meadow, N.Y.: Author.

Wong, G. (1998). The sports law decade. *Athletic Business, 22,* 33–37.

Youth Today. (1994). What price background checks? 1994 (March/April).

Appendix: Pronouncements of Professional Organizations Regarding Youth Sports

Organization	Year	Title	Purpose/Focus
American Academy of Pediatrics	1989	Organized Athletics for Pre-Adolescent Children	Lists the safeguards that should accompany children's sports.
American Academy of Pediatrics	1988	Recommendations for Participation in Competitive Sports	Lists medical conditions that would disqualify children from athletic competition.
American Academy of Pediatrics	1983	Weight Training and Weight Lifting: Information for the Pediatrician	A conservative assessment of the benefits and risks of weight lifting and weight training.
American Academy of Pediatrics	1982	Climatic Heat Stress and the Exercising Child	Documents the special problems of children when exercising in hot-humid-environment.
American Academy of Pediatrics	1982	Risks of Long-Distance Running for Children	Provides guidelines for involving children in long-distance running.
American Academy of Pediatrics	1981	Competitive Sports for Children of Elementary School Age	An update of their position statement in 1968.
American Academy of Pediatrics	1981	Injuries to Young Athletes	Presents the special problems of young athletes in competitive sports.

Organization	Year	Title	Purpose/Focus
American Academy of Pediatrics	1973	Athletic Activities for Children with Skeletal Abnormalities	Outlines the conditions under which children with specific conditions can and should not be involved in athletics.
American College of Sports Medicine	2000	Cocaine Abuse in Sports	Reviews the adverse effects of cocaine on physical and psychological health. Cites the behavioral changes including the deterioration of athletic performance in conjunction with the use of cocaine.
American College of Sports Medicine	2000	Exercise-Induced Asthma (EIA)	Discusses the symptoms of EIA and its underlying factors. Detection, medication and possible causes are discussed.
American College of Sports Medicine	2000	Preseason Conditioning of Young Athletes	Underscores the importance of a conditioning program that is designed to prepare the athlete for strenuous activity. Recommends that coaches take 6 to 8 weeks to prepare the athlete through activities that include strength, aerobic, anaerobic and flexibility training.
American College of Sports Medicine	2000	Stress Fractures	Lists the causes and mechanisms of stress fractures and recommends procedures to reduce the likelihood of acquiring stress fractures.
American College of Sports Medicine	1999	Anabolic Steroids	Updates the position stand issued in 1984. Traces the use of steroids since 1989 and suggests ways to combat the current rise in the use of steroids.

Organization	Year	Title	Purpose/Focus
American College of Sports Medicine	1999	Exercise and Age-Related Weight Gain	Primarily directed at the rise in obesity among adults, but applicable to youth, as well. Emphasizes the important role of exercise in controlling weight.
American College of Sports Medicine	1999	Explosive Exercise	Defines and describes explosive exercises and describes the types of training programs that are used to obtain maximum force.
American College of Sports Medicine	1999	Health-Related Fitness for Children and Adults With Cerebral Palsy	Discounts the former assumption that physical activity would increase spasticity and abnormal patterns of movement. Reviews newer therapeutic approaches that incorporate movement and physical fitness as an essential part of the exercise program, under the supervision of a professional educator/trainer/therapist.
American College of Sports Medicine	1999	Preparticipation Physical Examinations (PPE)	Lists objectives of the PPE and its contents. Provides a rationale for various portions of the exam and provides guidelines for restricting or disqualifying athletes from participation.
American College of Sports Medicine	1998	Creatine Supplementation	Provides a summary of the acute effects that creatine has on skeletal muscle and discusses its effectiveness and the incidence of potentially unknown side effects.

Organization	Year	Title	Purpose/Focus
American College of Sports Medicine	1998	Vitamin and Mineral Supplements and Exercise	Cautions against depending on supplements in lieu of a balanced diet. Warns athletes of the dangers associated with the consumption of megadoses of minerals and vitamins.
American College of Sports Medicine	1998	Youth Strength Training	Outlines the goals of strength training for children and describes the conditions under which safe and enjoyable programs should be conducted.
American College of Sports Medicine	1996	Anorexia and Bulimia	Defines the various eating disorders and suggests ways in which adults who supervise and coach athletes can detect and educate student-athletes who are suspected of having eating disorders.
American College of Sports Medicine	1996	Exercise and Fluid Replacement	Reviews the effects of dehydration and hydration on human performance.
American College of Sports Medicine and American College of Cardiology	1994	Recommendations for Determining Eligibility for Competition in Athletes with Cardiovascular Abnormalities	Provides an extensive set of papers that review the various abnormalities and makes recommendations to physicians.
American College of Sports Medicine	1993	The Prevention of Sports Injuries of Children and Adolescents	Suggests that fifty percent of current injuries could be prevented with proper techniques.
American College of Sports Medicine	1984	The Use of Anabolic-Androgenic Steroids in Sports	Documents the adverse effects of anabolic steroids on the human body.
American College of Sports Medicine	1982	The Use of Alcohol in Sports	Reviews the literature on the influence of alcohol on human performance.

Organization	Year	Title	Purpose/Focus
American College of Sports Medicine	1979	The Participation of the Female Athlete in Long-Distance Running	Documents that female athletes should not be denied opportunities for long-distance running.
American College of Sports Medicine	1976	Weight Loss in Wrestlers	Warns of the dangers of personal health when excessive weight loss is incurred.
American Heart Association	1986	Coronary Risk Factor Modification in Children: Exercise	Reviews ways to combat the sedentary lifestyles of children.
American Medical Association	1975	Female Athletes	An early and outdated version of athletic competition for girls and women.
International Federation of Sports Medicine	1991	Excessive Physical Training in Children and Adolescents	Provides guidelines and examples of activities that are to be avoided in children's training for athletic competition.
Michigan Governor's Council on Physical Fitness, Health and Sports	1995	The Importance of Physical Activity for Children and Youth (Pivarnik)	Provides the scientific basis for physical activity in childhood and adolescence; Advocates policies for families, communities, public health and schools.
National Strength and Conditioning Association	1985	Prepubescent Strength Training	Documents the benefits and risks of strength training for prepubescent children. Provides guidelines for parents and coaches.

Printed in the USA
CPSIA information can be obtained
at www.ICGtesting.com
JSHW061209011123
51254JS00004B/9

9 780787 282233